Feminist Frontiers II

Rethinking Sex, Gender, and Society

LAUREL RICHARDSON
Ohio State University

VERTA TAYLOR
Ohio State University

Random House New York

Second Edition

987654321

Copyright © 1986, 1989 by Newbery Award Records,
Inc.

Library of Congress Cataloging-in-Publication Data

Feminist frontiers II.

  Includes bibliographies.
  1. Feminism—United States.   2. Women—United
States. 3. Sex role—United States.   4. Women—Cross-
cultural studies.   I. Richardson, Laurel Walum.
II. Taylor, Verta A.   III. Title: Feminist frontiers two.
HQ1426.F472 1989   305.4'2   88-11664
ISBN 0-394-37399-5

Text and Cover Design: Lorraine Hohman

Manufactured in the United States of America

To our mothers
Rose Foreman Richardson and
Alice F. Houston
and to our "sisters"
Jessica Richardson Phillips and
Betty Jo Hudson

P R E F A C E

The first edition of *Feminist Frontiers* was conceived in the late 1970s, when large numbers of women inside and outside academia were recognizing and challenging the extent to which male dominance permeated the structure of societies around the world. The articles in the first edition reflected the newness of feminist thought and sought to document the nature and causes of women's subordinate status. The anthology was published in the early 1980s during a period that brought a backlash against feminism and witnessed the rise of movements seeking to reinstate traditional roles for and ideas about women and men. There is no doubt that the situation of women has changed since the 1970s. Gender inequality, however, has not disappeared. Over the past decade, feminists have refined and enlarged their understanding of the ways that gender inequality operates and is sustained. Embarking as we are on the last decade of the twentieth century, we are fortunate to be writing, teaching, and learning at a time when feminist thought and research are flourishing and deepening. It is simultaneously a time of enjoying the bounty of feminist scholarship and of sowing new feminist seeds.

Feminist thought seeks to transform in fundamentally profound ways all the old patriarchal ways of seeing, defining, thinking about, and understanding our experiences and the social world. Contemporary feminist thought views the accomplishment of this transformation as a global activity, and as one which must take account of differences and diversity. Class, ethnicity, race, sexual identity, age, and gender are all relevant to a feminist understanding of the social world. To present contemporary feminist scholarship to the student, we offer *Feminist Frontiers II: Rethinking Sex, Gender, and Society.*

This book can be used as the major or supplementary text in courses on the sociology of women, women's studies, sex roles, and the psychology of women. In addition, because the book offers a general framework of analysis, it can be used as a supplementary text in introductory sociology courses and in courses on social problems, foundations of society, comparative studies, and American studies.

The articles in *Feminist Frontiers II* underscore that cultural, racial, ethnic, and other differences are pervasive, and pervasively intersect with gender. Although we have retained some articles from the first edition, more than two-thirds of the readings are new to this edition. We have sought out many new cross-cultural and comparative articles. In selecting such works, we have looked for material that lends itself to discussion by people with no previous knowledge of the culture under consideration. In addition, we have added some early writings that have become feminist classics.

Feminist Frontiers II is organized into three parts, each introduced by a sociological-feminist analysis. Part One, "Learning Sex and Gender," has two sections, "Language and Images" and "Socialization." The six sections of Part Two, "Organization of Sex and Gender," provide theoretical explanations for sex-based inequality and discuss the social organization of work and family, sexuality and intimate relationships, medicine and science, politics, and violence against women. Part Three, "The Feminist Movement," documents the diversity of the feminist movement and looks toward its future.

This book begins with material that is easily apprehended because it deals with familiar socialization experiences. The more complex and theoretical material in Section Three, "Explanations of Sex-Based Inequality," may then be introduced as a framework for the later substantive articles—or may be postponed or omitted, according to the instructor's needs. The remaining sections lead students to consider concrete issues and to take part in the dialogue between social order and social change, with emphasis on the ways the social world is changed through individual, interpersonal, and collective action.

As we set about the task of selecting articles for this edition, we found an abundance of excellent ones on some topics and few or none on others. We established a set of criteria for choosing articles and for balancing the entire collection. First, we wanted each article to be well written and accessible in style and language; we wanted the articles to stimulate the reader's thought and vision. Second, we wanted the selections to explore contemporary theory and issues and to reflect the tremendous growth in depth and understanding of feminist scholarship. Third, we wanted to include materials on a diversity of racial, ethnic, generational, and cultural experiences. Fourth, we wanted the articles to represent the cross-disciplinary nature of gender research. And fifth, we wanted some of the articles to provide research models that students could replicate. When we could not locate an existing article that met our criteria on a particular topic, we asked colleagues to write or revise a work specifically for this volume. The result is a collection that links well-written and significant articles within a more general sociological and feminist perspective.

With the greatest pleasure we acknowledge the support, skill, and help of the many people who have made this volume a reality. We have found the contributing authors to be exceptionally generous, caring, and astute individuals. We are appreciative of their contributions. We especially thank Bert Lummus, our editor, for believing in and supporting this project, and we thank Pat Plunkett, Beena Kamlani, and Jennifer Sutherland for shepherding the book through its many restructurings.

Phyllis Gorman has been with this project from its inception. She has spent endless hours at the library tracking down articles and even more hours teaching the material to her women's studies classes and keeping us informed about its "teachability." Kelly McCormick joined the project for the second edition, and her aid in reading material, teaching it to her classes, and sharing her experiences with us has been invaluable. We thank our colleagues Claire Robinson and Leila Rupp for giving generously of their time and expertise by suggesting articles for the second edition. We are very grateful to Dianne Small and Annette Lendacki, who aided the revision project through their technical know-how and their good spirits, and to Gina Laudick, who helped in countless ways. We thank especially the students in our sociology of women and women's studies classes, who have contributed to the development of this book by their critical responses to articles. The following reviewers read the manuscript and improved it by their expert and generous comments:

Patricia Carter, University of Connecticut at Storrs;
Gayle Davis, Wichita State University;
Saul Feinman, University of Wyoming;
Saundra Gardner, University of Maine at Orono;
Linda Grant, University of Georgia at Athens;
Patricia Harvey, Colorado State University;
Marilyn Meyerson, University of South Florida;
Elizabeth Nelson, California State University at Fresno;
Cynthia Rexroat, University of Florida at Gainesville;
Karen Rosenblum, George Mason University;
Susan Shoemaker, Illinois State University at Normal; and
Kathryn Ward, Southern Illinois University.

Special thanks go to those close to us who inspired both the work and the authors. Ernest Lockridge has been steadfast in his belief in and support for the project. Leila Rupp critically reviewed the entire collection at various stages of revision and offered the friendship and support we needed to carry out this project. To them and to the many others who have touched our lives positively, we give our thanks.

Finally, we wish all to know that we are full co-editors. Our names are in alphabetical order.

Laurel Richardson
Verta Taylor

C O N T E N T S

SECTION FOUR: WORK AND FAMILY 159

SECTION FIVE: SEXUALITY AND INTIMATE RELATIONSHIPS 227

SECTION TEN: THE FUTURE OF FEMINISM

P A R T   O N E

Learning Sex and Gender

Everyone is born into a *culture*—a *set of shared ideas* about the nature of reality, the nature of right and wrong, *evaluation of what is good and desirable,* and the nature of the good and desirable versus the bad and nondesirable. These ideas are manifested in behaviors and artifacts. As totally dependent infants we are *socialized*—taught the rules, roles, and relationships of the social world we will inherit. We exchange our infant hedonism for the love, protection, and attention of others; in the process we learn to think, act, and feel as we are "supposed to."

One of the earliest and most deep-seated ideas to which we are socialized is that of gender identity: the *idea* that "I am a boy" or "I am a girl." Because the culture, moreover, has strong ideas about what boys are like and what girls are like, we learn to identify our gender identity (our "boyness" or "girlness") with behaviors and attitudes that are sex-assigned in our culture. Thus, for example, a girl who plays with dolls is viewed as behaving in an appropriate and "feminine" manner and a boy who plays with trucks as appropriately "masculine." Sometimes consciously and sometimes nonconsciously, children are categorized, differentially responded to and regarded, and encouraged to adopt behaviors and attitudes on the basis of their sex. We raise, in effect, two different kinds of children: boys and girls.

Parents (or surrogate parents) are strong socializing influences in that they provide the first and most deeply experienced socialization experiences. Despite claims to the contrary, parents treat their infant boys and girls differently. Boys have "boy names," "boy toys," "boy room decor," and are played with in more "boylike" ways than girls. Even if parents monitor their actions in the hope of preventing sexism from affecting their child, their endeavors will not succeed, because *other* socializing influences bear down on the child.

One of the primary socializing influences is the *language* we acquire. In learning to talk we acquire the thought patterns and communication styles of our culture. Those patterns and styles perpetuate and reinforce differentiation by sex and sex stereotyping. They are *unavoidable.* Embedded in the language are such ideas as "women are adjuncts to men" (e.g., the use of the generic "man" or "he"); women's aspirations are and should be different from men's (e.g., "The secretary . . . *she,*" "the pilot . . . *he*"); women remain immature and incompetent throughout adult life (e.g., "The girls [office staff] have gone to lunch"); women are defined in terms of their sexual desirability (to men) whereas men are defined in terms of their sexual prowess. (Contrast the meanings of the supposedly equivalent words *spinster* and *bachelor, mistress* and *master, courtesan* and *courtier,* etc.) As long as we speak the language we have acquired, we are not only speaking but also thinking in sex-stereotyping ways.

As our society becomes more complex, increasingly the mass media have become centralized agents for the transmission of cultural beliefs. The media present sex stereotypes in their purest and simplest forms. Children spend more time watching television than they spend in school or inter-acting with their parents and peers. Moreover, children tend to *believe* that what they see on tele-vision is an accurate representation of the way the world is and *should* be organized. Although the impact is not so great, other forms of mass media—comics, newspapers, advertisements, movies, music—reiterate the theme that (white middle-class) males are powerful and prestigious (and should be), and women are subordinate and without esteem.

The socialization effected by the family and by language (including the mass media) is supple-mented by the educational system. Educational institutions are formally charged with teaching the young. While teaching them reading, writing, and arithmetic, however, the schools also imbue them with sexist values. They do so through the pattern of staffing (male principals and custodians, female teachers and food servers), the curriculum materials, the sex segregation of sports and activities, and differential *expectations* of boys and girls. No child can avoid this socialization experience.

Through powerful social institutions, then, children learn a culture. The culture they learn is one that views malehood as superior to femalehood; it is a system that differentially assigns behaviors and attitudes to males and females.

Socialization—whether through the home, the school, language, or the mass media—creates and sustains gender differences. Boys are taught that they will inherit the privileges and prestige of manhood, and girls are taught that they are less socially valuable than boys. Both are expected to view their status as right, moral, and appropriate. Moreover, socialization never ends. As adults we continue to be resocialized by the books we read, the movies we see, and the people we spend time with.

The readings selected for this section, "Learning Sex and Gender," illustrate and explain different aspects of the socialization process and provide the reader with conceptual frameworks and per-spectives for understanding the implications of gender.

Language and Images

Language—both verbal and nonverbal—affects the way we view ourselves and our relationships, and reflects the values of a society. Our language teaches that males and male-associated behaviors, attitudes, and goals are more important and more valuable than females and female-associated behaviors, traits, and goals.

In the first selection, "Gender Stereotyping in the English Language," Laurel Richardson describes six major ways in which the English language perpetuates differential expectations of males and females. As we speak the language and hear it spoken, we unwittingly reinforce in ourselves gender stereotyping. Mary Brown Parlee, in "Conversational Politics," reviews some of the research on the ways in which power differences affect speech styles and conversational interactions between males and females.

Embedded in our language are ideas about beauty and sexuality. In many societies, male standards of beauty and eroticism require the physical mutilation of women. In "Gynocide: Chinese Foot-binding" Andrea Dworkin discusses a brutal form of mutilation that affected millions of Chinese women: the binding of a little girl's feet to force them into the tiny "lotus" shape erotically desired by men. Susan Squire in "Is the Binge-Purge Cycle Catching?" describes a dangerous practice in the United States which many young women have also adopted in order to meet idealized standards of beauty.

We cannot emphasize too strongly the importance of language, both verbal and nonverbal. We are continuously exposed to ideas and images of women as subordinate to men. Moreover, since the language we have acquired and the images we use are so deep-rooted and so omnipresent, it is very difficult for us to break from them, to see and describe the world and our experiences in nonsexist ways. The power to define—to decide whether, for example, a woman supervisor is "pushy" or "assertive," "energetic" or "a rate-buster," "cool headed" or "frigid"—has a major influence on our perception of ourselves and of others.

Gender Stereotyping in the English Language

LAUREL RICHARDSON

Everyone in our society, regardless of class, ethnicity, sex, age, or race, is exposed to the same language, the language of the dominant culture. Analysis of verbal language can tell us a great deal about a people's fears, prejudices, anxieties, and interests. A rich vocabulary on a particular subject indicates societal interests or obsessions (e.g., the extensive vocabulary about cars in America). And different words for the same subject (such as *freedom fighter* and *terrorist, passed away* and *croaked, make love* and *ball*) show that there is a range of attitudes and feelings in the society toward that subject.

It should not be surprising, then, to find differential attitudes and feelings about men and women rooted in the English language. Although the English language has not been completely analyzed, six general propositions concerning these attitudes and feelings about males and females can be made.

First, in terms of grammatical and semantic structure, women do not have a fully autonomous, independent existence; they are part of man. Our language is not divided into male and female with distinct conjugations and declensions, as many other languages are. Rather, *women* are included under the generic *man.* Grammar books specify that the pronoun *he* can be used generically to mean *he* or *she.* Further, *man,* when used as an indefinite pronoun, grammatically refers to both men and women. So, for example, when we read *man* in the following phrases we are to interpret it as applying to both men and women: "man the oars," "one small step for man, one giant step for mankind," "man, that's tough," "man overboard," "man the toolmaker," "alienated man," "garbageman." Our rules of etiquette complete the grammati-

cal presumption of inclusivity. When two persons are pronounced "man and wife," Miss Susan Jones changes her entire name to Mrs. Robert Gordon (Vanderbilt, 1972). In each of these correct usages, women are a part of man; they do not exist autonomously. The exclusion of women is well expressed in Mary Daly's ear-jarring slogan "the sisterhood of man" (1973:7–21).

However, there is some question as to whether the theory that *man* means everybody is carried out in practice (see Bendix, 1979; Martyna, 1980). For example, an eight-year-old interrupts her reading of "The Story of the Cavemen" to ask how we got here without cavewomen. A ten-year-old thinks it is dumb to have a woman post*man.* A beginning anthropology student believes (incorrectly) that all shamans ("witch doctors") are males because her textbook and professor use the referential pronoun *he.*

But beginning language learners are not the only ones who visualize males when they see the word *man.* Research has consistently demonstrated that when the generic *man* is used, people visualize men, not women (Schneider & Hacker, 1973; DeStefano, 1976; Martyna, 1978; Hamilton & Henley, 1982). DeStefano, for example, reports that college students choose silhouettes of males for sentences with the word *man* or *men* in them. Similarly, the presumably generic *he* elicits images of men rather than women. The finding is so persistent that linguists doubt whether there actually is a semantic generic in English (MacKay, 1983).

Man, then, suggests not humanity but rather male images. Moreover, over one's lifetime, an educated American will be exposed to the prescriptive *he* more than a million times (MacKay, 1983). One consequence is the exclusion of women in the visualization, imagination, and thought of males and females. Most likely this linguistic practice perpetuates in men their

Adapted from Laurel Richardson, *The Dynamics of Sex and Gender: A Sociological Perspective* (New York: Harper & Row, 1987), by permission of the author.

feelings of dominance over and responsibility for women, feelings that interfere with the development of equality in relationships.

Second, in actual practice, our pronoun usage perpetuates different personality attributes and career aspirations for men and women. Nurses, secretaries, and elementary school teachers are almost invariably referred to as *she;* doctors, engineers, electricians, and presidents as *he.* In one classroom, students referred to an unidentified child as *he* but shifted to *she* when discussing the child's parent. In a faculty discussion of the problems of acquiring new staff, all architects, engineers, security officers, faculty, and computer programmers were referred to as *he;* secretaries and file clerks were referred to as *she.* Martyna (1978) has noted that speakers consistently use *he* when the referent has a high-status occupation (e.g., doctor, lawyer, judge) but shift to *she* when the occupations have lower status (e.g., nurse, secretary).

Even our choice of sex ascription to nonhuman objects subtly reinforces different personalities for males and females. It seems as though the small (e.g., kittens), the graceful (e.g., poetry), the unpredictable (e.g., the fates), the nurturant (e.g., the church, the school), and that which is owned and/or controlled by men (e.g., boats, cars, governments, nations) represent the feminine, whereas that which is a controlling forceful power in and of itself (e.g., God, Satan, tiger) primarily represents the masculine. Even athletic teams are not immune. In one college, the men's teams are called the Bearcats and the women's teams the Bearkittens.

Some of you may wonder whether it matters that the female is linguistically included in the male. The inclusion of women under the pseudogeneric *man* and the prescriptive *he,* however, is not a trivial issue. Language has tremendous power to shape attitudes and influence behavior. Indeed, MacKay (1983) argues that the prescriptive *he* "has all the characteristics of a highly effective propaganda technique": frequent repetition, early age of acquisition (before age 6), covertness (*he* is not thought of as propaganda), use of high-prestige sources (including university texts and professors), and indirectness (presented as though it were a matter of common knowledge). As a result, the prescriptive affects females' sense of life options and feelings of well-being. For example, Adamsky (1981) found that women's sense of power and importance were enhanced when the prescriptive *he* was replaced by *she.*

Awareness of the impact of the generic *man* and prescriptive *he* has generated considerable activity to change the language. One change, approved by the Modern Language Association, is to replace the prescriptive *he* with the plural *they*—as was accepted practice before the 18th century. Another is the use of *he or she.* Although it sounds awkward at first, the *he or she* designation is increasingly being used in the media and among people who have recognized the power of the pronoun to perpetuate sex stereotyping. When a professor, for example, talks about "the lawyer" as "he or she," a speech pattern that counteracts sex stereotyping is modeled. This drive to neutralize the impact of pronouns is evidenced further in the renaming of occupations: a policeman is now a police officer, a postman is a mail carrier, a stewardess is a flight attendant.

Third, linguistic practice defines females as immature, incompetent, and incapable and males as mature, complete, and competent. Because the words *man* and *woman* tend to connote sexual and human maturity, common speech, organizational titles, public addresses, and bathroom doors frequently designate the women in question as *ladies.* Simply contrast the different connotations of *lady* and *woman* in the following common phrases:

Luck, be a lady (woman) tonight.
Barbara's a little lady (woman).
Ladies' (Women's) Air Corps.

In the first two examples, the use of *lady* desexualizes the contextual meaning of *woman.* So trivializing is the use of *lady* in the last phrase that the second is wholly anomalous. The male equivalent, *lord,* is never used; and its synonym, *gentleman,* is used infrequently. When *gentleman* is used, the assumption seems to be that certain culturally condoned aspects of masculinity (e.g., aggressivity, activity, and strength) should be set aside in the interests of maturity and order, as in the following phrases:

A gentlemen's (men's) agreement.
A duel between gentlemen (men).
He's a real gentleman (man).

Rather than feeling constrained to set aside the stereotypes associated with *man,* males frequently find the opposite process occurring. The contextual connotation of *man* places a strain on males to be continuously sexually and socially potent, as the following examples reveal:

I was not a man (gentleman) with her tonight.
This is a man's (gentleman's) job.
Be a man (gentleman).

Whether males, therefore, feel competent or anxious, valuable or worthless in particular contexts is influenced by the demands placed on them by the expectations of the language.

Not only are men infrequently labeled *gentlemen,* but they are infrequently labeled *boys.* The term *boy* is reserved for young males, bellhops, car attendants, and as a putdown to those males judged inferior. *Boy* connotes immaturity and powerlessness. Only occasionally do males "have a night out with the boys." They do not talk "boy talk" at the office. Rarely does our language legitimize carefreeness in males. Rather, they are expected, linguistically, to adopt the responsibilities of manhood.

On the other hand, women of all ages may be called *girls.* Grown females "play bridge with the girls" and indulge in "girl talk." They are encouraged to remain childlike, and the implication is that they are basically immature and without power. Men can become men, linguistically, putting aside the immaturity of childhood; indeed, for them to retain the openness and playfulness of boyhood is linguistically difficult.

Further, the presumed incompetence and immaturity of women are evidenced by the linguistic company they keep. Women are categorized with children ("women and children first"), the infirm ("the blind, the lame, the women"), and the incompetent ("women, convicts, and idiots"). The use of these categorical designations is not accidental happenstance; "rather these selectional groupings are powerful forces behind the actual expressions of language and are based on distinctions which are not regarded as trivial by the speakers of the language" (Key, 1975:82). A total language analysis of categorical groupings is not available, yet it seems likely that women tend to be included in groupings that designate incompleteness, ineptitude, and immaturity. On the other hand, it is difficult for us to conceive of the word *man* in any categorical grouping other than one that extends beyond humanity, such as "Man, apes, and angels" or "Man

and Superman." That is, men do exist as an independent category capable of autonomy; women are grouped with the stigmatized, the immature, and the foolish. Moreover, when men are in human groupings, males are invariably first on the list ("men and women," "he and she," "man and wife"). This order is not accidental but was prescribed in the 16th century to honor the worthier party.

Fourth, in practice women are defined in terms of their sexual desirability (to men); men are defined in terms of their sexual prowess (over women). Most slang words in reference to women refer to their sexual desirability to men (e.g., *dog, fox, broad, ass, chick*). Slang about men refers to their sexual prowess over women (e.g., *dude, stud, hunk*). The fewer examples given for men is not an oversight. An analysis of sexual slang, for example, listed more than 1,000 words and phrases that derogate women sexually but found "nowhere near this multitude for describing men" (Kramarae, 1975:72). Farmer and Henley (cited in Schulz, 1975) list 500 synonyms for *prostitute,* for example, and only 65 for *whoremonger.* Stanley (1977) reports 220 terms for a sexually promiscuous woman and only 22 for a sexually promiscuous man. Shuster (1973) reports that the passive verb form is used in reference to women's sexual experiences (e.g., *to be laid, to be had, to be taken*), whereas the active tense is used in reference to the male's sexual experience (e.g., *lay, take, have*). Being sexually attractive to males is culturally condoned for women and being sexually powerful is approved for males. In this regard, the slang of the street is certainly not countercultural; rather it perpetuates and reinforces different expectations in females and males as sexual objects and performers.

Further, we find sexual connotations associated with neutral words applied to women. A few examples should suffice. A male academician questioned the title of a new course, asserting it was "too suggestive." The title? "The Position of Women in the Social Order." A male tramp is simply a hobo, but a female tramp is a slut. And consider the difference in connotation of the following expressions:

It's easy.
He's easy.
She's easy.

In the first, we assume something is "easy to do"; in the second, we might assume a professor is an "easy grader" or a man is "easygoing." But when we read "she's easy," the connotation is "she's an easy lay."

In the world of slang, men are defined by their sexual prowess. In the world of slang and proper speech, women are defined as sexual objects. The rule in practice seems to be: If in doubt, assume that *any* reference to a women has a sexual connotation. For both genders, the constant bombardment of prescribed sexuality is bound to have real consequences.

Fifth, women are defined in terms of their relations to men; men are defined in terms of their relations to the world at large. A good example is seen in the words *master* and *mistress.* Originally these words had the same meaning—"a person who holds power over servants." With the demise of the feudal system, however, these words took on different meanings. The masculine variant metaphorically refers to power over something; as in "He is the master of his trade"; the feminine variant metaphorically (although probably not in actuality) refers to power over a man sexually, as in "She is Tom's mistress." Men are defined in terms of their power in the occupational world, women in terms of their sexual power over men.

The existence of two contractions for Mistress (*Miss* and *Mrs.*) and but one for Mister (*Mr.*) underscores the cultural concern and linguistic practice: women are defined in relation to men. Even a divorced women is defined in terms of her no-longer-existing relation to a man (she is still *Mrs. Man's Name*). But apparently the divorced state is not relevant enough to the man or to the society to require a label. A divorced woman is a *divorcee,* but what do you call a divorced man? The recent preference of many women to be called *Ms.* is an attempt to provide for women an equivalency title that is not dependent on marital status.

Sixth, a historical pattern can be seen in the meanings that come to be attached to words that originally were neutral: those that apply to women acquire obscene and/or debased connotations but no such pattern of derogation holds for neutral words referring to men. The processes of *pejoration* (the acquiring of an obscene or debased connotation) and *amelioration* (the reacquiring of a neutral or positive connotation) in the English language in regard to terms for males and females have been studied extensively by Muriel Schulz (1975).

Leveling is the least derogative form of pejoration.

Through leveling, titles that originally referred to an elite class of persons come to include a wider class of persons. Such democratic leveling is more common for female designates than for males. For example, contrast the following: *lord–lady (lady); baronet–dame (dame); governor–governess (governess).*

Most frequently what happens to words designating women as they become pejorated, however, is that they come to denote or connote sexual wantonness. *Sir* and *mister,* for example, remain titles of courtesy, but at some time *madam, miss,* and *mistress* have come to designate, respectively, a brothelkeeper, a prostitute, and an unmarried sexual partner of a male (Schulz, 1975:66).

Names for domestic helpers, if they are females, are frequently derogated. *Hussy,* for example, originally meant "housewife." *Laundress, needlewoman, spinster* ("tender of the spinning wheel"), and *nurse* all referred to domestic occupations within the home, and all at some point became slang expressions for prostitute or mistress.

Even kinship terms referring to women become denigrated. During the 17th century, *mother* was used to mean "a bawd"; more recently *mother (mothuh f———)* has become a common derogatory epithet (Cameron, 1974). Probably at some point in history every kinship term for females has been derogated (Schulz, 1975:66).

Terms of endearment for women also seem to follow a downward path. Such pet names as Tart, Dolly, Kitty, Polly, Mopsy, Biddy, and Jill all eventually became sexually derogatory (Schulz, 1975:67). *Whore* comes from the same Latin root as *care* and once meant "a lover of either sex."

Indeed, even the most neutral categorical designations—*girl, female, woman, lady*—at some point in their history have been used to connote sexual immorality. *Girl* originally meant "a child of either sex"; through the process of semantic degeneration it eventually meant "a prostitute." Although *girl* has lost this meaning, *girlie* still retains sexual connotations. *Woman* connoted "a mistress" in the early 19th century; *female* was a degrading epithet in the latter part of the 19th century; and when *lady* was introduced as a euphemism, it too became deprecatory. "Even so neutral a term as *person,* when it was used as substitute for *woman,* suffered [vulgarization]" (Mencken, 1963:350, quoted in Schulz, 1975:71).

Whether one looks at elite titles, occupational roles, kinship relationships, endearments, or age-sex categorical designations, the pattern is clear. Terms referring to females are pejorated—"become negative in the middle instances and abusive in the extremes" (Schulz, 1975:69). Such semantic derogation, however, is not evidenced for male referents. *Lord, baronet, father, brother, nephew, footman, bowman, boy, lad, fellow, gentleman, man, male,* and so on "have failed to undergo the derogation found in the history of their corresponding feminine designations" (Schulz, 1975:67). Interestingly, the male word, rather than undergoing derogation, frequently is replaced by a female referent when the speaker wants to debase a male. A weak man, for example, is referred to as a *sissy* (diminutive of *sister*), and an army recruit during basic training is called a *pussy*. And when one is swearing at a male, he is referred to as a *bastard* or a *son-of-a-*

bitch—both appellations that impugn the dignity of a man's mother.

In summary, these verbal practices are consistent with the gender stereotypes that we encounter in everyday life. Women are thought to be a part of man, nonautonomous, dependent, relegated to roles that require few skills, characteristically incompetent and immature, sexual objects, best defined in terms of their relations to men. Males are visible, autonomous and independent, responsible for the protection and containment of women, expected to occupy positions on the basis of their high achievement or physical power, assumed to be sexually potent, and defined primarily by their relations to the world of work. The use of the language perpetuates the stereotypes for both genders and limits the options available for self-definition.

REFERENCES

Adamsky, C. 1981. "Changes in pronominal usage in a classroom situation." *Psychology of Women Quarterly* 5:773–79.

Bendix, J. 1979. "Linguistic models as political symbols: Gender and the generic 'he' in English." In J. Orasanu, M. Slater, and L. L. Adler, eds., *Language, sex and gender: Does la différence make a difference?*, pp. 23–42. New York: New Academy of Science Annuals.

Cameron, P. 1974. "Frequency and kinds of words in various social settings, or What the hell's going on?" In M. Truzzi, ed., *Sociology for pleasure*, pp. 31–37. Englewood Cliffs, N.J.: Prentice-Hall.

Daly, M. 1973. *Beyond God the father.* Boston: Beacon Press.

DeStefano, J. S. 1976. Personal communication. Columbus: Ohio State University.

Hamilton, N., & Henley, N. 1982. "Detrimental consequences of the generic masculine usage." Paper presented to the Western Psychological Association meetings, Sacramento.

Key, M. R. 1975. *Male/female language.* Metuchen, N.J.: Scarecrow Press.

Kramarae, Cheris. 1975. "Woman's speech: Separate but unequal?" In Barrie Thorne and Nancy Henley, eds., *Language and sex: Difference and dominance*, pp. 43–56. Rowley, Mass.: Newbury House.

MacKay, D. G. 1983. "Prescriptive grammar and the pronoun problem." In B. Thorne, C. Kramarae, and N. Henley, eds., *Language, gender, and society*, pp. 38–53. Rowley, Mass.: Newbury House.

Martyna, W. 1978. "What does 'he' mean? Use of the generic masculine." *Journal of Communication* 28:131–38.

Martyna, W. 1980. "Beyond the 'he/man' approach: The case for nonsexist language." *Signs* 5:482–93.

Mencken, H. L. 1963. *The American language.* 4th ed. with supplements. Abr. and ed. R. I. McDavis. New York: Knopf.

Schneider, J., & Hacker, S. 1973. "Sex role imagery in the use of the generic 'man' in introductory texts: A case in the sociology of sociology." *American Sociologist* 8:12–18.

Schulz, M. R. 1975. "The semantic derogation of women." In B. Thorne and N. Henley, eds., *Language and sex: Difference and dominance*, pp. 64–75. Rowley, Mass.: Newbury House.

Shuster, Janet. 1973. "Grammatical forms marked for male and female in English." Unpublished paper. Chicago: University of Chicago.

Stanley, J. P. 1977. "Paradigmatic woman: The prostitute." In D. L. Shores, ed., *Papers in language variation.* Birmingham: University of Alabama Press.

Vanderbilt, A. 1972. *Amy Vanderbilt's etiquette.* Garden City, N.Y.: Doubleday.

Conversational Politics

MARY BROWN PARLEE

THE MALE CONVERSATIONAL STYLE: INTERRUPTIONS

Studies of sex as a variable in language have focused on the way conversations among males and among females differ from conversations between males and females. One striking set of findings concerns interruptions—which are violations of the general turn-taking rules. Sociologists Candace West and Donald Zimmerman, whose pioneering work at the University of California at Santa Barbara opened up the topic for scientific investigation, studied conversations in a variety of university settings (including a coffee shop, drugstore, and apartment). After recording and analyzing spontaneous conversations, they found that males interrupt females much more often than they interrupt other males, and more often than females interrupt either males or females. Here is a typical example of male interruptions, taken from the transcript of a conversation about term papers recorded by West and Zimmerman (the brackets indicate points when the man and woman are speaking at the same time):

FEMALE: How's your paper coming?
MALE: All right, I guess. *(pause)* I haven't done much in the past two weeks. *(pause)*
FEMALE: Yeah, know how that
$\begin{bmatrix} \text{can .} \end{bmatrix}$. .
MALE: $\begin{bmatrix} \text{Hey,} \end{bmatrix}$ ya got an extra cigarette? *(pause)*
FEMALE: Oh uh sure. *(hands him the pack)*
Like my $\begin{bmatrix} \text{pa . . .} \end{bmatrix}$
MALE: $\begin{bmatrix} \text{How bout} \end{bmatrix}$ a match?
FEMALE: 'Ere you go. Uh like my $\begin{bmatrix} \text{pa . . .} \end{bmatrix}$
MALE: $\begin{bmatrix} \text{Thanks.} \end{bmatrix}$ *(pause)*

FEMALE: Sure. *(pause)* I was gonna tell you $\begin{bmatrix} \text{my .} \\ \text{Hey,} \end{bmatrix}$. .
MALE: I'd really like ta talk but I gotta run. See you. *(long pause)*
FEMALE: Yeah.

The patterns of male–female interruptions were similar to those West and Zimmerman had observed in an earlier study between parents and children in a doctor's waiting room. Parents interrupted children much more often than the reverse. Perhaps, the investigators reasoned, they had biased their results by studying only conversations between persons who knew each other; people meeting each other for the first time might be more concerned with being polite, and any interruptions might be more evenly distributed between the sexes.

West and Zimmerman recorded conversations between pairs of previously unacquainted students, once again counting the interruptions in male–male, female–female, and male–female conversations. Concern over politeness apparently does not prevent violations of the turn-taking rules. In laboratory conversations between the sexes, males interrupted females more than females interrupted males. In the male–male and female–female conversations, the researchers frequently found that one partner interrupted the other more than vice versa.

West and Zimmerman argue that interruptions reflect and assert power differences, with the more powerful conversational partner interrupting the less powerful one more frequently. They define power not as an attribute of an individual but as something that is created in an interaction. The person who interrupts is creating and exercising power by violating the other's right to speak. The researchers believe, although they do not yet have data to prove it, that the display of power through interruptions will be found in other re-

lationships besides male–female and parent–child—
for example, in conversations between people who differ in race, class, or job status. In their view, such interruptions might be expected to occur even on a first
meeting—men might want to make a dominant first
impression to set the tone for any future relationship
that may occur.

West and Zimmerman's interpretation is similar to
one that psychologist Nancy Henley of the University
of Massachusetts in Lowell has offered concerning
body language. Henley studied couples in outdoor settings such as parks and zoos and found that men touch
women more frequently than the reverse. She proposes that touching, when it is not mutual, is a form
of body politics: the assertion of power is a significant
aspect of the nonverbal message. The nonverbal display of power is particularly important in hierarchical
relationships, she argues, because the message can be
denied verbally. Body politics thus represents a way in
which one group—defined by sex, race, class, job status—can exert control over another.

Sociologist Pamela Fishman has also studied sex
differences in male-female conversations, and found
that women "work" harder in conversations than
men, in the sense that they put more effort into keeping the conversation going even though they have less
control over what it is about. She placed tape recorders
in the homes of three couples and, with their consent,
recorded over 50 hours of naturally occurring conversations. All three couples described themselves
as being "liberated" from traditional sex-role
stereotypes.

Fishman analyzed the conversations to see how
often the men and women introduced topics that "succeeded" (were developed in further conversation between the partners) and how often they raised topics
that "failed" (the speaker was unable to get the listener
to pursue the subject). She found that topics introduced by men succeeded 96 percent of the time, while
topics introduced by women succeeded only 36 percent of the time (even though, overall, women initiated 62 percent of the topics in the conversations).

According to Fishman, the women used a number
of strategies to try to increase their chance of success,
strategies that men seldom used. Women asked questions (which in our culture demand an answer) nearly
three times as often as men did. They often used an
introductory attention-getter: "D'ya know what?" or
"This is really interesting." As a group, they said "you

know" ten times more than the men did, with the use
of the phrase increasing in individual conversations as
the man failed to respond to the topic.

One way men "killed" conversational topics introduced by women was to give a minimal response
("um"), sometimes after a pause, when the woman
had finished speaking. The minimal response prevents
the turn-taking rules from operating smoothly since
the topic is not jointly developed. Eventually, a topic
receiving only minimal response fails, and the conversation breaks down. By killing topics raised by
women, and by having their own topics almost always
succeed, men controlled the conversation with little effort, Fishman concluded. Women, on the other hand,
not only worked harder to have their own topics succeed, but also regularly took their turns talking about
a topic raised by the men.

The following two excerpts (slightly adapted for
readability) from dialogues recorded by Fishman illustrate the different treatment given a topic raised by a
man compared with the treatment of one raised by a
woman. In the first, the man begins by introducing the
topic of a newspaper article on Russian gymnast Olga
Korbut's visit to then-President Richard Nixon. The
woman responds with apparent interest, asking
questions:

MALE: What do you think your best weight is?
FEMALE: Ninety-five *heheheh*, Oh, I'd say 92.
MALE: I saw in the paper where Olga Korbut . . .
FEMALE: Yeah.
MALE: . . . went to see Dickie . . .
FEMALE: You're kidding! What for?
MALE: I don't know.
FEMALE: I can just imagine what she would go see
         Dick Nixon for. I don't get it.
MALE: I think she's on a tour of the United States.
FEMALE: Has he sat down and talked to her?
MALE: *(shows a picture in the paper) (conversation
         continues)*

The second full transcript is much longer than the
first. In it, the female "worked" for a full five minutes
to get a conversation going on an article she is reading.
The male responds minimally, and no conversation
develops.

FEMALE: I am really offended! That a magazine could
         publish this book. *(pause, during which male*

MUST WOMEN OPERATE FAMILY SWITCHBOARD?

ELLEN GOODMAN

BOSTON—The little girl doesn't understand.

A boy in her first-grade class has selected her as his recess quarry. All week he has pursued her, capturing her scarf, circling her with it, threatening to tie her up.

The look on her face as she tells us the story is puzzled and upset. She has brought home similar tales of playground encounters since Monday and laid them across the dinner table.

My friend, who is her mother, and amused by it all, explains again to the little girl, "That's because he likes you," But she still doesn't understand.

Finally, the mother turns to me, because I have been through it before, seen the tears of another first grader, offered the same explanations. "Tell her," says the mother in frustration.

I begin to form the analysis in my mind. I will tell her how the boy wants attention, doesn't know how to ask for it, only knows how to grab for it, confuses aggression with affection.

Suddenly I stop.

I hear an odd echo from the words inside my head. What is it? An echo of a hundred generations of women interpreting males to their daughters? An echo of a hundred generations of women teaching their daughters the fine art of understanding human behavior?

All at once I find myself reluctant to pass on that legacy. I am wary of teaching this little girl the way to analyze. I am not so sure we should raise more girls to be cultural interpreters for men, for families.

I look at my friend. This woman is admirably skilled in the task of transmitting one person's ideas and feelings to another. Indeed, she operates the switchboard of her family life.

The people in her home communicate with each other through her. She delivers peace messages

does not respond) That someone could put together this kind of book on muckraking sociology. This article I'm reading just *(pause)* just to aggravate myself, I guess, called *"(title of article)"* by Bill London. *(pause, no response from male)* It is the most sexist thing, overtly sexist-racist thing I have read in years.

MALE: Why?

Although the male's attention seems to be perking up, he in fact becomes less involved as the female continues to talk about the article. His responses become further apart and less conversational (*"umhum,"* grunts). At the end, it sounds as if she is talking to herself.

POWER AND GENDERLECTS

Some investigators think another area of sociolinguistic research also supports the idea that women's relative lack of power is reflected in their speech. Linguist Robin Lakoff has suggested that because their social roles are so different, men's and women's speech are almost different enough to be regarded as different dialects ("genderlects"). According to Lakoff, women's language (language used typically but not exclusively by women) has these characteristics:

1. Use of certain words rarely used by men (an example: *mauve*).
2. Use of "empty" adjectives (such as *divine* or *lovely*) that do not have connotations of power.

from one child to another; softens ultimatums from father to son; explains the daughter to her father. Under her constant monitoring, communication lines are kept open; one person stays plugged into the next.

Sometimes I wonder whether she has kept all these people together or kept them apart. Does she make it easier for them to understand each other, or does she stand between them, holding all the wires in her hands?

Last week, I watched Katharine Hepburn play the same role magnificently in *On Golden Pond.* She placed herself between the angry, acerbic, viciously amusing husband—Henry Fonda—and the world. She was his buffer and his interpreter—to gas station attendants, the postman, their daughter.

"He wasn't yelling at you," she tells the boy who comes to live with them. "He was yelling at life. Sometimes you have to look hard at a person and remember he's doing the best he can—just trying to find his way, like you."

Her caring was wondrous, inspiring, full of energy and love. But it was only when the boy confronted the old man, dialing directly, shortcutting the switchboard, that the man changed.

In Gail Godwin's new novel, *A Mother and Two Daughters,* there is another aging mother, still negotiating between her two "children" who are turning 40. She is like the woman in many of our autobiographies—the mother or grandmother behind the scenes.

How many families know each other only through such women? Some mothers, like the one in this movie and this book, have been forced to occupy the stormy fulcrum of family life. Others have chosen to be the power broker of human relationships. Some keep people at peace. Others keep them at bay. Sometimes the endless interpretation, especially of men by women, keeps couples together. Other times, it keeps men from explaining themselves.

I know it is a skill to be able to understand and analyze one person's motives and psyche to another. It requires time, attention and emotional dexterity to run these switchboards. Yet it also can overload the operator and cripple the people from talking across their own private lines.

Today, I feel peculiarly unwilling to explain the first-grade boy to the first-grade girl, peculiarly unwilling to initiate a six-year-old into this cult of communication.

I offer only friendship and sympathy. Those are things she doesn't have to struggle to understand.

---

3. Use of a questioning intonation at the end of a declarative statement (and more frequent use of tag questions as well).
4. Frequent use of modifiers or hedges ("sort of," "kind of," "I guess"). Such qualifiers, like the questioning intonation, decrease the assertiveness in the statement.
5. Intensive use of "so" with an adjective (as in "*so* many people").
6. Use of hypercorrect grammar and excessively polite speech.

All of these characteristics, Lakoff believes, render women's language expressive and polite rather than direct and informative. It is definitely nonassertive. Lakoff's conclusions were based largely on unsystem-atic observation and listening. But recent sociolinguistic research has provided evidence that her observations were, by and large, correct.

Cornell linguist Sally McConnell-Ginet has experimental evidence that women do use the diffident declarative (statements with a questioning tone) more often than do men. Her research involved asking men and women on the Cornell campus what the name of a particular building was. Women, she found, would answer with something that sounded like another question ("This is Olin Library?") more often than men.

Women, on the average, have been found to be less precise when describing the perceptual properties of a complex scene ("about six books" is a typical phrase); those differences may begin in children as young as four.

Psychologists Faye Crosby and Linda Nyquist, working at Boston University, directly tested Lakoff's hypothesis about the existence of "women's language." They developed a system for scoring speech on all six of the characteristics Lakoff proposed; the summary score could then be used to test whether women use "women's language" more than men do.

Crosby and Nyquist found that "women's language" was more frequently found, in a laboratory setting, in the speech of college women than in that of college men. In another experiment, Crosby and Nyquist studied the speech of police personnel and their clients in conversations at a police station. (Most of the clients came to the station with inquiries of one sort or another.) Crosby and Nyquist found that the clients—males and females—used "women's language more than the police personnel, who were both male and female." They suggest that "women's language" is used by people in particular roles—which tend to be those lacking power. Nothing is inherently female in "women's language."

If men's and women's speech styles are different in systematic ways, what are the social consequences? Recent research by Duke anthropologist William O'Barr suggests that people—male or female—who use the more tentative style of "women's language" are less likely to be believed by a jury. They lack the credibility of someone speaking in the "male" style. For much the same reasons, the British Broadcasting Corporation (BBC) for years prohibited women from reading the news over the air (and only recently broke with this tradition). Thus, speech may not only reflect power differences in the world, it may also create them through a self-fulfilling prophecy. (People who use the diffident declarative do not sound authoritative, therefore they should not be in positions of authority because they will not be believed. No one in a position of authority uses the diffident declarative. And so on.)

Research on how men and women talk to one another is only one example of a larger domain of study that is exploring the way power differences affect speaking styles and conversational interactions. Conversational politics, together with body language and the spoken word, may lie at the heart of the way we maintain roles, relationships, and the feelings that go with them. While researchers don't completely understand why we feel so one down when we're victims of conversational politics, sociolinguistic studies are providing at least the beginnings of some of the answers, don't you think?

A HANDSHAKE WILL DO

The International Federation in Zurich told soccer players Tuesday to act like men and stop hugging and kissing each other after scoring goals.

The Federation called on national soccer associations to take disciplinary measures against "unmanly behavior."

"The exultant outbursts of several players at

Reprinted from "A Handshake Will Do," compiled from staff and wire reports, Ohio State *Lantern*, November 17, 1980.

once jumping on top of each other, kissing and embracing is really excessive and inappropriate and should be banned from the football pitch," the Federation said in its September bulletin.

Supporting a call for sanctions made by its technical committee, the Federation said jubilation over a goal should be limited to congratulation by the team captain.

It conceded that top players get a lot of bonus money for scoring goals but said they should all the same be "reminded" to behave like adults.

Gynocide: Chinese Footbinding

ANDREA DWORKIN

FOOTBINDING EVENT

Instructions Before Reading Chapter

1. Find a piece of cloth 10 feet long and 2 inches wide
2. Find a pair of children's shoes
3. Bend all toes except the big one under and into the sole of the foot. Wrap the cloth around these toes and then around the heel. Bring the heel and toes as close together as possible. Wrap the full length of the cloth as tightly as possible
4. Squeeze foot into children's shoes
5. Walk
6. Imagine that you are 5 years old
7. Imagine being like this for the rest of your life

The origins of Chinese footbinding, as of Chinese thought in general, belong to that amorphous entity called antiquity. The 10th century marks the beginning of the physical, intellectual, and spiritual dehumanization of women in China through the institution of footbinding. That institution itself, the implicit belief in its necessity and beauty, and the rigor with which it was practiced lasted another 10 centuries. There were sporadic attempts at emancipating the foot—some artists, intellectuals, and women in positions of power were the proverbial drop in the bucket. Those attempts, modest as they were, were doomed to failure: footbinding was a political institution which reflected and perpetuated the sociological and psychological inferiority of women; footbinding cemented women to a certain sphere, with a certain function— women were sexual objects and breeders. Footbinding was mass attitude, mass culture—it was the key reality

in a way of life lived by real women—10 centuries times that many millions of them.

It is generally thought that footbinding originated as an innovation among the dancers of the Imperial harem. Sometime between the 9th and 11th centuries, Emperor Li Yu ordered a favorite ballerina to achieve the "pointed look." The fairy tale reads like this:

Li Yu had a favored palace concubine named Lovely Maiden who was a slender-waisted beauty and a gifted dancer. He had a six-foot-high lotus constructed for her out of gold; it was decorated lavishly with pearls and had a carmine lotus carpet in the center. Lovely Maiden was ordered to bind her feet with white silk cloth to make the tips look like the points of a moon sickle. She then danced in the center of the lotus, whirling about like a rising cloud.[1]

From this original event, the bound foot received the euphemism "Golden Lotus," though it is clear that Lovely Maiden's feet were bound loosely—she could still dance.

A later essayist, a true foot gourmand, described 58 varieties of the human lotus, each one graded on a 9-point scale. For example:

Type: Lotus petal, New moon, Harmonious bow, Bamboo shoot, Water chestnut
Specifications: plumpness, softness, fineness
Rank: Divine Quality (A-1), perfectly plump, soft and fine
Wondrous Quality (A-2), weak and slender
Immortal Quality (A-3), straight-boned, independent
Precious Article (B-1), peacocklike, too wide, disproportioned
Pure Article (B-2), gooselike, too long and thin

Seductive Article (B-3), fleshy, short, wide, round (the disadvantage of this foot was that its owner *could* withstand a blowing wind)

Excessive Article (C-1), narrow but insufficiently pointed

Ordinary Article (C-2), plump and common

False Article (C-3), monkeylike large heel (could climb)

The distinctions only emphasize that footbinding was a rather hazardous operation. To break the bones involved or to modify the pressure of the bindings irregularly had embarrassing consequences—no girl could bear the ridicule involved in being called a "large-footed demon" and the shame of being unable to marry.

Even the possessor of an A-1 Golden Lotus could not rest on her laurels—she had to observe scrupulously the taboo-ridden etiquette of bound femininity: (1) do not walk with toes pointed upwards; (2) do not stand with heels seemingly suspended in midair; (3) do not move skirt when sitting; (4) do not move feet when lying down. The same essayist concludes his treatise with this most sensible advice (directed to the gentlemen, of course):

> Do not remove the bindings to look at her bare feet, but be satisfied with its external appearance. Enjoy the outward impression, for if you remove the shoes and bindings the aesthetic feeling will be destroyed forever.[2]

Indeed. The real feet looked like Figure 1.

The physical process which created this foot is described by Howard S. Levy in *Chinese Footbinding: The History of a Curious Erotic Custom:*

> The success or failure of footbinding depended on skillful application of a bandage around each foot. The bandage, about two inches wide and ten feet long, was wrapped in the following way. One end was placed on the inside of the instep, and from there it was carried over the small toes so as to force the toes in and towards the sole. the large toe was left unbound. The bandage was then wrapped around the heel so forcefully that heel and toes were drawn closer together. The process was then repeated from the beginning until the entire bandage had been applied. The foot of the young child was

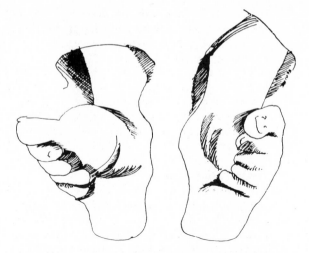

FIGURE 1   FEET: 3 TO 4 INCHES IN LENGTH

> subjected to a coercive and unremitting pressure, for the object was not merely to confine the foot but to make the toes bend under and into the sole and bring the heel and sole as close together as physically possible.[3]

A Christian missionary observed:

> The flesh often became putrescent during the binding and portions sloughed off from the sole; sometimes one or more toes dropped off.[4]

An elderly Chinese woman, as late as 1934, remembered vividly her childhood experience:

> Born into an old-fashioned family in P'ing-hsi, I was inflicted with the pain of footbinding when I was seven years old. I was an active child who liked to jump about, but from then on my free and optimistic nature vanished. Elder Sister endured the process from six to eight years of age [this means that it took Elder Sister two years to attain the 3-inch foot]. It was in the first lunar month of my seventh year that my ears were pierced and fitted with gold earrings. I was told that a girl had to suffer twice, through ear piercing and footbinding. Binding started in the second lunar month; mother consulted references in order to select an auspicious day for it. I wept and hid in a neighbor's home, but Mother found me, scolded me, and dragged me

home. She shut the bedroom door, boiled water, and from a box withdrew binding, shoes, knife, needle and thread. I begged for a one-day postponement, but Mother refused: "Today is a lucky day," she said. "If bound today, your feet will never hurt; if bound tomorrow they will." She washed and placed alum on my feet and cut the toenails. She then bent my toes toward the plantar with a binding cloth ten feet long and two inches wide, doing the right foot and then the left. She finished binding and ordered me to walk, but when I did the pain proved unbearable.

That night, Mother wouldn't let me remove the shoes. My feet felt on fire and I couldn't sleep; Mother struck me for crying. On the following days, I tried to hide but was forced to walk on my feet. Mother hit me on my hands and feet for resisting. Beatings and curses were my lot for covertly loosening the wrappings. The feet were washed and rebound after three or four days, with alum added. After several months, all toes but the big one were pressed against the inner surface. Whenever I ate fish or freshly killed meat, my feet would swell, and the pus would drip. Mother criticized me for placing pressure on the heel in walking, saying that my feet would never assume a pretty shape. Mother would remove the bindings and wipe the blood and pus which dripped from my feet. She told me that only with the removal of the flesh could my feet become slender. If I mistakenly punctured a sore, the blood gushed like a stream. My somewhat fleshy big toes were bound with small pieces of cloth and forced upwards, to assume a new-moon shape.

Every two weeks, I changed to new shoes. Each new pair was one- to two-tenths of an inch smaller than the previous one. The shoes were unyielding, and it took pressure to get into them. Though I wanted to sit passively by the K'ang, Mother forced me to move around. After changing more than ten pairs of shoes, my feet were reduced to a little over four inches. I had been in binding for a month when my younger sister started; when no one was around, we would weep together. In summer, my feet smelled offensively because of pus and blood; in winter, my feet felt cold because of lack of circulation and hurt if they got too near the K'ang and were struck by warm air currents. Four of the toes were curled in like so many dead caterpillars; no outsider would ever have believed that they be-

longed to a human being. It took two years to achieve the three-inch model. My toenails pressed against the flesh like thin paper. The heavily creased plantar couldn't be scratched when it itched or soothed when it ached. My shanks were thin, my feet became humped, ugly, and odiferous; how I envied the natural-footed![5]

Bound feet were crippled and excruciatingly painful. The woman was actually "walking" on the outside of toes which had been bent under into the sole of the foot. The heel and instep of the foot resembled the sole and heel of a high-heeled boot. Hard calloses formed; toenails grew into the skin; the feet were pus-filled and bloody; circulation was virtually stopped. The footbound woman hobbled along, leaning on a cane, against a wall, against a servant. To keep her balance she took very short steps. She was actually falling with every step and catching herself with the next. Walking required tremendous exertion.

Footbinding also distorted the natural lines of the female body. It caused the thighs and buttocks, which were always in a state of tension, to become somewhat swollen (which men called "voluptuous"). A curious belief developed among Chinese men that footbinding produced a most useful alteration of the vagina. A Chinese diplomat explained:

The smaller the woman's foot, the more wondrous become the folds of the vagina. (There was the saying: the smaller the feet, the more intense the sex urge.) Therefore marriages in Ta-t'ung (where binding is most effective) often take place earlier than elsewhere. Women in other districts can produce these folds artificially, but the only way is by footbinding, which concentrates development in this one place. There consequently develop layer after layer (of folds within the vagina); those who have personally experienced this (in sexual intercourse) feel a supernatural exaltation. So the system of footbinding was not really oppressive.[6]

Medical authorities confirm that physiologically footbinding had no effect whatsoever on the vagina, although it did distort the direction of the pelvis. The belief in the wondrous folds of the vagina of footbound woman was pure mass delusion, a projection of lust onto the feet, buttocks, and vagina of the crippled female. Needless to say, the diplomat's rationale for finding footbinding "not really oppressive" confused his "supernatural exaltation" with her misery and mutilation.

Bound feet, the same myth continues, "made the buttocks more sensual, [and] concentrated life-giving vapors on the upper part of the body, making the face more attractive."[7] If, due to a breakdown in the flow of these "life-giving vapors," an ugly woman was footbound and still ugly, she need not despair, for an A-1 Golden Lotus could compensate for a C-3 face and figure.

But to return to herstory, how did our Chinese ballerina become the millions of women stretched over 10 centuries? The transition from palace dancer to population at large can be seen as part of a class dynamic. The emperor sets the style, the nobility copies it, and the lower classes climbing ever upward do their best to emulate it. The upper class bound the feet of their ladies with the utmost severity. The Lady, unable to walk, remained properly invisible in her boudoir, an ornament, weak and small, a testimony to the wealth and privilege of the man who could afford to keep her—to keep her idle. Doing no manual labor, she did not need her feet either. Only on the rarest of occasions was she allowed outside of the incarcerating walls of her home, and then only in a sedan chair behind heavy curtains. The lower a woman's class, the less could such idleness be supported: the larger the feet. The women who had to work for the economic survival of the family still had bound feet, but the bindings were looser, the feet bigger—after all, she had to be able to walk, even if slowly and with little balance.

Footbinding was a visible brand. *Footbinding did not emphasize the differences between men and women—it created them,* and they were then perpetuated in the name of morality. Footbinding functioned as the Cerberus of morality and ensured female chastity in a nation of women who literally could not "run around." Fidelity, and the legitimacy of children, could be reckoned on.

The minds of footbound women were as contracted as their feet. Daughters were taught to cook, supervise the household, and embroider shoes for the Golden Lotus. Intellectual and physical restriction had the usual male justification. Women were perverse and sinful, lewd and lascivious, if left to develop naturally. The Chinese believed that being born a woman was payment for evils committed in a previous life. Foot-

binding was designed to spare a woman the disaster of another such incarnation.

Marriage and family are the twin pillars of all patriarchal cultures. Bound feet, in China, were the twin pillars of these twin pillars. Here we have the joining together of politics and morality, coupled to produce their inevitable offspring—the oppression of women based on totalitarian standards of beauty and a rampant sexual fascism. In arranging a marriage, a male's parents inquired first about the prospective bride's feet, then about her face. Those were her human, recognizable qualities. During the process of footbinding, mothers consoled their daughters by conjuring up the luscious marriage possibilities dependent on the beauty of the bound foot. Concubines for the Imperial harem were selected at tiny-foot festivals (forerunners of Miss America pageants). Rows upon rows of women sat on benches with their feet outstretched while audience and judges went along the aisles and commented on the size, shape and decoration of foot and shoes. No one, however, was ever allowed to touch the merchandise. Women looked forward to these festivals, since they were allowed out of the house.

The sexual aesthetics, literally the art of love, of the bound foot was complex. The sexual attraction of the foot was based on its concealment and the mystery surrounding its development and care. The bindings were unwrapped and the feet were washed in the woman's boudoir, in the strictest privacy. The frequency of bathing varied from once a week to once a year. Perfumes of various fragrances and alum were used during and after washing, and various kinds of surgery were performed on the calluses and nails. The physical process of washing helped restore circulation. The mummy was unwrapped, touched up, and put back to sleep with more preservatives added. The rest of the body was never washed at the same time as the feet, for fear that one would become a pig in the next life. Well-bred women were supposed to die of shame if men observed them washing their feet. The foot consisted, after all, of smelly, rotted flesh. This was naturally not pleasing to the intruding male, a violation of his aesthetic sensibility.

The art of the shoes was basic to the sexual aesthetics of the bound foot. Untold hours, days, months went into the embroidery of shoes. There were shoes for all occasions, shoes of different colors, shoes to hobble in, shoes to go to bed in, shoes for special occasions like birthdays, marriages, funerals, shoes which denoted age. Red was the favored color for bed shoes because it accentuated the whiteness of the skin of the calves and thighs. A marriageable daughter made about 12 pairs of shoes as a part of her dowry. She presented two specially made pairs to her mother-in-law and father-in-law. When she entered her husband's home for the first time, her feet were immediately examined by the whole family, neither praise nor sarcasm being withheld.

There was also the art of the gait, the art of sitting, the art of standing, the art of lying down, the art of adjusting the skirt, the art of every movement which involves feet. Beauty was the way feet looked and how they moved. Certain feet were better than other feet, more beautiful. Perfect three-inch form and utter uselessness were the distinguishing marks of the aristocratic foot. These concepts of beauty and status defined women: as ornaments, as sexual playthings, as sexual constructs. The perfect construct, even in China, was naturally the prostitute.

The natural-footed woman generated horror and repulsion in China. She was anathema, and all the forces of insult and contempt were used to obliterate her. Men said about bound feet and natural feet:

A tiny foot is proof of feminine goodness. . . .

Women who don't bind their feet look like men, for the tiny foot serves to show the differentiation. . . .

The tiny foot is soft and, when rubbed, leads to great excitement. . . .

The graceful walk gives the beholder mixed feelings of compassion and pity. . . .

Natural feet are heavy and ponderous as they get into bed, but tiny feet lightly steal under the coverlets. . . .

The large-footed woman is careless about adornment, but the tiny-footed frequently wash and apply a variety of perfumed fragrances, enchanting all who come into their presence. . . .

The natural foot looks much less aesthetic in walking. . . .

Everyone welcomes the tiny foot, regarding its smallness as precious. . . .

Men formerly so craved it that its possessor achieved harmonious matrimony. . . .

Because of its diminutiveness, it gives rise to a variety of sensual pleasures and love feelings. . . . [8]

Thin, small, curved, soft, fragrant, weak, easily inflamed, passive to the point of being almost inanimate—this was footbound woman. Her bindings created extraordinary vaginal folds; isolation in the bedroom increased her sexual desire; playing with the shriveled, crippled foot increased everyone's desire. Even the imagery of the names of various types of foot suggest, on the one hand, feminine passivity (lotuses, lilies, bamboo shoots, water chestnuts) and, on the other hand, male independence, strength, and mobility (lotus boats, large-footed crows, monkey foot). It was unacceptable for a woman to have those male qualities denoted by large feet. This fact conjures up an earlier assertion: footbinding did not formalize existing differences between men and women—it created them. One sex became male by virtue of having made the other sex some thing, something other, something completely polar to itself, something called female. In 1915, a satirical essay in defense of footbinding, written by a Chinese male, emphasized this:

The bound foot is the condition of a life of dignity for man, of contentment for woman. Let me make this clear. I am a Chinese fairly typical of my class. I pored too much over classic tests in my youth and dimmed my eyes, narrowed my chest, crooked my back. My memory is not strong, and in an old civilization there is a vast deal to learn before you can know anything. Accordingly among scholars I cut a poor figure. I am timid, and my voice plays me false in gatherings of men. But to my footbound wife, confined for life to her house except when I bear her in my arms to her palanquin, my stride is heroic, my voice is that of a roaring lion, my wisdom is of the sages. To her I am the world; I am life itself.[9]

Chinese men, it is clear, stood tall and strong on women's tiny feet.

The so-called art of footbinding was the process of taking the human foot, using it as though it were insensible matter, molding it into an inhuman form. Footbinding was the "art" of making living matter insensible, inanimate. We are obviously not dealing here with art at all, but with fetishism, with sexual psychosis. This fetish became the primary content of sexual experience for an entire culture for 1,000 years. The manipulation of the tiny foot was an indispensable prelude to all sexual experience. Manuals were written elaborating various techniques for holding and rubbing the Golden Lotus. Smelling the feet, chewing them, licking them, sucking them, all were sexually charged experiences. A woman with tiny feet was supposedly more easily maneuvered around in bed and this was no small advantage. Theft of shoes was commonplace. Women were forced to sew their shoes directly onto their bindings. Stolen shoes might be returned soaked in semen. Prostitutes would show their naked feet for a high price (there weren't many streetwalkers in China). Drinking games using cups placed in the shoes of prostitutes or courtesans were favorite pastimes. Tiny-footed prostitutes took special names like Moon Immortal, Red Treasure, Golden Pearl. No less numerous were the euphemisms for feet, shoes, and bindings. Some men went to prostitutes to wash the tiny foot and eat its dirt, or to drink tea made from the washing water. Others wanted their penises manipulated by the feet. Superstition also had its place— there was a belief in the curative powers of the water in which tiny feet were washed.

Lastly, footbinding was the soil in which sadism could grow and go unchecked—in which simple cruelty could transcend itself, without much effort, into atrocity. These are some typical horror stories of those times:

> A stepmother or aunt in binding the child's foot was usually much harsher than the natural mother would have been. An old man was described who delighted in seeing his daughters weep as the binding was tightly applied. . . . In one household, everyone had to bind. The main wife and concubines bound to the smallest degree, once morning and evening, and once before retiring. The husband and first wife strictly carried out foot inspections and whipped those guilty of having let the binding become loose. The sleeping shoes were so painfully small that the women had to ask the master to rub them in order to bring relief. Another rich man would flog his concubines on their tiny feet, one after another, until the blood flowed.[10]
>
> . . . About 1931 . . . bound-foot women unable to flee had been taken captive. The bandits, angered because of their captives' weak way of walking and inability to keep in file, forced the women to remove the bindings and socks and run about barefoot. They cried out in pain and were unable to move on in spite of the beatings. Each of the ban-

dits grabbed a woman and forced her to dance about on a wide field covered with sharp rocks. The harshest treatment was meted out to prostitutes. Nails were driven through their hands and feet; they cried aloud for several days before expiring. One form of torture was to tie up a woman so that her legs dangled in midair and place bricks around each toe, increasing the weight until the toes straightened out and eventually dropped off.[11]

END OF FOOTBINDING EVENT

One asks the same questions again and again, over a period of years, in the course of a lifetime. The questions have to do with people and what they do—the how and the why of it. How could the Germans have murdered 6,000,000 Jews, used their skins for lampshades, taken the gold out of their teeth? How could white people have bought and sold black people, hanged them and castrated them? How could "Americans" have slaughtered the Indian nations, stolen the land, spread famine and disease? How could the Indochina genocide continue, day after day, year after year? How is it possible? Why does it happen?

As a woman, one is forced to ask another series of hard questions: Why, everywhere, the oppression of women throughout recorded history? How could the Inquisitors torture and burn women as witches? How could men idealize the bound feet of crippled women? How and why?

The bound foot existed for 1,000 years. In what terms, using what measure, could one calculate the enormity of the crime, the dimensions of the transgression, the *amount* of cruelty and pain inherent in that 1,000-year herstory? In what terms, using what vocabulary, could one penetrate to the meaning, to the reality, of that 1,000-year herstory?

Here one race did not war with another to acquire food, or land, or civil power; one nation did not fight with another in the interest of survival, real or imagined; one group of people in a fever pitch of hysteria did not destroy another. None of the traditional explanations or justifications for brutality between or among peoples applies to this situation. On the contrary, here one sex mutilated (enslaved) the other in the interest of the *art* of sex, male–female *harmony*, role-definition, beauty.

Consider the magnitude of the crime.

CHINESE ARE KILLING NEWBORN GIRLS AT HIGH RATE

PEKING (UPI)—Chinese peasants are killing new-born girls at such a high rate that the nation's balance between males and females could be upset, an official publication said yesterday.

The *China Youth News* newspaper said female babies were being drowned or abandoned in the streets at such a rate that in 20 years Chinese men may have trouble finding women to marry.

In a study of rural communes, the report said three out of every five babies were boys. Because of reports of widespread killing and abandonment of unwanted female babies, the male to female ratio could be artificially damaged, it said.

"Is there anything on earth more heinous than this?" the report said.

China's tough birth control policy allows only one child per couple in urban areas and a maximum of two in the countryside without the risk of economic penalties and, in extreme cases, forced abortions.

For young couples clinging to "feudalistic thinking" that favors men over women, the pressure is to have a son even it if means killing a female baby born first, the newspaper said.

The Chinese traditionally believe a son can provide more labor as he grows up, take better care of his parents when they retire and carry on the family name.

A daughter often is viewed as a financial burden who eventually would change her name once married and care for her in-laws first.

Statistics of communes already indicate an imbalance in the sex ratio in the last two years because of the infanticide, *China Youth News* said.

"In two decades, if this phenomenon goes unchecked, there will appear a serious social problem in which a large group of men will be unable to find spouses."

"The law governing human development and propagation requires the rough balance between men and women in society," it said.

Men presently outnumber women 51 percent to 49 percent with 106 men to every 100 women in the nation of more than 1 billion people, according to census results announced last month.

The newspaper stressed the current marriage law demands both sons and daughters care for their parents and said in many cases the daughters provide better comfort and support.

Reprinted from the Columbus Citizen-Journal, *11 November 1982.*

Millions of women, over a period of 1,000 years, were brutally crippled, mutilated, in the name of erotica.

Millions of human beings, over a period of 1,000 years, were brutally crippled, mutilated, in the name of beauty.

Millions of men, over a period of 1,000 years, reveled in love-making devoted to the worship of the bound foot.

Millions of men, over a period of 1,000 years, worshiped and adored the bound foot.

Millions of mothers, over a period of 1,000 years, brutally crippled and mutilated their daughters for the sake of a secure marriage.

Millions of mothers, over a period of 1,000 years, brutally crippled and mutilated their daughters in the name of beauty.

But this thousand-year period is only the tip of an awesome, fearful iceberg: an extreme and visible expression of romantic attitudes, processes, and values organically rooted in all cultures, then and now. It demonstrates that man's love for woman, his sexual adoration of her, his human definition of her, his delight and pleasure in her, require her negation: physical crippling and psychological lobotomy. That is the very nature of romantic love, which is the love based on polar role definitions, manifest in herstory as well as in fiction—he glories in her agony, he adores her deformity, he annihilates her freedom, he will have her as sex object, even if he must destroy the bones in her feet to do it. Brutality, sadism, and oppression emerge as the substantive core of the romantic ethos. That ethos is the warp and woof of culture as we know it.

Women should be beautiful. All repositories of cultural wisdom from King Solomon to King Hefner agree: women should be beautiful. It is the reverence for female beauty which informs the romantic ethos, gives it its energy and justification. Beauty is transformed into that golden ideal, Beauty—rapturous and abstract. Women must be beautiful and Woman is Beauty.

Notions of beauty always incorporate the whole of a given societal structure, are crystallizations of its values. A society with a well-defined aristocracy will have aristocratic standards of beauty. In Western "democracy" notions of beauty are "democratic": even if a woman is not born beautiful, she can make herself *attractive*.

The argument is not simply that some women are not beautiful, therefore it is not fair to judge women on the basis of physical beauty; or that men are not judged on that basis, therefore women also should not be judged on that basis; or that men should look for character in women; or that our standards of beauty are too parochial in and of themselves; or even that judging women according to their conformity to a standard of beauty serves to make them into products, chattels, differing from the farmer's favorite cow only in terms of literal form. The issue at stake is different, and crucial. Standards of beauty describe in precise terms the relationship that an individual will have to her own body. They prescribe her mobility, spontaneity, posture, gait, the uses to which she can put her body. *They define precisely the dimensions of her physical freedom.* And, of course, the relationship between physical freedom and psychological development, intellectual possibility, and creative potential is an umbilical one.

In our culture, not one part of a woman's body is left untouched, unaltered. No feature or extremity is spared the art, or pain, of improvement. Hair is dyed, lacquered, straightened, permanented; eyebrows are plucked, penciled, dyed; eyes are lined, mascaraed, shadowed; lashes are curled, or false—from head to toe, every feature of a woman's face, every section of her body, is subject to modification, alteration. This alteration is an ongoing, repetitive process. It is vital to the economy, the major substance of male–female role differentiation, the most immediate physical and psychological reality of being a woman. From the age of 11 or 12 until she dies, a woman will spend a large part of her time, money, and energy on binding, plucking, painting, and deodorizing herself. It is commonly and wrongly said that male transvestites through the use of makeup and costuming caricature the women they would become, but any real knowledge of the romantic ethos makes clear that these men have penetrated to the core experience of being a woman, a romanticized construct.

The technology of beauty, and the message it carries, is handed down from mother to daughter. Mother teaches daughter to apply lipstick, to shave under her arms, to bind her breasts, to wear a girdle and high-heeled shoes. Mother teaches daughter concomitantly her role, her appropriate behavior, her place. Mother teaches daughter, necessarily, the psychology which defines womanhood: a woman must be beautiful, in order to please the amorphous and amorous Him. What we have called the romantic ethos operates as vividly in 20th-century America and Europe as it did in 10th-century China.

This cultural transfer of technology, role, and psychology virtually affects the emotive relationship between mother and daughter. It contributes substantially to the ambivalent love-hate dynamics of that relationship. What must the Chinese daughter/child have felt toward the mother who bound her feet? What does any daughter/child feel toward the mother who forces her to do painful things to her own body? The mother takes on the role of enforcer: she uses seduction, command, all manner of force to coerce the daughter to conform to the demands of the culture. It is because this role becomes her dominant role in the mother–daughter relationship that tensions and difficulties between mothers and daughters are so often unresolvable. The daughter who rejects the cultural norms enforced by the mother is forced to a basic rejection of her own mother, a recognition of the hatred and resentment she felt toward that mother, an alienation from mother and society so extreme that her own womanhood is denied by both. The daughter who internalizes those values and endorses those same processes is bound to repeat the teaching she was taught—

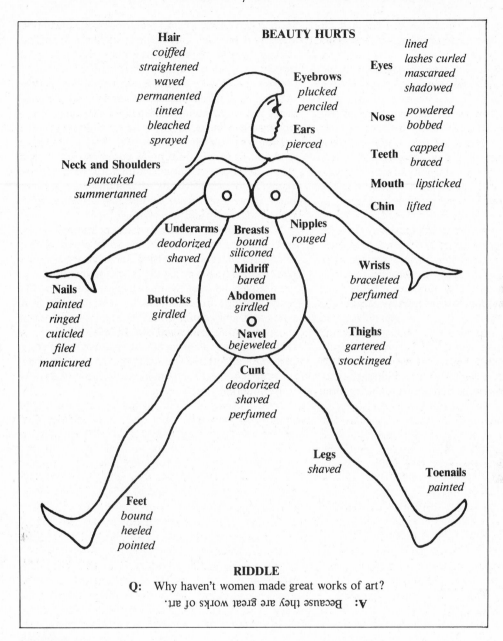

BEAUTY HURTS

Hair
coiffed
straightened
waved
permanented
tinted
bleached
sprayed

Eyebrows
plucked
penciled

Ears
pierced

Eyes
lined
lashes curled
mascaraed
shadowed

Nose
powdered
bobbed

Teeth
capped
braced

Mouth   *lipsticked*

Chin   *lifted*

Neck and Shoulders
pancaked
summertanned

Underarms
deodorized
shaved

Breasts
bound
siliconed

Nipples
rouged

Midriff
bared

Wrists
braceleted
perfumed

Nails
painted
ringed
cuticled
filed
manicured

Buttocks
girdled

Abdomen
girdled

Navel
bejeweled

Thighs
gartered
stockinged

Cunt
deodorized
shaved
perfumed

Legs
shaved

Toenails
painted

Feet
bound
heeled
pointed

RIDDLE

Q: Why haven't women made great works of art?

A: Because they are great works of art.

FIGURE 2

her anger and resentment remain subterranean, channeled against her own female offspring as well as her mother.

Pain is an essential part of the grooming process, and that is not accidental. Plucking the eyebrows, shaving under the arms, wearing a girdle, learning to walk in high-heeled shoes, having one's nose fixed, straightening or curling one's hair—these things *hurt.* The pain, of course, teaches an important lesson: no price is too great, no process too repulsive, no operation too painful for the woman who would be beautiful. *The tolerance of pain and the romanticization of that tolerance begins here,* in preadolescence, in socialization, and serves to prepare women for lives of childbearing, self-abnegation, and husband-pleasing. The adolescent experience of the "pain of being a woman" casts the feminine psyche into a masochistic mold and forces the adolescent to conform to a self-image which bases itself on mutilation of the body, pain happily suffered, and restricted physical mobility. It creates the masochistic personalities generally found in adult women: subservient, materialistic (since all value is placed on the body and its ornamentation), intellectually restricted, creatively impoverished. It forces women to be a sex of lesser accomplishment, weaker, as underdeveloped as any backward nation.

Indeed, the effects of that prescribed relationship between women and their bodies are so extreme, so deep, so extensive, that scarcely any area of human possibility is left untouched by it.

Men, of course, like a woman who "takes care of herself." The male response to the woman who is made up and bound is a learned fetish, societal in its dimensions. One need only refer to the male idealization of the bound foot and say that the same dynamic is operating here. Romance based on role differentiation, superiority based on a culturally determined and rigidly enforced inferiority, shame and guilt and fear of women and sex itself: all necessitate the perpetuation of these oppressive grooming imperatives.

The meaning of this analysis of the romantic ethos surely is clear. A first step in the process of liberation (women from their oppression, men from the unfreedom of their fetishism) is the radical redefining of the relationship between women and their bodies. The body must be freed, liberated, quite literally: from paint and girdles and all varieties of crap. Women must stop mutilating their bodies and start living in them. Perhaps the notion of beauty which will then organically emerge will be truly democratic and demonstrate a respect for human life in its infinite, and most honorable, variety.

NOTES

1. Howard S. Levy, *Chinese footbinding: The history of a curious erotic custom* (New York: W. Rawls, 1966), p. 39. Mr. Levy's book is the primary source for all the factual, historical information in this chapter.

2. Ibid., p. 112.

3. Ibid., pp. 25–26.

4. Ibid., p. 26.

5. Ibid., pp. 26–28.

6. Ibid., p. 141.

7. Ibid.

8. Ibid., p. 182.

9. Ibid., p. 89.

10. Ibid., p. 144.

11. Ibid., pp. 144–45.

Is the Binge-Purge Cycle Catching?

SUSAN SQUIRE

The college campus is surely the most fertile land of all for sowing the seeds of all types of chaotic eating behavior. Not only does college represent the challenge of separation—for many it means leaving home for the first time with all that that implies, from doing laundry to establishing your own curfew to selecting your own meals—but it also means an increase in social and academic pressures and a new anxiety about the future. In fact, the emotional stress of the experience causes an estimated 20 percent of college women to stop menstruating or have highly irregular menstrual periods.

The residential college environment itself, a community of peers with no parents around, provides endless opportunities for pass-along behaviors to soften classical collegiate depression. Drugs. Alcohol. Smoking. Dieting. Bingeing and vomiting. As the *Dartmouth Alumni Magazine* reported, "Inside a stall in a women's bathroom on campus, a woman wrote: 'I starve myself, then I gorge myself on garbage and make myself throw up afterward. I am getting out of control and am really disgusted with myself. Does anyone else have this problem?' In response, several others scrawled 'YES, YES, YES!'"

In an academically competitive college environment, the daily pressure and accompanying risk of developing a stress-related eating behavior mounts. A bingeing-and-dieting premed student at the Massachusetts Institute of Technology, where maybe 23 percent of the students are female, explained: "You can't come here and not know what you want to do. I know I can do the work required, but there are always those nagging doubts: Am I asking too much? Is this out of my range? At a place like this, with so many more men

than women, the pressure to look good in order to get your share of men may not be as intense, but the academic pressure causes lots of women I know to turn to food for alleviation. I'm certainly one of them."

David M. Garner and Paul E. Garfinkel, researchers at Toronto General Hospital, have surveyed thousands of women about eating behavior. Dr. Garner calculates that a significant percentage—about 12 percent—of college-age women have *serious* difficulties with their eating behavior. These women, Dr. Garner explains, worry about food almost constantly, and all use drastic weight-control techniques, including laxatives and diuretics, as well as vomiting.

Michael G. Thompson, Ph.D., and Donald M. Schwartz, Ph.D., surveyed "problem-free" and "anorexic-like" groups of normal-weight college women, and then compared the two groups with a third: women with anorexia nervosa. "The most dramatic finding," Thompson and Schwartz reported, "was the prevalence of anorexic-like behaviors among normally functioning college women. These women were not impaired in their work, though they often felt that they were struggling. The frequently intense feelings of inadequacy they reported appeared to arise from violation of high standards." As far as dieting goes, it was so widespread that the researchers found it impossible to measure. Almost all the anorexic-like women and many of the problem-free women simply said that they were *always* dieting. "The overall impression," the researchers wrote, "is of women—anorexic and anorexic-like and problem-free—experiencing their hunger as exaggerated and obscene, secretly wishing to gratify their impulse to eat, and constantly fighting this impulse."

In a study at Ohio State University at Columbus, Judith Cusin, M.S.W., and Dr. Dale Svendsen looked at three groups of female subjects: 944 sorority women, 38 upper-level dance majors, and 244 regular coeds. They found that 9 percent of the regulars, 16 percent of the sorority members, and 23 percent of the dance majors showed serious eating problems that indicated the symptoms of anorexia nervosa.

When they broke down the responses, the researchers found that 44.8 percent of the regular coeds, 53.5 percent of the sorority women, and 64.8 percent of the dancers answered "often," "very often," or "always" to "being preoccupied with a desire to be thinner."

It figures that sorority women, who have chosen a more socially oriented campus life and therefore tend to be even more appearance-conscious than other coeds, would score higher than the latter.

Holly, a member of a University of California at Berkeley sorority for three years, says that people often joke, "Oh, she's throwing up," when a member starts to lose weight. "I've walked into the bathroom at the sorority house and immediately had to leave because it smelled so bad from vomit." Though everyone in Holly's sorority worries about gaining weight, methods other than self-induced vomiting are frequently used to prevent the terror of fat. "A lot of us count calories, most everyone goes on fad diets, and people say things like, 'I wish I could have anorexia for just a week or two.'

"Drinking is big on campus," Holly adds, "and lots of girls save all their calories for drinking by taking diet pills so they don't eat. One girl passed out at a party because she'd taken so many diet pills and was drinking so much."

Renee, now a senior at the University of Arizona, says that she and other sorority members are open about their bulimic behavior, especially if they're bored. "We go out together and spend thirty dollars on food, knowing all the time that we'll throw it up. If we're somewhere with only one bathroom we take turns throwing up, but if there are stalls we'll do it at the same time."

Like most bulimic vomiters, between binges Renee tries to diet. On diet days, she avoids social eating whenever possible. Unlike others who engage in the behavior, Renee is not ashamed of it and is, in fact, completely open about it—with her boyfriends and family as well as with her sorority sisters. Once, her brother wanted her to join him and several other friends for dinner at a French restaurant. "I told him I was dieting and I couldn't go, but he insisted. I said okay, after I explained to him that I'd have to throw up the food. At the restaurant after the meal, I got up

and announced to the table that I was going off to vomit, and everyone applauded."

Renee doesn't binge and vomit every day; the longest she's gone without throwing up has been three weeks. But once she starts, often in response to being upset with her boyfriend and not being able to show her feelings, she usually repeats it three or four times, until she's so exhausted that she goes to sleep. Despite her efforts to control her weight, Renee now weighs 130 and she hates it. "I'm bothered more by being heavy than by bingeing and vomiting. My weight is my life, and when I'm fat, I'm completely miserable."

What does Renee plan to do about her problems? "Maybe once I graduate and get out of the sorority life, the bingeing and vomiting will go away. But I doubt it. The only real reason I want to stop is I'm afraid all the vomiting might affect my unborn children. Otherwise, I just want to be thin, whatever it takes."

Another high-risk area of college life where bingeing and vomiting is peer-approved is competitive athletics. Karen Lee-Benner, R.N., M.S.N., clinical coordinator of UCLA's Eating Disorders Clinic, treated two world-class gymnasts for bulimia. She says that at least one of those patients told her that the entire gymnastics team would binge and vomit together following a meet—a purely social thing.

One star gymnast on a major university's female team developed anorexia nervosa in conjunction with bingeing and vomiting up to 10 times a day and had to be hospitalized. She'd been in training since the age of 10. For all those years, keeping slim wasn't just desirable; her future as an athlete literally depended upon it. The day-in, day-out pressure to maintain control starting at such a young age, combined with a certain personality and family background, ultimately took a permanent toll.

Even without the intensified peer pressure that comes with sorority life or the performance pressure of competitive college athletics, there's always the famous "Freshman 10" to struggle with. It's the 10 pounds that so many women put on during their first year in college when they are separated from the family refrigerator and easy access to their mothers' marketing lists, and confront instead starch- and sugar-laden dorm food. Freshman men tend to lose weight that first year, which can be an annoyance to their female peers. "In a coed situation," says one Radcliffe sophomore, "you want to eat what the men eat, but you gain and they lose."

Jan had never had a weight or eating problem before entering college, but she slowly began to put on weight her first year at a large Midwestern university, where she lived on campus in a dorm. Jan went on a diet—lots of exercise and skipping meals—and dropped 15 pounds. Then the weight crept back on, the comments started from her mother, her sisters, and her boyfriend, and Jan began to binge regularly every time she was criticized about her weight. At a family picnic the summer before her junior year, "my cousin, who was anorexic, gave me the idea to vomit. She had learned it from her roommate, who'd heard it from her sister."

Once she'd learned about vomiting, Jan was eager to return to school where she could binge and vomit without her mother nosing around. She knew it was wrong, but thought it was a great way to be able to eat what she wanted. Ultimately, Jan's bingeing and vomiting severely disrupted her life.

Again, it was the combination of a stressful environment with a certain vulnerable personality and probably a particular family history *along with* constant indulgence in a potentially addictive behavior that created such danger for Jan. Relatively few college women would be suffering from all those factors at once; a far greater majority binge and diet or binge and vomit only on special occasions.

Overall, the very nature of the college lifestyle may create, especially for the female student, an upsetting tension between work orientation and dating concerns, says Dr. Raymond C. Hawkins, psychological consultant at the Austin (Texas) Stress Clinic. Interpersonal problems—such as rejection in love or academic difficulties—may precipitate overeating, with the expectation that "eating will make me feel better and who else cares about me anyway, so I might as well eat."

Dr. Hawkins's on-campus research shows a roller-coaster effect between interpersonal relationships, lack of self-esteem, and confusion over professional goals. Bingeing has a knockout effect on such conflicts. The feelings that follow the binge—guilt and self-deprecation, plus the fear of weight gain—distract the binger from the original problem. At this point, says Dr. Hawkins, the binger makes the logical error of redefining her problem as being the uncontrolled eating itself, or her overweight appearance.

Because Dr. Hawkins believes that working to clarify professional goals is a firmer ground on which to build self-esteem than romantic relationships, which tend to be much less controllable, he emphasizes career planning in treatment of college women with food-control problems. Feeling directed plays a crucial role in getting a college woman past chaotic eating behavior, Dr. Hawkins stresses. When she gets involved with a new idea or project, she relates to her body more positively, he says. The trick is to make that state of mind a permanent one by focusing closely on that idea or project—and channeling it to a viable direction for the future.

SECTION TWO
Socialization

We are born into a culture that has definite ideas about males and females—ideas about what is appropriate for males to do and what is appropriate for females to do. Further, our culture evaluates men's behaviors, occupations, and attitudes more highly than women's behaviors, occupations, and attitudes, and it assumes that what men do is what is right and normal. Women are judged in accordance with how well they do or do not conform to the male standard. This way of thinking is known as *androcentrism*.

Carol Gilligan, in "Woman's Place in Man's Life Cycle," shows how androcentrism has failed to take account of women's experiences. Theories of the "life cycle" have valued the autonomy and achievement associated with men's goals more highly than the attachment and intimacy associated with women's goals. To achieve a more balanced conception of human development, Gilligan suggests, both theory and research should direct more systematic attention to women's lives.

Learning about our culture begins in the family. We learn about gender not only from what our parents say but from what they do. Some theorists argue that women's universal mothering role has consequences both for the development of gender-related personality differences and for the unequal social status of women and men. Nancy Chodorow, in "Family Structure and Feminine Personality," proposes that as a result of the fact that women do the mothering, men are socioculturally superior but psychologically defensive and insecure, whereas women's secondary social value is somewhat countered by their gains in psychological strength and security.

Because the culture differentiates not only between males and females but between blacks and whites as well, the experiences of growing up as a black male, black female, white male, and white female differ. What a black mother, for example, needs to teach her sons and daughters to enable them to survive in a white-male-dominated society is different from what a white mother has to teach her children. The race differences are often compounded by class differences. In "'The Means to Put My Children Through': Child-Rearing Goals and Strategies among Black Female Domestic Servants," Bonnie Thornton Dill writes about the complexity of race and gender issues by focusing on the experiences of black female domestic workers. Contrasting the race and class advantages available to the white employers' children with the goals these women held for their own children, Dill outlines the reactions and responses of black female servants who reared white children to provide income and reared their own children to provide opportunities.

The family, then, provides an environment in which interactions establish deep-seated ideas about gender and gender-appropriate behavior. Today many parents claim that they raise their boys and girls without sex bias, but considerable evidence indicates that such claims have little validity. Letty Cottin Pogrebin, in "The Secret Fear

That Keeps Us from Raising Free Children," discusses a fear common to many parents: that if their children are allowed sex-role freedom, they may grow up to be gay. She presents evidence that such fears are groundless.

Gender socialization is carried out in schools as well as in homes. By the time children are in school, they not only have been socialized into their gender but are able to negotiate how and when gender will be socially salient. Barrie Thorne, in "Girls and Boys Together . . . But Mostly Apart," argues for this more complex idea of gender as a socially constructed variable. In her observations of elementary school children's social relations, she finds that the organization and definition of one's sex and gender depend on the particular situation, and that the children socialize each other.

Beyond the home, the school, and the peer group is a most important socialization agent: the mass media. Lessons are taught verbally and nonverbally. Children believe what they see and hear on television; indeed, they tend to believe that television characters are more real and more normal than the people they actually know. Thomas R. Forrest, in "Such a Handsome Face: Advertising Male Cosmetics," describes the burgeoning consumer market for male cosmetics and the advertising that sells them. Men are not expected to look "pretty" or "feminine," so the advertising campaigns stress *masculinity*—the products are intended for use "after shave," are a "workout for the face," "spell success," and so on.

Through the home, school, peers, and the mass media we are all continuously socialized and resocialized into our culture. Throughout our entire life span we are learning to be members of our society. We invite you to examine your own socialization experiences. How do the movies you see, the books you read, the music you listen to, the people you hang out with socialize you into particular ideas about sex and gender?

Woman's Place in Man's Life Cycle

CAROL GILLIGAN

In the second act of *The Cherry Orchard,* Lopakhin, the young merchant, describes his life of hard work and success. Failing to convince Madame Ranevskaya to cut down the cherry orchard to save her estate, he will go on, in the next act, to buy it himself. He is the self-made man, who, in purchasing "the estate where grandfather and father were slaves," seeks to eradicate the "awkward, unhappy life" of the past, replacing the cherry orchard with summer cottages where coming generations "will see a new life" (Act III). Elaborating this developmental vision, he describes the image of man that underlies and supports this activity: "At times when I can't go to sleep, I think: Lord, thou gavest us immense forests, unbounded fields and the widest horizons, and living in the midst of them we should indeed be giants." At which point, Madame Ranevskaya interrupts him, saying, "You feel the need for giants—They are good only in fairy tales, anywhere else they only frighten us" (Act II).

Conceptions of the life cycle represent attempts to order and make coherent the unfolding experiences and perceptions, the changing wishes and realities of everyday life. But the truth of such conceptions depends in part on the position of the observer. The brief excerpt from Chekhov's play (1904/1956) suggests that when the observer is a woman, the truth may be of a different sort. This discrepancy in judgment between men and women is the center of my consideration.

This essay traces the extent to which psychological theories of human development, theories that have informed both educational philosophy and classroom practice, have enshrined a view of human life similar to Lopakhin's while dismissing the ironic commentary

in which Chekhov embeds this view. The specific issue I address is that of sex differences, and my focus is on the observation and assessment of sex differences by life-cycle theorists. In talking about sex differences, however, I risk the criticism which such generalization invariably invites. As Virginia Woolf said, when embarking on a similar endeavor: "When a subject is highly controversial—and any question about sex is that—one cannot hope to tell the truth. One can only show how one came to hold whatever opinion one does hold" (1929:4).

At a time when efforts are being made to eradicate discrimination between the sexes in the search for equality and justice, the differences between the sexes are being rediscovered in the social sciences. This discovery occurs when theories formerly considered to be sexually neutral in their scientific objectivity are found instead to reflect a consistent observational and evaluative bias. Then the presumed neutrality of science, like that of language itself, gives way to the recognition that the categories of knowledge are human constructions. The fascination with point of view and the corresponding recognition of the relativity of truth that has informed the fiction of the twentieth century begin to infuse our scientific understanding as well when we begin to notice how accustomed we have become to seeing life through men's eyes.

A recent discovery of this sort pertains to the apparently innocent classic by Strunk and White (1959), *The Elements of Style.* The Supreme Court ruling on the subject of discrimination in classroom texts led one teacher of English to notice that the elementary rules of English usage were being taught through examples which counterposed the birth of Napoleon, the writings of Coleridge, and statements such as "He was an interesting talker, a man who had traveled all over the world and lived in half a dozen countries" (p. 7) with "Well, Susan, this is a fine mess you are in" (p.

Reprinted from *Harvard Educational Review* 49, no. 4 (November 1979):431–446.

3) or, less drastically, "He saw a woman accompanied by two children, walking slowly down the road" (p. 8).

Psychological theorists have fallen as innocently as Strunk and White into the same observational bias. Implicitly adopting the male life as the norm, they have tried to fashion women out of a masculine cloth. It all goes back of course, to Adam and Eve, a story which shows, among other things, that if you make a woman out of a man, you are bound to get into trouble. In the life cycle, as in the Garden of Eden, it is the woman who has been the deviant.

The penchant of developmental theorists to project a masculine image, and one that appears frightening to women, goes back at least to Freud (1905/1961), who built this theory of psychosexual development around the experiences of the male child that culminate in the Oedipus complex. In the 1920s, Freud struggled to resolve the contradictions posed for his theory by the different configuration of female sexuality and the different dynamics of the young girl's early family relationships. After trying to fit women into his masculine conception, seeing them as envying that which they missed, he came instead to acknowledge, in the strength and persistence of women's pre-Oedipal attachments to their mothers, a developmental difference. However, he considered this difference in women's development to be responsible for what he saw as women's developmental failure.

Deprived by nature of the impetus for a clear-cut Oedipal resolution, women's superego, the heir to the Oedipus complex, consequently was compromised. It was never, Freud observed, "so inexorable, so impersonal, so independent of its emotional origins as we require it to be in men" (1925/1961:257). From this observation of difference, "that for women the level of what is ethically normal is different from what it is in men" (p. 257), Freud concluded that "women have less sense of justice than men, that they are less ready to submit to the great exigencies of life, that they are more often influenced in their judgments by feelings of affection and hostility" (pp. 257–58).

Chodorow (1974, 1978) addresses this evaluative bias in the assessment of sex differences in her attempt to account for "the reproduction within each generation of certain general and nearly universal differences that characterize masculine and feminine personality and roles" (1974:43). Writing from a psychoanalytic perspective, she attributes these continuing differences between the sexes not to anatomy but rather to "the

fact that women, universally, are largely responsible for early child care and for (at least) later female socialization" (1974:43). Because this early social environment differs for and is experienced differently by male and female children, basic sex differences recur in personality development. As a result, "in any given society, feminine personality comes to define itself in relation and connection to other people more than masculine personality does. (In psychoanalytic terms, women are less individuated than men; they have more flexible ego boundaries)" (1974:44).

In her analysis, Chodorow relies primarily on Stoller's research on the development of gender identity and gender-identity disturbances. Stoller's work indicates that male and female identity, the unchanging core of personality formation, is "with rare exception firmly and irreversibly established for both sexes by the time a child is around three" (Chodorow, 1978:150). Given that for both sexes the primary caretaker in the first three years of life is typically female, the interpersonal dynamics of gender identity formation are different for boys and girls. Female identity formation takes place in a context of ongoing relationship as "mothers tend to experience their daughters as more like, and continuous with, themselves. Correspondingly, girls tend to remain part of the dyadic primary mother–child relationship itself. This means that a girl continues to experience herself as involved in issues of merging and separation, and in an attachment characterized by primary identification and the fusion of identification and object choice" (1978:166).

In contrast, "mothers experience their sons as a male opposite" and, as a result, "boys are more likely to have been pushed out of the preoedipal relationship and to have had to curtail their primary love and sense of empathic tie with their mother" (1978:166). Consequently, boys' development entails a "more emphatic individuation and a more defensive firming of ego boundaries." For boys, but not for girls, "issues of differentiation have become intertwined with sexual issues" (1978:167).

Thus Chodorow refutes the masculine bias of psychoanalytic theory, claiming that the existence of sex differences in the early experiences of individuation and relationship "does not mean that women have 'weaker ego boundaries' than men or are more prone to psychosis" (1978:167). What it means instead is that "the earliest mode of individuation, the primary construction of the ego and its inner object-world, the

earliest conflicts and the earliest unconscious definitions of self, the earliest threats to individuation, and
the earliest anxieties which call up defenses, all differ
for boys and girls because of differences in the character of the early mother–child relationship for each"
(1978:167). Because of these differences, "girls emerge
from this period with a basis for 'empathy' built into
their primary definition of self in a way that boys do
not" (1978:167). Chodorow thus replaces Freud's negative and derivative description of female psychology
with a more positive and direct account of her own:

> Girls emerge with a stronger basis for experiencing
> another's needs and feelings as one's own (or of
> thinking that one is so experiencing another's needs
> and feelings). Furthermore, girls do not define
> themselves in terms of the denial of preoedipal re-
> lational modes to the same extent as do boys.
> Therefore, regression to these modes tends not to
> feel as much a basic threat to their ego. From very
> early, then, because they are parented by a person
> of the same gender ... girls come to experience
> themselves as less differentiated than boys, as more
> continuous with and related to the external object
> world, and as differently oriented to their inner ob-
> ject-world as well. [1978:167]

Consequently, "issues of dependency, in particular,
are handled and experienced differently by men and
women" (Chodorow, 1974:44). For boys and men,
separation and individuation are critically tied to gender identity since separation from the mother is essential for the development of masculinity. "For girls and
women, by contrast, issues of femininity or feminine
identity are not problematic in the same way
(1974:44); they do not depend on the achievement of
separation from the mother or on the progress of individuation. Since, in Chodorow's analysis, masculinity is defined through separation while femininity is
defined through attachment, male gender identity will
be threatened by intimacy while female gender identity will be threatened by individuation. Thus males
will tend to have difficulty with relationships while females will tend to have problems with separation. The
quality of embeddedness in social interaction and personal relationships that characterizes women's lives in
contrast to men's, however, becomes not only a descriptive difference but also a developmental liability

when the milestones of childhood and adolescent development are described by markers of increasing separation. Then women's failure to separate becomes by
definition a failure to develop.

The sex differences in personality formation that
Chodorow delineates in her analysis of early childhood relationships, as well as the bias she points out
in the evaluation of these differences, reappear in the
middle childhood years in the studies of children's
games. Children's games have been considered by
Mead (1934) and Piaget (1932/1965) as the crucible of
social development during the school years. In games
children learn to take the role of the other and come
to see themselves through another's eyes. In games
they learn respect for rules and come to understand
the ways rules can be made and changed.

Lever (1976), considering the peer group to be the
agent of socialization during the elementary school
years and play to be a major activity of socialization
at that time, set out to discover whether there were sex
differences in the games that children play. Studying
181 fifth-grade, white, middle-class Connecticut children, ages 10 and 11, she observed the organization
and structure of their playtime activities. She watched
the children as they played during the school recess,
lunch, and in physical education class, and, in addition, kept diaries of their accounts as to how they
spent their out-of-school time.

From this study, Lever reports the following sex differences: boys play more out of doors than girls do;
boys more often play in large and age-heterogeneous
groups; they play competitive games more often than
girls do, and their games last longer than girls' games
(Lever, 1976). The last is in some ways the most interesting finding. Boys' games appeared to last longer not
only because they required a higher level of skill and
were thus less likely to become boring, but also because when disputes arose in the course of a game, the
boys were able to resolve the disputes more effectively
than the girls: "During the course of this study, boys
were seen quarrelling all the time, but not once was a
game terminated because of a quarrel and no game
was interrupted for more than seven minutes. In the
gravest debates, the final word was always to 'repeat
the play,' generally followed by a chorus of 'cheater's
proof'" (1976:482). In fact, it seemed that the boys enjoyed the legal debates as much as they did the game
itself, and even marginal players of lesser size or skill
participated equally in these recurrent squabbles. In

contrast, the eruption of disputes among girls tended to end the game.

Thus Lever extends and corroborates the observations reported by Piaget (1932/1965) in his naturalistic study of the rules of the game, where he found boys becoming increasingly fascinated with the legal elaboration of rules and the development of fair procedures for adjudicating conflicts, a fascination that, he noted, did not hold for girls. Girls, Piaget observed, had a more "pragmatic" attitude toward rules, "regarding a rule as good as long as the game repaid it" (p. 83). As a result, he considered girls to be more tolerant in their attitudes toward rules, more willing to make exceptions, and more easily reconciled to innovations. However, and presumably as a result, he concluded that the legal sense which he considered essential to moral development "is far less developed in little girls than in boys" (p. 77).

This same bias that led Piaget to equate male development with child development also colors Lever's work. The assumption that shapes her discussion of results is that the male model is the better one. It seems, in any case, more adaptive, since, as Lever points out, it fits the requirements Riesman (1961) describes for success in modern corporate life. In contrast, the sensitivity and care for the feelings of others that girls develop through their primarily dyadic play relationships have little market value and can even impede professional success. Lever clearly implies that, given the realities of adult life, if a girl does not want to be dependent on men, she will have to learn to play like a boy.

Since Piaget argues that children learn the respect for rules necessary for moral development by playing rule-bound games, and Kohlberg (1971) adds that these lessons are most effectively learned through the opportunities for role-taking that arise in the course of resolving disputes, the moral lessons inherent in girls' play appear to be fewer than for boys. Traditional girls' games like jump rope and hopscotch are turn-taking games where competition is indirect in that one person's success does not necessarily signify another's failure. Consequently, disputes requiring adjudication are less likely to occur. In fact, most of the girls whom Lever interviewed claimed that when a quarrel broke out, they ended the game. Rather than elaborating a system of rules for resolving disputes, girls directed their efforts instead toward sustaining affective ties.

Lever concludes that from the games they play boys learn both independence and the organizational skills necessary for coordinating the activities of large and diverse groups of people. By participating in controlled and socially approved competitive situations, they learn to deal with competition in a relatively forthright manner—to play with their enemies and compete with their friends, all in accordance with the rules of the game. In contrast, girls' play tends to occur in smaller, more intimate groups, often the best-friend dyad, and in private places. This play replicates the social pattern of primary human relationships in that its organization is more cooperative and points less toward learning to take the role of the generalized other than it does toward the development of the empathy and sensitivity necessary for taking the role of the particular other.

Chodorow's analysis of sex differences in personality formation in early childhood is thus extended by Lever's observations of sex differences in the play activities of middle childhood. Together these accounts suggest that boys and girls arrive at puberty with a different interpersonal orientation and a different range of social experiences. While Sullivan (1953), tracing the sequence of male development, posits the experience of a close same-sex friendship in preadolescence as necessary for the subsequent integration of sexuality and intimacy, no corresponding account is available to describe girls' development at this critical juncture. Instead, since adolescence is considered a crucial time for separation and individuation, the period of "the second individuation process" (Blos, 1967), it has been in adolescence that female development has appeared most divergent and thus most problematic.

"Puberty," Freud said, "which brings about so great an accession of libido in boys, is marked in girls by a fresh wave of repression" (1905/1961:220) necessary for the transformation of the young girls' "masculine sexuality" into the "specifically feminine" sexuality of her adulthood. Freud posits this transformation on the girl's acknowledgement and acceptance of "the fact of her castration." In his account puberty brings for girls a new awareness of "the wound to her narcissism" and leads her to develop, "like a scar, a sense of inferiority" (1925/1961:253). Since adolescence is, in Erikson's expansion of Freud's psychoanalytic account, the time when the ego takes on an identity which confirms the individual in relation to society, the girl arrives at this juncture in development either psychologically at risk or with a different agenda.

The problem that female adolescence presents for psychologists of human development is apparent in Erikson's account. Erikson (1950) charts eight stages of psychosocial development, in which adolescence is the fifth. The task of this stage is to forge a coherent sense of self, to verify an identity that can span the discontinuity of puberty and make possible the adult capacity to love and to work. The preparation for the successful resolution of the adolescent identity crisis is delineated in Erikson's description of the preceding four stages. If in infancy the initial crisis of trust versus mistrust generates enough hope to sustain the child through the arduous life cycle that lies ahead, the task at hand clearly becomes one of individuation. Erikson's second stage centers on the crisis of autonomy versus shame and doubt, the walking child's emerging sense of separateness and agency. From there, development goes on to the crisis of initiative versus guilt, successful resolution of which represents a further move in the direction of autonomy. Next, following the inevitable disappointment of the magical wishes of the Oedipal period, the child realizes with respect to his parents that to bear them he must first join them and learn to do what they do so well. Thus in the middle childhood years, development comes to hinge on the crisis of industry versus inferiority, as the demonstration of competence becomes critical to the child's developing self-esteem. This is the time when children strive to learn and master the technology of their culture in order to recognize themselves and be recognized as capable of becoming· adults. Next comes adolescence, the celebration of the autonomous, initiating, industrious self through the forging of an identity based on an ideology that can support and justify adult commitments. But about whom is Erikson talking?

Once again it turns out to be the male child—the coming generation of men like George Bernard Shaw, William James, Martin Luther, and Mahatma Gandhi—who provide Erikson with his most vivid illustrations. For the woman, Erikson says, the sequence is a bit different. She holds her identity in abeyance as she prepares to attract the man by whose name she will be known, by whose status she will be defined, the man who will rescue her from emptiness and loneliness by filling "the inner space" (Erikson, 1968). While for men, identity precedes intimacy and generativity in the optimal cycle of human separation and attachment, for women these tasks seem instead to be fused. Intimacy precedes, or rather goes along with, identity as the female comes to know herself as she is known, through her relationships with others.

Two things are essential to note at this point. The first is that, despite Erikson's observation of sex differences, his chart of life-cycle stages remains unchanged: identity continues to precede intimacy as the male diagonal continues to define his life-cycle conception. The second is that in the male life cycle there is little preparation for the intimacy of the first adult stage. Only the initial stage of trust versus mistrust suggests the type of mutuality that Erikson means by intimacy and generativity and Freud by genitality. The rest is separateness, with the result that development itself comes to be identified with separation and attachments appear as developmental impediments, as we have repeatedly found to be the case in the assessment of women.

Erikson's description of male identity as forged in relation to the world and of female identity as awakened in a relationship of intimacy with another person, however controversial, is hardly new. In Bettelheim's discussion of fairy tales in *The Uses of Enchantment* (1976) an identical portrayal appears. While Bettelheim argues, in refutation of those critics who see in fairy tales a sexist literature, that opposite models exist and could readily be found, nevertheless the ones upon which he focues his discussion of adolescence conform to the pattern we have begun to observe.

The dynamics of male adolescence are illustrated archetypically by the conflict between father and son in "The Three Languages" (Bettelheim, 1976). Here a son, considered hopelessly stupid by his father, is given one last chance at education and sent for a year to study with a famous master. But when he returns, all he has learned is "what the dogs bark" (p. 97). After two further attempts of this sort, the father gives up in disgust and orders his servants to take the child into the forest and kill him. The servants, however, those perpetual rescuers of disowned and abandoned children, take pity on the child and decide simply to leave him in the forest. From there, his wanderings take him to a land beset by furious dogs whose barking permits nobody to rest and who periodically devour one of the inhabitants. Now it turns out that our hero has learned just the right thing: he can talk with the dogs and is able to quiet them, thus restoring peace to the land. The other knowledge he acquires serves him equally well, and he emerges triumphant from his adolescent confrontation with his father, a giant of the life-cycle conception.

In contrast, the dynamics of female adolescence are depicted through the telling of a very different story. In the world of the fairy tale, the girl's first bleeding is followed by a period of intense passivity in which nothing seems to be happening. Yet in the deep sleep of Snow White and Sleeping Beauty, Bettelheim sees that inner concentration which he considers to be the necessary counterpart to the activity of adventure. The adolescent heroines awaken from their sleep not to conquer the world but to marry the prince. Their feminine identity is inwardly and interpersonally defined. As in Erikson's observation, for women, identity and intimacy are more intricately conjoined. The sex differences depicted in the world of the fairy tales, like the fantasy of the woman warrior in Maxine Hong Kingston's (1977) autobiographical novel (which in turn echoes the old stories of Troilus and Cressida and Tancred and Chlorinda) indicate repeatedly that active adventure is a male activity, and if women are to embark on such endeavors, they must at least dress like men.

These observations about sex difference support the conclusion reached by McClelland, that "sex role turns out to be one of the most important determinants of human behavior. Psychologists have found sex differences in their studies from the moment they started doing empirical research" (1975:81). But since it is difficult to say "different" without saying "better" or "worse," and since there is a tendency to construct a single scale of measurement, and since that scale has been derived and standardized on the basis of men's observations and interpretations of research data predominantly or exclusively drawn from studies of males, psychologists have tended, in McClelland's words, "to regard male behavior as the 'norm' and female behavior as some kind of deviation from that norm" (p. 81). Thus when women do not conform to the standards of psychological expectation, the conclusion has generally been that something is wrong with the women.

What Horner (1972) found to be wrong with women was the anxiety they showed about competitive achievement. From the beginning, research on human motivation using the Thematic Apperception Test (TAT) was plagued by evidence of sex differences which appeared to confuse and complicate data analysis. The TAT presents for interpretation an ambiguous cue—a picture about which a story is to be written or a brief story stem to be completed. Such stories in reflecting projective imagination are considered to reveal the ways in which people construe what they perceive—that is, the concepts and interpretations they bring to their experience and thus presumably the kind of sense that they make of their lives. Prior to Horner's work, it was clear that women made a different kind of sense than men of situations of competitive achievement, that in some way they saw the situation differently or the situation aroused in them some different response.

On the basis of his studies of men, McClelland (1961) had divided the concept of achievement motivation into what appeared to be its two logical components, a motive to approach success ("hope success") and a motive to avoid failure ("fear failure"). When Horner (1972) began to analyze the problematic projective data on female achievement motivation, she identified as a third category the unlikely motivation to avoid success ("fear success"). Women appeared to have a problem with competitive achievement, and that problem seemed, in Horner's interpretation, to emanate from a perceived conflict between femininity and success, the dilemma of the female adolescent who struggles to integrate her feminine aspirations and the identifications of her early childhood with the more masculine competence she has acquired at school. Thus Horner reports, "When success is likely or possible, threatened by the negative consequences they expect to follow success, young women become anxious and their positive achievement strivings become thwarted" (1972:171). She concludes that this fear exists because for most women, the anticipation of success in competitive achievement activity, especially against men, produces anticipation of certain negative consequences, for example, threat of social rejection and loss of femininity."

It is, however, possible to view such conflicts about success in a different light. Sassen (forthcoming), on the basis of her reanalysis of the data presented in Horner's thesis, suggests that the conflicts expressed by the women might instead indicate "a heightened perception of the 'other side' of competitive success, that is, the great emotional costs of success achieved through competition, or an understanding which, while confused, indicates an awareness that something is rotten in the state in which success is defined as having better grades than everyone else." Sassan points out that Horner found success anxiety to be present in women only when achievement was directly competitive, that is, when one person's success was at the expense of another's failure.

From Horner's examples of fear of success, it is impossible to differentiate between neurotic or realistic anxiety about the consequences of achievement, the questioning of conventional definitions of success, and the discovery of personal goals other than conventional success. The construction of the problem posed by success as a problem of identity and ideology that appears in Horner's illustrations, if taken at face value rather than assumed to be derivative, suggests Erikson's distinction between a conventional and neohumanist identity, or, in cognitive terms, the distinction between conventional and postconventional thought (Loevinger & Wessler, 1970; Inhelder & Piaget, 1958; Kohlberg, 1971; Perry, 1968).

In his elaboration of the identity crisis, Erikson discusses the life of George Bernard Shaw to illustrate the young person's sense of being co-opted prematurely by success in a career he cannot wholeheartedly endorse. Shaw at seventy, reflecting upon his life, describes his crisis at the age of twenty as one caused not by lack of success or the absence of recognition, but by too much of both:

> I made good in spite of myself, and found, to my dismay, that Business, instead of expelling me as the worthless imposter I was, was fastening upon me with no intention of letting me go. Behold me, therefore, in my twentieth year, with a business training, in an occupation which I detested as cordially as any sane person lets himself detest anything he cannot escape from. In March, 1876, I broke loose. [Quoted in Erikson, 1968:143]

At which point Shaw settled down to study and to write as he pleased. Hardly interpreted as evidence of developmental difficulty, of neurotic anxiety about achievement and competition, Shaw's refusal suggested to Erikson "the extraordinary workings of an extraordinary personality coming to the fore" (1968:144).

We might on these grounds begin to ask not why women have conflicts about succeeding but why men show such readiness to adopt and celebrate a rather narrow vision of success. Remembering Piaget's observation, corroborated by Lever, that boys in their games are concerned more with rules while girls are more concerned with relationships, often at the expense of the game itself; remembering also that, in Chodorow's analysis, men's social orientation is positional and women's orientation is personal, we begin to understand why, when Anne becomes John in Horner's tale of competitive success and the stories are written by men, fear of success tends to disappear. John is considered by other men to have played by the rules and won. He has the *right* to feel good about his success. Confirmed in his sense of his own identity as separate from those who, compared to him, are less competent, his positional sense of self is affirmed. For Anne, it is possible that the position she could obtain by being at the top of her medical school class may not, in fact, be what she wants.

"It is obvious," Virginia Woolf said, "that the values of women differ very often from the values which have been made by the other sex" (1929:76). Yet, she adds, it is the masculine values that prevail. As a result, women come to question the "normality" of their feelings and to alter their judgments in deference to the opinion of others. In the nineteenth-century novels written by women, Woolf sees at work "a mind slightly pulled from the straight, altering its clear vision in the anger and confusion of deference to external authority" (1929:77). The same deference that Woolf identifies in nineteenth-century fiction can be seen as well in the judgments of twentieth-century women. Women's reluctance to make moral judgments, the difficulty they experience in finding or speaking publicly in their own voice, emerge repeatedly in the form of qualification and self-doubt, in intimations of a divided judgment, in public and private assessments which are fundamentally at odds (Gilligan, 1977).

Yet the deference and confusion that Woolf criticizes in women derive from the values she sees as their strength. Women's deference is rooted not only in their social circumstances but also in the substance of their moral concern. Sensitivity to the needs of others and the assumption of responsibility for taking care lead women to attend to voices other than their own and to include in their judgment other points of view. Women's moral weakness, manifest in an apparent diffusion and confusion of judgment, is thus inseparable from women's moral strength, an overriding concern with relationships and responsibilities. The reluctance to judge can itself be indicative of the same care and concern for others that infuses the psychology of women's development and is responsible for what is characteristically seen as problematic in its nature.

Thus women not only define themselves in a context of human relationship but also judge themselves in terms of their ability to care. Woman's place in man's life cycle has been that of nurturer, caretaker, and helpmate, the weaver of those networks of relationships on which she in turn relies. While women have thus taken care of men, however, men have in their theories of psychological development tended either to assume or devalue that care. The focus on individuation and individual achievement that has dominated the description of child and adolescent development has recently been extended to the depiction of adult development as well. Levinson, in his study *The Seasons of a Man's Life* (1978), elaborates a view of adult development in which relationships are portrayed as a means to an end of individual achievement and success. In the critical relationships of early adulthood, the "Mentor" and the "Special Woman" are defined by the role they play in facilitating the man's realization of his "Dream." Along similar lines Vaillant (1977), in his study of men, considers altruism a defense, characteristic of mature ego functioning and associated with successful "adaptation to life," but conceived as derivative rather than primary, in contrast to Chodorow's analysis, in which empathy is considered "built in" to the woman's primary definition of self.

The discovery now being celebrated by men in midlife of the importance of intimacy, relationships, and care is something that women have known from the beginning. However, because that knowledge has been considered "intuitive" or "instinctive," a function of anatomy coupled with destiny, psychologists have neglected to describe its development. In my research, I have found that women's moral development centers on the elaboration of that knowledge. Women's moral development thus delineates a critical line of psychological development whose importance for both sexes becomes apparent in the intergenerational

framework of a life-cycle perspective. While the subject of moral development provides the final illustration of the reiterative pattern in the observation and assessment of sex differences in the literature on human development, it also indicates more particularly why the nature and significance of women's development has for so long been obscured and considered shrouded in mystery.

The criticism that Freud (1961) makes of women's sense of justice, seeing it as compromised in its refusal to blind impartiality, reappears not only in the work of Piaget (1934) but also in that of Kohlberg (1958). While girls are an aside in Piaget's account of *The Moral Judgment of the Child* (1932), an odd curiosity to whom he devotes four brief entries in an index that omits "boys" altogether because "the child" is assumed to be male, in Kohlberg's research on moral development, females simply do not exist. Kohlberg's six stages that describe the development of moral judgment from childhood to adulthood were derived empirically from a longitudinal study of eighty-four boys from the United States. While Kohlberg (1973) claims universality for his stage sequence and considers his conception of justice as fairness to have been naturalistically derived, those groups not included in his original sample rarely reach his higher stages (Edwards, 1975; Gilligan, 1977). Prominent among those found to be deficient in moral development when measured by Kohlberg's scale are women whose judgments on his scale seemed to exemplify the third stage in his six-stage sequence. At this stage morality is conceived in terms of relationships, and goodness is equated with helping and pleasing others. This concept of goodness was considered by Kohlberg and Kramer (1969) to be functional in the lives of mature women insofar as those lives took place in the home and thus were relationally bound. Only if women were to go out of the house to enter the arena of male activity would they realize the inadequacy of their Stage Three perspective and progress like men toward higher stages where morality is societally or universally defined in accordance with a conception of justice as fairness.

In this version of human development, however, a particular conception of maturity is assumed, based on the study of men's lives and reflecting the importance of individuation in their development. When one begins instead with women and derives developmental constructs from their lives, then a different conception of development emerges, the expansion and elaboration of which can also be traced through stages that comprise a developmental sequence. In Loevinger's (1966) test for measuring ego development that was drawn from studies of females, fifteen of the thirty-six sentence stems to complete begin with the subject of human relationships (for example, "Raising a family . . . ; If my mother . . . ; Being with other people . . . ; When I am with a man . . . ; When a child won't join in group activities . . . ") (Loevinger & Wessler, 1970:141). Thus ego development is described and measured by Loevinger through the conception of relationships as well as by the concept of identity that measures the progress of individuation.

Research on moral judgment has shown that when the categories of women's thinking are examined in detail (Gilligan, 1977) the outline of a moral conception different from that described by Freud, Piaget, or Kohlberg begins to emerge and to inform a different description of moral development. In this conception, the moral problem is seen to arise from conflicting responsibilities rather than from competing rights and to require for its resolution a mode of thinking that is contextual and inductive rather than formal and abstract.

This conception of morality as fundamentally concerned with the capacity for understanding and care also develops through a structural progression of increasing differentiation and integration. This progression witnesses the shift from an egocentric through a societal to the universal moral perspective that Kohlberg described in his research on men, but it does so in different terms. The shift in women's judgment from an egocentric to a conventional to a principled ethical understanding is articulated through their use of a distinct moral language, in which the terms "selfishness" and "responsibility" define the moral problem as one of care. Moral development then consists of the progressive reconstruction of this understanding toward a more adequate conception of care.

The concern with caring centers moral development around the progressive differentiation and integration that characterize the evolution of the understanding of relationships just as the conception of fairness delineates the progressive differentiation and balancing of individual rights. Within the responsibility orientation, the infliction of hurt is the center of moral concern and is considered immoral whether or not it can otherwise be construed as fair or unfair. The reiterative use of the language of selfishness and re-

sponsibility to define the moral problem as a problem of care sets women apart from the men whom Kohlberg studied and from whose thinking he derived his six stages. This different construction of the moral problem by women may be seen as the critical reason for their failure to develop within the constraints of Kohlberg's system.

Regarding all constructions of responsibility as evidence of a conventional moral understanding, Kohlberg defines the highest stages of moral development as deriving from a reflective understanding of human rights. That the morality of rights differs from the morality of responsibility in its emphasis on separation rather than attachment, in its consideration of the individual rather than the relationship as primary, is illustrated by two quotations that exemplify these different orientations. The first comes from a twenty-five-year-old man who participated in Kohlberg's longitudinal study. The quotation itself is cited by Kohlberg to illustrate the principled conception of morality that he scores as "integrated [Stage] Five judgment, possibly moving to Stage Six."

[What does the word morality mean to you?] Nobody in the world knows the answer. I think it is recognizing the right of the individual, the rights of other individuals, not interfering with those rights. Act as fairly as you would have them treat you. I think it is basically to preserve the human being's right to existence. I think that is the most important. Secondly, the human being's right to do as he pleases, again without interfering with somebody else's rights.

[How have your views on morality changed since the last interview?] I think I am more aware of an individual's rights now. I used to be looking at it strictly from my point of view, just for me. Now I think I am more aware of what the individual has a right to. [Note 1, p. 29]

"Clearly," Kohlberg states,

these responses represent attainment of the third level of moral theory. Moving to a perspective outside of that of his society, he identifies morality with justice (fairness, rights, the Golden Rule), with recognition of the rights of others as these are defined naturally or intrinsically. The human's right to do as he pleases without interfering with some-body else's rights is a formula defining rights prior to social legislation and opinion which defines what society may expect rather than being defined by it. [Note 1, pp. 29–30]

The second quotation comes from my interview with a woman, also twenty-five years old and at the time of the interview a third-year student at Harvard Law School. She described her conception of morality as follows:

[Is there really some correct solution to moral prob-lems or is everybody's opinion equally right?] No, I don't think everybody's opinion is equally right. I think that in some situations . . . there may be opin-ions that are equally valid and one could consci-entiously adopt one of several courses of action. But there are other situations which I think there are right and wrong answers, that sort of inhere in the nature of existence, of all individuals here who need to live with each other to live. We need to de-pend on each other and hopefully it is not only a physical need but a need of fulfillment in ourselves, that a person's life is enriched by cooperating with other people and striving to live in harmony with everybody else, and to that end, there are right and wrong, there are things which promote that end and that move away from it, and in that way, it is pos-sible to choose in certain cases among different courses of action, that obviously promote or harm that goal.

[Is there a time in the past when you would have thought about these things differently?] Oh, yah. I think that I went through a time when I thought that things were pretty relative, that I can't tell you what to do and you can't tell me what to do, be-cause you've got your conscience and I've got mine. . . .

[When was that?] When I was in high school. I guess that it just sort of dawned on me that my own ideas changed and because my own judgments changed, I felt I couldn't judge another person's judgment . . . but now I think even when it is only the person himself who is going to be affected, I say

it is wrong to the extent it doesn't cohere with what I know about human nature and what I know about you, and just from what I think is true about the operation of the universe, I could say I think you are making a mistake.

[What led you to change, do you think?] Just seeing more of life, just recognizing that there are an awful lot of things that are common among people . . . there are certain things that you come to learn pro-mote a better life and better relationships and more personal fulfillment than other things that in gen-eral tend to do the opposite and the things that promote these things, you would call morally right.

These responses also represent a reflective recon-struction of morality following a period of relativistic questioning and doubt, but the reconstruction of moral understanding is based not on the primacy and universality of individual rights, but rather on what she herself describes as a "very strong sense of being responsible to the world." Within this construction, the moral dilemma changes from how to exercise one's rights without interfering with the rights of oth-ers to how "to lead a moral life which includes obli-gations to myself and my family and people in gen-eral." The problem then becomes one of limiting responsibilities without abandoning moral concern. When asked to describe herself, this woman says that she values

having other people that I am tied to and also hav-ing people that I am responsible to. I have a very strong sense of being responsible to the world, that I can't just live for my enjoyment, but just the fact of being in the world gives me an obligation to do what I can to make the world a better place to live in, no matter how small a scale that may be on.

Thus while Kohlberg's subject worries about people interfering with one another's rights, this woman wor-ries about "the possibility of omission, of your not helping others when you could help them."

The issue this law student raises is addressed by Loevinger's fifth "autonomous" stage of ego develop-ment. The terms of its resolution lie in achieving partial autonomy from an excessive sense of responsibility by recognizing that other people have responsibility for their own destiny (Loevinger, 1968). The autonomous stage in Loevinger's account witnesses a relinquishing of moral dichotomies and their replacement with "a feeling for the complexity and multifaceted character of real people and real situations" (1970:6).

Whereas the rights conception of morality that informs Kohlberg's principled level (Stages Five and Six) is geared to arriving at an objectively fair or just resolution to the moral dilemmas to which "all rational men can agree" (Kohlberg, 1976), the responsibility conception focuses instead on the limitations of any particular resolution and describes the conflicts that remain. This limitation of moral judgment and choice is described by a woman in her thirties when she says that her guiding principle in making moral decisions has to do with "responsibility and caring about yourself and others, not just a principle that once you take hold of, you settle [the moral problem]. The principle put into practice is still going to leave you with conflict."

Given the substance and orientation of these women's judgments, it becomes clear why a morality of rights and noninterference may appear to women as frightening in its potential justification of indifference and unconcern. At the same time, however, it also becomes clear why, from a male perspective, women's judgments appear inconclusive and diffuse, given their insistent contextual relativism. Women's moral judgments thus elucidate the pattern that we have observed in the differences between the sexes, but provide an alternative conception of maturity by which these differences can be developmentally considered. The psychology of women that has consistently been described as distinctive in its greater orientation toward relationships of interdependence implies a more contextual mode of judgment and a different moral understanding. Given the differences in women's conceptions of self and morality, it is not surprising that women bring to the life cycle a different point of view and that they order human experience in terms of different priorities.

The myth of Demeter and Persephone, which McClelland cites as exemplifying the feminine attitude toward power, was associated with the Eleusinian Mysteries, celebrated in ancient Greece for over two thousand years (1975:96). As told in *The Homeric Hymn* (1971), the story of Persephone indicates the strengths of "interdependence, building up resources and giving" (McClelland, 1975:96) that McClelland found in his research on power motivation to characterize the mature feminine style. Although, McClelland says, "it is fashionable to conclude that no one knows what went on in the Mysteries, it is known that they were probably the most important religious ceremonies, even partly on the historical record, which were organized by and for women, especially at the onset before men by means of the cult of Dionysus began to take them over" (p. 96). Thus McClelland regards the myth as "a special presentation of feminine psychology." It is, as well, a life-cycle story par excellence.

Persephone, the daughter of Demeter, while out playing in the meadows with her girl friends, sees a beautiful narcissus which she runs to pick. As she does so, the earth opens and she is snatched away by Pluto, who takes her to his underworld kingdom. Demeter, goddess of the earth, so mourns the loss of her daughter that she refuses to allow anything to grow. The crops that sustain life on earth shrivel and dry up, killing men and animals alike, until Zeus takes pity on man's suffering and persuades his brother to return Persephone to her mother. But before she leaves, Persephone eats some pomegranate seeds which ensures that she will spend six months of every year in the underworld.

The elusive mystery of women's development lies in its recognition of the continuing importance of attachment in the human life cycle. Woman's place in man's life cycle has been to protect this recognition while the developmental litany intones the celebration of separation, autonomy, individuation, and natural rights. The myth of Persephone speaks directly to the distortion in this view by reminding us that narcissism leads to death, that the fertility of the earth is in some mysterious way tied to the continuation of the mother–daughter relationship, and that the life cycle itself arises from an alternation between the world of women and that of men. My intention in this essay has been to suggest that only when life-cycle theorists equally divide their attention and begin to live with women as they have lived with men will their vision encompass the experience of both sexes and their theories become correspondingly more fertile.

REFERENCES

Bettelheim, B. 1976. *The uses of enchantment*. New York: Knopf.

Blos, P. 1967. "The second individuation process of adolescence." In A. Freud, ed., *The psychoanalytic study of the child*, vol. 22. New York: International Universities Press.

Chekhov, A. 1904/1956. *The cherry orchard*. Stark Young, trans. New York: Modern Library.

Chodorow, N. 1974. Family structure and feminine personality. In M. Rosaldo and L. Lamphere, eds., *Women, culture, and society*. Stanford, Calif.: Stanford University Press.

Chodorow, N. 1978. *The reproduction of mothering*. Berkeley: University of California Press.

Edwards, C. P. 1975. "Societal complexity and moral development: A Kenyan study." *Ethos* 3:505–527.

Erikson, E. 1950. *Childhood and society*. New York: Norton.

Erikson, E. 1968. *Identity: Youth and crisis*. New York: Norton.

Freud, S. 1931/1961. "Female sexuality." In J. Strachey, ed., *The standard edition of the complete psychological works of Sigmund Freud*, vol. 21. London: Hogarth Press.

Freud, S. 1925/1961. "Some psychical consequences of the anatomical distinction between the sexes." In J. Strachey, ed., *The standard edition of the complete psychological works of Sigmund Freud*, vol. 19. London: Hogarth Press.

Freud, S. 1905/1961. "Three essays on sexuality." In J. Strachey, ed., *The standard edition of the complete psychological works of Sigmund Freud*, vol. 7., London: Hogarth Press.

Gilligan, C. 1977. "In a different voice: Women's conceptions of the self and of morality." *Harvard Educational Review* 47:481–517.

The Homeric Hymn. 1971. C. Boer, trans. Chicago: Swallow Press.

Horner, M. 1972. "Toward an understanding of achievement-related conflicts in women." *Journal of Social Issues* 28:157–74.

Inhelder, B., & Piaget, J. 1958. *The growth of logical thinking from childhood to adolescence*. New York: Basic Books.

Kingston, M. H. 1977. *The woman warrior*. New York: Vintage Books.

Kohlberg, L. 1971. "From is to ought: How to commit the naturalistic fallacy and get away with it in the study of moral development." In T. Mischel, ed., *Cognitive development and epistemology*. New York: Academic Press.

Kohlberg, L. 1973. "Continuities and discontinuities in childhood and adult moral development revisited." Unpublished manuscript, Harvard University.

Kohlberg, L., & Kramer, R. 1969. "Continuities and discontinuities in childhood and adult moral development." *Human Development* 12:93–120.

Lever, J. 1976. "Sex differences in the games children play." *Social Problems* 23:478–87.

Levinson, D. 1978. *The seasons of a man's life*. New York: Knopf.

Loevinger, J., & Wessler, R. 1970. *The meaning and measurement of ego development*. San Francisco: Jossey-Bass.

McClelland, D. 1961. *The achieving society*. New York: Van Nostrand.

McClelland, D. 1975. *Power: The inner experience*. New York: Irvington.

Mead, G. H. 1934. *Mind, self, and society*. Chicago: University of Chicago Press.

Perry, W. 1968. *Forms of intellectual and ethical development in the college years*. New York: Holt, Rinehart & Winston.

Piaget, J. 1932/1965. *The moral judgment of the child*. New York: Free Press.

Riesman, D. 1961. *The lonely crowd*. New Haven: Yale University Press.

Sassen, G. "Success-anxiety in women: A constructivist theory of its sources and its significance." *Harvard Educational Review*.

Strunk, W., & White, E. B. 1959. *The elements of style*. New York: Macmillan.

Sullivan, H. S. 1953. *The interpersonal theory of psychiatry*. New York: Norton.

Vaillant, G. 1977. *Adaptation to life*. Boston: Little, Brown.

Woolf, V. 1929. *A room of one's own*. New York: Harcourt, Brace.

READING 6

Family Structure and Feminine Personality
NANCY CHODOROW

I propose here[1] a model to account for the reproduction within each generation of certain general and nearly universal differences that characterize masculine and feminine personality and roles. My perspective is largely psychoanalytic. Cross-cultural and social-psychological evidence suggests that an argument drawn solely from the universality of biological sex differences is unconvincing.[2] At the same time, explanations based on patterns of deliberate socialization (the most prevalent kind of anthropological, sociological, and social-psychological explanation) are in themselves insufficient to account for the extent to which psychological and value commitments to sex differences are so emotionally laden and tenaciously maintained, for the way gender identity and expectations about sex roles and gender consistency are so deeply central to a person's consistent sense of self.

This paper suggests that a crucial differentiating experience in male and female development arises out of the fact that women, universally, are largely responsible for early child care and for (at least) later female socialization. This points to the central importance of the mother–daughter relationship for women, and to a focus on the conscious and unconscious effects of early involvement with a female for children of both sexes. The fact that males and females experience this social environment differently as they grow up accounts for the development of basic sex differences in personality. In particular, certain features of the mother–daughter relationship are internalized universally as basic elements of feminine ego structure (although not necessarily what we normally mean by "femininity").

Specifically, I shall propose that, in any given society, feminine personality comes to define itself in relation and connection to other people more than masculine personality does. (In psychoanalytic terms, women are less individuated than men; they have more flexible ego boundaries.)[3] Moreover, issues of dependency are handled and experienced differently by men and women. For boys and men, both individuation and dependency issues become tied up with the sense of masculinity, or masculine identity. For girls and women, by contrast, issues of femininity, or feminine identity, are not problematic in the same way. The structural situation of child rearing, reinforced by female and male role training, produces these differences, which are replicated and reproduced in the sexual sociology of adult life.

The paper is also a beginning attempt to rectify certain gaps in the social-scientific literature, and a contribution to the reformulation of psychological anthropology. Most traditional accounts of family and socialization tend to emphasize only role training, and not unconscious features of personality. Those few that rely on Freudian theory have abstracted a behaviorist methodology from this theory, concentrating on isolated "significant" behaviors like weaning and toilet training. The paper advocates instead a focus on the ongoing interpersonal relationships in which these various behaviors are given meaning.[4]

More empirically, most social-scientific accounts of socialization, child development, and the mother–child relationship refer implicitly or explicitly only to the development and socialization of boys and to the mother–son relationship. There is a striking lack of systematic description about the mother–daughter relationship, and a basic theoretical discontinuity between, on the one hand, theories about female development, which tend to stress the development of "feminine" qualities in relation to and comparison with men, and on the other hand, theories about women's ultimate mothering role. This final lack is particularly crucial, because women's motherhood and mothering role seem to be the most important features in accounting for the universal secondary status of women (Chodorow, 1971; Ortner, Rosaldo, this volume). The present paper describes the development of psychological qualities in women that are central to the perpetuation of this role.

In a formulation of this preliminary nature, there is not a great body of consistent evidence to draw upon. Available evidence is presented that illuminates aspects of the theory—for the most part psychoanalytic and social-psychological accounts based almost entirely on highly industrialized Western society. Because aspects of family structure are discussed that are universal, however, I think it is worth considering the theory as a general model. In any case, this is in some sense a programmatic appeal to people doing research. It points to certain issues that might be especially important in investigations of child development and family relationships, and suggests that researchers look explicitly at female vs. male development, and that they consider seriously mother–daughter relationships even if these are not of obvious "structural importance" in a traditional anthropological view of that society.

THE DEVELOPMENT OF GENDER PERSONALITY

According to psychoanalytic theory,[5] personality is a result of a boy's or girl's social-relational experiences from earliest infancy. Personality development is not the result of conscious parental intention. The nature and quality of the social relationships that the child experiences are appropriated, internalized, and organized by her/him and come to constitute her/his personality. What is internalized from an ongoing relationship continues independent of that original relationship and is generalized and set up as a permanent feature of the personality. The conscious self is usually not aware of many of the features of personality, or of its total structural organization. At the same time, these are important determinants of any person's behavior, both that which is culturally expected and that which is idiosyncratic or unique to the individual. The conscious aspects of personality, like

a person's general self-concept and, importantly, her/his gender identity, require and depend upon the consistency and stability of its unconscious organization. In what follows I shall describe how contrasting male and female experiences lead to differences in the way the developing masculine or feminine psyche resolves certain relational issues.

Separation and individuation (preoedipal development). All children begin life in a state of "infantile dependence" (Fairbairn, 1952) upon an adult or adults, in most cases their mother. This state consists first in the persistence of primary identification with the mother: the child does not differentiate herself/himself from her/his mother but experiences a sense of oneness with her. (It is important to distinguish this from later forms of identification, from "secondary identification," which presuppose at least some degree of experienced separateness by the person who identifies.) Second, it includes an oral-incorporative mode of relationship to the world, leading, because of the infant's total helplessness, to a strong attachment to and dependence upon whoever nurses and carries her/him.

Both aspects of this state are continuous with the child's prenatal experience of being emotionally and physically part of the mother's body and of the exchange of body material through the placenta. That this relationship continues with the natural mother in most societies stems from the fact that women lactate. For convenience, and not because of biological necessity, this has usually meant that mothers, and females in general, tend to take all care of babies. It is probable that the mother's continuing to have major responsibility for the feeding and care of the child (so that the child interacts almost entirely with her) extends and intensifies her/his period of primary identification with her more than if, for instance, someone else were to take major or total care of the child. A child's earliest experience, then, is usually of identity with and attachment to a single mother, and always with women.

For both boys and girls, the first few years are preoccupied with issues of separation and individuation. This includes breaking or attenuating the primary identification with the mother and beginning to develop an individuated sense of self, and mitigating the totally dependent oral attitude and attachment to the mother. I would suggest that, contrary to the traditional psychoanalytic model, the preoedipal experience is likely to differ for boys and girls. Specifically, the experience of mothering for a woman involves a double identification (Klein & Rivière, 1937). A woman identifies with her own mother and, through identification with her child, she (re)experiences herself as a cared-for child. The particular nature of this double identification for the individual mother is closely bound up with her relationship to her own mother. As Deutsch expresses it, "In relation to her own child, woman repeats her own mother–child history" (1944:205). Given that she was a female child, and that identification with her mother and mothering are so bound up with her being a woman, we might expect that a woman's identification with a girl child might be stronger; that a mother, who is, after all, a person who is a woman and not simply the performer of a formally defined role, would tend to treat infants of different sexes in different ways.

There is some suggestive sociological evidence that this is the case. Mothers in a women's group in Cambridge, Massachusetts (see note 1), say that they identified more with their girl children than with boy children. The perception and treatment of girl vs. boy children in high-caste, extremely patriarchal, patrilocal communities in India are in the same vein. Families express preference for boy children and celebrate when sons are born. At the same time, Rajput mothers in North India are "as likely as not" (Minturn & Hitchcock, 1963) to like girl babies better than boy babies once they are born, and they and Havik Brahmins in South India (Harper, 1969) treat their daughters with greater affection and leniency than their sons. People in both groups say that this is out of sympathy for the future plight of their daughters, who will have to leave their natal family for a strange and usually oppressive postmarital household. From the time of their daughters' birth, then, mothers in these communities identify anticipatorily, by reexperiencing their own past, with the experiences of separation that their daughters will go through. They develop a particular attachment to their daughters because of this and by imposing their own reaction to the issue of separation on this new external situation.

It seems, then, that a mother is more likely to identify with a daughter than with a son, to experience her daughter (or parts of her daughter's life) as herself. Fliess's description (1961) of his neurotic patients who were the children of ambulatory psychotic mothers presents the problem in its psychopathological extreme. The example is interesting, because, although Fliess claims to be writing about people defined only by the fact that their problems were tied to a particular kind of relationship to their mothers, an overwhelmingly large proportion of the cases he presents are women. It seems, then, that this sort of disturbed mother inflicts her pathology predominantly on daughters. The mothers Fliess describes did not allow their daughters to perceive themselves as separate people, but simply acted as if their daughters were narcissistic extensions or doubles of themselves, extensions to whom were attributed the mothers' bodily feelings and who became physical vehicles for their mothers' achievement of autoerotic gratification. The daughters were bound into a mutually dependent "hypersymbiotic" relationship. These mothers, then, perpetuate a mutual relationship with their daughters of both primary identification and infantile dependence.

A son's case is different. Cultural evidence suggests that insofar as a mother treats her son differently, it is usually by emphasizing his masculinity in opposition to herself and by pushing him to assume, or acquiescing in his assumption of, a sexually toned male-role relation to her. Whiting (1959) and Whiting et al. (1958) suggest that mothers in societies with mother–child sleeping arrangements and postpartum sex taboos may be seductive toward infant sons. Slater (1968) describes the socialization of precarious masculinity in Greek males of the classical period through their mothers' alternation of sexual praise and seductive behavior with hostile deflation and ridicule. This kind of behavior contributes to the son's differentiation from his mother and to the formation of ego boundaries (I will later discuss certain problems that result from this).

Neither form of attitude or treatment is what we would call "good mothering." However, evidence of differentiation of a pathological nature in the mother's behavior toward girls and boys does highlight tendencies in "normal" behavior. It seems likely that from their children's earliest childhood, mothers and women tend to identify more with daughters and to help them to differentiate less, and that processes of separation and individuation are made more difficult for girls. On the other hand, a mother tends to identify less with her son, and to push him toward differentiation and the taking on of a male role unsuitable to his age, and undesirable at any age in his relationship to her.

For boys and girls, the quality of the preoedipal relationship to the mother differs. This, as well as differences in development during the oedipal period, accounts for the persisting importance of preoedipal issues in female development and personality that many psychoanalytic writers describe.[6] Even before the establishment of gender identity, gender personality differentiation begins.

Gender identity (oedipal crisis and resolution). There is only a slight suggestion in the psychological and sociological literature that preoedipal development differs for boys and girls. The pattern becomes explicit at the next developmental level. All theoretical and empirical accounts agree that after about age three (the beginning of the "oedipal" period, which focuses on the attainment of a stable gender identity) male and female development becomes radically different. It is at this stage that the father, and men in general, begin to become important in the child's primary object world. It is, of course, particularly difficult to generalize about the attainment of gender identity and sex-role assumption, since there is such wide variety in the sexual sociology of different societies. However, to the extent that in all societies women's life tends to be more private and domestic, and men's more public and social (Rosaldo, this volume), we can make general statements about this kind of development.

In what follows, I shall be talking about the development of gender personality and gender identity in the tradition of psychoanalytic theory. Cognitive psychologists have established that by the age of three, boys and girls have an irreversible conception of what their gender is (see Kohlberg, 1966). I do not dispute these findings. It remains true that children (and adults) may know definitely that they are boys (men) or girls (women), and at the same time experience conflicts or uncertainty about "masculinity" or "femininity," about what these identities require in behavioral or emotional terms, etc. I am discussing the development of "gender identity" in this latter sense.

A boy's masculine gender identification must come to replace his early primary identification with his mother. This masculine identification is usually based on identification with a boy's father or other salient adult males. However, a boy's father is relatively more remote than his mother. He rarely plays a major caretaking role even at this period in his son's life. In most societies, his work and social life take place farther from the home than do those of his wife. He is, then, often relatively inaccessible to his son, and performs his male role activities away from where the son spends most of his life. As a result, a boy's male gender identification often becomes a "positional" identification, with aspects of his father's clearly or not-so-clearly defined male role, rather than a more generalized "personal" identification—a diffuse identification with his father's personality, values, and behavioral traits—that could grow out of a real relationship to his father.[7]

Mitscherlich (1963), in his discussion of Western advanced capitalist society, provides a useful insight into the problem of male development. The father, because his work takes him outside of the home most of the time, and because his active presence in the family has progressively decreased, has become an "invisible father." For the boy, the tie between affective relations and masculine gender identification and role learning (between libidinal and ego development) is relatively attenuated. He identifies with a fantasied masculine role, because the reality constraint that contact with his father would provide is missing. In all societies characterized by some sex segregation (even those in which a son will eventually lead the same sort of life as his father), much of a boy's masculine identification must be of this sort, that is, with aspects of his father's role, or what he fantasies to be a male role, rather than with his father as a person involved in a relationship to him.

There is another important aspect to this situation, which explains the psychological dynamics of the universal social and cultural devaluation and subordination of women.[8] A boy, in his attempt to gain an elusive masculine identification, often comes to define this masculinity largely in negative terms, as that which is not feminine or involved with women. There is an internal and external aspect to this. Internally, the boy tries to reject his mother and deny his attachment to her and the strong dependence upon her that he still feels. He also tries to deny the deep personal identification with her that has developed during his early years. He does this by repressing whatever he takes to be feminine inside himself, and, importantly, by denigrating and devaluing whatever he considers to be feminine in the outside world. As a societal member, he also appropriates to himself and defines as superior particular social activities and cultural (moral, religious, and creative) spheres—possibly, in fact, "society" and "culture" themselves.[9]

Freud's description of the boy's oedipal crisis speaks to the issues of rejection of the feminine and identification with the father. As his early attachment to his mother takes on phallic-sexual overtones, and his father enters the picture as an obvious rival (who, in the son's fantasy, has apparent power to kill or castrate his son), the boy must radically deny and repress his attachment to his mother and replace it with an identification with his loved and admired, but also potentially punitive, therefore feared, father. He internalizes a superego.[10]

To summarize, four components of the attainment of masculine gender identity are important. First, masculinity becomes and remains a problematic issue for a boy. Second, it involves denial of attachment or relationship, particularly of what the boy takes to be dependence or need for another, and differentiation of himself from another. Third, it involves the repression and devaluation of femininity on both psychological and cultural levels. Finally, identification with his father does not usually develop in the context of a satisfactory affective relationship, but consists in the attempt to internalize and learn components of a not immediately apprehensible role.

The development of a girl's gender identity contrasts with that of a boy. Most important, femininity and female role activities are immediately apprehensible in the world of her daily life. Her final role identification is with her mother and women, that is, with the person or people with whom she also has her earliest relationship of infantile dependence. The development of her gender identity does not involve a rejection of this early identification, however. Rather, her later identification with her mother is embedded in and influenced by their ongoing relationship of both primary identification and preoedipal attachment. Because her mother is around, and she has had a genuine relationship to her as a person, a girl's gender and gender-role identification are mediated by and depend upon real affective relations. Identification with her mother is not positional—the narrow learning of particular role behaviors—but rather a personal identification with her mother's general traits of character and values. Feminine identification is based not on fantasied or externally defined characteristics and negative identification, but on the gradual learning of a way of being familiar in everyday life, and exemplified by the person (or kind of people—women) with whom she has been most involved. It is continuous with her early childhood identifications and attachments.

The major discontinuity in the development of a girl's sense of gender identity, and one that has led Freud and other early psychoanalysts to see female development as exceedingly difficult and tortuous, is that at some point she must transfer her primary sexual object choice from her mother and females to her father and males, if she is to attain her expected heterosexual adulthood. Briefly, Freud considers that all children feel that mothers give some cause for complaint and unhappiness: they give too little milk; they have a second child; they arouse and then forbid their child's sexual gratification in the process of caring for her/him. A girl receives a final blow, however: her discovery that she lacks a penis. She blames this lack on her mother, rejects her mother, and turns to her father in reaction.

Problems in this account have been discussed extensively in the general literature that has grown out of the women's movement, and within the psychoanalytic tradition itself. These concern Freud's misogyny and his obvious assumption that males possess physiological superiority, and that a woman's personality is inevitably determined by her lack of a penis.[11] The psychoanalytic account is not completely unsatisfactory, however. A more detailed consideration of several theorists[12] reveals important features of female development, especially about the mother–daughter relationship, and at the same time contradicts or mitigates the absoluteness of the more general Freudian outline.

These psychoanalysts emphasize how, in contrast to males, the female oedipal crisis is not resolved in the same absolute way. A girl cannot and does not completely reject her mother in favor of men, but continues her relationship of dependence upon and attachment to her. In addition, the strength and quality of her relationship to her father is completely dependent upon the strength and quality of her relationship to her mother. Deutsch suggests that a girl wavers in a "bisexual triangle" throughout her childhood and into puberty, normally making a very tentative resolution in favor of her father, but in such a way that issues of separation from and attachment to her mother remain important throughout a woman's life (1944:205):

It is erroneous to say that the little girl gives up her first mother relation in favor of the father. She only gradually draws him into the alliance, develops from the mother–child exclusiveness toward the triangular parent–child relationship and continues the latter, just as she does the former, although in a weaker and less elemental form, all her life. Only the principal part changes: now the mother, now the father plays it. The ineradicability of affective constellations manifests itself in later repetitions.

We might suggest from this that a girl's internalized and external object-relations become and remain more complex, and at the same time more defining of her, than those of a boy. Psychoanalytic preoccupation with constitutionally based libidinal development, and with a normative male model of development, has obscured this fact. Most women are genitally heterosexual. At the same time, their lives always involve other sorts of equally deep and primary relationships, especially with their children, and, importantly, with other women. In these spheres also, even more than in the area of heterosexual relations, a girl imposes the sort of object-relations she has internalized in her preoedipal and later relationship to her mother.

Men are also for the most part genitally heterosexual. This grows directly out of their early primary attachment to their mother. We know, however, that in many societies their heterosexual relationships are not embedded in close personal relationship but simply in relations of dominance and power. Furthermore, they do not have the extended personal relations women have. They are not so connected to children, and their relationships with other men tend to be based not on particularistic connection or affective ties, but rather on abstract, universalistic role expectations.

Building on the psychoanalytic assumption that unique individual experiences contribute to the formation of individual personality, culture and personality theory has held that early experiences common to members of a particular society contribute to the formation of "typical" personalities organized around and preoccupied with certain issues: "Prevailing patterns of child-rearing must result in similar internalized situations in the unconscious of the majority of individuals in a culture, and these will be externalized back into the culture again to perpetuate it from generation to generation" (Guntrip, 1961:378). In a similar vein, I have tried to show that to the extent males and females, respectively, experience similar interpersonal environments as they grow up, masculine and feminine personality will develop differently.

I have relied on a theory which suggests that features of adult personality and behavior are determined, but which is not biologically determinist. Culturally expected personality and behavior are not simply "taught," however. Rather, certain features of social structure, supported by cultural beliefs, values, and perceptions, are internalized through the family and the child's early social object-relationships. This largely unconscious organization is the context in which role training and purposive socialization take place.

SEX-ROLE LEARNING AND ITS SOCIAL CONTEXT

Sex-role training and social interaction in childhood build upon and reinforce the largely unconscious development I have described. In most societies (ours is a complicated exception) a girl is usually with her mother and other female relatives in an interpersonal situation that facilitates continuous and early role learning and emphasizes the mother–daughter identification and particularistic, diffuse, affective relationships between women. A boy, to a greater or lesser extent, is also with women for a large part of his childhood, which prevents continuous or easy masculine role identification. His development is characterized by discontinuity.

Ariès (1962:61), in his discussion of the changing concept of childhood in modern capitalist society, makes a distinction that seems to have more general applicability. Boys, he suggests, became "children" while girls remained "little women." "The idea of childhood profited the boys first of all, while the girls persisted much longer in the traditional way of life which confused them with the adults: we shall have cause to notice more than once this delay on the part of the women in adopting the visible forms of the essentially masculine civilization of modern times." This took place first in the middle classes, as a situation developed in which boys needed special schooling in order to prepare for their future work and could not begin to do this kind of work in childhood. Girls (and working-class boys) could still learn work more directly from their parents, and could begin to participate in the adult economy at an earlier age. Rapid economic change and development have exacerbated the lack of male generational role continuity. Few fathers now have either the opportunity or the ability to pass on a profession or skill to their sons.

Sex-role development of girls in modern society is more complex. On the one hand, they go to school to prepare for life in a technologically and socially complex society. On the other, there is a sense in which this schooling is a pseudo-training. It is not meant to interfere with the much more important training to be "feminine" and a wife and mother, which is embedded in the girl's unconscious development and which her mother teaches her in a family context where she is clearly the salient parent.

This dichotomy is not unique to modern industrial society. Even if special, segregated schooling is not necessary for adult male work (and many male initiation rites remain a form of segregated role training), boys still participate in more activities that characterize them as a category apart from adult life. Their activities grow out of the boy's need to fill time until he can begin to take on an adult male role. Boys may withdraw into isolation and self-involved play or join together in a group that remains more or less unconnected with either the adult world of work and activity or the familial world.

Jay (1969) describes this sort of situation in rural Modjokuto, Java. Girls, after the age of five or so, begin gradually to help their mothers in their work and spend time with their mothers. Boys at this early age begin to form bands of age mates who roam and play about the city, relating neither to adult men nor to their mothers and sisters. Boys, then, enter a temporary group based on universalistic membership criteria, while girls continue to participate in particularistic role relations in a group characterized by continuity and relative permanence.

The content of boys' and girls' role training tends in the same direction as the context of this training and its results. Barry, Bacon, and Child, in their well-known study (1957), demonstrate that the socialization of boys tends to be oriented toward achievement and self-reliance and that of girls toward nurturance and responsibility. Girls are thus pressured to be involved with and connected to others, boys to deny this involvement and connection.

ADULT GENDER PERSONALITY AND SEX ROLE

A variety of conceptualizations of female and male personality all focus on distinctions around the same issue, and provide alternative confirmation of the developmental model I have proposed. Bakan (1966:15) claims that male personality is preoccupied with the "agentic," and female personality with the "communal." His expanded definition of the two concepts is illuminating:

> I have adopted the terms "agency" and "communion" to characterize two fundamental modalities in the existence of living forms, agency for the existence of an organism as an individual and communion for the participation of the individual in some larger organism of which the individual is a part. Agency manifests itself in self-protection, self-assertion, and self-expansion; communion manifests itself in the sense of being at one with other organisms. Agency manifests itself in the formation of separations; communion in the lack of separations. Agency manifests itself in isolation, alienation, and aloneness; communion in contact, openness, and union. Agency manifests itself in the urge to master; communion in noncontractual cooperation. Agency manifests itself in the repression of thought, feeling, and impulse; communion in the lack and removal of repression.

Gutmann (1965) contrasts the socialization of male personalities in "allocentric" milieux (milieux in which the individual is part of a larger social organization and system of social bonds) with that of female personalities in "autocentric" milieux (in which the individual herself/himself is a focus of events and ties).[13] Gutmann suggests that this leads to a number of systematic differences in ego functioning. Female ego qualities, growing out of participation in autocentric milieux, include more flexible ego boundaries (i.e., less insistent self–other distinctions), present orientation rather than future orientation, and relatively greater subjectivity and less detached objectivity.[14]

Carlson (1971) confirms both characterizations. Her tests of Gutmann's claims lead her to conclude that "males represent experiences of self, others, space, and time in individualistic, objective, and distant ways, while females represent experiences in relatively interpersonal, subjective, immediate ways" (p. 270). With reference to Bakan, she claims that men's descriptions of affective experience tend to be in agentic terms and women's in terms of communion, and that an examination of abstracts of a large number of social-psychological articles on sex differences yields an overwhelming confirmation of the agency/communion hypothesis.

Cohen (1969) contrasts the development of "analytic" and "relational" cognitive style, the former characterized by a stimulus-centered, parts-specific orientation to reality, the latter centered on the self and responding to the global characteristics of a stimulus in reference to its total context. Although focusing primarily on class differences in cognitive style, she also points out that girls are more likely to mix the two types of functioning (and also to exhibit internal conflict about this). Especially, they are likely to exhibit at the same time both high field dependence and highly developed analytic skills in other areas. She suggests that boys and girls participate in different sorts of interactional subgroups in their families: boys experience their family more as a formally organized primary group; girls experience theirs as a group characterized by shared and less clearly delineated functions. She concludes (p. 836): "Since embedded responses covered the gamut from abstract categories, through language behaviors, to expressions of embeddedness in their social environments, it is possible that embeddedness may be a distinctive characteristic of female sex-role learning in this society regardless of social class, native ability, ethnic differences, and the cognitive impact of the school."

Preliminary consideration suggests a correspondence between the production of feminine personalities organized around "communal" and "autocentric" issues and characterized by flexible ego boundaries, less detached objectivity, and relational cognitive style, on the one hand, and important aspects of feminine as opposed to masculine social roles, on the other.

Most generally, I would suggest that a quality of embeddedness in social interaction and personal relationships characterizes women's life relative to men's. From childhood, daughters are likely to participate in an intergenerational world with their mother, and often with their aunts and grandmothers, whereas boys are on their own or participate in a single-generation world of age mates. In adult life, women's interaction with other women in most societies is kin-based and cuts across generational lines. Their roles tend to be particularistic, and to involve diffuse relationships and responsibilities rather than specific ones. Women in most societies are *defined* relationally (as someone's wife, mother, daughter, daughter-in-law; even a nun

becomes the bride of Christ). Men's association (although it too may be kin-based and intergenerational) is much more likely than women's to cut across kinship units, to be restricted to a single generation, and to be recruited according to universalistic criteria and involve relationships and responsibilities defined by their specificity.

EGO BOUNDARIES AND THE MOTHER–DAUGHTER RELATIONSHIP

The care and socialization of girls by women ensures the production of feminine personalities founded on relation and connection, with flexible rather than rigid ego boundaries, and with a comparatively secure sense of gender identity. This is one explanation for how women's relative embeddedness is reproduced from generation to generation, and why it exists within almost every society. More specific investigation of different social contexts suggests, however, that there are variations in the kind of relationship that can exist between women's role performance and feminine personality.

Various kinds of evidence suggest that separation from the mother, the breaking of dependence, and the establishment and maintenance of a consistently individuated sense of self remain difficult psychological issues for Western middle-class women (i.e., the women who become subjects of psychoanalytic and clinical reports and social-psychological studies). Deutsch (1944, 1945) in particular provides extensive clinical documentation of these difficulties and of the way they affect women's relationships to men and children and, because of their nature, are reproduced in the next generation of women. Mothers and daughters in the women's group mentioned in note 1 describe their experiences of boundary confusion or equation of self and other, for example, guilt and self-blame for the other's unhappiness; shame and embarrassment at the other's actions; daughters' "discovery" that they are "really" living out their mothers' lives in their choice of career; mothers' not completely conscious reactions to their daughters' bodies as their own (overidentification and therefore often unnecessary concern with supposed weight or skin problems, which the mother is really worried about in herself); etc.

A kind of guilt that Western women express seems

to grow out of and to reflect lack of adequate self/other distinctions and a sense of inescapable embeddedness in relationships to others. Tax describes this well (1970:2; italics mine):

> Since our awareness of others is considered our duty, the price we pay when things go wrong is guilt and self-hatred. And things always go wrong. We respond with apologies; we continue to apologize long after the event is forgotten—and *even if it had no causal relation to anything we did to begin with.* If the rain spoils someone's picnic, we apologize. We apologize for taking up space in a room, for living.

As if the woman does not differentiate herself clearly from the rest of the world, she feels a sense of guilt and responsibility for situations that did not come about through her actions and without relation to her actual ability to determine the course of events. This happens, in the most familiar instance, in a sense of diffuse responsibility for everything connected to the welfare of her family and the happiness and success of her children. This loss of self in overwhelming responsibility for and connection to others is described particularly acutely by women writers (in the work, for instance, of Simone de Beauvoir, Kate Chopin, Doris Lessing, Tillie Olsen, Christina Stead, Virginia Woolf).

Slater (1961) points to several studies supporting the contention that Western daughters have particular problems about differentiation from their mother. These studies show that though most forms of personal parental identification correlate with psychological adjustment (i.e., freedom from neurosis or psychosis, *not* social acceptability), personal identification of a daughter with her mother does not. The reason is that the mother–daughter relation is the one form of personal identification that, because it results so easily from the normal situation of child development, is liable to be excessive in the direction of allowing no room for separation or difference between mother and daughter.

The situation reinforces itself in circular fashion. A mother, on the one hand, grows up without establishing adequate ego boundaries or a firm sense of self. She tends to experience boundary confusion with her daughter, and does not provide experiences of differentiating ego development for her daughter or encourage the breaking of her daugher's dependence. The daughter, for her part, makes a rather unsatisfactory and artificial attempt to establish boundaries: she projects what she defines as bad within her onto her mother and tries to take what is good into herself. (This, I think, is the best way to understand the girl's oedipal "rejection" of her mother.) Such an arbitrary mechanism cannot break the underlying psychological unity, however. Projection is never more than a temporary solution to ambivalence or boundary confusion.

The implication is that, contrary to Gutmann's suggestion (see note 3), "so-called ego pathology" may not be "adaptive" for women. Women's biosexual experiences (menstruation, coitus, pregnancy, childbirth, lactation) all involve some challenge to the boundaries of her body ego ("me"/"not-me" in relation to her blood or milk, to a man who penetrates her, to a child once part of her body). These are important and fundamental human experiences that are probably intrinsically meaningful and at the same time complicated for women everywhere. However, a Western woman's tenuous sense of individuation and of the firmness of her ego boundaries increases the likelihood that experiences challenging these boundaries will be difficult for her and conflictive.

Nor is it clear that this personality structure is "functional" for society as a whole. The evidence presented in this paper suggests that satisfactory mothering, which does not reproduce particular psychological problems in boys and girls, comes from a person with a firm sense of self and of her own value, whose care is a freely chosen activity rather than a reflection of a conscious and unconscious sense of inescapable connection to and responsibility for her children.

SOCIAL STRUCTURE AND THE MOTHER–DAUGHTER RELATIONSHIP

Clinical and self-analytic descriptions of women and of the psychological component of mother–daughter relationships are not available from societies and subcultures outside of the Western middle class. However, accounts that are primarily sociological about women in other societies enable us to infer certain aspects of their psychological situation. In what follows, I am not claiming to make any kind of general statement about what constitutes a "healthy society," but only to examine and isolate specific features of social life that seem to contribute to the psychological strength of some members of a society. Consideration of three groups with matrifocal tendencies in their family structure (Tanner, 1971) highlights several dimensions of importance in the developmental situation of the girl.

Young and Willmott (1957) describe the daily visiting and mutual aid of working-class mothers and daughters in East London. In a situation where household structure is usually nuclear, like the Western middle class, grown daughters look to their mothers for advice, for aid in childbirth and child care, for friendship and companionship, and for financial help. Their mother's house is the ultimate center of the family world. Husbands are in many ways peripheral to family relationships, possibly because of their failure to provide sufficiently for their families as men are expected to do. This becomes apparent if they demand their wife's disloyalty toward or separation from her mother: "The great triangle of childhood is mother–father–child; in Bethnal Green the great triangle of adult life is Mum–wife–husband" (p. 64).

Geertz (1961)[15] and Jay (1969) describe Javanese nuclear families in which women are often the more powerful spouse and have primary influence upon how kin relations are expressed and to whom (although these families are formally centered upon a highly valued conjugal relationship based on equality of spouses). Financial and decision-making control in the family often rests largely in the hands of its women. Women are potentially independent of men in a way that men are not independent of women. Geertz points to a woman's ability to participate in most occupations, and to own farmland and supervise its cultivation, which contrasts with a man's inability, even if he is financially independent, to do his own household work and cooking.

Women's kin role in Java is important. Their parental role and rights are greater than those of men; children always belong to the woman in case of divorce. When extra members join a nuclear family to constitute an extended family household, they are much more likely to be the wife's relatives than those of the husband. Formal and distant relations between men in a family, and between a man and his children (especially his son), contrast with the informal and close relations between women, and between a woman and her children. Jay and Geertz both emphasize the continuing closeness of the mother–daughter relation-

ship as a daughter is growing up and throughout her married life. Jay suggests that there is a certain amount of ambivalence in the mother–daughter relationship, particularly as a girl grows toward adulthood and before she is married, but points out that at the same time the mother remains a girl's "primary figure of confidence and support" (1969:103).

Siegel (1969) describes Atjehnese families in Indonesia in which women stay on the homestead of their parents after marriage and are in total control of the household. Women tolerate men in the household only as long as they provide money, and even then treat them as someone between a child and a guest. Women's stated preference would be to eliminate even this necessary dependence on men: "Women, for instance, envision paradise as the place where they are reunited with their children and their mothers; husbands and fathers are absent, and yet there is an abundance all the same. Quarrels over money reflect the women's idea that men are basically adjuncts who exist only to give their families whatever they can earn" (p. 177). A woman in this society does not get into conflicts in which she has to choose between her mother and her husband, as happens in the Western working class (see above; also Komarovsky, 1962), where the reigning ideology supports the nuclear family.

In these three settings, the mother–daughter tie and other female kin relations remain important from a woman's childhood through her old age. Daughters stay closer to home in both childhood and adulthood, and remain involved in particularistic role relations. Sons and men are more likely to feel uncomfortable at home, and to spend work and play time away from the house. Male activities and spheres emphasize universalistic, distancing qualities: men in Java are the bearers and transmitters of high culture and formal relationships; men in East London spend much of their time in alienated work settings; Atjehnese boys spend their time in school, and their fathers trade in distant places.

Mother–daughter ties in these three societies, described as extremely close, seem to be composed of companionship and mutual cooperation, and to be positively valued by both mother and daughter. The ethnographies do not imply that women are weighed down by the burden of their relationships or by overwhelming guilt and responsibility. On the contrary, they seem to have developed a strong sense of self and self-worth, which continues to grow as they get older and take on their maternal role. The implication is that "ego strength" is not completely dependent on the firmness of the ego's boundaries.

Guntrip's distinction between "immature" and "mature" dependence clarifies the difference between mother–daughter relationships and women's psyche in the Western middle class and in the matrifocal societies described. Women in the Western middle class are caught up to some extent in issues of infantile dependence, while the women in matrifocal societies remain in definite connection with others, but in relationships characterized by mature dependence. As Guntrip describes it (1961:291): "*Mature dependence* is characterized by full differentiation of ego and object (emergence from primary identification) and therewith a capacity for valuing the object for its own sake and for giving as well as receiving; a condition which should be described not as independence but as mature dependence." This kind of mature dependence is also to be distinguished from the kind of forced independence and denial of need for relationship that I have suggested characterizes masculine personality, and that reflects continuing conflict about infantile dependence (Guntrip, 1961:293; my italics): "Maturity is not equated with independence though it includes a certain capacity for independence.... The independence of the mature person is simply that he does not collapse when he has to stand alone. It is not an independence of needs for other persons with whom to have relationship: *that would not be desired by the mature.*"

Depending on its social setting, women's sense of relation and connection and their embeddedness in social life provide them with a kind of security that men lack. The quality of a mother's relationship to her children and maternal self-esteem, on the one hand, and the nature of a daughter's developing identification with her mother, on the other, make crucial differences in female development.

Women's kin role, and in particular the mother role, is central and positively valued in Atjeh, Java, and East London. Women gain status and prestige as they get older; their major role is not fulfilled in early motherhood. At the same time, women may be important contributors to the family's economic support, as in Java and East London, and in all three societies they have control over real economic resources. All these factors give women a sense of self-esteem independent of their relationship to their children. Finally, strong relationships exist between women in these societies, expressed in mutual cooperation and frequent contact. A mother, then, when her children are young, is likely to spend much of her time in the company of other women, not simply isolated with her children.

These social facts have important positive effects on female psychological development. (It must be emphasized that all the ethnographies indicate that these same social facts make male development difficult and contribute to psychological insecurity and lack of ease in interpersonal relationships in men.) A mother is not invested in keeping her daughter from individuating and becoming less dependent. She has other ongoing contacts and relationships that help fulfill her psychological and social needs. In addition, the people surrounding a mother while a child is growing up become mediators between mother and daughter, by providing a daughter with alternative models for personal identification and objects of attachment, which contribute to her differentiation from her mother. Finally, a daughter's identification with her mother in this kind of setting is with a strong woman with clear control over important spheres of life, whose sense of self-esteem can reflect this. Acceptance of her gender identity involves positive valuation of herself, and not an admission of inferiority. In psychoanalytic terms, we might say it involves identification with a preoedipal, active, caring mother. Bibring points to clinical findings supporting this interpretation: "We find in the analysis of the women who grew up in this 'matriarchal' setting the rejection of the feminine role less frequently than among female patients coming from the patriarchal family culture" (1953:281).

There is another important aspect of the situation in these societies. The continuing structural and practical importance of the mother–daughter tie not only ensures that a daughter develops a positive personal and role identification with her mother, but also requires that the close psychological tie between mother and daughter become firmly grounded in real role expectations. These provide a certain constraint and limitation upon the relationship, as well as an avenue for its expression through common spheres of interest based in the external social world.

All these societal features contrast with the situation of the Western middle-class woman. Kinship relations in the middle class are less important. Kin are not likely to live near each other, and, insofar as husbands are able to provide adequate financial support for their families, there is no need for a network of mutual aid among related wives. As the middle-class woman gets older and becomes a grandmother, she cannot look forward to increased status and prestige in her new role.

The Western middle-class housewife does not have an important economic role in her family. The work she does and the responsibilities that go with it (household management, cooking, entertaining, etc.) do not seem to be really necessary to the economic support of her family (they are crucial contributions to the maintenance and reproduction of her family's class position, but this is not generally recognized as important either by the woman herself or by the society's ideology). If she works outside the home, neither she nor the rest of society is apt to consider this work to be important to her self-definition in the way that her housewife role is.

Child care, on the other hand, is considered to be her crucially important responsibility. Our post-Freudian society in fact assigns to parents (and especially to the mother)[16] nearly total responsibility for how children turn out. A middle-class mother's daily life is not centrally involved in relations with other women. She is isolated with her children for most of her workday. It is not surprising, then, that she is likely to invest a lot of anxious energy and guilt in her concern for her children and to look to them for her own self-affirmation, or that her self-esteem, dependent on the lives of others than herself, is shaky. Her life situation leads her to an overinvolvement in her children's lives.

A mother in this situation keeps her daughter from differentiation and from lessening her infantile dependence. (She also perpetuates her son's dependence, but in this case society and his father are more likely to interfere in order to assure that, behaviorally, at least, he doesn't *act* dependent.) And there are no other people around to mediate in the mother–daughter relationship. Insofar as the father is actively involved in a relationship with his daughter and his daughter develops some identification with him, this helps her individuation, but the formation of ego autonomy through identification with and idealization of her father may be at the expense of her positive sense of feminine self. Unlike the situation in matrifocal families, the continuing closeness of the mother–daughter relationship is expressed only on a psychological, interpersonal level. External role expectations do not ground or limit it.

It is difficult, then, for daughters in a Western middle-class family to develop self-esteem. Most psychoanalytic and social theorists[17] claim that the mother inevitably represents to her daughter (and son) regression, passivity, dependence, and lack of orientation to reality, whereas the father represents progression, activity, independence, and reality orientation.[18] Given the value implications of this dichotomy, there are advantages for the son in giving up his mother and identifying with his father. For the daughter, feminine gender identification means identification with a devalued, passive mother, and personal maternal identification is with a mother whose own self-esteem is low. Conscious rejection of her oedipal maternal identification, however, remains an unconscious rejection and devaluation of herself, because of her continuing preoedipal identification and boundary confusion with her mother.

Cultural devaluation is not the central issue, however. Even in patrilineal, patrilocal societies in which women's status is very low, women do not necessarily translate this cultural devaluation into low self-esteem, nor do girls have to develop difficult boundary problems with their mother. In the Moslem Moroccan family, for example, a large amount of sex segregation and sex antagonism gives women a separate (domestic) sphere in which they have a real productive role and control, and also a life situation in which any young mother is in the company of other women.[19] Women do not need to invest all their psychic energy in their children, and their self-esteem is not dependent on their relationship to their children. In this and other patrilineal, patrilocal societies, what resentment women do have at their oppressive situation is more often expressed toward their sons, whereas daughters are seen as allies against oppression. Conversely, a daughter develops relationships of attachment to and identification with other adult women. Loosening her tie to her mother therefore does not entail the rejection of all women. The close tie that remains between mother and daughter is based not simply on mutual overinvolvement but often on mutual understanding of their oppression.

CONCLUSION

Women's universal mothering role has effects both on the development of masculine and feminine personality and on the relative status of the sexes. This paper has described the development of relational personality in women and of personalities preoccupied with the denial of relation in men. In its comparison of different societies it has suggested that men, while guaranteeing to themselves sociocultural superiority over women, always remain psychologically defensive and insecure. Women, by contrast, although always of secondary social and cultural status, may in favorable circumstances gain psychological security and a firm sense of worth and importance in spite of this.

Social and psychological oppression, then, is perpetuated in the structure of personality. The paper enables us to suggest what social arrangements contribute (and could contribute) to social equality between men and women and their relative freedom from certain sorts of psychological conflict. Daughters and sons must be able to develop a personal identification with more than one adult, and preferably one embedded in a role relationship that gives it a social context of expression and provides some limitation upon it. Most important, boys need to grow up around men who take a major role in child care, and girls around women who, in addition to their child-care responsibilities, have a valued role and recognized spheres of legitimate control. These arrangements could help to ensure that children of both sexes develop a sufficiently individuated and strong sense of self, as well as a positively valued and secure gender identity that does not bog down either in ego-boundary confusion, low self-esteem, and overwhelming relatedness to others or in compulsive denial of any connection to others or dependence upon them.

NOTES

1. My understanding of mother–daughter relationships and their effect on feminine psychology grows out of my participation beginning in 1971 in a women's group that discusses mother–daughter relationships in particular and family relationships in general. All the women in this group have contributed to this understanding. An excellent dissertation by Marcia Millman (1972) first suggested to me the importance of boundary issues for women and became a major organizational focus for my subsequent work. Discussions with Nancy Jay, Michelle Rosaldo, Philip Slater, Barrie Thorne, Susan Weisskopf, and Beatrice Whiting have been central to the development of the ideas presented here. I am grateful to George Goethals, Edward Payne, and Mal Slavin for their comments and suggestions about earlier versions of this paper.

2. Margaret Mead provides the most widely read and earliest argument for this viewpoint (cf., e.g., 1935 and 1949); see also Chodorow (1971) for another discussion of the same issue.

3. Unfortunately, the language that describes personality structure is itself embedded with value judgment. The implication in most studies is that it is always better to have firmer ego boundaries, that "ego strength" depends on the degree of individuation. Gutmann, who recognizes the linguistic problem, even suggests that "so-called ego pathology may have adaptive implications for women" (1965:231). The argument can be made that extremes in either direction are harmful. Complete lack of ego boundaries is clearly pathological, but so also, as critics of contemporary Western men point out (cf., e.g., Bakan, 1966, and Slater, 1970), is individuation gone wild, what Bakan calls "agency unmitigated by communion," which he takes to characterize, among other things, both capitalism based on the Protestant ethic and aggressive masculinity. With some explicit exceptions that I will specify in context, I am using the concepts solely in the descriptive sense.

4. Slater (1968) provides one example of such an investigation. LeVine's recent work on psychoanalytic anthropology (1971a, b) proposes a methodology that will enable social scientists to study personality development in this way.

5. Particularly as interpreted by object-relations theorists (e.g., Fairbairn, 1952, and Guntrip, 1961) and, with some similarity, by Parsons (1964) and Parsons and Bales (1955).

6. See, e.g., Brunswick, 1940; Deutsch, 1932, 1944; Fliess, 1948; Freud, 1931; Jones, 1927; and Lampl-de Groot, 1927.

7. The important distinction between "positional" and "personal" identification comes from Slater, 1961, and Winch, 1962.

8. For more extensive arguments concerning this, see, e.g., Burton & Whiting (1961), Chodorow (1971), and Slater (1968).

9. The processes by which individual personal experiences and psychological factors contribute to or are translated into social and cultural facts, and, more generally, the circularity of explanations in terms of socialization, are clearly very complicated. A discussion of these issues, however, is not within the scope of this paper.

10. The question of the universality of the oedipus com-

plex as Freud describes it is beyond the scope of this paper. Bakan (1966, 1968) points out that in the original Oedipus myth, it was the father who first tried to kill his son, and that the theme of paternal infanticide is central to the entire Old Testament. He suggests that for a variety of reasons, fathers probably have hostile and aggressive fantasies and feelings about their children (sons). This more general account, along with a variety of psychological and anthropological data, convinces me that we must take seriously the notion that members of both generations may have conflicts over the inevitable replacement of the elder generation by the younger, and that children probably feel both guilt and (rightly) some helplessness in this situation.

11. These views are most extreme and explicit in two papers (Freud, 1925, 1933) and warrant the criticism that has been directed at them. Although the issue of penis envy in women is not central to this paper, it is central to Freud's theory of female development. Therefore I think it worthwhile to mention three accounts that avoid Freud's ideological mistakes while allowing that his clinical observations of penis envy might be correct.

Thompson (1943) suggests that penis envy is a symbolic expression of women's culturally devalued and underprivileged position in our patriarchal society; that possession of a penis symbolizes the possession of power and privilege. Bettelheim (1954) suggests that members of either sex envy the sexual functions of the other, and that women are more likely to express this envy overtly, because, since men are culturally superior, such envy is considered "natural." Balint (1954) does not rely on the fact of men's cultural superiority, but suggests that a little girl develops penis envy when she realizes that her mother loves people with penises, i.e., her father, and thinks that possession of a penis will help her in her rivalry for her mother's attentions.

12. See, e.g., Brunswick, 1940; Deutsch, 1925, 1930, 1932, 1944; Freedman, 1961; Freud, 1931; Jones, 1927.

13. Following Cohen (1969), I would suggest that the external structural features of these settings (in the family or in school, for instance) are often similar or the same for boys and girls. The different kind and amount of adult male and female participation in these settings accounts for their being experienced by children of different sexes as different sorts of milieux.

14. Gutmann points out that all these qualities are supposed to indicate lack of adequate ego strength, and suggests

that we ought to evaluate ego strength in terms of the specific demands of different people's (e.g., women's as opposed to men's) daily lives. Bakan goes even further and suggests that modern male ego qualities are a pathological extreme. Neither account is completely adequate. Gutmann does not consider the possibility (for which we have good evidence) that the everyday demands of an autocentric milieu are unreasonable: although women's ego qualities may be "functional" for their participation in these milieux, they do not necessarily contribute to the psychological strength of the women themselves. Bakan, in his (legitimate) preoccupation with the lack of connection and compulsive independence that characterize Western masculine success, fails to recognize the equally clear danger (which, I will suggest, is more likely to affect women) of communion unmitigated by agency—of personality and behavior with no sense of autonomous control or independence at all.

I think this is part of a more general social-scientific mistake, growing out of the tendency to equate social structure and society with male social organization and activities within a society. This is exemplified, for instance, in Erikson's idealistic conception of maternal qualities in women (1965) and, less obviously, in the contrast between Durkheim's extensive treatment of "anomic" suicide (1897) and his relegation of "fatalistic" suicide to a single footnote (p. 276).

15. This ethnography and a reading of it that focuses on strong female kin relations (Siegel, 1969) were brought to my attention by Tanner (1971).

16. See Slater (1970) for an extended discussion of the implications of this.

17. See, e.g., Deutsch, 1944, *passim;* Erikson, 1964:162; Klein & Rivière, 1937:18; Parsons, 1964, *passim;* Parsons & Bales, 1955, *passim.*

18. Their argument derives from the universal fact that a child must outgrow her/his primary identification with and total dependence upon the mother. The present paper argues that the value implications of this dichotomy grow out of the particular circumstances of our society and its devaluation of relational qualities. Allied to this is the suggestion that it does not need to be, and often is not, relationship to the father that breaks the early maternal relationship.

19. Personal communication from Fatima Mernissi, based on her experience growing up in Morocco and her sociological fieldwork there.

REFERENCES

Ariès, P. 1962. *Centuries of childhood: A social history of family life.* New York.

Bakan, D. 1966. *The duality of human existence: Isolation and communion in Western man.* Boston.

————. 1968. *Disease, pain, and sacrifice: Toward a psychology of suffering.* Boston.

Balint, A. 1954. *The early years of life: A psychoanalytic study.* New York.

Barry, H., Bacon, M., & I. Child. 1957. "A cross-cultural survey of some sex differences in socialization." *Journal of Abnormal and Social Psychology* 55:327–32.

Bettelheim, B. 1954. *Symbolic wounds: Puberty rites and the envious male.* New York.

Bibring, G. 1953. "On the 'passing of the Oedipus complex' in a matriarchal family setting." In R. Lowenstein, ed., *Drives, affects and behavior: Essays in honor of Marie Bonaparte,* pp. 278–84. New York.

Brunswick, R. 1940. "The preoedipal phase of the libido development." In R. Fliess, ed., pp. 231–53.

Burton, R., & Whiting, J. 1961. "The absent father and cross-sex identity." *Merrill-Palmer Quarterly of Behavior and Development* 7 (2):85–95.

Carlson, R. 1971. "Sex differences in ego functioning: Exploratory studies of agency and communion." *Journal of Consulting and Clinical Psychology* 37:267–77.

Chodorow, N. 1971. "Being and doing. A cross-cultural examination of the socialization of males and females." In V. Gornick & B. Moran, eds., *Woman in sexist society: Studies in power and powerlessness.* New York.

Cohen, R. 1969. "Conceptual styles, culture conflict, and nonverbal tests of intelligence." *American Anthropologist* 71:828–56.

Deutsch, H. 1925. "The psychology of woman in relation to the functions of reproduction." In R. Fliess, ed., pp. 165–79.

————. 1930. "The significance of masochism in the mental life of women." In R. Fliess, ed., pp. 195–207.

————. 1932. "On female homosexuality." In R. Fliess, ed., pp. 208–30.

————. 1944, 1945. *Psychology of women.* Vols. I & II. New York.

Durkheim, E. 1897. *Suicide.* New York, 1968.

Erikson, E. 1964. *Insight and responsibility.* New York.

————. 1965. "Womanhood and the inner space." In R. Lifton, ed., *The woman in America.* Cambridge, Mass.

Fairbairn, W. 1952. *An object-relations theory of the personality.* New York.

Fliess, R. 1948. "Female and preoedipal sexuality: A historical survey." In R. Fliess, ed., pp. 159–64.

————. 1961. *Ego and body ego: Contributions to their psychoanalytic psychology.* New York, 1970.

Fliess, R., Ed. 1969. *The psychoanalytic reader: An anthology of essential papers with critical introductions.* New York. Originally published in 1948.

Freedman, D. 1961. "On women who hate their husbands." In H. Ruitenbeek, ed., pp. 221–37.

Freud, S. 1925. "Some psychological consequences of the anatomical distinction between the sexes." In J. Strachey, ed., *The standard edition of the complete psychological works of Sigmund Freud,* Vol. XIX, pp. 248–58. London.

————. 1931. "Female sexuality." In H. Ruitenbeek, ed., pp. 88–105.

————. 1933. "Femininity." In *New introductory lectures in psychoanalysis,* pp. 112–35. New York, 1961.

Geertz, H. 1961. *The Javanese family: A study of kinship and socialization.* New York.

Guntrip, H. 1961. *Personality structure and human interaction: The developing synthesis of psycho-dynamic theory.* New York.

Gutmann, D. 1965. "Women and the conception of ego strength." *Merrill-Palmer Quarterly of Behavior and Development* 2:229–40.

Harper, E. 1969. "Fear and the status of women." *Southwestern Journal of Anthropology* 25:81–95.

Jay, R. 1969. *Javanese villagers: Social relations in rural Modjokuto.* Cambridge, Mass.

Jones, E. 1927. "The early development of female sexuality." In H. Ruitenbeek, ed., pp. 21–35.

Klein, M., & Rivière, J. 1937. *Love, hate and reparation.* New York, 1964.

Kohlberg, L. 1966. "A cognitive-developmental analysis of children's sex-role concepts and attitudes." In E. Maccoby, ed., *The development of sex differences,* pp. 82–173. Stanford, Calif.

Komarovsky, M. 1962. *Blue-collar marriage,* New York, 1967.

Lampl-de Groot, J. 1927. "The evolution of the Oedipus complex in women." In R. Fliess, ed., pp. 180–94.

LeVine, R. 1971a. "The psychoanalytic study of lives in natural social settings." *Human Development* 14:100–109.

————. 1971b. "Re-thinking psychoanalytic anthropology." Paper presented at the Institute on Psychoanalytic Anthropology, 70th Annual Meeting of the American Anthropological Association, New York.

Mead, M. 1935. *Sex and temperament in three primitive societies.* New York, 1963.

————. 1949. *Male and female: A study of sexes in a changing world.* New York, 1968.

Millman, M. 1972. "Tragedy and exchange: Metaphoric understandings of interpersonal relationships." Ph.D. dissertation, Department of Sociology, Brandeis University.

Minturn, L., & Hitchcock, J. 1963. "The Rajputs of Khalapur, India." In B. Whiting, ed., *Six cultures: Studies in child rearing.* New York.

Mitscherlich, A. 1963. *Society without the father.* New York, 1970.

Parsons, T., 1964. *Social structure and personality.* New York.

Parsons, T., & Bales, R. 1955. *Family, socialization and interaction process.* New York.

Ruitenbeek, H., Ed. 1966. *Psychoanalysis and female sexuality.* New Haven.

Siegel, J. 1969. *The rope of God.* Berkeley, Calif.

Slater, P. 1961. "Toward a dualistic theory of identification." *Merrill-Palmer Quarterly of Behavior and Development* 7:113–26.

———. 1968. *The glory of Hera: Greek mythology and the Greek family.* Boston.

———. 1970. *The pursuit of loneliness: American culture at the breaking point.* Boston.

Tanner, N. 1971. "Matrifocality in Indonesia and among Black Americans." Paper presented at the 70th Annual Meeting of the American Anthropological Association, New York.

Tax, M. 1970. *Woman and her mind: The story of daily life.* Boston.

Thompson, C. 1943. "'Penis envy' in women." In H. Ruitenbeek, ed., pp. 246–51.

Whiting, J. 1959. "Sorcery, sin and the superego: A cross-cultural study of some mechanisms of social control." In C. Ford, ed., *Cross-cultural approaches: Readings in comparative research,* pp. 147–68. New Haven, 1967.

Whiting, J., Kluckhohn, R., & Anthony, A. 1958. "The function of male initiation rites at puberty." In E. Maccoby, T. Newcomb, & E. Hartley, eds., *Readings in social psychology,* pp. 359–70. New York.

Winch, R. 1962. *Identification and its familial determinants.* New York.

Young, M., & Willmott, P. 1957. *Family and kinship in East London.* London, 1966.

R E A D I N G 7

"The Means to Put My Children Through":
Child-Rearing Goals and Strategies Among Black Female
Domestic Servants

BONNIE THORNTON DILL

This essay explores the family and child-rearing strategies presented by a small group of Afro-American women who held jobs as household workers while raising their children. The data are drawn from a study of the relationship of work and family among American-born women of African descent who were private household workers (domestic servants) for most of their working lives.

The primary method of data collection was life histories, collected through open-ended, in-depth interviews with 26 women living in the northeastern United States. All participants were between 60 and 80 years old. A word of caution in reading this essay: The

Reprinted from La Frances Rodgers-Rose, ed., *The Black Woman* (Beverly Hills, Calif.: Sage, 1980), pp. 107–23. Copyright © 1980 by Sage Publications, Inc. Reprinted by permission of Sage Publications, Inc.

conclusions are not meant to apply to all Black female domestic servants, but represent only my interpretation of the experiences of these 26 women.

The life history method is particularly useful in studying Black female domestic workers whose stories and experiences have largely been distorted or ignored in the social science literature.[1] According to Denzin (1970:220), the method "presents the experiences and definitions held by one person, group or organization as that person, group or organization interprets those experiences." As such, it provides a means of exploring the processes whereby people construct, endure, and create meaning in both the interactional and structural aspects of their lives. It aids in the identification and definition of concepts appropriate to a sociological understanding of the subject's experience, and moves toward building theory that is grounded in imagery and meanings relevant to the subject. Collected through in-depth interviews, life histories are active processes of rendering meaning to one's life— its conflicts, ambiguities, crises, successes, and significant interpersonal relationships. Subjects are not merely asked to "report" but rather to reconstruct and interpret their choices, situations and experiences.[2] The study of Black Americans cries out for such a sensitized approach to their lives.

The child-rearing goals and strategies adopted by the women who participated in this study are particularly revealing of the relationship of work and family. As working mothers, they were concerned with providing safe and secure care for their children while they were away from home. As working-class people, seeking to advance their children beyond their own occupational achievements, they confronted the problem of guiding them toward goals that were outside of their own personal experience. These issues, as well as others, take on a particular form for women who were household workers primarily because of the nature of their work.

Unlike many other occupations, domestic work brings together, in a closed and intimate sphere of human interaction, people whose paths would never cross were they to conduct their lives within the socioeconomic boundaries to which they were ascribed. These intimate interactions across the barriers of income, ethnicity, religion, and race occur within a sphere of life that is private and has little public exposure—the family.

As household workers, these women often become vital participants in the daily lives of two separate families: their employer's and their own. In fact, they have often been described as being "like one of the family" (Childress, 1956), and yet the barriers between them and their employers are real and immutable ones. In addition, working-class Black women employed by middle- and upper-class white families observe and experience vast differences in the material quality of life in the two homes. With regard to child-rearing, employers could provide luxuries and experiences for their children that were well beyond the financial means of the employee.

This essay, therefore, presents some of the ways in which the women talked about their reactions and responses to the discrepancies in life chances between those of their children and those of their employers. To some extent, these discrepancies became the lens through which we viewed their goals for their children

and their child-rearing practices. At the same time, the contrast in objective conditions provides a background against which the women's perceptions of similarities between themselves and their employers are made more interesting.

The data from this study indicate that the relationship between the employee's family life and her work was shaped by four basic factors. First, there was the structure of the work. Whether she worked full-time or part-time and lived in, lived out, or did day work determined the extent to which she became involved in the employer's day-to-day life. It also determined the amount of time she had to share with her own family. Second were the tasks and duties she was assigned. With regard to her own child-rearing goals and strategies, the intermingling of employer and employee lifestyles occurred most frequently among those women who took care of the employer's children. It is through their discussion of these activities that the similarities and differences between the two families are most sharply revealed. A third factor is the degree of employer–employee intimacy. An employee who cared for the employer's children was more likely to have an intimate relationship with her employing family, but not always. Though the employer–employee relationship in domestic service is characterized as a personalized one when compared with other work relationships, this does not presume intimacy between the two parties; that is, a reciprocal exchange of interests and concerns. Among the women who participated in this study, those who did not share much of their own life with their employers appeared to minimize the interaction of work and family. Finally were the employee's goals for her children. Those women who felt that their employers could aid them in achieving the educational or other goals they had set for their children were more likely to encourage an intermingling of these two parts of their lives.

On domestic work and upward mobility:

Strangely enough, I never intended for my children to have to work for anybody in the capacity that I worked. Never. And I never allowed my children to do any babysitting or anything of the sort. I figured it's enough for the mother to do it and in this day and time you don't have to do that. . . . So they never knew anything about going out to work or anything. They went to school.

Given the low social status of the occupation, the ambivalent and defensive feelings many of the women expressed about their work and the eagerness with which women left the occupation when other opportunities were opened to them, it is not at all surprising that most of the women in this study said they did not want their children to work in domestic service. Their hopes were centered upon "better" jobs for their children: jobs with more status, income, security, and comfort. Pearl Runner[3] recalled her goals for her children:

> My main goal was I didn't want them to follow in my footsteps as far as working. I always wanted them to please go to school and get a good job because it's important. That was really my main object.

Lena Hudson explained her own similar feelings this way:

> They had a better chance than I had, and they shouldn't look back at what I was doing. They had a better chance and a better education than I had, so look out for something better than I was doing. And they did. I haven't had a one that had to do any housework or anything like that. So I think that's good.

The notion of a better chance is a dominant one in the women's discussions of their goals for their children. They portray themselves as struggling to give their children the skills and training they did not have; and as praying that opportunities which had not been open to them would be open to their children. In their life histories, the women describe many of the obstacles they encountered in this quest. Nevertheless, there are dilemmas which, though not discussed explicitly, are implicit in their narratives and a natural outgrowth of their aspirations.

First of these is the task of guiding children toward a future over which they had little control and toward occupational objectives with which they had no direct experience. Closely tied to this problem was their need to communicate the undesirability of household work and at the same time maintain their personal dignity despite the occupation. While these two problems are not exceptional for working-class parents in an upwardly mobile society, they were mediated for Black domestic workers through the attitudes toward house-

hold work held by members of the Black communities in which the women lived and raised their children.

Had domestic work not been the primary occupation of Black women and had racial and sexual barriers not been so clearly identifiable as the reason for their concentration in this field of employment, these problems might have been viewed more personally and the women's histories might have been more self-deprecating than in fact they were. This particular set of circumstances would suggest that the women at least had the option of directing their anger and frustration about their situation outward upon the society rather than turning it inward upon themselves. Drake and Cayton (1945) confirm this argument in their analysis of domestic work, saying that "colored girls are often bitter in their comments about a society which condemns them to the 'white folks' kitchen'" (p. 246). In addition, attitudes in the Black community toward domestic service work mediated some of the more negative attitudes which were prevalent in the wider society. Thus, the community could potentially become an important support in the child-rearing process, reinforcing the idea that while domestic service was low-status work, the people who did it were not necessarily low-status people.

The data in this study do not include the attitudes of the children of domestic servants toward their mothers' occupation. To my knowledge, there has been no systematic study of this issue. However, some biographies and community studies have provided insight into the range of feelings children express. Drake and Cayton (1945), for example, cite one woman who described her daughter as being "bitter against what she calls the American social system." DuBois talks about feeling an instinctive hatred toward the occupation (1920:110). I have had employers tell me that their domestics' children hated their children because the employer's kids got the best of their mother's time. I have also heard Black professionals speak with a mixture of pride, anger, and embarrassment about the fact that their mother worked "in the white folks' kitchen" so that they could get an education. Clearly, these issues deserve further study.

Throughout these histories, the women identified education as the primary means through which mobility could be achieved. As with many working-class people, education was seen as a primary strategy for upward mobility; a means to a better-paying and more prestigious job. Most of the women who participated in this study had not completed high school (the mean years of schooling completed for the group was 9.2 years). They reasoned that their limited education in combination with racial discrimination had hindered their own chances for upward mobility. Zenobia King explained her attitudes toward education in this way:

> In my home in Virginia, education, I don't think, was stressed. The best you could do was be a school teacher. It wasn't something people impressed upon you you could get. I had an aunt and cousin who were trained nurses and the best they could do was nursing somebody at home or something. They couldn't get a job in a hospital. . . . I didn't pay education any mind really until I came to New York. I'd gotten to a certain stage in domestic work in the country and I didn't see the need for it. When I came, I could see opportunities that I could have had if I had a degree. People said it's too bad I didn't have a diploma.

From Mrs. King's perspective and from those of some of the other women, education for a Black woman in the South before World War II did not seem to offer any tangible rewards. She communicates the idea that an education was not only unnecessary but could perhaps have been a source of even greater frustration and dissatisfaction. This idea was reemphasized by other women who talked about college-educated women they knew who could find no work other than domestic work. In fact, both Queenie Watkins and Corrinne Raines discussed their experiences as trained teachers who could not find suitable jobs and thus took work in domestic service. Nevertheless, Corrinne Raines maintained her belief in education as a means of upward mobility, a belief that was rooted in her family of orientation. She said:

> I am the 12th child [and was] born on a farm. My father was—at that day, you would call him a successful farmer. He was a man who was eager for his children to get an education. Some of the older ones had gotten out of school and were working and they were able to help the younger ones. That's how he was able to give his children as much education as he gave them, because the older ones helped him out.

Given this mixed experience with education and social mobility, it might be expected that many of the women would have expressed reservations about the value of an education for their children's mobility. However, this was not the case. Most of them, reflecting on their goals for their children, expressed sentiments similar to Pearl Runner's:

> This is the reason why I told them to get an education. . . . If they want to go to college it was fine because the higher you go the better jobs you get. They understood that because I always taught that into them. Please try to get an education so you can get a good job 'cause it was hard for colored girls to get jobs, period. They had to have an education.

Mrs. Runner's statement is important because it contains the rudiments of an explanation for why she and other women stressed education in the face of discriminatory practices that frequently discounted even their best efforts. Opallou Tucker elaborates on this theme and provides a somewhat more detailed explanation:

> It's [domestic work] all right if you want to do it and if you can't do anything else, but it's not necessary now. If you prepare yourself for something that's better, the doors are open now. I know years ago there was no such thing as a Black typist. I remember girls who were taking typing when I was going to school. They were never able to get a job at it. So it really [was] for their own personal use. My third child, and a niece, after they got up some size, started taking typing. And things began to open up after she got grown up. But in my day and time you could have been the greatest typist in the world, but you would never have gotten a job. It's fine to prepare yourself so that when opportunity knocks, you'll be able to catch up.

In these statements, Mrs. Runner and Mrs. Tucker convey a complex and subtle understanding of the interaction of racism and opportunity. They recognize the former as a real and tangible barrier, but they do not give in to it. They describe themselves as having taught their children to be prepared. Education was seen as a means of equipping oneself for whatever breaks might occur in the nation's patterns of racial exclusion. Thus, key to their aspirations for their children was the hope and belief that opportunities would eventually open and permit their children to make full use of the skills and knowledge they encouraged them to attain.

Nevertheless, maintaining these hopes could not

have been as easy and unproblematic as hindsight makes it seem. The fact that many of the women who expressed this strong commitment to education at the time of the interview had seen their children complete a number of years of schooling and enter jobs which would never have been open to them when they were young was clearly a source of pride and satisfaction which could only have strengthened their beliefs. Thus, as they recalled their goals and aspirations for their children, they tended to speak with a sense of self-affirmation about their choices; confidence that may not have been present years earlier. As Mrs. Runner expressed,

> I tell you I feel really proud and I really feel that with all the struggling that I went through, I feel happy and proud that I was able to keep helping my children, that they listened and that they all went to high school. So when I look back, I really feel proud, even though at times the work was very hard and I came home very tired. But now, I feel proud about it. They all got their education.

Perhaps reflective of their understanding of the complex interaction of racism and opportunity, most of the women described limited and general educational objectives for their children. Although a few women said they had wanted their children to go to college and one sent her son to a private high school with the help of scholarships, most women saw high school graduation as the concrete, realizable objective which they could help their children attain. Willie Lee Murray's story brings out a theme that was recurrent in several other histories:

> My children did not go to college. I could not afford to send them to college. And they told me, my younger one especially, he said: Mommy, I don't want to go to college at your expense. When I go to college, I'll go on my own. I would not think of you workin' all your days—sometimes you go sick and I don't know how you gonna get back. You put us through school and you gave us a beautiful life. We'll get to college on our own.

Mrs. Murray seems to indicate that while she would have liked her children to go to college, she limited her goals and concentrated her energies upon their completing high school.

In addition to limited educational objectives, most of the women did not describe themselves as having had a specific career objective in mind for their children. They encouraged the children to get an education in order to get a better job. Precisely what those jobs would be was left open, to be resolved through the interaction of their son or daughter's own luck, skill, perseverance, and the overall position of the job market vis-à-vis Black entrants.

Closely related to the goals the women expressed about their children's future position in society were their goals relative to their child's development as a person. Concern that their children grow up to be good, decent, law-abiding citizens was a dominant theme in these discussions. Most of the women in the study described their employers as having very specific career goals for their children, usually goals that would have the children following their parents' professional footsteps. In characterizing the differences between their goals and those of their employers, the women stressed the differences in economic resources. Johnnie Boatwright was quite explicit on this point:

> There was a lot of things they [employers] did that I wanted to do for mine, but I just couldn't afford it. . . . Like sending them to school. Then they could hire somebody; child slow, they could hire a tutor for the child. I wish I could have been able to do what they done. And then too, they sent them to camps, nice camps, not any camp but one they'd pick out. . . . So that's what I wished I could had did for him [her son]. . . . See whether it was right or wrong, mines I couldn't do it because I didn't have the money to do it. I wasn't able to do it. So that's the way it was. I did what I could and that was better than nothing.

In light of these discrepancies in resources, personal development was an important and realizable goal which may have been an adaptive response to the barriers which constricted the women's range of choices. This was an area over which the women had greater influence and potential control. It was also an area in which they probably received considerable community support, since values in the Black community, as pointed out above, attribute status to success along personal and family dimensions in addition to the basic ones of occupation, education, and income.

While Mrs. Boatwright conveys a sense of resignation and defeat in discussing her inability to do for her son what the employers did for theirs, Pearl Runner is more optimistic and positive about what she was able to do for her children.

> Their money may be a little more, but I felt my goal was just as important as long as they [the children] got their education. They [employers] had the money to do lots more than I did, but I felt that if I kept working, my goals was just as important. I felt my children were just as important.

Feelings like those expressed by both Mrs. Runner and Mrs. Boatwright are reflected throughout the data in the women's comparisons of their aspirations and expectations for their children's future with those of their employers. However, it also seems apparent that their intimate participation in families in which the husbands were doctors, lawyers, stockbrokers, college professors, writers, and housewives provided considerable support for their more limited educational objectives. While not everyone had the specific experience of Lena Hudson, whose employer provided an allowance for her daughter which permitted the girl to stay in high school, the model of the employer's life with regard to the kinds of things they were able to give their children was a forceful one and is repeatedly reflected in the women's discussions of their child-rearing goals.

When asked: "What do you think were the goals that the Wallises [her employers] had for their children? What did they want for their children? What did they want them to become in life?" Lena Hudson replied:

> Well, for *their* children, I imagine they wanted them to become like they were, educators or something that like. What they had in mind for *my* children, they saw in me that I wasn't able to make all of that mark. But raised my children in the best method I could. Because I wouldn't have the means to put *my* children through like they could for *their* children. And they see I wasn't the worst person in the world, and they saw I meant *some* good to my family, you see, so I think that was the standard with them and my family.

Her answers provide insight into the personal and social relationship between the two families and into her recognition of the points of connectedness and distance between them. The way in which she chose to answer the question reflects her feelings about working for the Wallis family and how that helped her accomplish the goals which she had set for her own family.

MRS. HUDSON: And in the meantime, they owned a big place up in Connecticut. And they would take my children, and she, the madam, would do for my children just what she did for theirs.

INTERVIEWER: What kinds of things do you think your children learned from that, from the time that they spent with them?

MRS. HUDSON: Well, I think what they learnt from them, to try to live a decent life themselves, and try to make the best out of their life and the best out of the education they had. So I think that's what they got from them.

INTERVIEWER: What would you say you liked most about the work that you did?

MRS. HUDSON: Well, what I liked most about it, the things that I weren't able to go to school to do for my children. I could kinda pattern from the families that I worked for, that I could give my children the best of my abilities. And I think that's the thing I got from them, though they [her children] couldn't become professors, but they could be good in whatever they did.

The warm personal relationship between the two families was based not only on the direct assistance which the Wallises gave Mrs. Hudson, but also on the ways in which she was able to utilize her position in their family to support and sustain her personal goals. Thus, we can understand why she saw work as an ability rather than a burden. Work was a means for attaining her goals; it provided her with the money she needed to be an independent person, and it exposed her and her children to "good" things—values and a style of life which she considered important. To some extent, Lena Hudson found the same things in her work that she found in her church; reinforcement for the standards which she held for her children and for herself.

The women who stressed education for their children and saw their children attain it were most frequently women like Mrs. Hudson who were closely tied to one or two employing families for a long period of time. For the most part, they were the women who had careers in domestic service. However, ties with employers were not crucial even within this small group, because some women said they had received very little support from their employers along these lines. Several women, as indicated above, pointed to a strong emphasis upon education in their families of orientation. Additionally, education as a means of upward mobility is a fundamental element in American social ideology. It appears, therefore, that the importance of the employer–employee relationship was in the support and reinforcement these middle-class families' goals, aspirations, and style of life provided the women. The amount of support varied, of course, with the particular relationship the employee had with her employer's family and the degree of the employer's interest in and commitment to the employee's personal life. On the spectrum presented by the women in this study, Mrs. Hudson's relationship with the Wallis family would be at one end; the relationship between Georgia Sims and the family for whom she worked longest at the other. The following segment of the interview with Mrs. Sims is a good example of a minimally interactive employer–employee relationship:

INTERVIEWER: What were your goals for your children?

MRS. SIMS: Well, to be decent, law-abiding men. That's all.

INTERVIEWER: Do you think there were any similarities between your goals for your children and the goals your employers, the Peters, had for their children?

MRS. SIMS: On, sure! Oh, yes, because I mean you must remember, they had the money; now I didn't have it. Oh, definitely there was different goals between us. [*Note:* Mrs. Sims obviously understood the question to be about *differences* rather than similarities, so the question was asked again.]

INTERVIEWER: Do you think there were any things that were alike in terms of your goals for your children and their goals for their children?

MRS: SIMS: No. Nothing.

INTERVIEWER: Nothing at all?

MRS. SIMS: No.

INTERVIEWER: What kinds of goals did they have for their children?

MRS. SIMS: Oh, I mean education, going on to be, you know, upstanding citizens, and they had the jobs—My children couldn't get up, I mean when they become 20, 21, they couldn't get up and go out and say, well, I'm gonna get an office job, I'm gonna get this kind of job. No. The best thing they could do is go and be a porter in the subway.

Mrs. Sims was very detached from her occupation. She was not a career household worker. In fact, she described herself as having had very limited contact with her employers, arriving when they were all on their way to work and school and often departing before they returned home. She said that she had no specific child-care duties. Thus, her description of the employers' goals for their children is probably more of a projection on her part than it is based on discussion or direct participation in the employers' life.

Two types of child-rearing goals have been identified thus far: goals regarding the child's future position in the society and goals regarding his or her personal development. In addition to these two types of goals, the women aspired to provide their children with some accoutrements of a middle-class lifestyle. Their discussion of these desires often reflects the discrepancies between their lives and those of their employers. Jewell Prieleau describes her employer's children as follows:

Her children always dress nice. Whenever her daughter was going to music school or anyplace, I had to take her in a taxi. Whenever she finish, she had to be picked up. I had to go get her.

In describing her own grandchildren, she said:

I went to three nice department stores and I opened up credit for them so I could send them to school looking nice. I got up early in the morning and sent them off to school. After school I would pick them up in a taxi and bring them here [the job].

Mrs. Prieleau is not the only woman in this study who talked about going into debt to give her children some of the material things that she never had and that were part of her image of a "better life" for her children. Willa Murray told the following story:

I remember when my sons wanted that record player. I said I'm gonna get a record player; I'm gonna do days work. But I had to get AC current for this record player. I called up this lady [her employer] and I said, I'm goin' to Household Finance this morning. If they call you for a reference would you give me some reference. She said, sure. I sat down and the man said come in. He said, Miz Murray, do you have a co-signer. I said, no. He said, well what's your collateral? I said something about the furniture. He said, do you work? I said, yeah, I do days work. He said, days work? You don't have a steady job? I said yes sir, days work. He said, who do you work for? I told him. He said, we'll see what we can do. He gave the hundred and fifty dollars. I came home, phone the electric company, told them they could send the man to put the current in.

In these statements and some of the ones quoted earlier, we begin to see how the employer's style of life influenced these women. However, it cannot be assumed that the women's desires were merely an outgrowth of the employer–employee relationship. The material products which they sought are so widely available in the culture that they are considered general symbols of upward mobility. Upward mobility for their children was the basic goal of most of the women who participated in this study. It was a goal which seems to have existed prior to and apart from their work situation and the values of their employers. Nevertheless, in some cases the women found reinforcement for and regeneration of these goals within the work situation, just as they found supports within their community and family lives.

RAISING THE "WHITE FOLKS'" CHILDREN

The women's discussion of child-rearing strategies, particularly such issues as discipline, exemplify both the class and cultural differences between employer and employee. For private household workers, these differences are expressed within a relationship of inequality. The data collected in this study permitted an examination of employer parent–child interactions as it was perceived and constructed by the household workers. This has benefits as well as liabilities. As outsiders whose child-rearing practices and lifestyle differed from those of the employers, the women in this study provide a particularly revealing picture of parent–child relationships in the employing family. However, they were not mere observers of the process; they participated in it and thereby restructured it. The women's insights, therefore, offer a unique critical perspective that is found only in subordinates' characterizations of their superiors. However, as participants in the process, their observations are limited to the time frame in which they were present and make it virtually impossible to assess the women's impact on the process. Nevertheless, their stories about their own role in rearing the employer's children provide considerable understanding of how they saw their work and, more importantly, how their work affected their own style of parenting. Willa Murray's comments illuminate this:

> Throughout, the people that I worked for taught their children that they can talk back. They would let them [the children] say anything they wanted to say to them. I noticed a lot of times they [the children] would talk back or something and they [the parents] would be hurt. They would say to me, I wish they [the children] wouldn't. I wish they were more like your children. They allowed them to do so much. But they taught them a lot of things. I know one thing, I think I got a lot of things from them. . . . I think I've learnt a lot about [how to do] with my children by letting them do and telling them—like the whites would tell them—that I trust you. I think a lot of Black mothers when we come along, they didn't trust us. They were telling us what we were gonna do. . . . But I think they [whites] talk to their children about what's in life, what's for them, what not to do. And they let them talk, they tell them all the things that we didn't tell our children. We're beginning to tell our children. . . . The alternative is that I told my children straight, that if a boy and a girl have sexual intercourse—I learned that from the white people—and you don't have anything to protect it, that girl will get a baby. So my children were looking out for that. I learned that from my people. I listened to what they tell [their children].

Talk between parents and children is a dominant theme of Mrs. Murray's comments. She is critical of her employers for permitting their children to "talk back" to them; to question their instructions, to respond impertinently or otherwise mock or demean the parents' authority. Yet, talking *with* the children, reasoning with them, explaining things and hearing their thoughts and opinions on various matters, is behavior which she admired enough to try to emulate. Telling the children that you "trust them" places greater emphasis upon self-direction than upon following orders. Clearly, the line between letting the children talk and permitting them to "talk back" is a difficult one to draw, yet Mrs. Murray draws it in transferring her work-learned behavior to her own child-rearing circumstances.

It should not be surprising that there would be behavioral characteristics which employers would admire in employee children, just as there were traits which Mrs. Murray and others admired in their employers' interactions with their children. In fact, it is striking that each would admire aspects of the other and seek to incorporate them within their own lives while the circumstances that generated those particular patterns were quite different. Nevertheless, reorienting the parent–child relationship in the employer's family was frequently described as a regular part of the worker's child-care activity. In fact, the women's discussions of their experiences in caring for their employers' children are variations upon the stories of resistance which characterized their establishing themselves in the employer–employee relationship. Queenie Watkins' description of the following child-care incident provides a good example:

One morning I was feeding Stevie oatmeal and I was eating oatmeal. His uncle, the little girl and I were all sitting at the table together eating. He said, I don't want this and I'm gonna spit it out. I said, you better not, Stevie. With that he just let it all come into my face. I took myself a big mouthful and let it go right back in his face. He screamed, and his uncle said, what did you do that for? I said, you fight fire with fire. My psychology is to let a child know he can't do to you what you can't do to him. The mother came running. I said, this ends my work here but she said, just wash Stevie's face. I said, I'm not gonna wash it; let him wash it himself—he wasn't two years old. Finally, I said, I'll take him and wash his face but who's gonna wash my face? His mother started to laugh and said,

you're some character. And you know what, he never did that again. He ate his food and I never had to chastise Stevie about anything after that.

Zenobia King told a slightly different story about the way in which she inserted her values into the parent–child relationship of an employing family:

One time the daughter went out and she stayed all day. She didn't tell her mother where she was. And when she came back, her mother jumped on her in a really bad way. She told her she wished she had died out there, etc., etc., and her daughter said if her mother had loved her she would have asked where she was going. So, I separated them. I sent the daughter to one room and the mother to the other and talked to both of them and I brought them back together.

In both of these stories, as in others in this genre, the women see themselves as the instructor of both the children and the parents. They characterize themselves as helping the parent learn how to parent while simultaneously setting rules and regulations as to the kind of treatment they should expect from the children. Queenie Watkins' philosophy of fighting fire with fire was reiterated by Oneida Harris in describing her relations with one of the children whom she cared for:

He was nine years old and he rate me the worst maid they'd ever had because I wouldn't take any of his foolishness. If he kicked me in the shins, I'd kick him back. . . . I said he hasn't any bringing up, and if I stay here he's gonna listen. I said to his mother, if you don't want me, tell me tomorrow and I'll go. So anyway, the next day he would bring me up a little bit; she's the next-to-the-worst maid we ever had. Each week I came up till I was the best one.

As in the stories of resistance, both Queenie Watkins and Oneida Harris depict themselves as setting guidelines for respect from the children in the same way respect was established in the employer–employee relationship. The additional dimension of instructing parents in the ways of handling their children was another recurrent theme in the life histories.

Through these and other similar anecdotes which

the women used to describe their participation in caring for their employers' children, they communicate a perception of their employers as uncomfortable in exercising the power associated with the parenting role. To a large degree, they depict their employers as either inconsistent and afraid of their children or ignorant of child-rearing strategies that would develop obedience and respect. The women see this as their forte; in many instances they describe themselves as exercising power on behalf of the parents and teaching the children to obey them and respect their parents. In so doing, they also present themselves as teaching the parents. Willa Murray is keenly aware of the paradoxical nature of this situation when she says: "Now I'm the maid, not the mistress." In the maid–mistress relationship, the latter gives instructions which the former carries out. In a sense, Willa Murray's story presents a role reversal, one which she finds both surprising and amusing but also appropriate. It is akin to the anecdote in which she described herself telling her employers that they had more education than she did but their behavior was not intelligent. These presentations suggest that despite stereotypic conceptions of the maid–mistress relationship, women in these roles could gain considerable power and influence within a family, particularly where they had worked for a number of years and had considerable responsibility.

The household worker's impact on the parent–child relationship is only one aspect of their child-care role. The other, equally important, aspect of this role is their relationship with the children they cared for and the fact, implicit in our earlier discussion, that they describe themselves as surrogate mothers for these children:

There's a long time she [the child] use to thought I was her mamma. She would ask me why is my skin white and yours brown, you my mamma? I tell her I'm not your mamma and I see the hurt coming in her eye. You know like she didn't want me to say that. I said there's your mamma in there, I'm just your nurse. She said no, you my mamma. [Mattie Washington]

I took care of the children. In fact, the children would call me when they had a problem or something, before they would call her [their mother]. [Zenobia King]

He [the boy] looked at me as a mother. When he went away to school he just would not come home if I wasn't there. And even when he was at home, if he was out playing with the boys he'd come in, his mother, grandmother and father would be sitting around, he'd say, where is everybody? His mother would look around and say well if you mean Oneida, I think she's upstairs. Upstairs he'd come. And they couldn't get that. It was sad, you see. They give him everything in the world but love. [Oneida Harris]

I was more like a mother to them, and you see she didn't have to take too much time as a mother should to know her children. They were more used to me because I put them to bed. The only time she would actually be with them was like when I'm off Thursday and on Sundays. They would go out sometime, but actually I was really the mother because I raised them from little. [Pearl Runner]

Without exception, the women in this study who had child-care responsibilities talked about themselves as being "like a mother" to the employers' children. Their explanations of the development of this kind of relationship tended to follow those of Oneida Harris and Pearl Runner: their employers were frequently unavailable and spent less time with the children than they did. Because they interacted with the children on a daily basis and often had responsibility for their care, discipline, play, and meals, their role was a vital and important one in the eyes of both child and parent. This explains, in part, some of their power in affecting the parent–child relationship, as discussed above. The fact that the women had such an important and pivotal role in the development of the employer's children and at the same time held a job in which they could be replaced gave the entire relationship of parent, child, and housekeeper a particularly intense quality. For the most part, workers developed their strongest emotional ties to the children in the employing family.

Because the women saw themselves as surrogate mothers, the children whom they cared for could easily become their surrogate children. This is particularly apparent when we compare their comments and discussions about their own and their employers' children. One of the most prevalent patterns was to talk with pride and satisfaction about the accomplishments of their surrogate children. In general, the women would talk about how frequently they heard from these children and whether they got cards, letters, or money at Mothers' Day or Christmas. In addition, they would describe the (now grown) children's occupation and family and, if they had pictures available, they would show them to me. This type of commentary provided an interesting parallel to their discussions of their own children. But even more important, it was designed to communicate the closeness that they felt existed between them and the children they had raised; closeness which was maintained over a number of years even after the children were grown.

Surrogate mothering, as pointed out in Opallou Tucker's case study, had the prospect of tying the worker into the emotional life of the employing family. For the women who lived outside the employer's household and were actively engaged in rearing their own children and caring for their own families, as were most of the women in this study, the prospect was minimized. However, for a woman like Mattie Washington, who lived in for most of the 30 years that she

worked for one family, the potential for becoming enveloped in their life, at the expense of her own, was much greater.

In most instances, the women described themselves as caretakers, playmates, disciplinarians, confidantes, and friends of the employer's children. Nevertheless, it is clear from their discussions that in most cases the real ties of affection between themselves and their employer came through the children.

The children, therefore, provided the ties that bound the women to their employers as well as the mark of their difference. The role of surrogate mother allowed the women to cross these barriers and, for a fleeting moment, express their love and concern for a child without regard to the obstacles that lay ahead. Also, because most young children readily return love that is freely given and are open and accepting of people without regard to status factors that have meaning for their parents, the workers probably felt that they were treated with greater equality and more genuine acceptance by the children of the household.

NOTES

1. There is a very limited body of literature directly focused upon Black women in domestic service in the United States. Many of these studies are confined to the Southern experience. Among the most important containing data on Black women in northern cities are Haynes (1923), Eaton (1967), and Chaplin (1964). Some discussion of the subject was also found in community studies, particularly those conducted before World War II (Drake & Cayton, 1945; Oving-

ton, 1969). Labor studies provided a third source of data (among these were Green & Woodson, 1930, and Haynes, 1912).

2. This discussion is largely drawn from a paper by Dill and Joselin (1977).

3. The names used for the participants in the study are fictitious.

REFERENCES

Chaplin, D. 1964. "Domestic service and the Negro." In A. Shostak and W. Gamberg, eds., *Blue Collar World.* Englewood Cliffs, N.J.: Prentice-Hall.

Childress, A. 1956. *Like one of the family.* Brooklyn: Independence Publishers.

Denzin, N. K. 1970. *The research act.* Chicago: AVC.

Dill, B. T., & Joselin, D. 1977. "The limit of quantitative

methods: The need of life histories." Paper presented at the Society for the Study of Social Problems Annual Meetings, Chicago.

Drake, S. C., & Cayton, H. 1945. *Black metropolis.* New York: Harper & Row.

DuBois, W. E. B. 1920. *Darkwater.* New York: Harcourt Brace.

Eaton, I. 1967. "Negro domestic service in Seventh Ward Philadelphia." In W. E. B. DuBois, *The Philadelphia Negro.* New York: Schocken.

Green, L. J., & Woodson, C. G. 1930. *The Negro wage earner.* Washington, D.C.: Association for the Study of Negro Life and History.

Haynes, G. 1912. *The Negro at work in New York City: A study in economic progress.* New York: Longmans.

Haynes, G. 1923. "Negroes in domestic service in the United States." *Journal of Negro History* 8:384–442.

Ovington, M. W. 1969. *Half a man.* New York: Schocken.

R E A D I N G 8

The Secret Fear That Keeps Us from Raising Free Children

LETTY COTTIN POGREBIN

In the 19th century when women of all races began their drive for the vote, what was the argument most often used against them?

That voting was a masculine concern, and that therefore women who attempted it would become (or already were) "mannish," "unwomanly," and "unnatural." In short, sexually suspect.

In the 20th century when young men objected to the rationale for the American military presence in Vietnam, what was the argument most used to discredit their protest?

That refusing a masculine enterprise like war made them "like a women," "soft," "scared," and therefore sexually suspect.

It's time we faced head-on the most powerful argument that authoritarian forces in any society use to keep people—male or female—in line: the idea that you are not born with gender but must earn it, and thus the threat that if you don't follow orders you will not be a "real man" or "real woman."

Even those of us who have long since stopped worrying about this conformity for ourselves may find

that our own deepest conditioning takes over in the emotional landscape inhabited by our children and our feelings about child-rearing. It is this conditioning that the right wing plays on to prevent change, no matter how life-enhancing. And it is these fears that sometimes inhibit pro-child attitudes in the most well-intentioned parents; the fear

1. that sex roles determine sexuality;
2. that specific ingredients *make* a child homosexual; and
3. that homosexuality is one of the worst things that can happen.

ASSUMPTION I: SEX ROLES DETERMINE SEXUALITY

It was inevitable that the cult of sex differences would lead us to the familiar romantic bromide—*opposites attract.* Most people truly believe that the more "masculine" you are, the more you'll love and be loved by females, and the more "feminine" you are, the more you'll love and be loved by males.

If you believe this quid pro quo, you will systematically raise your daughters and sons differently so that they become magnets for their "opposites," and you will fear that resistance to stereotyped sex roles might distort their behavior in bed as adults.

Clever, this patriarchy. In return for conformity, it promises a "normal" sex life for our children. But it can't deliver on that promise, because all available evidence proves that *sex role does not determine sexual orientation.*

During the last decade thousands of homosexual men and women have "come out" from behind their "straight" disguises, and we discovered that except for choice of sex partner, they look and act so much the same as everyone else that as sexologist Dr. Wainright Churchill put it, "they may not be identified as homosexuals even by experts." Most female and male homosexuals have tried heterosexual intercourse; many have been married and have children; and sometimes they are remarkable only for being so *unlike* the "gay" stereotype.

Take a quintessential "man's man," David Kopay—six feet one, 205 pounds, 10-year veteran of pro football. "I was the typical jock," writes Kopay in his autobiography (*The David Kopay Story;* Bantam). "I was tough. I was successful. And all the time I knew I preferred sex with men."

And great beauties, such as Maria Schneider, the sex bomb of *Last Tango in Paris;* "feminine-looking" women, married women, mothers of many children have, for centuries, had lesbian love affairs with one another, disproving the opposites-attract theory with a vengeance, and reminding us again that sex roles do not determine sexuality.

ASSUMPTION 2: SPECIFIC INGREDIENTS MAKE A CHILD HOMOSEXUAL

Although no one knows what causes homosexuality, there is no shortage of theories on the subject. Sociobiologists and other behavioral scientists pursue the idea that "genetic loading" can create a predisposition toward homosexuality, a theory that will remain farfetched until researchers find many sets of identical twins both members of which became homosexual although reared separately.

Proponents of *hormone theory* have tried to find a definitive connection between testosterone level and homosexual orientation. However, various biochemical studies of the last decade show directly contradictory results, and even when hormonal differences are found, no one knows whether hormones cause the homosexuality, or the homosexual activities cause the hormone production.

The biochemical "explorers," like the geneticists, perpetuate the idea that homosexuals are a different species with a hormonal disturbance that chemistry might "cure." So far, attempts to alter sexual orientation with doses of hormones have only succeeded in increasing the *amount* of sex drive, not in changing its direction.

The *conditioned-response theory* holds that sexual orientation depends not on biology or "instincts" but on learning from experience, from the same reward-and-punishment process as any other acquired behavior, and from sexual trigger mechanisms, such as pictures, music, or certain memories, that set off homosexual or heterosexual responses the way the bell set off Pavlov's dog salivating.

The conditioning theory, logical as far as it goes, leads us down several blind alleys. Why might one child experience a certain kind of stroking as pleasurable when a same-sex friend does it but *more* pleasurable when a friend of the other sex does it, while another child feels the reverse? Why do some children "learn to" overcome the effects of a frightening early sexual experience, while others may be hurt by it forever, and still others "learn" to merge pain with pleasure?

Doesn't cultural pressure itself "teach" children to avoid a particular sexual response, no matter what the body has learned to like? Otherwise, how do millions of adolescents move from masturbation to homosexual experimentation—often the *only* interpersonal sexual pleasure they have known—to heterosexuality?

Perhaps the conditioned-response theory can explain the man who has felt homosexual since childhood, but how does it account for the woman who, after 20 years as an orgasmic, exclusive heterosexual, had a lesbian encounter and found she didn't have to "learn" to like it?

One research psychiatrist reminds us that we don't yet understand the basic mechanism of sexual arousal in the human central nervous system, and until we do, questions about homosexual or heterosexual arousal are entirely premature.

Psychoanalytic theory, the most steadfast and intimidating of all the causation theories, is the one that "blames" homosexuality on the family. To challenge it, we must begin at the beginning.

In 1905, Sigmund Freud declared that human beings are innately *bisexual* at birth and their early psychosexual experiences tip the scales one way or the other.

To ensure a heterosexual outcome, the child is supposed to identify with the same-sex parent, to "kill them off," so to speak, as an object of sexual interest. For example, a girl's psychodynamic is "I become like Mother, therefore I no longer desire Mother; I desire Father, but I can't have him so I desire those who are like him."

If instead the girl identifies with the other-sex parent ("I become like Father"), he is killed off as object choice ("therefore I do not desire Father"), and the girl will be a lesbian ("I desire Mother or those who are like her"). For the boy, obviously, the same psychodynamic is true in reverse.

According to this theory, female homosexuality derived mainly from too much *hostility* toward the mother for passing on her inferior genital equipment. The lesbian girl identifies with the Father and compensates for her hatred of the inferior mother by loving women, while rejecting "femininity" (meaning passivity, masochism, inferiority) for herself.

Male homosexuality derives mainly from too much *attachment* to the mother, i.e., a Momma's Boy can't be a woman's man.

Although many contemporary psychologists now believe otherwise, and despite the fact that Freud's views are unsupported by objective evidence, it is his ideas that millions of lay people have accepted—the view that human beings grow "healthy" by the Oedipal resolution: fearing and thus respecting one parent (Dad) and disdaining the other (Mom). Since our parents stand as our first models of male and female, this primal fear and disdain tends to form a paradigm for lifelong sexual enmity, suspicion, betrayal, and rejection.

Father is supposed to represent reality and Mother is associated with infant dependency. In order to gain their independence, both girls and boys must form an alliance with Father against Mother. Politically, this translates to male supremacy ("alliance with Father") and cultural misogyny ("against Mother"). Psychologically, the message is conform or you might turn out "queer."

The hitch is, as we've noted, that sex role and sexual orientation have been shown to be totally unrelated. Modern practitioners may know this, but since they have not loudly and publicly revised psychoanalytic theories on homosexuality, they are in effect supporting the old lies. What's more, their silence leaves unchallenged these contradictions within psychoanalytic theory itself:

- A human *instinct,* by definition, should be the same for everyone, everywhere; yet in societies where sex stereotypes do not exist, the supposedly instinctual Oedipal psychodrama doesn't exist either.
- If the castration complex, the fear of losing the penis, is the founding element of "masculinity," how is it that Dr. Robert Stoller, professor of psychiatry at UCLA Medical School, found boys who were born without penises believed themselves boys anyway?
- How do we account for millions of children who become heterosexual though raised in father-absent homes? How do these mothers arouse fear and respect in the boy and the requisite penis envy in the girl?
- Why do batteries of psychological tests *fail to show any significant difference* between lesbians and heterosexuals on the psychological criteria that are supposed to "cause" female homosexuality?
- How can one say that male homosexuals identify with Mother and take on "feminine" ways, when mothers of homosexuals are supposedly "masculine," dominant, and aggressive?
- If a woman's compensation for her missing penis is a baby boy, then of course she'll overprotect her son as a hedge against a *second* castration—losing him. It's a cruel tautology to posit motherhood in these terms and, at the same time, to hold Mother responsible for overprotection of the one treasure she's supposedly spent her whole life seeking.
- Could it be that girls and women envy the *privileges* that accrue to people whose distinguishing feature happens to be the penis, without envying the penis?
- Freud declared the "vaginal orgasm" to be the diploma of heterosexual maturity, yet in *Human Sexual Response,* William Masters and Virginia Johnson have proved the clitoris to be the physiological source of all female orgasms. Why require a girl to unlearn clitoral pleasure when in every other instance Freud believed that "urges dissipate when they become satisfied"? Is it because the clitoral or-

gasm is active, not receptive; because it doesn't require a penis and it doesn't result in procreation?
Was the promotion of the "vaginal orgasm" patriarchy's way of keeping females passive, male-
connected, and frequently pregnant?

We could devote pages and pages to poking holes in
psychoanalytic theory, but these final points should do
the trick: studies show that the classic "homosexual-
inducing" family produces plenty of "straight" children; other kinds of families raise both heterosexual
and homosexual siblings under the same roof; and totally "straight" family constellations rear homosexual
kids.

And so, all speculations have been found wanting,
and we are left with one indisputable fact: *no one
knows what causes homosexuality.*

ASSUMPTION 3: HOMOSEXUALITY IS ONE OF THE WORST THINGS THAT CAN HAPPEN TO ANYONE

Studies show that the majority of American people
want homosexuality "cured." Yet the facts—when
this volatile subject can be viewed factually—prove
that homosexuality is neither uncommon, abnormal,
nor harmful to its practitioners or anyone else.

When the "naturalness" of heterosexuality is
claimed via examples in the animal kingdom, one can
point to recorded observations of homosexuality
among seagulls, cows, mares, sows, primates, and
many other mammals. But more important, among
humans, "there is probably no culture from which homosexuality has not been reported," according to Drs.
Clellan Ford and Frank Beach in *Patterns of Sexual
Behavior* (Harper). And no matter what moral or legal
prohibitions have been devised through the ages, none
has ever eliminated homosexuality. In fact, the incidence of homosexuality is greater in countries that forbid it than in those that don't. With all the fluctuations
of public morality, many sources confirm that 10 percent of the entire population consider themselves exclusively homosexual at any given place and time.

Aside from choosing to love members of their own
sex, lesbians and homosexual males have been found
no different from heterosexuals in gender identity or
self-esteem, in drinking, drug use, suicide rates, relationships with parents and friends, and general life sat-

isfaction. One study actually found lower rates of
depression among lesbians; another study measured
higher competence and intellectual efficiency; still another found more lesbians (87 percent) than heterosexual women (18 percent) experienced orgasm "almost
always"; and two important recent reports revealed
that homosexuals seem clearly far *less* likely than heterosexuals to commit child abuse or other sexual
crimes. In short, many homosexuals "could very well
serve as models of social comportment and psychological maturity." And yet, parents feel obliged to protect
their children from it.

Why?

In a word, *homophobia*—fear and intolerance of
homosexuality. Despite the facts just enumerated,
millions still believe homosexuality *is* the worst thing.
In one study, nearly half of the college students questioned labeled it more deviant than murder and drug
addiction. Others reveal their homophobia by sitting
an average of 10 inches further away from an interviewer of the same sex wearing a "gay and proud" button than from an interviewer wearing no button. Another group said they wouldn't be able to form a close
friendship with a gay person.

In a society that works as hard as ours does to convince everyone that Boys are Better, homosexual
taunts whether "sissy" or "faggot," say *nonboy*. In
pure form, the worst insult one boy can scream at another is "You girl!" That curse is the coming home to
roost of the cult of sex differences. Indeed, sexism and
homophobia go hand in hand. The homophobic male
needs sharp sex-role boundaries to help him avoid
transgressing to the "other side." His terror is that he
is not different enough from the "opposite" sex, and
that his "masculine" facade may not always protect
him from the "femininity" within himself that he
learned as a boy to hate and repress. Among men, homophobia is rooted in contempt for everything
female.

A homophobic man cannot love a woman with
abandon, for he might reveal his vulnerability; he cannot adore and nurture his children because being
around babies is "sissy" and child care is "women's
work." According to his perverse logic, making
women pregnant is "masculine," but making children
happy is a betrayal of manhood. One man complained
that his child wouldn't shake hands and was getting
too old for father–son kissing. How old was "too old"?
Three.

Homophobia, the malevolent enforcer of sex-role behavior, is the enemy of children because it doesn't care about children, it cares about conformity, differences, and divisions.

If women seem to be less threatened by homosexuality than men and less obsessed with latent homosexual impulses, it's because the process of "becoming" a woman is considered less arduous for the female and less important to society than the process of "proving" one's manhood. "Masculinity" once won is not to be lost. But a girl needn't guard against losing that which is of little value.

Like male homosexuals, the lesbian doesn't need the other sex for physical gratification. But the lesbian's crime goes beyond sex: she doesn't need men at all. Accordingly, despite the relative unimportance of female sexuality, lesbianism is seen as a hostile alternative to heterosexual marriage, family, and patriarchal survival.

Before children have the vaguest idea about who or what is a homosexual, they learn that homosexuality is something frightening, horrid, and nasty. They be-

come homophobic long before they understand what it is they fear. They learn that "What are you, a sissy?" is the fastest way to coerce a boy into self-destructive exploits.

While homophobia cannot prevent homosexuality, its power to destroy female assertiveness and male sensitivity is boundless. For children who, for whatever reason, would have been homosexual no matter what, homophobia only adds external cruelty to their internal feelings of alienation. And for those who become the taunters, the ones who mock and harass "queers," homophobia is a clue to a disturbed sense of self.

It's all so painful. And so unnecessary. Eliminate sex-role stereotypes and you eliminate homophobia. Eliminate homophobia and you eliminate the power of words to wound and the power of stigma to mold a person into something she or he was never meant to be. So here's my best advice on the subject: *Don't worry how to raise a heterosexual child; worry about how not to be a homophobic parent.*

R E A D I N G 9

Girls and Boys Together . . . But Mostly Apart:
Gender Arrangements in Elementary Schools

BARRIE THORNE

Throughout the years of elementary school, children's friendships and casual encounters are strongly separated by sex. Sex segregation among children, which

Reprinted from Willard W. Hartup and Zick Rubin, eds., *Relationships and Development* (Hillsdale, N.J.: Lawrence Erlbaum Associates, 1986). Volume sponsored by the Social Science Research Council. Copyright © 1986 by Lawrence Erlbaum Associates. Reprinted by permission of the publisher and author.

starts in preschool and is well established by middle childhood, has been amply documented in studies of children's groups and friendships (e.g., Eder & Hallinan, 1978; Schofield, 1981) and is immediately visible in elementary school settings. When children choose seats in classrooms or the cafeteria, or get into line, they frequently arrange themselves in same-sex clusters. At lunchtime, they talk matter-of-factly about "girls' tables" and "boys' tables." Playgrounds have gendered turfs, with some areas and activities, such as large playing fields and basketball courts, controlled mainly by boys, and others—smaller enclaves like jungle-gym areas and concrete spaces for hopscotch or jumprope—more often controlled by girls. Sex segregation is so common in elementary schools that it is meaningful to speak of separate girls' and boys' worlds.

Studies of gender and children's social relations have mostly followed this "two worlds" model, separately describing and comparing the subcultures of girls and of boys (e.g., Lever, 1976; Maltz & Borker, 1983). In brief summary: Boys tend to interact in larger, more age-heterogeneous groups (Lever, 1976; Waldrop & Halverson, 1975; Eder & Hallinan, 1978). They engage in more rough and tumble play and physical fighting (Maccoby & Jacklin, 1974). Organized sports are both a central activity and a major metaphor in boys' subcultures; they use the language of "teams" even when not engaged in sports, and they often construct interaction in the form of contests. The shifting hierarchies of boys' groups (Savin-Williams, 1976) are evident in their more frequent use of direct commands, insults, and challenges (Goodwin, 1980).

Fewer studies have been done of girls' groups (Foot, Chapman, & Smith, 1980; McRobbie & Garber, 1975), and—perhaps because categories for description and analysis have come more from male than female experience—researchers have had difficulty seeing and analyzing girls' social relations. Recent work has begun to correct this skew. In middle childhood, girls' worlds are less public than those of boys; girls more often interact in private places and in smaller groups or friendship pairs (Eder & Hallinan, 1978; Waldrop & Halverson, 1975). Their play is more cooperative and turn-taking (Lever, 1976). Girls have more intense and exclusive friendships, which take shape around keeping and telling secrets, shifting alliances, and indirect ways of expressing disagreement (Goodwin, 1980; Lever, 1976; Maltz & Borker, 1983). Instead of direct commands, girls more often use directives which merge speaker and hearer, e.g., "let's" or "we gotta" (Goodwin, 1980).

Although much can be learned by comparing the social organization and subcultures of boys' and of girls' groups, the separate worlds approach has eclipsed full, contextual understanding of gender and social relations among children. The separate worlds model essentially involves a search for group sex differences, and shares the limitations of individual sex

difference research. Differences tend to be exaggerated and similarities ignored, with little theoretical attention to the integration of similarity and difference (Unger, 1979). Statistical findings of difference are often portrayed as dichotomous, neglecting the considerable individual variation that exists; for example, not all boys fight, and some have intense and exclusive friendships. The sex difference approach tends to abstract gender from its social context, to assume that males and females are qualitatively and permanently different (with differences perhaps unfolding through separate developmental lines). These assumptions mask the possibility that gender arrangements and patterns of similarity and difference may vary by situation, race, social class, region, or subculture.

Sex segregation is far from total, and is a more complex and dynamic process than the portrayal of separate worlds reveals. Erving Goffman (1977) has observed that sex segregation has a "with-then-apart" structure; the sexes segregate periodically, with separate spaces, rituals, groups, but they also come together and are, in crucial ways, part of the same world. This is certainly true in the social environment of elementary schools. Although girls and boys do interact as boundaried collectivities—an image suggested by the separate worlds approach—there are other occasions when they work or play in relaxed and integrated ways. Gender is less central to the organization and meaning of some situations than others. In short, sex segregation is not static, but is a variable and complicated process.

To gain an understanding of gender which can encompass both the "with" and the "apart" of sex segregation, analysis should start not with the individual, nor with a search for sex differences, but with social relationships. Gender should be conceptualized as a system of relationships rather than as an immutable and dichotomous given. Taking this approach, I have organized my research on gender and children's social relations around questions like the following: How and when does gender enter into group formation? In a given situation, how is gender made more or less salient or infused with particular meanings? By what rituals, processes, and forms of social organization and conflict do "with-then-apart" rhythms get enacted? How are these processes affected by the organization of institutions (e.g., different types of schools, neighborhoods, or summer camps), varied settings (e.g., the constraints and possibilities governing interaction on playgrounds vs. classrooms), and particular encounters?

METHODS AND SOURCES OF DATA

This study is based on two periods of participant observation. In 1976–1977 I observed for 8 months in a largely working-class elementary school in California, a school with 8% Black and 12% Chicana/o students. In 1980 I did fieldwork for 3 months in a Michigan elementary school of similar size (around 400 students), social class, and racial composition. I observed in several classrooms—a kindergarten, a second grade, and a combined fourth–fifth grade—and in school hallways, cafeterias, and playgrounds. I set out to follow the round of the school day as children experience it, recording their interactions with one another, and with adults, in varied settings.

Participant observation involves gaining access to everyday, "naturalistic" settings and taking systematic notes over an extended period of time. Rather than starting with preset categories for recording, or with fixed hypotheses for testing, participant observers record detail in ways which maximize opportunities for discovery. Through continuous interaction between observation and analysis, "grounded theory" is developed (Glaser & Strauss, 1967).

The distinctive logic and discipline of this mode of inquiry emerges from: (1) theoretical sampling—being relatively systematic in the choice of where and whom to observe in order to maximize knowledge relevant to categories and analysis which are being developed; and (2) comparing all relevant data on a given point in order to modify emerging propositions to take account of discrepant cases (Katz, 1983). Participant observation is a flexible, open-ended and inductive method, designed to understand behavior within, rather than stripped from, social context. It provides richly detailed information which is anchored in everyday meanings and experience.

DAILY PROCESSES OF SEX SEGREGATION

Sex segregation should be understood not as a given, but as the result of deliberate activity. The outcome is dramatically visible when there are separate girls' and boys' tables in school lunchrooms, or sex-separated groups on playgrounds. But in the same lunchroom one can also find tables where girls and boys eat and talk together, and in some playground activities the sexes mix. By what processes do girls and boys separate into gender-defined and relatively boundaried collectivities? And in what contexts, and through what processes, do boys and girls interact in less gender-divided ways?

In the school settings I observed, much segregation happened with no mention of gender. Gender was implicit in the contours of friendship, shared interest, and perceived risk which came into play when children chose companions—in their prior planning, invitations, seeking of access, saving of places, denials of entry, and allowing or protesting of "cuts" by those who violated the rules for lining up. Sometimes children formed mixed-sex groups for play, eating, talking, working on a classroom project, or moving through space. When adults or children explicitly invoked gender—and this was nearly always in ways which separated girls and boys—boundaries were heightened and mixed-sex interaction became an explicit arena of risk.

In the schools I studied, the physical space and curricula were not formally divided by sex, as they have been in the history of elementary schooling (a history evident in separate entrances to old school buildings, where the words "Boys" and "Girls" are permanently etched in concrete). Nevertheless, gender was a visible marker in the adult-organized school day. In both schools, when the public address system sounded, the principal inevitably opened with: "Boys and girls ... ," and in addressing clusters of children, teachers and aides regularly used gender terms ("Heads down, girls"; "The girls are ready and the boys aren't"). These forms of address made gender visible and salient, conveying an assumption that the sexes are separate social groups.

Teachers and aides sometimes drew upon gender as a basis for sorting children and organizing activities. Gender is an embodied and visual social category which roughly divides the population in half, and the separation of girls and boys permeates the history and lore of schools and playgrounds. In both schools—although through awareness of Title IX, many teachers had changed this practice—one could see separate girls' and boys' lines moving, like caterpillars, through the school halls. In the fourth–fifth-grade classroom the teacher frequently pitted girls against boys for spelling and math contests. On the playground in the Michigan school, aides regarded the space close to the building as girls' territory, and the playing fields "out there" as boys' territory. They sometimes shooed children of the other sex away from those spaces, especially boys who ventured near the girls' area and seemed to have teasing in mind.

In organizing their activities, both within and apart from the surveillance of adults, children also explicitly invoked gender. During my fieldwork in the Michigan school, I kept daily records of who sat where in the lunchroom. The amount of sex segregation varied: it was least at the first-grade tables and almost total among sixth-graders. There was also variation from classroom to classroom within a given age, and from day to day. Actions like the following heightened the gender divide: In the lunchroom, when the two second-grade tables were filling, a high-status boy walked by the inside table, which had a scattering of both boys and girls, and said loudly, "Oooo, too many girls," as he headed for a seat at the far table. The boys at the inside table picked up their trays and moved, and no other boys sat at the inside table, which the pronouncement had effectively made taboo. In the end, that day (which was not the case every day), girls and boys ate at separate tables.

Eating and walking are not sex-typed activities, yet in forming groups in lunchrooms and hallways children often separated by sex. Sex segregation assumed added dimensions on the playground, where spaces, equipment, and activities were infused with gender meanings. My inventories of activities and groupings on the playground showed similar patterns in both schools: boys controlled the large fixed spaces designated for team sports (baseball diamonds, grassy fields used for football or soccer); girls more often played closer to the building, doing tricks on the monkey bars (which, for sixth-graders, became an area for sitting and talking) and using cement areas for jumprope, hopscotch, and group games like four-square. (Lever, 1976, provides a good analysis of sex-divided play.) Girls and boys most often played together in kickball, and in group (rather than team) games like four-square, dodgeball, and handball. When children used gender to exclude others from play, they often drew upon beliefs connecting boys to some activities and girls to others: A first-grade boy avidly watched an all-female game of jumprope. When the girls began to shift positions, he recognized a means of access to the

play and he offered, "I'll swing it." A girl responded, "No way, you don't know how to do it, to swing it. You gotta be a girl." He left without protest. Although children sometimes ignored pronouncements about what each sex could or could not do, I never heard them directly challenge such claims.

When children had explicitly defined an activity or a group as gendered, those who crossed the boundary—especially boys who moved into female-marked space—risked being teased. ("Look! Mike's in the girls' line!"; "That's a girl over there," a girl said loudly, pointing to a boy sitting at an otherwise all-female table in the lunchroom.) Children, and occasionally adults, used teasing—especially the tease of "liking" someone of the other sex, or of "being" that sex by virtue of being in their midst—to police gender boundaries. Much of the teasing drew upon heterosexual romantic definitions, making cross-sex interaction risky, and increasing social distance between boys and girls.

RELATIONSHIPS BETWEEN THE SEXES

Because I have emphasized the "apart" and ignored the occasions of "with," this analysis of sex segregation falsely implies that there is little contact between girls and boys in daily school life. In fact, relationships between girls and boys—which should be studied as fully as, and in connection with, same-sex relationships—are of several kinds:

1. "Borderwork," or forms of cross-sex interaction which are based upon and reaffirm boundaries and asymmetries between girls' and boys' groups.
2. Interactions which are infused with heterosexual meanings.
3. Occasions where individuals cross gender boundaries to participate in the world of the other sex.
4. Situations where gender is muted in salience, with girls and boys interacting in more relaxed ways.

Borderwork

In elementary school settings boys' and girls' groups are sometimes spatially set apart. Same-sex groups sometimes claim fixed territories such as the basketball court, the bars, or specific lunchroom tables. However, in the crowded, multifocused, and adult-controlled environment of the school, groups form and disperse at a rapid rate and can never stay totally apart. Contact between girls and boys sometimes lessens sex segregation, but gender-defined groups also come together in ways which emphasize their boundaries.

"Borderwork" refers to interaction across, yet based upon and even strengthening gender boundaries. I have drawn this notion from Fredrik Barth's (1969) analysis of social relations which are maintained across ethnic boundaries without diminishing dichotomized ethnic status.¹ His focus is on more macro, ecological arrangements; mine is on face-to-face behavior. But the insight is similar: groups may interact in ways which strengthen their borders, and the maintenance of ethnic (or gender) groups can best be understood by examining the boundary that defines the groups, "not the cultural stuff that it encloses" (Barth, 1969:15). In elementary schools there are several types of borderwork: contests or games where gender-defined teams compete; cross-sex rituals of chasing and pollution; and group invasions. These interactions are asymmetrical, challenging the separate-but-parallel model of "two worlds."

Contests Boys and girls are sometimes pitted against each other in classroom competitions and playground games. The fourth–fifth-grade classroom had a boys' side and a girls' side, an arrangement that reemerged each time the teacher asked children to choose their own desks. Although there was some within-sex shuffling, the result was always a spatial moiety system—boys on the left, girls on the right—with the exception of one girl (the "tomboy" whom I'll describe later), who twice chose a desk with the boys and once with the girls. Drawing upon and reinforcing the children's self-segregation, the teacher often pitted the boys against the girls in spelling and math competitions, events marked by cross-sex antagonism and within-sex solidarity. The teacher introduced a math game; she would write addition and subtraction problems on the board, and a member of each team would race to be the first to write the correct answer. She wrote two score-keeping columns on the board: "Beastly Boys" ... "Gossipy Girls." The boys yelled out, as several girls laughed, "Noisy girls! Gruesome girls!" The girls sat in a row on top of their desks; sometimes they moved collectively, pushing their hips or whispering "Pass it on." The boys stood along the wall, some reclining against desks. When members of

either group came back victorious from the front of the room, they would do the "giving five" hand-slapping ritual with their team members.

On the playground a team of girls occasionally played a team of boys, usually in kickball or team two-square. Sometimes these games proceeded matter-of-factly, but if gender became the explicit basis of team solidarity, the interaction changed, becoming more antagonistic and unstable. Two fifth-grade girls played against two fifth-grade boys in a team game of two-square. The game proceeded at an even pace until an argument ensued about whether the ball was out or on the line. Karen, who had hit the ball, became annoyed, flashed her middle finger at the other team, and called to a passing girl to join their side. The boys then called out to other boys, and cheered as several arrived to play. "We got five and you got three!" Jack yelled. The game continued, with the girls yelling, "Bratty boys! Sissy boys!" and the boys making noises—"Weee haw," "Ha-ha-ha"—as they played.

Chasing Cross-sex chasing dramatically affirms boundaries between girls and boys. The basic elements of chase and elude, capture and rescue (Sutton-Smith, 1971) are found in various kinds of tag with formal rules, and in informal episodes of chasing which punctuate life on playgrounds. These episodes begin with a provocation (taunts like "You can't get me!" or "Slobber monster!"; bodily pokes or the grabbing of possessions). A provocation may be ignored, or responded to by chasing. Chaser and chased may then alternate roles. In an ethnographic study of chase sequences on a school playground, Christine Finnan (1982) observes that chases vary in number of chasers to chased (e.g., one chasing one or five chasing two); form of provocation (a taunt or a poke); outcome (an episode may end when the chased outdistances the chaser, or with a brief touch, being wrestled to the ground, or the recapturing of a hat or a ball); and in use of space (there may or may not be safety zones).

Like Finnan (1982) and Sluckin (1981), who studied a playground in England, I found that chasing has a gendered structure. Boys frequently chase one another, an activity which often ends in wrestling and mock fights. When girls chase girls, they are usually less physically aggresssive; they less often, for example, wrestle one another to the ground.

Cross-sex chasing is set apart by special names—"girls chase the boys"; "boys chase the girls"; "the chase"; "chasers"; "chase and kiss"; "kiss chase";

"kissers and chasers"; "kiss or kill"—and by children's animated talk about the activity. The names vary by region and school, but contain both gender and sexual meanings (this form of play is mentioned, but only briefly analyzed, in Finnan, 1982; Sluckin, 1981; Parrott, 1972; and Borman, 1979).

In "boys chase the girls" and "girls chase the boys" (the names most frequently used in both the California and Michigan schools) boys and girls become, by definition, separate teams. Gender terms override individual identities, especially for the other team ("Help, a girl's chasin' me!"; "C'mon, Sarah, let's get that boy"; "Tony, help save me from the girls"). Individuals may also grab someone of their sex and turn them over to the opposing team: Ryan grabbed Billy from behind, wrestling him to the ground. "Hey, girls, get 'im," Ryan called.

Boys more often mix episodes of cross-sex with same-sex chasing. Girls more often have safety zones, places like the girls' restroom or an area by the school wall, where they retreat to rest and talk (sometimes in animated postmortems) before new episodes of cross-sex chasing begin.

Early in the fall in the Michigan school, where chasing was especially prevalent, I watched a second-grade boy teach a kindergarten girl how to chase. He slowly ran backwards, beckoning her to pursue him, as he called, "Help, a girl's after me." In the early grades chasing mixes with fantasy play, e.g., a first-grade boy who played "sea monster," his arms outflung and his voice growling, as he chased a group of girls. By third grade, stylized gestures—exaggerated stalking motions, screams (which only girls do), and karate kicks—accompany scenes of chasing.

Names like "chase and kiss" mark the sexual meanings of cross-sex chasing, a theme I return to later. The threat of kissing—most often girls threatening to kiss boys—is a ritualized form of provocation. Cross-sex chasing among sixth-graders involves elaborate patterns of touch and touch avoidance, which adults see as sexual. The principal told the sixth-graders in the Michigan school that they were not to play "pom-pom," a complicated chasing game, because it entailed "inappropriate touch."

Rituals of Pollution   Cross-sex chasing is sometimes entwined with rituals of pollution, as in "cooties," where specific individuals or groups are treated as contaminating or carrying "germs." Children have rituals

for transfering cooties (usually touching someone else and shouting, "You've got cooties!"), for immunization (e.g., writing "CV" for "cootie vaccination" on their arms), and for eliminating cooties (e.g., saying "no gives" or using "cootie catchers" made of folded paper) (described in Knapp & Knapp, 1976). While girls may give cooties to girls, boys do not generally give cooties to one another (Samuelson, 1980).

In cross-sex play, either girls or boys may be defined as having cooties, which they transfer through chasing and touching. Girls give cooties to boys more often than vice versa. In Michigan, one version of cooties is called "girl stain"; the fourth-graders whom Karkau (1973) describes used the phrase "girl touch." "Cootie queens" or "cootie girls" (there are no "kings" or "boys") are female pariahs, the ultimate school untouchables, seen as contaminating not only by virtue of gender, but also through some added stigma such as being overweight or poor.[2] That girls are seen as more polluting than boys is a significant asymmetry, which echoes cross-cultural patterns, although in other cultures female pollution is generally connected to menstruation, and not applied to prepubertal girls.

Invasions   Playground invasions are another asymmetric form of borderwork. On a few occasions I saw girls invade and disrupt an all-male game, most memorably a group of tall sixth-grade girls who ran onto the playing field and grabbed a football which was in play. The boys were surprised and frustrated, and, unusual for boys this old, finally tattled to the aide. But in the majority of cases, boys disrupt girls' activities rather than vice versa. Boys grab the ball from girls playing four-square, stick feet into a jumprope and stop an ongoing game, and dash through the area of the bars where girls are taking turns performing, sending the rings flying. Sometimes boys ask to join a girls' game and then, after a short period of seemingly earnest play, disrupt the game. Two second-grade boys begged to "twirl" the jumprope for a group of second-grade girls who had been jumping for some time. The girls agreed, and the boys began to twirl. Soon, without announcement, the boys changed from "seashells, cockle bells" to "hot peppers" (spinning the rope very fast), and tangled the jumper in the rope. The boys ran away laughing.

Boys disrupt girls' play so often that girls have developed almost ritualized responses: they guard their ongoing play, chase boys away, and tattle to the aides.

In a playground cycle which enhances sex segregation, aides who try to spot potential trouble before it occurs sometimes shoo boys away from areas where girls are playing. Aides do not anticipate trouble from girls who seek to join groups of boys, with the exception of girls intent on provoking a chase sequence. And indeed, if they seek access to a boys' game, girls usually play with boys in earnest rather than breaking up the game.

A close look at the organization of borderwork—or boundaried interactions between the sexes—shows that the worlds of boys and girls may be separate, but they are not parallel, nor are they equal. The worlds of girls and boys articulate in several asymmetric ways:

1. On the playground, boys control as much as ten times more space than girls, when one adds up the area of large playing fields and compares it with the much smaller areas where girls predominate. Girls, who play closer to the building, are more often watched over and protected by the adult aides.

2. Boys invade all-female games and scenes of play much more than girls invade boys. This, and boys' greater control of space, correspond with other findings about the organization of gender, and inequality, in our society: compared with men and boys, women and girls take up less space, and their space and talk are more often violated and interrupted (Greif, 1982; Henley, 1977; West & Zimmerman, 1983).

3. Although individual boys are occasionally treated as contaminating (e.g., a third-grade boy who both boys and girls said was "stinky" and "smelled like pee"), girls are more often defined as polluting. This pattern ties to themes that I discuss later: it is more taboo for a boy to play with (as opposed to invade) girls, and girls are more sexually defined than boys.

A look at the boundaries between the separated worlds of girls and boys illuminates within-sex hierarchies of status and control. For example, in the sex-divided seating in the fourth–fifth-grade classroom, several boys recurringly sat near "female space": their desks were at the gender divide in the classroom, and they were more likely than other boys to sit at a predominantly female table in the lunchroom. These boys—two nonbilingual Chicanos and an overweight "loner" boy who was afraid of sports—were at the bottom of the male hierarchy. Gender is sometimes used as a metaphor for male hierarchies; the inferior status of boys at the bottom is conveyed by calling them "girls." Seven boys and one girl were playing basket-

ball. Two younger boys came over and asked to play. While the girl silently stood, fully accepted in the company of players, one of the older boys disparagingly said to the younger boys, "You girls can't play."[3]

In contrast, the girls who more often travel in the boys' world, sitting with groups of boys in the lunchroom or playing basketball, soccer, and baseball with them, are not stigmatized. Some have fairly high status with other girls. The worlds of girls and boys are asymmetrically arranged, and spatial patterns map out interacting forms of inequality.

Heterosexual Meanings

The organization and meanings of gender (the social categories "woman/man," "girl/boy") and of sexuality vary cross-culturally (Ortner & Whitehead, 1981)—and, in our society, across the life course. Harriet Whitehead (1981) observed that in our (Western) gender system, and that of many traditional North American Indian cultures, one's choice of a sexual object, occupation, and dress and demeanor are closely associated with gender. However, the "center of gravity" differs in the two gender systems. For Indians, occupational pursuits provide the primary imagery of gender; dress and demeanor are secondary, and sexuality is least important. In our system, at least for adults, the order is reversed: heterosexuality is central to our definitions of "man" and "woman" ("masculinity/femininity") and the relationships that obtain between them, whereas occupation and dress/demeanor are secondary.

Whereas erotic orientation and gender are closely linked in our definitions of adults, we define children as relatively asexual. Activities and dress/demeanor are more important than sexuality in the cultural meanings of "girl" and "boy." Children are less heterosexually defined than adults, and we have nonsexual imagery for relations between girls and boys. However, both children and adults sometimes use heterosexual language—"crushes," "like," "goin' with," "girlfriends," and "boyfriends"—to define cross-sex relationships. This language increases through the years of elementary school; the shift to adolescence consolidates a gender system organized around the institution of heterosexuality.

In everyday life in the schools, heterosexual and romantic meanings infuse some ritualized forms of interaction between groups of boys and girls (e.g., "chase and kiss") and help maintain sex segregation. "Jimmy likes Beth" or "Beth likes Jimmy" is a major form of teasing, which a child risks in choosing to sit by or walk with someone of the other sex. The structure of teasing and children's sparse vocabulary for relationships between girls and boys are evident in the following conversation which I had with a group of third-grade girls in the lunchroom. Susan asked me what I was doing, and I said I was observing the things children do and play. Nicole volunteered, "I like running, boys chase all the girls. See Tim over there? Judy chases him all around the school. She likes him." Judy, sitting across the table, quickly responded, "I hate him. I like him for a friend." "Tim loves Judy," Nicole said in a loud, sing-song voice.

In the younger grades, the culture and lore of girls contains more heterosexual romantic themes than that of boys. In Michigan, the first-grade girls often jumped rope to a rhyme which began: "Down in the valley where the green grass grows, there sat Cindy [name of jumper], as sweet as a rose. She sat, she sat, she sat so sweet. Along came Jason, and kissed her on the cheek. First comes love, then comes marriage, then along comes Cindy with a baby carriage." Before a girl took her turn at jumping, the chanters asked her, "Who do you want to be your boyfriend?" The jumper always proffered a name, which was accepted matter-of-factly. In chasing, a girl's kiss carried greater threat than a boy's kiss; "girl touch," when defined as contaminating, had sexual connotations. In short, starting at an early age, girls are more sexually defined than boys.

Through the years of elementary school, and increasing with age, the idiom of heterosexuality helps maintain the gender divide. Cross-sex interactions, especially when children initiate them, are fraught with the risk of being teased about "liking" someone of the other sex. I learned of several close cross-sex friendships, formed and maintained in neighborhoods and church, which went underground during the school day.

By the fifth grade a few children began to affirm, rather than avoid, the charge of having a girlfriend or a boyfriend; they introduced the heterosexual courtship rituals of adolescence. In the lunchroom in the Michigan school, as the tables were forming, a high-status fifth-grade boy called out from his seat at the table: "I want Trish to sit by me." Trish came over, and almost like a king and queen, they sat at the gender divide—a row of girls down the table on her side,

a row of boys on his. In this situation, which inverted earlier forms, it was not a loss but a gain in status to publicly choose a companion of the other sex. By affirming his choice, the boy became unteasable (note the familiar asymmetry of heterosexual courtship rituals: the male initiates). This incident signals a temporal shift in arrangements of sex and gender.

Traveling in the World of the Other Sex

Contests, invasions, chasing, and heterosexually defined encounters are based upon and reaffirm boundaries between girls and boys. In another type of cross-sex interaction, individuals (or sometimes pairs) cross gender boundaries, seeking acceptance in a group of the other sex. Nearly all the cases I saw of this were tomboys—girls who played organized sports and frequently sat with boys in the cafeteria or classroom. If these girls were skilled at activities central in the boys' world, especially games like soccer, baseball, and basketball, they were pretty much accepted as participants.

Being a tomboy is a matter of degree. Some girls seek access to boys' groups but are excluded; other girls limit their "crossing" to specific sports. Only a few—such as the tomboy I mentioned earlier, who chose a seat with the boys in the sex-divided fourth–fifth grade—participate fully in the boys' world. That particular girl was skilled at the various organized sports which boys played in different seasons of the year. She was also adept at physical fighting and at using the forms of arguing, insult, teasing, naming, and sports-talk of the boys' subculture. She was the only Black child in her classroom, in a school with only 8% Black students; overall that token status, along with unusual athletic and verbal skills, may have contributed to her ability to move back and forth across the gender divide. Her unique position in the children's world was widely recognized in the school. Several times, the teacher said to me, "She thinks she's a boy."

I observed only one boy in the upper grades (a fourth-grader) who regularly played with all-female groups, as opposed to "playing at" girls' games and seeking to disrupt them. He frequently played jump-rope and took turns with girls doing tricks on the bars, using the small gestures—for example, a helpful push on the heel of a girl who needed momentum to turn her body around the bar—which mark skillful and earnest participation. Although I never saw him play in other than an earnest spirit, the girls often chased him away from their games, and both girls and boys teased him. The fact that girls seek and have more access to boys' worlds than vice versa, and the fact that girls who travel with the other sex are less stigmatized for it, are obvious asymmetries, tied to the asymmetries previously discussed.

Relaxed Cross-Sex Interactions

Relationships between boys and girls are not always marked by strong boundaries, heterosexual definitions, or interacting on the terms and turfs of the other sex. On some occasions girls and boys interact in relatively comfortable ways. Gender is not strongly salient nor explicitly invoked, and girls and boys are not organized into boundaried collectivities. These "with" occasions have been neglected by those studying gender and children's relationships, who have emphasized either the model of separate worlds (with little attention to their articulation) or heterosexual forms of contact.

Occasions when boys and girls interact without strain, when gender wanes rather than waxes in importance, frequently have one or more of the following characteristics:

1. The situations are organized around an absorbing task, such as a group art project or creating a radio show, which encourages cooperation and lessens attention to gender. This pattern accords with other studies finding that cooperative activities reduce group antagonism (e.g., Sherif & Sherif, 1953, who studied divisions between boys in a summer camp; and Aronson et al., 1978, who used cooperative activities to lessen racial divisions in a classroom).

2. Gender is less prominent when children are not responsible for the formation of the group. Mixed-sex play is less frequent in games like football, which require the choosing of teams, and more frequent in games like handball or dodgeball, which individuals can join simply by getting into a line or a circle. When adults organize mixed-sex encounters—which they frequently do in the classroom and in physical education periods on the playground—they legitimize cross-sex contact. This removes the risk of being teased for choosing to be with the other sex.

3. There is more extensive and relaxed cross-sex interaction when principles of grouping other than gen-

der are explicitly invoked—for example, counting off to form teams for spelling or kickball, dividing lines by hot lunch or cold lunch, or organizing a work group on the basis of interests or reading ability.

4. Girls and boys may interact more readily in less public and crowded settings. Neighborhood play, depending on demography, is more often sex and age integrated than play at school, partly because with fewer numbers, one may have to resort to an array of social categories to find play partners or to constitute a game. And in less crowded environments there are fewer potential witnesses to "make something of it" if girls and boys play together.

Relaxed interactions between girls and boys often depend on adults to set up and legitimize the contact.[4] Perhaps because of this contingency—and the other, distancing patterns which permeate relations between girls and boys—the easeful moments of interaction rarely build to close friendship. Schofield (1981) makes a similar observation about gender and racial barriers to friendship in a junior high school.

IMPLICATIONS FOR DEVELOPMENT

I have located social relations within an essentially spatial framework, emphasizing the organization of children's play, work, and other activities within specific settings and in one type of institution, the school. In contrast, frameworks of child development rely upon temporal metaphors, using images of growth and transformation over time. Taken alone, both spatial and temporal frameworks have shortcomings; fitted together, they may be mutually correcting.

Those interested in gender and development have relied upon conceptualizations of "sex-role socialization" and "sex differences." Sexuality and gender, I have argued, are more situated and fluid than these individualist and intrinsic models imply. Sex and gender are differently organized and defined across situations, even within the same institution. This situational variation (e.g., in the extent to which an encounter heightens or lessens gender boundaries, or is infused with sexual meanings) shapes and constrains individual behavior. Features which a developmental perspective might attribute to individuals and understand as relatively internal attributes unfolding over time may, in fact, be highly dependent on context. For example, children's avoidance of cross-sex friendship may be attributed to individual gender development in middle childhood. But attention to varied situations may show that this avoidance is contingent on group size, activity, adult behavior, collective meanings, and the risk of being teased.

A focus on social organization and situation draws attention to children's experiences in the present. This helps correct a model like "sex-role socialization" which casts the present under the shadow of the future, or presumed "endpoints" (Speier, 1976). A situated analysis of arrangements of sex and gender among those of different ages may point to crucial disjunctions in the life course. In the fourth and fifth grades, culturally defined heterosexual rituals ("goin' with") begin to suppress the presence and visibility of other types of interaction between girls and boys, such as nonsexualized and comfortable interaction and traveling in the world of the other sex. As "boyfriend/ girlfriend" definitions spread, the fifth-grade tomboy I described had to work to sustain "buddy" relationships with boys. Adult women who were tomboys often speak of early adolescence as a painful time when they were pushed away from participation in boys' activities. Other adult women speak of the loss of intense, even erotic ties with other girls when they entered puberty and the rituals of dating, that is, when they became absorbed into the situation of heterosexuality (Rich, 1980). When Lever (1976) describes best-friend relationships among fifth-grade girls as preparation for dating, she imposes heterosexual ideologies onto a present which should be understood on its own terms.

As heterosexual encounters assume more importance, they may alter relations in same-sex groups. For example, Schofield (1981) reports that for sixth- and seventh-grade children in a middle school, the popularity of girls with other girls was affected by their popularity with boys, while boys' status with other boys did not depend on their relations with girls. This is an asymmetry familiar from the adult world; men's relationships with one another are defined through varied activities (occupations, sports), while relationships among women—and their public status—are more influenced by their connections to individual men.

A full understanding of gender and social relations should encompass cross-sex as well as within-sex interactions. "Borderwork" helps maintain separate, gender-linked subcultures, which, as those interested in development have begun to suggest, may result in

different milieux for learning. Daniel Maltz and Ruth Borker (1983), for example, argue that because of different interactions within girls' and boys' groups, the sexes learn different rules for creating and interpreting friendly conversation, rules which carry into adulthood and help account for miscommunication between men and women. Carol Gilligan (1982) fits research on the different worlds of girls and boys into a theory of sex differences in moral development. Girls develop a style of reasoning, she argues, which is more personal and relational; boys develop a style which is more positional, based on separateness. Eleanor Maccoby (1982), also following the insight that because of sex segregation, girls and boys grow up in different environments, suggests implications for gender-differentiated prosocial and antisocial behavior.

This separate worlds approach, as I have illustrated, also has limitations. The occasions when the sexes are together should also be studied, and understood as contexts for experience and learning. For example, asymmetries in cross-sex relationships convey a series of messages: that boys are more entitled to space and to the nonreciprocal right of interrupting or invading the activities of the other sex; that girls are more in need of adult protection, lower in status, more defined by sexuality, and may even be polluting. Different types of cross-sex interaction—relaxed, boundaried, sexualized, or taking place on the terms of the other sex—provide different contexts for development.

By mapping the array of relationships between and within the sexes, one adds complexity to the overly static and dichotomous imagery of separate worlds. Individual experiences vary, with implications for development. Some children prefer same-sex groupings; some are more likely to cross the gender boundary and participate in the world of the other sex; some children (e.g., girls and boys who frequently play "chase and kiss") invoke heterosexual meanings, while others avoid them.

Finally, after charting the terrain of relationships, one can trace their development over time. For example, age variation in the content and form of borderwork, or of cross- and same-sex touch, may be related to differing cognitive, social, emotional, or physical capacities, as well as to age-associated cultural forms. I earlier mentioned temporal shifts in the organization of cross-sex chasing, from mixing with fantasy play in the early grades to more elaborately ritualized and sexualized forms by the sixth grade. There also appear to be temporal changes in same- and cross-sex touch. In kindergarten, girls and boys touch one another more freely than in fourth grade, when children avoid relaxed cross-sex touch and instead use pokes, pushes, and other forms of mock violence, even when the touch clearly expresses affection. This touch taboo is obviously related to the risk of seeming to *like* someone of the other sex. In fourth grade, same-sex touch begins to signal sexual meanings among boys as well as between boys and girls. Younger boys touch one another freely in cuddling (arm around shoulder) as well as mock-violence ways. By fourth grade, when homophobic taunts like "fag" become more common among boys, cuddling touch begins to disappear for boys, but less for girls.

Overall, I am calling for more complexity in our conceptualizations of gender and of children's social relationships. Our challenge is to retain the temporal sweep, looking at individual and group lives as they unfold over time, while also attending to social structure and context and to the full variety of experiences in the present.

ACKNOWLEDGMENTS

I would like to thank Jane Atkinson, Nancy Chodorow, Arlene Daniels, Peter Lyman, Zick Rubin, Malcolm Spector, Avril Thorne, and Margery Wolf for comments on an earlier version of this paper. Conversations with Zella Luria enriched this work.

NOTES

1. I am grateful to Frederick Erickson for suggesting the relevance of Barth's analysis.

2. Sue Samuelson (1980) reports that in a racially mixed playground in Fresno, California, Mexican-American but not Anglo children gave cooties. Racial as well as sexual inequality may be expressed through these forms.

3. This incident was recorded by Margaret Blume, who, for an undergraduate research project in 1982, observed in the California school where I earlier did fieldwork. Her observations and insights enhanced my own, and I would like to thank her for letting me cite this excerpt.

4. Note that in daily school life, depending on the individual and the situation, teachers and aides sometimes lessened and at other times heightened sex segregation.

REFERENCES

Aronson, E., et al. 1978. *The jigsaw classroom.* Beverly Hills, Calif.: Sage.

Barth, F., Ed. 1969. *Ethnic groups and boundaries.* Boston: Little, Brown.

Borman, K. M. 1979. "Children's interactions in playgrounds." *Theory into Practice* 18:251–57.

Eder D., & Hallinan, M. T. 1978. "Sex differences in children's friendships." *American Sociological Review* 43:237–50.

Finnan, C. R. 1982. "The ethnography of children's spontaneous play." In G. Spindler, ed., *Doing the ethnography of schooling,* pp. 358–80. New York: Holt, Rinehart & Winston.

Foot, H. C.; Chapman, A. J.; & Smith, J. R. 1980. "Introduction." *Friendship and social relations in children,* pp. 1–14. New York: Wiley.

Gilligan, C. 1982. *In a different voice: Psychological theory and women's development.* Cambridge: Harvard University Press.

Glaser, B. G., & Strauss, A. L. 1967. *The discovery of grounded theory.* Chicago: Aldine.

Goffman, E. 1977. "The arrangement between the sexes." *Theory and Society* 4:301–36.

Goodwin, M. H. 1980. "Directive-response speech sequences in girls' and boys' task activities." In S. McConnell-Ginet, R. Borker, & N. Furman, eds., *Women and language in literature and society,* pp. 157–73. New York: Praeger.

Greif, E. B. 1982. "Sex differences in parent–child conversations." *Women's Studies International Quarterly* 3:253–58.

Henley, N. 1977. *Body politics: Power, sex, and nonverbal communication.* Englewood Cliffs, N.J.: Prentice-Hall.

Karkau, K. 1973. *Sexism in the fourth grade.* Pittsburgh: KNOW, Inc. (pamphlet).

Katz, J. 1983. "A theory of qualitative methodology: The social system of analytic fieldwork." In R. M. Emerson, ed., *Contemporary field research,* pp. 127–48. Boston: Little, Brown.

Knapp, M., & Knapp, H. 1976. *One potato, two potato: The secret education of American children.* New York: W. W. Norton.

Lever, J. 1976. "Sex differences in the games children play." *Social Problems* 23:478–87.

Maccoby, E. 1982. "Social groupings in childhood: Their relationship to prosocial and antisocial behavior in boys and girls." Paper presented at conference on The Development of Prosocial and Antisocial Behavior, Voss, Norway.

Maccoby, E., & Jacklin, C. 1974. *The psychology of sex differences.* Stanford, Calif.: Stanford University Press.

McRobbie, A., & Garber, J. 1975. "Girls and subcultures." In S. Hall & T. Jefferson, eds., *Resistance through rituals,* pp. 209–23. London: Hutchinson.

Maltz, D. N., & Borker, R. A. 1983. "A cultural approach to male–female miscommunication." In J. J. Gumperz, ed., *Language and social identity,* pp. 195–216. New York: Cambridge University Press.

Ortner, S. B., & Whitehead, H. 1981. *Sexual meanings.* New York: Cambridge University Press.

Parrott, S. 1972. "Games children play: Ethnography of a second-grade recess." In J. P. Spradley & D. W McCurdy, eds., *The cultural experience,* pp. 206–19. Chicago: Science Research Associates.

Rich, A. 1980. "Compulsory heterosexuality and lesbian existence." *Signs,* 5:631–60.

Samuelson, S. 1980. "The cooties complex." *Western Folklore* 39:198–210.

Savin-Williams, R. C. 1976. "An ethological study of dominance formation and maintenance in a group of human adolescents." *Child Development* 47:972–79.

Schofield, J. W. 1981. "Complementary and conflicting identities: Images and interaction in an interracial school." In S. R. Asher & J. M. Gottman, eds., *The development of children's friendships,* pp. 53–90. New York: Cambridge University Press.

Sherif, M., & Sherif, C. 1953. *Groups in harmony and tension.* New York: Harper.

Sluckin, A. 1981. *Growing up in the playground.* London: Routledge & Kegan Paul.

Speier, M. 1976. "The adult ideological viewpoint in studies of childhood." In A. Skolnick, ed., *Rethinking childhood,* pp. 168–86. Boston: Little, Brown.

Sutton-Smith, B. 1971. "A syntax for play and games." In R. E. Herron and B. Sutton-Smith, eds., *Child's play,* pp. 298–307. New York: Wiley.

Unger, R. K. 1979. "Toward a redefinition of sex and gender." *American Psychologist* 34:1085–94.

Waldrop, M. F., & Halverson, C. F. 1975. "Intensive and extensive peer behavior: Longitudinal and cross-sectional analysis." *Child Development* 46:19–26.

West, C., & Zimmerman, D. H. 1983. "Small insults: A study of interruptions in cross-sex conversations between unacquainted persons." In B. Thorne, C. Kramarae, & N. Henley, eds., *Language, gender, and society.* Rowley, Mass.: Newbury House.

Whitehead, H. 1981. "The bow and the burden strap: A new look at institutionalized homosexuality in Native America." In S. B. Ortner & H. Whitehead, eds., *Sexual meanings,* pp. 80–115. New York: Cambridge University Press.

READING 10

Such a Handsome Face: Advertising Male Cosmetics

THOMAS R. FORREST

Gender-role changes initiated by the women's movement have become both comic and serious subjects to the media. Television sitcoms depict struggling couples working out egalitarian relationships; movies show fathers actively raising children and women pursuing professional careers; and mass advertising uses these new images to sell products. Cosmetics manufacturers have recently capitalized on this increasingly fluid gender environment to target a new market: men. Only a few years ago male cosmetics were relegated to obscure drugstore shelves. With changing gender roles, however, advertising campaigns have proliferated in an attempt to convince men of the importance of personal appearance. The effectiveness of the campaigns is evidenced by the counter space now devoted to male cosmetics in any prestigious department store.

The role of advertising has been sharply debated. Advertisers argue that they perform an important service to our economy by presenting consumers with product information in a persuasive manner that acknowledges and reflects public needs, attitudes, values, and behavior (Katona, 1971; Atwan, McQuade, & Wright, 1979; Berman, 1981). Critics charge that advertising is a somewhat cynical force that shapes, molds, and manipulates public opinion for the purpose of creating passive, obedient consumers (Komisar, 1971; Ewen, 1976; Cagen, 1978). Investigators of the subject tend to believe that advertising both reflects and influences social trends. They see advertising as socializing "individuals in a way that roughly resembles education, providing them with ideas, images, and examples of cultural expectations" (Berman, 1981:32). In this sense, advertising helps to tell us who we are.

As a major market-expansion mechanism of capitalism, advertising carefully monitors social change as

Reprinted by permission of Thomas R. Forrest.

fertile ground for potential new markets. In the continual search for greater sales and profits, changes in gender roles present an exciting and challenging environment in which to develop and sell to one sex products previously marketed only to the other. Insurance, investments, sports equipment, cars, liquor, business suits, and briefcases, for example, are now being marketed to women; cologne, jewelry, hair dryers, hair spray, colored underwear, and cosmetics are being sold to men. Male cosmetics extend beyond simple aftershave preparations and cologne to encompass a wide range of products that enhance and alter facial appearance.

An estimated $45 million was spent on male cosmetics in 1986, up 28 percent from the previous year. Market experts predict an annual growth rate of 20 to 30 percent for the foreseeable future (Small, 1986:146). While the new products for men constitute only a small fraction of the output of the cosmetics industry, their sales are expanding more rapidly than those of either male cologne and aftershave products or women's cosmetics. This emerging market has captured the attention of many cosmetics manufacturers. Most major women's cosmetics firms have developed or are developing skin-care products for men. Estée Lauder has cornered roughly three-quarters of the men's market with products under the Lauder, Aramis, and Clinique labels. Two companies, Jan Stuart and Interface, have been formed for the sole purpose of marketing cosmetics to men. Millions of dollars are to be made by people clever enough to convince men that personal appearance is a vital part of today's masculine image (Adler et al., 1986).

Acceptance of cosmetics for men has not come overnight. In 1960 a man who used any fragrance other than Aqua Velva or Old Spice found his masculinity suspect. Rigid standards loosened with the rise of the counterculture of the late 1960s and early

1970s. Young men embraced a natural, unkempt look with long hair, denim jeans, work shirts, sandals, and love beads, all in the interest of appearing "hip." To some observers this fashion statement was a flamboyant and outrageous affront to convention, marking a direct challenge to established political and social orthodoxy. To others it was merely a fashion change. The more enduring change, though, was men's increased focus on personal appearance. The hair tends to be well groomed now and the love beads have been put away, but bolder styles in clothing have settled in for a long run.

To help men cope with the new emphasis on appearance, new products began to appear, particularly hair dryers and hair spray. In earlier years these products had been associated primarily with women. In order to introduce these "women's products" to men, advertisers and market experts developed strategies that removed any hint of femininity from their products. Men would run no risk of being labeled "sissy." So hair dryers were marketed as "hair stylers" and hair spray became "hair control." Instructional advertising showed men how to use these products. After extensive experimentation with format and copy, advertising campaigns today have taken on misogynistic undertones and explicitly disassociate their products from anything considered remotely feminine. When traditionally male products—cars, investments, insurance, liquor—are marketed to women, though, it is considered quite acceptable to emphasize the standard male traits of success, achievement, competition, and independence.

A campaign designed to acquaint men with cosmetics has to address the male fear of effeminacy. This is a most interesting challenge. Careful analysis of print media advertising provides insights into how advertisers meet that challenge.

Making men conscious that their skin needs care and protection is the first task. Linking skin care to an activity comfortable and familiar to most men, such as shaving, establishes this association in a nonthreatening context. As one marketing manager commented, "You have to lead a person [man] into these products. You must lead him from something he knows to something he doesn't. You first start off with an aftershave balm or shave cream" (Sexton, 1985:17). Many makers of shaving creams today advertise skin conditioners as important ingredients; ads for preshave and aftershave products emphasize preparation and pro-

tection of facial skin. Exposure to natural elements, too, is proclaimed to be damaging to skin. Like shaving, it makes skin flaky and dry, bringing premature aging. Shaving products that help protect facial skin seem simple and logical enough, and coupling skin care with shaving is a clever way to incorporate skin care into daily grooming habits. A man needs only to reach for the right product. Aramis' Moisturizing After Shave, for example, advertises:

> Some of the worst problems of shaving come after shaving. First, you scrape, nick and irritate your skin. Then, the environment dries, chaps and pollutes it. Moisturizing After Shave rescues it. Soothes and helps heal irritation. Relieves dryness. The fluid formula sinks in instantly. Actually improves your skin.

Once men acknowledge a need to protect their skin, they must be persuaded to invest in specific skin-care products unrelated to shaving. Advertising campaigns designed to convince men of the importance of a "skin-care program" are now common. Many of these products are identical to their counterparts for women, but their presentation undergoes a radical change to make them distinctly masculine. A change in the product's name is the most obvious alteration. Astringents become scruffing lotion, face scrub, facial cellular scrub, hydro-elastic cleanser; moisturizers become M Lotion, moisture lock, nutrient moisture lock, skin comfort lotion, soothing moisture balm, double-action moisture cream. All are no-nonsense, hard-hitting action names for common-sense, results-oriented products. Concurrently, the product's package is redesigned, with attention given to size, shape, and subdued masculine colors, either white or shades of gray or tan. Lightweight plastic containers make products suitable for travel, while the ability to stand freely on their caps helps ensure speed, efficiency, and ease in application. Busy, ever-striving males can ill afford to waste excessive time primping, if we are to believe the hidden message. Emphasis on the male consumer's limited time further removes products from women, who stereotypically spend hours making themselves up. Copy headlines proclaim:

> It only takes a minute.

> A three-minute workout for your face.

In just two minutes this man's face is going to look terrific.

Once a product's name and packaging are settled, further advertising themes are selected. Traditional dimensions of masculinity dramatically surface. Physical fitness is a popular theme for skin-care products.

You take care of your body, you ought to take care of your skin.

A fitness program for your skin.

Don't just wash your face—give it a workout!

Interface manufactures a "workout kit" that includes a deep cleanser, a toner, a moisturizer, and a "gripper workout mask" that "not only feeds and nourishes the skin with lost COLLAGEN and ELASTIN but also penetrates and isometrically 'WORKS-OUT' the facial muscles to keep the face healthy and youthful."

Association of products with sports and sports figures is a proven tactic to induce males to try new products, as witness the success of a popular baseball player in selling colored and patterned underwear. A locker room and a playing field are contexts in which masculinity is seldom questioned. Similarly, at a time when physical fitness is equated with good health, the care and conditioning of the skin can readily be presented as sound, even essential practice.

Success and achievement in business or professional life are central features of masculinity. It is not surprising that efforts are made to couple personal appearance with a competitive edge in business. Advertising copy emphasizes:

Put your best foot forward to win.

Success—it's written all over your face.

During those face-to-face encounters the quality of your skin can give away more than just your age. At times, your skin's color and tone can reflect poor care, lack of nourishment and an overall unhealthy appearance. Whether it's business or pleasure, your face is your most valuable calling card!

The message is clear: Competition in business is tough, and a man needs all the resources he can mus-ter. A man who looks good, feels good, and has the confidence of a winner receives the fruits of victory. The attention he pays to his personal appearance, particularly to his face, is another "asset" in his race to be a winner.

Competition with younger men for professional and sexual success puts further emphasis on the importance of a youthful appearance and generates products to resist aging. It has been estimated that 10 to 15 percent of all cosmetic surgery is performed on men. A less dramatic alternative to surgery is a product gaining some popularity, the face mask. Again no-nonsense, tough brand names are devised to present the product in a masculine context: Skin Tight, Firming Mask, Facial Cellular Booster, Face Fitness Mask, Ponce de Leon 28. An advertisement for this last product shows a man who appears to be in his mid-30s but who is identified as 47 years old. The product, the advertisement asserts, is a nonsurgical face lift that "takes only minutes a day." It promises

a whole new you. Ponce de Leon 28 can mean a younger, more vital you. When you look younger, you feel younger . . . you act younger, and people think you are years younger than you are. It works no matter what your age. If you start using it when you are young, Ponce de Leon 28 helps maintain your youthful good looks.

Body lotions, too, and night creams, under-eye conditioners, and antiwrinkle creams are all being marketed to men to retard aging.

The most startling aspect of the introduction of cosmetics for men is the marketing of cosmetics in the traditional sense: makeup. Spearheading this effort is Clinique's Non-Streak Bronzer:

In just one minute, this man's tan will look new again. His face will get a fresh-looking glow. A smooth, even tone. A believably sunned and healthy look. . . . Non-Streak Bronzer is transparent. Spreads easily. Produces the perfect natural sun color—not a jolting orange. Has no perfume, no alcohol. Stays put through rain and swimming. Use Non-Streak Bronzer when there is no sun. Or when you could have used more sleep. Or to renew a fading tan. Or simply to look your best. . . . Non-Streak Bronzer is a year-round reviver. Great as all outdoors.

EXERCISES FOR MEN

WILLAMETTE BRIDGE/LIBERATION NEWS SERVICE

1. Sit down in a straight chair. Cross your legs at the ankles and keep your knees pressed together. Try to do this while you're having a conversation with someone, but pay attention at all times to keeping your knees pressed tightly together.

2. Bend down to pick up an object from the floor. Each time you bend remember to bend your knees so that your rear end doesn't stick up, and place one hand on your shirtfront to hold it to your chest. This exercise simulates the experience of a woman in a short, low-necked dress bending over.

3. Run a short distance, keeping your knees together. You'll find you have to take short, high steps if your run this way. Women have been taught it is unfeminine to run like a man with long, free strides. See how far you get running this way for 30 seconds.

Reprinted from Willamette Bridge/Liberation News Service, "Exercises for Men," in *The Radical Therapist* (forerunner of *State and Mind*), December–January 1971, by permission of the publisher, New Directions in Psychology, Inc., The State and Mind Collective.

4. Sit comfortably on the floor. Imagine that you are wearing a dress and that everyone in the room wants to see your underwear. Arrange your legs so that no one can see. Sit like this for a long time without changing your position.

5. Walk down a city street. Pay a lot of attention to your clothing: make sure your pants are zipped, shirt tucked in, buttons done. Look straight ahead. Every time a man walks past you, avert your eyes and make your face expressionless. Most women learn to go through this act each time we leave our houses. It's a way to avoid at least some of the encounters we've all had with strange men who decided we looked available.

6. Walk around with your stomach pulled in tight, your shoulders thrown back, and your chest thrust out. Pay attention to keeping this posture at all times. Notice how it changes your breathing. Try to speak loudly and aggressively in this posture.

90

Notice that nowhere does the word *makeup* appear. Yet here is a product that alters appearance and promises men "the perfect natural sun color." Men can now hide pale skin that shows anxiety, too much partying, or lack of sleep. An interesting psychological ploy is being used here. Men are encouraged to take a positive attitude, to put their best face forward to win. A positive attitude along with the benefits of cosmetics gives a man full access to additional tools to manage and control the impression he makes.

Most American men still seem to be oblivious to these changes. If manufacturers can persuade them to purchase and use skin-care products and appearance-altering cosmetics, however, they will have created a billion-dollar market. But what of the implications for men? Is a more insidious process occurring? As we have seen, concern for personal appearance does not seriously negate any traditional aspects of American masculinity. In fact, a deliberate effort is being made to translate concern for personal appearance into a distinctly masculine context. Success, achievement, physical fitness, efficiency, competition, managing and controlling one's presentation of self are all themes used to make personal appearance a significant component of the masculine mystique. To feel good about oneself, it will soon not be enough to be a successful achiever; a man will also have to look young, energetic, and healthy.

Women have long been subjected to the tyranny of appearance. According to Dr. Jean Kilbourne in her film *Killing Us Softly: Advertising's Image of Women,* American women spend more than $1 million on cosmetics every hour. Many eating disorders, such as an-

orexia and bulimia, are attributed to women's desire to attain an unrealistic standard of beauty. Is this what awaits men?

What man will not find himself lacking when he measures himself against these new role models? Will he then suffer low self-esteem and a feeling of inadequacy? Ironically, it is precisely this sense of inadequacy that gets translated into the motivating force to use appearance-enhancing products. A vicious cycle is set up: the more inadequate a man feels when he compares himself with a media-created image, the more effort he exerts to attain that image; the more effort he exerts in pursuit of the image, the more inadequate he feels. Although purchasing cosmetics may temporarily soothe newly created insecurities, emergent role models that equate appearance with masculinity only lead to further entrapment.

An original goal of the women's movement was to free both women and men from artificial cultural values and restrictions that limited all people's ability to develop their talents and put them to full use. Yet as men and women break from their traditional roles, enterprising entrepreneurs jump in and ultimately subvert the situation. Ever ready to exploit social trends, alert market analysts are quick to recognize a potential new market. Cosmetics for men is only one such market. Nothing is done to disturb masculine hegemony. As long as traditional masculine prescriptions are not altered or threatened, tremendous opportunities exist for more and bigger male markets. The question remains whether concern for personal appearance and use of cosmetics will suffuse postliberation masculinity so that the only real winner is the economic system.

REFERENCES

Adler, J., et al. 1986. "You're so vain." *Newsweek,* April 14, pp. 48–55.

Atwan, R.; McQuade, D.; & Wright, J. W. 1979. *Edsels, Luckies, and Frigidaires: Advertising the American way.* New York: Dell.

Berman, R. 1981. *Advertising and social change.* Beverly Hills, Calif.: Sage.

Cagen, E. 1978. "The selling of the women's movement." *Social Policy* 9:4–12.

Ewen, S. 1976. *Captains of consciousness.* New York: McGraw-Hill.

Katona, G. 1971. *The mass consumption society.* New York: McGraw-Hill.

Komisar, L. 1971. "The image of woman in advertising." In V. Gornick & B. Moran, eds., *Women in sexist society.* New York: New American Library.

Sexton, N. 1985. "Segment puts new wrinkle in toiletries industry." *Advertising Age,* March 14, p. 17.

Small, M. 1986. "Men save face! Sissy creams are in as real guys get beautified." *People,* December 15, pp. 146–47.

P A R T   T W O

Organization of Sex and Gender

In our investigation of how male domination is perpetuated and why it is so resistant to change, the readings up to now have focused primarily on the ways in which women and men are inducted into the stratification system at the individual level. Socialization of the young, as we have seen, is a powerful force directed toward creating sex differences and sex inequalities. If maintaining the culture's ideology and social institutions depended only on the inculcation of values, attitudes, and behaviors in children, the task of maintaining the status quo would be easy for those who embrace traditionalism. However, in one important sense socialization is never completed: adults, especially in complex societies, continue to have new experiences and new ideas; that is, they are constantly "desocialized" and "resocialized." Change and growth within an individual is a *continuing* process: heretical thoughts, atypical experiences, and system-altering activities are not only possible but probable. Society requires, however, that the adults be kept in line—not only so that they will appropriately socialize the young but also so that they will fulfill their own mandated social roles.

In this section we turn our attention to the *structural* bases of gender inequality. We shall be looking at the ways in which societies are organized so as to create a pattern of male dominance and female subordination. A society's pattern of gender roles and relationships is a part of its system of social stratification or inequality.

All societies have stratification systems; that is, systems for categorizing and ranking individuals and groups in accordance with the extent to which they possess characteristics that are highly valued by the society. Members can be differentiated either on the basis of *ascribed* characteristics (those that befall individuals regardless of their efforts, such as sex, race, age, and family background) or on the basis of *achieved* characteristics (those attained by individuals because of their own efforts, such as education, occupation, and marital status). However, no matter which criteria are used to evaluate people, social stratification functions to ensure that those persons with characteristics more highly valued by a particular society will be given superior access to whatever rewards and scarce resources the society has to offer; and, conversely, that those with less valued characteristics will be deprived of those advantages. Social stratification is, in essence, society's institutionalized pattern of social inequality.

When sex is a fundamental basis for social stratification—when the distribution of society's scarce goods and services is profoundly related to, if not determined by, whether one is male or female—then sex-based inequality exists. Most scholars agree that sex-based inequality is a fundamental and universal feature of all social life. Indeed, no society exists that does not assume that men and women are "different" in a variety of ways, and that it is these "differences" that account for and necessitate women's subordinate position in the society. True, considerable diversity can be found in the specific roles performed by men and women in various cultures throughout the world; in most societies, however, the roles assigned to men, whatever they may be, are generally valued more highly than those assigned to women.

Like other forms of social inequality, sex-based inequality generally can be viewed as arising from an unequal distribution of rights to control three kinds of valued commodities: power, or the ability to carry out one's will despite opposition; prestige, or the ability to command respect, honor, and deference; and wealth, or economic and material compensation. Because these commodities—or rewards—are closely and reciprocally linked, sex-based inequality perpetuates itself through a kind of built-in feedback process. Quite obviously, those who are more highly situated are more likely to be in control of the distribution of these scarce rewards. Such control, in turn, further reinforces and heightens their dominance. In American society, as in other industrialized societies, power, prestige, and wealth belong to those who control the distribution of resources outside the home; that is, in the extradomestic institutions of work and politics. The assignment of extradomestic tasks to men and domestic tasks to women—or the ideology that "woman's place is in the home"— is, therefore, one of the primary means by which men have achieved and maintained dominance. When women enter the extradomestic arena, moreover, they are channeled into occupations that involve doing the "domestic" work of the society. Fully one-fourth of employed women are concentrated in five occupations that are consistent with prevailing cultural definitions of "femininity": secretary, bookkeeper, elementary school teacher, waitress, and retail salesclerk. These are jobs that confer neither prestige nor great financial reward. Men, by contrast, are spread out among a greater number of occupations that are better paid than the categories dominated by women.

Thus to unravel the complex structural basis of sex-based inequality we must examine the interplay between what scholars refer to as the private or domestic sphere and the public or extradomestic sphere of social life. We must also recognize the extent to which gender inequality is reflected in and perpetuated by the structures of all the major social institutions—the economy, family, religion, medicine and science, and politics and the law. Furthermore, we shall see that these institutions are linked to one another in such a way that male superiority becomes in fact dependent on female subordination. For example, the sexual division of labor in the traditional family benefits men because it gives them access to the nonsalaried domestic services of women, such as cooking, cleaning, and child-rearing. This social arrangement at the same time weakens women's position in the labor force and provides justification for segregating or slotting women into low-paying, seasonal, and "fringe" occupations with little opportunity for advancement. Occupational sex segregation, in turn, functions not only to keep women dependent on men and marriage for economic support but to ensure higher wages for men. In addition, by providing a class of easily exploitable female laborers, occupational sex segregation increases profits—thereby serving the larger economic system of capitalism.

In short, we have reached the point in our analysis where we must take into account the full and awesome reality of the power of social institutions and the ways in which they are intricately interrelated to serve and to perpetuate the interests of powerful segments in society. To illuminate how this situation came about, this section begins with readings that propose different theoretical explanations for the widespread existence of gender inequality. Subsequent readings illustrate the ways in which major institutions of society reflect patriarchal ideology and androcentric practices.

Explantions of Sex - Based Inequality

Scholars have struggled to understand why sex-based stratification is so ubiquitous. Their explanations fall into two basic schools of thought: the *biogenetic* and the *biocultural*. The biogenetic argument holds that the behaviors of men and women are rooted in biological and genetic factors—the differences in hormonal patterns, physical size, and aggressiveness, the propensity to "bond" with members of the same sex, the capacity to rear children or to lead. Whether they view such differences as innate or as a natural outgrowth of human evolution, biogeneticists contend that sex-based inequality and the natural superiority of the male are inevitable, immutable, and necessary for the survival of the species. For the biogeneticist, the sexual division of labor in human societies is rooted, then, in the sexual determination to be found in all species, from ants to felines to deer to primates.

The second school of thought, the biocultural approach, bases its position on a growing body of historical and anthropological research that points to wide variations in gender-based behavior and in the sexual division of labor among human societies throughout time. Bioculturalists contend that the diversity of cultural adaptations to biological differences in the sexes is so great that biological factors do not sufficiently explain universal male dominance. They argue that one of the reasons that the

superiority of males appears so inevitable is that in societies of all types—capitalist and communist, democratic and authoritarian, industrial and preindustrial—a cultural idea or belief has arisen to justify and to perpetuate sex-based stratification systems that entitle men to greater power, prestige, and wealth. This ideology is patriarchalism. Why it arose in the first place is difficult to answer, but social scientists have long understood that it is common for groups to propagate beliefs that aggrandize themselves, and it is equally common for the subordinate group to accept the dominant group's definition as natural and inevitable. The important point is that ideas are culturally produced and therefore are always subject to revision. If, however, we are to refute the inevitability of male dominance, we must understand the structures through which it is perpetuated. The biocultural perspective holds that it is within the context of universal social stratification, or institutionalized social inequality, that sex-based inequality occurs and can be understood.

In this section we examine a variety of theories of gender inequality. We begin with anthropological perspectives that challenge the biological explanation of gender differences in power and privilege. In the first reading, "'Universals' and Male Dominance Among Primates: A Critical Examination," Lila Leibowitz looks at various assumptions of traditional primatology and the more recent ideas of sociobiology, and discusses how the actual social arrangements of primates contradict the view that there are innate biological explanations for the unequal distribution of social privileges between females and males.

The next two selections exemplify contemporary sociological perspectives on gender stratification. In "Gender and Parenthood: An Evolutionary Perspective," Alice S. Rossi holds that current social science explanations of gender differences are inadequate. She considers child-rearing and parenting the key elements in women's subordination. Rossi considers the ways in which demographic trends in longevity and the sex ratio, marriage and fertility, and household composition affect parenting at both the macro and micro levels and offers an explanatory model of gender stratification that draws heavily on bio-evolutionary theory and the neurosciences.

In "A Theory of Gender Stratification," Joan Huber agrees that traditional stratification theories in the social sciences, by defining women only as appendages to men, do not adequately address the question of gender inequality. Huber's evolutionary analysis emphasizes the effect that subsistence technology has had on the evolution of the division of labor between women and men. Three principles form the core of Huber's theory of gender stratification: (1) family members who produce goods have more power and prestige than those who consume them; (2) women's tasks must be compatible with pregnancy and lactation if societies are to replace themselves; and (3) the people who control the distribution of valued resources outside the family have the greatest power and prestige.

In "Compulsory Heterosexuality and Lesbian Existence," Adrienne Rich argues that one of the primary means of perpetuating male dominance is what she conceptualizes as the social institution of heterosexuality. The main contribution of this article is its power to force us to consider heterosexuality as a cultural ideology and social institution that proscribes and devalues all forms of female friendship and community as it perpetuates women's subordination to men.

The last two readings in this section focus on gender stratification in different cultural contexts. Evelyn Blackwood, in "Sexuality and Gender in Certain Native American Tribes: The Case of Cross-Gender Females," examines a subsistence-level economy with an egalitarian kinship system in which some women assumed the male role permanently and were allowed to marry other women. Blackwood demonstrates in a striking way the cultural basis of sex and gender and provides evidence that not all societies conceive of male and female gender as dictating invariably opposed roles. "'The Status of Women' in Indigenous African Societies," by Niara Sudarkasa, demonstrates that in some precolonial societies, although they assigned different roles to women and men, the statuses of the sexes were not unequal. Sudarkasa examines the roles of women in precolonial African society—in families and descent groups, in the economy, and in the political process—and concludes that gender was not a basis for inequality. Rather, the colonial experience was significant in creating female and male as separate roles and in establishing hierarchical relations between the sexes.

"Universals" and Male Dominance Among Primates: A Critical Examination

LILA LEIBOWITZ

The genetic basis of behavioral traits is usually argued from the claim that a behavior pattern is universal or nearly universal within a species. The notion that among humans sex roles are very standardized and certain traits are universally those of one sex or the other is not a new one. Nor is the notion that such traits are genetically programmed or "instinctive" a new one. In fact, for the century or so that anthropologists have been investigating other cultures systematically, these two intertwined notions have been tested time and again. Much evidence has accumulated about some of the behaviors that were once considered part of the genetic heritage of one sex or the other, and, as a result, the hypotheses generally have been rejected because universals have not been found. Nevertheless, there are still a few anthropologists who see in the tremendously varied sex role assignments of men and women a pervasive pattern of male dominance, and some among them who regard what they perceive as male dominance to be biologically determined. The majority of social anthropologists, however, regard sex roles and statuses among humans as varied, learned, and the product of socioeconomic and cultural forces.

It is obvious to most students of other cultures that how labor is divided differs from one society or place to another. Who sews, or cooks, or hews wood, or draws water, or engages in market bargaining, or works in the fields, or produces the greater portion of subsistence foods are matters so varied as to defy sim-

Reprinted from Lila Leibowitz, "'Universals' and Male Dominance Among Primates: A Critical Examination," in *Pitfalls in Research on Sex and Gender*, ed. Ethel Tobach and Betty Rosoff, Genes and Gender Series, no. 2 (Staten Island, NY: Gordian Press, 1978), by permission of the publisher and author.

ple sexual classifications. Societies also differ as to whether a biological mother is expected to nurse her infant or assume the major burden of caring for it, a fact which seems to surprise many Westerners who themselves belong to a tradition in which wet nurses and nannies are not long a thing of the past. Societies differ as to whether all husbands are men (West African peoples do not regard maleness as a prerequisite for husbandness). Societies differ as to whether spouses of either sex or both are taken one at a time or several at once; whether or not they live together, and whether or not they work with and for each other. More important in a discussion of sex roles and "dominance," and the degree—if any—to which they are biologically determined, are the different ways resources are controlled in different societies.

Data collected over the past hundred years show that there are quite a few variations as to who is in charge of collecting and distributing ordinary and special foods even in simple foraging societies. When women of particular kin or class or caste groups in more complex societies are in the position to allocate land or work or other valued goods to other members of their society, we are directly confronted with the problem of analyzing what sorts of control women and men exercise over the things which give people the power to negotiate decisions. Are Iroquois women who withhold the special dried foods men need for a war party exercising control over the domestic or political arena?[1] Is their veto power over men's decisions a form of dominance? Cultural variables in the control of strategic resources indicate that power relationships among humans, inter- and intrasexual, cannot be reduced to the simple notion of "dominance" nor to its presumed biological components. As we shall see, oversimplification and vagueness as to what is meant by "dominance" are significant factors in the revival of the argument that male dominance is universal among humans, and among primate species generally.

Interestingly, the revival of the argument that sex roles among humans are genetically programmed was stimulated by several scientists who do not specialize in studying human behavior but who did not regard this as a drawback for the purposes of producing popular books on animal behavior and human evolution and behavior.[2] Nonscientists and social scientists then hastened to get in on their act and benefit from the rich market they uncovered among Americans.[3] After questions were raised about the scientific validity, political bias and sexist prejudice of these popularized books, the argument was moved into the arena of "serious" scientific scholarship with the publication in 1975 of E. O. Wilson's *Sociobiology,*[4] a text that received the prepublication treatment usually reserved for more readable books designed to reach general audiences.

In a major work intended to lay the scholarly foundation for a "new" and innovative *science* of social behavior that he predicts will soon replace the softness of sociology and anthropology with the hardness of more rigorous biological subdisciplines, E. O. Wilson, a noted authority on social insects, states that "aggressive dominance systems with males generally dominant over females"[5] are characteristic of the order Primates, the taxonomic order which includes monkeys, apes and humans. Coming as it does from a highly prestigious biologist in a text that addresses the issue of the evolution of social behavior, this statement has implications which are unavoidable for the conscientious student of human societies and cultures. If true, it implies that the observed range of human behavioral variability is either a departure from, or a conquest of, pre- or protohuman behavioral patterns, programs, or predispositions. An important question, then, is, "Is this statement true?"

There are two ways in which I will address the question of the validity of the proposal that dominance systems and male dominance over females characterize primate social behavior. First, I will examine whether the statement represents an accurate generalization drawn from the evidence which its author cites to support it. Secondly, I will examine the concept of "dominance" on which this author's analysis is built and which allows him to underwrite "scientifically" the notion that male dominance among

humans is universal, biologically determined and hence difficult to overcome at best.

The text in which the above statement appears provides extended descriptions of the social arrangements of a number of primate species. The social arrangements that are described not only fail to justify the claim of widespread or near universal male dominance but are also somewhat confusing. Let me summarize some of the problems a reader encounters with regard to these descriptions.[6]

The mouse lemur is characterized as "an essentially solitary animal," although, we discover, mouse lemur females nest in groups. Evidently it is the *males* that are solitary. Whom or what they dominate in their solitary state is not clear. It appears that female nest groups are made up of mothers and daughters and their young who "displace" sons and brothers. "Dominant" males are characterized as those who manage to breed. Dominant males sometimes join females in their nests when the females are in estrus. Several males may join a nest when the females have passed out of estrus. The author notes, "the males evidently become more tolerant toward one another." Yet, who is becoming tolerant of whom is perhaps debatable, since all males usually are displaced to the outskirts of favored habitats.

Orangutans, the next species described, are designated as maintaining "nuclear groups," which consist of females and their young—occasionally accompanied by a usually solitary male. (In fact, the term "matri-centered group" seems more appropriate than "nuclear group" in this context, since the term "nuclear family" is used to describe the male/female/young family form among humans. But that's not the main issue just yet.) The author notes that "aggression within the society is quite rare, and nothing resembling a dominance system has been established in studies to date." Wilson cites a single instance of a female driving another female from a tree as the only clear episode of open hostility reported by observers. However, he states that males "probably do repel one another" because "a few pieces of indirect evidence suggest that such intrasexual conflict does exist." That indirect evidence consists of the fact that male orangutans are much larger than females and have vocal pouches that make their calls extremely loud. By reading from morphology to behavior, the author presumes that large noisy males win out in "intrasexual conflicts" over females, though open conflicts between males were not observed. Reading from morphology to behavior is a dangerous business, it turns out. Early on in the description of orangutans we find the statement, "As the orangs' unusual body form testifies, they are exclusively arboreal." Recent observers have learned, "The orangutan, studied in a rain forest in Indonesian Borneo, is not a tree dweller, contrary to popular belief, but does almost 100 percent of its long-distance traveling on the ground."[7] Indirect evidence of body form probably tells us very little about the nature of intrasexual conflict between males, and certainly tells us even less about whether the normally solitary males are "generally dominant over females" with whom they rarely associate.

The dusky titis of the Amazon-Orinoco region and the white-handed gibbons of Malaya and Sumatra are next discussed in sequence. Dusky titis live in small groups which consist of a female, her young and a male. These mated pairs and their young are referred to as "one of the simplest familial forms of society." The titis, it is noted, share this societal form with, among others, the white-handed gibbons whose social arrangement is described as "identical to family." In the gibbon pair "the female plays an equal role in territorial defense and in precoital sexual behavior," though it is especially, though not always, the female who emits territorial calls. While "the mother takes care of the infant ... " a lone gibbon male who allowed a small juvenile to adopt him and thereafter "carried the smaller animal in the maternal position during much of the day," indicates that, "the male is also prepared to assume the role of the mother when she falls ill or dies."

Though it is tempting to regard the parenting capacities and pair mating arrangements of titis and gibbons in terms of the particular nuclear family form Americans have recently come to idealize, the extension of the term to nonhuman mating and nurturing arrangements violates the common practice of ethologists. It is important to note that in Wilson's descriptions the term is used with reference to a form of animal grouping which resembles only one of the many kinds of groupings that are called "family" in human societies.[8] The use of the term "family" when referring to pair bond arrangements among nonhuman primates implies a biological basis for a familiar human social convention.

The mantled howlers who are described next are "of special sociobiological interest because a high level of individual tolerance permits the formation of large multimale societies." In addition, it is noted, they exhibit "the *unusual* circumstance of a species that appears to alternate between multimale and unimale organization and even has solitary males." The variability of howler social arrangements is clearly acknowledged. Conflict within troops is uncommon and almost never entails fighting. Not too surprisingly we learn that in this species dominance orders are "weakly defined." Despite extensive observations by the seven researchers cited, "It has not yet been established whether the troops are age-graded-male, with one dominant individual controlling younger animals, or whether the troops contain multiple high-ranking males." The possibility that there might be no hierarchy is not entertained. No mention is made in the description of behaviors that indicate that males are "dominant over females." The author simply assumes that in species where males are larger than females, as is the case among mantled howlers, the males must be dominant over the females. (The dangers of reading from morphology to behavior have already been pointed out.)

Ring-tailed lemurs also live in troops in which "fighting is rare." Yet their society is regarded as "aggressively organized." More notably we find that "adult females are dominant over males," which is "a reversal of an otherwise nearly universal primate pattern." While a linear hierarchy is observed among ring-tailed males, Wilson considers it "odd" that dominance in this hierarchy "seems to have no influence on access to estrous females." (Note that in the mouse lemur, which is "solitary" and lacks a male hierarchy, "dominance" is attributed to males who have access to estrous females.)

It is hard to see on what grounds the claim for male dominance as a nearly universal primate pattern is being made, since up to this point in the argument Wilson has cited social organizations in which females seem to exclude males, social organizations in which males may or may not fight with each other, and social organizations which may or may not have male hierarchies, while no social organizations in which males determine or control female behavior have been described.

The other three primate species discussed in some detail are the hamadryas baboons, Eastern mountain gorillas, and chimpanzees. All three are treated as giving evidence of "male dominance," although consistent criteria of dominance are not established. The hamadryas males of the small "single-male" units, found in Ethiopia, herd and nip at females, effectively determining what the females will do. Among the peaceful gorillas who live in multimale groups, "most dominance interactions consist of a mere acknowledgment of precedence," which is to say that an animal, male or female, who gives up space to another is regarded as subdominant. In loosely structured groups of chimpanzees we are told that "dominance behavior is well developed." Yet dominance behavior usually involves interactions which are "subtle," again usually just giving way. "Overt threats and retreats are uncommon." Among chimpanzees we once again find that "*curiously* . . . [my emphasis] the dominance system appears to have no influence on access to females," who appear to solicit whom they please when they please. An estrous female who stopped grooming a dominant male to copulate with a subadult male exemplifies the situation.

Wilson's evidence to support the view that male dominance is universal among *all primates* is furthered with his description of the following human situation.

Within a small tribe of Kung bushmen can be found individuals who are acknowledged as the "best people"; the leaders and outstanding specialists among the hunters and healers. Even with an emphasis on sharing goods, some are exceptionally able entrepreneurs and unostentatiously acquire a certain amount of wealth. Kung men no less than men in advanced industrial societies generally establish themselves by their mid-thirties or else accept a lesser status for life. There are some who never try to make it, live in rundown huts and show little pride in themselves and their work.[9]

To set the record straight, Kung are not tribal.[10] They live in camps of transient populations,[11] accumulate as little as possible to allow movement from camp to camp, and exchange and circulate materials and tools as well as food.[12] Camps include huts that are built—by the women, incidentally—at different times.[13] Leadership is ephemeral and task-oriented, depending on who is in the camp and what has to be done.[14] There are no specialists other than shamans,

some of whom are women.[15] The Kung have only recently become articulated with an entrepreneurial market economy, have no native category of "best people," and until recently, that is to say, the past decade, discouraged competitiveness and pride.[16]

As we look over the evidence that's offered, it becomes pretty clear that the generalization that primate males are usually dominant over females is arrived at by treating a minority of the species described as evolutionarily important and the majority of them as unimportant. No statistical survey of the admittedly incomplete data on nonhuman primates is presented, although a series of tables summarizing some of the data on nonhuman primate social organization is offered. How reliable that data is with respect to "dominance" is another question, for clearly, there is considerable ambiguity and inconsistency just in the way the term itself is used.

Before examining the concept of dominance closely, however, let me point out that the order in which Wilson describes the social arrangements of the primates reflects his evolutionary model of "grades of sociality." Wilson explicitly rejects evolutionary models of behavior which stress either the biological relationships between primate species or focus on primate social organizational patterns as responses to ecological circumstances. Wilson's model is built on the notion that social evolution among primates involves a development from no-male, to one-male, to multimale groups, but more significantly he assumes that social relationships evolve around males and male behaviors. Increases in male-to-male tolerance are at the heart of group development. That males are usually dominant over females in the no-male, one-male, and multimale situations alike is expressly stated, although we've seen that this is not clearly the case. Furthermore, Wilson's notions about one-male–multimale groups are fuzzy; for example, one-male hamadryas groups are not truly comparable to the one-male groups of patas monkeys where the member male is peripheral both socially and in space.[17] Males are emphasized as central in evolution because it is commonly assumed that while all females usually have infants, not all males have the same chance to breed. The idea that "dominant" males father more offspring than subdominant ones is so pervasive that it is said to be "odd" or "curious" when evidence to the contrary is found. Yet there is no doubt "dominant" males don't have special sexual prerogatives in many, and perhaps most, species other than those Wilson regards as "curious" and "odd" (e.g., gorillas,[18] Japanese macaques,[19] cynocephalous baboons in forested areas,[20] chimps, and others). Newer field studies clearly show that in many primates and in many situations social dominance is no guarantee of success with the ladies. That the text ignores such data and rejects the examination of how primate social patterns are related to ecological settings and/or vary within species reflects the author's underlying premise that social behavior and social arrangements are genetically determined. Wilson's model of "grades of sociality" thus disregards evidence which suggests that there is an evolutionary trajectory involving increased reliance on learned and socially transmitted behaviors in the primate order and makes more of the ill-defined notion of "dominance" than the data warrant.

To return to the uses and meaning of the term "dominance," the most thorough discussion of the concept of "dominance" and of primate behavior and social organization I have seen is that of Thelma Rowell.[21] Her review of the literature shows that whereas hierarchy and dominance-subordinance relationships have been considered the most important aspects of social behavior in animal groups, these concepts have been casually handled. Rarely have objective descriptions of social interactions been attached to statements about dominance, and predigested generalized observations make it impossible to compare studies by different observers who do not state how they define and interpret the phenomenon. Despite this obvious difficulty there is widespread agreement that hierarchical relationships occur frequently among caged animals and are less clearly discernible or absent in noncaged groups of animals. (The reasons for hierarchy in caged groups are complex. Such things as where food is placed, whether the animals were originally strange to each other, the age and prior experiences of the animals, and the nature of first encounters—all play a part in the formation and maintenance of hierarchies.) Studies which attempt to unravel the complex of factors usually associated with dominance have, therefore, been made on caged animals.

In a 1970 paper I. S. Bernstein[22] identified three dominance-related behaviors: aggression, mounting, and being groomed. For the study six species of monkeys were observed in groups living in large enclosures. Five of the six groups showed stable hierarchical relationships over several months with respect to the patterning of aggressive or agonistic encounters. In the sixth, a group of guenons, animals reversed their relationships several times during a year. Mounting relationships, and the hierarchies based on them, proved less stable than aggression hierarchies in all six species, and grooming relationships proved to be nondirectional and reciprocal. Bernstein found no correlation between the hierarchies obtained from the three kinds of relationships and concluded that they were not determined by a single social mechanism, were independent of one another, and not necessarily determined the same way in each of the groups observed. In a later study Bernstein and his associates[23] attempted to correlate aggressiveness and testosterone levels in an all-male group of rhesus monkeys and discovered that very high-ranking males—those who easily displaced all others—were neither very aggressive nor high in testosterone. A general correlation between aggressiveness and testosterone level, however, was found in lower-ranking males, who were under constant stress, leading Bernstein et al. to suggest that output of the hormone is determined by an animal's behavioral context, since the lowest-ranking socially active males in this study had higher testosterone levels than males living in isolation. A key issue in the dominance-aggression-hierarchy equation appears to be stress.

Rowell examines the possibility that what is often discussed as "dominance" behavior is in reality "subordinance" behavior. Ultimately, she notes, the outcome of approach-retreat interactions are decided by the behavior of the potential retreater. Animals under stress tend to avoid interactions which may have unpredictable or negative results and hesitate to initiate them. Secure animals are far less cautious. Researchers tend to attribute high rank to those who approach others, whether or not they do so in an "aggressive" or agonistic manner, especially if they displace an animal which is avoiding them. Cages induce both high levels of stress and high interaction rates which may be why dominance is so evident in the caged setting and why in these circumstances hierarchies become stabilized. In any event, "agonistic" hierarchies do not coincide with grooming or mounting hierarchies.

Rowell finds there are several reasons for asking whether the concept of dominance is a useful one in discussing the evolution of primate social behavior:

1. "Dominance hierarchies" are not consistent when determined for different types of behavior, so that the "top" animal is not the same in all situations.
2. Among primates group behavior is rarely determined by coercion, so that a "top" animal does not in fact lead or control the group.
3. Dominance has not been correlated with food-finding abilities or with danger avoidance; therefore, one cannot assume that dominance leads to significant survival advantages.
4. Dominance by some may be an expression of the subordinance of others, which results from stress. Thus it is either an ephemeral or a long-lived result of situational settings rather than an independent trait, much less a genetically determined one.
5. The males who mate are by no means always dominant. Furthermore, although Rowell does not directly address the issue of whether male dominance is universal or nearly universal among primates, it is relevant that among monkeys she finds significant variations regarding the sex of those who constitute the core of particular social groups.

Jane Lancaster[24] also has recorded some interesting observations that raise yet other questions about what is meant by male dominance. Her work on vervet monkeys shows that coalitions of females were easily formed against the top three males of the group she studied. If these offended some females by trying to monopolize a food source or by frightening an infant, even females of the lowest rank would band together to chase them. While a male's rank never changed as a result of such an encounter, his ability to bully others was curbed, and he learned to be very careful about frightening an infant. Several times Lancaster saw all the nearby adult males leave the vicinity when an infant screamed. Though they in fact were not what had frightened the infant, their behavior clearly revealed their anxiety that the females would form a coalition directed against them.

It is hardly necessary to point out that Wilson's use of the term "dominance" as applied to primate societies reflects few of the caveats and cautions Rowell and Lancaster express about the behaviors subsumed under the notion of dominance. Furthermore, it is self-evident that he uses the term inconsistently: a

male who breeds more than other males is defined as dominant on the basis of his breeding activities in a "solitary" species, yet in a more social arrangement a male who stands at the apex of a displacement hierarchy is called dominant though he does not breed more than other males. Such inconsistencies—as well as the inaccuracies—in the use of a term do not inspire much confidence in Wilson's claim that one of sociobiology's virtues is that it will introduce behavioral and social scientists to the analytic vigorousness of biology.

It is eminently clear that the recent contention that male dominance is universal or nearly universal among primates is unfounded. All it is is a new version of one of many pseudo-biological arguments that are used to justify social arrangements in our society. By claiming that these arrangements are found in our animal relatives, it suggests that these arrangements are the result of our genetic heritage. Now, as always, some researchers are trying to explain social traits among humans by attributing them to our innate biology. For the most part, however, such traits are no longer regarded as universal. Instead of talking about "instinctive, universal traits," researchers have been forced to talk about predilections or potentials for frequent or nearly universal traits. They therefore use vague notions such as "programmed potential" and "perceptual predisposition" to justify the conclusion that such traits are genetically determined. But like its other deterministic antecedents, this device ignores the history of changing human societies; just as it ignores the variety and variability of monkeys, it also ignores the fact that the *alternatives* to such frequent or nearly universal traits are also part of our human potential, and that "predispositions," "propensities," and "potentials" are developed in the contexts that favor them. The device of looking upon "near universals" as though they were therefore genetic seems to be a new way of minimizing the need for analyzing the social contexts in which traits have developed. This is particularly insidious if these traits reflect social privileges for some people and result from the unequal distribution of social privileges among the different social classes, races, or the sexes. Incorrectly attributing to primates, in general, the male dominance which is nurtured and relished in our own society is not science; it is political propaganda.

NOTES

1. M. Kay Martin and Barbara Voorhies, *The Female of the Species* (New York: Columbia U. Press, 1975), pp. 225–227.

2. See, for instance, Konrad Lorenz, *On Aggression* (New York: Harcourt, Brace and World, 1966), or Desmond Morris, *The Naked Ape* (New York: McGraw-Hill, 1968).

3. Nonsocial scientist, Robert Ardrey, published *The Territorial Imperative* (New York: Atheneum) in 1966, his *African Genesis* (London: Collins) had appeared in 1961. Lionel Tiger's *Men in Groups* (New York: Vintage Books, 1920) was one of the first of the popular books by a social scientist to exploit this market.

4. E. O. Wilson, *Sociobiology: The New Synthesis* (Cambridge: The Belknap Press of Harvard University Press, 1975).

5. Ibid., p. 551.

6. In the next few paragraphs of this paper a number of words, phrases, and sentences are cited verbatim from the above text. Rather than providing the reader with a long list of "ibids" and page references, I am noting here that these citations come from pages 514–546, a chapter entitled "The Nonhuman Primates."

7. *Science News,* Vol. 113, No. 12, 1978, p. 178.

8. Lila Leibowitz, *Females, Males, Families: A Biosocial Approach* (North Scituate, Mass.: Duxbury Press, 1978), pp. 6–9.

9. Wilson, 1975, p. 549.

10. R. B. Lee, "The Kung Bushman of Botswana," in *Hunters and Gatherers Today,* ed. M. Bicchieri (New York: Holt, Rinehart and Winston, 1972).

11. R. B. Lee, "What Hunters Do for a Living, or, How to Make Out on Scarce Resources," in *Man the Hunter,* ed. R. B. Lee and I. DeVore (Chicago: Aldine, 1968).

12. L. Marshall, "Sharing, Talking and Growing; Relief of Social Tensions among Kung Bushman of the Kalahari," *Africa,* Vol. 31, 1961.

13. F. Plog, C. J. Jolly, and D. G. Bates, *Anthropology: Decisions, Adaptations and Evolution* (New York: Alfred A. Knopf, 1976), p. 486.

14. Plog, Jolly, and Bates, *Anthropology,* 1976, p. 425.

15. R. B. Lee, personal communication.

16. R. B. Lee, "Eating Christmas in the Kalahari," *Natural History,* Vol. 77, No. 10 (Dec.), 1969, pp. 14–19.

17. Thelma Rowell, *The Social Behavior of Monkeys* (Harmondsworth, England: Penguin Books, 1972), p. 63.

18. George B. Schaller, *The Mountain Gorilla: Ecology and Behavior* (Chicago: University of Chicago Press, 1963).

19. G. Gray Eaton, "The Social Order of Japanese Macaques," *Scientific American,* October 1976, Vol. 235, No. 4, pp. 96–107.

20. Rowell, *Social Behavior of Monkeys,* pp. 46–66.

21. Ibid., pp. 159–164.

22. I. S. Bernstein, "Primate Status Hierarchies," in *Primate Behavior*, ed. L. A. Rosenblum (New York: Academic Press, 1970). Cited in Rowell, pp. 161–162.

23. R. M. Rose, J. W. Holaday, and I. S. Bernstein, "Plasma Testosterone, Dominance Rank, and Aggressive Behavior in Male Rhesus Monkeys." *Nature,* Vol. 231, 1971, pp. 366–71. Cited in Rowell.

24. Jane B. Lancaster, *Primate Behavior and the Emergence of Human Culture* (New York: Holt, Rinehart and Winston, 1975).

Gender and Parenthood: An Evolutionary Perspective
ALICE S. ROSSI

Parenting styles show the same gender differences found in contexts other than the family, which refutes the idea that there is something particular to pregnancy and birthing that "predisposes" or "triggers" maternal attachment to the newborn. It is not to a "maternal instinct" or "hormonal priming" at birth that one should look, but to gender differences that are in place long before a first pregnancy. This makes very dubious a view prevalent in the infant development literature in the last decade that close contact of the mother with her newborn during the first hours after birth, when hormonal levels are still very high, is important to subsequent mother-infant attachment. Lamb and Hwang's (1982) review of this literature concludes that the post-birth period is neither a critical nor a sensitive period[1] for maternal attachment.[2]

Indeed, a rethinking of this issue from an evolutionary perspective suggests it is highly unlikely that small variations in early contact could be critical to human attachment to infants. For a complex organism like a human being, fixing of an essential bond is not likely to be dependent on a brief period or specific experience following childbirth. There will be considerable redundancy in the processes that assure activation of parental attachment to a child, and this will take place over a considerably longer period than a few hours or days after birth.

Animal research shows that it is possible experimentally to invoke nurturant behavior toward the young through the administration of female sex hormones to virgin, prepubescent males and females, so some hormonal factors implicit in sex dimorphism are

implicated (Moltz et al., 1970; Rosenblatt, 1967, 1969; Terkel & Rosenblatt, 1968). It is also the case that normal males show nurturant behavior if exposed to pups for a period of time. Adler (1973) suggests that hormones may *prime* nurturant behavior, but continuous proximity is necessary to *maintain* that behavior and may even stimulate it in the absence of hormonal priming.

For most primate species and most of human history, lactation assured the maintenance of proximity between mother and newborn. Then too, the mother-infant dyad is not isolated but enmeshed in a group, whether a baboon troop, hunter-gatherer band or contemporary family. Support by the group is enhanced by the general affiliative, socially responsive qualities of the female, since these qualities elicit aid from the group and assure persistence in providing nurturant care to the young by all the females in the group.[3]

Thus an evolutionary perspective suggests not only that no specific experience will be critical for parental attachment to and care of the young. It also argues against the possibility of leaving to a late stage of development, close to or following a pregnancy, the acquisition of qualities necessary for so important a function as reproduction. The attributes of mothering and fathering are inherent parts of the sex differentiation that paves the way to reproduction. This is where the sociological analogy so often drawn between race and sex breaks down in the most fundamental sense. Genetic assimilation is possible through interracial mating, and we can envisage a society that is color-blind. But genetic assimilation of male and female is impossible, and no society will be sex-blind. Except for a small minority, awareness of and attraction to differences between male and female are essential features of the species.

If the parenting styles of men and women build

Adapted from *American Sociological Review* 49 (February 1984):1–19. Reprinted by permission of the author and the American Sociological Association. Notes have been renumbered.

upon underlying features rooted in basic sexual dimorphism, then increased male involvement in primary care of the very young child will not have the effect that some theorists expect. For example, Chodorow (1974, 1978) argues that gender differences are themselves the consequence of the fact that it is women who do the parenting of both sons and daughters. By this thesis, if fathers had primary care responsibility for their same-sex child, boys, like girls today, would grow up with less individuation, greater relational affiliation, less clearly marked-off ego boundaries.

But there is no evidence from the studies of solo or co-parenting fathers to date to suggest this is a likely outcome. Men bring their maleness to parenting, as women bring their femaleness. Hence the effect of increased male investment in primary care of sons is not to produce sons who would be more like daughters, but either to enhance gender differences or, if there is significant co-parenting, to enlarge the range of characteristics shown by both sons and daughters.

BIOLOGICAL COMPONENTS OF GENDER

It is one thing to criticize psychosocial theories for their inadequacy in explaining empirical findings on gender differences in parenting. It is quite another to supplement them with biological factors. Sociologists share enough ground in theory and method with psychologists to work readily across both disciplines. This is not the case where biological contributions to gender differences are concerned. My treatment must be very selective, but it is nonetheless necessary to make a few general points.

One, it makes no sense to view biology and social experience as separate domains contesting for election as "primary causes." Biological processes unfold in a cultural context, and are themselves malleable, not stable and inevitable. So, too, cultural processes take place within and through the biological organism; they do not take place in a biological vacuum.

Second, there is a good deal of ferment in the biological sciences these days in opposition to the Cartesian reductionism that has characterized Western science for three centuries.[4] That model worked well in physics and chemistry and the technology they spawned. It has not worked well in embryology and the brain sciences. Reductionism in the biomedical fields works via the experimental mode in which one perturbs the normal working of the system under study, but as a consequence it runs the risk of confusing the nature of the perturbation with the cause of the system's normal functioning. An example from medical research illustrates this point: if you give patients the drug dopamine and it reduces Parkinsonian tremors, then Parkinson's disease is thought to be "caused" by a deficiency of dopamine (Lewontin, 1983). Sociobiologists rely on the same reductionist model: they consider properties of society to be determined by intrinsic properties of individual human beings; individuals in turn are expressions of their genes, and genes are self-replicating molecules. Following this logic leads to such claims as Dawkins's (1976) for a "selfish gene," others for an "altruistic gene." Under fire from social scientists, Edward Wilson has revised his earlier gene-determinist theory to include the evolution of culture itself, using the concept of "gene-culture co-evolution" to explain the emergence of "mind" (Lumsden & Wilson, 1981, 1982). But the revised theory remains a reductionist theory.[5]

The challenge to the reductionist model has come from biological scientists here and in western Europe, particularly among Marxist biologists, who argue in favor of a dialectical model. This is based on an interesting set of assumptions: one, organisms grow and change throughout their life spans through an interplay of biological, psychological and sociocultural processes (Parsons, 1982; Petersen, 1980; Riegel, 1976; Rose, 1982a, 1982b). Second, biological processes are assumed to have greater influence at some points in the life span than at others. For example, they are critical in fetal development, at puberty, during pregnancy, but less potent during latency or early middle age. Thus, for example, there are quite high correlations between testosterone level and aggression among young men, but no significant correlations among older men, since the latter's greater social maturation permits higher levels of impulse control (Persky et al., 1971). So, too, Gutmann's theory of the parental imperative (1975) is illuminated by an awareness of the ebb and flow along the life span in the significance of hormonal processes: childbearing and -rearing take place during that phase of the life span with the greatest sex dimorphism in hormonal secretion and body morphology, and with very great pressure to perform in culturally specified ways in adult male and female roles. Along with the relaxation of social pressure from middle age on, there is also a change in body, a blurring of sexual and hormonal differences between men and women. It is the interaction of lowered inner hormonal pressures and lowered external social pressures, combined with psychologically coming to terms with a shortened life span, that I believe produces the sex-role involution noted in studies of personality in the later years.

In sum, organisms are not passive objects acted upon by internal genetic forces, as some sociobiologists claim, nor are they passive objects acted upon by external environmental forces, as some social scientists claim. Genes, organisms and environment interpenetrate and mutually determine each other. To discuss biological predispositions is to attempt a specification of biological processes, in the same way sociologists try to specify social processes. Awareness of *both* social and biological processes adds a synergistic increment to knowledge, knowledge that can then be used to provide the means for modification and change; they do not imply that we are locked into an unchangeable body or social system. *Ignorance of biological processes may doom efforts at social change to failure because we misidentify what the targets for change should be, and hence what our means should be to attain the change we desire.*

But for social scientists to specify what biological processes are relevant to the phenomena they study can easily lead to flimsy argument by selective analogy, of the aggressive-territorial-male-animal variety. One must adhere to some guidelines in exploring whether and in what specific way gender differences may be shaped by biological processes. The biological factors relevant to gender differences in social behavior will be located at some point on the chain of development that runs from genetic sex at conception (a female XX chromosome or a male XY chromosome), through gonadal differentiation during the first trimester of fetal development, to hormones produced by the gonads and related pituitary glands, to neural organization of the brain, and from there to social behavior.

We can study the effect of variation at any one of these points on the chain for subsequent social behavior of the organism. For example, a normal conceptus has two sex chromosomes (XX or XY), but occasionally may have three, either an extra X (XXY) or an extra Y (XYY). The Y chromosome is critical in gonadal differentiation of the male and the level of androgenic hormones the gonads produce. If androgens

affect behavior, as they do, then we can see what social behavior and physical characteristics vary between, say, a normal XY male and an XYY male or an XXY male. Compared to a normal male, the XYY male, with his extra dose of maleness if you will, will be taller than average, more muscular, have more body hair, higher activity levels, more impulsivity, and more acute visual-spatial abilities. A male with an extra dose of femaleness, the XXY male with Klinefelter's Syndrome, is shorter and less muscular, has less body hair and smaller testicles, lower sexual arousability, and is more timid and passive in behavior than the average male. Family and social circumstances will obviously affect how and the extent to which the behavioral characteristics are shown, but we have identified a very specific and important biological component in the behavior of such males.

Sex hormones affect social behavior in one of two ways: they can have *direct* effects—what biologists call activational effects—or *indirect* effects—what biologists call inductive or organizational effects (Goy & McEwen, 1980; Hoyenga & Hoyenga, 1979). A direct effect means secretion level, hormone production rate or type of hormone is a *proximate* contributor to behavior. Think of the contrast in behavior of a 10-year-old and an 18-year-old male; one contributor to the different social behavior they show is androgens: the older boy will have on average an eight times higher level of androgen secretion than the younger (Ellis, 1982), and a good deal of the behavior of the two males is affected by that difference.

The indirect or organizational effect of sex hormones refers to the influence of hormones during the critical phase of neural development in the third trimester of pregnancy when the brain is undergoing rapid development and differentiation. Hormonal influence at this critical stage is important for gender differentiation, since brain cells acquire a "set" (like a thermostat setting), highly resistant to change after birth. It is this organizational effect of hormones on neural circuitry that led neuroscientists to speak of a "male" or a "female" brain at birth. Note, too, that the amount of androgens circulating in a male fetus during the first trimester of pregnancy is the equivalent by body weight to four times the amount he will have from birth to approximately 10 years of age (Ellis, 1982). Hormones, then, have powerful effects during fetal development, go into a relatively quiescent period for the first decade of life, and then rapidly increase again during the second decade of life. To the extent that hormones affect behavior, it is simply not true that an absence of a gender difference in behavior at age 4 and the emergence of such a difference at 14 means the difference is culturally produced, because the adolescent's behavior is strongly influenced by the activational effects of sex hormones.

With these comments as background, we can specify the criteria for determining whether biology is involved in a gender difference in social behavior. Parsons (1982) suggests four such criteria and proposes that if two or more of them are met, there is strong evidence implicating biology in the observed gender difference. Slightly modified from those Parsons proposed,[6] the criteria are: (1) consistent correlations between social behavior and a physiological sex attribute (body morphology, sex chromosome type, hormonal type and secretion level, neural organization in the brain); (2) the pattern is found in infants and young children prior to major socialization influences, or the pattern emerges with the onset of puberty, when body morphology and hormonal secretion change rapidly; (3) the pattern is stable across cultures; and (4) similar behavior is noted across species, particularly the higher primates most genetically similar to the human species.

Using these four criteria, sex dimorphism with biological contributions can be claimed in four areas: (1) sensory sensitivity (sight, hearing, smell, touch) and body morphology; (2) aggression or, more aptly, general activity level; (3) cognitive skills in spatial visualization, mathematical reasoning, and to a lesser extent verbal fluency; and (4) parenting behavior (Petersen, 1980).

Parenting as a sex-dimorphic pattern clearly meets two of the four criteria: in almost all cultures and most species, it is primarily a female responsibility to care for the young. In most cultures, siblings provide more caregiving to the very young than fathers do (Weisner, 1982; Whiting & Whiting, 1975). Paternal caregiving among nonhuman primates tends to be among New World monkeys, who typically have multiple litters, unlike large apes and humans, who typically have one infant at a time and a prolonged period of immature dependency (Redican, 1976).

Redican's review of the structural conditions that predict paternal involvement among nonhuman primates is remarkably similar to a comparable review by West and Konner (1976) of the conditions that predict human paternal involvement. For nonhuman primate males, paternal involvement is high when there is a monogamous social organization, and paternity is readily identifiable when males are not needed for the role of warrior-hunter and when females are permissive and encourage paternal caregiving. For human males, West and Konner observe that men take care of their children if they are sure they are the fathers, if they are not needed as warriors and hunters, if mothers contribute to food resources, and if male parenting is encouraged by women.

The structural conditions specified by Redican, West and Konner apply for the most part to modern societies. There are limits of course on confidence in paternity, but sharing of the economic provider role is increasingly the pattern and spills over to rising pressure from women for greater participation by their husbands in child care. We can assume, then, that structural conditions are ripe for higher levels of paternal involvement in the future. Two criteria remain at issue concerning biological implications: do the differences between male and female in hormones, sensory sensitivity, activity level or social and cognitive skills lead one to predict different styles of parenting on the part of men compared to women as they move toward greater co-parenting? It is my working hypothesis that all sexually dimorphic characteristics contribute to the species function of reproduction, and hence have persisted as biological predispositions across cultures and through historical time.

A profile of gender differences in sensory modalities reads like this:[7] females show greater sensitivity to touch, sound and odor; have greater fine motor coordination and finger dexterity. Sounds are judged to be twice as loud by women as men; women pick up nuances of voice and music more readily, and are six times more likely to sing in tune as men. The sense modality in which men show greater acuity than women is vision: men show greater sensitivity to light, responding more quickly to changes in light intensity than women do. At birth, females are four to six weeks more mature neurologically than males, which persists in their earlier acquisition of language, verbal fluency, and memory retention. Language disabilities like stuttering and dyslexia are several times more prevalent among males than females.

Gender differences in social and cognitive skills are also found: females are more sensitive to context, show greater skill in picking up peripheral information and process information faster; they are more attracted to human faces and respond to nuances of facial expression as they do to nuances of sound. Males are better at object manipulation in space, can rotate objects in their mind, read maps and perform in mazes better, and show a better sense of direction. Males are more rule-bound, less sensitive to situational nuance. Most of these differences meet the criterion of precultural influence in that they show up at very early ages. Male infants are more attracted to the movement of objects, females to the play of expression on human faces. Girl babies startle to sound more quickly than boy babies, and respond to the soothing effect of a human voice, while boys respond to physical contact and movement.

Viewed as a composite profile, there is some predisposition in the female to be responsive to people and sounds, an edge in receiving, interpreting and giving back communication. Males have an edge on finer differentiation of the physical world through better spatial visualization and physical object manipulation. The female combination of sensitivity to sound and face and rapid processing of peripheral information implies a quicker judgment of emotional nuance, a profile that carries a putdown tone when labeled "female intuition." It also suggests an easier connection between feelings and their expression in words among women. Spatial perception, good gross motor control, visual acuity, and a more rigid division between emotional and cognitive responsivity combine in a counterpart profile of the male.

One ingenious study illustrates both the greater sound acuity of women and greater spatial perception ability of men. The test was simply to mentally search the alphabet for two types of capital letters: those with a curve in their shape like an "S," and those with a long "ee" sound like a "Z." As predicted, men were faster and made fewer errors than women on the letter *shape* task, while women were faster and more accurate on the verbal *sound* task (Coltheart et al., 1975).

When these gender differences are viewed in connection with caring for a nonverbal, fragile infant, then women have a head start in easier reading of an infant's facial expressions, smoothness of body motions, greater ease in handling a tiny creature with tactile gentleness and in soothing through a high, soft, rhythmic use of the voice. By contrast, men have tendencies more congenial to interaction with an older child, with whom rough-and-tumble physical play,

physical coordination, teaching of object manipulation are easier and more congenial. Note, however, that these are general tendencies, many of them exaggerated through sex-differentiated socialization practices; they should not be taken to mean they are either biologically immutable or invariant across individuals or cultures. Some cultures may reinforce these predispositions, as ours does, while others may socialize against or reverse them.

There is, however, a good deal of evidence in animal and human research to support the view that sex hormones and sex differentiation in neurological organization of the brain contribute to these differences. Androgens have been the most intensively studied for their effects on spatial visualization, maze running, aggression and sexual behavior. Animals given androgen either neonatally or as adults show improvement in complex maze scores, while the administration of the female hormone, estrogen, depresses maze learning. Sons of diabetic mothers who were given estrogen during pregnancy show reduced spatial ability and more field dependence than control males. Turner's-syndrome women, genetic females with only one sex chromosome (XO type), do not develop ovaries and hence are deprived of fetal androgens, and they show poor spatial and numerical ability.

As noted earlier, hormones can operate in either an activational or organizational manner. There is evidence that certain of the gender differences cited above are not acquired after birth, when they could be the result of the interactive effect of both biological and social factors, but before birth, in the organization of the brain under the influence of gonadal hormones. Neuroscience research has established that the right hemisphere of the brain is dominant in emotions, facial recognition, music, visual tasks and identification of spatial relationships, while language skills are dominant in the left hemisphere of the brain (Kinsbourne, 1978; Goy & McEwen, 1980). Human males show more rigid separation of function between the two brain hemispheres, while the female brain is less lateralized, less tightly organized than the male. Thus the brains of 4-year-old girls show more advanced cell growth in the left, language-dominant hemisphere, boys in the right, spatial-perception-dominant hemisphere.[8]

Anatomical research further established that a larger proportion of space in the right hemisphere is devoted to the visual-spatial function in males than females. McGuinness (1976) suggests that as a consequence males have more restricted verbal access to their emotions than females (Durden-Smith & De-Simone, 1983). Brain lateralization differences between men and women also suggest that one reason males show greater mathematical ability than females is that females approach mathematical problems through left-hemisphere *verbal* means, while males rely more directly on right-hemisphere *symbols,* which is a more efficient route to problem solving.

Until 1982, a prevalent interpretation for why and how gender differentiation in hemisphere organization occurs was linked to the earlier maturation of girls generally. Lateralization, beginning earlier in girls, might give them an advantage in verbal skills, while delayed lateralization gives males an advantage in spatial skills (Harris, 1978). This interpretation has been challenged by new research that found the divider between the brain hemispheres called the *corpus callosum* (a bundle of fibers that carries information between the two halves of the brain) was larger and more bulbous in females than in males, suggesting greater ease and frequency of communication between the two hemispheres in females (De La Coste-Utamsing & Holloway, 1982; Durden-Smith & DeSimone, 1983).

If further research substantiates these findings, they do not mean we simply accept a gender difference in spatial visualization and mathematical ability as immutable. A postindustrial society in which an increasing proportion of occupations rely on mathematical and spatial skills, coupled with these findings, can as readily lead to a shift in mathematical training of girls away from dealing narrowly with their assumed "math anxiety," to biofeedback training to encourage greater direct reliance on symbols rather than words in problem solving.

CONCLUSION

Let us assume that the neurosciences continue to affirm what is a growing accumulation of evidence of biological processes that differentiate the sexes, and let us assume further that the social trend toward greater co-parenting continues in the future. What are the likely outcomes in gender characteristics of a future generation of children?

I take the research findings to mean that at birth the child brings gender predispositions that interact with gender differences in the parents, whose own differences reflect biological predispositions either reinforced or downplayed by adult socialization and role pressure. Biological predispositions in the child do not preclude their supplementation by psychological qualities of the parents or encouraged in the child by parents who do not themselves possess a given characteristic. Quite traditional parents encourage children to develop in ways they perceive to be useful when their children are adults, even when they themselves do not possess the qualities they encourage in their children. Differences between parents and children do not mean that parental influence is nil, nor that children have rebelled under peer pressure. The qualities in question may have been actively encouraged by the parent.

If you assume further, as I do, that there are many socially desirable attributes among traditional male and female traits, then an equal exposure of children to them from parents who both invest a great deal in caregiving could have the effect of encouraging more androgyny in the children. Several researchers have shown that cognitive ability and even scientific productivity are higher when subjects are neither strongly feminine nor strongly masculine, but possess in equal measure the socially desirable traits of both sexes. Spence and Helmreich (1978) show that when socially desirable attributes of men and women are measured, they vary independently of each other within each sex. In other words, masculine qualities and feminine qualities do not preclude each other in the same person, although that combination is still not prevalent in American society. Furthermore, those with the highest levels of self-esteem and self-confidence were subjects *high* on *both sets* of attributes.

Spence and Helmreich used their masculinity–femininity scales in a study of established scientists that also included measures of work commitment, subject mastery, degree of overall competitiveness in work, and productivity. The measure of scientific productivity was an external criterion, the number of references to their subjects' publications in the Science Citation Index. They found that those scientists *high on both* the masculinity and the femininity scales were the *most* scientifically productive. Further analysis found the highest scientific attainment to be among those *high* in subject mastery and work commitment and *lowest* in competitiveness, a profile that again combines traditionally feminine with masculine characteristics.

Productive labor in all sectors of the occupational system and creativity in critical professions may therefore benefit by a blending of the attributes traditionally associated with male and female. That blending may be encouraged by movement away from sex-segregated occupations with token minority representation of one sex, toward compositional sex parity, on the assumption of an eventual reciprocal influence on each other of equal numbers of men and women incumbents.

But in the long run, on an individual as well as societal level, the socially desirable attributes of both sexes can be acquired by each sex only if we properly identify their sources in both biology and culture. Biological predispositions make certain things easier for one sex to learn than the other; knowing this in advance would permit a specification of how to provide compensatory training for each sex, in rearing children within families, in teaching children in schools, or in training adults on the job. No individual and no society can benefit from a circumstance in which men fear intimacy and women fear impersonality.

As adults, there are limits on the extent to which we can change our deeply ingrained characteristics. But a first step is to understand and to respect the qualities of each sex, and to actively encourage children to absorb the socially desirable attributes of both sexes. To the extent this is done, whether by solo fathers, solo mothers, or egalitarian co-parents, a future generation of boys and men may temper competitive self-interest with affiliative concern for the welfare of others and skills in intimate relations, and girls and women may temper their affiliative concern for others with a sense of effective, actualized selves.

No society on this tiny planet provides a model for us to emulate. It was my hope in recent years that feminism provided a guide to such a future, as it had been earlier that socialism did. But neither Marxism nor feminism, to say nothing of mainstream social science, has yet taken up the challenge of the biological component to human behavior, despite the fact that sex dimorphism is central to both production and reproduction. An ideology that does not confront this basic issue is an exercise in wishful thinking, and a social science that does not confront it is sterile. Whether one's motivation as a sociologist is rooted in passionate commitment to social change or passionate commitment to scientific advance, or both, it is my firm conviction, and conclusion, that the goals we seek are best approached through an integrated biosocial science.

NOTES

1. A "critical" period refers to a discrete phase of development during which specific events *must* occur if development is to proceed normally, while a "sensitive" period refers to a phase of development during which an aspect of development may be *more readily* influenced than at other stages. Contact with the newborn in the hours after birth is neither a "must" in the critical period sense nor even "facilitative" in the sensitive period sense.

2. The best-known work in this area is that by Klaus and Kennell (1976), whose findings have not been replicated. Klaus and Kennell used poor young clinic patients, who may have been more affected by the projected model of good parenting behavior when they were marked off for special treatment by having more time with their newborn infants (Hawthorne effect). Studies with middle-class women at Stanford and in Sweden did not show any comparable effect of increased time with neonates for subsequent mother-infant attachment that Klaus and Kennell claim to have established. See Lamb and Hwang (1982) for a detailed review.

3. Gender-differentiated persistence in seeking contact with the newborn is found among siblings in both monkey and human groups. In monkey groups, mothers often try to keep both male and female siblings away from the newborn, but pubescent females *persist* in seeking proximity while males do not (Suomi, 1982). Human toddlers show similar behavior, with girls seeking contact, while boys go off more readily when the mother is with a newborn (Dunn and Kendrick, 1982; Nadelman and Begun, 1982). Ember (1973) found that helping to care for younger children increased nurturing and socially responsible behavior in boys.

4. Two books of essays, from a 1980 conference in Bressanone, Italy, are a useful introduction to the dialectic per-

spective in biology (Rose, 1982a, 1892b). For a brief overview of the major ideas from this conference, see Lewontin's review of these books (Lewontin, 1983).

5. See Gould (1983) for a review of Lumsden and Wilson's book, *Promethean Fire* (1982). A critical review of the companion volume, *Genes, Mind, Culture* (Lumsden & Wilson, 1981), can be found in Smith and Warre (1982).

6. I have expanded Parsons's criterion "1" from just hormones to the factors cited in the text, and modified criterion "2" by including pubertal change.

7. Several sources contribute to this overview profile: Durden-Smith and DeSimone, 1983; Gove and Carpenter, 1982; Hoyenga and Hoyenga, 1979; Parsons, 1980, 1982.

8. Male victims whose left brain hemispheres were affected by stroke or epileptic seizure show more language impairment during recovery than female victims, because of the much greater male reliance on the left hemisphere for language; female victims compensate by relying on their unimpaired right hemisphere.

REFERENCES

Adler, N. 1973. "The biopsychology of hormones and behavior." In D. A. Dewbery & D. A. Rethlingshafer, eds., *Comparative psychology: A modern survey,* pp. 301–43. New York: McGraw-Hill.

Chodorow, N. 1974. "Family structure and feminine personality." In M. Z. Rosaldo & L. Lamphere, eds., *Women, culture, and society,* pp. 43–66. Palo Alto: Stanford University Press. [Reading 6 in this volume.]

Chodorow, N. 1978. *The reproduction of mothering: Psychoanalysis and the sociology of gender.* Los Angeles: University of California Press.

Coltheart, M.; Hull, E.; & Slater, D. 1975. "Sex differences in imagery and reading." *Nature* 253:438–40.

Dawkins, R. 1976. *The selfish gene.* London: Oxford University Press.

De La Coste-Utamsing, C., & Holloway, R. 1982. "Sexual dimorphism in the human corpus callosum." *Science* 216:431–32.

Dunn, J., & Kendrick, C. 1982. "Siblings and their mothers: Developing relationships within the family." In M. E. Lamb & B. Sutton-Smith, eds., *Sibling relationships: Their nature and significance across the lifespan.* Hillsdale, N.J.: Lawrence Erlbaum.

Durden-Smith, J., & DeSimone, D. 1983. *Sex and the brain.* New York: Arbor House.

Ellis, L. 1982. "Developmental androgen fluctuations and the five dimensions of mammalian sex (with emphasis upon the behavioral dimension and the human species)." *Ethology and Sociobiology* 3:171–97.

Ember, C. R. 1973. "The effects of feminine task assignment on the social behavior of boys." *Ethos* 1:424–39.

Gould, S. J. 1983. "Genes on the brain." *New York Review of Books* 30 (11): 5–6, 10.

Gove, W. R., & Carpenter, G. R. 1982. *The fundamental connection between nature and nurture.* Lexington, Mass.: Lexington Books.

Goy, R. W., & McEwen, B. S. 1980. *Sexual differentiation of the brain.* Cambridge: M.I.T. Press.

Gutmann, D. 1975. "Parenthood: A key to the comparative study of the life cycle." In N. Datan & L. H. Ginsberg, eds., *Life span development and psychology: Normative life crises,* pp. 167–84. New York: Academic Press.

Harris, L. J. 1978. "Sex differences in spatial ability: Possible environmental, genetic, and neurological factors." In M. Kinsbourne, ed., *Asymmetrical functions of the brain,* pp. 405–522. Cambridge: Cambridge University Press.

Hoyenga, K. B., & Hoyenga, K. T. 1979. *The question of sex differences: Psychological, cultural, and biological issues.* Boston: Little, Brown.

Kinsbourne, M., ed. 1978. *Asymmetrical functions of the brain.* Cambridge: Cambridge University Press.

Klaus, M. H., & Kennell, J. H. 1976. *Maternal-infant bonding: The impact of early separation or loss on family development.* St. Louis: C. V. Mosby.

Lamb, M. E., & Hwang, C. P. 1982. "Maternal attachment and mother-neonate bonding: A critical review." In M. E. Lamb & A. L. Brown, eds., *Advances in developmental psychology,* 2:1–38. Hillsdale, N. J.: Lawrence Erlbaum.

Lewontin, R. 1983. "The corpse in the elevator." *New York Review of Books* 29 (21 and 22): 34–37.

Lumsden, C. J., & Wilson, E. O. 1981. *Genes, mind, culture.* Cambridge: Harvard University Press.

Lumsden, C. J., & Wilson, E. O. 1982. *Promethean fire: Reflections on the origin of mind.* Cambridge: Harvard University Press.

McGuinness, D. 1976. "Away from a unisex psychology: Individual differences in visual, sensory, and perceptual processes." *Perception* 5:279–94.

Moltz, H.; Lubin, M.; Leon, M.; & Numan, M. 1970. "Hormonal induction of maternal behavior in the ovariectomized nulliparous rat." *Physiology and Behavior* 5:1373–77.

Nadelman, L., & Begun, A. 1982. "The effect of the newborn on the older sibling: Mothers' questionnaires." In M. E. Lamb & B. Sutton-Smith, eds., *Sibling relationships: Their nature and significance across the lifespan.* Hillsdale, N.J.: Lawrence Erlbaum.

Parsons, J. E., ed. 1980. *The psychobiology of sex differences and sex roles.* Washington, D.C.: Hemisphere.

Parsons, J. E. 1982. "Biology, experience, and sex dimorphic behaviors." In W. R. Gove & G. R. Carpenter, eds., *The fundamental connection between nature and nurture,* pp. 137–70. Lexington, Mass.: Lexington Books.

Persky, H.; Smith, K. D.; & Basu, G. K. 1971. "Relation of psychologic measures of aggression and hostility to testosterone production in man." *Psychosomatic Medicine* 33:265–77.

Petersen, A. C. 1980. "Biopsychosocial processes in the development of sex-related differences." In J. E. Parsons, ed., *The psychology of sex differences and sex roles,* pp. 31–56. Washington, D.C.: Hemisphere.

Redican, W. K. 1976. "Adult male-infant interactions in nonhuman primates." In M. E. Lamb, ed., *The role of the father in child development.* New York: Wiley.

Riegel, K. F. 1976. "The dialectics of human development." *American Psychologist* 31:689–700.

Rose, S., ed. 1982a. *Against biological determinism.* New York: Schocken.

Rose, S., ed. 1982b. *Towards a liberatory biology.* New York: Schocken.

Rosenblatt, J. S. 1967. "Nonhormonal basis of maternal behavior in the rat." *Science* 156:1512–14.

Rosenblatt, J. S. 1969. "The development of maternal responsiveness in the rat." *American Journal of Orthopsychiatry* 39:36–56.

Smith, J. M., & Warre, N. 1982. "Models of cultural and genetic change." *Evolution* 36:620–21.

Spence, J. T., & Helmreich, R. L. 1978. *Masculinity and femininity: Their psychological dimensions, correlates and antecedents.* Austin: University of Texas Press.

Suomi, S. J. 1982. "Sibling relationships in nonhuman primates." In M. E. Lamb & B. Sutton-Smith, eds., *Sibling relationships: Their nature and significance across the lifespan.* Hillsdale, N.J.: Lawrence Erlbaum.

Terkel, J., & Rosenblatt, J. S. 1968. "Maternal behavior induced by maternal blood plasma injected into virgin rats." *Journal of Comparative and Physiological Psychology* 65:479–82.

Weisner, T. S. 1982. "Sibling interdependence and child caretaking: A cross-cultural view." In M. E. Lamb & B. Sutton-Smith, eds., *Sibling relationships: Their nature and significance across the lifespan.* Hillsdale, N.J.: Lawrence Erlbaum.

West, M. M., & Konner, M. L. 1976. "The role of the father: An anthropological perspective." In M. E. Lamb, ed., *The role of the father in child development,* pp. 185–218. New York: Wiley.

Whiting, B., & Whiting, J. W. 1975. *Children of six cultures: A psycho-cultural analysis.* Cambridge: Harvard University Press.

R E A D I N G   1 3

A Theory of Gender Stratification

JOAN HUBER

In the long view of history, most theories of social stratification have been theological. The world was thus because God (or the gods) wanted it that way. In the words of a popular hymn,

The rich man in his castle,
The poor man at his gate,
God made them high and lowly
And ordered man's estate.

By the time that stanza was dropped from the hymn about all creatures great and small, God was being given less credit for stratal design than he used to be. Industrialization in Europe and North America during the nineteenth century had spawned grand theories about class differences in power and prestige. These theories came to permeate twentieth-century consciousness.

Gender differences in power and privilege, in contrast, were still taken for granted. Before 1970 the major theory of gender stratification was biological: sex differences in power and prestige stemmed from inborn characteristics. One was categorical: no man could bear or breastfeed a child. Other differences overlapped. Men tended to come in larger sizes with heavier muscles. Many mental differences also overlapped. The extent to which they were inborn or the result of experience was (and still is) unknown.

Industrialization reduced the functional importance of many sex differences. The importance of men's inability to breastfeed a child diminished after 1910, when techniques of sterilization enabled babies to survive on bottled milk. Women's lesser muscular strength mattered less as machines increasingly replaced human power. Today, for example, a man's brawn gives him little advantage in a white-collar job, the kind where brains count. Brawn still gives marginal advantage in such activities as shoveling heavy wet snow, but prudent men do not press it too hard. They tend to suffer vascular problems earlier than women do.

Industrialization also lessened the credibility of some alleged sex differences. Myths about women's mental weakness which justified their exclusion from positions of power were thwarted by the spread of compulsory education. It became harder to define women as less able than men when girls did as well as boys in school. In fact, they often did better. Ever since colleges admitted women, it has been hard to preserve a balanced sex ratio when the same admission standards are applied to both sexes. Historically, many colleges separated the applicant pools, reserving a larger quota for men. Some used the same yardstick but required higher scores for girls. In the 1960s, for example, the New York City Colleges required a grade average of 85 for men but 90 for women lest the system be swamped with women. Using the same yardstick for both sexes, North Carolina at Chapel Hill now has more women undergraduates than men, a development that has alarmed some of the trustees (Greene, 1987).

The need to replace biological theories of sex stratification became apparent around 1970 (Huber, 1986). A new wave of the women's movement threw into relief many anomalies that had surfaced in the wake of industrialization. Sex-role behaviors clearly followed no logical pattern based on biological differences. Even though men possessed the requisite skills, for example, they were much less likely than women to bottle-feed babies. Similarly, the hours that fully employed wives spent washing dishes and cleaning toilets stemmed from no demonstrable biological imperative. It dawned on scholars that gender stratification was a form of social stratification to which biology contributed but which biology alone could not explain.

In 1970, however, the data needed for a theory were hard to find in the relevant disciplines (Huber & Spitze, forthcoming). Anthropologists had long gathered data on foraging and hoe cultures, but most anthropologists, being men, had not been able to mix freely with native women going about their work. In consequence, the data about women's behavior and beliefs were sketchy. Moreover, interpretations tended to stem from the Western sex-role ideologies that male anthropologists carried in their heads as part of their intellectual equipment.

Historians had long studied the great men and great events of diplomatic history to the neglect of social history, the study of the daily lives of ordinary people. Since the historical record included few great queens and female warriors, women were nearly invisible.

Sociologists had analyzed women as wives and mothers in the study of the family or as prostitutes in the study of deviance. The literature on stratification defined women only as appendages to their husbands. A basic problem was that stratification theories, whether influenced by Karl Marx or Max Weber, defined social class as a market relationship. The household was a black box. Neither Marx nor Weber (nor, for that matter, Emile Durkheim) had conceptualized the household division of labor as part of the division of labor in society. In consequence, neither European nor American theories of society had much to contribute to a theory of gender stratification.

Nonetheless, the earliest social theories of gender stratification were the work of scholars who were influenced by Marx or Weber. The focus was primarily on occupations. Little attention was given to the long-term changes in fertility that had greatly altered women's life chances. The theories influenced by Marx were almost entirely the work of women scholars. They were the first to appear.

Marxism had been rather isolated from social science in the United States until the late 1960s, when some of the under-thirties crowd rediscovered an extensive literature. A common thread was the idea that the working class had been done in by the capitalists. Early Marxist feminists, invoking the concept of patriarchal capitalism, tried to show that working-class women had been done in even more thoroughly than working-class men. Over time, however, Marxist feminist thought divided into two identifiable streams.

One view implicitly or explicitly held that women are subordinated only in class societies; gender is simply an aspect of class stratification. The other held that sex was the original and basic class division. Marx was not incorrect but incomplete (Crompton, 1986). In point of fact, patriarchal socialism strongly resembles patriarchal capitalism. The position of women relative to men in the people's democracies of Eastern Europe seems remarkably akin to that in the Western democracies.

In the early 1970s the Weberian tradition in U.S. sociology was making its way through a new and quite different channel: measuring the effects of fathers' educational and occupational attainment on the attainment of their sons had come to dominate stratification research. When the models were extended to women in the mid-1970s, it was found that both sexes experienced similar rates of occupational mobility but, anomalously, women earned less. Later it was reported that the standard indicators of socioeconomic status do not tap the attributes of sex-typed occupations (Bose & Rossi, 1983). In sum, neither Marxist nor Weberian theories could adequately explain women's status in industrial societies. A basic problem was that neither theorist, understandably, had perceived the part that a dramatic decline in fertility would play in determining women's life chances. In consequence, the study of occupations was conceptualized as being quite apart from the study of fertility.

The interaction of occupations and fertility became more evident during the 1970s. New data appeared, a result of interest in the trends that had stimulated a massive expansion of the women's movement. Historical demography and sociology, social history, and anthropology greatly enriched knowledge about fertility and women's labor-force participation. One research stream culminated in the life-course perspec-

tive, a mix of history, social psychology, and demography that addressed events of the industrial period. Sophisticated analytic techniques and large longitudinal data sets enabled researchers to address previously unanswerable questions.

Another stream was influenced by comparative sociology—or social anthropology, which was separated artificially from sociology in those Western countries where preindustrial peoples were wiped out (e.g., native Americans) or incorporated much earlier (e.g., European peasants) (Goody, 1982:2). This stream includes the work of the anthropologists Ernestine Friedl (1975) and Jack Goody (1976); the sociologists Gerhard Lenski (1970), Rae Lesser Blumberg (1978, 1984), and Janet Saltzman Chafetz (1984); the demographers Ron Lesthaeghe (1980) and John Caldwell (1980); and the economist Ester Boserup (1970).

The theory outlined below draws heavily on this second stream. It obviously needs to be fleshed out with more data. Its purpose is not to lay out a tidy set of answers but rather to suggest the potential of this research strategy.

Gender stratification is a subset of social stratification. A theory of stratification must begin with what men and women do each day to secure food, clothing, and shelter, analyzing how their work is organized around the tools available to do it. It must also consider the physical conditions that affect human ability to sustain life—climate, soil, temperature, and other ecological variables. This approach is not new. Although such factors are often overshadowed by the abiding fascination with personal interactions as prime movers in human affairs, from its very beginnings much sociological analysis has implicitly or explicitly stressed the importance of ecology and technology.[1]

This view of the importance of subsistence technology is not deterministic. A given technology only permits certain events to occur; it does not require that they occur. Nor can this approach claim to answer all the significant questions about the human condition. But it is a necessary first step. Analyses that focus primarily on thought, feeling, and belief can yield important knowledge but they are unlikely to provide much insight into the causes and effects of stratification systems, which are inextricably intertwined with material reality (Harris, 1979). Humankind does not live by bread alone, but without bread no one can live at all.

The most complete analysis of the anthropological literature showing the interaction of ecology, technology, and the organization of work is in Lenski's *Power and Privilege* (1966) and his macrosociology text (1970), indebted to Gordon Childe (1951) and Walter Goldschmidt (1959). The approach is called evolutionary because improvements in tool efficiency result in an increase in food supply.

The anthropologist Ernestine Friedl (1975) used an ecological approach to examine the effect of subsistence tools on gender stratification in hunting-and-gathering and hoe cultures, thereby suggesting two principles of gender stratification. The following three principles represent a modification of her analysis. First, at the family level, the people who produce goods tend to have more power and prestige than those who consume them. It is better to be able to give than to have to receive.

But what determines who gets to do the most productive work in a given society? Men and women can perform a wide range of tasks, yet in all societies most tasks are allocated by sex. The answer stems from the fact that one sex cannot perform two tasks central to group survival: no man can bear or breastfeed a child. If societies are to survive, most women must bear and suckle children. This fact suggests a second principle: women's tasks must be compatible with pregnancy and lactation if the population is to be replaced.

The emphasis on population replacement makes my formulation differ somewhat from Friedl's (1975) and Blumberg's (1984) dictum that the work women do shapes the mode of child-rearing and not the other way round. Their view has merit in that it corrects for the tendency to assume that throughout human history child-rearing activities have comprised women's primary task, a common mistake in postwar American sociology. Also, it is probably true that the lower the level of living, the more women must perform certain tasks, no matter how these activities affect population replacement. It is not widely known, for example, that early in the nineteenth century the work that many French wives had to do in order to feed their families significantly increased infant mortality.

French cities had grown quickly because of rapid rural population increase, as Sussman (1982) has shown. But industrialization was slow, and the resulting high rents, low working-class incomes, and persistence of the household as the unit of production imposed more work on wives. Since safe methods of

artificial infant feeding had not yet been invented, wet-nursing was widely adopted (hiring another woman to suckle one's child for pay). Working-class families followed the examples of the nobility, who for a century or more and for different reasons had put their children out to nurse. Early in the nineteenth century the majority of Lyonnais babies were sent out (Garden, 1975); only one Parisian baby in 30 was nursed by its own mother (Sussman, 1982:183). Even though the death rate was much higher among wetnursed babies than among babies nursed by their mothers, the custom ceased only when household production of textiles became unprofitable.

The third principle in my gender theory comes from general stratification theory: in any society the most power and prestige accrue to the people who control the distribution of valued goods beyond the family. In foraging societies, for example, these are the hunters; in plow societies, the warrior nobility; and in industrial societies, the top bureaucrats in the political, economic, and military arenas.

Together, these principles comprise a theory that can explain how ecological conditions and tool use interacted with childbearing and suckling to shape gender stratification in five of the most important of the ten basic types of societies that Lenski (1970) analyzed. The oldest type was based on hunting and gathering. Throughout most of our species' history, the entire human population lived in such societies. This period of relative technological uniformity ended only within the last 10,000 to 12,000 years (Lenski & Lenski, 1982:87). Hoe cultures first appeared in the Middle East about 9,000 years ago. Plow societies appeared about 5,000 years ago, with herding societies somewhere in between. The most modern type of society is based on industrial technology.

In hunting-and-gathering societies the tools consisted of wooden spears, rocks, and human hands. As such tools yielded a meager food supply, these groups were small, averaging about 50. The level of equality was high. Slim pickings flatten the distribution of power and privilege. Men hunted large animals. Women and children gathered nuts, berries, insects, and small animals. A woman could typically gather enough nuts and berries to feed only her immediate family. The hunters, in contrast, could distribute a large animal to the entire group. Men therefore tended to have more power and prestige than women did. Their dominance was greatest when hunting was almost the only source of food, as in Eskimo societies. Men and women were more equal when both sexes contributed to subsistence tasks (Friedl, 1975:32).

Polygyny was permitted in most of these societies but it was rare. Food was too scarce to enable a hunter to supply more than one set of affinal relatives. Divorce was fairly common, since it had little effect on the subsistence of either spouse or of the children. Premarital sexual relations were usually permitted.

Why didn't women hunt? They could readily master the necessary skills. Success in hunting depended far more on cooperation, patience, and dexterity than on brute strength. The functional requirements of hunting, however, conflicted with those of child-rearing. A hunt requires an uncertain number of days away from camp. To offset the wastage of a high death rate, women were pregnant or breastfeeding during most of their productive years. Children were breastfed to age 4 to increase the probability of their survival. A woman could not carry a suckling on a hunt nor could she readily return to camp to feed it. Thus the need for population replacement ultimately excluded women from the task that yielded the most power and prestige.

What induced a shift to plant cultivation as the basis for subsistence? Gerhard and Jean Lenski (1982:135) observe that until recently it was thought that the benefits of a more advanced technology were obvious to early peoples. New evidence, however, shows that between 22,000 and 7,000 years ago the number of large animals declined and human diet shifted. In North America, for example, 32 genera of large animals became extinct, including horses, giant bison, oxen, elephants, camels, and giant rodents. The pattern was similar in northern Europe, where the woolly mammoth, woolly rhinoceros, steppe bison, and giant elk vanished. People in these areas increasingly relied on fish, crabs, birds, snails, nuts, and wild grains and legumes. The shift may have resulted from the striking advances in weapons technology that began 20,000 years ago. The increase in kills of large animals led, in turn, to an increasing human population, which had a feedback effect on the big-game kills. In consequence (and perhaps in combination with a climate change), large mammals' reproductive rates could no longer match kill rates. One species after another was exterminated. The resulting food shortage induced peoples to opt for a more sedentary lifestyle wherever plants and animals could be domesticated.

Despite the extra work, plant cultivation was attractive because it yielded so much more food per unit of land.

Simple hoe cultures appeared in the area where Eurasia abuts Africa about 9,000 years ago. The major tool, a wooden digging stick, did not dig deeply enough to raise soil nutrients or eradicate weeds. Consequently, groups had to move every few years to find fertile soil. Subsistence was supplemented by hunting, herding, or gathering in various combinations. Nonetheless, the digging stick produced enough surplus to enable these groups to number about 95 persons (Lenski & Lenski, 1982:91). The only such societies that remain today are on Pacific islands and in pockets of the New World.

Advanced hoe cultures appeared about 6,000 years ago, when the invention of metallurgy permitted the making of metal tools and weapons. Such societies appeared in North and South America (the Aztecs, Mayas, and Incas), Asia, and Europe. Today almost all remaining ones are in sub-Saharan Africa, where they are in transitional status (Robertson, 1984). Metal tools and weapons were so much more efficient than wooden ones that a greatly increased food surplus enabled these societies to be about 60 times larger than their predecessors.

Thus the introduction of the hoe, especially with a metal tip, marked the beginnings of modern social stratification. The hoe enabled people to settle in one place and thus to accumulate more goods. Dwellings became more substantial, settlements grew larger and more dense, and the creation of a stable economic surplus made occupational specialization common, which in turn increased the level of social inequality. Kinship systems, which represented social security, became extremely complex. Since the use of metal made weapons more effective, for the first time in human history war became a profitable alternative to technological innovation as a means of increasing a surplus.

For our purposes the most important aspect of hoe technology is that women on average produce about half of the food, giving them half the economic power (Blumberg, 1984:29). Care of a garden-size plot meshes readily with pregnancy and lactation. There is no simple division of labor, however, with men producing one kind of food and women another, and no universal pattern of women's producing one type of craft object and men another, except that routine domestic cooking tends to be women's work and metallurgy men's. Men monopolized land clearing in simple hoe cultures. In advanced hoe cultures they monopolized war (Friedl, 1975:53–60), thus gaining an advantage over women in the right to distribute valued goods beyond the family.

One would expect women's substantial contribution to food production to improve their status in relation to men. Indeed, the data show that the incidence of matrilineality (the tracing of descent in the mother's line) and matrilocality (newlyweds move in with her family) is greater in hoe cultures, although such practices occur only in a minority of them. Both practices improve women's status. The extent to which a woman must operate as an initially powerless bride in her husband's extended kin household, isolated from support from her natal kin, tends to depress her status (Mason, 1984:72).

Women's contribution to food production also affects the divorce rate. In hoe cultures it tends to be high, higher on average than in the United States today. A high divorce rate is more common when the dissolution of a marriage does not interfere with the subsistence of either spouse or of their children.

Women's ability to feed their children also permits what I have elsewhere called populist polygyny (Huber & Spitze, forthcoming), as in sub-Saharan Africa. In this type of polygyny, nearly everyone marries. Such societies solve the sex-ratio problem by having women marry young and men marry when they are older. A postpartum taboo on sexual relations decreases child mortality by ensuring longer birth intervals. As an appropriation of female labor and sexual gratification by those who by virtue of age, sex, and descent form the ruling group, the system serves male gerontocratic control (Lesthaeghe, 1980:531). The need for women's productive work, however, ensures the wives a measure of freedom of movement.

Herding societies are found where mountains, low rainfall, or a short season makes agriculture impractical, as in Central Asia and the Middle East. The roles, norms, and ideologies of such societies have acquired importance because the Jewish, Christian, and Muslim religions originally developed in herding cultures; their beliefs and rules affect communities all over the world. The need for water and grazing rights made war an important means of acquiring a surplus and enabled elites to control economy and polity. Since warfare and herding both involve absence from home

over long periods, they are incompatible with pregnancy and nursing. Women therefore lack access to the major tools of food production. These circumstances make it possible to practice elite polygyny—only rich men have plural wives (Huber & Spitze, forthcoming). In contrast to the sub-Saharan African women, the wives of elite polygynists tend to be secluded, free to interact only with other wives and children, as in much of the Arab world.

Plow societies are of special importance because they immediately preceded the industrial societies that developed in Europe and Asia. The laws, customs, and beliefs that have governed men's and women's behavior in all of the industrialized societies were therefore directly inherited from those of the plow kingdoms and empires of Eurasia.

The earliest plows were made of wood. After the invention of techniques to smelt iron, which was commonly available, the plow was equipped with an iron blade, which greatly increased its efficiency. The effect on the food supply was fantastic. The plow could dig much deeper than the hoe, bringing plant nutrients to the surface and killing weeds. It stimulated the domestication of draft animals. Confining oxen in stalls to prevent their wandering away in turn encouraged the collection of manure to fertilize fields, further increasing food production. Eurasian stratification patterns assumed the pyramidal form that characterized feudal societies: a tiny political and economic elite, artisans and craftworkers of lesser rank, and swarms of peasants, serfs, or slaves. The plow's effect on the status of ordinary people was devastating. The presence of a food surplus in the countryside coupled with the availability of iron weapons tempted elites to extract as much as possible from impoverished peasants. The flatter and richer the land, the worse off the common people, probably worse off than their hunting-and-gathering ancestors (Lenski & Lenski, 1978:206).

For two reasons the plow had an enormous effect on patterns of gender stratification. First, whenever it was introduced, men monopolized its use—as they do in Africa today (Boserup, 1970). Larger fields a substantial distance from home make it hard to arrange work to suit a nursing baby (Blumberg, 1978:50). Women therefore supplied a much lower proportion of food in plow than in hoe cultures (Giele & Smock, 1977).

The effect of the plow on women's status, however, went well beyond what was implied by women's reduced participation in food production. The basic reason was that the use of the plow required a particular kind of inheritance pattern, which in turn affected marriage and sexual behavior. Landownership became the basis for social stratification. The plow makes land the chief form of wealth because its use permits land to be used indefinitely and so increases its value. Hoe peoples, by contrast, had to move when the soil's fertility was exhausted.

Unlike gold and silver trinkets, cowrie beads, or money, land is an impartible inheritance. At a given level of technology a piece of land can support only a given number of persons. Therefore, the number of legal heirs must be controlled. The dominant form of marriage must be monogamy because polygyny permits the uncontrolled proliferation of legal heirs. Divorce must become difficult or impossible because serial monogamy regulates the number of legal heirs less efficiently than does lifetime marriage. Women's premarital and marital sexual behavior must be governed by law and custom lest a man's property go to another man's child. Wealthy Eurasian men can in effect practice polygyny by keeping mistresses or concubines whose children have few or no inheritance rights. The concern with women's sexual purity derives from their status as transmitters of male property (Goody, 1976:97, 15). Friedrich Engels' insight about the effect of private property on women's status still rings true.

Severe constraints, such as footbinding and suttee, governed women's behavior in Asian plow kingdoms. Clitoridectomy occurs in Muslim countries of mixed plow and herding culture.[2]

The custom of binding a little girl's feet arose about a thousand years ago, during a period marked by change in the direction of controlling women's behavior. An emperor was said to have admired a dancer's feet. Loosely bound in linen cloths, they resembled those of a ballerina (Levy, 1966). The rationale for the custom was that the resulting hobbled gait so tightened the muscles in the genital region that sleeping with a woman with bound feet was like sleeping with a virgin. Western physicians report that no evidence supports such a belief. Whatever the rationale, women with bound feet certainly did little running around.

The mother applied the bindings when the little girl was three to five years old, depending on how small a foot was desired. The richer the girl's family, the less work she would have to do, and the smaller the foot could be. Rich women were so crippled that they could not walk at all. The pain resulted primarily from bend-

ing the four smaller toes underneath the foot, then successively tightening the bindings until the toes were broken and, finally, atrophied.

The custom was widespread in China (Gamble, 1943), especially in the colder and drier regions of the north, where wheat was the main crop. In the south, where rice, a much more labor-intensive crop, was the main staple, the entire family was needed to work in the paddies—work that girls and women with crippled feet could not do. Early in the industrial period, opposition to the custom increased. Footbinding was outlawed in 1911.

The Hindu custom of suttee requires a widow to be burned alive on her husband's funeral pyre. Some widows climbed up willingly. Others had to be tied down. The rationalization was that a widow, by sinning in a previous life, caused her husband to die first. Her death also gave the husband's male relatives undisputed influence over the children and precluded her lifetime rights in the estate. The incidence of suttee was low in comparison with that of footbinding, as only rich women were at risk.

Clitoridectomy, apparently widespread in Egypt, Yemen, Ethiopia, Somalia, Sudan, Kenya, and Muslim West Africa (Hosken, 1979; El Saadawi, 1982), shows the importance of protecting a daughter's reputation for chastity (Paige, 1982). It is often called female circumcision, but this is a euphemism because it is like slicing off the glans penis or the entire penis. The operation, extremely painful, is practiced on prepubertal girls. Its purpose is to prevent sexual pleasure so that women will find it easier to remain chaste. A popular belief holds that women by nature are so lascivious that chastity is inordinately difficult for them.

The operation takes three forms. In traditional circumcision the clitoral prepuce and tip of the clitoris are removed. In excision, the entire clitoris is removed. Infibulation involves removal of the clitoris, the labia minora, and part of the labia majora. The two sides of the vulva are partially sliced or scraped raw and then sewn together, so that the entrance to the vagina is closed except for a tiny posterior opening to allow urine and, later, menstrual blood to drain. Primary fatalities result from hemorrhage, shock, and septicemia. Long-term problems include urinary disturbance due to chronic infection and difficulties in coitus and childbirth.

So far as I know, European women during the plow era suffered no restraints that were so severe or that affected so many women. But if not, why not? Recent work of the anthropologist Jack Goody (1983) suggests that European women's greater freedom may have been an unplanned outcome of efforts by the Roman Catholic church to increase its wealth. The church sought to influence inheritance patterns by instituting controls on marriage and the legitimation of children. After A.D. 325 it established a series of measures that reduced a person's supply of close relatives in an effort to persuade the pious to bequeath it their land. The church encouraged celibacy, prohibited close cousin marriage and adoption (both widespread in biblical and Roman times), condemned polygyny and divorce, and discouraged remarriage. The church also emphasized mutual consent as a requirement for valid marriage, which decreased the incidence of child marriage and also reduced the probability that a marriage would serve family interests. Furthermore, unlike Chinese or Indian women, European women could avoid marriage altogether by entering the cloister, a possibility that tended to increase their control over property.

Such measures arguably gave European women more freedom than Asian women for more than a millennium before the Industrial Revolution. In principle, this relative freedom should have made European women better able than Asian women to adapt to new circumstances and seize new opportunities. It would be ironic were historians one day to find that the spirit of capitalism in Europe was spurred less by the Protestant ethic than by a Catholic ethic that incidentally permitted women a modest measure of control over property.

Industrialization ended the plow era in Europe during the nineteenth century. The primary event was the invention of machines that made cheap cotton cloth. Rapid acceleration in the development of machines that replaced human labor stimulated a train of events that sharply altered the work men and women did. Over time, changes in behavior led to changes in beliefs.

Men's work behavior changed first. The factory system transformed erstwhile peasants, serfs, and slaves into urban wage workers, giving rise to a series of men's movements that voiced the claims of ordinary men for a fair share of a rapidly increasing surplus. These movements represented men's response to the changes that industrialization had wrought in the conditions of their lives. However, historians do not refer to these struggles as the men's movement. They write instead about the socialist and labor movements that swept nineteenth-century Europe, labels that tend to obscure the fact that women played little part in them. A mass movement that would represent women's occupational claims would appear only after women had entered the labor market in large numbers. They could not do so until three trends spawned by industrialization had irrevocably altered the conditions of their lives: the first two, a decrease in mortality and the attainment of widespread literacy, preceded the third, a decrease in fertility. The stage is set for a massive increase in the labor-force participation of married women only when these three trends are well under way.

Mortality, primarily of infants, declined in response to improved nutrition, reduced exposure to disease, and (in the twentieth century) medical measures (Collins, 1982). The mortality decline reduced the average number of births per woman needed to ensure population replacement. Then after 1910 the invention of sterilization techniques permitted safe bottle-feeding; for the first time in history artificially fed babies had the same survival probabilities as babies nursed by their mothers. Population replacement now poses few constraints on women's work.

Education was compulsory in most Western countries by 1880. As John Caldwell (1980) notes, education restructures family relations by redirecting generational wealth flows and thereby profoundly affects fertility. In preindustrial societies family wealth flowed from children to parents. Mass education redirects these flows by reducing the child's potential for employment outside the home. When children cannot earn, the cost of raising them is increased far beyond the fees that must be paid. Schools place indirect demands on families. The children's appearance must enable them to participate equally with others. Third, schooling speeds cultural change by propagating the values not of local families but of the Western middle classes. The main message of schooling is not spelled out in textbooks. It is assumed. Schools destroy the corporate identity of the family for those members previously the most submissive: children and women (Caldwell, 1980:241). Schooling causes parents to lose control over their children's labor (Lesthaeghe, 1980).

The fertility decline was triggered by the mortality decline, the spread of mass education, and rapid economic growth. A rapid increase in real income—it doubled in the West between 1860 and 1910—fuels individual aspirations and opens up new opportunities, creating an impression of lowered economic vulnerability. This self-confidence in turn allows individuals to be more independent. The net outcome is an alteration in preference maps. Since the new maps require legitimation, periods of economic growth also generate various emancipation movements (Lesthaeghe, 1983:430).

Fertility declined from more than seven to fewer than three children with the use of methods that required considerable self-discipline and courage: abstinence, withdrawal, and abortion, which has been a major means of birth control in nearly all industrializing societies until women learn other means of fertility control (Mohr, 1978). The decline also occurred despite massive opposition from church and state. When people are motivated to reduce fertility, they find ways of doing so.

From early in the industrial period women had worked for pay, but the typical worker was either young and unmarried or poor. Young women who expect to be briefly employed are unlikely to be aware of discrimination. Moreover, young women and poor women lack political clout. What matters politically is the participation of educated women who expect to remain in the work force. Such women entered the labor force in ever larger numbers after 1950 in response to strong demand for female labor (Blau & Ferber, 1986), and their rates of participation are still rising (Mott, 1982). Although most women work in heavily feminized occupations (Rytina & Bianchi, 1984), the wage gap is beginning to close. A generation ago most highly educated men were employed and most of their female counterparts were housewives. This pattern is reversing. The higher a woman's level of education, the more likely she is to be employed. From now to the end of the century young women's wage rates are expected to rise about 15 percent faster than young men's (Smith & Ward, 1984).

In sum, these trends have irrevocably altered the social stratification systems of plow societies. Declines in mortality and fertility have reduced the proportion of time the average woman spends in pregnancy or breastfeeding. Increases in educational levels and employment rates have enabled women to provide a sizable share of family income. These trends increased the centrality of individual goal attainment in the Western ideational system (Lesthaeghe, 1983:429). The ideology of equal opportunity which pervades all modern societies finally applies to women too.

Still in question is the extent to which women will hold a fair share of top positions, those whose incumbents control the distribution of valued goods. The outcome will hinge on the division of household labor. Housework is to gender stratification as market work is to class stratification. Women cannot become men's social equals until the most talented women can aspire as realistically as their male counterparts to contribute in proportion to their talents.

To date, the household division of labor has changed little, but I predict substantial change on the basis of American beliefs about fairness. A generation or two ago husbands did not want their wives to be employed, hence wives' household obligations seemed fair. Today men like their wives to work for pay. This change gives wives leverage for a little friendly persuasion.

Incentives to share housework should be strongest for highly paid doctors, lawyers, and merchant chiefs who are married to highly paid doctors, lawyers, and merchant chiefs. People who think great thoughts and push paper all day need the healthful relaxation that comes from scrubbing kitchen floors, cleaning up after the dog, and preparing meals that contain all four essential nutrients. Housework may even improve mental health. Ross and colleagues (1983) report that the more spouses share housework, the lower their depression scores. Housework may even account for women's longevity: its varied physical activities lower cholesterol, keep the arteries free of crud, and increase cardiac output. If housework be the perfect form of exercise, surely equity requires that it be equally shared.

NOTES

1. O. D. Duncan's (1964) statement remains the best description of this perspective in modern sociology.

2. These discussions follow the accounts in Huber and Spitze (1983). Footbinding is also discussed at length in Andrea Dworkin's "Gynocide: Chinese Footbinding," [Reading 3 in this volume].

REFERENCES

Blau, F., & Ferber, M. 1986. *The economics of women, men, and work.* Englewood Cliffs, N.J.: Prentice-Hall.

Blumberg, R. L. 1978. *Stratification: Socioeconomic and sexual inequality.* Dubuque: William C Brown.

Blumberg, R. L. 1984. "A general theory of gender stratification." In R. Collins, ed., *Sociological theory.* San Francisco: Jossey-Bass.

Bose, C., & Rossi, P. 1983. "Gender and jobs: Prestige standings of occupations and gender." *American Journal of Sociology* 48:316–330.

Boserup, E. 1970. *Women's role in economic development.* London: George Allen & Unwin.

Caldwell, J. 1980. "Mass education as a determinant of fertility decline timing." *Population and Development Review* 6:225–256.

Chafetz, J. S. 1984. *Sex and advantage.* Towtowa, N.J.: Rowman & Allenheld.

Childe, G. 1951. *Man makes himself.* New York: Mentor.

Collins, J. 1982. "The contribution of modern medicine to mortality decline." *Demography* 19:409–427.

Crompton, R. 1986. "Women and the 'service class.'" In R. Crompton and M. Mann, eds., *Gender stratification.* Oxford: Polity Press.

Duncan, O. D. 1964. "Social organization and the ecosystem." In R. E. L. Faris, ed., *Handbook of modern sociology.* Chicago: Rand McNally.

El Saadawi, N. 1982. *The hidden face of Eve.* Boston: Beacon Press.

Friedl, E. 1975. *Women and men: An anthropologist's view.* New York: Holt, Rinehart & Winston.

Gamble, S. 1943. "The disappearance of footbinding in Tinghsien." *American Journal of Sociology* 49:181–183.

Garden, M. 1975. *Lyon et les lyonnais au XVIIIe siècle.* Paris: Flammarion.

Giele, J. Z., & Smock, A. C. 1977. *Women: Roles and status in eight countries.* New York: Wiley.

Goldschmidt, W. 1959. *Man's way.* New York: Holt.

Goody, J. 1976. *Production and reproduction.* Cambridge: Cambridge University Press.

Goody, J. 1982. *Cooking, cuisine, and class.* Cambridge: Cambridge University Press.

Goody, J. 1983. *The development of family and marriage in Europe.* Cambridge: Cambridge University Press.

Greene, E. 1987. "Too many women?" *Chronicle of Higher Education* 28 (January 28, 1987):27–28.

Harris, M. 1979. *Cultural materialism.* New York: Random House.

Hosken, F. 1979. *The Hosken report.* Lexington, Mass.: Women's Network News.

Huber, J. 1986. "Trends in gender stratification, 1970–1985." *Sociological Forum* 1:476–495.

Huber, J., & Spitze, G. 1983. *Sex stratification.* New York: Academic Press.

Huber, J., & Spitze, G. Forthcoming. "Family sociology." In N. Smelser & R. Burt, eds., *The revised handbook of sociology.* Beverly Hills: Sage.

Lenski, G. 1966. *Power and privilege.* New York: McGraw-Hill.

Lenski, G. 1970. *Human societies.* New York: McGraw-Hill.

Lenski, G., & Lenski, J. 1978. *Human societies,* 3rd ed. New York: McGraw-Hill.

Lesthaeghe, R. 1980. "On the social control of reproduction." *Population and Development Review* 6:527–548.

Lesthaeghe, R. 1983. "A century of demographic and cultural change in Western Europe." *Population and Development Review* 9:411–435.

Levi, H. 1966. *Chinese footbinding.* New York: Walton Rawls.

Mason, K. 1984. *The status of women: A review of its relationships to fertility and mortality.* New York: Rockefeller Foundation.

Mohr, J. 1978. *Abortion in America.* New York: Oxford University Press.

Mott, F. 1982. *The employment revolution.* Cambridge: MIT Press.

Paige, K. 1982. "Patterns of excision and excision rationale in Egypt." Mimeo. University of California at Davis.

Robertson, C. 1984. *Sharing the same bowl: A history of women and class in Accra, Ghana.* Bloomington: Indiana University Press.

Ross, C., Mirowsky, J., & Huber, J. 1983. "Marriage patterns and depression." *American Sociological Review* 48:809–823.

Rytina, N., & Bianchi, S. 1984. "Occupational reclassification and changes in distribution by gender." *Monthly Labor Review* 107:11–17.

Smith, J., & Ward, M. 1984. *Women's wages and work in the twentieth century.* Santa Monica: Rand Corporation.

Sussman, G. 1982. *Selling mothers' milk: The wet-nursing business in France 1715–1914.* Urbana: University of Illinois Press.

Compulsory Heterosexuality and Lesbian Existence

ADRIENNE RICH

FOREWORD

I want to say a little about the way "Compulsory Heterosexuality" was originally conceived and the context in which we are now living. It was written in part to challenge the erasure of lesbian existence from so much of scholarly feminist literature, an erasure which I felt (and feel) to be not just antilesbian but antifeminist in its consequences, and to distort the experience of heterosexual women as well. It was not written to widen divisions but to encourage heterosexual feminists to examine heterosexuality as a political institution which disempowers women—and to change it. I also hoped that other lesbians would feel the depth and breadth of woman identification and woman bonding that has run like a continuous though stifled theme through the heterosexual experience, and that this would become increasingly a politically activating impulse, not simply a validation of personal lives. I wanted the essay to suggest new kinds of criticism, to incite new questions in classrooms and academic journals, and to sketch, at least, some bridge over the gap between *lesbian* and *feminist*. I wanted, at the very least, for feminists to find it less possible to read, write, or teach from a perspective of unexamined heterocentricity.

Within the three years since I wrote "Compulsory Heterosexuality"—with this energy of hope and desire—the pressures to conform in a society increasingly conservative in mood have become more intense. The New Right's messages to women have been, precisely, that we are the emotional and sexual property of men, and that the autonomy and equality of women threaten family, religion, and state. The institutions by which women have traditionally been controlled—patriarchal motherhood, economic exploitation, the nuclear family, compulsory heterosexuality—are being strengthened by legislation, religious fiat, media imagery, and efforts at censorship. In a worsening economy, the single mother trying to support her children confronts the feminization of poverty which Joyce Miller of the National Coalition of Labor Union Women has named one of the major issues of the 1980s. The lesbian, unless in disguise, faces discrimination in hiring and harassment and violence in the street. Even within feminist-inspired institutions such as battered-women's shelters and Women's Studies programs, open lesbians are fired and others warned to stay in the closet. The retreat into sameness—assimilation for those who can manage it—is the most passive and debilitating of responses to political repression, economic insecurity, and a renewed open season on difference.

I want to note that documentation of male violence against women—within the home especially—has been accumulating rapidly in this period (see note 9). At the same time, in the realm of literature which depicts woman bonding and woman identification as essential for female survival, a steady stream of writing and criticism has been coming from women of color in general and lesbians of color in particular—the latter group being even more profoundly erased in academic feminist scholarship by the double bias of racism and homophobia.[1]

There has recently been an intensified debate on female sexuality among feminists and lesbians, with lines often furiously and bitterly drawn, with *sado-masochism* and *pornography* as key words, which are

Originally written in 1978 for the "Sexuality" issue of *Signs,* this essay was published there in 1980. In 1982 Antelope Publications reprinted it as part of a feminist pamphlet series. The foreword was written for the pamphlet. Reprinted from *Blood, Bread, and Poetry, Selected Prose, 1979–1985,* by Adrienne Rich, by permission of the author and the publisher, W. W. Norton & Company, Inc. Copyright © 1986 by Adrienne Rich.

variously defined according to who is talking. The depth of women's rage and fear regarding sexuality and its relation to power and pain is real, even when the dialogue sounds simplistic, self-righteous, or like parallel monologues.

Because of all these developments, there are parts of this essay that I would word differently, qualify, or expand if I were writing it today. But I continue to think that heterosexual feminists will draw political strength for change from taking a critical stance toward the ideology which *demands* heterosexuality, and that lesbians cannot assume that we are untouched by that ideology and the institutions founded upon it. There is nothing about such a critique that requires us to think of ourselves as victims, as having been brainwashed or totally powerless. Coercion and compulsion are among the conditions in which women have learned to recognize our strength. Resistance is a major theme in this essay and in the study of women's lives, if we know what we are looking for.

I

Biologically men have only one innate orientation—a sexual one that draws them to women—while women have two innate orientations, sexual toward men and reproductive toward their young.[2]

I was a woman terribly vulnerable, critical, using femaleness as a sort of standard or yardstick to measure and discard men. Yes—something like that. I was an Anna who invited defeat from men without ever being conscious of it. (But I am conscious of it. And being conscious of it means I shall leave it all behind me and become—but what?) I was stuck fast in an emotion common to women of our time, that can turn them bitter, or Lesbian, or solitary. Yes, that Anna during that time was . . .

[Another blank line across the page:][3]

The bias of compulsory heterosexuality, through which lesbian experience is perceived on a scale ranging from deviant to abhorrent or simply rendered invisible, could be illustrated from many texts other than the two just preceding. The assumption made by Rossi, that women are "innately" sexually oriented only toward men, and that made by Lessing, that the lesbian is simply acting out of her bitterness toward

men, are by no means theirs alone; these assumptions are widely current in literature and in the social sciences.

I am concerned here with two other matters as well: first, how and why women's choice of women as passionate comrades, life partners, co-workers, lovers, community has been crushed, invalidated, forced into hiding and disguise; and second, the virtual or total neglect of lesbian existence in a wide range of writings, including feminist scholarship. Obviously there is a connection here. I believe that much feminist theory and criticism is stranded on this shoal.

My organizing impulse is the belief that it is not enough for feminist thought that specifically lesbian texts exist. Any theory of cultural/political creation that treats lesbian existence as a marginal or less "natural" phenomenon, as mere "sexual preference," or as the mirror image of either heterosexual or male homosexual relations is profoundly weakened thereby, whatever its other contributions. Feminist theory can no longer afford merely to voice a toleration of "lesbianism" as an "alternative life style" or make token allusion to lesbians. A feminist critique of compulsory heterosexual orientation for women is long overdue. In this exploratory paper, I shall try to show why.

I will begin by way of examples, briefly discussing four books that have appeared in the last few years, written from different viewpoints and political orientations, but all presenting themselves, and favorably reviewed, as feminist.[4] All take as a basic assumption that the social relations of the sexes are disordered and extremely problematic, if not disabling, for women; all seek paths toward change. I have learned more from some of these books than from others, but on this I am clear: each one might have been more accurate, more powerful, more truly a force for change had the author dealt with lesbian existence as a reality and as a source of knowledge and power available to women, or with the institution of heterosexuality itself as a beachhead of male dominance.[5] In none of them is the question ever raised as to whether, in a different context or other things being equal, women would *choose* heterosexual coupling and marriage; heterosexuality is presumed the "sexual preference" of "most women," either implicitly or explicitly. In none of these books, which concern themselves with mothering, sex roles, relationships, and societal prescriptions for women, is compulsory heterosexuality ever examined as an institution powerfully affecting all these, or the idea of "preference" or "innate orientation" even indirectly questioned.

In *For Her Own Good: 150 Years of the Experts' Advice to Women* by Barbara Ehrenreich and Deirdre English, the authors' superb pamphlets *Witches, Midwives and Nurses: A History of Women Healers and Complaints and Disorders: The Sexual Politics of Sickness* are developed into a provocative and complex study. Their thesis in this book is that the advice given to American women by male health professionals, particularly in the areas of marital sex, maternity, and child care, has echoed the dictates of the economic marketplace and the role capitalism has needed women to play in production and/or reproduction. Women have become the consumer victims of various cures, therapies, and normative judgments in different periods (including the prescription to middle-class women to embody and preserve the sacredness of the home—the "scientific" romanticization of the home itself). None of the "experts' " advice has been either particularly scientific or women-oriented; it has reflected male needs, male fantasies about women, and male interest in controlling women—particularly in the realms of sexuality and motherhood—fused with the requirements of industrial capitalism. So much of this book is so devastatingly informative and is written with such lucid feminist wit that I kept waiting as I read for the basic proscription against lesbianism to be examined. It never was.

This can hardly be for lack of information. Jonathan Katz's *Gay American History*[6] tells us that as early as 1656 the New Haven Colony prescribed the death penalty for lesbians. Katz provides many suggestive and informative documents on the "treatment" (or torture) of lesbians by the medical profession in the nineteenth and twentieth centuries. Recent work by the historian Nancy Sahli documents the crackdown on intense female friendships among college women at the turn of the present century.[7] The ironic title *For Her Own Good* might have referred first and foremost to the economic imperative to heterosexuality and marriage and to the sanctions imposed against single women and widows—both of whom have been and still are viewed as deviant. Yet, in this often enlightening Marxist-feminist overview of male prescriptions for female sanity and health, the economics of prescriptive heterosexuality go unexamined.[8]

Of the three psychoanalytically based books, one,

Jean Baker Miller's *Toward a New Psychology of Women,* is written as if lesbians simply do not exist, even as marginal beings. Given Miller's title, I find this astonishing. However, the favorable reviews the book has received in feminist journals, including *Signs* and *Spokeswoman,* suggest that Miller's heterocentric assumptions are widely shared. In *The Mermaid and the Minotaur: Sexual Arrangements and the Human Malaise,* Dorothy Dinnerstein makes an impassioned argument for the sharing of parenting between women and men and for an end to what she perceives as the male/female symbiosis of "gender arrangements," which she feels are leading the species further and further into violence and self-extinction. Apart from other problems that I have with this book (including her silence on the institutional and random terrorism men have practiced on women—and children—throughout history,[9] and her obsession with psychology to the neglect of economic and other material realities that help to create psychological reality), I find Dinnerstein's view of the relations between women and men as "a collaboration to keep history mad" utterly ahistorical. She means by this a collaboration to perpetuate social relations which are hostile, exploitative, and destructive to life itself. She sees women and men as equal partners in the making of "sexual arrangements," seemingly unaware of the repeated struggles of women to resist oppression (their own and that of others) and to change their condition. She ignores, specifically, the history of women who—as witches, *femmes seules,* marriage resisters, spinsters, autonomous widows, and/or lesbians—have managed on varying levels *not* to collaborate. It is this history, precisely, from which feminists have so much to learn and on which there is overall such blanketing silence. Dinnerstein acknowledges at the end of her book that "female separatism," though "on a large scale and in the long run wildly impractical," has something to teach us: "Separate, women could in principle set out to learn from scratch—undeflected by the opportunities to evade this task that men's presence has so far offered—what intact self-creative humanness is."[10] Phrases like "intact self-creative humanness" obscure the question of what the many forms of female separatism have actually been addressing. The fact is that women in every culture and throughout history *have* undertaken the task of independent, nonheterosexual, woman-connected existence, to the extent made possible by their context, often in the belief that they were the "only ones" ever to have done so. They have undertaken it even though few women have been in an economic position to resist marriage altogether, and even though attacks against unmarried women have ranged from aspersion and mockery to deliberate gynocide, including the burning and torturing of millions of widows and spinsters during the witch persecutions of the 15th, 16th, and 17th centuries in Europe.

Nancy Chodorow does come close to the edge of an acknowledgment of lesbian existence. Like Dinnerstein, Chodorow believes that the fact that women, and women only, are responsible for child care in the sexual division of labor has led to an entire social organization of gender inequality, and that men as well as women must become primary carers for children if that inequality is to change. In the process of examining, from a psychoanalytic perspective, how mothering by women affects the psychological development of girl and boy children, she offers documentation that men are "emotionally secondary" in women's lives, that "women have a richer, ongoing inner world to fall back on . . . men do not become as emotionally important to women as women do to men."[11] This would carry into the late 20th century Smith-Rosenberg's findings about 18th- and 19th-century women's emotional focus on women. "Emotionally important" can, of course, refer to anger as well as to love, or to that intense mixture of the two often found in women's relationships with women—one aspect of what I have come to call the "double life of women" (see below). Chodorow concludes that because women have women as mothers, "the mother remains a primary internal object [sic] to the girl, so that heterosexual relationships are on the model of a nonexclusive, second relationship for her, whereas for the boy they re-create an exclusive, primary relationship." According to Chodorow, women "have learned to deny the limitations of masculine lovers for both psychological and practical reasons."[12]

But the practical reasons (like witch burnings, male control of law, theology, and science, or economic nonviability within the sexual division of labor) are glossed over. Chodorow's account barely glances at the constraints and sanctions which historically have enforced or ensured the coupling of women with men and obstructed or penalized women's coupling or allying in independent groups with other women. She dismisses lesbian existence with the comment that

"lesbian relationships do tend to re-create mother-daughter emotions and connections, but most women are heterosexual" (implied: more mature, having developed beyond the mother-daughter connection?). She then adds: "This heterosexual preference and taboos on homosexuality, in addition to objective economic dependence on men, make the option of primary sexual bonds with other women unlikely—though more prevalent in recent years."[13] The significance of that qualification seems irresistible, but Chodorow does not explore it further. Is she saying that lesbian existence has become more *visible* in recent years (in certain groups), that economic and other pressures have changed (under capitalism, socialism, or both), and that consequently more women are rejecting the heterosexual "choice"? She argues that women want children because their heterosexual relationships lack richness and intensity, that in having a child a woman seeks to re-create her own intense relationship with her mother. It seems to me that on the basis of her own findings, Chodorow leads us implicitly to conclude that heterosexuality is *not* a "preference" for women, that, for one thing, it fragments the erotic from the emotional in a way that women find impoverishing and painful. Yet her book participates in mandating it. Neglecting the covert socializations and the overt forces which have channeled women into marriage and heterosexual romance, pressures ranging from the selling of daughters to the silences of literature to the images of the television screen, she, like Dinnerstein, is stuck with trying to reform a man-made institution—compulsory heterosexuality—as if, despite profound emotional impulses and complementarities drawing women toward women, there is a mystical/biological heterosexual inclination, a "preference" or "choice" which draws women toward men.

Moreover, it is understood that this "preference" does not need to be explained unless through the tortuous theory of the female Oedipus complex or the necessity for species reproduction. It is lesbian sexuality which (usually, and incorrectly, "included" under male homosexuality) is seen as requiring explanation. This assumption of female heterosexuality seems to me in itself remarkable: it is an enormous assumption to have glided so silently into the foundations of our thought.

The extension of this assumption is the frequently heard assertion that in a world of genuine equality, where men are nonoppressive and nurturing, everyone would be bisexual. Such a notion blurs and sentimentalizes the actualities within which women have experienced sexuality; it is a liberal leap across the tasks and struggles of here and now, the continuing process of sexual definition which will generate its own possibilities and choices. (It also assumes that women who have chosen women have done so simply because men are oppressive and emotionally unavailable, which still fails to account for women who continue to pursue relationships with oppressive and/or emotionally unsatisfying men.) I am suggesting that heterosexuality, like motherhood, needs to be recognized and studied as a *political institution*—even, or especially, by those individuals who feel they are, in their personal experience, the precursors of a new social relation between the sexes.

II

If women are the earliest sources of emotional caring and physical nurture for both female and male children, it would seem logical, from a feminist perspective at least, to pose the following questions: whether the search for love and tenderness in both sexes does not originally lead toward women; *why in fact women would ever redirect that search;* why species survival, the means of impregnation, and emotional/erotic relationships should ever have become so rigidly identified with each other; and why such violent strictures should be found necessary to enforce women's total emotional, erotic loyalty and subservience to men. I doubt that enough feminist scholars and theorists have taken the pains to acknowledge the societal forces which wrench women's emotional and erotic energies away from themselves and other women and from woman-identified values. These forces, as I shall try to show, range from literal physical enslavement to the disguising and distorting of possible options.

I do not assume that mothering by women is a "sufficient cause" of lesbian existence. But the issue of mothering by women has been much in the air of late, usually accompanied by the view that increased parenting by men would minimize antagonism between the sexes and equalize the sexual imbalance of power of males over females. These discussions are carried on without reference to compulsory heterosexuality as a phenomenon, let alone as an ideology. I do not wish to psychologize here but rather to identify sources of male power. I believe large numbers of men could, in fact, undertake child care on a large scale without radically altering the balance of male power in a male-identified society.

In her essay "The Origin of the Family," Kathleen Gough lists eight characteristics of male power in archaic and contemporary societies which I would like to use as a framework: "men's ability to deny women sexuality or to force it upon them; to command or exploit their labor to control their produce; to control or rob them of their children; to confine them physically and prevent their movement; to use them as objects in male transactions; to cramp their creativeness; or to withhold from them large areas of the society's knowledge and cultural attainments."[14] (Gough does not perceive these power characteristics as specifically enforcing heterosexuality, only as producing sexual inequality.) Below, Gough's words appear in italics; the elaboration of each of her categories, in brackets, is my own.

Characteristics of male power include *the power of men*

1. *to deny women* [their own] *sexuality*—[by means of clitoridectomy and infibulation; chastity belts; punishment, including death, for female adultery; punishment, including death, for lesbian sexuality; psychoanalytic denial of the clitoris; strictures against masturbation; denial of maternal and post-menopausal sensuality; unnecessary hysterectomy; pseudolesbian images in the media and literature; closing of archives and destruction of documents relating to lesbian existence]
2. *or to force it* [male sexuality] *upon them*—[by means of rape (including marital rape) and wife beating; father-daughter, brother-sister incest; the socialization of women to feel that male sexual "drive" amounts to a right;[15] idealization of heterosexual romance in art, literature, the media, advertising, etc.; child marriage; arranged marriage; prostitution; the harem; psychoanalytic doctrines of frigidity and vaginal organism; pornographic depictions of women responding pleasurably to sexual violence and humiliation (a subliminal message being that sadistic heterosexuality is more "normal" than sensuality between women)]
3. *to command or exploit their labor to control their produce*—[by means of the institutions of marriage and motherhood as unpaid production; the hori-

zontal segregation of women in paid employment; the decoy of the upwardly mobile token woman; male control of abortion, contraception, sterilization, and childbirth; pimping; female infanticide, which robs mothers of daughters and contributes to generalized devaluation of women]

4. *to control or rob them of their children*—[by means of father right and "legal kidnaping";[16] enforced sterilization; systematized infanticide; seizure of children from lesbian mothers by the courts; the malpractice of male obstetrics; use of the mother as "token torturer"[17] in genital mutilation or in binding the daughter's feet (or mind) to fit her for marriage]

5. *to confine them physically and prevent their movement*—[by means of rape as terrorism, keeping women off the streets; purdah; foot binding; atrophying of women's athletic capabilities; high heels and "feminine" dress codes in fashion; the veil; sexual harassment on the streets; horizontal segregation of women in employment; prescriptions for "full-time" mothering at home; enforced economic dependence of wives]

6. *to use them as objects in male transactions*—[use of women as "gifts"; bride price; pimping; arranged marriage; use of women as entertainers to facilitate male deals—e.g., wife-hostess, cocktail waitress required to dress for male sexual titillation, call girls, "bunnies," geisha, *kisaeng* prostitutes, secretaries]

7. *to cramp their creativeness*—[witch persecutions as campaigns against midwives and female healers, and as pogrom against independent, "unassimilated" women;[18] definition of male pursuits as more valuable than female within any culture, so that cultural values become the embodiment of male subjectivity; restriction of female self-fulfillment to marriage and motherhood; sexual exploitation of women by male artists and teachers; the social and economic disruption of women's creative aspirations;[19] erasure of female tradition][20]

8. *to withhold from them large areas of the society's knowledge and cultural attainments*—[by means of noneducation of females; the "Great Silence" regarding women and particularly lesbian existence in history and culture;[21] sex-role tracking which deflects women from science, technology, and other "masculine" pursuits; male social/professional bonding which excludes women; discrimination against women in the professions]

These are some of the methods by which male power is manifested and maintained. Looking at the schema, what surely impresses itself is the fact that we are confronting not a simple maintenance of inequality and property possession, but a pervasive cluster of forces, ranging from physical brutality to control of consciousness, which suggests that an enormous potential counterforce is having to be restrained.

Some of the forms by which male power manifests itself are more easily recognizable as enforcing heterosexuality on women than are others. Yet each one I have listed adds to the cluster of forces within which women have been convinced that marriage and sexual orientation toward men are inevitable—even if unsatisfying or oppressive—components of their lives. The chastity belt; child marriage; erasure of lesbian existence (except as exotic and perverse) in art, literature, film; idealization of heterosexual romance and marriage—these are some fairly obvious forms of compulsion, the first two exemplifying physical force, the second two control of consciousness. While clitoridectomy has been assailed by feminists as a form of woman torture,[22] Kathleen Barry first pointed out that it is not simply a way of turning the young girl into a "marriageable" woman through brutal surgery. It intends that women in the intimate proximity of polygynous marriage will not form sexual relationships with each other, that—from a male, genital-fetishist perspective—female erotic connections, even in a sex-segregated situation, will be literally excised.[23]

The function of pornography as an influence on consciousness is a major public issue of our time, when a multibillion-dollar industry has the power to disseminate increasingly sadistic, women-degrading visual images. But even so-called soft-core pornography and advertising depict women as objects of sexual appetite devoid of emotional context, without individual meaning or personality—essentially as a sexual commodity to be consumed by males. (So-called lesbian pornography, created for the male voyeuristic eye, is equally devoid of emotional context or individual personality.) The most pernicious message relayed by pornography is that women are natural sexual prey to men and love it, that sexuality and violence are congruent, and that for women sex is essentially masochistic, humiliation pleasurable, physical abuse erotic. But along with this message comes another, not always recognized: that enforced submission and the use of cruelty, if played out in heterosexual pairing, is sexually "normal," while sensuality between women, including erotic mutuality and respect, is "queer," "sick," and either pornographic in itself or not very exciting compared with the sexuality of whips and bondage.[24] Pornography does not simply create a climate in which sex and violence are interchangeable; *it widens the range of behavior considered acceptable from men in heterosexual intercourse*—behavior which reiteratively strips women of their autonomy, dignity, and sexual potential, including the potential of loving and being loved by women in mutuality and integrity.

In her brilliant study *Sexual Harassment of Working Women: A Case of Sex Discrimination,* Catharine A. MacKinnon delineates the intersection of compulsory heterosexuality and economics. Under capitalism, women are horizontally segregated by gender and occupy a structurally inferior position in the workplace. This is hardly news, but MacKinnon raises the question why, even if capitalism "requires some collection of individuals to occupy low-status, low-paying positions ... such persons must be biologically female," and goes on to point out that "the fact that male employers often do not hire qualified women, *even when they could pay them less than men,* suggests that more than the profit motive is implicated" [emphasis added].[25] She cites a wealth of material documenting the fact that women are not only segregated in low-paying service jobs (as secretaries, domestics, nurses, typists, telephone operators, child-care workers, waitresses), but that "sexualization of the woman" is part of the job. Central and intrinsic to the economic realities of women's lives is the requirement that women will "market sexual attractiveness to men, who tend to hold the economic power and position to enforce their predilections." And MacKinnon documents that "sexual harassment perpetuates the interlocked structure by which women have been kept sexually in thrall to men at the bottom of the labor market. Two forces of American society converge: men's control over women's sexuality and capital's control over employees' work lives."[26] Thus, women in the workplace are at the mercy of sex as power in a vicious circle. Economically disadvantaged, women—whether waitresses or professors—endure sexual harassment to keep their jobs and learn to behave in a complaisantly and ingratiatingly heterosexual manner because they discover this is their true qualification for employment, whatever the job description. And,

MacKinnon notes, the woman who too decisively resists sexual overtures in the workplace is accused of being "dried up" and sexless, or lesbian. This raises a specific difference between the experiences of lesbians and homosexual men. A lesbian, closeted on her job because of heterosexist prejudice, is not simply forced into denying the truth of her outside relationships or private life. Her job depends on her pretending to be not merely heterosexual, but a heterosexual *woman* in terms of dressing and playing the feminine, deferential role required of "real" women.

MacKinnon raises radical questions as to the qualitative differences between sexual harassment, rape, and ordinary heterosexual intercourse. ("As one accused rapist put it, he hadn't used 'any more force than is usual for males during the preliminaries.'") She criticizes Susan Brownmiller[27] for separating rape from the mainstream of daily life and for her unexamined premise that "rape is violence, intercourse is sexuality," removing rape from the sexual sphere altogether. Most crucially she argues that "taking rape from the realm of 'the sexual,' placing it in the realm of 'the violent,' allows one to be against it without raising any questions about the extent to which the institution of heterosexuality has defined force as a normal part of 'the preliminaries.'"[28] "Never is it asked whether, under conditions of male supremacy, the notion of 'consent' has any meaning."[29]

The fact is that the workplace, among other social institutions, is a place where women have learned to accept male violation of their psychic and physical boundaries as the price of survival; where women have been educated—no less than by romantic literature or by pornography—to perceive themselves as sexual prey. A woman seeking to escape such casual violations along with economic disadvantage may well turn to marriage as a form of hoped-for protection, while bringing into marriage neither social nor economic power, thus entering that institution also from a disadvantaged position. MacKinnon finally asks:

What if inequality is built into the social conceptions of male and female sexuality, of masculinity and femininity, of sexiness and heterosexual attractiveness? Incidents of sexual harassment suggest that male sexual desire itself may be aroused by female vulnerability.... Men feel they can take advantage, so they want to, so they do. Examination of sexual harassment, precisely because the episodes appear commonplace, forces one to confront the fact that sexual intercourse normally occurs between economic (as well as physical) unequals . . . the apparent legal requirement that violations of women's sexuality appear out of the ordinary before they will be punished helps prevent women from defining the ordinary conditions of their own consent.[30]

Given the nature and extent of heterosexual pressures—the daily "eroticization of women's subordination," as MacKinnon phrases it[31]—I question the more or less psychoanalytic perspective (suggested by such writers as Karen Horney, H. R. Hayes, Wolfgang Lederer, and, most recently, Dorothy Dinnerstein) that the male need to control women sexually results from some primal male "fear of women" and of women's sexual insatiability. It seems more probable that men really fear not that they will have women's sexual appetites forced on them or that women want to smother and devour them, but that women could be indifferent to them altogether, that men could be allowed sexual and emotional—therefore economic—access to women *only* on women's terms, otherwise being left on the periphery of the matrix.

The means of assuring male sexual access to women have recently received searching investigation by Kathleen Barry.[32] She documents extensive and appalling evidence for the existence, on a very large scale, of international female slavery, the institution once known as "white slavery" but which in fact has involved, and at this very moment involves, women of every race and class. In the theoretical analysis derived from her research, Barry makes the connection between all enforced conditions under which women live subject to men: prostitution, marital rape, father-daughter and brother-sister incest, wife beating, pornography, bride price, the selling of daughters, purdah, and genital mutilation. She sees the rape paradigm—where the victim of sexual assault is held responsible for her own victimization—as leading to the rationalization and acceptance of other forms of enslavement where the woman is presumed to have "chosen" her fate, to embrace it passively, or to have courted it perversely through rash or unchaste behavior. On the contrary, Barry maintains, "female sexual slavery is present in ALL situations where women or girls can- not change the conditions of their existence; where re-

gardless of how they got into those conditions, e.g., social pressure, economic hardship, misplaced trust or the longing for affection, they cannot get out; and where they are subject to sexual violence and exploitation."[33] She provides a spectrum of concrete examples, not only as to the existence of a widespread international traffic in women, but also as to how this operates—whether in the form of a Minnesota pipeline" funneling blonde, blue-eyed midwestern runaways to Times Square, or the purchasing of young women out of rural poverty in Latin America or Southeast Asia, or the providing of *maisons d'abattage* for migrant workers in the eighteenth arrondissement of Paris. Instead of "blaming the victim" or trying to diagnose her presumed pathology, Barry turns her floodlight on the pathology of sex colonization itself, the ideology of "cultural sadism" represented by the pornography industry and by the overall identification of women primarily as "sexual beings whose responsibility is the sexual service of men."[34]

Barry delineates what she names a "sexual domination perspective" through whose lens sexual abuse and terrorism of women by men has been rendered almost invisible by treating it as natural and inevitable. From its point of view, women are expendable as long as the sexual and emotional needs of the male can be satisfied. To replace this perspective of domination with a universal standard of basic freedom for women from gender-specific violence, from constraints on movement, and from male right of sexual and emotional access is the political purpose of her book. Like Mary Daly in *Gyn/Ecology,* Barry rejects structuralist and other cultural-relativist rationalizations for sexual torture and antiwoman violence. In her opening chapter, she asks of her readers that they refuse all handy escapes into ignorance and denial. "The only way we can come out of hiding, break through our paralyzing defenses, is to know it all—the full extent of sexual violence and domination of women. . . . In *knowing,* in facing directly, we can learn to chart our course out of this oppression, by envisioning and creating a world which will preclude sexual slavery."[35]

"Until we name the practice, give conceptual definition and form to it, illustrate its life over time and in space, those who are its most obvious victims will also not be able to name it or define their experience."

But women are all, in different ways and to different degrees, its victims; and part of the problem with naming and conceptualizing female sexual slavery is, as Barry clearly sees, compulsory heterosexuality.[36] Compulsory heterosexuality simplifies the task of the procurer and pimp in worldwide prostitution rings and "eros centers," while, in the privacy of the home, it leads the daughter to "accept" incest/rape by her father, the mother to deny that it is happening, the battered wife to stay on with an abusive husband. "Befriending or love" is a major tactic of the procurer, whose job it is to turn the runaway or the confused young girl over to the pimp for seasoning. The ideology of heterosexual romance, beamed at her from childhood out of fairy tales, television, films, advertising, popular songs, wedding pageantry, is a tool ready to the procurer's hand and one which he does not hesitate to use, as Barry documents. Early female indoctrination in "love" as an emotion may be largely a Western concept; but a more universal ideology concerns the primacy and uncontrollability of the male sexual drive. This is one of many insights offered by Barry's work:

> As sexual power is learned by adolescent boys through the social experience of their sex drive, so do girls learn that the locus of sexual power is male. Given the importance placed on the male sex drive in the socialization of girls as well as boys, early adolescence is probably the first significant phase of male identification in a girl's life and development. . . . As a young girl becomes aware of her own increasing sexual feelings . . . she turns away from her heretofore primary relationships with girlfriends. As they become secondary to her, recede in importance in her life, her own identity also assumes a secondary role and she grows into male identification.[37]

We still need to ask why some women never, even temporarily, turn away from "heretofore primary relationships" with other females. And why does male identification—the casting of one's social, political, and intellectual allegiances with men—exist among lifelong sexual lesbians? Barry's hypothesis throws us among new questions, but it clarifies the diversity of forms in which compulsory heterosexuality presents itself. In the mystique of the overpowering, all-conquering male sex drive, the penis-with-a-life-of-its-own, is rooted the law of male sex right to women, which justifies prostitution as a universal cultural assumption on the one hand, while defending sexual

slavery within the family on the basis of "family privacy and cultural uniqueness" on the other.[38] The adolescent male sex drive, which, as both young women and men are taught, once triggered cannot take responsibility for itself or take no for an answer, becomes, according to Barry, the norm and rationale for adult male sexual behavior: a condition of *arrested sexual development*. Women learn to accept as natural the inevitability of this "drive" because they receive it as dogma. Hence, marital rape; hence, the Japanese wife resignedly packing her husband's suitcase for a weekend in the *kisaeng* brothels of Taiwan; hence, the psychological as well as economic imbalance of power between husband and wife, male employer and female worker, father and daughter, male professor and female student.

The effect of male identification means

> internalizing the values of the colonizer and actively participating in carrying out the colonization of one's self and one's sex. . . . Male identification is the act whereby women place men above women, including themselves, in credibility, status, and importance in most situations, regardless of the comparative quality the women may bring to the situation. . . . Interaction with women is seen as a lesser form of relating on every level.[39]

What deserves further exploration is the doublethink many women engage in and from which no woman is permanently and utterly free: However woman-to-woman relationships, female support networks, a female and feminist value system are relied on and cherished, indoctrination in male credibility and status can still create synapses in thought, denials of feeling, wishful thinking, a profound sexual and intellectual confusion.[40] I quote here from a letter I received the day I was writing this passage: "I have had very bad relationships with men—I am now in the midst of a very painful separation. I am trying to find my strength through women—without my friends, I would not survive." How many times a day do women speak words like these or think them or write them, and how often does the synapse reassert itself?

Barry summarizes her findings:

> Considering the arrested sexual development that is understood to be normal in the male population, and considering the numbers of men who are

pimps, procurers, members of slavery gangs, corrupt officials participating in this traffic, owners, operators, employees of brothels and lodging and entertainment facilities, pornography purveyors, associated with prostitution, wife beaters, child molesters, incest perpetrators, johns (tricks) and rapists, one cannot but be momentarily stunned by the enormous male population engaging in female sexual slavery. The huge number of men engaged in these practices should be cause for declaration of an international emergency, a crisis in sexual violence. But what should be cause for alarm is instead accepted as normal sexual intercourse.[41]

Susan Cavin, in a rich and provocative, if highly speculative, dissertation, suggests that patriarchy becomes possible when the original female band, which includes children but ejects adolescent males, becomes invaded and outnumbered by males; that not patriarchal marriage, but the rape of the mother by the son, becomes the first act of male domination. The entering wedge, or leverage, which allows this to happen is not just a simple change in sex ratios; it is also the mother-child bond, manipulated by adolescent males in order to remain within the matrix past the age of exclusion. Maternal affection is used to establish male right of sexual access, which, however, must ever after be held by force (or through control of consciousness) since the original deep adult bonding is that of woman for woman.[42] I find this hypothesis extremely suggestive, since one form of false consciousness which serves compulsory heterosexuality is the maintenance of a mother-son relationship between women and men, including the demand that women provide maternal solace, nonjudgmental nurturing, and compassion for their harassers, rapists, and batterers (as well as for men who passively vampirize them).

But whatever its origins, when we look hard and clearly at the extent and elaboration of measures designed to keep women within a male sexual purlieu, it becomes an inescapable question whether the issue feminists have to address is not simple "gender inequality" nor the domination of culture by males nor mere "taboos against homosexuality," but the enforcement of heterosexuality for women as a means of assuring male right of physical, economic, and emotional access.[43] One of many means of enforcement is, of course, the rendering invisible of the lesbian possibility, an engulfed continent which rises fragmentedly

into view from time to time only to become submerged again. Feminist research and theory that contribute to lesbian invisibility or marginality are actually working against the liberation and empowerment of women as a group.[44]

The assumption that "most women are innately heterosexual" stands as a theoretical and political stumbling block for feminism. It remains a tenable assumption partly because lesbian existence has been written out of history or catalogued under disease, partly because it has been treated as exceptional rather than intrinsic, partly because to acknowledge that for women heterosexuality may not be a "preference" at all but something that has had to be imposed, managed, organized, propagandized, and maintained by force is an immense step to take if you consider yourself freely and "innately" heterosexual. Yet the failure to examine heterosexuality as an institution is like failing to admit that the economic system called capitalism or the caste system of racism is maintained by a variety of forces, including both physical violence and false consciousness. To take the step of questioning heterosexuality as a "preference" or "choice" for women—and to do the intellectual and emotional work that follows—will call for a special quality of courage in heterosexually identified feminists, but I think the rewards will be great: a freeing-up of thinking, the exploring of new paths, the shattering of another great silence, new clarity in personal relationships.

III

I have chosen to use the terms *lesbian existence* and *lesbian continuum* because the word *lesbianism* has a clinical and limiting ring. *Lesbian existence* suggests both the fact of the historical presence of lesbians and our continuing creation of the meaning of that existence. I mean the term *lesbian continuum* to include a range—through each woman's life and throughout history—of woman-identified experience, not simply the fact that a woman has had or consciously desired genital sexual experience with another woman. If we expand it to embrace many more forms of primary intensity between and among women, including the sharing of a rich inner life, the bonding against male tyranny, the giving and receiving of practical and political support, if we can also hear it in such associations as *marriage resistance* and the "haggard" behavior identified by Mary Daly (obsolete meanings: "intractable," "willful," "wanton," and "unchaste," "a woman reluctant to yield to wooing"),[45] we begin to grasp breadths of female history and psychology which have lain out of reach as a consequence of limited, mostly clinical, definitions of *lesbianism*.

Lesbian existence comprises both the breaking of a taboo and the rejection of a compulsory way of life. It is also a direct or indirect attack on male right of access to women. But it is more than these, although we may first begin to perceive it as a form of naysaying to patriarchy, an act of resistance. It has, of course, included isolation, self-hatred, breakdown, alcoholism, suicide, and intrawoman violence; we romanticize at our peril what it means to love and act against the grain, and under heavy penalties; and lesbian existence has been lived (unlike, say, Jewish or Catholic existence) without access to any knowledge of a tradition, a continuity, a social underpinning. The destruction of records and memorabilia and letters documenting the realities of lesbian existence must be taken very seriously as a means of keeping heterosexuality compulsory for women, since what has been kept from our knowledge is joy, sensuality, courage, and community, as well as guilt, self-betrayal, and pain.[46]

Lesbians have historically been deprived of a political existence through "inclusion" as female versions of male homosexuality. To equate lesbian existence with male homosexuality because each is stigmatized is to erase female reality once again. Part of the history of lesbian existence is, obviously, to be found where lesbians, lacking a coherent female community, have shared a kind of social life and common cause with homosexual men. But there are differences: women's lack of economic and cultural privilege relative to men; qualitative differences in female and male relationships—for example, the patterns of anonymous sex among male homosexuals, and the pronounced ageism in male homosexual standards of sexual attractiveness. I perceive the lesbian experience as being, like motherhood, a profoundly *female* experience, with particular oppressions, meanings, and potentialities we cannot comprehend as long as we simply bracket it with other sexually stigmatized existences. Just as the term *parenting* serves to conceal the particular and significant reality of being a parent who is actually a mother, the term *gay* may serve the purpose of blurring the very outlines we need to discern, which

are of crucial value for feminism and for the freedom of women as a group.[47]

As the term *lesbian* has been held to limiting, clinical associations in its patriarchal definition, female friendship and comradeship have been set apart from the erotic, thus limiting the erotic itself. But as we deepen and broaden the range of what we define as lesbian existence, as we delineate a lesbian continuum, we begin to discover the erotic in female terms: as that which is unconfined to any single part of the body or solely to the body itself; as an energy not only diffuse but, as Audre Lorde has described it, omnipresent in "the sharing of joy, whether physical, emotional, psychic," and in the sharing of work; as the empowering joy which "makes us less willing to accept powerlessness, or those other supplied states of being which are not native to me, such as resignation, despair, self-effacement, depression, self-denial."[48] In another context, writing of women and work, I quoted the autobiographical passage in which the poet H. D. described how her friend Bryher supported her in persisting with the visionary experience which was to shape her mature work:

> I knew that this experience, this writing-on-the-wall before me, could not be shared with anyone except the girl who stood so bravely there beside me. This girl said without hesitation, "Go on." It was she really who had the detachment and integrity of the Pythoness of Delphi. But it was I, battered and dissociated . . . who was seeing the pictures, and who was reading the writing or granted the inner vision. Or perhaps, in some sense, we were "seeing" it together, for without her, admittedly, I could not have gone on.[49]

If we consider the possibility that all women—from the infant suckling at her mother's breast, to the grown woman experiencing orgasmic sensations while suckling her own child, perhaps recalling her mother's milk smell in her own, to two women, like Virginia Woolf's Chloe and Olivia, who share a laboratory,[50] to the woman dying at ninety, touched and handled by women—exist on a lesbian continuum, we can see ourselves as moving in and out of this continuum, whether we identify ourselves as lesbian or not.

We can then connect aspects of woman identification as diverse as the impudent, intimate girl friendships of eight or nine year olds and the banding together of those women of the 12th and 15th centuries known as Beguines who "shared houses, rented to one another, bequeathed houses to their room-mates . . . in cheap subdivided houses in the artisans' area of town," who "practiced Christian virtue on their own, dressing and living simply and not associating with men," who earned their livings as spinsters, bakers, nurses, or ran schools for young girls, and who managed—until the Church forced them to disperse—to live independent both of marriage and of conventual restrictions.[51] It allows us to connect these women with the more celebrated "Lesbians" of the women's school around Sappho of the 7th century B.C., with the secret sororities and economic networks reported among African women, and with the Chinese marriage-resistance sisterhoods—communities of women who refused marriage or who, if married, often refused to consummate their marriages and soon left their husbands, the only women in China who were not footbound and who, Agnes Smedley tells us, welcomed the births of daughters and organized successful women's strikes in the silk mills.[52] It allows us to connect and compare disparate individual instances of marriage resistance: for example, the strategies available to Emily Dickinson, a 19th-century white woman genius, with the strategies available to Zora Neale Hurston, a 20th-century Black woman genius. Dickinson never married, had tenuous intellectual friendships with men, lived self-convented in her genteel father's house in Amherst, and wrote a lifetime of passionate letters to her sister-in-law Sue Gilbert and a smaller group of such letters to her friend Kate Scott Anthon. Hurston married twice but soon left each husband, scrambled her way from Florida to Harlem to Columbia University to Haiti and finally back to Florida, moved in and out of white patronage and poverty, professional success, and failure; her survival relationships were all with women, beginning with her mother. Both of these women in their vastly different circumstances were marriage resisters, committed to their own work and selfhood, and were later characterized as "apolitical." Both were drawn to men of intellectual quality; for both of them women provided the ongoing fascination and sustenance of life.

If we think of heterosexuality as *the* natural emotional and sensual inclination for women, lives such as these are seen as deviant, as pathological, or as emotionally and sensually deprived. Or, in more recent and permissive jargon, they are banalized as "life

styles." And the work of such women, whether merely the daily work of individual or collective survival and resistance or the work of the writer, the activist, the reformer, the anthropologist, or the artist—the work of self-creation—is undervalued, or seen as the bitter fruit of "penis envy" or the sublimation of repressed eroticism or the meaningless rant of a "man-hater." But when we turn the lens of vision and consider the degree to which and the methods whereby heterosexual "preference" has actually been imposed on women, not only can we understand differently the meaning of individual lives and work, but we can begin to recognize a central fact of women's history: that women have always resisted male tyranny. A feminism of action, often though not always without a theory, has constantly re-emerged in every culture and in every period. We can then begin to study women's struggle against powerlessness, women's radical rebellion, not just in male-defined "concrete revolutionary situations"[53] but in all the situations male ideologies have not perceived as revolutionary—for example, the refusal of some women to produce children, aided at great risk by other women,[54] the refusal to produce a higher standard of living and leisure for men (Leghorn and Parker show how both are part of women's unacknowledged, unpaid, and ununionized economic contribution). We can no longer have patience with Dinnerstein's view that women have simply collaborated with men in the "sexual arrangements" of history. We begin to observe behavior, both in history and in individual biography, that has hitherto been invisible or misnamed, behavior which often constitutes, given the limits of the counterforce exerted in a given time and place, radical rebellion. And we can connect these rebellions and the necessity for them with the physical passion of woman for woman which is central to lesbian existence: the erotic sensuality which has been, precisely, the most violently erased fact of female experience.

Heterosexuality has been both forcibly and subliminally imposed on women. Yet everywhere women have resisted it, often at the cost of physical torture, imprisonment, psychosurgery, social ostracism, and extreme poverty. "Compulsory heterosexuality" was named as one of the "crimes against women" by the Brussels International Tribunal Crimes against Women in 1976. Two pieces of testimony from two very different cultures reflect the degree to which persecution of lesbians is a global practice here and now.

A report from Norway relates:

> A lesbian in Oslo was in a heterosexual marriage that didn't work, so she started taking tranquillizers and ended up at the health sanatorium for treatment and rehabilitation. . . . The moment she said in family group therapy that she believed she was a lesbian, the doctor told her she was not. He knew from "looking into her eyes," he said. She had the eyes of a woman who wanted sexual intercourse with her husband. So she was subjected to so-called "couch therapy." She was put into a comfortably heated room, naked, on a bed, and for an hour her husband was to . . . try to excite her sexually. . . . The idea was that the touching was always to end with sexual intercourse. She felt stronger and stronger aversion. She threw up and sometimes ran out of the room to avoid this "treatment." The more strongly she asserted that she was a lesbian, the more violent the forced heterosexual intercourse became. This treatment went on for about six months. She escaped from the hospital, but she was brought back. Again she escaped. She has not been there since. In the end she realized that she had been subjected to forcible rape for six months.

And from Mozambique:

> I am condemned to a life of exile because I will not deny that I am a lesbian, that my primary commitments are, and will always be to other women. In the new Mozambique, lesbianism is considered a left-over from colonialism and decadent Western civilization. Lesbians are sent to rehabilitation camps to learn through self-criticism the correct line about themselves. . . . If I am forced to denounce my own love for women, if I therefore denounce myself, I could go back to Mozambique and join forces in the exciting and hard struggle of rebuilding a nation, including the struggle for the emancipation of Mozambiquan women. As it is, I either risk the rehabilitation camps, or remain in exile.[55]

Nor can it be assumed that women like those in Carroll Smith-Rosenberg's study, who married, stayed married, yet dwelt in a profoundly female emotional and passional world, "preferred" or "chose" heterosexuality. Women have married because it was necessary, in order to survive economically, in order to have children who would not suffer economic deprivation or social ostracism, in order to remain respectable, in order to do what was expected of women, because coming out of "abnormal" childhoods they wanted to feel "normal" and because heterosexual romance has been represented as the great female adventure, duty, and fulfillment. We may faithfully or ambivalently have obeyed the institution, but our feelings—and our sensuality—have not been tamed or contained within it. There is no statistical documentation of the numbers of lesbians who have remained in heterosexual marriages for most of their lives. But in a letter to the early lesbian publication *The Ladder,* the playwright Lorraine Hansberry had this to say:

> I suspect that the problem of the married woman who would prefer emotional-physical relationships with other women is proportionally much higher than a similar statistic for men. (A statistic surely no one will ever really have.) This because the estate of women being what it is, how could we ever begin to guess the numbers of women who are not prepared to risk a life alien to what they have been taught all their lives to believe was their "natural" destiny—AND—their only expectation for ECONOMIC security. It seems to be that this is why the question has an immensity that it does not have for male homosexuals. . . . A woman of strength and honesty may, if she chooses, sever her marriage and marry a new male mate and society will be upset that the divorce rate is rising so—but there are few places in the United States, in any event, where she will be anything remotely akin to an "outcast." Obviously this is not true for a woman who would end her marriage to take up life with another woman.[56]

This *double life*—this apparent acquiescence to an institution founded on male interest and prerogative—has been characteristic of female experience: in motherhood and in many kinds of heterosexual behavior, including the rituals of courtship; the pretense of asexuality by the 19th-century wife; the simulation of orgasm by the prostitute, the courtesan, the 20th-century "sexually liberated" woman.

Meridel LeSueur's documentary novel of the depression, *The Girl,* is arresting as a study of female double life. The protagonist, a waitress in a St. Paul working-class speakeasy, feels herself passionately attracted to the young man Butch, but her survival relationships are with Clara, an older waitress and prostitute, with Belle, whose husband owns the bar, and with Amelia, a union activist. For Clara and Belle and the unnamed protagonist, sex with men is in one sense an escape from the bedrock misery of daily life, a flare of intensity in the gray, relentless, often brutal web of day-to-day existence:

> It was like he was a magnet pulling me. It was exciting and powerful and frightening. He was after me too and when he found me I would run, or be petrified, just standing in front of him like a zany. And he told me not to be wandering with Clara to the Marigold where we danced with strangers. He said he would knock the shit out of me. Which made me shake and tremble, but it was better than being a husk full of suffering and not knowing why.[57]

Throughout the novel the theme of double life emerges; Belle reminisces about her marriage to the bootlegger Hoinck:

> You know, when I had that black eye and said I hit it on the cupboard, well he did it the bastard, and then he says don't tell anybody.... He's nuts, that's what he is, nuts, and I don't see why I live with him, why I put up with him a minute on this earth. But listen kid, she said, I'm telling you something. She looked at me and her face was wonderful. She said, Jesus Christ, Goddam him I love him that's why I'm hooked like this all my life, Goddam him I love him.[58]

After the protagonist has her first sex with Butch, her women friends care for her bleeding, give her whiskey, and compare notes.

> My luck, the first time and I got into trouble. He gave me a little money and I come to St. Paul where for ten bucks they'd stick a huge vet's needle into you and you start it and then you were on your own.... I never had no child. I've just had Hoinck to mother, and a hell of a child he is.[59]

> Later they made me go back to Clara's room to lie down.... Clara lay down beside me and put her arms around me and wanted me to tell me about it

but she wanted to tell about herself. She said she started it when she was twelve with a bunch of boys in an old shed. She said nobody had paid any attention to her before and she became very popular.... They like it so much, she said, why shouldn't you give it to them and get presents and attention? I never cared anything for it and neither did my mama. But it's the only thing you got that's valuable.[60]

Sex is thus equated with attention from the male, who is charismatic though brutal, infantile, or unreliable. Yet it is the women who make life endurable for each other, give physical affection without causing pain, share, advise, and stick by each other. *(I am trying to find my strength through women—without my friends, I could not survive.)* LeSueur's *The Girl* parallels Toni Morrison's remarkable *Sula,* another revelation of female double life:

> Nel was the one person who had wanted nothing from her, who had accepted all aspects of her.... Nel was one of the reasons Sula had drifted back to Medallion.... The men ... had merged into one large personality: the same language of love, the same entertainments of love, the same cooling of love. Whenever she introduced her private thoughts into their rubbings and goings, they hooded their eyes. They taught her nothing but love tricks, shared nothing but worry, gave nothing but money. She had been looking all along for a friend, and it took her a while to discover that a lover was not a comrade and could never be—for a woman.

But Sula's last thought at the second of her death is "Wait'll I tell Nel." And after Sula's death, Nel looks back on her own life:

> "All that time, all that time, I thought I was missing Jude." And the loss pressed down on her chest and came up into her throat. "We was girls together," she said as though explaining something. "O Lord, Sula," she cried, "Girl, girl, girlgirlgirl!" It was a fine cry—loud and long—but it had no bottom and it had no top, just circles and circles of sorrow.[61]

The Girl and *Sula* are both novels which examine what I am calling the lesbian continuum, in contrast to the shallow or sensational "lesbian scenes" in recent commercial fiction.[62] Each shows us woman identification untarnished (till the end of LeSueur's novel) by romanticism; each depicts the competition of heterosexual compulsion for women's attention, the diffusion and frustration of female bonding that might, in a more conscious form, reintegrate love and power.

IV

Woman identification is a source of energy, a potential springhead of female power, curtailed and contained under the institution of heterosexuality. The denial of reality and visibility to women's passion for women, women's choice of women as allies, life companions, and community, the forcing of such relationships into dissimulation and their disintegration under intense pressure have meant an incalculable loss to the power of all women *to change the social relations of the sexes, to liberate ourselves and each other*. The lie of compulsory female heterosexuality today afflicts not just feminist scholarship but every profession, every reference work, every curriculum, every organizing attempt, every relationship or conversation over which it hovers. It creates, specifically, a profound falseness, hypocrisy, and hysteria in the heterosexual dialogue, for every heterosexual relationship is lived in the queasy strobe light of that lie. However we choose to identify ourselves, however we find ourselves labeled, it flickers across and distorts our lives.[63]

The lie keeps numberless women psychologically trapped, trying to fit mind, spirit, and sexuality into a prescribed script because they cannot look beyond the parameters of the acceptable. It pulls on the energy of such women even as it drains the energy of "closeted" lesbians—the energy exhausted in the double life. The lesbian trapped in the "closet," the woman imprisoned in prescriptive ideas of the "normal" share the pain of blocked options, broken connections, lost access to self-definition freely and powerfully assumed.

The lie is many-layered. In Western tradition, one layer—the romantic—asserts that women are inevitably, even if rashly and tragically, drawn to men; that even when that attraction is suicidal (e.g., *Tristan and Isolde*, Kate Chopin's *The Awakening*), it is still an organic imperative. In the tradition of the social sciences it asserts that primary love between the sexes is "normal"; that women *need* men as social and economic protectors, for adult sexuality, and for psychological

completion; that the heterosexually constituted family is the basic social unit, that women who do not attach their primary intensity to men must be, in functional terms, condemned to an even more devastating outsiderhood than their outsiderhood as women. Small wonder that lesbians are reported to be a more hidden population than male homosexuals. The Black lesbian-feminist critic Lorraine Bethel, writing on Zora Neale Hurston, remarks that for a Black woman—already twice an outsider—to choose to assume still another "hated identity" is problematic indeed. Yet the lesbian continuum has been a life line for Black women both in Africa and the United States.

> Black women have a long tradition of bonding together . . . in a Black/women's community that has been a source of vital survival information, psychic and emotional support for us. We have a distinct Black woman-identified folk culture based on our experiences as Black women in this society; symbols, language and modes of expression that are specific to the realities of our lives. . . . Because Black women were rarely among those Blacks and females who gained access to literary and other acknowledged forms of artistic expression, this Black female bonding and Black woman-identification has often been hidden and unrecorded except in the individual lives of Black women through our own memories of our particular Black female tradition.[64]

Another layer of the lie is the frequently encountered implication that women turn to women out of hatred for men. Profound skepticism, caution, and righteous paranoia about men may indeed be part of any healthy woman's response to the misogyny of male-dominated culture, to the forms assumed by "normal" male sexuality, and to *the failure even of "sensitive" or "political" men to perceive or find these troubling*. Lesbian existence is also represented as mere refuge from male abuses, rather than as an electric and empowering charge between women. One of the most frequently quoted literary passages on lesbian relationship is that in which Colette's Renée, in *The Vagabond*, describes "the melancholy and touching image of two weak creatures who have perhaps found shelter in each other's arms, there to sleep and weep, safe from man who is often cruel, and there to taste *better than any pleasure, the bitter happiness of feeling themselves akin, frail and forgotten* [emphasis added]."[65] Colette is often considered a lesbian writer. Her popular reputation has, I think, much to do with the fact that she writes about lesbian existence as if for a male audience; her earliest "lesbian" novels, the Claudine series, were written under compulsion for her husband and published under both their names. At all events, except for her writings on her mother, Colette is a less reliable source on the lesbian continuum than, I would think, Charlotte Brontë, who understood that while women may, indeed must, be one another's allies, mentors, and comforters in the female struggle for survival, there is quite extraneous delight in each other's company and attraction to each others' minds and character, which attend a recognition of each others' strengths.

By the same token, we can say that there is a *nascent* feminist political content in the act of choosing a woman lover or life partner in the face of institutionalized heterosexuality.[66] But for lesbian existence to realize this political content in an ultimately liberating form, the erotic choice must deepen and expand into conscious woman identification—into lesbian feminism.

The work that lies ahead, of unearthing and describing what I call here "lesbian existence," is potentially liberating for all women. It is work that must assuredly move beyond the limits of white and middle-class Western Women's Studies to examine women's lives, work, and groupings within every racial, ethnic, and political structure. There are differences, moreover, between "lesbian existence" and the "lesbian continuum," differences we can discern even in the movement of our own lives. The lesbian continuum, I suggest, needs delineation in light of the "double life" of women, not only women self-described as heterosexual but also of self-described lesbians. We need a far more exhaustive account of the forms the double life has assumed. Historians need to ask at every point how heterosexuality as institution has been organized and maintained through the female wage scale, the enforcement of middle-class women's "leisure," the glamorization of so-called sexual liberation, the withholding of education from women, the imagery of "high art" and popular culture, the mystification of the "personal" sphere, and much else. We need an economics which comprehends the institution of heterosexuality, with its doubled workload for women and its sexual divisions of labor, as the most idealized of economic relations.

The question inevitably will arise: Are we then to condemn all heterosexual relationships, including those which are least oppressive? I believe this question, though often heartfelt, is the wrong question here. We have been stalled in a maze of false dichotomies which prevents our apprehending the institution as a whole: "good" versus "bad" marriages; "marriage for love" versus arranged marriage; "liberated" sex versus prostitution; heterosexual intercourse versus rape; *Liebeschmerz* versus humiliation and dependency. Within the institution exist, of course, qualitative differences of experience; but the absence of choice remains the great unacknowledged reality, and in the absence of choice, women will remain dependent upon the chance or luck of particular relationships and will have no collective power to determine the meaning and place of sexuality in their lives. As we address the institution itself, moreover, we begin to perceive a history of female resistance which has never fully understood itself because it has been so fragmented, miscalled, erased. It will require a courageous grasp of the politics and economics, as well as the cultural propaganda, of heterosexuality to carry us beyond individual cases or diversified group situations into the complex kind of overview needed to undo the power men everywhere wield over women, power which has become a model for every other form of exploitation and illegitimate control.

AFTERWORD

In 1980, Ann Snitow, Christine Stansell, and Sharon Thompson, three Marxist-feminist activists and scholars, sent out a call for papers for an anthology on the politics of sexuality. Having just finished writing "Compulsory Heterosexuality" for *Signs,* I sent them that manuscript and asked them to consider it. Their anthology, *Powers of Desire,* was published by the Monthly Review Press New Feminist Library in 1983 and included my paper. During the intervening period, the four of us were in correspondence, but I was able to take only limited advantage of this dialogue due to ill health and resulting surgery. With their permission, I reprint here excerpts from that correspondence as a way of indicating that my essay should be read as one contribution to a long exploration in progress, not as my own "last word" on sexual politics. I also refer interested readers to *Powers of Desire* itself.

Dear Adrienne,

... In one of our first letters, we told you that we were finding parameters of left-wing/feminist sexual discourse to be far broader than we imagined. Since then, we have perceived what we believe to be a crisis in the feminist movement about sex, an intensifying debate (although not always an explicit one), and a questioning of assumptions once taken for granted. While we fear the link between sex and violence, as do Women Against Pornography, we wish we better understood its sources in ourselves as well as in men. In the Reagan era, we can hardly afford to romanticize any old norm of a virtuous and moral sexuality.

In your piece, you are asking the question, what would women choose in a world where patriarchy and capitalism did *not* rule? We agree with you that heterosexuality is an institution created between these grind stones, but we don't conclude, therefore, that it is entirely a male creation. You only allow for female historical agency insofar as women exist on the lesbian continuum while we would argue that women's history, like men's history, is created out of a dialectic of necessity and choice.

All three of us (hence one lesbian, two heterosexual women) had questions about your use of the term "false consciousness" for women's heterosexuality. In general, we think the false-consciousness model can blind us to the necessities and desires that comprise the lives of the oppressed. It can also lead to the too easy denial of others' experience when that experience is different from our own. We posit, rather, a complex social model in which all erotic life is a continuum, one which therefore includes relations with men.

Which brings us to this metaphor of the continuum. We know you are a poet, not an historian, and we look forward to reading your metaphors all our lives—and standing straighter as feminists, as women, for having read them. But the metaphor of the lesbian continuum is open to all kinds of misunderstandings, and these sometimes have odd political effects. For ex-

ample, Sharon reports that at a recent meeting around the abortion-rights struggle, the notions of continuum arose in the discussion several times and underwent divisive transformation. Overall, the notion that two ways of being existed on the same continuum was interpreted to mean that those two ways were the *same*. The sense of range and gradation that your description evokes disappeared. Lesbianism and female friendship became exactly the same thing. Similarly, heterosexuality and rape became the same. In one of several versions of the continuum that evolved, a slope was added, like so:

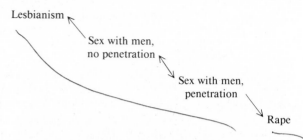

This sloped continuum brought its proponents to the following conclusion: An appropriate, workable abortion-rights strategy is to inform all women that heterosexual penetration is rape, whatever their subjective experiences to the contrary. All women will immediately recognize the truth of this and opt for the alternative of nonpenetration. The abortion-rights struggle will thus be simplified into a struggle against coercive sex and its consequences (since no enlightened woman would voluntarily undergo penetration unless her object was procreation—a peculiarly Catholic-sounding view).

The proponents of this strategy were young women who have worked hard in the abortion-rights movement for the past two or more years. They are inexperienced but they are dedicated. For this reason, we take their reading of your work seriously. We don't think, however, that it comes solely, or even at all, from the work itself. As likely a source is the tendency to dichotomize that has plagued the women's movement. The source of that tendency is harder to trace.

In that regard, the hints in "Compulsory" about the double life of women intrigue us. You define the double life as "the apparent acquiescence to an institution founded on male interest and prerogative." But that definition doesn't really explain your other references—to, for instance, the "intense mixture" of love and anger in lesbian relationships and to the peril of romanticizing what it means "to love and act against the grain." We think these comments raise extremely important issues for feminists right now; the problem of division and anger among us needs airing and analysis. Is this, by any chance, the theme of a piece you have in the works?

. . . We would still love it if we could have a meeting with you in the next few months. Any chance? . . . Greetings and support from us—in all your undertakings.

We send love,
Sharon, Chris, and Ann

New York City
April 19, 1981

Dear Ann, Chris, and Sharon,

. . . It's good to be back in touch with you, you who have been so unfailingly patient, generous, and persistent. Above all, it's important to me that you know that ill health, not a withdrawal because of political differences, delayed my writing back to you. . . .

"False consciousness" can, I agree, be used as a term of dismissal for any thinking we don't like to adhere to. But, as I tried to illustrate in some detail, there is a real, identifiable system of heterosexual propaganda, of defining women as existing for the sexual use of men, which goes beyond "sex role" or "gender" stereotyping or "sexist imagery" to include a vast number of verbal and nonverbal messages. And this I call "control of consciousness." The possibility of a woman who does not exist sexually for men—the lesbian possibility—is buried, erased, occluded, distorted, misnamed, and driven underground. The feminist books—Chodorow, Dinnerstein, Ehrenreich and English, and others—which I discuss at the beginning of my essay contribute to this invalidation and erasure, and as such are part of the problem.

My essay is founded on the belief that we all think from within the limits of certain solipsisms—usually linked with privilege, racial, cultural, and economic as well as sexual—which present themselves as "the universal," "the way things are," "all women," etc., etc. I wrote it equally out of the belief that in becoming conscious of our solipsisms we have certain kinds of

choices, that we can and must re-educate ourselves. I never have maintained that heterosexual feminists are walking about in a state of "brainwashed" false consciousness. Nor have such phrases as "sleeping with the enemy" seemed to me either profound or useful. *Homophobia* is too diffuse a term and does not go very far in helping us identify and talk about the sexual solipsism of heterosexual feminism. In this paper I was trying to ask heterosexual feminists to examine their experience of heterosexuality critically and antagonistically, to critique the institution of which they are a part, to struggle with the norm and its implications for women's freedom, to become more open to the considerable resources offered by the lesbian-feminist perspective, to refuse to settle for the personal privilege and solution of the individual "good relationship" within the institution of heterosexuality.

As regards "female historical agency," I wanted, precisely, to suggest that the victim model is insufficient; that there *is* a history of female agency and choice which has actually challenged aspects of male supremacy; that, like male supremacy, these can be found in many different cultures. . . . It's not that I think all female agency has been solely and avowedly lesbian. But by erasing lesbian existence from female history, from theory, from literary criticism . . . from feminist approaches to economic structure, ideas about "the family," etc., an enormous amount of female agency is kept unavailable, hence unusable. I wanted to demonstrate that that kind of obliteration continues to be acceptable in seriously regarded feminist texts. What surprised me in the responses to my essay, including your notes, is how almost every aspect of it has been considered, except this—to me—central one. I was taking a position which was neither lesbian/ separatist in the sense of dismissing heterosexual women nor a "gay civil rights" plea for . . . openness to lesbianism as an "option" or an "alternate life style." I was urging that lesbian *existence* has been an unrecognized and unaffirmed claiming by women of their sexuality, thus a pattern of resistance, thus also a kind of borderline position from which to analyze and challenge the relationship of heterosexuality to male supremacy. And that lesbian existence, when recognized, demands a conscious restructuring of feminist analysis and criticism, not just a token reference or two.

I certainly agree with you that the term *lesbian con-*

tinuum can be misused. It was, in the example you report of the abortion-rights meeting, though I would think anyone who had read my work from *Of Woman Born* onward would know that my position on abortion and sterilization abuse is more complicated than that. My own problem with the phrase is that it can be, is, used by women who have not yet begun to examine the privileges and solipsisms of heterosexuality, as a safe way to describe their felt connections with women, without having to share in the risks and threats of lesbian existence. What I had thought to delineate rather complexly as a continuum has begun to sound more like "life-style shopping." *Lesbian continuum*—the phrase—came from a desire to allow for the greatest possible variation of female-identified experience, while paying a different kind of respect to *lesbian existence*—the traces and knowledge of women who have made their primary erotic and emotional choices for women. If I were writing the paper today, I would still want to make this distinction, but would put more caveats around *lesbian continuum*. I fully agree with you that Smith-Rosenberg's "female world" is not a social ideal, enclosed as it is within prescriptive middle-class heterosexuality and marriage.

My own essay could have been stronger had it drawn on more of the literature by Black women toward which Toni Morrison's *Sula* inevitably pointed me. In reading a great deal more of Black women's fiction I began to perceive a different set of valences from those found in white women's fiction for the most part: a different quest for the woman hero, a different relationship both to sexuality with men and to female loyalty and bonding. . . .

You comment briefly on your reactions to some of the radical-feminist works I cited in my first footnote.[67] I am myself critical of some of them even as I found them vitally useful. What most of them share is a taking seriously of misogyny—of organized, institutionalized, normalized hostility and violence against women. I feel no "hierarchy of oppressions" is needed in order for us to take misogyny as seriously as we take racism, anti-Semitism, imperialism. To take misogyny seriously needn't mean that we perceive women merely as victims, without responsibilities or choices; it does mean recognizing the "necessity" in that "dialectic of necessity and choice"—identifying, describing, refusing to turn aside our eyes. I think that some of the apparent reductiveness, or even obsessiveness, of some white radical-feminist theory derives from racial and/or class solipsism, but also from the immense effort of trying to render women hating visible amid so much denial. . . .

Finally, as to poetry and history: I want both in my life; I need to see through both. If metaphor can be misconstrued, history can also lead to misconstrual when it obliterates acts of resistance or rebellion, wipes out transformational models, or sentimentalizes power relationships. I know you know this. I believe we are all trying to think and write out of our best consciences, our most open consciousness. I expect that quality in this book which you are editing, and look forward with anticipation to the thinking—and the actions—toward which it may take us.

In sisterhood,
Adrienne

Montague, Massachusetts
November 1981

NOTES

1. See, for example, Paula Gunn Allen, *The Sacred Hoop: Recovering the Feminine in American Indian Traditions* (Boston: Beacon, 1986); Beth Brant, ed., *A Gathering of Spirit: Writing and Art by North American Indian Women* (Montpelier, Vt.: Sinister Wisdom Books, 1984); Gloria Anzaldúa and Cherríe Moraga, eds., *This Bridge Called My Back: Writings by Radical Women of Color* (Watertown, Mass.: Persephone, 1981; distributed by Kitchen Table/ Women of Color Press, Albany, N.Y.); J. R. Roberts, *Black Lesbians: An Annotated Bibliography* (Tallahassee, Fla.: Naiad, 1981); Barbara Smith, ed., *Home Girls: A Black Feminist Anthology* (Albany, N.Y.: Kitchen Table/Women of Color Press, 1984). As Lorraine Bethel and Barbara Smith pointed out in *Conditions 5: The Black Women's Issue* (1980), a great deal of fiction by Black women depicts primary relationships between women. I would like to cite here

the work of Ama Ata Aidoo, Toni Cade Bambara, Buchi Emecheta, Bessie Head, Zora Neale Hurston, Alice Walker. Donna Allegra, Red Jordan Arobateau, Audre Lorde, Ann Allen Shockley, among others, write directly as Black lesbians. For fiction by other lesbians of color, see Elly Bulkin, ed., *Lesbian Fiction: An Anthology* (Watertown, Mass.: Persephone, 1981).

See also, for accounts of contemporary Jewish-lesbian existence, Evelyn Torton Beck, ed., *Nice Jewish Girls: A Lesbian Anthology* (Watertown, Mass.: Persephone, 1982; distributed by Crossing Press, Trumansburg, N.Y. 14886); Alice Bloch, *Lifetime Guarantee* (Watertown, Mass.: Persephone, 1982); and Melanie Kaye-Kantrowitz and Irena Klepfisz, eds., *The Tribe of Dina: A Jewish Women's Anthology* (Montpelier, Vt.: Sinister Wisdom Books, 1986).

The earliest formulation that I know of heterosexuality as an institution was in the lesbian-feminist paper *The Furies,* founded in 1971. For a collection of articles from that paper, see Nancy Myron and Charlotte Bunch, eds., *Lesbianism and the Women's Movement* (Oakland, Calif.: Diana Press, 1975; distributed by Crossing Press, Trumansburg, N.Y. 14886).

2. Alice Rossi, "Children and Work in the Lives of Women," paper delivered at the University of Arizona, Tucson, February 1976.

3. Doris Lessing, *The Golden Notebook,* 1962 (New York: Bantam, 1977), p. 480.

4. Nancy Chodorow, *The Reproduction of Mothering* (Berkeley: University of California Press, 1978); Dorothy Dinnerstein, *The Mermaid and the Minotaur: Sexual Arrangements and the Human Malaise* (New York: Harper & Row, 1976); Barbara Ehrenreich and Deirdre English, *For Her Own Good: 150 Years of the Experts' Advice to Women* (Garden City, N.Y.: Doubleday, Anchor, 1978); Jean Baker Miller, *Toward a New Psychology of Women* (Boston: Beacon, 1976).

5. I could have chosen many other serious and influential recent books, including anthologies, which would illustrate the same point: e.g., *Our Bodies, Ourselves,* the Boston Women's Health Book Collective's best seller (New York: Simon and Schuster, 1976), which devotes a separate (and inadequate) chapter to lesbians, but whose message is that heterosexuality is most women's life preference; Berenice Carroll, ed., *Liberating Women's History: Theoretical and Critical Essays* (Urbana: University of Illinois Press, 1976), which does not include even a token essay on the lesbian presence in history, though an essay by Linda Gordon, Persis Hunt, et al. notes the use by male historians of "sexual deviance" as a category to discredit and dismiss Anna Howard Shaw, Jane Addams, and other feminists ("Historical Phallacies: Sexism in American Historical Writing"); and Renate Bridenthal and Claudia Koonz, eds., *Becoming Visible: Women in European History* (Boston: Houghton Mifflin, 1977), which contains three mentions of male homosexuality

but no materials that I have been able to locate on lesbians. Gerda Lerner, ed., *The Female Experience: An American Documentary* (Indianapolis: Bobbs-Merrill, 1977), contains an abridgment of two lesbian-feminist–position papers from the contemporary movement but no other documentation of lesbian existence. Lerner does note in her preface, however, how the charge of deviance has been used to fragment women and discourage women's resistance. Linda Gordon, in *Woman's Body, Woman's Right: A Social History of Birth Control in America* (New York: Viking, Grossman, 1976), notes accurately that "it is not that feminism has produced more lesbians. There have always been many lesbians, despite the high levels of repression; and most lesbians experience their sexual preference as innate" (p. 410).

[A. R., 1986: I am glad to update the first annotation in this footnote. *"The New" Our Bodies, Ourselves* (New York: Simon and Schuster, 1984) contains an expanded chapter on "Loving Women: Lesbian Life and Relationships" and furthermore emphasizes *choices* for women throughout—in terms of sexuality, health care, family, politics, etc.]

6. Jonathan Katz, ed., *Gay American History: Lesbians and Gay Men in the U.S.A.* (New York: Thomas Y. Crowell, 1976).

7. Nancy Sahli, "Smashing Women's Relationships before the Fall," *Chrysalis: A Magazine of Women's Culture* 8 (1979): 17–27.

8. This is a book which I have publicly endorsed. I would still do so, though with the above caveat. It is only since beginning to write this article that I fully appreciated how enormous is the unasked question in Ehrenreich and English's book.

9. See, for example, Kathleen Barry, *Female Sexual Slavery* (Englewood Cliffs, N.J.: Prenctice-Hall, 1979); Mary Daly, *Gyn/Ecology: The Metaethics of Radical Feminism* (Boston: Beacon, 1978); Susan Griffin, *Woman and Nature: The Roaring inside Her* (New York: Harper & Row, 1978); Diana Russell and Nicole van de Ven, eds., *Proceedings of the International Tribunal of Crimes against Women* (Millbrae, Calif.: Les Femmes, 1976); and Susan Brownmiller, *Against Our Will: Men, Women and Rape* (New York: Simon and Schuster, 1975); *Aegis: Magazine on Ending Violence against Women* (Feminist Alliance against Rape, P.O. Box 21033, Washington, D.C. 20009).

[A. R., 1986: Work on both incest and on woman battering has appeared in the 1980s which I did not cite in the essay. See Florence Rush, *The Best-kept Secret* (New York: McGraw-Hill, 1980); Louise Armstrong, *Kiss Daddy Goodnight: A Speakout on Incest* (New York: Pocket Books, 1979); Sandra Butler, *Conspiracy of Silence: The Trauma of Incest* (San Francisco: New Glide, 1978); F. Delacoste and F. Newman, eds., *Fight Back!: Feminist Resistance to Male Violence* (Minneapolis: Cleis Press, 1981); Judy Freespirit, *Daddy's Girl: An Incest Survivor's Story* (Langlois, Ore.: Diaspora Distribution, 1982); Judith Herman, *Father-Daughter Incest* (Cambridge, Mass.: Harvard University Press, 1981); Toni McNaron and Yarrow Morgan, eds., *Voices in the Night: Women Speaking about Incest* (Minneapolis: Cleis Press, 1982); and Betsy Warrior's richly informative, multipurpose compilation of essays, statistics, listings, and facts, the *Battered Women's Directory* (formerly entitled *Working on Wife Abuse),* 8th ed. (Cambridge, Mass.: 1982).]

10. Dinnerstein, p. 272.

11. Chodorow, pp. 197–198.

12. Ibid., pp. 198–199.

13. Ibid., p. 200.

14. Kathleen Gough, "The Origin of the Family," in *Toward an Anthropology of Women,* ed. Rayna [Rapp] Reiter (New York: Monthly Review Press, 1975), pp. 69–70.

15. Barry, pp. 216–219.

16. Anna Demeter, *Legal Kidnapping* (Boston: Beacon, 1977), pp. xx, 126–128.

17. Daly, pp. 139–141, 163–165.

18. Barbara Ehrenreich and Deirdre English, *Witches, Midwives and Nurses: A History of Women Healers* (Old Westbury, N.Y.: Feminist Press, 1973); Andrea Dworkin, *Woman Hating* (New York: Dutton, 1974), pp. 118–154; Daly, pp. 178–222.

19. See Virginia Woolf, *A Room of One's Own* (London: Hogarth, 1929), and ibid., *Three Guineas* (New York: Harcourt Brace, [1938] 1966); Tillie Olsen, *Silences* (Boston: Delacorte, 1978); Michelle Cliff, "The Resonance of Interruption" *Chrysalis: A Magazine of Women's Culture* 8 (1979): 29–37.

20. Mary Daly, *Beyond God the Father* (Boston: Beacon, 1973), pp. 347–351; Olsen, pp. 22–46.

21. Daly, *Beyond God the Father,* p. 93.

22. Fran P. Hosken, "The Violence of Power: Genital Mutilation of Females," *Heresies: A Feminist Journal of Art and Politics* 6 (1979): 28–35; Russell and van de Ven, pp. 194–195.

[A. R., 1986: See especially "Circumcision of Girls," in Nawal El Saadawi, *The Hidden Face of Eve: Women in the Arab World* (Boston: Beacon, 1982), pp. 33–43.]

23. Barry, pp. 163–164.

24. The issue of "lesbian sadomasochism" needs to be examined in terms of dominant cultures' teachings about the relation of sex and violence. I believe this to be another example of the "double life" of women.

25. Catharine A. MacKinnon, *Sexual Harassment of Working Women: A Case of Sex Discrimination* (New Haven, Conn.: Yale University Press, 1979), pp. 15–16.

26. Ibid., p. 174.

27. Brownmiller, *Against Our Will.*

28. MacKinnon, p. 219. Susan Schecter writes: "The push for heterosexual union at whatever cost is so intense that . . . it has become a cultural force of its own that creates

battering. The ideology of romantic love and its jealous possession of the partner as property provide the masquerade for what can become severe abuse" (*Aegis: Magazine on Ending Violence against Women* [July–August 1979]: 50–51).

29. Mackinnon, p. 298.

30. Ibid., p. 220.

31. Ibid. p. 221.

32. Barry, *Female Sexual Slavery.*

[A. R., 1986: See also Kathleen Barry, Charlotte Bunch, and Shirley Castley, eds., *International Feminism: Networking against Female Sexual Slavery* (New York: International Women's Tribune Center, 1984).]

33. Barry, p. 33.

34. Ibid., p. 103.

35. Ibid., p. 5.

36. Ibid., p. 100.

[A. R., 1986: This statement has been taken as claiming that "all women are victims" purely and simply, or that "all heterosexuality equals sexual slavery." I would say, rather, that all women are affected, though differently, by dehumanizing attitudes and practices directed at women as a group.]

37. Ibid., p. 218.

38. Ibid., p. 140.

39. Ibid., p. 172.

40. Elsewhere I have suggested that male identification has been a powerful source of white women's racism and that it has often been women already seen as "disloyal" to male codes and systems who have actively battled against it (Adrienne Rich, "Disloyal to Civilization: Feminism, Racism, Gynephobia," in *On Lies, Secrets, and Silence: Selected Prose, 1966–1978* [New York: W. W. Norton, 1979]).

41. Barry, p. 220.

42. Susan Cavin, "Lesbian Origins" (Ph.D. diss., Rutgers University, 1978), unpublished, ch. 6.

[A. R., 1986: This dissertation was recently published as *Lesbian Origins* (San Francisco: Ism Press, 1986).]

43. For my perception of heterosexuality as an economic institution I am indebted to Lisa Leghorn and Katherine Parker, who allowed me to read the unpublished manuscript of their book *Woman's Worth: Sexual Economics and the World of Women* (London and Boston: Routledge & Kegan Paul, 1981).

44. I would suggest that lesbian existence has been most recognized and tolerated where it has resembled a "deviant" version of heterosexuality—e.g., where lesbians have, like Stein and Toklas, played heterosexual roles (or seemed to in public) and have been chiefly identified with male culture. See also Claude E. Schaeffer, "The Kuterai Female Berdache: Courier, Guide, Prophetess and Warrior," *Ethnohistory* 12, no. 3 (Summer 1965): 193–236. (Berdache: "an individual of a definite physiological sex [m. or f.] who assumes the role and status of the opposite sex and who is viewed by the community as being of one sex physiologically but as having as-

sumed the role and status of the opposite sex" [Schaeffer, p. 231].) Lesbian existence has also been relegated to an upperclass phenomenon, an elite decadence (as in the fascination with Paris salon lesbians such as Renée Vivien and Natalie Clifford Barney), to the obscuring of such "common women" as Judy Grahn depicts in her *The Work of a Common Woman* (Oakland, Calif.: Diana Press, 1978) and *True to Life Adventure Stories* (Oakland, Calif.: Diana Press, 1978).

45. Daly, *Gyn/Ecology*, p. 15.

46. "In a hostile world in which women are not supposed to survive except in relation with and in service to men, entire communities of women were simply erased. History tends to bury what it seeks to reject" (Blanche W. Cook, "'Women Alone Stir My Imagination': Lesbianism and the Cultural Tradition," *Signs: Journal of Women in Culture and Society* 4, no. 4 [Summer 1970]: 719–720). The Lesbian Herstory Archives in New York City is one attempt to preserve contemporary documents on lesbian existence—a project of enormous value and meaning, working against the continuing censorship and obliteration of relationships, networks, communities in other archives and elsewhere in the culture.

47. [A.R., 1986: The shared historical and spiritual "crossover" functions of lesbians and gay men in cultures past and present are traced by Judy Grahn in *Another Mother Tongue: Gay Words, Gay Worlds* (Boston: Beacon, 1984). I now think we have much to learn both from the uniquely female aspects of lesbian existence and from the complex "gay" identity we share with gay men.]

48. Audre Lorde, "Uses of the Erotic: The Erotic as Power," in *Sister Outsider* (Trumansburg, N.Y.: Crossing Press, 1984).

49. Adrienne Rich, "Conditions for Work: The Common World of Women," in *On Lies, Secrets, and Silence*, p. 209; H. D., *Tribute to Freud* (Oxford: Carcanet, 1971), pp. 50–54.

50. Woolf, *A Room of One's Own*, p. 126.

51. Gracia Clark, "The Beguines: A Mediaeval Women's Community," *Quest: A Feminist Quarterly* 1, no. 4 (1975): 73–80.

52. See Denise Paulmé, ed., *Women of Tropical Africa* (Berkeley: University of California Press, 1963), pp. 7, 266–267. Some of these sororities are described as "a kind of defensive syndicate against the male element," their aims being "to offer concerted resistance to an oppressive patriarchate," "independence in relation to one's husband and with regard to motherhood, mutual aid, satisfaction of personal revenge." See also Audre Lorde, "Scratching the Surface: Some Notes on Barriers to Women and Loving" in *Sister Outsider*, pp. 45–52; Marjorie Topley, "Marriage Resistance in Rural Kwangtung," in *Women in Chinese Society*, ed. M. Wolf and R. Witke (Stanford, Calif.: Stanford University Press, 1978), pp. 67–89; Agnes Smedley, *Portraits of Chinese Women in Revolution*, ed. J. MacKinnon and S. MacKinnon (Old Westbury, N.Y.: Feminist Press, 1976), pp. 103–110.

53. See Rosalind Petchesky, "Dissolving the Hyphen: A Report on Marxist-Feminist Groups 1–5," in *Capitalist Patriarchy and the Case for Socialist Feminism*, ed. Zillah Eisenstein (New York: Monthly Review Press, 1979), p. 387.

54. [A. R., 1986: See Angela Davis, *Women, Race and Class* (New York: Random House, 1981), p. 102; Orlando Patterson, *Slavery and Social Death: A Comparative Study* (Cambridge: Harvard University Press, 1982), p. 133.]

55. Russell and van de Ven, pp. 42–43, 56–57.

56. I am indebted to Jonathan Katz's *Gay American History* for bringing to my attention Hansberry's letters to *The Ladder* and to Barbara Grier for supplying me with copies of relevant pages from *The Ladder*, quoted here by permission of Barbara Grier. See also the reprinted series of *The Ladder*, ed. Jonathan Katz et al. (New York: Arno, 1975), and Deirdre Carmody, "Letters by Eleanor Roosevelt Detail Friendship with Lorena Hickok." *New York Times* (October 21, 1979).

57. Meridel LeSueur, *The Girl* (Cambridge, Mass.: West End Press, 1978), pp. 10–11. LeSueur describes, in an afterword, how this book was drawn from the writings and oral narrations of women in the Workers Alliance who met as a writers' group during the depression.

58. Ibid., p. 20.

59. Ibid., pp. 53–54.

60. Ibid., p. 55.

61. Toni Morrison, *Sula* (New York: Bantam, 1973), pp. 103–104, 149. I am indebted to Lorraine Bethel's essay "'This Infinity of Conscious Pain': Zora Neale Hurston and the Black Female Literary Tradition," in *All the Women Are White, All the Blacks Are Men, but Some of Us Are Brave: Black Women's Studies*, ed. Gloria T. Hull, Patricia Bell Scott, and Barbara Smith (Old Westbury, N.Y.: Feminist Press, 1982).

62. See Maureen Brady and Judith McDaniel, "Lesbians in the Mainstream: The Image of Lesbians in Recent Commercial Fiction," *Conditions* 6 (1979): 82–105.

63. See Russell and van de Ven, p. 40: "Few heterosexual women realize their lack of free choice about their sexuality, and few realize how and why compulsory heterosexuality is also a crime against them."

64. Bethel, "'This Infinity of Conscious Pain.'"

65. Dinnerstein, the most recent writer to quote this passage, adds ominously: "But what has to be added to her account is that these 'women enlaced' are sheltering each other not just from what men want to do to them, but also from what they want to do to each other" (Dinnerstein, p. 103). The fact is, however, that woman-to-woman violence is a minute grain in the universe of male-against-female violence perpetuated and rationalized in every social institution.

66. Conversation with Blanche W. Cook, New York City, March 1979.

67. See note 9, above.

Sexuality and Gender in Certain Native American Tribes: The Case of Cross-Gender Females

EVELYN BLACKWOOD

Ideological concepts of gender and sexuality arise from cultural constructions and vary from culture to culture. The female cross-gender role in certain Native American tribes constituted an opportunity for women to assume the male role permanently and to marry women. Its existence challenges Western assumptions about gender roles. Some feminist anthropologists assume that it is in the nature of sex and gender systems to create asymmetry in the form of male dominance and female subservience and to enforce corresponding forms of sexual behavior.[1] Because kinship and marriage are closely tied to gender systems, these social structures are implicated in the subordination of women. The existence of the female cross-gender role, however, points to the inadequacies of such a view and helps to clarify the nature of sex and gender systems.

This study closely examines the female cross-gender role as it existed historically in several Native American tribes, primarily in western North America and the Plains. It focuses on western tribes that shared a basically egalitarian mode of production in precolonial times,[2] and for which sufficient data on the female role exist. Although there were cultural differences among these groups, prior to the colonial period they all had subsistence-level economies that had not developed significant forms of wealth or rank. These tribes include the Kaska of the Yukon Territory, the Klamath of southern Oregon, and the Mohave, Maricopa, and Cocopa of the Colorado River area in the Southwest. The Plains tribes, by contrast, are noteworthy for the relative absence of the female cross-gender role. Conditions affecting the tribes of the Plains varied from those of the western tribes, and thus analysis of historical-cultural contexts will serve to illuminate the differing constraints on sex and gender systems in these two areas.

Ethnographic literature has perpetuated some misconceptions about the cross-gender role. Informants frequently describe the institution in negative terms, stating that berdache were despised and ridiculed.[3] But ethnographers collected much of the data in this century; it is based on informants' memories of the mid- to late 1800s. During this period the cross-gender institution was disappearing rapidly. Thus, twentieth-century informants do not accurately represent the institution in the precontact period. Alfred Kroeber found that "while the [berdache] institution was in full bloom, the Caucasian attitude was one of repugnance and condemnation. This attitude . . . made subsequent personality inquiry difficult, the later berdache leading repressed or disguised lives."[4] Informants' statements to later ethnographers or hostile white officials were far different from the actual attitude toward the role that prevailed in the precolonial period. An analysis of the cross-gender role in its proper historical context brings to light the integral nature of its relationship to the larger community.

CULTURAL SIGNIFICANCE OF THE FEMALE CROSS-GENDER ROLE

Most anthropological work on the cross-gender role has focused on the male berdache, with little recognition given to the female cross-gender role. Part of the problem has been the much smaller data base available for a study of the female role. Yet anthropologists have overlooked even the available data. This over-

Reprinted from *Signs: Journal of Women in Culture and Society* 10, no. 1 (1984): 27–42. Copyright © 1984 by The University of Chicago. All rights reserved. Some footnotes have been renumbered.

sight has led to the current misconception that the cross-gender role was not feasible for women. Harriet Whitehead, in a comprehensive article on the berdache, states that, given the small number of cross-gender females, "the gender-crossed status was more fully instituted for males than for females."[5] Charles Callender and Lee Kochems, in a well-researched article, base their analysis of the role predominantly on the male berdache.[6] Evidence from thirty-three Native American tribes indicates that the cross-gender role for women was as viable an institution as was the male berdache role.[7]

The Native American cross-gender role confounded Western concepts of gender. Cross-gender individuals typically acted, sat, dressed, talked like, and did the work of the other sex. Early Western observers described the berdache as half male and half female, but such a description attests only to their inability to accept a male in a female role or vice versa. In the great majority of reported cases of berdache, they assumed the social role of the other sex, not of both sexes.[8] Contemporary theorists, such as Callender and Kochems and Whitehead, resist the idea of a complete social role reclassification because they equate gender with biological sex. Native gender categories contradict such definitions.

Although the details of the cross-gender females' lives are scant in the ethnographic literature, a basic pattern emerges from the data on the western tribes. Recognition and cultural validation of the female cross-gender role varied slightly from tribe to tribe, although the social role was the same. Among the Southwestern tribes, dream experience was an important ritual aspect of life and provided success, leadership, and special skills for those who sought it. All cross-gender individuals in these tribes dreamed about their role change. The Mohave hwame dreamed of becoming cross-gender while still in the womb.[9] The Maricopa kwiraxame dreamed too much as a child and so changed her sex.[10] No information is available for the development of the female cross-gender role (tw!nnaek) among the Klamath. It was most likely similar to the male adolescent transformative experience, which was accomplished through fasting or diving.[11] Dreaming provided an avenue to special powers and also provided sanction for the use of those powers. In the same way, dreams about the cross-gender role provided impetus and community sanction for assumption of the role.

The female candidate for cross-gender status displayed an interest in the male role during childhood. A girl avoided learning female tasks. Instead, as in the case of the Cocopa warrhameh, she played with boys and made bows and arrows with which to hunt birds and rabbits.[12] The Mohave hwame "[threw] away their dolls and metates, and [refused] to shred bark or perform other feminine tasks."[13] Adults, acknowledging the interests of such girls, taught them the same skills the boys learned. Among the Kaska, a family that had all female children and desired a son to hunt for them would select a daughter (probably the one who showed the most inclination) to be "like a man." When she was five, the parents tied the dried ovaries of a bear to her belt to wear for life as protection against conception.[14] Though in different tribes the socializing processes varied, girls achieved the cross-gender role in each instance through accepted cultural channels.

Upon reaching puberty, the time when girls were considered ready for marriage, the cross-gender female was unable to fulfill her obligations and duties as a woman in marriage, having learned the tasks assigned to men. Nonmarriageable status could have presented a disadvantage both to herself and to her kin, who would be called upon to support her in her later years. But a role transfer allowed her to enter the marriage market for a wife with whom she could establish a household. The Mohave publicly acknowledged the new status of the woman by performing an initiation ceremony. Following this ceremony she assumed a name befitting a person of the male sex and was given marriage rights.[15] At puberty, the Cocopa warrhameh dressed her hair in the male style and had her nose pierced like the men, instead of receiving a chin tattoo like other women.[16] These public rites validated the cross-gender identity, signifying to the community that the woman was to be treated as a man.

In adult life cross-gender females performed the duties of the male gender role. Their tasks included hunting, trapping, cultivating crops, and fighting in battles. For example, the Cocopa warrhameh established households like men and fought in battle.[17] The Kaska cross-gender female "dressed in masculine attire, did male allocated tasks, often developing great strength and usually becoming an outstanding hunter."[18] The Mohave hwame were known as excellent providers, hunting for meat, working in the fields, and caring for the children of their wives.[19] Cross-gender females also adhered to male ritual obligations. A Klamath *tw!nnaek* observed the usual mourning when her long-time female partner died, wearing a bark belt as did a man.[20] Mohave *hwame* were said to be powerful shamans, in this case especially good at curing venereal disease.[21] Many other cross-gender females were considered powerful spiritually, but most were not shamans, even in the Southwest. Cross-gender females did not bear children once they took up the male role. Their kin considered them nonreproductive and accepted the loss of their childbearing potential, placing a woman's individual interests and abilities above her value as a reproducer.[22]

In most cases ethnographers do not discuss the ability of cross-gender females to maintain the fiction of their maleness. Whitehead suggests that women were barred from crossing over unless they were, or at least pretended to be, deficient physically.[23] However, despite some reports that cross-gender women in the Southwest had muscular builds, undeveloped secondary sexual characteristics, and sporadic or absent menstruation,[24] convincing physical evidence is noticeably lacking. In fact, the Mohave *hwame* kept a husband's taboos with regard to her menstruating or pregnant wife and ignored her own menses.[25] That such may have been the case in other tribes as well is borne out by the practice of the Ingalik cross-gender female. Among the Alaskan Ingalik, the *kashim* was the center of men's activities and the place for male-only sweat baths. The cross-gender female participated in the activities of the *kashim,* and the men were said not to perceive her true sex.[26] Cornelius Osgood suggests that she was able to hide her sex, but, as with the Mohave, the people probably ignored her physical sex in favor of her chosen role. Through this social fiction, then, cross-gender females dismissed the physiological functions of women and claimed an identity based on their performance of a social role.

GENDER EQUALITY

Women's ability to assume the cross-gender role arose from the particular conditions of kinship and gender in these tribes. The egalitarian relations of the sexes were predicated on the cooperation of autonomous individuals who had control of their productive activities. In these tribes women owned and distributed the articles they produced, and they had equal voice in matters affecting kin and community. Economic strat-

egies depended on collective activity. Lineages or individuals had no formal authority; the whole group made decisions by consensus. People of both sexes could achieve positions of leadership through skill, wisdom, and spiritual power. Ultimately, neither women nor men had an inferior role but rather had power in those spheres of activity specific to their sex.[27]

Among these tribes, gender roles involved the performance of a particular set of duties. Most occupations necessary to the functioning of the group were defined as either male or female tasks. A typical division of labor allocated responsibilities for gathering, food preparation, child rearing, basket weaving, and making clothes to women, while men hunted, made weapons, and built canoes and houses. The allocation of separate tasks to each sex established a system of reciprocity that assured the interdependence of the sexes. Because neither set of tasks was valued more highly than the other, neither sex predominated.

Gender-assigned tasks overlapped considerably among these people. Many individuals engaged in activities that were also performed by the other sex without incurring disfavor. The small game and fish that Kaska and Klamath women hunted on a regular basis were an important contribution to the survival of the band. Some Klamath women made canoes, usually a man's task, and older men helped women with food preparation.[28] In the Colorado River area, both men and women collected tule pollen.[29] Engaging in such activities did not make a woman masculine or a man feminine because, although distinct spheres of male and female production existed, a wide range of tasks was acceptable for both sexes. Because there was no need to maintain gender inequalities, notions of power and prestige did not circumscribe the roles. Without strict gender definitions, it was then possible for some Native American women to take up the male role permanently without threatening the gender system.

Another factor in creating the possibility of the cross-gender role for women was the nature of the kinship system. Kinship was not based on hierarchical relations between men and women; it was organized in the interest of both sexes. Each sex had something to gain by forming kin ties through marriage,[30] because of the mutual assistance and economic security marital relations provided.[31] Marriage also created an alliance between two families, thereby broadening the network of kin on whom an individual could rely.

Thus, marriage promoted security in a subsistence-level economy.

The marriage customs of these tribes reflected the egalitarian nature of their kinship system. Since status and property were unimportant, marriage arrangements did not involve any transfer of wealth or rank through the female. The small marriage gifts that were exchanged served as tokens of the woman's worth in the marriage relationship.[32] Furthermore, because of the unimportance of property or rank, individuals often had a series of marriages, rather than one permanent relationship; divorce was relatively easy and frequent for both women and men.[33] Marriages in these tribes became more permanent only when couples had children. Women were not forced to remain in a marriage, and either partner had the right to dissolve an unhappy or unproductive relationship.

This egalitarian kinship system had important ramifications for the cross-gender female. A daughter's marriage was not essential for maintenance of family rank; that is, a woman's family did not lose wealth if she abandoned her role as daughter. As a social male, she had marriage rights through which she could establish a household and contribute to the subsistence of the group. Additionally, because of the frequency of divorce, it was possible for a married cross-gender female to raise children. Evidence of cross-gender females caring for their wives' offspring is available only for the Mohave hwame. Women in other tribes, however, could also have brought children into a cross-gender marriage, since at least younger offspring typically went with the mother in a divorce.[34] A cross-gender woman might acquire children through marriage to a pregnant woman, or possibly through her wife's extramarital relationships with men. Cross-gender couples probably also adopted children, a practice common among heterosexual couples in many tribes.

Details from the Mohave help to illuminate the cross-gender parent/child relationship. The Mohave believed that the paternity of an unborn child changed if the pregnant woman had sex with another partner; thus, the cross-gender female claimed any child her wife might be carrying when they married. George Devereux states that such children retained the clan affiliation of the previous father.[35] But the clan structure of the Mohave was not strongly organized and possessed no formal authority or ceremonial functions.[36] The significant relationships were those developed through residence with kin. Thus, children raised in a cross-gender household established strong ties with those parents. The investment of parental care was reciprocated when these children became adults. In this way the cross-gender female remained a part of the network of kin through marriage.

SEXUAL RELATIONS IN THE CROSS-GENDER ROLE

Sexual behavior was part of the relationship between cross-gender females and the women they married. Although the cross-gender female was a social male, Native Americans did not consider her sexual activity an imitation of heterosexual behavior. Her sexual behavior was recognized as lesbian—that is, as female homosexuality. The Mohave were aware of a range of sexual activities between the cross-gender female and her partner—activities that were possible only between two physiological females. Devereux recorded a Mohave term that referred specifically to the lesbian love-making of the hwame and her partner.[37] The Native American acceptance of lesbian behavior among cross-gender females did not depend on the presence of a male role-playing person; their acceptance derived instead from their concept of sexuality.

Native American beliefs about sexuality are reflected in the marriage system. Theorists such as Gayle Rubin have implicated marriage as one of the mechanisms that enforce and define women's sexuality. According to Rubin, the division of labor "can ... be seen as a taboo against sexual arrrangements other than those containing at least one man and one woman, thereby enjoining heterosexual marriage."[38] Yet in certain Native American tribes other sexual behavior, both heterosexual and homosexual, was available and permissible within and outside of marriage. Homosexual behavior occurred in contexts within which neither individual was cross-gender, nor were such individuals seen as expressing cross-gender behavior.[39] Premarital and extramarital sexual relations were also permissible.[40] Furthermore, through the cross-gender role, women could marry one another. Sexuality clearly was not restricted by the institution of marriage.

Native American ideology disassociated sexual behavior from concepts of male and female gender roles and was not concerned with the identity of the sexual partner. The status of the cross-gender female's partner is telling in this respect. She was always a tradi-tional female; that is, two cross-gender females did not marry. Thus, a woman could follow the traditional fe-male gender role, yet marry and make love with an-other woman without being stigmatized by such be-havior. Even though she was the partner of a cross-gender female, she was not considered homosexual or cross-gender. If the relationship ended in divorce, het-erosexual marriage was still an option for the ex-wife. The traditional female gender role did not restrict her choice of marital/sexual partners. Consequently, in-dividuals possessed a gender identity, but not a cor-responding sexual identity, and thus were allowed sev-eral sexual options. Sexuality itself was not embedded in Native American gender ideology.

WOMEN ON THE PLAINS

The conditions that supported the development and continuation of the cross-gender role among certain western tribes were not replicated among the Plains tribes. Evidence of cross-gender females there is scant while reports of male berdache are numerous. White-head suggests that the absence of cross-gender females resulted from the weakness of the cross-gender insti-tution for women.[41] A more plausible explanation in-volves the particular historical conditions that differ-entiate the Plains tribes from the western tribes. Yet it is precisely these conditions that make accurate inter-pretation of women's roles and the female cross-gen-der role much more difficult for the Plains tribes.

The Plains Indian culture of nomadic buffalo hunt-ing and frequent warfare did not develop until the late eighteenth and early nineteenth centuries as tribes moved west in response to the expansion and devel-opment of colonial America. The new mode of life represented for many tribes a tremendous shift from an originally settled and horticultural or hunting and gathering life-style. With the introduction of the horse and gun, the growth of the fur trade, and pressure from westward-moving white settlers, tribes from the east and north were displaced onto the Plains in the late 1700s.[42] As the importance of hide trade with Euro-Americans increased in the early 1800s, it altered the mode of production among Plains tribes. Increased wealth and authority were accessible through trade and warfare. Individual males were able to achieve greater dominance while women's social and eco-

nomic autonomy declined.[43] With the growing impor-tance of hides for trade, men who were successful hunters required additional wives to handle the tan-ning. Women's increasing loss of control in this pro-ductive sphere downgraded their status and tied them to marital demands. Recent work on the Plains tribes, however, indicates that this process was not consis-tent; women maintained a degree of autonomy and power not previously acknowledged.[44]

Early ethnographic descriptions of Plains Indian women were based on a Western gender ideology that was contradicted by actual female behavior. Although traditional Plains culture valued quiet, productive, nonpromiscuous women, this was only one side of the coin. There was actually a variability in female roles that can only be attributed to women's continued au-tonomy. Beatrice Medicine provides an excellent dis-cussion of the various roles open to women among the Blackfoot and Lakota. Such roles included the "manly-hearted woman," the "crazy woman" (who was sexually promiscuous), the Sun Dance woman, and the chief woman or favorite wife.[45] According to Ruth Landes, Lakota women served in tribal govern-ment and were sometimes appointed marshals to han-dle problems among women. Most Plains tribes had women warriors who accompanied war parties for limited purposes on certain occasions, such as aveng-ing the death of kin, and who received warrior honors for their deeds.[46] As Medicine states, "These varied role categories . . . suggest that the idealized behavior of women was not as rigidly defined and followed as has been supposed."[47]

The presence of a variety of socially approved roles also suggests that these were normative patterns of be-havior for women that need not be construed as "con-trary" to their gender role. Warrior women were not a counterpart of the male berdache, nor were they con-sidered cross-gender.[48] Ethnographers' attributions of masculinity to such behavior seem to be a product of Western beliefs about the rigid dichotomization of gender roles and the nature of suitable pursuits for women. That men simply accepted females as war-riors and were not threatened by such behavior con-tradicts the notion that such women were even tem-porarily assuming the male role.[49] The men's acceptance was based on recognition of the women warriors' capabilities as women.

There were individual Plains women in the nine-teenth century whose behavior throughout their lives exemplified a cross-gender role. They did not always cross-dress, but, like Woman Chief of the Crow, neither did they participate in female activities. They took wives to handle their households and were highly successful in hunting and raiding activities. They were also considered very powerful. Of these women, the Kutenai cross-gender woman always dressed in male attire and was renowned for her exploits as warrior and mediator and guide for white traders. Running Eagle of the Blackfoot lived as a warrior and married a young widow. Woman Chief became the head of her father's lodge when he died and achieved the third highest rank among the Crow. She took four wives.[50] Particularly since no records of earlier cross-gender women have been found, these few examples seem to constitute individual exceptions. What then was the status of the female cross-gender role among Plains tribes?

Part of the difficulty with answering this question stems from the nature of the data itself. Nineteenth-century observers rarely recorded information on Plains Indian women, "considering them too insignificant to merit special treatment."[51] These observers knew few women and only the more successful males. "Those who did become known were women who had acted as go-betweens for the whites and Indians,"[52] such as the Kutenai cross-gender female. Running Eagle and Woman Chief were also exceptional enough to be noticed by white traders. Except for the Kutenai woman, none of the women are identified as berdache in nineteenth-century reports, although all were cross-gender. Observers seem to have been unable to recognize the female cross-gender role. Indeed, no nineteenth-century reports mention cross-gender females among even the western tribes, although later ethnographers found ample evidence of the role.

Ethnographers had no solid evidence of the female cross-gender role among Plains Indians. Several factors may help to explain this discrepancy. White contact with Plains tribes came earlier than with the western tribes and was more disruptive. The last cross-gender females seem to have disappeared among Plains tribes by the mid-nineteenth century, while in the Southwest this did not occur until the end of the century, much closer to the time when ethnographers began to collect data. Discrepancies also arise in informants' stories. The Kutenai denied the existence of cross-gender females among them, in contradiction with earlier evidence, and yet willingly claimed that

such women lived among the Flathead and Blackfoot.[53] The Arapaho told Alfred Kroeber that the Lakota had female berdache, but there is no corroborating evidence from the Lakota themselves.[54] Informants were clearly reticent or unwilling to discuss cross-gender women. In her article on Native American lesbians, Paula Gunn Allen suggests that such information was suppressed by the elders of the tribes.[55] Most information on Plains Indian women was transmitted from elder tribesmen to white male ethnographers. But men were excluded from knowledge of much of women's behavior;[56] in this way much of the data on cross-gender females may have been lost.

The record of Plains cross-gender females remains limited. Certain social conditions may have contributed to the small number of women who assumed the role in the nineteenth century. During the 1800s the practice of taking additional wives increased with the men's need for female labor. This phenomenon may have limited women's choice of occupation. The pressures to marry may have barred women from a role that required success in male tasks only. The practice of sororal polygyny particularly would have put subtle pressures on families to assure that each daughter learned the traditional female role. Indeed, there were said to be no unmarried women among the Lakota.[57] Furthermore, given the constant state of warfare and loss of able-bodied men, the tribes were under pressure merely to survive. Such conditions in the 1800s discouraged women from abandoning their reproductive abilities through the cross-gender role. In fact, among the Lakota, women who insisted on leading men's lives were ostracized from the group and forced to wander by themselves.[58] Knowledge of the female

DEAR ABBY: We have two baby girls. One is 3 and the other is 2. My wife is pregnant and will have the baby in January. We are now thinking that if we should get another girl baby, we should get a sex-change operation for her that is now possible.

How much would it cost?—**No more girls in British Columbia** cross-gender role may have persisted, but those few who actually lived out the role were exceptions in a changing environment.

THE DEMISE OF THE CROSS-GENDER ROLE

By the late nineteenth century the female cross-gender role had all but disappeared among Native Americans. Its final demise was related to a change in the construction of sexuality and gender in these tribes. The dominant ideology of Western culture, with its belief in the inferior nature of the female role and its insistence on heterosexuality, began to replace traditional Native American gender systems.

Ideological pressures of white culture encouraged Native American peoples to reject the validity of the cross-gender role and to invoke notions of "proper" sexuality that supported men's possession of sexual rights to women. Communities expressed disapproval by berating the cross-gender female for not being a "real man" and not being properly equipped to satisfy her wife sexually. In effect, variations in sexual behavior that had previously been acceptable were now repudiated in favor of heterosexual practices. Furthermore, the identity of the sexual partner became an important aspect of sexual behavior.

The life of the last cross-gender female among the Mohave, Sahaykwisa, provides a clear example of this process. According to Devereux, "Sahaykwisa . . . was born toward the middle of the last century and killed . . . at the age of 45. Sahaykwisa had at a certain time a very pretty wife. Other men desired the woman and tried to lure her away from the *hwame*." The men teased Sahaykwisa in a derogatory manner, suggesting that her love-making was unsatisfactory to her wife in comparison to that of a "real man." They ridiculed her wife and said, "Why do you want a transvestite for your husband who has no penis and pokes you with the finger?"[59] Such derision went beyond usual joking behavior until finally Sahaykwisa was raped by a man who was angered because his wife left him for Sahaykwisa. The community no longer validated the cross-gender role, and Sahaykwisa herself eventually abandoned it, only to be killed later as a witch. By accusing the cross-gender female of sexual inadequacy, men of the tribe claimed in effect that they had sole rights to women's sexuality, and that sexuality was appropriate only between men and women.

CONCLUSION

In attempting to fit the Native American cross-gender role into Western categories, anthropologists have disregarded the ways in which the institution represents native categories of behavior. Western interpretations dichotomize the two sexes' gender roles because of erroneous assumptions about, first, the connection between biology and gender and, second, the nature of gender roles. Callender and Kochems state, "The transformation of a berdache was not a complete shift from his or her *biological* gender to the opposite one, but rather an approximation of the latter in some of its social aspects."[60] They imply that anatomy circumscribed the berdache's ability to function in the gender role of the other sex. Whitehead finds the anatomical factor particularly telling for women, who were supposedly unable to succeed in the male role unless deficient physically as females.[61] These theorists, by claiming a mixed gender status for the berdache, confuse a social role with a physical identity that remained unchanged for the cross-gender individual.

Knowing the true sex of the berdache, Native Americans accepted them on the basis of their social attributes; physiological sex was not relevant to the gender role. The Mohave, for example, did not focus on the biological sex of the berdache. Nonberdache were said to "feel toward their possible transvestite mate as they would feel toward a true woman, [or] man."[62] In response to a newly initiated berdache, the Yuma "began to feel toward him as to a woman."[63] These tribes concurred in the social fiction of the cross-gender role despite the obvious physical differences, indicating the unimportance of biological sex to the gender role.[64]

Assumptions regarding the hierarchical nature of Native American gender relations have created serious problems in the analysis of the female cross-gender role. Whitehead claims that few females could have been cross-gender because she assumes the asymmetrical nature of gender relations.[65] In cultures with an egalitarian mode of production, however, gender does not create an imbalance between the sexes. In the western North American tribes discussed above, neither gender role nor sexuality was associated with an ideology of male dominance. Women were not barred from the cross-gender role by rigid gender definitions; instead, they filled the role successfully. Although cross-gender roles are not limited to egalitarian societies, the historical conditions of nonegalitarian societies, in which increasing restrictions are placed on women's productive and reproductive activities, strongly discourage them from taking on the cross-gender role.

Anthropologists' classification of gender roles as dichotomous has served to obscure the nature of the Native American cross-gender role. For Whitehead, the male berdache is "less than a full man" but "more than a mere woman,"[66] suggesting a mixed gender role combining elements of both the male and the female. Similarly, Callender and Kochems suggest that the berdache formed an intermediate gender status.[67] Native conceptualizations of gender, particularly in the egalitarian tribes, do not contain an invariable opposition of two roles. The Western ideology of feminine and masculine traits actually has little in common with these Native American gender systems, within which exist large areas of overlapping tasks.

The idea of a mixed gender role is particularly geared to the male berdache and assumes the existence of a limited traditional female role. Such a concept does not account for the wide range of behaviors possible for both the male and female gender roles. By contrast, the term "cross-gender" defines the role as a set of behaviors typifying the attributes of the other sex, but not limited to an exact duplication of either role. Attributes of the male berdache that are not typical of the female role—for example, certain ritual activities—do not indicate a mixed gender category. These activities are specialized tasks that arise from the spiritual power of the cross-gender individual.

The term "cross-gender," however, is not without its problems. Sue-Ellen Jacobs suggests that a person who from birth or early childhood fills this variant role may not be "crossing" a gender boundary. She prefers the term "third gender" because, as among the Tewa, the berdache role may not fit either a male or female gender category but may be conceived instead as another gender.[68] Kay Martin and Barbara Voorheis also explore the possibility of more than two genders.[69] Certainly the last word has not been spoken about a role that has confounded researchers for at least one hundred years. But it is imperative to develop an analysis of variant gender roles based on the historical conditions that faced particular tribes, since gender systems vary in different cultures and change as modes of production change.

ACKNOWLEDGMENTS

I am particularly grateful to Naomi Katz, Mina Caulfield, and Carolyn Clark for their encouragement, support, and suggestions during the development of this article. I would also like to thank Gilbert Herdt, Paula Gunn Allen, Sue-Ellen Jacobs, Walter Williams, Luis Kemnitzer, and Ruby Rohrlich for their insightful comments on an earlier version.

NOTES

1. Sherry B. Ortner and Harriet Whitehead, eds., *Sexual Meanings: The Cultural Construction of Gender and Sexuality* (Cambridge: Cambridge University Press, 1981); Gayle Rubin, "The Traffic in Women: Notes on the 'Political Economy' of Sex," in *Toward an Anthropology of Women,* ed. Rayna R. Reiter (New York: Monthly Review Press, 1975), pp. 157–210.

2. Much feminist debate has focused on whether male dominance is universal, or whether societies with egalitarian relations exist. For a more comprehensive discussion of egalitarian societies, see Mina Davis Caulfield, "Equality, Sex and Mode of Production," in *Social Inequality: Comparative and Developmental Approaches,* ed. Gerald D. Berreman (New York: Academic Press, 1981), pp. 201–19; Mona Etienne and Eleanor Leacock, eds., *Women and Colonization: Anthropological Perspectives* (New York: J. F. Bergin, 1980); Eleanor Burke Leacock, *Myths of Male Dominance: Collected Articles on Women Cross-Culturally* (New York: Monthly Review Press, 1981); Karen Sacks, *Sisters and Wives: The Past and Future of Sexual Inequality* (Westport,

Conn.: Greenwood Press, 1979); Rayna R. Reiter, ed., *Toward an Anthropology of Women* (New York: Monthly Review Press, 1975); and Eleanor Burke Leacock and Nancy O. Lurie, eds., *North American Indians in Historical Perspective* (New York: Random House, 1971).

3. The term "berdache" is the more common term associated with the cross-gender role. It was originally applied by Europeans to Native American men who assumed the female role, and was derived from the Arabic *bardaj,* meaning a boy slave kept for sexual purposes. I prefer the term "cross-gender," first used by J. M. Carrier, particularly for the female role. See J. M. Carrier, "Homosexual Behavior in Cross-Cultural Perspective," in *Homosexual Behavior: A Modern Reappraisal,* ed. Judd Marmor (New York: Basic Books, 1980), pp. 100–122.

4. Alfred L. Kroeber, "Psychosis or Social Sanction," *Character and Personality* 8, no. 3 (1940); 204–15, quote on p. 209.

5. Harriet Whitehead, "The Bow and the Burden Strap: A New Look at Institutionalized Homosexuality in Native North America," in Ortner and Whitehead, eds. (n. 1 above), pp. 80–115, quote on p. 86.

6. Charles Callender and Lee M. Kochems, "The North American Berdache," *Current Anthropology* 24, no. 4 (1983): 443–56.

7. These tribes by area are as follows: Subarctic—Ingalik, Kaska; Northwest—Bella Coola, Haisla, Lillooet, Nootka, Okanagon, Queets, Quinault; California/Oregon—Achomawi, Atsugewi, Klamath, Shasta, Wintu, Wiyot, Yokuts, Yuki; Southwest—Apache, Cocopa, Maricopa, Mohave, Navajo, Papago, Pima, Yuma; Great Basin—Ute, Southern Ute, Shoshoni, Southern Paiute, Northern Paiute; Plains—Blackfoot, Crow, Kutenai.

8. See S. C. Simms, "Crow Indian Hermaphrodites," *American Anthropologist* 5, no. 3 (1903): 580–81; Alfred L. Kroeber, "The Arapaho," *American Museum of Natural History Bulletin* 18, no. 1 (1902): 1–150; Royal B. Hassrick, *The Sioux: Life and Customs of a Warrior Society* (Norman: University of Oklahoma Press, 1964); Ronald L. Olson, *The Quinault Indians* (Seattle: University of Washington Press, 1936); Ruth Murray Underhill, *Social Organization of the Papago Indians* (1939; reprint, New York: AMS Press, 1969).

9. George Devereux, "Institutionalized Homosexuality of the Mohave Indians," *Human Biology* 9, no. 4 (1937): 498–527.

10. Leslie Spier, *Yuman Tribes of the Gila River* (Chicago: University of Chicago Press, 1933).

11. Leslie Spier, *Klamath Ethnography,* University of California Publications in American Archaeology and Ethnology, vol. 30 (Berkeley: University of California Press, 1930).

12. E. W. Gifford, *The Cocopa,* University of California Publications in American Archaeology and Ethnology, vol. 31, no. 6 (Berkeley: University of California Press, 1933).

13. Devereux (n. 9 above), p. 503.

14. John J. Honigmann, *The Kaska Indians: An Ethnographic Reconstruction,* Yale University Publications in Anthropology, no. 51 (New Haven, Conn.: Yale University Press, 1954), p. 130.

15. Devereux (n. 9 above), pp. 508–9.

16. Gifford (n. 12 above).

17. Ibid., p. 294.

18. Honigmann (n. 14 above), p. 130.

19. Devereux (n. 9 above).

20. Spier, *Klamath Ethnography* (n. 11 above), p. 53.

21. Devereux (n. 9 above).

22. Ibid.; Gifford (n. 12 above); Honigmann (n. 14 above).

23. Whitehead (n. 5 above), pp. 92–93.

24. C. Daryll Forde, *Ethnography of the Yuma Indians,* University of California Publications in American Archaeology and Ethnology, vol. 28, no. 4 (Berkeley: University of California Press, 1931), p. 157; Gifford (n. 12 above), p. 294; Devereux (n. 9 above), p. 510.

25. Devereux (n. 9 above), p. 515.

26. Cornelius Osgood, *Ingalik Social Culture,* Yale University Publications in Anthropology, no. 53 (New Haven, Conn.: Yale University Press, 1958).

27. Based on ethnographic data in Honigmann (n. 14 above); Gifford (n. 12 above); Leslie Spier, *Cultural Relations of the Gila and Colorado River Tribes,* Yale University Publications in Anthropology, no. 3 (New Haven, Conn.: Yale University Press, 1936), *Klamath Ethnography* (n. 11 above), and *Yuman Tribes* (n. 10 above); Theodore Stern, *The Klamath Tribe* (Seattle: University of Washington Press, 1966); Alfred L. Kroeber, *Mohave Indians: Report on Aboriginal Territory and Occupancy of the Mohave Tribe,* ed. David Horr (New York: Garland Publishing, 1974), and *Handbook of the Indians of California,* Bureau of American Ethnology Bulletin no. 78 (Washington, D.C.: Government Printing Office, 1925); William H. Kelly, *Cocopa Ethnography,* Anthropological Papers of the University of Arizona, no. 29 (Tucson: University of Arizona Press, 1977); Lorraine M. Sherer, *The Clan System of the Fort Mohave Indians* (Los Angeles: Historical Society of Southern California, 1965).

28. Julie Cruikshank, *Athapaskan Women: Lives and Legends* (Ottawa: National Museums of Canada, 1979); Spier, *Klamath Ethnography* (n. 11 above).

29. Gifford (n. 12 above).

30. The five tribes discussed here varied in forms of kinship, but this variation did not have a significant effect on the relations between the sexes. Lacking rank or wealth, kinship groups were not the focus of power or authority, hence whether a tribe was matrilineal or patrilineal was not as important as the overall relationship with kin on either side.

31. John J. Honigmann, *Culture and Ethos of Kaska Society,* Yale University Publications in Anthropology, no. 40 (New Haven, Conn.: Yale University Press, 1949), and *Kaska Indians* (n. 14 above).

32. Spier, *Klamath Ethnography* (n. 11 above); J. A. Teit,

"Field Notes on the Tahltan and Kaska Indians: 1912–15," *Anthropologica* 3, no. 1 (1956): 39–171; Kroeber, *Handbook* (n. 27 above); Gifford (n. 12 above).

33. Kelly (n. 27 above); Spier, *Klamath Ethnography* (n. 11 above).

34. Kelly (n. 27 above).

35. Devereux (n. 9 above), p. 514.

36. Kelly (n. 27 above); Forde (n. 24 above).

37. Devereux (n. 9 above), pp. 514–15.

38. Rubin (n. 1 above), p. 178.

39. See Forde (n. 24 above), p. 157; Honigmann, *Kaska Indians* (n. 14 above), 127.

40. Spier, *Klamath Ethnography* (n. 11 above), and *Yuman Tribes* (n. 10 above); Kroeber, *Handbook* (n. 27 above).

41. Whitehead (n. 5 above), p. 86.

42. Gene Weltfish, "The Plains Indians: Their Continuity in History and Their Indian Identity," in Leacock and Lurie, eds. (n. 2 above).

43. Leacock and Lurie, eds. (n. 2 above); Alan Klein, "The Political Economy of Gender: A 19th-Century Plains Indian Case Study," in *The Hidden Half: Studies of Plains Indian Women,* ed. Patricia Albers and Beatrice Medicine (Washington, D.C.: University Press of America, 1983), pp. 143–73.

44. See Albers and Medicine, eds.

45. Beatrice Medicine, "'Warrior Women'—Sex Role Alternatives for Plains Indian Women," in Albers and Medicine, eds., pp. 267–80; see also Oscar Lewis, "Manly-Hearted Women among the North Piegan," *American Anthropologist* 43, no. 2 (1941): 173–87.

46. Ruth Landes, *The Mystic Lake Sioux* (Madison: University of Wisconsin Press, 1968).

47. Medicine, p. 272.

48. Sue-Ellen Jacobs, "The Berdache," in *Cultural Diversity and Homosexuality,* ed. Stephen Murray (New York: Irvington Press, in press); Medicine, p. 269.

49. On male acceptance of women warriors, see Landes.

50. Edwin Thompson Denig, *Of the Crow Nation,* ed. John C. Ewers, Smithsonian Institution, Bureau of American Ethnology, Bulletin no. 151, Anthropology Papers no. 33 (Washington, D.C.: Government Printing Office, 1953), and *Five Indian Tribes of the Upper Missouri,* ed. John C. Ewers (Norman: University of Oklahoma Press, 1961); Claude E. Schaeffer, "The Kutenai Female Berdache: Courier, Guide,

Prophetess, and Warrior," *Ethnohistory* 12, no. 3 (1965): 193–236.

51. Patricia Albers, "Introduction: New Perspectives on Plains Indian Women," in Albers and Medicine, eds. (n. 43 above), pp. 1–26, quote on p. 3.

52. Katherine Weist, "Beasts of Burden and Menial Slaves: Nineteenth Century Observations of Northern Plains Indian Women," in Albers and Medicine, eds. (n. 43 above), pp. 29–52, quote on p. 39.

53. Harry H. Turney-High, *Ethnography of the Kutenai,* Memoirs of the American Anthropological Association, no. 56 (1941; reprint, New York: Kraus Reprint, 1969), and *The Flathead Indians of Montana,* Memoirs of the American Anthropological Association, no. 48 (1937; reprint, New York: Kraus Reprint, 1969).

54. Kroeber, "The Arapaho" (n. 8 above), p. 19.

55. Paula Gunn Allen, "Beloved Women: Lesbians in American Indian Cultures," *Conditions: Seven* 3, no. 1 (1981): 67–87.

56. Alice Kehoe, "The Shackles of Tradition," in Albers and Medicine, eds. (n. 43 above), pp. 53–73.

57. Hassrick (n. 8 above).

58. Jeannette Mirsky, "The Dakota," in *Cooperation and Competition among Primitive Peoples,* ed. Margaret Mead (Boston: Beacon Press, 1961), p. 417.

59. Devereux (n. 9 above), p. 523.

60. Callender and Kochems (n. 6 above), p. 453 (italics mine).

61. Whitehead (n. 5 above), p. 92.

62. Devereux (n. 9 above), p. 501.

63. Forde (n. 24 above), p. 157.

64. Data on the Navajo *nadle* are not included in this article because the Navajo conception of the berdache was atypical. The *nadle* was considered a hermaphrodite by the Navajo—i.e., of both sexes physically—and therefore did not actually exemplify a cross-gender role. See W. W. Hill. "The Status of the Hermaphrodite and Transvestite in Navaho Culture." *American Anthropologist* 37, no. 2 (1935): 273–79.

65. Whitehead (n. 5 above), p. 86.

66. Ibid., p. 89.

67. Callender and Kochems (n. 6 above), p. 454.

68. Sue-Ellen Jacobs, personal communication, 1983, and "Comment on Callender and Kochems," *Current Anthropology* 24, no. 4 (1983): 459–60.

69. M. Kay Martin and Barbara Voorheis, *Female of the Species* (New York: Columbia University Press, 1975).

"The Status of Women" in Indigenous African Societies

NIARA SUDARKASA

INTRODUCTION

Long before the women's movement ushered in an era of renewed concern with the "status of women" in various societies and cultures, a number of writers had addressed the question of the "status of women" in various African societies.[1] Some writers characterized women in African societies as "jural minors" for most of their lives, falling under the guardianship first of their fathers and then of their husbands. Other writers stressed the independence of African women, noting their control over their own lives and resources.

From my own readings on Africa and my research among the Yoruba in Nigeria and other parts of West Africa, it appears that except for the highly Islamized societies in Sub-Saharan Africa, in this part of the world more than any other, in precolonial times women were conspicuous in "high places." They were queen-mothers; queen-sisters; princesses, chiefs, and holders of other offices in towns and villages; occasional warriors; and, in one well-known case, that of the Lovedu, the supreme monarch. Furthermore, it was almost invariably the case that African women were conspicuous in the economic life of their societies, being involved in farming, trade, or craft production.

The purviews of female and male in African societies were often described as separate and complementary.[2] Yet, whenever most writers compared "the lot" of women and men in Africa, they ascribed to men a "better" situation, a "higher" status. Women were depicted as "saddled" with home and domesticity; men were portrayed as enjoying the exhilaration of life in the "outside" world. For me, the pieces of the portrait

Reprinted from *Feminist Studies* 12, no. 1 (Spring 1986): 91–103, by permission of the publisher, Feminist Studies, Inc., c/o Women's Studies Program, University of Maryland, College Park, MD 20742. Some notes have been renumbered.

did not ring true, Not only was there an obvious distortion of the ethnographic reality—women were "outside the home" as well as in it—but there was also something inappropriate about the notion that women and men were everywhere related to each other in a hierarchical fashion, as was implied in the most common usage of the concept of "status of women."

The "status" of women is often used simultaneously in the two conceptual meanings that it has in social science. On the one hand, the term is used in Ralph Linton's sense to mean "the collection of rights and duties" that attach to particular positions. According to this usage, "status," which refers to a particular position itself, contrasts with "role," which refers to the behavior appropriate to a given status.[3] On the other hand, the concept of the "status of women" is also used to refer to the placement of females relative to males in a two-leveled hierarchy. In this sense, the term "status" connotes stratification and invites comparison with other systems of stratification. It was this notion of sexual stratification that seemed inappropriate for describing the relationship of female and male in most of the African societies I had studied.

Martin K. Whyte concludes his cross-cultural survey of *The Status of Women in Preindustrial Societies* with a similar observation. After discussing the status of women in the hierarchical sense used above, Whyte's first major finding is that there is a general absence of covariation among the different indicators of status in this hierarchical usage. He notes that one cannot assume "that a favorable position for women in any particular area of social life will be related to favorable positions in other areas." Similarly, there is no "best indicator" or "key variable" that will yield an overall assessment of the status of women relative to men.[4]

More to the point of the present argument is Whyte's observation that this lack of covariation in the indicators of the status of women signals a difference between this area and other areas where stratification is a known feature of the social structure. "This lack of association between different measures of the role and status of women relative to men still constitutes something of a puzzle. . . . In the study of stratification we ordinarily expect indicators of status at the individual level to be positively, although not perfectly, associated with one another." Drawing on Simone de Beauvoir's distinction between the position of women and that of oppressed national or racial groups, Whyte concludes that "powerful factors" in all preindustrial societies lead to the perception by females and males that women's statuses differ from those of men but in a manner that does not imply the hierarchical relationship characteristic of those linking occupational and ethnic groups. Going further, Whyte states that "the lack of association between different aspects of the role and status of women relative to men is due largely to the fact that women as a group [in preindustrial societies] are fundamentally different from status groups and classes."[5]

This observation by Whyte seems to make sense of the data from most African societies. Although his cross-cultural study dispels a number of treasured notions about "*the* status of women," it points to a critical research problem that should be pursued, namely, the problem of determining the conditions under which women's relationship to men *does* take on the characteristics of a hierarchical relationship. I should hasten to point out that conceptually this is a *different* problem from that which seeks to ascertain when an "egalitarian" relationship between the sexes gives way to a subordinate/superordinate relationship. The very concept of an "egalitarian" relationship between women and men implies that the "female" and "male" are unitary categories that are "measured" or "sized up" one against the other in the societies described. In this article, I will attempt to show that there are societies for which such a conceptualization does not accurately reflect the social and ideological reality of the peoples concerned. The data gathered from some African societies suggest a reason for this. As I will attempt to demonstrate, "female" and "male" are not so much statuses, in Linton's sense, as they are clusters of statuses for which gender is only one of the defining characteristics. Women and men might be hierarchically related to each other in one or more of their reciprocal statuses, but not in others. Be-

cause contradiction as much as congruence characterized the status-clusters termed "female" and "male," many African societies did not or could not consistently stratify the categories one against the other, but, rather, codified the ambiguities.

The argument put forth in this article suggests that Engels and a number of his adherents may have missed the mark in arguing, if I may simplify, that private property and production for exchange served to lower the status of women. It also suggests that Karen Sacks's reformulation of Engels, which, in any case, rests on a controversial interpretation of the African data, also misses the mark by arguing that the critical or key variable in the subordination of women in class societies was their confinement to production within the "domestic sphere" and their exclusion from "social production for exchange."[6] I am suggesting here that various conditions, including, most probably, the development of private property and the market or exchange economy, *created conditions where female and male became increasingly defined as unitary statuses that were hierarchically related to one another.* Such conditions appear to have been absent in various precolonial African societies and possibly other parts of the world as well.[7]

In recent years, the postulation of separate nonhierarchically related (complementary) domains for women and men has been disputed by anthropologists who argued that women occupied the "domestic" domain and men the "public" domain and that, because power and authority were vested in the public domain, women had *de facto* lower status than men. It has always seemed to me that in many African societies a more appropriate conception—and by that I mean one that makes sense of more of the realities of those societies—was to recognize two domains, one occupied by men and another by women, both of which were internally ordered in a hierarchical fashion and both of which provided "personnel" for domestic and extradomestic (or public) activities. I have already argued elsewhere that there was considerable overlap between the "public" and "domestic" domains in preindustrial African societies.[8]

In the remainder of this article, I will examine the roles of women in families and descent groups, in the economy, and in the political process in West Africa. Potentially nonhierarchical models of relationships between female and male are indicated and contrasted with ones that are hierarchical. Data will be used from stateless societies (such as the Ibo and Tallensi) and from preindustrial state societies such as the Asante (Ashanti), Nupe, and Yoruba. The ideas presented here are tentative and subject to reformulation. Eventually I hope to subject this schema to the scrutiny of data from societies throughout the African continent and in other parts of the world as well.

Before turning to the data, let me make one other prefatory remark. There is no question that status, in the hierarchical sense, attaches to sex (or gender) in contemporary Africa. Ester Boserup is the best known exponent of the view that the forces of "modernization" and "development" have denied African women equal access to formal education and have undermined their contribution to the political and economic arenas of their countries.[9] Annie M. D. Lebeuf was one of the first writers to make this point and was the one who demonstrated it most conclusively for the political sphere;[10] other scholars have taken up and elaborated the same theme. The fact of the present day linkage between gender and stratification in West Africa and elsewhere on the continent, and the realization that most of the studies from which we have to take our data were carried out *after* the onset of the colonial period, should be borne in mind as the following discussion unfolds.[11]

WOMEN IN AFRICAN KIN GROUPS

In West Africa, as in most parts of the continent, the three basic kin groups to which females and males belong are (1) corporate unilineal descent groups, which we term lineages; (2) domiciled extended families made up of certain lineage members and their spouses and dependent children; and (3) conjugally based family units which are subdivisions of the extended family and within which procreation and primary responsibilities for socialization rest.[12] Within their lineages, African women have rights and responsibilities toward their kinsmen and kinswomen that are independent of males. As far as their responsibilities are concerned, female members of the lineage are expected to meet certain obligations in the same way that males are. For example, women offer material assistance to their sisters and brothers; they also "do their part" (that is, they make the appropriate financial or material outlay) at the time of important "rites of passage" such as naming ceremonies, marriages, and funerals.

Within patrilineages, women, as father's sisters, sisters, and daughters, generally do not hold formal leadership positions—although they do take part in most discussions of lineage affairs, and the more advanced in age they are, the more influence they wield. As mothers, sisters, and daughters within the matrilineages, some women hold leadership positions and exercise authority equivalent to that of men.[13]

In both patrilineages and matrilineages, interpersonal relations on a daily basis tend to be regulated by seniority as determined by order of birth rather than by gender. Hence, senior sisters outrank junior brothers. Where males prostrate before their elders, they do so for females as well as males. In the extended family, women occupy roles defined by consanguinity as well as conjugality. They are mothers and daughters as well as wives and cowives. The position of "wife" refers not only to the conjugal relationship to a husband, but also to the affinal (or in-law) relationship to all the members—female as well as male—in the husband's compound and lineage. (Among the Yoruba, for example, female members of a lineage refer to their brother's wives as their own "wives," a formulation which signals that certain reciprocal responsibilities and behavior are entailed in the relationship of the women to each other.)

If there is one thing that is conspicuous in discussions of "the status of women" in Africa (and elsewhere in the world), it is the tendency to assess that status only in relation to the conjugal role of wife or cowife. Interestingly, in Whyte's cross-cultural study of the status of women in ninety-three societies, of the twenty-seven indicators of status as related to gender and the family, twenty (74 percent) of the variables had to do specifically with behavior and/or rights within or related to the conjugal (marital) relationship. The focus on the conjugal roles of women to the near exclusion of analyses of their functioning in consanguineal roles derives, as I have tried to show elsewhere, from the obsession of Western scholars with analyses of the nuclear family and the operation of the principle of conjugality in determining kin relations. In other words, the emphasis derives from an attempt to analyze kinship in other societies from the viewpoint of and with paradigms appropriate to Western kin groups.[14] African *extended* families, which are the normal coresidential form of family in indigenous precolonial African societies, are *built around* consanguineal relationships; failure to recognize this has led to misrepresentation of many aspects of African kinship. One consequence of the focus on conjugal families and the concern with breaking down polygynous families into "constituent nuclear families" is the distortion of an understanding of the roles of women as wives, co-wives, and mothers.[15]

Women as *wives* generally exhibit overt signals of deference to their husbands in patrilineal African societies. In matrilineal societies, the patterns may not be as pronounced, but wives still defer to their husbands. In other kinship roles, especially those of mother and senior consanguineal kinswoman, women are the recipients of deference and the wielders of power and authority.

Western students of African societies have not only focused unduly on the husband–wife relationship in describing African kinship, they have also sought to define that conjugal relationship in terms of parameters found in Western societies. This has led to a misrepresentation of the essence and implications of what is generally called "woman-to-woman" marriage. This complex institution cannot be described at length here, but I would make the following observations: First, the institution of "woman marriage" signifies most of all that gender is not the sole basis for recruitment to the "husband" role in Africa; hence, the authority that attaches to that role is not gender-specific. Second, the institution must be understood in the context of the meaning of the concepts of husband and wife in African societies, not in Western societies. Third, in African societies, the term "wife" has two basic referents: female married to a given male (or female) and female married into a given compound or lineage. Thus, for example, among the Yoruba, a husband refers to his spouse as "wife"; a woman refers to her cowife as "wife" or "mate," and, as noted earlier, female as well as male members of the lineage refer to the in-marrying spouses as their "wives." The term "husband" refers specifically to a woman's spouse but also generally to the males (and females) in her husband's lineage. Again, among the Yoruba, a woman refers to her own spouse, and in certain contexts to his lineage members, including her own children, as "husband."

Given these usages, it is important to recognize that the terms "husband" and "wife" connote certain clusters of affinal relations, and in "woman marriage," the principles concerned emphasize certain *jural* relations. (They do not, as all writers point out, imply a

sexual component to the relationship as in heterosexual conjugal unions.)

If the concept of conjugal relations in Africa were not circumscribed to those common in the West, it would be appreciated that the unifying factor in the various "types" of woman-to-woman marriage is that everywhere it serves a procreative function, either on behalf of the female husband herself, or on behalf of her male spouse or male kinsmen. Because marriage is the institution and the idiom through which procreation is legitimated in Africa, it must be entered into by women (as by men) who want to acquire rights over a woman's childbearing capacity.[16] The existence of woman-to-woman marriage in Africa is consistent with a general deemphasis on gender and an emphasis on seniority and personal "standing" (usually but not always determined by wealth) in recruitment to positions of authority.

This brief discussion of African families and kin groups is intended to suggest that male gender predictably calls forth deferential behavior only within the conjugal relationship. The case of woman-to-woman marriage demonstrates, however, that male gender does not exclusively determine entry into the husband role, which is the more authoritative of the two conjugal roles. But even though patterns of deference emphasize subordination of the wife's role, the decision-making process and the control over resources within the conjugal relationship in many West African societies, including those of the Yoruba, Ibo, Ashanti, and Nupe, indicate parallel and complementary control by husbands and wives. In the consanguineal aspects of African kinship, as I have indicated, seniority and personal attributes (especially accumulated resources) rather than gender serve as the primary basis of status in the hierarchical sense.

WOMEN IN THE POLITICAL PROCESS IN INDIGENOUS AFRICAN SOCIETIES

Any investigation of women in the political process in precolonial Africa should begin with the excellent article by Annie Lebeuf in Denise Paulme's *Women of Tropical Africa*.[17] Here I only want to highlight certain facts that might aid in addressing the question of whether the relationship of females and males within the political domain is most appropriately conceptualized as a hierarchical one.

Africa is noted for the presence of women in very high positions in the formal governmental structure.[18] Africa is also noted for having parallel chieftaincies, one line made up of males, the other of females. One way of interpreting these facts has been to dismiss the female chieftaincies as simply women controlling women (and after all, if women are subordinate anyway, of what significance is it that they have chieftaincies or sodalities among themselves?). The presence of women at the highest levels of indigenous government has been similarly dismissed as an instance of women distinguishing themselves individually by entering the "public world of men."[19] I would suggest that a formulation that makes an *a priori judgment* that any participation of women in the public sphere represents entry into the world of men simply begs the question. For in West Africa, the "public domain" was not conceptualized as "the world of men." Rather, the public domain was one in which both sexes were recognized as having important roles to play.[20]

Indeed, the positing of distinct public and domestic domains does not hold true for precolonial West Africa. The distinction is also not very useful for looking at the rest of the continent. As many writers on African political structure have shown, even in states in which monarchs were elevated to statuses "removed from their kin groups," the lineage and the compound remained important aspects of political organization in all localities where they existed.[21] Compounds were generally the courts of the first instance and the bases for mobilizing people for public works and public service; lineages were the units through which land was allocated and were the repositories of titles to offices in many African societies. Women held formal leadership roles in matrilineages and were influential in decision-making patrilineages. Their participation in the affairs of their affinal compounds (within which women in patrilineal societies lived most of their adult lives) was channeled through an organizational structure in which the women were most often ranked according to order of marriage into the group.

To answer the question of whether women's participation in the political process should be conceptualized as subordinate to that of men, I would propose that we look at the type of political decisions and activities in which they were involved and ask from what types they were excluded. Throughout most of West Africa, women controlled their own worlds. For example, they had trade and craft guilds, and they spoke on matters of taxation and maintenance of public facilities (such as markets, roads, wells, and streams). They also testified on their own behalf in any court or hearing. Thus, in internal political affairs, women were generally consulted and had channels through which they were represented. External affairs were largely in the hands of men, but in any crisis, such as war, women were always involved: they served minimally as suppliers of rations for troops but in some instances acted as leaders of armies and as financiers of campaigns.[22]

The question then arises, from what political processes were they excluded? They could not participate in the male secret societies that were important in the political process in some Western African states. They were also excluded from certain councils of chiefs, although this was rare. Much more common was representation on the councils by one or more of the women who headed the hierarchy of women chiefs. In all cases, however, it seems that women were consulted on most governmental affairs. Their participation through their spokespersons paralleled the participation of males through theirs. And of course in cases in which the chief rulers were female and male (for example, the queen-mother and monarch-son), the complementarity of the relationship between the sexes was symbolized and codified in the highest offices of the land.

THE INVOLVEMENT OF WOMEN IN PRODUCTION AND DISTRIBUTION IN AFRICAN SOCIETIES

It is well known that African women were farmers, traders, and crafts producers in different parts of the continent. It is equally well documented that their economic roles were at once "public" and "private." Women worked in order to meet the responsibilities placed upon them in their roles as mothers, wives, sisters, daughters, members of guilds, chiefs, or citizens.[23] In the economic sphere more than in any other it is easy to show that women's activities were complementary to those of men and that women producers and traders were not subordinate to men. In most African societies, as elsewhere, the division of labor along sexual lines promoted a reciprocity of effort. If men were farmers, women were food processors and traders. Where women and men were engaged in the same productive activity (such as farming or weaving), they produced different items. Among the Ibo, females and males grew different crops; among the Yoruba, the female and male weavers produced different types of cloth on different types of looms. Where both females and males traded, there was usually a sexual bifurcation along commodity lines. Normally, too, men predominated in long-distance trade, and women were predominant in local markets. I have never heard of an indigenous African society in which differential value was attached to the labor of women and men working at the same tasks or in which women and men were differentially rewarded for the products of their labor.

In the management and disposal of their incomes, the activities of African women and men were also separate but coordinated. Within the conjugal family unit, women and men had different responsibilities which were met from the proceeds of their separate economic pursuits. A husband might be primarily responsible for the construction and upkeep of the home and the provision of staple foods, and the wife (or more probably the wives) assumed responsibility for nonstaple foods and the daily needs of her/their children.

> The separate management of "the family purse" definitely appeared to be a response to a situation in which the members of conjugal units had independent obligations to persons outside these groups. However, it was also a way of minimizing the risks involved in the expenditure [of resources] by disbursing [them] among potentially beneficial investment options, as perceived from the vantage point of the different persons concerned.[24]

CONCLUSION

In this article, I have tried to show that a "neutral" complementarity, rather than a superordination/subordination, more accurately describes the relationship between certain female and male roles in various precolonial African societies. In the process, I have argued that the preconceived notion of a unitary status for female and male, respectively, is probably what led many students of African societies to paint such misleading pictures of *the* status of African women.

The data presented in this brief discussion are only an indication of those that must be considered in any serious research into the issues raised here. I have always been intrigued by what appear to be linguistic clues to the "neutrality" of gender in many African societies. The absence of gender in the pronouns of many African languages and the interchangeability of first names among females and males strike me as possibly related to a societal deemphasis on gender as a designation for behavior. Many other areas of traditional culture, including personal dress and adornment, religious ceremonials, and intragender patterns of comportment, suggest that Africans often deemphasize gender in relation to seniority and other insignia of status.

Only brief mention can be made of the fact that in contemporary Africa, the relationship between women and men has moved decidedly in the direction of a hierarchical one. In understanding the change in the nature of these relationships from the precolonial, preindustrial context to the present, it is important that we not presume the movement from an egalitarian relationship to a nonegalitarian one. Rather, it has been suggested that the domains of women and men in many indigenous African societies should not be conceptualized in terms of ranking all (which is implied in the concept of egalitarianism because each concept entails its opposite). It is suggested that the changes that occurred with the onset of colonialism (and capitalism, its economic correlate) were ones that created hierarchical relations between the sexes. It is therefore appropriate in the modern context to investigate causes and characteristics of "the status of *women*" in Africa.

NOTES

1. M. Perlman and M. P. Moal, in *Women of Tropical Africa*, ed. Denise Paulme, trans. H. M. Wright (Berkeley: University of California Press, 1963), 231–93.

2. Paulme, ed., *Women of Tropical Africa*, Introduction, 1–16.

3. Ralph Linton, *The Study of Man* (New York: Appleton-Century, 1936), 113–31.

4. Martin K. Whyte, *The Status of Women in Preindustrial Societies* (Princeton, N.J.: Princeton University Press, 1978), 170.

5. Ibid., 176, 179–80.

6. Karen Sacks, "Engels Revisted: Women, the Organization of Production, and Private Property," in *Woman, Culture, and Society,* ed. Michelle Z. Rosaldo and Louise Lamphere (Stanford: Stanford University Press, 1974), 207–22.

7. Here the term "precolonial" refers to the period before the mid- and late-nineteenth century from which European colonization is conventionally dated. Some information concerning African social life in precolonial times is gleaned from contemporaneous written sources, but most information comes from anthropological constructions of "traditional life," using oral history and ethnographic techniques. Due allowance must be made for possible distortions in these ethnographies, but, for the most part, they are all we have to rely on for descriptions of Africa's socio-cultural past.

8. Gloria Marshall [Niara Sudarkasa], "In a World of Women: Field Work in a Yoruba Community," in *Women in the Field,* ed. Peggy Golde (Chicago: Aldine, 1970); Niara Sudarkasa, *Where Women Work: A Study of Yoruba Women in the Market Place and in the Home* (Ann Arbor: Museum of Anthropology, University of Michigan, 1973); Niara Sudarkasa, "Female Employment and Family Organization in West Africa," in *The Black Woman Cross-Culturally,* ed. Filomena C. Steady (Cambridge, Mass.: Schenkman, 1981), 49–64.

9. Ester Boserup, *Women's Role in Economic Development* (London: Allen & Unwin, 1970).

10. Annie M. D. Lebeuf, "The Role of Women in the Political Organization of African Societies," in *Women of Tropical Africa.*

11. Margorie Mbilinyi, "The 'New Woman' and Traditional Norms in Tanzania," *Journal of Modern African Studies* 10 (January 1972): 57–72; Judith Van Allen, "Women in Africa: Modernization Means More Dependency," *Center Magazine* 7 (March 1974): 60–67; Audrey Smock, "The Impact of Modernization on Women's Position in the Family in Ghana," in *Sexual Stratification: A Cross-Cultural View,* ed. Alice Schlegel (New York: Columbia University Press, 1977), 192–214; Niara Sudarkasa, "The Effects of Twentieth-Century Social Change, Especially of Migration, on Women of West Africa," in *Proceedings of the West Africa Conference,* ed. Patricia Paylore and Richard Haney (Tucson: Office of Arid Lands Studies, University of Arizona, 1976), 102–10; Niara Sudarkasa, "Sex Roles, Education, and Development in Africa," *Anthropology and Education Quarterly* 13 (Fall 1982): 279–89.

12. Niara Sudarkasa, "African and Afro-American Family Organization," in *Anthropology for the Eighties: Introductory Readings,* ed. Johnetta B. Cole (New York: Free Press, 1982), 132–60.

13. Sudarkasa, "Female Employment and Family Organization in West Africa," 49–64. See these authors on Asante: K. A. Busia, *The Position of the Chief in the Modern Political System of the Ashanti* (London: Oxford University Press, 1951); Meyer Fortes and E. E. Evans-Pritchard, eds., *African Political Systems* (Oxford: Oxford University Press, 1980); R. S. Rattray, *Ashanti Law and Constitution* (Oxford: Clarendon Press, 1929).

14. Niara Sudarkasa, "An Exposition on the Value Premise Underlying Black Family Studies," *Journal of the National Medical Association* 67 (March 1975): 235–39; Niara Sudarkasa, "African and Afro-American Family Organization," in *Anthropology for the Eighties,* 132–60.

15. Sudarkasa, "An Exposition on the Value Premise Underlying Black Family Studies"; "Female Employment and Family Organization in West Africa"; and "African and Afro-American Family Organization."

16. Bamidele Agbasegbe, "Is There Marriage between Women in Africa?" in *Sociological Research Symposium V,* ed. J. S. Williams et al. (Richmond: Virginia Commonwealth University Department of Sociology, 1975); and Denise O'Brien, "Female Husbands in Southern Bantu Societies," in *Sexual Stratification: A Cross-Cultural View.*

17. See n. 10.

18. Ibid.

19. Michelle Z. Rosaldo, "Women, Culture, and Society: A Theoretical Overview," in *Woman, Culture, and Society.*

20. Sudarkasa, "Female Employment and Family Organization in West Africa."

21. See Fortes and Evans-Pritchard.

22. Paulme, *Women of Tropical Africa;* Sudarkasa, *Where Women Work;* Victor Uchendu, *The Igbo (Ibo) of Southeast Nigeria* (New York: Holt, Rinehart & Winston, 1965); Bolanle Awe, "The Iyalode in the Traditional Yoruba Political System," in *Sexual Stratification: A Cross-Cultural View.*

23. Sudarkasa, *Where Women Work;* "Female Employment and Family Organization in West Africa."

24. Sudarkasa, "Female Employment and Family Organization in West Africa," 60.

SECTION FOUR

Work and Family

If you were to be asked, "What are the most important things in your life?" chances are you would name your family and your work, though not necessarily in that order. These are the social institutions in which we spend the major part of our lives from day to day, month to month, and year to year. Both work and family are situated in a larger context, a context in which, as we have seen, gender stereotypes and inequalities abound. These stereotypes and inequalities have serious consequences for contemporary men and women as they struggle to create lives in which both work and family bring them satisfaction.

Although researchers in the past defined work and family as opposites—work having to do with the public sphere and family with the private sphere, work being the man's responsibility and the family the woman's—the actual experiences of women and men do not support such a naively dualistic conception. Work affects family life and family life affects work; the two are inseparable. In "The Work–Family Role System" Joseph H. Pleck identifies the components of this system as the female family role, the female work role, the male family role, and the male work role. He discusses how sex-segregated labor markets and asymmetrically permeable boundaries between work and family affect the various work–family roles. Arguing that family needs should have priority, Pleck proposes a new, less segregated work–family role system.

The way the work–family role system differen-

tially impinges on men and women is examined in Kathleen Gerson's "Briefcase, Baby, or Both?" In interviews with women who look forward to motherhood and with others who are apprehensive about it, she explores the frequent failure of childhood expectations to mesh with career aspirations. The demands of the workplace still conflict with those of the home, and Gerson concludes that until social changes produce gender equality, women will continue to have hard choices to make in regard to careers and motherhood.

As we know, though, gender intersects with age, race, and ethnicity, and what works for a young two-career couple may be impossible for a differently structured family. Many Americans live in families or family-like groupings with different problems and solutions. Melba Sánchez-Ayéndez describes in "Puerto Rican Elderly Women: Shared Meanings and Informal Support Networks" the interplay between behavior and values in family and community. She explores how the Puerto Rican values of family interdependence and sex-segregated roles have shaped elderly women's behavior in family and community networks.

Gay men and lesbians also construct alternative family structures, and their relation to work tends to differ from that of heterosexual couples. John D'Emilio argues in "Capitalism and Gay Identity" that the chance for wage labor, with the possibility it offers of a life apart from the family, has permitted the rise of homosexuality as a social category, an urban subculture, and a political force. He summarizes the history and structure of capitalism and the changing meanings of homosexual identity, and argues for the importance of the "affectional community" as an alternative to the traditional family.

Women's historical relation to the world of work is described by Alice Kessler-Harris in "Women, Work, and the Social Order." The pattern of women's participation in the labor force is shaped by assumptions in respect to social roles in the labor market, by the changing economic needs of employers, and by sociocultural perceptions of women's roles, from the perspectives of both the family and the society. Beverly W. Jones sheds additional light on the historical pattern by considering race and class as well as gender in "Race, Sex, and Class: Black Female Tobacco Workers in Durham, North Carolina, 1920–1940, and the Development of Female Consciousness." Jones describes how black women were restricted to unhealthful working conditions because of their race and to the lowest-paying jobs because of their sex. These ex-

tremely negative conditions forged a class identity, and from it emerged a sisterhood of struggle, support, dignity, and resistance. Mary Margaret Fonow provides further insight into women's work lives in "Occupation/Steelworker: Sex/Female." Using interview data, she uncovers the problems encountered by women who work in a male-dominated occupation.

Lesbians face special problems in the workplace because of "heterosexual privilege" and the "heterosexual assumption." The assumption is that all men and all women are heterosexually paired, or desire to be so. This assumption has served to rationalize lower salaries for women than for men, because it has supported the further assumption that a woman will be financially supported by a man. In "Peril and Promise: Lesbians' Workplace Participation," Beth Schneider discusses specific problems of and pressures on lesbians at work and the strategies they use to integrate their social and work lives.

The Work–Family Role System

JOSEPH H. PLECK

The study of work and the study of the family have traditionally constituted separate subdisciplines in sociology. Rapoport and Rapoport (1965) and Kanter (1976), among others, have aptly stressed the need for greater examination of work and family roles in relation to each other. Such joint consideration is necessary to describe how individuals' functioning in either of these spheres is affected by their involvement in the other. Further, the current examination of sex roles bring added impetus to the analysis of work–family interrelationships. A major part of what is usually meant by change in "sex roles" is specifically change in the traditional allocation of work and family roles between men and women. Traditional sex role norms prescribed the specialization of work and family responsibilities by sex, but a new option for each sex to integrate roles in both work and the family is now emerging.

This paper analyzes some aspects of what I term the "work–family role system." The work–family role system is composed of the male work role, the female work role, the female family role, and the male family role. Each of these roles may be fully actualized, or may be only partly actualized or latent, as is often the case with the female work role and the male family role. The analysis of these four roles as a system provides a useful way of organizing research about the relations among these roles, and suggests new relations to be examined. It also makes possible some inferences about the dynamics of future changes in women's and men's roles in work and the family.

Analyzing men's and women's work and family roles as components of a role system involves specifying how each role articulates with the others to which it is linked, and how variations in the nature of

Reprinted from *Social Problems* 24, no. 4 (April 1977): 417–427, by permission. Copyright © 1977 by the Society for the Study of Social Problems.

each role, or whether the role is actualized at all, affects the others. For example, to describe the link between the female work and the female family roles, we consider how the extent of the female work role (ranging from no paid work at all to the most demanding and highest status full time work) both affects and is affected by the extent of the female family role. These links can be considered at two conceptual levels. They can be analyzed at the level of the individual couple, e.g., the relation between wives' employment status and wives' role performance in the family. Each link can also be considered at the aggregate or macrosocial level, e.g., the relation between married women's labor force participation rate and married women's level of household work and childcare (expressed, for example, in mean hours per day).

FEMALE WORK AND FAMILY ROLES

Let us start with the link between the female work and female family roles, and move clockwise around Figure 1. Research on the effects of married female employment on the family (see Hoffman & Nye, 1974; Howell, 1973a, 1973b) contains much information relevant to this link. The three major topics in this research have been the effects of wives' employment on children's psychological well-being, marital satisfaction and happiness, and marital power. The consensus today appears to be that when other variables are controlled, wives' employment has no clear positive or negative effect on children's well-being, and when freely chosen, has no negative effect on marital happiness and satisfaction. Most reviews (e.g., Bahr, 1974) conclude that wives' employment is associated with some increase in wives' marital power (primarily assessed by wives' reports of how the couple would make various hypothetical decisions). However, Safi-

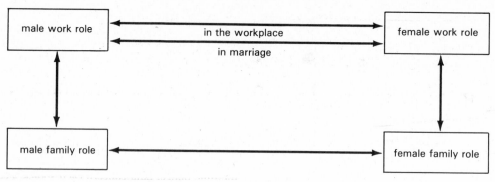

FIGURE 17.1   THE WORK–FAMILY ROLE SYSTEM

lios-Rothschild (1970) has questioned the support for this and other aspects of the "resource" theory of marital power.

The most important aspect of married females' employment in the present analysis is simply its effect on the level of wives' performance of family roles. Blood and Wolfe's (1960) examination of the relation between household division of labor and wives' employment indicated that when wives held paid jobs, they reported doing a lower proportion of the work performed by the couple on eight household tasks (not including childcare). Several analyses of time budget data (Walker, 1969; Meissner et al., 1975; Robinson, Juster & Stafford, 1976) have likewise shown, predictably enough, that wives holding paid jobs outside the family spend less time performing family tasks than wives not so employed. In Walker's data, for example, wives' average time in family tasks was 8.1 hours per day when not employed and declined, through several intermediate categories of part-time employment, to 4.8 hours per day when the wife was employed 30 or more hours per week.

Two observations should be made about this inverse relationship between wives' performance of work roles and family roles. First, it is not clear as yet whether the composition of wives' family role performance changes when they hold paid work. The various time budget analyses do not indicate a consistent reduction in wives' family work disproportionately greater in some categories than others. But the categories for family tasks used in these analyses may be too broad. Second, it should be emphasized that the overall reduction in employed wives' time in family work is not fully commensurate to their increased time in paid employment. The total burden of work and family roles combined is substantially greater for the employed than the non-employed wife.

FEMALE AND MALE FAMILY ROLES

The first and most obvious feature of the articulation between females' and males' family roles is that women and men generally perform different family tasks.[1] That is, there is a marital division of family labor. There is no single accepted way of quantifying how far family tasks are segregated by sex, and any quantitative index would be strongly dependent on which tasks were selected for study, and how narrowly or broadly each was defined. In an analysis of eight household tasks (not including childcare) in a 1955 Detroit sample, Blood and Wolfe (1960) found that six were performed predominately by one or the other spouse, and only two were performed relatively equally by both spouses. Duncan et al. (1974), replicating these items in a similarly drawn Detroit sample in 1971, concluded the general principle that household tasks should be segregated by sex had been maintained with only slight adjustments on particular tasks since the earlier study.

Ideological support for the traditional division of family labor by sex remains quite strong. Robinson, Yerby, Feiweger, and Sommerick (1976) note that in their national sample of married women in 1965–66, only 19 percent responded yes to the question "Do you wish your husband would give you more help with the household chores?" When the question was repeated in a 1973 national survey, the percentage of agreement rose only 4 points, to 23 percent. The increase in the percentage of wives wanting more help from their husbands in household work was considerably greater in certain subgroups, however. There was, for example, an increase of 23 percent for black women and 20 percent for women who graduated from college. The increase in these groups may presage a challenge to the traditional division of household labor which will become more widespread in the future.

A second important feature of the link between male and female family roles concerns simply the relation between the overall levels of each. Though no direct analyses of this relation have been located, it can be inferred from the relation between males' family role performance and wives' employment status, since the latter is associated with variations in females' family role performance. Walker's (1970) time budget data indicate that, on average, there is *no* variation in husband's mean time in family roles (about 1.6 hours per day) associated with their wives' employment status. That is, husbands contribute about the same time to family tasks whether their wives are employed (and doing an average of 4.8 hours of family work per day) or are not employed (and doing an average of 1.8 hours of family work per day). Other time budget studies (Meissner et al., 1975; Robinson, Juster & Stafford, 1976) confirm Walker's general findings. In Walker's data, husbands' family time does increase slightly, to 2.1 hours per day, when their wives are employed if a child under 2 is present, but otherwise the independence of husbands' family time from wives' employment status holds true when age and number of children are controlled.

Blood and Wolfe (1960:62–68) and later studies using their methods (see Bahr, 1974), however, find an increase in the proportion of household work performed by husbands when their wives are employed. At least two factors may account for the discrepancy between Blood and Wolfe's and the time budget findings. First, Blood and Wolfe's measure sampled only a few household tasks, and expressly excluded childcare. It may be that the particular tasks Blood and Wolfe sampled are ones in which husbands do increase their participation when their wives are employed, but this explanation seems unlikely. The time budget analyses do not indicate any change in the composition of husbands' unvarying family time according to wives' employment status, though the categories of family tasks used in these analyses may be

too broad. In small-sample British and American studies, Oakley (1970) and Lein et al. (1974) suggest that husbands of working wives are more likely to increase their participation in childcare than in other household work. But if so, then it is quite paradoxical that Blood and Wolfe's measure, which does not include childcare, shows an increase in husbands' family role performance in response to wives' employment, while the time budget measures, which do include childcare, do not indicate such an increase.

A more likely accounting for the discrepancy is that the time budget data concern each spouse's contribution to family work in absolute terms, while Blood and Wolfe's measure indicates only the relative division of labor between husband and wife. If the husband's absolute time in family tasks remains constant when his wife is employed, and if his wife spends less time in family work, the husband's *relative* share of family work increases. Thus, Blood and Wolfe's results and the time budget data are not inconsistent.

The two most significant features of the relation between husbands' and wives' family role performance are, then, that family tasks are strongly segregated by sex, and that husbands' time in family tasks does not vary in response to the changes in wives' family work resulting from wives' paid employment. Note that the time budget data indicating that husbands do not increase their family role performance when their wives are employed are cross-sectional rather than longitudinal in nature. It is possible that longitudinal analysis might find changes in husbands' level of family work as their wives enter the labor force, leave it during childbearing, and then re-enter it, in the family life cycle pattern so frequent today. Further, although there is no average increase in husbands' family time when their wives have paid jobs, this average lack of response may conceal subgroups of husbands who do take on a significantly greater family role. If so, there must be subgroups of husbands who actually decrease their family role when their wives work. More needs to be known about the determinants of individual variation in husbands' family role performance and in their responsiveness to their wives' paid employment.

MALE FAMILY AND WORK ROLES

The effect of the male work role on the family is receiving increasing attention. Scanzoni (1970) notes that functionalist theory emphasizes how the family is linked to the larger society through the husband-father's occupational role, and how this extrafamilial link affects family relationships. A number of studies and reviews (Aberle & Naegele, 1952; Dyer, 1956, 1965; Miller & Swanson, 1958; Scanzoni, 1965, 1970; Aldous, 1969; Gronseth, 1971, 1972; Pearlin, 1974) have considered how characteristics of the male's occupational role (especially his occupational status) affect the family and particularly the socialization of children.

The most obvious and direct effect of the male occupational role on the family, however, has so far received little analytical attention: the restricting effect of the male occupational role on men's family role. Again using time budget and division of labor measures, data from Walker (1974) and Blood and Wolfe (1960) indicate that role performance in work and family are inversely related to each other for husbands as they are for wives.

While the extent of the husband's family role covaries with the extent of his work role, variation in the extent of the husband's family role occurs around a low baseline *not* accounted for by the demands of his work role. Rather, men's family role varies within the limits imposed by the traditional division of family labor by sex. Though both men's and women's family roles vary according to their employment status, fully employed men still do only a fraction of the family work that fully employed women do—about one-third, according to Walker's data. To put it another way, though employment status has a significant main effect on family work, sex has a stronger effect and accounts for much more of the variance in an individual's time in family work than does his or her employment status.

Thus, it would be misleading to state that men's work role is the primary determinant of the limited family role men typically hold at present. It would be more accurate to say that the objective demands of the male work role are now a latent and secondary constraint, but will emerge as the primary constraint on men's family role if and when ideological support for the traditional division of family labor by sex is weakened. Until then, reduction in the demands of the male work role (for example, shortening the workweek) may not lead to much of an increase in males' family role, as compared to increases in overtime work, the holding of two jobs, and leisure.

Several other aspects of the relation between male work and family roles can be considered. When the methods and assumptions traditionally used in the analysis of married females' employment and its relation to the family are applied to married men, it becomes apparent that many important questions have not yet been asked. For example, economic literature on the "labor supply response" (Mincer, 1962; Cain, 1966) uses slightly different analytic models for husbands and wives. Wives are assumed to allocate time among paid market work, "home market" work (i.e., housework and childcare), and leisure. The parallel analytical equations for men, however, omit "home market" work and include as dependent variables only paid market work and leisure. That is, men's actual participation in family roles is analytically invisible. Such analytical formulations reflect an assumption that men's contribution to family roles is unvarying and of little conceptual significance.[2] For another example, maternal employment has long, and incorrectly, been thought to harm children psychologically. Despite decades of clinical stereotypes about psychologically absent or "weak, passive" fathers, it was rarely asked whether or how *paternal* employment might harm children.

There has been considerable research on the effects of husbands' occupational status and, to a lesser extent, other occupational characteristics on marital satisfaction and marital power (see Scanzoni, 1970). Of particular note are two recent studies on the effects of a previously overlooked aspect of men's occupational role: the overall salience of men's occupational role in comparison to their family role as a source of satisfaction. Bailyn (1971) classified husbands as oriented primarily to work or to the family, according to their self-rating of which gave them more satisfaction. In marriages where wives held paid employment and valued it positively, marital satisfaction was high if the husband was family-oriented, but markedly low if the husband was work-oriented. Husband's orientation was not associated with marital satisfaction, however, in other marriages. Rapoport et al. (1974), classifying husbands in the same way, found that both husbands and wives reported greater enjoyment of everyday activities with their spouses if the husband was family-oriented than if he was not. Interestingly, both studies noted that husbands' orientation to work or family appeared to have a stronger effect on marital variables than did wives' orientation.

MALE AND FEMALE WORK ROLES

There are two distinct contexts in which male and female work roles articulate with each other: in work environments themselves and in marriage. In the workplace, the most significant feature of the articulation of male and female work roles is the high degree of occupational segregation by sex (Waldman & McEaddy, 1974; Blaxall & Reagan, 1976), with females concentrated in lower-paying, lower-status occupations. Within this overall occupational segregation, two dominant patterns for the articulation of male and female work roles can be distinguished. In the older pattern, typical in much blue-collar employment, women and men work in entirely separate settings, and do not generally interact with each other in their work roles. Females are completely excluded from male workplaces. Males are not completely excluded from female workplaces, since women work under the authority and control of male employers. However, this control is largely administered through a cadre of female supervisors, thus greatly minimizing male–female contact.

A major source of this pattern of occupational segregation historically has been men's desire to exclude women in order to keep their own wages up (Hartmann, 1976). This pattern may derive from non-economic sources as well. Caplow (1954) proposed that a fundamental norm that women and men should not interact with each other except in romantic and kinship relationships underlies the sex segregation of the workplace. Caplow speculatively argued that a major psychological source of this norm is that aggression toward females is severely punished in male childhood socialization, and is therefore highly anxiety-provoking to males. Since interaction with work partners inevitably entails some degree of competition and aggression, Caplow argues, interacting with women in the workplace makes men anxious. We can also note similarities between these traditional norms prescribing complete segregation of male and female work roles and what anthropologists term "pollution ideology" (Douglas, 1970). According to pollution ideology, if certain categories of social objects (e.g., menstrual blood) are not segregated or handled in special ways, the order of the world is disturbed and catastrophe will result. In similar fashion, many miners and seamen in the past have resisted the introduction of women as co-workers because they superstitiously believed that women would be a "jinx" or "bad luck," bringing on mining disasters and shipwrecks.

The more recent pattern for the articulation of male and female work roles, whose ideal type is the modern office, is the integration of women into mixed-sex workplaces, but in roles that are segregated from and clearly subordinate to men's. Thus, women and men do not compete for the same jobs, and do not have to interact with each other as peers. In this pattern, the potential for interacting with members of the other sex, particularly if unmarried, has almost attained the status of a fringe benefit. The shift from the first pattern of work organization to the second has not received sufficient attention. Several studies have examined how certain previously male occupations became female ones (Prather, 1972; Davies, 1974), but that these occupational shifts transformed previously all-male work environments into mixed-sex ones has not been adequately analyzed as yet.

The second context for the articulation of male and female work roles is marriage. The critical factor affecting this link is primarily psychological in nature, based on men's investment in their performance of the paid breadwinner role as uniquely validating their masculinity. Yankelovich (1974:44–45) has suggested that for the large majority of men whose jobs are not inherently psychologically satisfying, daily work is made worthwhile by pride in hard work. The sacrifices made to provide for their families' needs validate them as men. Wives working thus takes away a major source of these men's identity, and is psychologically threatening.

Two dominant patterns for the articulation between male and female roles in marriage are apparent, corresponding to the two patterns noted in the workplace. In the more traditional pattern, husbands cannot tolerate their wives taking or holding any paid employment. Supporting this pattern, in many workplaces married women were ineligible for employment, and single women were dismissed if they married. In the more recent pattern, husbands can accept their wives' employment as long as it does not come too close to, or worse surpass, their own in prestige, earnings, or psychological commitment. The segregation of women in lower-paying, lower-status occupations helps insure that this limit is not breached. Further, husbands' acceptance of their wives' work in this pattern is conditional on their wives' continuing to meet their traditional family responsibilities.

Taking an overview of the workplace and marriage, the second pattern for the articulation of male and female work roles in each is not necessarily more equitable or less restrictive to women than the first. The emergence of the second pattern was, however, inevitable as the married female labor force has expanded over the course of this century. The question now is whether a third pattern can emerge on a wide scale in which wives can have work roles of equal or greater status than their husbands' (Rapoport & Rapoport, 1971), and in which female workers can interact with male workers as equals in the workplace.

STRUCTURAL "BUFFERS" IN THE WORK–FAMILY ROLE SYSTEM

What are the more general characteristics of the links in the work–family role system? How do these links affect whether change in one role does or does not lead to accommodating change in the other roles to which it is linked? We consider here two structural "buffers" in the links among these roles, limiting how much change in one role affects the others.

The first kind of buffer is *sex-segregated market mechanisms* for both paid work and family work. A sex-segregated, dual market for paid work means that women and men do not compete for the same jobs. As a result, changes in the level of female employment occur neither at the expense nor to the benefit of male employment. Further, since women are segregated into not only different but inferior jobs, women will rarely have jobs of equal or greater status than men's, psychologically threatening their husbands or co-workers. In these ways, the dual market for paid work insulates the male work role from the changes in the female work role that have occurred so far in our society.

Household work and childcare can likewise be conceptualized as allocated by a sex-segregated, dual market mechanism. This market mechanism is supported by ideology concerning the appropriate household activities of the two sexes as well as by differential training in family tasks. The result is that the husband's family role is generally unresponsive to changes in the wife's family role. If a wife's employment requires her to reduce the level of her family role performance, the husband is unlikely to increase his. He may perceive that family work needs doing, but he will not perceive

the kind of work that needs to be done as appropriate or suitable to him. The dual market for household work and childcare thus has insulated men's family role from the changes in the female family role resulting so far from paid employment.

The second kind of structural buffer in the work–family role system is *asymmetrically permeable boundaries between work and family roles* for both men and women. For women, the demands of the family role are permitted to intrude into the work role more than vice versa. Though working mothers try to devise schedules to accommodate the demands of both roles, if an emergency or irregularity arises requiring a choice between the two, the family will often take priority. For example, when there is a crisis for a child in school, it is the child's working mother rather than working father who will be called to take responsibility. This vulnerability of the female work role to family demands is an important part of negative stereotypes about women workers. It is also a major source of stress for women on the job, since the sex role norm that women take responsibility for the family conflicts with the norms of the job role.

For husbands, the work–family role boundary is likewise asymmetrically permeable, but in the other direction. Many husbands literally "take work home" with them or need to use family time simply to recuperate from the stresses they face in their work role. Husbands are expected to manage their families so that their family responsibilities do not interfere with their work efficiency, and so that families will make any adjustments necessary to accommodate the demands of husbands' work roles.

CHANGE IN THE WORK–FAMILY ROLE SYSTEM

As is well known, over the course of this century there has been a major increase in married women's rate of labor force participation (Oppenheimer, 1970). Married women's increased employment has induced a partially accommodating reduction in women's family role, but as yet almost no increase in husbands' family role, as indicated by the time budget data considered earlier. In consequence, employed wives face considerable problems of strain and exhaustion in both their work and family roles. As Rapoport and Rapoport (1972) have formulated it, there is a psychosocial lag between the changes occurring for women in the macrosocial world of work and changes in the microsocial world of family. In their analysis, this psychosocial lag generates transitional problems of adjustment, but these will be resolved as the family "catches up" to changes in the workplace. Young and Willmott (1973) have likewise argued that the family is becoming more "symmetrical," that is, evolving toward a pattern where each marital partner has a significant role in both paid work and the family. The analysis of the work–family role system developed here makes possible a more specific consideration of the issues these social changes will involve.

First, it is clear that one of the most pressing changes needed in the work–family role system is an end to the traditional norms prescribing the sex-segregated and unequal division of household work and childcare. As noted earlier, however, if and when these norms break down, the demands of the male work role will emerge as the crucial constraint on how much men can increase their family role. Expansion of the scope of the male family role without accommodating changes in the male work role will lead to role strain in men similar to the strains now faced by working wives. While this distribution of strain throughout the role system will be more equitable than the current one, it will continue to be a source of instability. Husbands who are committed to equal sharing of household work and childcare will find that the demands of their jobs make this quite difficult, and that a diversion of their energy from work into the family will penalize them in the competition for job advancement. The idea of paternity leave—admittedly only beginning to be raised in labor negotiations, and not widely taken advantage of in the few places where it has been implemented—is perhaps the first indication of the kind of workplace practices needed to legitimate a shift of husbands' energies from work to the family.

A second potential future change in the work–family role system is the breakdown of occupational sex segregation. Recent progress toward reducing occupational segregation, when it has been evident at all, has been dishearteningly slow (Waldman & McEaddy, 1974; Blaxall & Reagan, 1976). If occupational segregation is significantly reduced, major adjustments will be required in men's self-conceptions as primary family breadwinners and in the norms governing male–female interaction on the job. In addition, women holding higher-status jobs may give added impetus to

the desegregation of family work and the enlargement of the male family role. First, women holding higher-status jobs may require that women's boundary between their work and family roles become more like men's, that is, their work role will more often need to take priority over their family role, and they will be able to do less family work. Second, women holding jobs more equal in status to their husbands' will give greater legitimation to the demand for a more equal sharing of family work. Contrary to these two effects, however, the increased income provided by women's holding higher-status jobs may make it more possible for families to purchase goods and services to compensate for the reduction in women's family role than is possible now where women are in relatively low-paying jobs. If these goods and services are available, purchasing them may be less stressful than trying to increase men's family role.

Third, if the sex segregation of both family work and paid work is significantly reduced, a fundamental change in the nature of the work role may be necessary, not just for men but for both sexes. As the paid work role has evolved in modern society, it has come to call for full time, continuous work from the end of one's education to retirement, desire to actualize one's potential to the fullest, and subordination of other roles to work. This conception of the work role has been, in effect, the male model of the work role. Women, because of the family responsibilities traditionally assigned to them, have had considerable difficulty fitting themselves to this male model of work. To a large extent, it has been possible for men in modern society to work according to this model precisely because women have subordinated their own potential work role and accepted such an extensive role in the family. In doing so, wives take on the family responsibilities that husbands might otherwise have to fill, and in additional emotionally, and often practically, support their husbands in their work role.[3]

In the past, it has been possible for families to function, though not without strain, with one marital partner, the husband, performing according to this male work model. Families have also been able to function, though with even more strain, with one partner conforming to the male work model and with the other partner in a less demanding job role. Though it is stressful, especially for the wife, this kind of two-job family is on the verge of being the statistically dominant pattern (Hayghe, 1976). However, it does not seem possible for large numbers of families to function with *both* partners following the traditional male work model. Such a pattern could become widespread only if fertility dropped significantly further or if household work and childcare services became inexpensive, widely available, and socially accepted on a scale hith-

erto unknown.[4] In the absence of such developments, greater equality in the sharing of work and family roles by women and men will ultimately require the development of a new model of the work role and a new model for the boundary between work and the family which gives higher priority to family needs.

ACKNOWLEDGMENTS

This is a revised version of a paper given at the 1975 Annual Meeting of the American Sociological Association. I would like to thank Arlie Hochschild, Jeylan Mortimer, and Elizabeth Pleck for their comments on earlier drafts.

NOTES

1. Glazer-Malbin (1976) provides a useful analysis of current theoretical approaches to household work.

2. The present analysis, it should be noted, omits consideration of children's family role performance. Walker and Gauger (1973) found that children aged 12–17 contribute an average of slightly over an hour a day to family tasks.

3. Mortimer et al. (1976) have drawn attention to the extent to which wives can directly contribute to their hus-

bands' work as an alternative to holding paid work of their own, a further indication of the demanding nature of the male work role.

4. Safilios-Rothschild (1976) has analyzed in a somewhat different way the structural changes that may occur to accommodate families in which both parents have high-status jobs.

REFERENCES

Aberle, D., & Naegele, K. 1952. "Middle-class fathers' occupational role and attitudes toward children." *American Journal of Orthopsychiatry* 22:366–78.

Aldous, J. 1969. "Occupational characteristics and males' role performance in the family." *Journal of Marriage and the Family* 31:707–12.

Bahr, S. 1974. "Effects on power and division of labor in the family." In L. W. Hoffman & F. Ivan Nye, eds., *Working mothers*, pp. 167–85. San Francisco: Jossey-Bass.

Bailyn, L. 1971. "Career and family orientations of husbands and wives in relation to marital happiness." *Human Relations* 23:97–113.

Blaxall, M., & Reagan, B., eds. 1976. "Women and the work-

place: The implications of occupational segregation." *Signs* 1 (3, pt. 2): entire.

Blood, R. O., & Wolfe, D. 1960. *Husbands and wives.* New York: Free Press.

Cain, G. 1966. *Married women in the labor force: An economic analysis.* Chicago: University of Chicago Press.

Caplow, T. 1954. *The sociology of work.* Minneapolis: University of Minnesota Press.

Davies, M. 1974. "Women's place is at the typewriter: The feminization of the clerical labor force." *Radical America* 8 (4):1–37.

Douglas, M. 1970. *Purity and danger: An analysis of concepts of pollution and taboo.* Baltimore: Penguin.

Dyer, W. 1956. "The interlocking of work and family social systems among lower occupational families." *Social Forces* 34:230–33.

Dyer, W. 1965. "Family reactions to the father's job." In A. Shostak & W. Gomberg, eds., *Blue-collar world,* pp. 86–91. Englewood Cliffs, N.J.: Prentice-Hall.

Duncan, O. D.; Schuman, H.; & Duncan, B. 1974. *Social change in a metropolitan community.* New York: Russell Sage.

Glazer-Malbin, N. 1976. "Housework." *Signs* 1:905–22.

Gronseth, E. 1971. "The husband-provider role: A critical appraisal." In A. Michel, ed., *Family issues of employed women in Europe and America,* pp. 11–31. Leiden: E. J. Brill.

Gronseth, E. 1972. "The breadwinner trap." In L. K. Howe, ed., *The future of the family,* pp. 175–91. New York: Simon & Schuster.

Hayghe, H. 1976. "Families and the rise of working wives: An overview." *Monthly Labor Review* 99 (5):12–19.

Hartmann, H. 1976. "Capitalism, patriarchy, and job segregation by sex." *Signs* 1 (3, pt. 2):137–70.

Hoffman, L. W., & Nye, F. I., eds. 1974. *Working mothers.* San Francisco: Jossey-Bass.

Howell, M. 1973a. "Employed mothers and their families (I)." *Pediatrics* 52:252–63.

Howell, M. 1973b. "Effects of maternal employment on the child (II)." *Pediatrics* 52:327–43.

Kanter, R. 1976. *Work and family in America: A critical review and research agenda.* Social Science Frontiers Monograph Series. New York: Russell Sage.

Lein, L.; Durham, M.; Pratt, M.; Schudson, M.; Thomas, R.; & Weiss, H. 1974. *Final report: Work and family life.* National Institute of Education Project no. 3-3094. Cambridge, Mass.: Center for the Study of Public Policy.

Meissner, M.; Humphreys, E.; Meis, S.; & Scheu, W. 1975. "No exit for wives: Sexual division of labor and the cumulation of household demands." *Canadian Review of Sociology and Anthropology* 12:424–39.

Miller, D. R., & Swanson, G. E. 1958. *The changing American parent.* New York: Wiley.

Mincer, J. 1962. "Labor force participation of married women." In National Bureau of Economic Research, *Aspects of labor economics,* pp. 63–97. Princeton: Princeton University Press.

Mortimer, J.; Hall, R.; & Hill, R. 1976. "Husbands' occupational attributes as constraints on wives' employment." Paper given at the Annual Meeting of the American Sociological Association.

Oakley, A. 1970. "Are husbands good housewives?" *New Society* 112:377–79.

Oppenheimer, V. K. 1970. *The female labor force in the United States.* Population Monograph Series no. 3. Berkeley: University of California Press.

Pearlin, L. I. 1974. *Class context and family relations.* Boston: Little, Brown.

Prather, J. 1972. "When the girls move in: A sociological analysis of the feminization of the bank teller's job." *Journal of Marriage and the Family* 33:777–82.

Rapoport, R., & Rapoport, R. 1965. "Work and family in modern society." *American Sociological Review* 30:381–94.

Rapoport, R., & Rapoport, R. 1971. *Dual-career families.* Baltimore: Penguin.

Rapoport, R., & Rapoport, R. 1972. "The working woman and the enabling role of the husband." Paper given at the XIIth International Family Research Seminar, International Sociological Association, Moscow.

Rapoport, R.; Rapoport, R.; & Thiessen, V. 1974. "Couple symmetry and enjoyment." *Journal of Marriage and the Family* 36:588–91.

Robinson, J.; Juster, T., & Stafford, F. 1976. *Americans' use of time.* Ann Arbor, Mich.: Institute for Social Research.

Robinson, J.; Yerby, J.; Feiweger, M.; & Sommerick, N. 1976. "Time use as an indicator of sex territoriality." Unpublished paper.

Safilios-Rothschild, C. 1970. "The study of family power structure: A review, 1960–1969." *Journal of Marriage and the Family* 32:539–52.

Safilios-Rothschild, C. 1976. "Dual linkages between the occupational and family systems: A macrosociological analysis." *Signs* 1 (3, pt. 2): 51–60.

Scanzoni, J. 1965. "Resolution of occupational-conjugal role conflict in clergy marriages." *Journal of Marriage and the Family* 27:396–402.

Scanzoni, J. 1970. *Opportunity and the family.* New York: Free Press.

Waldman, E. & McEaddy, B. 1974. "Where women work: An analysis by industry and occupation." *Monthly Labor Review* 95 (5): 3–13.

Walker, K.E. 1969. "Time spent in household work by homemakers." *Family Economics Review* 3:5–6.

Walker, K. E. 1970. "Time spent by husbands in household work." *Family Economics Review* 4:8–11.

Walker, K. E. 1974. Unpublished data.

Walker, K. E., & Gauger, W. 1973. "Time and its dollar value in household work." *Family Economics Review* 7:8–13.

Yankelovich, D. 1974. "The meaning of work." In J. M. Rosow, ed., *The worker and the job,* pp. 19–48. Englewood Cliffs, N.J.: Prentice-Hall.

Young, M., & Willmott, P. 1973. *The symmetrical family.* New York: Pantheon.

READING 18

Briefcase, Baby, or Both?

KATHLEEN GERSON

It is no coincidence that as more women are employed, they're having fewer babies. Women's work and family decisions have always been closely connected, and recent changes simply underscore their interaction. To explore this important link, I have studied a strategic group of women now in their prime childbearing years. They are of the generation that is particularly responsible for recent changes in women's employment and childbearing patterns, and as such, they are especially well positioned to illuminate the causes, consequences and meaning of the subtle revolution now under way. By understanding the forces that have shaped the decisions of these women, we can also learn how women, in general, choose between work and family commitments.

Women who came of age during the last decade or so have responded in many ways to the historic conflict between work and family. Some have embraced the domestic patterns of an earlier historical period. They have married, borne children and committed themselves to full-time mothering. These "traditional" women have worked outside the home only intermittently, if at all, and have taken care to subordinate work to family pursuits.

But many other women—I'll call them "nontraditional"—have veered off this time-honored path. They have postponed, and even forgone, motherhood; they have developed committed, permanent ties to the workplace that resemble the pattern once reserved for men alone. When they have had children, they have tried to combine careers with motherhood. In short, they have rejected the domestic path that places children, family and home above all else. While there have always been some "career" women, today their numbers are growing at an unprecedented rate. For some, it is the culmination of childhood hopes and dreams; for others, it is a very unexpected and usually rewarding development.

Consider, for example, the very different paths taken by Joanne and Jane, composites of a number of women in the group I interviewed:

Joanne grew up in a "typical" American family. Although her father earned only a modest wage as a repairman, her mother stayed at home to rear their four children because both parents believed that full-time mothering for the children was more important than added income. They nevertheless hoped that Joanne would educate herself for a better life.

Joanne, however, was more interested in dating than in schoolwork or her job as a fast-food waitress. When she became pregnant at 17, she was happy to marry her boyfriend and settle down to full-time mothering.

Two children, several brief and disheartening sales jobs and ten years later, Joanne still finds satisfaction in full-time mothering. She sometimes feels social and financial pressure to give up homemaking for paid work and resents feeling snubbed when she says her family is her career. But every time she searches the want ads, she remembers how much she disliked her few temporary jobs. And since her husband earns enough money as a mechanic to make ends meet, the urge to work quickly passes. Instead, she is considering having another child.

Joanne's life history illustrates the traditional model of female development: An adult woman chooses the domestic life for which she was prepared emotionally and practically since childhood. About 20 percent of the women I interviewed, from a wide variety of class and family backgrounds, followed a similar life course. These women were insulated from events that might have steered them off their expected paths. They were neither pushed out of the home by economic necessity or marital instability nor pulled into the workplace by enticing opportunities. Instead, they remained committed to the domestic niche that they assumed was a woman's proper and "natural" place.

In contrast, consider Jane's life path:

Like Joanne, Jane just assumed as a child that she would grow up to marry, have numerous children and "live happily ever after" as a housewife. She vaguely wished to go to college, but her father thought it inappropriate for women to do so, and as a low-paid laborer he could not have paid her way in any case.

Jane worked after high school as a filing clerk and married Frank, a salesman, two years later. Within six months of the ceremony, she was pregnant and planning to stay home with her young child. But things changed shortly after her daughter was born. Unlike Joanne, she became bored and unhappy as a full-time mother. Taking care of the baby was just not the ultimate fulfillment she had anticipated. Instead, she found motherhood to be a decidedly mixed experience—alternately rewarding and frustrating, joyful and depressing. Despite her reluctance to admit these feelings to herself or others, a growing sense of emptiness, added to the need for additional income, spurred her to look for paid work.

Jane took a job as a bank teller. She thought of it as a temporary way to boost the family income, but the right time to quit never seemed to arrive. Frank's income consistently fell short of their needs, and as his work frustrations mounted, the marriage began to falter. When Frank began to pressure Jane to have another child, she wondered whether she might be happier without Frank than with him.

Just when the marriage had begun to seem unbearable, Jane's boss offered her a chance to advance. Faced with affirmative-action pressures, the bank had initiated a program designed to move qualified women—including those who, like Jane, lacked college degrees—into management. She worried about the pressures of a higher-level job but was eager for the greater pay, respect and control that upward mobility promised. She accepted the advancement and decided to divorce Frank.

Today, more than a decade later, Jane is dedicated to her career, aspires to upper-level management and does not plan to remarry or expand her family beyond her only child. She is convinced that her daughter is better off being cared for primarily by a woman who, unlike herself, really enjoys full-time childrearing. When Jane looks back over her life, she wonders how she could have come so far.

Jane's life illustrates an emerging and increasingly common pattern among both middle- and working-class women—one of rising work aspirations and ambivalence toward motherhood. Like their traditional counterparts, these women (about one-third of the total group I studied) also grew up wanting and preparing for domesticity, only to find that events prompted them to move in a different direction. Compared with their domestic counterparts, members of this group were more likely to experience unstable relationships with men, unanticipated opportunities for job advancement, economic squeezes at home and disappointment with mothering and full-time homemaking. As a result, heightened work ambitions replaced their earlier home-centered orientation. Although Joanne and Jane shared similar childhood backgrounds and aspirations, their lives diverged increasingly as they encountered a different set of opportunities and constraints in adulthood.

Now consider the lives of two other women, Gail and Susan—also composites—who, unlike Joanne and Jane, shared a quite different set of expectations in childhood:

As a child, Gail looked on motherhood with ambivalence and doubt. Her own mother had relinquished a promising career to raise three children and never seemed to recover from this sacrifice. As Gail watched her mother slip deeper and deeper into depression, she resolved to avoid her mother's fate.

Gail's father, a successful businessman, encouraged all his children to aim for whatever they wanted in life, and for as long as she could remember, Gail wanted to be a lawyer. At the time the law was an unusual career choice for a girl, but the social pressure against it only fueled her determination.

Gail has not wavered from her early plans. She did well in college, went to law school, joined a small law firm and was eventually made a partner. Throughout this period, she had a few serious relationships but never found the time nor felt the inclination to marry or have a child.

Now in her mid-30s and secure in her career, Gail has begun to consider having a child. But she feels that time is running out, and no partner is in sight. All her previous relationships ended badly, and she has begun to doubt that she can or should commit herself exclusively to one person for life. Because having a child outside a committed relationship seems unfair to herself and the child, Gail acknowledges with mild regret that, despite her wish to "have it all," she probably will never bear children.

Gail represents a group of women (slightly less than 20 percent of those in the study) who, even as children, viewed exclusive motherhood with apprehension and hoped for something different out of life. Like Joanne, Gail and her counterparts realized their early life goals and did not change significantly in adulthood. Because their childhood aspirations differed from those of traditional women, however, they rejected full-time homemaking, part-time or interrupted employment, and often motherhood as well, in favor of permanent, committed employment. Circumstances supported their career goals and enabled them to follow a non-traditional path.

Finally, there is the case of Susan, who shared Gail's early work ambitions and apprehensions about motherhood but encountered quite different circumstances as an adult:

Susan's father, an airline pilot, was often away from home, and her mother doted on her in his absence. She encouraged Susan in her studies, and Susan developed high hopes for a professional career. Indeed, she earned a scholarship to college and considered going to medical school.

Unlike Gail, however, Susan married in her senior year of college and found that her own career plans collided with those of John, her husband. They needed an income while he earned a professional degree, and her college counselors frowned on her own career aspirations. Under these pressures, she grudgingly became a preschool teacher.

Over the years, Susan has grown increasingly impatient with the low salary, lack of advancement opportunities and low prestige that accompany her demanding work. In contrast, John has finished his graduate training and begun a lucrative career. He intensely wants children and has started pressuring Susan to start a family. While she is still unsure about having children, she has begun to view motherhood as her best chance to escape from an alienating job. Since she can now depend on John for financial support, she plans to resign and start a family. Now she worries that if, like many other marriages, hers does not hold together, she will be forced to return to the workplace.

Susan represents a group of women (about one in three in our study) who developed career aspirations as children but later gave them up for home and children. They had joined the labor force with high hopes, only to meet stifling workplace experiences and roadblocks to upward mobility. Over time, as career ambitions were thwarted or employment commitments threatened to undermine a valued personal relationship, they came to view motherhood as their best hope for fulfillment and their only escape from alienating paid work.

Like members of this group, many other women choose motherhood not to fulfill a deep-seated need to mother but rather as the best option among a number of unappealing alternatives. Their apparent lack of ambition may actually be a well-founded concern for preserving a stable private life. For women like Susan and Joanne, who find work a dead-end street, the erosion of the domestic option poses a threat. But for women like Gail and Jane, who find work rewarding, the same trend is a boon.

Each of these life histories illustrates the powerful, interactive link between women's work and family decisions. They also illustrate the varied paths women negotiate through adulthood. Regardless of their social-class origins, women differed in their early childhood expectations. Exposed to a diverse, complex set of experiences as children, they formed a variety of conscious and unconscious hopes long before they were able to act on them as adults. When these early aspirations were then subjected to the real constraints and opportunities of adulthood, many followed their initial goals, but most met unanticipated social circumstances that encouraged, and often required, them to change, sometimes dramatically.

What explains the divergent paths of these women? The usual theories cannot account for their contrasting experiences and choices. The "childhood socialization" models, which focus on how psychological predispositions instilled in early childhood produce adult outcomes, are particularly ill equipped to explain these findings. These women's goals, capacities and outlooks were not irrevocably fixed at an early age, nor were they stable over time. While many maintained their early orientations, the majority went through changes that childhood expectations, taken alone, could never have predicted.

Similarly, a "feminine personality" did not lead most of these women to prefer motherhood to work.

Although some theorists propose that the vast majority of women share the desire and ability to devote themselves to mothering, the women I interviewed expressed quite varied views of motherhood and work. While many embraced motherhood and domesticity with enthusiasm, others were motivated not so much by an abstract "mothering need" as by stifling work experiences that led them to view mothering as preferable to paid work. As a disillusioned ex-teacher explained about her first pregnancy, "I reached a point in the job where I was just hating it daily. [So] we went and got pregnant. It was a relief not working, not having that pressure."

Women who were commited to work viewed childbearing and primary caregiving with ambivalence. Those who rejected or lost faith in the viability of marriage even chose, in some cases, to remain permanently childless. Others, in response to husbands eager to have children, moved slowly and reluctantly toward motherhood, while struggling to allay their own doubts and fears. These "reluctant" mothers then pressured their husbands to share child care and revised their own beliefs about proper child-rearing practices. They typically concluded that working mothers make better mothers than those at home full-time. As one put it, "Before, I felt a mother, to be a good mother, should be home with her children. Not only is it not necessary, but it might not even be best."

Other theorists stress that male coercion, or "patriarchy," is the major determinant of women's work and family decisions. But of the women I studied, most actively and creatively constructed their own lives within the context of social constraint. Most domestic women supported the traditional structure of female homemaking and male breadwinning. Indeed, given their limited options in the paid labor force, they felt protective of their right not to do paid work outside the home; they feared that social changes such as the rising instability of marriage and the increasing devaluation of domestic work were already eroding that right. In contrast, nondomestic women opposed and resisted patriarchal authority at home and work.

Unanticipated encounters with changing work and family structures prompted some women to veer toward domesticity and others to veer away from it. These two groups disagreed with each other because each faced different dilemmas and responded in different ways to contrasting social circumstances. Domestic women thus concluded that children suffer when their mothers pursue careers and that childless career women are "selfish" and "unfulfilled." Career women, for their part, viewed homemakers as "boring" and "underdeveloped." Many aspects of today's battles over abortion, child care and equal rights for women reflect these deepening social divisions between work-committed and domestically oriented women.

Because current changes in women's lives have underlying sources in our social structure, the changes are probably here to stay. Women are likely to become even more diverse as they attempt in a variety of ways to reconcile the conflict between work and domestic responsibilities. These issues will continue to reverberate well beyond women's lives into those of fathers, children, employers and fellow workers.

Thirty years ago, women had few choices. Today, they must make hard choices, in large part because social changes still have not produced gender equality. Men and women will not be equal until women have equal opportunity in the workplace and men share equal responsibility in the home. Only then will women and men face the same choices between their work and domestic lives.

Perhaps one day neither women nor men will face the dilemma of having to choose between commitment to parenting and a satisfying work career. Such a future will require a transformation in both the workplace and the parental division of labor—an even more revolutionary change than those now taking place in women's lives.

If, however, we fail to achieve gender equality and do not reduce the barriers that now put work and parenting in conflict for both sexes, then the diversity of alternatives for women still will not reduce the difficulties they face. Instead, whether confronted with full-time parenting, strong work commitment or juggling the demands of both, women will continue to face hard choices.

Puerto Rican Elderly Women: Shared Meanings and Informal Supportive Networks

MELBA SÁNCHEZ-AYÉNDEZ

INTRODUCTION

Studies of older adults' support systems have seldom taken into account how values within a specific cultural context affect expectations of support and patterns of assistance in social networks. Such networks and supportive relations have a cultural dimension reflecting a system of shared meanings. These meanings affect social interaction and the expectations people have of their relationships with others.

Ethnicity and gender affect a person's adjustment to old age. Although sharing a "minority" position produces similar consequences among members of different ethnic minority groups, the groups' diversity lies in their distinctive systems of shared meanings. Studies of older adults in ethnic minority groups have rarely focused on the cultural contents of ethnicity affecting the aging process, particularly of women (Barth, 1969). Cultural value orientations are central to understanding how minority elders approach growing old and how they meet the physical and emotional changes associated with aging.

This article describes the interplay between values and behavior in family and community of a group of older Puerto Rican women living on low incomes in Boston.[1] It explores how values emphasizing family interdependence and different roles of women and men shape the women's expectations, behavior, and supportive familial and community networks.

BEING A WOMAN IS DIFFERENT FROM BEING A MAN

The women interviewed believe in a dual standard of conduct for men and women. This dual standard is apparent in different attributes assigned to women and men, roles expected of them, and authority exercised by them.

The principal role of men in the family is viewed as that of provider; their main responsibility is economic in nature. Although fathers are expected to be affectionate with their children, child care is not seen to be a man's responsibility. Men are not envisioned within the domestic sphere.

The "ideal" man must be the protector of the family, able to control his emotions and be self-sufficient. Men enjoy more freedom in the public world than do women. From the women's perspective, the ideal of maleness is linked to the concept of *machismo*. This concept assumes men have a stronger sexual drive than women, a need to prove virility by the conquest of women, a dominant position in relation to females, and a belligerent attitude when confronted by male peers.

The women see themselves as subordinate to men and recognize the preeminence of male authority. They believe women ought to be patient and largely forbearing in their relations with men, particularly male family members. Patience and forbearance, however, are not confused with passivity or total submissiveness. The elderly Puerto Rican women do not conceive of themselves or other women as "resigned females" but as dynamic beings, continually devising strategies to improve everyday situations within and outside the household.

Rosa Mendoza,[2] now sixty-five, feels no regrets for having decided at thirty years of age and after nine years of marriage not to put up with her husband's heavy drinking any longer. She moved out of her house and went to live with her mother.

> I was patient for many years. I put up with his drunkenness and worked hard to earn money. One day I decided I'd be better off without him. One thing is to be patient, and another to be a complete fool. So I moved out.

Although conscious of their subordinate status to their husbands, wives are also aware of their power and the demands they can make. Ana Fuentes recalls when her husband had a mistress. Ana was thirty-eight.

> I knew he had a mistress in a nearby town. I was patient for a long time, hoping it would end. Most men, sooner or later, have a mistress somewhere. But when it didn't end after quite a time and everyone in the neighborhood knew about it, I said "I am fed up!" He came home one evening and the things I told him! I even said I'd go to that woman's house and beat her if I had to. . . . He knew I was not bluffing; that this was not just another argument. He tried to answer back and I didn't let him. He remained silent. . . . And you know what? He stopped seeing her! A woman can endure many things for a long time, but the time comes when she has to defend her rights.

These older Puerto Rican women perceive the home as the center around which the female world revolves. Home is the woman's domain; women generally make decisions about household maintenance and men seldom intervene.

Family relations are considered part of the domestic sphere and therefore a female responsibility. The women believe that success in marriage depends on the woman's ability to "make the marriage work."

> A marriage lasts as long as the woman decides it will last. It is us who make a marriage work, who put up with things, who try to make ends meet, who yield.

The norm of female subordination is evident in the view that marriage will last as long as the woman "puts up with things" and deals with marriage from her subordinate status. Good relations with affinal kin are also a woman's responsibility. They are perceived as relations between the wife's domestic unit and other women's domestic units.

Motherhood

Motherhood is seen by these older Puerto Rican women as the central role of women. Their concept of motherhood is based on the female capacity to bear children and on the notion of *marianismo,* which presents the Virgin Mary as a role model (Stevens, 1973). *Marianismo* presupposes that it is through motherhood that a woman realizes herself and derives her life's greatest satisfactions.

A woman's reproductive role is viewed as leading her toward more commitment to and a better understanding of her children than is shown by the father. One of the women emphasized this view:

> It is easier for a man to leave his children and form a new home with another woman, or not to be as forgiving of children as a mother is. They will never know what it is like to carry a child inside, feel it growing, and then bring that child into the world. This is why a mother is always willing to forgive and make sacrifices. That creature is a part of you; it nourished from you and came from within you. But it is not so for men. To them, a child is a being they receive once it is born. The attachment can never be the same.

The view that childrearing is their main responsibility in life comes from this conceptualization of the mother–child bond. For the older women, raising children means more than looking after the needs of offspring. It involves being able to offer them every possible opportunity for a better life, during childhood or adulthood, even if this requires personal sacrifices.

As mother and head of the domestic domain, a woman is also responsible for establishing the bases for close and good relations among her children. From childhood through adulthood, the creation and maintenance of family unity among offspring is considered another female responsibility.

FAMILY UNITY AND INTERDEPENDENCE

Family Unity

Ideal family relations are seen as based on two inter-related themes, family unity and family interdependence. Family unity refers to the desirability of close and intimate kin ties, with members getting along well and keeping in frequent contact despite dispersal.

Celebration of holidays and special occasions are seen as opportunities for kin to be together and strengthen family ties. Family members, particularly grandparents, adult children, and grandchildren, are often reunited at Christmas, New Year's, Mother's and Father's days, Easter, and Thanksgiving. Special celebrations like weddings, baptisms, first communions, birthdays, graduations, and funerals occasion reunions with other family members. Whether to celebrate happy or sad events, the older women encourage family gatherings as a way of strengthening kinship ties and fostering family continuity.

The value the women place on family unity is also evident in their desire for frequent interaction with kin members. Visits and telephone calls demonstrate a caring attitude by family members which cements family unity.

Family unity is viewed as contributing to the strengthening of family interdependence. Many of the older women repeat a proverb when referring to family unity: *En la unión está la fuerza.* ("In union there is strength.") They believe that the greater the degree of unity in the family, the greater the emphasis family members will place on interdependence and familial obligation.

Family Interdependence

Despite adaptation to life in a culturally different society, Puerto Rican families in the United States are still defined by strong norms of reciprocity among family members, especially those in the immediate kinship group (Cantor, 1979; Carrasquillo, 1982; Delgado, 1981; Donaldson & Martínez, 1980; Sánchez-Ayéndez, 1984). Interdependence within the Puerto Rican symbolic framework "fits an orientation to life that stresses that the individual is not capable of doing everything and doing it well. Therefore, he should rely on others for assistance" (Bastida, 1979:70). Individualism and self-reliance assume a different meaning from the one prevailing in the dominant U.S. cultural

tradition. Individuals in Puerto Rican families will expect and ask for assistance from certain people in their social networks without any derogatory implications for self-esteem.

Family interdependence is a value to which these older Puerto Rican women strongly adhere. It influences patterns of mutual assistance with their children as well as expectations of support. The older women expect to be taken care of during old age by their adult children. The notion of filial duty ensues from the value orientation of interdependence. Adult children are understood to have a responsibility toward their aged parents in exchange for the functions that parents performed for them throughout their upbringing. Expected reciprocity from offspring is intertwined with the concept of filial love and the nature of the parent–child relationship.

Parental duties of childrearing are perceived as inherent in the "parent" role and also lay the basis for long-term reciprocity with children, particularly during old age. The centrality that motherhood has in the lives of the older women contributes to creating great expectations among them of reciprocity from children. More elderly women than men verbalize disappointment when one of their children does not participate in the expected interdependence ties. Disappointment is unlikely to arise when an adult child cannot help due to financial or personal reasons. However, it is bound to arise when a child chooses not to assist the older parent for other reasons.

These older Puerto Rican women stress that good offspring ought to help their parents, contingent upon available resources. Statements such as the following are common:

> Of course I go to my children when I have a problem! To whom would I turn? I raised them and worked very hard to give them the little I could. Now that I am old, they try to help me in whatever they can. . . . Good offspring should help their aged parents as much as they are able to.

Interdependence for Puerto Rican older parents also means helping their children and grandchildren. Many times they provide help when it is not explicitly requested. They are happy when they can perform supportive tasks for their children's families. The child who needs help, no matter how old, is not judged as dependent or a failure.

Reciprocity is not based on strictly equal exchanges. Due to the rapid pace of life, lack of financial resources, or personal problems, adult children are not always able to provide the care the elder parent needs. Many times, the older adults provide their families with more financial and instrumental assistance than their children are able to provide them. Of utmost importance to the older women is not that their children be able to help all the time, but that they visit or call frequently. They place more emphasis on emotional support from their offspring than on any other form of support.

Gloria Santos, for example, has a son and a daughter. While they do not live in the same state as their mother, they each send her fifty to seventy dollars every month. Yet she is disappointed with her children and explains why:

> They both have good salaries but call me only once or twice a month. I hardly know my grandchildren. All I ask from them is that they be closer to me, that they visit and call me more often. They only visit me once a year and only for one or two days. I've told my daughter that instead of sending me money she could call me more often. I was a good mother and worked hard in order for them to get a good education and have everything. All I expected from them was to show me they care, that they love me.

The importance that the older women attach to family interdependence does not imply that they constantly require assistance from children or that they do not value their independence. They prefer to live in their own households rather than with their adult children. They also try to solve as many problems as possible by themselves. But when support is needed, the adult children are expected to assist the aged parent to the degree they are able. This does not engender conflict or lowered self-esteem for the aged adult. Conflict and dissatisfaction are caused when adult children do not offer any support at all.

SEX ROLES AND FAMILIAL SUPPORTIVE NETWORKS

The family is the predominant source of support for most of these older women, providing instrumental and emotional support in daily life as well as assistance during health crises or times of need. Adult children play a central role in providing familial support

to old parents. For married women, husbands are also an important component of their support system. At the same time, most of the older women still perform functional roles for their families.

Support from Adult Children

The support and helpfulness expected from offspring is related to perceptions of the difference between men and women. Older women seek different types of assistance from daughters than from sons. Daughters are perceived as being inherently better able to understand their mothers due to their shared status and qualities as women; they are also considered more reliable. Sons are not expected to help as much as daughters or in the same way. When a daughter does not fulfill the obligations expected of her, complaints are more bitter than if the same were true of a son: "Men are different; they do not feel as we feel. But she is a woman; she should know better." Daughters are also expected to visit and/or call more frequently than are sons. As women are linked closely to the domestic domain, they are held responsible for the care of family relations.

Motherhood is perceived as creating an emotional bond among women. When daughters become mothers, the older women anticipate stronger ties and more support from them.

> Once a daughter experiences motherhood, she understands the suffering and hardships you underwent for her. Sons will never be able to understand this.

> My daughter always helped me. But when she became a mother for the first time, she grew much closer to me. It was then she was able to understand how much a mother can love.

Most of the older women go to a daughter first when confronted by an emotional problem. Daughters are felt to be more patient and better able to understand them as women. It is not that older women never discuss their emotional problems with their sons, but they prefer to discuss them with their daughters. For example, Juana Rivera has two sons who live in the same city as she and a daughter who resides in Puerto Rico. She and her sons get along well and see each other often. The sons stop by their mother's house every day after work, talk about daily happenings, and assist her with some tasks. However, when a physical exam revealed a breast tumor thought to be malignant, it was to her daughter in Puerto Rico that the old woman expressed her worries. She recalls that time of crisis:

> Eddie was with me when the doctor told me of the possibility of a tumor. I was brave. I didn't want him to see me upset. They [sons] get nervous when I get upset or cry.... That evening I called my daughter and talked to her.... She was very understanding and comforted me. I can always depend on her to understand me. She is the person who better understands me. My sons are also understanding, but she is a woman and understands more.

Although adult children are sources of assistance during the illnesses of their mothers, it is generally daughters from whom more is expected. Quite often daughters take their sick parents into their homes or stay overnight in the parental household in order to provide better care. Sons, as well as daughters, take the aged parent to the hospital or doctors' offices and buy medicines if necessary. However, it is more often daughters who check on their parents, provide care, and perform household chores when the parent is sick.

When the old women have been hospitalized, adult children living nearby tend to visit the hospital daily. Daughters and daughters-in-law sometimes cook special meals for the sick parent and bring the meals to the hospital. Quite often, adult children living in other states or in Puerto Rico come to help care for the aged parent or be present at the time of an operation. When Juana Rivera had exploratory surgery on her breast, her daughter came from Puerto Rico and stayed with her mother throughout the convalescence. Similarly, when Ana Toledo suffered a stroke and remained unconscious for four days, three of her six children residing in other states came to be with her and their siblings. After her release from the hospital, a daughter from New Jersey stayed at her mother's house for a week. When she left, the children who live near the old woman took turns looking after her.

Most adult children are also helpful in assisting with chores of daily living. At times, offspring take their widowed mothers grocery shopping. Other times, the older women give their children money to do the shopping for them. Daughters are more often asked to do these favors and to also buy personal care items and clothes for their mothers. Some adult offspring also assist by depositing Social Security checks, checking post office boxes, and buying money orders.

Support from Elderly Mothers

The Puerto Rican older women play an active role in providing assistance to their adult children. Gender affects the frequency of emotional support offered as well as the dynamics of the support. The older women offer advice more often to daughters than to sons on matters related to childrearing. And the approach used differs according to the children's gender. For example, one older woman stated,

> I never ask my son openly what is wrong with him. I do not want him to think that I believe he needs help to solve his problems; he is a man.... Yet, as a mother I worry. It is my duty to listen and offer him advice. With my daughter it is different; I can be more direct. She doesn't have to prove to me that she is self-sufficient.

Another woman expressed similar views:

> Of course I give advice to my sons! When they have had problems with their wives, their children, even among themselves, I listen to them, and tell them what I think. But with my daughters I am more open. You see, if I ask one of my sons what is wrong and he doesn't want to tell me, I don't insist too much; I'll ask later, maybe in a different way; and they will tell me sooner or later. With my daughters, if they don't want to tell me, I insist. They know I am a mother and a woman like them and that I can understand.

Older mothers perceive sons and daughters as in equal need of support. Daughters, however, are understood to face additional problems in areas such as conjugal relations, childrearing, and sexual harrassment, due to their status as women.

Emotional support to daughters-in-law is also offered, particularly when they are encountering marriage or childrearing problems. Josefina Montes explains the active role she played in comforting her daughter-in-law, whose husband was having an extramarital affair.

I told her not to give up, that she had to defend what was hers. I always listened to her and tried to offer some comfort. . . . When my son would come to my home to visit I would ask him "What is wrong with you? Don't you realize what a good mother and wife that woman is?" . . . I made it my business that he did not forget the exceptional woman she is. . . . I told him I didn't want to ever see him with the other one and not to mention her name in front of me. . . . I was on his case for almost two years. . . . All the time I told her to be patient. . . . It took time but he finally broke up with the other one.

When relations between mother and daughters-in-law are not friendly, support is not usually present. Eulalia Valle says that when her son left his wife and children to move in with another woman, there was not much she could do for her daughter-in-law.

There was not much I could do. What could I tell him? I couldn't say she was nice to me. . . . Once I tried to make him see how much she was hurting and he replied: "Don't defend her. She has never been fond of you and you know it." What could I reply to that? All I said was, "That's true but, still, she must be very hurt." But there was nothing positive to say about her!

Monetary assistance generally flows from the older parent to the adult children, although few old people are able to offer substantial financial help. Direct monetary assistance, rarely exceeding fifty dollars, is less frequent than gift-giving. Gift-giving usually takes the form of monetary contributions for specific articles needed by their children or children's families. In this way the older people contribute indirectly to the maintenance of their children's families.

The older women also play an active role in the observance of special family occasions and holidays. On the days preceding the celebration, they are busy cooking traditional Puerto Rican foods. It is expected that those in good health will participate in the preparation of foods. This is especially true on Christmas and Easter, when traditional foods are an essential component of the celebrations.

Cooking for offspring is also a part of everyday life. In many of the households, meals prepared in the Puerto Rican tradition are cooked daily "in case children or grandchildren come by." Josefina Montes, for example, cooks a large quantity of food every day for herself, her husband, and their adult children and grandchildren. Her daughters come by after work to visit and pick up their youngest children, who stay with grandparents after school. The youngest daughter eats dinner at her parents' home. The oldest takes enough food home to serve her family. Doña[3] Josefina's sons frequently drop by after work or during lunch and she always insists that they eat something.

The older women also provide assistance to their children during health crises. When Juana Rivera's son was hospitalized for a hernia operation, she visited the hospital every day, occasionally bringing food she had prepared for him. When her son was released, Doña Juana stayed in his household throughout his convalescence, caring for him while her daughter-in-law went off to work.

The aged women also assist their children by taking care of grandchildren. Grandchildren go to their grandmother's house after school and stay until their parents stop by after work. If the children are not old enough to walk home by themselves, the grandparent waits for them at school and brings them home. The women also take care of their grandchildren when they are not old enough to attend school or are sick. They see their role as grandmothers as a continuation or reenactment of their role as mothers and childrearers.

The women, despite old age, have a place in the functional structure of their families. The older women's assistance is an important contribution to their children's households and also helps validate the women's sense of their importance and helpfulness.

Mutual Assistance in Elderly Couples

Different conceptions of women and men influence interdependence between husband and wife as well as their daily tasks. Older married women are responsible for domestic tasks and perform household chores. They also take care of grandchildren, grocery shopping, and maintaining family relations. Older married men have among their chores depositing Social Security checks, going to the post office, and buying money orders. Although they stay in the house for long periods, the men go out into the community more often than do their wives. They usually stop at the *bodegas,*[4] which serve as a place for socializing and exchange of information, to buy items needed at home and newspapers from Puerto Rico.

Most married couples have a distinctive newspaper reading pattern. The husband comments on the news to his wife as he reads or after he has finished. Sometimes, after her husband finishes reading and commenting on the news, the older woman reads about it herself. Husbands also inform their wives of ongoing neighborhood events learned on their daily stops at the *bodegas*. Wives, on the other hand, inform husbands of familial events learned through their daily telephone conversations and visits from children and other kin members.

The older couple escort each other to service-providing agencies, even though they are usually accompanied by an adult child, adolescent grandchild, or social worker serving as translator. An older man still perceives himself in the role of "family protector" by escorting the women in his family, particularly his wife.

Older husbands and wives provide each other with emotional assistance. They are daily companions and serve as primary sources of confidence for each other, most often sharing children's and grandchildren's problems, health concerns, or financial worries. The couple do not always agree on solutions or approaches for assisting children when sharing their worries about offspring. Many times the woman serves as a mediator in communicating her husband's problems to adult children. The men tend to keep their problems, particularly financial and emotional ones, to themselves or tell their wives but not their children. This behavior rests upon the notion of men as financially responsible for the family, more self-sufficient, and less emotional than women.

Among the older couples, the husband or wife is generally the principal caregiver during the health crises of their spouse. Carmen Ruiz, for example, suffers from chronic anemia and tires easily. Her husband used to be a cook and has taken responsibility for cooking meals and looking after the household. When Providencia Cruz's husband was hospitalized she spent many hours each day at the hospital, wanting to be certain he was comfortable. She brought meals she had cooked for him, arranged his pillows, rubbed him with bay leaf rubbing alcohol, or watched him as he slept. When he was convalescing at home, she was his principal caregiver. Doña Providencia suffers from osteoarthritis and gastric acidity. When she

is in pain and spends the day in bed, her husband provides most of the assistance she needs. He goes to the drugstore to buy medicine or ingredients used in folk remedies. He knows how to prepare the mint and chamomile teas she drinks when not feeling well. He also rubs her legs and hands with ointments when the arthritic pain is more intense than usual. Furthermore, during the days that Doña Providencia's ailments last, he performs most of the household chores.

While both spouses live, the couple manages many of their problems on their own. Assistance from other family members with daily chores or help during an illness is less frequent when the woman still lives with her husband than when she lives alone. However, if one or both spouses is ill, help from adult children is more common.

FRIENDS AND NEIGHBORS AS COMMUNITY SOURCES OF SUPPORT

Friends and neighbors form part of the older women's support network. However, the women differentiate between "neighbors" and "friends." Neighbors, unlike kin and friends, are not an essential component of the network which provides emotional support. They may or may not become friends. Supportive relations with friends involve being instrumental helpers, companions, and confidants. Neighbors are involved only in instrumental help.

Neighbors as Sources of Support

Contact with neighbors takes the form of greetings, occasional visits, and exchanges of food, all of which help to build the basis for reciprocity when and if the need arises. The establishment and maintenance of good relations with neighbors is considered to be important since neighbors are potentially helpful during emergencies or unexpected events. Views such as the following are common: "It is good to get acquainted with your neighbors; you never know when you might need them."

Josefina Rosario, a widow, has lived next door to an older Puerto Rican couple for three years. Exchange of food and occasional visits are part of her interaction with them. Her neighbor's husband, in his mid-sixties, occasionally runs errands for Doña Josefina, who suffers from rheumatoid arthritis and needs a walker to move around. If she runs out of a specific food item, he goes to the grocery store for her. Other times, he buys stamps, mails letters, or goes to the drugstore to pick up some medicines for her. Although Doña Josefina cannot reciprocate in the same way, she repays her neighbors by visiting every other week and exchanging food. Her neighbors tell her she is to call them day or night if she ever feels sick. Although glad to have such "good neighbors," as she calls them, she stresses she does not consider them friends and therefore does not confide her personal problems to them.

Supportive Relationships Among Friends

Although friends perform instrumental tasks, the older women believe that a good friend's most important quality is being able to provide emotional support. A friend is someone willing to help during the "good" and "bad" times, and is trustworthy and reserved. Problems may be shared with a friend with the certainty that confidences will not be betrayed. A friend provides emotional support not only during a crisis or problem, but in everyday life. Friends are companions, visiting and/or calling on a regular basis.

Friendship for this group of women is determined along gender lines. They tend to be careful about men. Relationships with males outside the immediate familial group are usually kept at a formal level. Mistrust of men is based upon the women's notion of *machismo*. Since men are conceived of as having a stronger sexual drive, the women are wary of the possibility of sexual advances, either physical or verbal. None of the women regards a male as a confidant friend. Many even emphasize the word *amiga* ("female friend") instead of *amigo* ("male friend"). Remarks such as the following are common:

I've never had an *amigo*. Men cannot be trusted too much. They might misunderstand your motives and some even try to make a pass at you.

The few times the women refer to a male as a friend they use the term *amigo de la familia* ("friend of the family"). This expression conveys that the friendly relations are not solely between the woman and the man. The expression is generally used to refer to a close friend of the husband. *Amigos de la familia* may perform instrumental tasks, be present at family gatherings and unhappy events, or drop by to chat with the respondent's husband during the day. However, relations are not based on male–female relationships.

Age similarity is another factor that seems to affect selection of friends. The friendship networks of the older women are mainly composed of people sixty years of age and older. Friends who fill the role of confidant are generally women of a similar age. The women believe that younger generations, generally, have little interest in the elders. They also state that people their own age are better able to understand their problems because they share many of the same difficulties and worries.

Friends often serve as escorts, particularly in the case of women who live alone. Those who know some English serve as translators on some occasions. Close friends also help illiterate friends by reading and writing letters.

Most of the support friends provide one another is of an emotional nature, which involves sharing personal problems. Close friends entrust one another with family and health problems. This exchange occurs when friends either visit or call each other on the telephone. A pattern commonly observed between dyads of friends is daily calls. Many women who live alone usually call the friend during the morning hours, to make sure she is all right and to find out how she is feeling.

Another aspect of the emotional support the older women provide one another is daily companionship, occurring more often among those who live alone. For example, Hilda Montes and Rosa Mendoza sit together from 1:00 to 3:00 in the afternoon to watch soap operas and talk about family events, neighborhood happenings, and household management. At 3:00 P.M., whoever is at the other's apartment leaves because their grandchildren usually arrive from school around 4:00 P.M.

Friends are also supportive during health crises. If they cannot come to visit, they inquire daily about their friend's health by telephone. When their health permits, some friends perform menial household chores and always bring food for the sick person. If the occasion requires it, they prepare and/or administer home remedies. Friends, in this sense, alleviate the stress adult children often feel in assisting their aged mothers, particularly those who live by themselves. Friends take turns among themselves or with kin in taking care of the ill during the daytime. Children generally stay throughout the night.

Exchange ties with female friends include instrumental support, companionship, and problem sharing. Friends, particularly age cohorts, play an important role in the emotional well-being of the elders.

The relevance of culture to the experience of old age is seen in the influence of value orientations on the expectations these Puerto Rican women have of themselves and those in their informal support networks. The way a group's cultural tradition defines and interprets relationships influences how elders use their networks to secure the support needed in old age. At the same time, the extent to which reality fits culturally based expectations will contribute, to a large extent, to elders' sense of well-being.

NOTES

1. The article is based on a nineteen-month ethnographic study. The research was supported by the Danforth Foundation; Sigma Xi; the Scientific Research Society; and the Delta Kappa Gamma Society International.

2. All names are fictitious.

3. The deference term *Doña* followed by the woman's first name is a common way by which to address elderly Puerto Rican women and the one preferred by those who participated in the study.

4. Neighborhood grocery stores, generally owned by Puerto Ricans or other Hispanics, where ethnic foods can be purchased.

REFERENCES

Barth, F. 1969. Introduction to F. Barth, ed., *Ethnic groups and boundaries*. Boston: Little, Brown.

Bastida, E. 1979. "Family integration and adjustment to aging among Hispanic American elderly." Ph.D. dissertation, University of Kansas.

Cantor, M. H. 1979. "The informal support system of New York's inner city elderly: Is ethnicity a factor?" In D. L. Gelfand & A. J. Kutzik, eds., *Ethnicity and aging*. New York: Springer.

Carrasquillo, H. 1982. "Perceived social reciprocity and self-esteem among elderly barrio Antillean Hispanics and their familial informal networks." Ph.D. dissertation, Syracuse University.

Delgado, M. 1981. "Hispanic elderly and natural support systems: A special focus on Puerto Ricans." Paper presented at the Scientific Meeting of the Boston Society for Gerontological Psychiatry, November, Boston.

Donaldson, E., & Martínez, E. 1980. "The Hispanic elderly of East Harlem." *Aging* 305–306:6–11.

Sánchez-Ayéndez, M. 1984. "Puerto Rican elderly women: Aging in an ethnic minority group in the United States." Ph.D. dissertation, University of Massachusetts at Amherst.

Stevens, E. P. 1973. "Marianismo: The other face of machismo in Latin America." In A. Pescatello, ed., *Female and male in Latin America*. Pittsburgh: University of Pittsburgh Press.

READING 20

Capitalism and Gay Identity

JOHN D'EMILIO

For gay men and lesbians, the 1970s were years of significant achievement. Gay liberation and women's liberation changed the sexual landscape of the nation. Hundreds of thousands of gay women and men came out and openly affirmed same-sex eroticism. We won repeal of sodomy laws in half the states, a partial lifting of the exclusion of lesbians and gay men from federal employment, civil rights protection in a few dozen cities, the inclusion of gay rights in the platform of the Democratic Party, and the elimination of homosexuality from the psychiatric profession's list of mental illnesses. The gay male subculture expanded and became increasingly visible in large cities, and lesbian feminists pioneered in building alternative institutions and an alternative culture that attempted to embody a liberatory vision of the future.

In the 1980s, however, with the resurgence of an active right wing, gay men and lesbians face the future warily. Our victories appear tenuous and fragile; the relative freedom of the past few years seems too recent to be permanent. In some parts of the lesbian and gay male community, a feeling of doom is growing: analogies with McCarthy's America, when "sexual perverts" were a special target of the Right, and with Nazi Germany, where gays were shipped to concentration camps, surface with increasing frequency. Everywhere there is the sense that new strategies are in order if we want to preserve our gains and move ahead.

I believe that a new, more accurate theory of gay history must be part of this political enterprise. When the gay liberation movement began at the end of the 1960s, gay men and lesbians had no history that we could use to fashion our goals and strategy. In the en-

Reprinted from Ann Snitow, Christine Stansell, and Sharon Thompson, eds., *Powers of Desire: The Politics of Sexuality* (New York: Monthly Review Press, 1983), by permission of the Monthly Review Foundation. Copyright © 1983 by Ann Snitow, Christine Stansell, and Sharon Thompson.

suing years, in building a movement without a knowledge of our history, we instead invented a mythology. This mythical history drew on personal experience, which we read backward in time. For instance, most lesbians and gay men in the 1960s first discovered their homosexual desires in isolation, unaware of others, and without resources for naming and understanding what they felt. From this experience, we constructed a myth of silence, invisibility, and isolation as the essential characteristics of gay life in the past as well as the present. Moreover, because we faced so many oppressive laws, public policies, and cultural beliefs, we projected this into an image of the abysmal past: until gay liberation, lesbians and gay men were always the victims of systematic, undifferentiated, terrible oppression.

These myths have limited our political perspective. They have contributed, for instance, to an overreliance on a strategy of coming out—if every gay man and lesbian in America came out, gay oppression would end—and have allowed us to ignore the institutionalized ways in which homophobia and heterosexism are reproduced. They have encouraged, at times, an incapacitating despair, especially at moments like the present: How can we unravel a gay oppression so pervasive and unchanging?

There is another historical myth that enjoys nearly universal acceptance in the gay movement, the myth of the "eternal homosexual." The argument runs something like this: Gay men and lesbians always were and always will be. We are everywhere; not just now, but throughout history, in all societies and all periods. This myth served a positive political function in the first years of gay liberation. In the early 1970s, when we battled an ideology that either denied our existence or defined us as psychopathic individuals or freaks of nature, it was empowering to assert that "we are everywhere." But in recent years it has confined us as surely as the most homophobic medical theories, and locked our movement in place.

Here I wish to challenge this myth. I want to argue that gay men and lesbians have *not* always existed. Instead, they are a product of history, and have come into existence in a specific historical era. Their emergence is associated with the relations of capitalism; it has been the historical development of capitalism—more specifically, its free labor system—that has allowed large numbers of men and women in the late twentieth century to call themselves gay, to see themselves as part of a community of similar men and women, and to organize politically on the basis of that identity.[1] Finally, I want to suggest some political lessons we can draw from this view of history.

What, then, are the relationships between the free labor system of capitalism and homosexuality? First, let me review some features of capitalism. Under capitalism, workers are "free" laborers in two ways. We have the freedom to look for a job. We own our ability to work and have the freedom to sell our labor power for wages to anyone willing to buy it. We are also freed from the ownership of anything except our labor power. Most of us do not own the land or the tools that produce what we need, but rather have to work for a living in order to survive. So, if we are free to sell our labor power in the positive sense, we are also freed, in the negative sense, from any other alternative. This dialectic—the constant interplay between exploitation and some measure of autonomy—informs all of the history of those who have lived under capitalism.

As capital—money used to make more money—expands, so does this system of free labor. Capital expands in several ways. Usually it expands in the same place, transforming small firms into larger ones, but it also expands by taking over new areas of production: the weaving of cloth, for instance, or the baking of bread. Finally, capital expands geographically. In the United States, capitalism initially took root in the Northeast, at a time when slavery was the dominant system in the South and when noncapitalist Native American societies occupied the western half of the continent. During the nineteenth century, capital spread from the Atlantic to the Pacific, and in the twentieth, U.S. capital has penetrated almost every part of the world.

The expansion of capital and the spread of wage labor have effected a profound transformation in the structure and functions of the nuclear family, the ideology of family life, and the meaning of heterosexual relations. It is these changes in the family that are most directly linked to the appearance of a collective gay life.

The white colonists in seventeenth-century New England established villages structured around a household economy, composed of family units that were basically self-sufficient, independent, and patriarchal. Men, women, and children farmed land owned by the male head of household. Although there was a division of labor between men and women, the family was truly an interdependent unit of production: the survival of each member depended on the cooperation of all. The home was a workplace where women processed raw farm products into food for daily consumption, where they made clothing, soap, and candles, and where husbands, wives, and children worked together to produce the goods they consumed.

By the nineteenth century, this system of household production was in decline. In the Northeast, as merchant capitalists invested the money accumulated through trade in the production of goods, wage labor became more common. Men and women were drawn out of the largely self-sufficient household economy of the colonial era into a capitalist system of free labor. For women in the nineteenth century, working for wages rarely lasted beyond marriage; for men, it became a permanent condition.

The family was thus no longer an independent unit of production. But although no longer independent, the family was still interdependent. Because capitalism had not expanded very far, because it had not yet taken over—or socialized—the production of consumer goods, women still performed necessary productive labor in the home. Many families no longer produced grain, but wives still baked into bread the flour they bought with their husbands' wages; or, when they purchased yarn or cloth, they still made clothing for their families. By the mid-1800s, capitalism had destroyed the economic self-sufficiency of many families, but not the mutual dependence of the members.

This transition away from the household family-based economy to a fully developed capitalist free labor economy occurred very slowly, over almost two centuries. As late as 1920, 50 percent of the U.S. population lived in communities of fewer than 2,500 people. The vast majority of blacks in the early twentieth century lived outside the free labor economy, in a system of sharecropping and tenancy that rested on the family. Not only did independent farming as a way of life still exist for millions of Americans, but even in towns and small cities women continued to grow and process food, make clothing, and engage in other kinds of domestic production.

But for those people who felt the brunt of these changes, the family took on new significance as an affective unit, an institution that produced not goods but emotional satisfaction and happiness. By the 1920s among the white middle class, the ideology surrounding the family described it as the means through which men and women formed satisfying, mutually enhancing relationships and created an environment that nurtured children. The family became the setting for a "personal life," sharply distinguished and disconnected from the public world of work and production.[2]

The meaning of heterosexual relations also changed. In colonial New England, the birthrate averaged over seven children per woman of childbearing age. Men and women needed the labor of children. Producing offspring was as necessary for survival as producing grain. Sex was harnessed to procreation. The Puritans did not celebrate *hetero*sexuality but rather marriage; they condemned *all* sexual expression outside the marriage bond and did not differentiate sharply between sodomy and heterosexual fornication.

By the 1970s, however, the birthrate had dropped to under two. With the exception of the post–World War II baby boom, the decline has been continuous for two centuries, paralleling the spread of capitalist relations of production. It occurred even when access to contraceptive devices and abortion was systematically curtailed. The decline has included every segment of the population—urban and rural families, blacks and whites, ethnics and WASPs, the middle class and the working class.

As wage labor spread and production became socialized, then, it became possible to release sexuality from the "imperative" to procreate. Ideologically, heterosexual expression came to be a means of establishing intimacy, promoting happiness, and experiencing pleasure. In divesting the household of its economic independence and fostering the separation of sexuality from procreation, capitalism has created conditions that allow some men and women to organize a personal life around their erotic/emotional attraction to their own sex. It has made possible the formation of urban communities of lesbians and gay men and, more recently, of a politics based on a sexual identity.

Evidence from colonial New England court records and church sermons indicates that male and female homosexual behavior existed in the seventeenth century. Homosexual *behavior,* however, is different from homosexual *identity.* There was, quite simply, no "social space" in the colonial system of production that allowed men and women to be gay. Survival was structured around participation in a nuclear family. There were certain homosexual acts—sodomy among men, "lewdness" among women—in which individuals engaged, but family was so pervasive that colonial society lacked even the category of homosexual or lesbian to describe a person. It is quite possible that some men and women experienced a stronger attraction to their own sex than to the opposite sex—in fact, some colonial court cases refer to men who persisted in their "unnatural" attractions—but one could not fashion out of that preference a way of life. Colonial Massachusetts even had laws prohibiting unmarried adults from living outside family units.[3]

By the second half of the nineteenth century, this situation was noticeably changing as the capitalist system of free labor took hold. Only when *individuals* began to make their living through wage labor, instead of as parts of an interdependent family unit, was it possible for homosexual desire to coalesce into a personal identity—an identity based on the ability to remain outside the heterosexual family and to construct a personal life based on attraction to one's own sex. By the end of the century, a class of men and women existed who recognized their erotic interest in their own sex, saw it as a trait that set them apart from the majority, and sought others like themselves. These early gay lives came from a wide social spectrum: civil servants and business executives, department store clerks and college professors, factory operatives, ministers, lawyers, cooks, domestics, hoboes, and the idle rich: men and women, black and white, immigrant and native born.

In this period, gay men and lesbians began to invent ways of meeting each other and sustaining a group life. Already, in the early twentieth century, large cities contained male homosexual bars. Gay men staked out cruising areas, such as Riverside Drive in New York City and Lafayette Park in Washington. In St. Louis and the nation's capital, annual drag balls brought together large numbers of black gay men. Public bathhouses and YMCAs became gathering spots for male homosexuals. Lesbians formed literary societies and private social clubs. Some working-class women "passed" as men to obtain better paying jobs and lived with other women—lesbian couples who appeared to the world as husband and wife. Among the faculties of women's colleges, in the settlement houses, and in the professional associations and clubs that women formed one could find lifelong intimate relationships supported by a web of lesbian friends. By the 1920s and 1930s, large cities such as New York and Chicago contained lesbian bars. These patterns of living could evolve because capitalism allowed individuals to survive beyond the confines of the family.[4]

Simultaneously, ideological definitions of homosexual behavior changed. Doctors developed theories about homosexual*ity,* describing it as a condition, something that was inherent in a person, a part of his or her "nature." These theories did not represent scientific breakthroughs, elucidations of previously undiscovered areas of knowledge; rather, they were an ideological response to a new way of organizing one's personal life. The popularization of the medical model, in turn, affected the consciousness of the women and men who experienced homosexual desire, so that they came to define themselves through their erotic life.[5]

These new forms of gay identity and patterns of group life also reflected the differentiation of people according to gender, race, and class that is so pervasive in capitalist societies. Among whites, for instance, gay men have traditionally been more visible than lesbians. This partly stems from the division between the public male sphere and the private female sphere. Streets, parks, and bars, especially at night, were "male space." Yet the greater visibility of white gay men also reflected their larger numbers. The Kinsey studies of the 1940s and 1950s found significantly more men than women with predominantly homosexual histories, a situation caused, I would argue, by the fact that capitalism had drawn far more men than women into the labor force, and at higher wages. Men could more easily construct a personal life independent of attachments to the opposite sex, whereas women were more likely to remain economically dependent on men. Kinsey also found a strong positive correlation between years of schooling and lesbian activity. College-educated white women, far more able than their working-class sisters to support themselves, could survive more easily without intimate relationships with men.[6]

Among working-class immigrants in the early twentieth century, closely knit kin networks and an ethic of family solidarity placed constraints on individual autonomy that made gayness a difficult option

to pursue. In contrast, for reasons not altogether clear, urban black communities appeared relatively tolerant of homosexuality. The popularity in the 1920s and 1930s of songs with lesbian and gay male themes—"B. D. Woman," "Prove It on Me," "Sissy Man," "Fairey Blues"—suggests an openness about homosexual expression at odds with the mores of whites. Among men in the rural West in the 1940s, Kinsey found extensive incidence of homosexual behavior, but, in contrast with the men in large cities, little consciousness of gay identity. Thus even as capitalism exerted a homogenizing influence by gradually transforming more individuals into wage laborers and separating them from traditional communities, different groups of people were also affected in different ways.[7]

The decisions of particular men and women to act on their erotic/emotional preference for the same sex, along with the new consciousness that this preference made them different, led to the formation of an urban subculture of gay men and lesbians. Yet at least through the 1930s this subculture remained rudimentary, unstable, and difficult to find. How, then, did the complex, well-developed gay community emerge that existed by the time the gay liberation movement exploded? The answer is to be found during World War II, a time when the cumulative changes of several decades coalesced into a qualitatively new shape.

The war severely disrupted traditional patterns of gender relations and sexuality, and temporarily created a new erotic situation conducive to homosexual expression. It plucked millions of young men and women, whose sexual identities were just forming, out of their homes, out of towns and small cities, out of the heterosexual environment of the family, and dropped them into sex-segregated situations—as GIs, as WACs and WAVEs, in same-sex rooming houses for women workers who relocated to seek employment. The war freed millions of men and women from the settings where heterosexuality was normally imposed. For men and women already gay, it provided an opportunity to meet people like themselves. Others could become gay because of the temporary freedom to explore sexuality that the war provided.[8]

Lisa Ben, for instance, came out during the war. She left the small California town where she was raised, came to Los Angeles to find work, and lived in a women's boarding house. There she met for the first time lesbians who took her to gay bars and introduced her to other gay women. Donald Vining was a young man with lots of homosexual desire and few gay experiences. He moved to New York City during the war and worked at a large YMCA. His diary reveals numerous erotic adventures with soldiers, sailors, marines, and civilians at the Y where he worked, as well as at the men's residence club where he lived, and in parks, bars, and movie theaters. Many GIs stayed in port cities like New York, at YMCAs like the one where Vining worked. In his oral histories of gay men in San Francisco, focusing on the 1940s, Allan Bérubé has found that the war years were critical in the formation of gay male *community* in the city. Places as different as San Jose, Denver, and Kansas City had their first gay bars in the 1940s. Even severe repression could have positive side effects. Pat Bond, a lesbian from Davenport, Iowa, joined the WACs during the 1940s. Caught in a purge of hundreds of lesbians from the WACs in the Pacific, she did not return to Iowa. She stayed in San Francisco and became part of a community of lesbians. How many other women and men had comparable experiences? How many other cities saw a rapid growth of lesbian and gay male communities?[9]

The gay men and women of the 1940s were pioneers. Their decisions to act on their desires formed the underpinnings of an urban subculture of gay men and lesbians. Throughout the 1950s and 1960s, the gay subculture grew and stabilized so that people coming out then could more easily find other gay women and men than in the past. Newspapers and magazines published articles describing gay male life. Literally hundreds of novels with lesbian themes were published.[10] Psychoanalysts complained about the new ease with which their gay male patients found sexual partners. And the gay subculture was not just to be found in the largest cities. Lesbian and gay male bars existed in places like Worcester, Massachusetts, and Buffalo, New York; in Columbia, South Carolina, and Des Moines, Iowa. Gay life in the 1950s and 1960s became a nationwide phenomenon. By the time of the Stonewall Riots in New York City in 1969—the event that ignited the gay liberation movement—our situation was hardly one of silence, invisibility, and isolation. A massive, grass-roots liberation movement could form almost overnight precisely because communities of lesbians and gay men existed.

Although gay community was a precondition for a mass movement, the oppression of lesbians and gay men was the force that propelled the movement into existence. As the subculture expanded and grew more visible in the post–World War II era, oppression by the state intensified, becoming more systematic and inclusive. The Right scapegoated "sexual perverts" during the McCarthy era. Eisenhower imposed a total ban on the employment of gay women and men by the federal government and government contractors. Purges of lesbians and homosexuals from the military rose sharply. The FBI instituted widespread surveillance of gay meeting places and of lesbian and gay organizations, such as the Daughters of Bilitis and the Mattachine Society. The Post Office placed tracers on the correspondence of gay men and passed evidence of homosexual activity on to employers. Urban vice squads invaded private homes, made sweeps of lesbian and gay male bars, entrapped gay men in public places, and fomented local witch hunts. The danger involved in being gay rose even as the possibilities of being gay were enhanced. Gay liberation was a response to this contradiction.

Although lesbians and gay men won significant victories in the 1970s and opened up some safe social space in which to exist, we can hardly claim to have dealt a fatal blow to heterosexism and homophobia. One could even argue that the enforcement of gay oppression has merely changed locales, shifting somewhat from the state to the arena of extralegal violence in the form of increasingly open physical attacks on lesbians and gay men. And, as our movements have grown, they have generated a backlash that threatens to wipe out our gains. Significantly, this New Right opposition has taken shape as a "pro-family" movement. How is it that capitalism, whose structure made possible the emergence of a gay identity and the creation of urban gay communities, appears unable to accept gay men and lesbians in its midst? Why do heterosexism and homophobia appear so resistant to assault?

The answers, I think, can be found in the contradictory relationship of capitalism to the family. On the one hand, as I argued earlier, capitalism has gradually undermined the material basis of the nuclear family by taking away the economic functions that cemented the ties between family members. As more adults have been drawn into the free labor system, and as capital has expanded its sphere until it produces as commodities most goods and services we need for our survival, the forces that propelled men and women into families and kept them there have weakened. On the other hand, the ideology of capitalist society has enshrined the family as the source of love, affection, and emotional security, the place where our need for stable, intimate human relationships is satisfied.

This elevation of the nuclear family to preeminence in the sphere of personal life is not accidental. Every society needs structures for reproduction and child-rearing, but the possibilities are not limited to the nuclear family. Yet the privatized family fits well with capitalist relations of production. Capitalism has socialized production while maintaining that the products of socialized labor belong to the owners of private property. In many ways, childrearing has also been progressively socialized over the last two centuries, with schools, the media, peer groups, and employers taking over functions that once belonged to parents. Nevertheless, capitalist society maintains that reproduction and childrearing are private tasks, that children "belong" to parents, who exercise the rights of ownership. Ideologically, capitalism drives people into heterosexual families: each generation comes of age having internalized a heterosexist model of intimacy and personal relationships. Materially, capitalism weakens the bonds that once kept families together so that their members experience a growing instability in the place they have come to expect happiness and emotional security. Thus, while capitalism has knocked the material foundation away from family life, lesbians, gay men, and heterosexual feminists have become the scapegoats for the social instability of the system.

This analysis, if persuasive, has implications for us today. It can affect our perception of our identity, our formulation of political goals, and our decisions about strategy.

I have argued that lesbian and gay identity and communities are historically created, the result of a process of capitalist development that has spanned many generations. A corollary of this argument is that we are *not* a fixed social minority composed for all time of a certain percentage of the population. *There are more of us* than one hundred years ago, more of us than forty years ago. And there may very well be more gay men and lesbians in the future. Claims made by gays and nongays that sexual orientation is fixed at an early age, that large numbers of visible gay men and lesbians in society, the media, and the schools will have no influence on the sexual identities of the young, are wrong. Capitalism has created the material

conditions for homosexual desire to express itself as a central component of some individuals' lives; now, our political movements are changing consciousness, creating the ideological conditions that make it easier for people to make that choice.

To be sure, this argument confirms the worst fears and most rabid rhetoric of our political opponents. But our response must be to challenge the underlying belief that homosexual relations are bad, a poor second choice. We must not slip into the opportunistic defense that society need not worry about tolerating us, since only homosexuals become homosexuals. At best, a minority group analysis and a civil rights strategy pertain to those of us who already are gay. It leaves today's youth—tomorrow's lesbians and gay men—to internalize heterosexist models that it can take a lifetime to expunge.

I have also argued that capitalism has led to the separation of sexuality from procreation. Human sexual desire need no longer be harnessed to reproductive imperatives, to procreation; its expression has increasingly entered the realm of choice. Lesbians and homosexuals most clearly embody the potential of this split, since our gay relationships stand entirely outside a procreative framework. The acceptance of our erotic choices ultimately depends on the degree to which society is willing to affirm sexual expression as a form of play, positive and life-enhancing. Our movement may have begun as the struggle of a "minority," but what we should now be trying to "liberate" is an aspect of the personal lives of all people—sexual expression.[11]

Finally, I have suggested that the relationship between capitalism and the family is fundamentally contradictory. On the one hand, capitalism continually weakens the material foundation of family life, making it possible for individuals to live outside the family, and for a lesbian and gay male identity to develop. On the other, it needs to push men and women into families, at least long enough to reproduce the next generation of workers. The elevation of the family to ideological preeminence guarantees that capitalist society will reproduce not just children, but heterosexism and homophobia. In the most profound sense, capitalism is the problem.[12]

How do we avoid remaining the scapegoats, the political victims of the social instability that capitalism generates? How can we take this contradictory relationship and use it to move toward liberation?

Gay men and lesbians exist on social terrain beyond the boundaries of the heterosexual nuclear family. Our communities have formed in that social space. Our survival and liberation depend on our ability to defend and expand that terrain, not just for ourselves but for everyone. That means, in part, support for issues that broaden the opportunities for living outside traditional heterosexual family units: issues like the availability of abortion and the ratification of the Equal Rights Amendment, affirmative action for people of color and for women, publicly funded daycare and other essential social services, decent welfare payments, full employment, the rights of young people—in other words, programs and issues that provide a material basis for personal autonomy.

The rights of young people are especially critical. The acceptance of children as dependents, as belonging to parents, is so deeply ingrained that we can scarcely imagine what it would mean to treat them as autonomous human beings, particularly in the realm of sexual expression and choice. Yet until that happens, gay liberation will remain out of our reach.

But personal autonomy is only half the story. The instability of families and the sense of impermanence and insecurity that people are now experiencing in their personal relationships are real social problems that need to be addressed. We need political solutions for these difficulties of personal life. These solutions should not come in the form of a radical version of the pro-family position, of some left-wing proposals to strengthen the family. Socialists do not generally respond to the exploitation and economic inequality of industrial capitalism by calling for a return to the fam-ily farm and handicraft production. We recognize that the vastly increased productivity that capitalism has made possible by socializing production is one of its progressive features. Similarly, we should not be trying to turn back the clock to some mythic age of the happy family.

We do need, however, structures and programs that will help to dissolve the boundaries that isolate the family, particularly those that privatize childrearing. We need community- or worker-controlled daycare, housing where privacy and community coexist, neighborhood institutions—from medical clinics to performance centers—that enlarge the social unit where each of us has a secure place. As we create structures beyond the nuclear family that provide a sense of belonging, the family will wane in significance. Less and less will it seem to make or break our emotional security.

In this respect gay men and lesbians are well situated to play a special role. Already excluded from families as most of us are, we have had to create, for our survival, networks of support that do not depend on the bonds of blood or the license of the state, but that are freely chosen and nurtured. The building of an "affectional community" must be as much a part of our political movement as are campaigns for civil rights. In this way we may prefigure the shape of personal relationships in a society grounded in equality and justice rather than exploitation and oppression, a society where autonomy and security do not preclude each other but coexist.

ACKNOWLEDGMENTS

This essay is a revised version of a lecture given before several audiences in 1979 and 1980. I am grateful to the following groups for giving me a forum in which to talk and get feedback: the Baltimore Gay Alliance, the San Francisco Lesbian and Gay History Project, the organizers of Gay Awareness Week 1980 at San Jose State University and the University of California at Irvine, and the coordinators of the Student Affairs Lectures at the University of California at Irvine.

Lisa Duggan, Estelle Freedman, Jonathan Katz, Carole Vance, Paula Webster, Bert Hansen, and the editors of *Powers of Desire* provided helpful criticisms of an earlier draft. I especially want to thank Allan Bérubé and Jonathan Katz for generously sharing with me their own research, and Amber Hollibaugh for many exciting hours of nonstop conversation about Marxism and sexuality.

NOTES

1. I do not mean to suggest that no one has ever proposed that gay identity is a product of historical change. See, for instance, Mary McIntosh, "The Homosexual Role," *Social Problems* 16 (1968): 182–92; Jeffrey Weeks, *Coming Out: Homosexual Politics in Britain* (New York: Quartet Books, 1977). It is also implied in Michel Foucault, *The History of Sexuality,* vol. 1: *An Introduction,* tr. Robert Hurley (New York: Pantheon, 1978). However, this does represent a minority viewpoint and the works cited above have not specified how it is that capitalism as a system of production has allowed for the emergence of a gay male and lesbian identity. As an example of the "eternal homosexual" thesis, see John Boswell, *Christianity, Social Tolerance, and Homosexuality* (Chicago: University of Chicago Press, 1980), where "gay people" remains an unchanging social category through fifteen centuries of Mediterranean and Western European history.

2. See Eli Zaretsky, *Capitalism, the Family, and Personal Life* (New York: Harper & Row, 1976); and Paul Fass, *The Damned and the Beautiful: American Youth in the 1920s* (New York: Oxford University Press, 1977).

3. Robert F. Oaks, "'Things Fearful to Name': Sodomy and Buggery in Seventeenth-Century New England," *Journal of Social History* 12 (1978): 268–81; J. R. Roberts, "The Case of Sarah Norman and Mary Hammond," *Sinister Wisdom* 24 (1980): 57–62; and Jonathan Katz, *Gay American History* (New York: Crowell, 1976), pp. 16–24, 568–71.

4. For the period from 1870 to 1940 see the documents in Katz, *Gay American History,* and idem, *Gay/Lesbian Almanac* (New York: Crowell, 1983). Other sources include Allan Bérubé, "Lesbians and Gay Men in Early San Francisco: Notes Toward a Social History of Lesbians and Gay Men in America," unpublished paper, 1979; Vern Bullough and Bonnie Bullough, "Lesbianism in the 1920s and 1930s: A Newfound Study," *Signs* 2 (Summer 1977): 895–904.

5. On the medical model see Weeks, *Coming Out,* pp. 23–32. The impact of the medical model on the consciousness of men and women can be seen in Louis Hyde, ed., *Rat and the Devil: The Journal Letters of F. O. Matthiessen and Russell Cheney* (Hamden, Conn.: Archon, 1978), p. 47, and in the story of Lucille Hart in Katz, *Gay American History,* pp. 258–79. Radclyffe Hall's classic novel about lesbianism, *The Well of Loneliness,* published in 1928, was perhaps one of the most important vehicles for the popularization of the medical model.

6. See Alfred Kinsey et al., *Sexual Behavior in the Human Male* (Philadelphia: W. B. Saunders, 1948) and *Sexual Behavior in the Human Female* (Philadelphia: W. B. Saunders, 1953).

7. On black music, see "AC/DC Blues: Gay Jazz Reissues," Stash Records, ST-106 (1977), and Chris Albertson, *Bessie* (New York: Stein & Day, 1974); on the persistence of kin networks in white ethnic communities see Judith Smith, "Our Own Kind: Family and Community Networks in Providence," in *A Heritage of Her Own,* ed. Nancy F. Cott and Elizabeth H. Pleck (New York: Simon & Schuster, 1979), pp. 393–411; on differences between rural and urban male homoeroticism see Kinsey et al., *Sexual Behavior in the Human Male,* pp. 455–57, 630–31.

8. The argument and the information in this and the following paragraphs come from my book *Sexual Politics, Sexual Communities: The Making of a Homosexual Minority in the United States, 1940–1970* (Chicago: University of Chicago Press, 1983). I have also developed it with reference to San Francisco in "Gay Politics, Gay Community: San Francisco's Experience," *Socialist Review* 55 (January–February 1981): 77–104.

9. Donald Vining, *A Gay Diary, 1933–1946* (New York: Pepys Press, 1979); "Pat Bond," in Nancy Adair and Casey Adair, *Word Is Out* (New York: New Glide Publications, 1978), pp. 55–65; and Allan Bérubé, "Marching to a Different Drummer: Coming Out During World War II," a slide/talk presented at the annual meeting of the American Historical Association, December 1981, Los Angeles. A shorter version of Bérubé's presentation can be found in *The Advocate,* October 15, 1981, pp. 20–24.

10. On lesbian novels see *The Ladder,* March 1958, p. 18; February 1960, pp. 14–15; April 1961, pp. 12–13; February 1962, pp. 6–11; January 1963, pp. 6–13, February 1964, pp. 12–19, February 1965, pp. 19–23; March 1966, pp. 22–26; and April 1967, pp. 8–13. *The Ladder* was the magazine published by the Daughters of Bilitis.

11. This especially needs to be emphasized today. The 1980 annual conference of the National Organization for Women, for instance, passed a lesbian rights resolution that defined the issue as one of "discrimination based on affectional/sexual preference/orientation," and explicitly disassociated the issue from other questions of sexuality such as pornography, sadomasochism, public sex, and pederasty.

12. I do not mean to suggest that homophobia is "caused" by capitalism, or is to be found only in capitalist societies. Severe sanctions against homoeroticism can be found in European feudal society and in contemporary socialist countries. But my focus in this essay has been the emergence of a gay identity under capitalism, and the mechanisms specific to capitalism that made this possible and that reproduce homophobia as well.

Women, Work, and the Social Order

ALICE KESSLER-HARRIS

In colonial New England, women routinely kept taverns, worked as compositors, operated printing presses, and ran their husbands' business affairs. Not infrequently, they also ran mills, served apprenticeships, and worked in saw mills. Yet in 1825, a young farm girl who wished to earn extra money by working in a textile mill had to board in a house where she was governed by stringent rules. Each girl had to sit at table during meals at a place assigned her according to the length of time she had worked in the factory. Doors were closed at 10 P.M. and boarders expected to retire then. Anyone "habitually absent from public worship on the Sabbath" was subject to discharge.[1] Not long thereafter, women were told by Sara Jane Clarke that the "true feminine genius is ever timid, doubtful, and clingingly dependent; a perpetual childhood."[2]

"Acceptable employments," pointed out one prominent ladies' magazine, were to be pursued only before marriage and in case of dire need.[3] But in World War I women successfully replaced male trolley drivers who had joined the army. Shortly after the men returned, they went out on strike to protest the fact that the women had not immediately been fired. During World War II, women "ran lathes, cut dies, read blueprints, and serviced airplanes. They maintained roadbeds, greased locomotives . . . worked as stevedores, blacksmiths, . . . and drill press operators."[4] After the war, a best-selling book proposed government programs to bolster the family, encourage women to bear children and revive the lost arts of canning, preserving, and interior decorating. In contrast, the contemporary women's liberation movement insists on equal opportunity, an end to the sex-stereotyp-

Reprinted from Berenice Carroll, ed., *Liberating Women's History* (Urbana: University of Illinois Press, 1976), by permission of the author. Copyright © 1976 by Alice Kessler-Harris.

ing of jobs, and changes in family structure which would free all women who want to work outside the home.

How can we explain these dramatic changes in the kinds of work done by women? How can we understand accompanying shifts in attitudes toward working women? What are the relationships of these two to the work that men do? This essay will explore the interaction between ideas about women and their labor force participation. It will consider women's work in the context of changing economic needs, and explore the relationship between work outside the home and changing family functions. For each economic stage in America's past, it will attempt to understand both the ways in which women have participated in the labor force, and the ways in which working women of different classes and ethnic groups perceive their experiences.

The relationships among these factors are complex. While ideas about women's proper roles have historically confined women to work within the home and community, to exclude them from paid labor altogether would have deprived the industrializing process of workers badly needed in an American labor market characterized by chronic scarcity until the closing decades of the 19th century. For all women to work would threaten the integrity of home and family on which social order was believed to rest. Clearly some women had to be socialized into staying at home while others were encouraged to work. The varying needs of the economy as well as the changing functions of families have increasingly led women into the labor force. The resulting tension between family and work roles has been resolved historically in a variety of ways and with different consequences for women of various classes and ethnic groups. At the same time, women as a group have always worked in the lowest-paid, least prestigious sectors of the work force. This essay will attempt to comprehend both the unity and the diversity of women's work experiences by exploring the interaction between the changing labor-force requirements of employers and the family's relationship to society.

The family had been a keystone of social order in Puritan New England. The Massachusetts Bay Colony self-consciously encouraged families to be "little cells of righteousness where the mother and father disciplined not only their children, but also their servants and any boarders they might take in."[5] Unmarried men and women were required to place themselves in the home of a family in order to be guided by them. Family members were encouraged to supervise each other to guard the morals of the community as a whole. John Demos sums up his study of the Plymouth colony by noting that the family functioned as a business, a school, a training institution, a church, and often as a welfare institution. "Family and community . . . ," he concludes, "formed part of the same moral equation. The one supported the other and they became in a sense indistinguishable."[6]

While the functions of the family changed toward the end of the 18th century, certain assumptions remained. A pre-industrial society assumed that, except among the aristocracy, all family members would work as a matter of course. So widely accepted was this practice that colonial widows almost routinely took over businesses left by their deceased husbands, and in at least one instance the Plymouth Colony General Court revoked the license of an innkeeper whose wife had recently died. The court judged that without her services, the husband was not capable of keeping a public house.[7] But work for women was inseparable from the home and family. When Alexander Hamilton argued that putting women and children to work in incipient manufacturing enterprises would save them from the curse of idleness, his idea was scorned.

As the agrarian 18th-century society moved into the early industrialization of the 19th century, a growing mythology confirmed women's attachment to their homes. On a functional level, this is readily explained. Industrialization and concurrent urbanization increased the number of men who worked in impersonal factories beyond the immediate surroundings of home and community. With men removed from contact with children during the lengthy and exhausting day, women had to fill the breach. Simultaneously, laissez-faire economic policies which emphasized individu-

alism, success, and competition, replaced the old Puritan ethic which emphasized morality, hard work, and community. Men who worked hard and strove for success required wives who could competently supervise the household and exercise supportive roles as well. Ideas about what women should do conformed to these new societal requirements. In what Bernard Wishy calls a reappraisal of family life that took place after 1830, motherhood rose to new heights, and children became the focus of womanly activity. Mothers were asked to give up wealth, frivolity, and fashion in order to prepare themselves for a great calling. "The mother was the obvious source of everything that would save or damn the child; the historical and spiritual destiny of America lay in her hands."[8]

Simultaneously, the woman became a lady. Meek and submissive, modest and silent, women were expected to submerge their wills into those of husbands and fathers. Piety, purity, and submissiveness became the ideal. The art of homemaking now reached mystical proportions, with some educators arguing that women must be trained to that end. Homemaking became a profession. There could be no higher calling.[9] Girls of all classes went to school to learn to read, write, and do simple math; but those whose parents aspired to the middle class were treated differently from their brothers. Since they inhabited "a realm different from that of men, their education must also be different."[10] For the affluent, a little music, literature, and embroidery added to the three R's were enough. "Home, duty to the family, and religion" were the only concerns fit for women.

For a woman to neglect her duty meant social chaos. As one popular 19th-century schoolbook argued, "when a woman quits her own department . . . she departs from that sphere which is assigned to her in the order of society, because she neglects her duty and leaves her own department vacant. . . . "[11] Consistent with this feeling, one state after another, beginning in New York in 1778, and ending with New Jersey in 1844, deprived women of the suffrage rights they had possessed in the early years after the revolution. When the suffragists asked for their lost political rights in 1848, they were met with ridicule and antagonism. As Aileen Kraditor has argued, "it was not that social order required the subordination of women, rather . . . it required a family structure that involved the subordination of women."[12] Until 1850, the decennial census recorded all data by families. In 1850, the name of each person was enumerated, but only the occupations of males over 15 were recorded. Finally, in 1860, occupations of females were included.[13]

Women became factory workers at a time when the family was understood as the basic social unit, essential to social order. Millowners, like most other Americans, had a large stake in preserving social order, and removing women from their homes did not prove appealing to an affluent and largely agrarian population with a coherent conception of woman's role. But the need for labor was undeniable. In the early years after the revolution, New England millowners hired whole families, many of whom worked only during slack seasons on the farm. Independent farmers were reluctant to adapt to the discipline of the factory, and proved to be an unsatisfactory labor supply.[14]

The unmarried daughters of New England farmers seemed to be the only alternative. Could one reconcile the moral imperative of the home with the use of these young women in factories? It was the genius of Francis Cabot Lowell to conceive of a way of doing so. He appealed to the young single daughters of farm families in a way that played into both their sense of family responsibility and into the ethic of hard work. For the mill which finally opened in Lowell, Massachusetts, in 1821, he proposed carefully supervised boarding houses for girls who would spend a few years before marriage at the mills, and he offered salaries which were to be saved for their trousseaux, or used to help pay off mortgages, or send a brother through college. At the same time, parents were assured that their daughters would be given both hard work and discipline, experiences that would make them into better wives and mothers. The mills attracted a reliable labor force, easily disciplined in industrial routines, and far less expensive than male breadwinners. In return, they promised a training ground in morality.

The millowners' needs conspired with their conviction that they were providing a service for the nation. Millowners repeatedly stated "that one of their prime purposes in launching the textile industry was to give employment to respectable women to save them from poverty and idleness."[15] They argued that they were in fact preserving republican virtues of hard work and raising the moral and intellectual tone of the country.[16] The mill girls themselves, at least in the early years, seemed to believe the rationale. In a manner reminiscent of the early Puritans, they "supervised" one another, ostracizing those whose morals were in question.[17] They were said to read poetry and to study together. The factory became a reputed cultural oasis.

For a variety of technological and economic reasons, employers could not long maintain high wages and good working conditions. Within 20 years after the mill's opening, the Lowell women complained of excessively long hours, wage cuts, and extra work. These complaints were echoed in textile mills throughout New England. Workers who had country homes to return to refused to work under deteriorating conditions. When Lowell operatives organized themselves into the Female Labor Reform Association in 1845, the millowners deserted their moral stance. Taking advantage of increasing Irish immigration, they rapidly eliminated the old work force. As late as 1845, only 7 percent of the employees in the eight Lowell mills were Irish. By 1852, the old New England mill girl had gone. The pages of the *Lowell Offering,* a worker-run but factory-supported paper, reveal the degree to which employers had chosen to place a cheap labor supply above their previous moral convictions. Some operators still continued to believe in 1849 that corporation owners would raise wages so as "to attract once more the sort of girl who had made the industry what it was."[18] Skeptics felt that the mills had lost the respect of the community because standards of morality and the old spirit of mutual surveillance had declined. Caroline Ware, historian of the textile industry, assesses the position of the employers: "Necessity had forced them to gain and hold the respect of the community in order to attract the requisite workers, and they were only too eager to be relieved of that necessity by the advent of a class of labor which had no standing in the community and no prejudice against mill-work."[19]

The rapid replacement of New England women by lower paid and more tractable Irish male and female workers illustrates the double uses of the moral code by channeling the labor force as the 19th century progressed. By the mid 1850s, "respectable" women would not work in factories or as servants. The only sanctioned occupations for women were teaching and, when genteel poverty struck, dressmaking. The labor force needs of employers encouraged class divisions which were reflected in the prevailing myths about women. None of the extensive and elaborate network aimed at preventing the middle-class woman from leaving her sphere applied to immigrants, working-class, or black women. These women constituted the growing number who, from 1850 on, took jobs in expanding industries.[20] While financial need drove them into the labor force, their practical exclusion from the moral code which defined a woman's role had a number of tangible benefits for employers.

In the first place, the existence of the moral code and the middle-class feminine ideal of domesticity provided employers with a labor force of women who, for the most part, were convinced that their real calling lay in marriage and child-rearing and had only a transient interest in their jobs. The drive toward respectability provided working women with a set of aspirations (equivalent to upward mobility for men) which mitigated class consciousness and complaints about present exploitation. For those who were married and working, the desire to stay home provided a goad to prod unfortunate husbands into working harder and earning more.

Second, insisting that women belonged at home permitted employers to exploit working women by treating them as though their earnings were merely supplemental. Any examination of women's wages, which were always substantially below those of men and seldom sufficient even for a single woman to support herself, reveals that this was the common practice of employers. Thus, John Commons estimated that while in 1914 a living wage for a single person was defined as eight dollars per week, 75 percent of all female wage earners received less than that, and 50 percent received less than six dollars per week. A 20 percent unemployment rate further reduced these wages.[21] The assumption that women belonged at home occasionally led employers to ask that the help received by women living at home be taken into account in calculating "living wages."[22] The same assumption led employers to refuse to train women to perform skilled jobs and to deny their aspirations for upward mobility.[23]

A third effect of the domestic code was to keep women out of unions. Since many felt their work life to be temporary, women had little incentive to join one another in a struggle for better conditions. Employers clearly felt this to be a tangible benefit, for in the few instances in the 19th century where women created successful unions, they were quickly crushed. Because unions would negate the advantages of low wages and docility they could not be tolerated.[24]

Fourth, employers gained an inestimable advantage from the dual work force in their relationships with male workers. Working men argued that women

workers held wages down. Repeatedly in the 1830s they insisted that wages paid to them would be higher if women were excluded from the work force. In 1836, a National Trades Union Committee urged that female labor be excluded from factories. After explaining that the natural responsibility and moral sensibility of women best suited them to domesticity, the report argued that female labor produced "ruinous competition, . . . to male labor" whose end finally would be that "the workman is discharged or reduced to a corresponding rate of wages with the female operative."[25] The report continued:

> One thing . . . must be apparent to every reflecting female, that all her exertions are scarce sufficient to keep her alive; that the price of her labor each year is reduced; and that she in a measure stands in the way of the male when attempting to raise his prices or equalize his labor, and that her efforts to sustain herself and family, are actually the same as tying a stone around the neck of her natural protector, Man, and destroying him with the weight she has brought to his assistance. This is the true and natural consequence of female labor when carried beyond the family.[26]

The president of the Philadelphia Trades Association advised women to withdraw altogether from the work force: " . . . the less you do, the more there will be for the men to do and the better they will be paid for doing it, and ultimately you will be what you ought to be, free from the performance of that kind of labor which was designed for man alone to perform."[27]

Male fears of displacement and of wage reductions seemed justified. While men and women normally did not compete for the same jobs, employers often substituted one for the other, over a period of time. The work force in New England textile factories, which was 90 percent female in 1828, was only 69 percent female in 1848.[28] In Massachusetts, 61 percent of the teachers were male in 1840; by 1865, 86 percent were female.[29]

Finally, the "cult of true womanhood" glorified a family structure and stability that encouraged, even coerced the male head to work harder, in order to support his family and provide for his wife. For one's wife to be working meant that the husband had failed. The need to preserve the wife's position on a pedestal pushed men into an endless search for upward mobility and financial success. Sacrificing for one's family

A WOMAN IN A MAN'S WORLD: DEAR ABBY

DEAR ABBY: Should you ever doubt women are paid less than men for doing the same job, let me assure you my personal experience will confirm that fact.

I was born a male and trained to be a computer programmer. I am also a transsexual and have had sex-reassignment surgery. I am now a female, physically and legally.

After my sex change, I took a job doing exactly the same work I had done as a man, but as a woman, I am paid $10,000 a year less!—**A woman in a man's world**

became a pattern still prevalent among working-class Americans. The idea that women should be able to stay at home, the better to mother their children, justified hard work, long hours, economic exploitation, and a host of other evils for male workers.

The moral injunction that confined women to their homes served many purposes. It maintained social order by providing stable families. It kept most married women out of the labor force, confining them to supportive roles in relation to the male work force. It divided women from each other along class lines and helped to ensure that those women who did work would stay in the labor force only briefly, remaining primarily committed to their families and satisfied with low-paying jobs. The special position of women as the least-paid and least-skilled members of the work force induced hostility from unskilled male labor. Afraid that women might take their jobs, some workingmen might have hesitated to demand justice from intransigent employers.

For most of the 19th century, the tension between the need for labor and the need for social order was contained by the domestic code. Toward the end of the century, a number of factors operated to break down the code so that it could no longer contain the underlying contradiction. The industrial strife that enveloped America in the late 19th century led many contemporary observers to fear that social order was giving way. Under these conditions several factors seem to have had special significance for women.

Increasing immigration had provided a plentiful labor supply of precisely the kinds of men and women who fell outside the moral code.[30] But as employers took advantage of the labor supply to lower wages and

to coerce hard work out of this group of people, strikes spread and public attention was drawn to their grievances. Newspaper exposes and government investigations noted the injurious effects on all workers, but especially on women, of harsh working conditions and of wages insufficient to keep body and soul together. Some investigators pointed to spreading prostitution as one consequence of low industrial wages.[31] Others argued that stunted and warped mothers endangered the health of the unborn, and objected to "latchkey" children. Pressure for legislation to "protect" these women began to build up.

Simultaneously, it became apparent both to the investigators and to male workers that women were finding it increasingly necessary to work. Sickness, accident, and death rates among industrial workers reached all-time highs between 1903 and 1907. Unemployment fluctuated cyclically. Despite rises in real wages after 1897, wages remained too low to meet normal family needs. Whether consequentially or not, the proportion of married women in the nonagricultural work force almost doubled between 1890 and 1920.[32] Workingmen now voiced new fears that women would undermine the male labor force. While a few made sporadic attempts to organize women into trade unions, most supported legislation that would effectively limit women's participation in the labor force by raising their wages, limiting the hours they could work, and prescribing the kinds of jobs in which they could be employed.

A further breakdown in the moral code and an explanation for women's increasing participation in the work force lay in the character of the immigrant population. Ambitious and anxious to fulfill the American

FACTS ABOUT PAY EQUITY

What Is Pay Equity?

Pay equity seeks to eliminate race and sex discrimination in the wage setting process by basing pay on the skill, effort and responsibility a job requires rather than on the sex or race of its workers. By requiring that employers use sex- and race-neutral criteria to set wages, pay equity would mean equal wages for workers in different but equally demanding occupations. Because pay equity calls for equal wages for jobs of comparable value, it has also been called *comparable worth.*

Why Do We Need Pay Equity?

Most of the 50 million employed women of all races and many male racial minorities work in low-paying jobs. In 1985 the earnings of women who worked full time year round averaged less than two-thirds of what men earned. This wage gap persists despite women's educational level: in 1982, on average, a male high school dropout earned more than a female college graduate. The Equal Pay Act outlaws paying women less than men who do essentially the same job, and Title VII prohibits wage discrimination on the basis of sex or race. However, employers may pay lower wages to workers in jobs in which women or minorities predominate compared to wages for predominantly white male jobs. Although considerable evidence suggests that

Reprinted with permission of Sociologists for Women in Society.

traditionally female jobs pay less because it is women rather than men who do them[9], the law does not presently view such differences as discrimination. Table 1 provides some typical examples.

There are two general strategies to reduce the wage gaps between men and women, and between members of different racial groups:

- Reduce the sex and race segregation of jobs.
- Through pay equity, raise the wages of predominantly female and minority jobs to reflect the skill, effort and responsibility these jobs require.

While it has declined slightly in the 1970s, considerable sex segregation and some race segregation remain in the workplace. Women are still concentrated in predominantly female occupations, and most men still work in occupations dominated by men. We need to continue to press for programs that guarantee people's access to all jobs, regardless of the sex or race of the worker. However, most new jobs are expected in traditionally female occupations, so experts predict limited progress in integrating occupations over the next decade[1]. Pay equity would reduce the wage gap between the sexes and races because workers in predominantly female or minority occupations would be paid as much as workers in predominantly white male occupations when their work requires equivalent skill, effort and responsibility.

TABLE I   EXAMPLES OF WAGES IN SEX AND RACE SEGREGATION OCCUPATIONS

Employer	Occupation	Predominant Sex/Race	Pay
Yale University	Administrative assistant	Female	$13,000/yr.
	Truck driver	Male	18,000/yr.
State of Minnesota	Registered nurse	Female	20,676/yr.
	Vocational education teacher	Male	27,120/yr.
County of Los Angeles	Health technician	Minority	13,380/yr.
	Evidence and property custodian	White	16,812/yr.

Who Will Decide the Value of a Job?

Employers would set their own pay scales, but pay scales would be based on the work itself. They would do this by using *job evaluation systems*. In job evaluation, the employer, employees (and union when there is a collective bargaining agreement) select the criteria on which wages should be based—such as skill, effort, responsibility, working conditions—and decide how much to weigh each factor. Participants must guard against sex bias in the criteria selected and how they are weighed, to avoid building sex or race biases into the job evaluation system[9]. Points are assigned for every job in a company according to its evaluation system, so that a job's total score represents its worth to the employer. Very different jobs in the same company may have similar scores. These scores are used to set a *salary range* for each job, so that jobs with the same score fall into the same salary range. The actual salary for any worker might take into account other legitimate, sex- and race-neutral criteria, such as seniority. The idea of job evaluations is not new; at present about two-thirds of all U.S. workers are employed in establishments that use some form of job evaluation to set wages[8].

If Job Evaluation Is Common, Why Is Pay Equity Necessary?

Employers often use separate wage scales for predominantly male and predominantly female jobs. In their job evaluation systems, all three of the employers in Table 1 assigned the predominantly female or minority job point scores as high as or higher than the predominantly male or white job. For example, Minnesota's evaluation system assigned 275 points to both registered nurses—overwhelmingly female—and vocational education teachers—predominantly male—but they paid vocational education teachers $6444 a year more than nurses.

Is Pay Equity Fair?

The point of pay equity is not to eliminate inequality in wages, but to eliminate wage inequality that is based on sex or race. Jobs that are more difficult or valuable should be rewarded accordingly. However, job evaluation studies by employers and state civil service systems have repeatedly shown that women's jobs are underpaid relative to their evaluation scores. Basing wages on workers' personal characteristics rather than on the worth of the job is unfair.

Will Pay Equity Cost So Much It Will Weaken the Economy?

Implementing pay equity will cost less than many fear. For example, the cost of doing so in Minnesota was less than 4% of the state's payroll budget[4]. Moreover, taxpayers already share the cost of women's artificially low wages. A Department of Labor study[10] calculated that about half of the families living in poverty would not be poor if their female wage-earners were paid as much as similarly qualified men. Pay equity will save tax dollars spent assisting employed women and minorities whose wages are lowered by discrimination.

Will Pay Equity Mean Government Interference in Private Firms?

Pay equity would *not* require national or state-wide wage-setting systems. Employers would continue to set wages, but they would have to do so in a non-discriminatory way according to their own job evaluation systems.

Will Implementing Pay Equity Lower White Men's Wages?

Under the Equal Pay Act and Title VII, courts have consistently held that an employer may not lower any employee's pay to eliminate wage discrimination. Pay equity will mean raises for *all* workers who work in occupations that have been underpaid. Since these tend to be women, pay equity will reduce the wage gap between predominantly male and female occupations.

Why Don't Women and Minorities Change to Higher Paying Jobs?

Race and sex discrimination continue to exclude women and minorities from many jobs. Moreover, jobs traditionally reserved for white men could not begin to absorb the millions of women and minorities who work in sex- and race-segregated jobs. Even if enough jobs existed, many mature workers lack the credentials or specific skills they require. Schools and the media continue to channel young people into occupations that have been labelled "appropriate" for their sex and race[7].

What Can You Do to Promote Pay Equity?

• Inform yourself (see organizations and references below). Work to inform others, in the classroom, through letters to the editor, and talks to community groups. Write your legislators, supporting your opinions with facts.

• If you do research on race or sex segregation or wage differences, share your findings with the public legislators.

• Organize workshops, conferences, letter-writing campaigns.

• Press for job evaluation studies and pay equity on your job, in your union or employees' organization, and in your city and state government.

• Contact and support labor, women's and civil rights organizations working for pay equity. These include the American Association of University Women; the American Civil Liberties Union; the American Federation of State, County and Municipal Employees; the Business and Professional Women's Foundation; the Coalition of Labor Union Women; the League of Women Voters; the Mexican-American Women's National Association; the National Conference of Puerto Rican Women; the National Education Association; the National Organization for Women; 9 to 5; the National Association of Working Women; the Service Employees International Union.

These and other groups belong to the National Committee of Pay Equity (N.C.P.E.). For further information, contact the N.C.P.E. at 1201 Six-teenth Street, N.W., Washington, D.C. 20036, 202/822-7304.

BIBLIOGRAPHY

1. Beller, Andrea H., & Kee-ok Kim Han. "Occupational segregation by sex: Prospects for the 1980s." In Barbara F. Reskin, ed., *Sex segregation in the workplace: Trends, explanations, remedies.* Washington, D.C.: National Academy Press, 1984.

2. Cook, Alice. "Comparable worth: The problem and states' approaches to wage equity." University of Hawaii at Manoa, 1983.

3. Feldberg, Roslyn. "Comparable worth: Toward theory and practice in the United States," *Signs* 10 (2) (1984):311–28.

4. Minnesota Commission on the Economic Status of Women. *Pay equity: The Minnesota experience.* St. Paul, August 1985.

5. National Committee on Pay Equity. "The wage gap: Myths and facts." Washington, D.C., n.d.

6. Remick, Helen. *Comparable worth and wage discrimination.* Philadelphia: Temple University Press, 1984.

7. Reskin, Barbara F., & Heidi Hartmann. *Women's work, men's work: Sex segregation on the job.* Washington, D.C.: National Academy Press, 1985.

8. Steinberg, Ronnie, & Lois Haigner. "Separate but equivalent: Equal pay for work of comparable worth." In *Gender at work.* Washington, D.C.: Women's Research and Education Institute, 1984.

9. Treiman, Donald, & Heidi Hartmann. *Women, work and wages.* Washington, D.C.: National Academy Press, 1981.

10. U.S. Department of Labor, Employment and Training Administration. *Women and work.* R&D Monograph 46, prepared by Patricia Cayo Sexton. Washington, D.C., 1977.

Dream, women from pre-industrial origins whose traditions incorporated both strong family loyalty and strong work orientations saw little need to play confined roles. Though the kinds of jobs they would take often depended on their ethnic origins, they were both willing and eager to work at least before marriage and often before having children.[33] To convince them of their errors, movements to "Americanize" the immigrant, of which the social settlement was a prime example, appeared in the 1890s. Those movements continued through the 1920s and were often directed at teaching the immigrant woman the arts of homemaking, bathing and caring for children, sewing, and cooking. All seemed designed to convince immigrant women that in America women stayed at home.

But probably the most telling failure of the moral code to contain the contradictions between the need for social order and the need for labor lies in its rejection by some middle-class women. While social values dictated leisure and an absence of work for women, these things themselves bred a challenge to social order. The number of women by the end of the 19th century exceeded the number of men. What were spinsters to do? For wealthy married women, affluence, servants, and a decline in the birth rate all added up to boredom. Excess energies spent themselves in ways which often had significance for working women. Some women, seeking the suffrage, allied themselves with working women, thus momentarily breaking down class barriers that had consistently divided them. Their involvement in the trade-union movement not only contributed markedly to the success of women attempting to organize themselves but revealed the common disabilities of the two groups. Other women became reformers, investigating and exposing conditions of child labor and the abuse of women, and as a consequence, publicizing the conditions on which their own leisure rested.

Still a third group crossed class lines more dramatically, attracted by new jobs opening in offices. Between 1890 and 1920, the percentage of women employed as clerks, saleswomen, stenographers, typists, bookkeepers, cashiers, and accountants increased from 5.3 percent of the nonagricultural female work force to 25.6 percent.[34] During the same period, among the women who worked, the proportion who were born in America of native parents also increased rapidly (35.3 percent to 43.8 percent); the percentage of native-born women of foreign parents increased

slightly (20.9 percent to 24.9 percent); the percentage of foreign-born women dropped slightly (19.8 percent to 18.8 percent), and that of Negro women dropped markedly (23.4 percent to 17.6 percent).[35] Increases were accompanied by enormous shifts to the clerical sectors of the work force.[36] The needs of employers for people who were both relatively well educated and willing to work for relatively low pay seem to have encouraged the creation of a new market. In part this was met by rising educational levels among immigrant daughters who had traditionally worked. But in part it was met by native white women entering the labor market for the first time.

Changing needs of employers, on the one hand (which encouraged the influx of native Americans into the labor force), and an overabundant labor supply of unskilled and semiskilled workers on the other (providing leisure for the middle class and encouraging exploitation of immigrants) seem together to have cracked the moral code which had served so many useful functions in the 19th century. The compromises which emerged from this period of uncertainty indicate new attempts to preserve social order in some sectors while providing new freedom to work in others. They are best seen in the context of broader value changes then affecting the whole society.

In the early 1900s America moved from laissez-faire economic policies to government regulation in a corporate state. The change reflected growing public willingness to accept corporate efficiency and rationality as the basis for industrial society. Large-scale industry encouraged both the homogenization of the labor force (by devaluing and removing control from skilled labor) and the artificial creation of distinctions among workers (by emphasizing expertise, credentials, and ethnic and sexual characteristics).[37] The division of the labor force in this way, effectively limiting occupational mobility for many groups, was sanctioned by legislation which legitimized these new hierarchies. State licensing requirements for medicine and social work as well as for many technical training schools illustrate this trend. So does protective labor legislation for women.

"Protective" legislation served the twofold function of segmenting the labor force and of returning some women to their homes by regulating the kinds of jobs they could hold. From about 1900 into the middle 1920s women found themselves subject to an increasing barrage of legislation limiting their working hours, establishing minimum wages, and defining the sanitary conditions under which they could work. Whatever its real value in eliminating the most gruesome abuses against a large working population, legislation effectively served to channel women into selected areas of the labor force.

Many women even then declared that protective legislation discriminated against working women. Supporters quite specifically argued that these laws were in the best interests of the state. Oregon, for example, preceded its minimum wage law with a preamble: "The welfare of the State of Oregon requires that women and minors should be protected from conditions of labor which have a pernicious effect on their health and morals, and inadequate wages ... have such a pernicious effect."[38] John Commons interpreted the principle as follows: "In proportion as certain classes of laborers ... are recognized by the courts as suffering an injury, and in proportion as the injured persons are deemed to be of importance to the public as well as unable to protect themselves, then legislation requiring the employer to remove the injury and prohibiting the laborer from even voluntarily consenting to the injury ... begins to be sustained as 'reasonable.'"[39] Men did not benefit from minimum wage laws in this period, and courts repeatedly struck down legislative restrictions on hours which applied to men. Clearly the state's vital interest in women placed them in a special category. Protective legislation affected deeply the unskilled poor working woman, while it had minimal effect on the new office clerk. Workingmen favored minimum wage legislation for women because it effectively reduced a downward pull on their wages.[40] As one authority phrased it, "The wage bargaining power of men is weakened by the competition of women and children, hence a law restricting the hours of women and children may also be looked upon as a law to protect men in their bargaining power."[41]

In other ways too, legislation recognized the needs of employers. A Federal Vocational Education Act passed in 1917 which provided for both men and women was widely supported by educators, manufacturers, trades unionists, businessmen, social workers, and philanthropists. Schools and professional agencies opened their doors to women who were encouraged to become teachers and social workers. Corporations and the state took over some social-insurance functions formerly provided by the family. Women got the vote.

The 1920s witnessed an elaborate reappraisal of the free-spirited, now middle-class, office girl *cum* flapper. But married women and poor women were encouraged not to work unless absolutely necessary, and employers, discouraged by minimum wage rules and short hours, often looked elsewhere for labor. That compromise satisfied both employers with an abundance of immigrant labor and workingmen. It maintained the tenuous compromise between social order vested in the home and passed down by women, and the need for labor, by arguing that women's place was in the home, most of the time. Between 1900 and 1940, the percentage of women participating in the work force rose only very slowly.[42] When it increased dramatically under the impetus of war in the 1940s, it was accompanied by elaborate justifications.

Since World War II, changing economic needs have simultaneously opened new jobs and altered the nature of families and of women's functions within them. Job structures have shifted dramatically from primarily blue-collar and manual labor before World War II to white-collar and service work in the postwar period. Teaching, social work, the human services, health, publishing, advertising: these expanding sectors have long been considered the preserves of women. While the spread of mass education and the demand for office workers of various kinds have encouraged women to enter the labor force, the concomitant need that these workers not seek advancement or high compensation has nevertheless encouraged the belief that their work experience is and ought to be secondary to their home roles.[43] Popular magazines, advertising, prevalent truths about child-rearing, and the glorification of femininity have conspired to support this belief. Together they add up to what Betty Friedan has called the "feminine mystique": the belief that a woman's satisfaction rests in competently and creatively running the household. For the most part the myth has served its purpose. Until the present, women have not agitated for more responsible jobs, higher wages, or release from their family roles. Even professional women who are married had until recently routinely accepted channeling that kept them out of the top reaches of their professions.

But the feminine mystique seems no longer able to contain the contradictions that have emerged from the ongoing tension between the need for labor on the one hand and the belief that social order is vested in the family on the other. Large numbers of women, as opposed to the relatively few turn-of-the-century pioneers for women's rights, seem dissatisfied with their family roles.[44] Increased affluence and improved household technology as well as expanding consumer services have reduced the need for women to work at home. Longer life spans for men and women and declining birth rates have reduced the proportion of a lifetime spent in child-rearing. Changes in life styles raise questions about how to socialize children and what values to instill in them.

As the family changes, more and more women begin to work.[45] Working women as a group are becoming older, better educated, less likely to take time off for babies, and more likely to be married and to have children. Available job opportunities raise questions about proper roles for women. The expansion of jobs in precisely those sectors in which women have been working leads to demands for upward mobility. Women with seniority rights and prior experience become discontented when they are consistently overlooked for top jobs.

Changes in the family as well as changes in perceptions of jobs seem to have produced the women's liberation movement. Its demands for more jobs and equal opportunities may help to satisfy the needs of the expanding service sector of the labor market for secretaries, clerks, and assistants of various kinds. There is some evidence that jobs for women are opening faster than they can be filled by the available pool of single or childless women.[46] Short of a dramatic rechanneling of men toward secretarial and low-level office jobs (which would involve major adjustments in social values), large-scale bureaucracies will have to make allowances for women with children if they wish to fill jobs. In some ways, these women may be ideal candidates for the secondary labor force. Their education and values have groomed them for office jobs, yet their primary commitments to children forestall claims to advancement. There is little evidence that the number of women holding prestige jobs has increased or that women's wages have risen in comparison with those of men. Moreover, government responses to working women seem to preserve class lines. Recent federal legislation encourages women who can afford the cost of child care or household help to work, while current executive action deprives those who are poor of federally financed day-care centers.

The enormous number of women now working prompts questions about whether their commitments to jobs will undermine the basis of the family and whether the family is any longer crucial to maintaining social order. Rising divorce rates, the recent Supreme Court decision on abortion, and public affirmations of homosexuality all testify to increasing conflict about the traditional role of the family. Attempts to alter sex-role stereotypes and to create communal shopping, child-care, and housework facilities; questions about mass-consumption psychology and the rejection of material goods; demands for individual fulfillment and authenticity—all emerge from the changing function of the family and challenge its relationship to prevalent ideology. Because the leaders of the current movement question the ideology that upholds the family, women's liberation may have the potential for long-term change.

Changes in women's participation in the work force must be understood partly as a function of the ideology of the family and therefore of the roles that women, like men, are convinced they must play. That ideology emerges both from the objective needs of families and from a complex of societal goals which derive from a changing political economy. Women are used in the work force in ways which encompass the ideological justifications of a whole society and its immediate labor-force needs. These together provide part of the complex reality that translates back into class divisions among working and nonworking women and into specific policies as they affect women workers.

NOTES

1. Edith Abbott, *Women in Industry* (New York: Appleton, 1910), pp. 374–76.

2. Barbara Welter, "The Cult of True Womanhood, 1820–1860," *American Quarterly* XVIII (Summer 1964): 160.

3. Glenda Gates Riley, "The Subtle Subversion:

Changes in the Traditionalist Image of the American Woman," *The Historian* XXXII (February 1970): 220.

4. William Chafe, *The American Woman: Her Changing Social Economic and Political Roles, 1920–1970* (New York: Oxford University Press, 1972).

5. Edmund Morgan, *The Puritan Dilemma* (Boston: Little, Brown, 1958), p. 71; see also John Demos, *A Little Commonwealth: Family Life in Plymouth Colony* (New York: Oxford University Press, 1970), p. 78.

6. Demos, *A Little Commonwealth*, p. 186.

7. Ibid., p. 89.

8. Bernard Wishy, *The Child and the Republic: The Dawn of Modern American Child Nurture* (Philadelphia: University of Pennsylvania Press, 1972), p. 28.

9. Ruth Miller Elson, *Guardians of Tradition: American Schoolbooks of the Nineteenth Century* (Lincoln: University of Nebraska Press, 1964), p. 309; Siegfried Giedion, *Mechanization Takes Command: A Contribution to Anonymous History* (New York: Norton, 1969 [1948]), p. 514; for discussions of the 19th-century woman, see also Welter, "The Cult of True Womanhood," and Riley, "The Subtle Subversion."

10. Elson, *Guardians of Tradition*, p. 309; Gerda Lerner, "Women's Rights and American Feminism," *American Scholar* (Spring 1971): 238.

11. Quoted in Elson, *Guardians of Tradition*, p. 309.

12. Aileen Kraditor, *Up from the Pedestal* (New York: Quadrangle, 1968), p. 13. Kraditor continued: "The home was the bulwark against social disorder, and woman was the creator of the home . . . she occupied a desperately necessary place as symbol and center of the one institution that prevented society from flying apart."

13. Joseph A. Hill, *Women in Gainful Occupations, 1870–1920*, Census Monographs IX (U.S. Government Printing Office, 1929), p. 3.

14. Caroline T. Ware, *The Early New England Cotton Manufactures: A Study in Industrial Beginnings* (Boston: Houghton Mifflin, 1931), p. 198. Hannah Josephson, *The Golden Threads: New England's Mill Girls and Magnates* (New York: Duell, Sloan and Pearce, 1949), p. 22; Oscar Handlin, *Boston's Immigrants: 1790–1880* (New York: Atheneum, 1971 [1941]), pp. 74–76; Reinhard Bendix, *Work and Authority in Industry: Ideologies of Management* (New York: Wiley, 1956), p. 39.

15. Josephson, *The Golden Threads*, pp. 63, 23; see also John Kasson, "Civilizing the Machine: Technology, Aesthetics, and Society in Nineteenth Century American Thought," Ph.D. dissertation, Yale University, 1971; and see also Holland Thompson, *From the Cotton Field to the Cotton Mill: A Study of the Industrial Transition in North Carolina* (Freeport, N.Y.: Books for Libraries Press, 1971 [1906]), p. 52, for a similar example of paternal employment in the South. About one-half of the employees in the New England textile mills were recruited this way.

16. Kasson, "Civilizing the Machine," p. 41.

17. Ibid., pp. 53–55.

18. Ware, *Early New England Cotton Manufactures*, p. 231.

19. Ibid., p. 234.

20. Handlin, *Boston's Immigrants*, p. 82.

21. John R. Commons et al., eds., *A Documentary History of American Industrial Society*, vol. VI, *The Labor Movement* (Cleveland, Ohio: Arthur H. Clark Co., 1910), p. 195; Emilie Josephine Hutchinson, *Women's Wages: A Study of the Wages of Industrial Women and Measures Suggested to Increase Them* (New York: AMS Press, 1968), pp. 24, 25. Handlin, *Boston's Immigrants*, p. 81, notes that women earned an average of $1.50 to $3.00 per week, while men earned from $4.50 to $5.50.

22. Commons, *A Documentary History*, p. 210.

23. The constant employment of women at low-skilled jobs bears this out.

24. Hutchinson, *Women's Wages*, pp. 159–60. See Alice Kessler-Harris, "Where Are the Organized Women Workers?" *Feminist Studies* III (Fall 1975): 92–110, for an elaboration on this point.

25. Commons, *A Documentary History*, p. 282.

26. Ibid ., p. 284.

27. Hutchinson, *Women's Wages*, p. 159, quoted from *The Report on the Conditions of Women and Child Wage Earners*, X, p. 48.

28. Elizabeth F. Baker, *Technology and Women's Work* (New York: Columbia University Press, 1964), p. 17.

29. Michael Katz, *The Irony of Early School Reform* (Cambridge, Mass.: Harvard University Press, 1968), p. 12; and Hutchinson, *Women's Wages*, pp. 34, 158.

30. The increasing percentage of women workers was especially significant. In nonagricultural occupations, the percentage of women workers increased from 12.8 of all women over 15 to 21.3 in 1920. There was only a slight increase from 1920 to 1930. Hill, *Women in Gainful Occupations*, p. 19. In 1920, 20 percent of native-born women of native parents were working; 47.8 percent of those women who were foreign-born or born of foreign parents were working; and 43 percent of Negro women were working. Ibid., p. 11. Between 1890 and 1930, the proportion of women over 15 who were employed increased by one-third. Donald Lescohier, "Working Conditions," in John Commons, *History of Labor in the United States: 1896–1932* (New York: Macmillan, 1935), III, p. 37.

31. See *Report on Conditions of Women and Child Wage Earners*, V, p. 70; XV, p. 93.

32. The percentage of married women among those who worked increased from 12.1 in 1890 to 19.8 in 1910. The percentage of married women who worked increased from 3.3 in 1890 to 6.8 in 1910. Lescohier, "Working Conditions," p. 37; and Hill, *Women in Gainful Occupations*, pp. 76, 77.

33. Caroline Manning, *The Immigrant Woman and Her Job* (New York: Arno Press, 1970 [1930]), *passim*.

34. Hill, *Women in Gainful Occupations,* pp. 39–41. The percentage of women employed in factories increased from 17.6 in 1870 to 23.8 in 1920.

35. Ibid., pp. 85, 94, 102, 110.

36. Ibid., pp. 90, 96. See also Margery Davies, "The Feminization of the Clerical Labor Force," paper given at the Conference on Labor Market Segmentation, Harvard University, Cambridge, Mass., March 17, 1973.

37. See David M. Gordon, Richard Edwards, and Michael Reich, "Labor Market Segmentation in American Capitalism," paper given at the Conference on Labor Market Segmentation, Harvard University, March 16, 1973, which outlines the historical development of the segmentation process. Kathy Stone, "The Origins of Job Structures in the Steel Industry," in a paper given at the same conference and subsequently published in *Radical America* VII (November–December 1973), traces motivation for segmentation in one industry.

38. Hutchinson, *Women's Wages,* p. 81.

39. John R. Commons and John B. Andrews, *Principles of Labor Legislation,* rev. ed. (New York: Harper, 1927), p. 30.

40. Hutchinson, *Women's Wages,* p. 161.

41. Commons and Andrews, *Principles of Labor Legislation,* p. 69.

42. See the extended discussion of this question in Valerie Kincaide Oppenheimer, *The Female Labor Force in the United States: Demographic and Economic Factors Governing Its Growth and Changing Composition,* Population Monograph Series, no. 5 (Berkeley: University of California Press, 1970), pp. 1–5.

43. Michael J. Piore's "The Dual Labor Market: Theory and Implications," in *Problems in Political Economy: An Urban Perspective,* ed. David Gordon (Lexington, Mass.: D. C. Heath, 1971), pp. 90–94, is a concise statement of the way these divisions in the labor force work.

44. See, for example, Susan Jacoby, "What Do I Do for the Next 20 Years?" *New York Times Magazine,* June 17, 1973, p. 10.

45. Cf. Alice Harris and Bertram Silverman, "Notes on Women in Advanced Capitalism," *Social Policy* (June–July 1973), for elaboration.

46. Valerie Kincaide Oppenheimer, "Demographic Influences on Female Employment and the Status of Women," *American Journal of Sociology* LXXVIII (January 1973).

R E A D I N G   2 2

Race, Sex, and Class: Black Female Tobacco Workers in Durham, North Carolina, 1920–1940, and the Development of Female Consciousness

BEVERLY W. JONES

This article examines how race, sex, and class affected the lives and consciousness of black female tobacco workers in Durham, North Carolina, and how they conceptualized work and its meaning in their lives. The research was based on 15 interviews. The interviewees fall into three broad age categories: five were

Reprinted from *Feminist Studies* 10, no. 3 (Fall 1984): 441–51, by permission of the publisher, Feminist Studies, Inc., c/o Women's Studies Program, University of Maryland, College Park, MD 20742.

born before 1908, seven between 1908 and 1916, and three between 1916 and 1930. All were born in the rural South. The majority migrated to Durham in the 1920s, subsequently entering the labor force.

Historically, black labor of both females and males has been critical to the tobacco manufacturing industry. As cigarette manufacture became mechanized, blacks were hired as stemmers, sorters, hangers, and pullers. These "dirty" jobs were seen as an extension of field labor and therefore as "Negro work" for which whites would not compete.[1] The rapidly expanding number of tobacco factories employed the thousands of black females and males migrating from the rural South. The pull of better paying jobs and the push of falling farm prices, perennial pests, and hazardous weather induced a substantial number of black share-croppers, renters, and landowners to seek refuge in Durham.

Charlie Necoda Mack, the father of three future female tobacco workers, remembered the difficulties of making an adequate living out of farming in Manning, South Carolina. "I was a big cotton farmer; I made nine bales of cotton one year. Next year I made, I think, one or two, and the next year I didn't make none. I left in July, I had to leave. I borrowed money to get up here—Durham. I had six children and I know no jobs available. Well, then I came up here in July in 1922 and got a job at the factory. And by Christmas I had all my children with clothes and everything." Unlike the Mack family, who were pushed out of South Carolina, others were pulled into the city. Dora Miller, after marrying in 1925, left Apex, North Carolina, because she heard of the "better paying jobs in Durham." Mary Dove, at age 10 and accompanied by her family, left Roxboro, North Carolina, because a "Duke agent told us that a job in the factory at Liggett Myers was waiting for my daddy." Rosetta Branch, age eighteen and single, left Wilmington, North Carolina, because her mother had died, and "there were no other kinfolks."[2]

Thus, Durham's gainfully employed black population swelled from 6,869 in 1910 to 12,402 in 1930.

TABLE I   TOBACCO INDUSTRY EMPLOYMENT BY RACE AND GENDER

DURHAM COUNTY: 1930			
WHITE		NEGRO	
Male	Female	Male	Female
2,511	2,932	1,336	1,979

NORTH CAROLINA: 1940			
WHITE		NEGRO	
Male	Female	Male	Female
6,517	3,175	5,899	5,898

Source: U.S. Bureau of the Census, *Population: 1930* (Washington, D.C.: GPO, 1930), vol. 3, pt. 2, pp. 355, 378; *Labor Force: 1940* (Washington, D.C.: GPO, 1940), vol. 3, pt. 4, p. 566.

(The city's total black population in 1930 was 23,481.) According to the census, the number of black female tobacco workers in 1930 was 1,979 out of a total black female population of 12,388. (See table 1.) Durham and Winston-Salem tobacco factories employed more black females than other cities: one-half of the number of women employed in tobacco factories in 1930 in these cities were black compared with the 19.7 in Petersburg and Richmond in Virginia.[3]

Upon disembarking at the central train station, the newly arrived southern migrants were immediately faced with race restrictions. Rigidly segregated communities were the dominant feature of Durham's black life. Many of the migrants settled in the dilapidated housing in the larger communities of East End and Hayti, a bustling commercial district of black businesses, and in the smaller areas of Buggy Bottom and Hickstown. Almost all black workers rented either from the company and white landlords or from black real estate agents. The comments of Annie Barbee, the daughter of Necoda Mack, reflect her first impressions of Durham.

> We were renting in the southern part of Durham—the Negro section—on Popular Street, second house from the corner, across the railroad tracks. The house was small, two rooms, but somehow we managed. The street was not paved and when it rained it got muddy and in the fall, the wind blew all the dust into your eyes and face. There were no private family bathrooms. But it was an exciting life. See, in the country things were so dull—no movie houses.... Up here people were always fighting and going on all the time.[4]

Despite the exploitive living conditions described by Barbee, urban employment did have some liberating consequences for rural daughters.

Race restricted the black population to segregated neighborhoods and also determined the kinds of jobs black females could get. Black female tobacco workers also faced discrimination as poor people and as females. Although class and sex restraints punctuated the lives of white female tobacco workers, their impact was reinforced by management policies. Although white females' wages were a fraction of white males' and inadequate to support a family, black females' wages were even lower. According to some black female tobacco workers, the wage inequity led many white women to consider black women inferior. This in turn led to an atmosphere of mistrust between black and white females. Management strengthened racial and class inequities in hiring practices, working conditions, and spatial organization of the factory, and therefore impeded the formation of gender bonds among working-class women.

Black females were usually hired as if they were on an auction block. "Foremen lined us up against the walls," one worker stated, "and chose the sturdy robust ones." Mary Dove recalled that she had "to hold up one leg at a time and then bend each backwards and forwards."[5] Once hired, black and white women were separated on different floors at the American Tobacco Company and in entirely different buildings at the Liggett & Myers Tobacco Company. In the 1920s and 1930s, according to a report by the Women's Bureau (the federal agency created in 1920), and confirmed by my interviews, 98 percent of these black females were confined to the prefabrication department, where they performed the "dirty" jobs—sorting, cleaning, and stemming tobacco.[6] White females had the "cleaner" jobs in the manufacturing and packing department as they caught, inspected, and packed the tobacco. However, both jobs were defined by the sex division of labor—jobs to be performed by women. Black men moved between the areas pushing 500-pound hogsheads of tobacco while white men worked as inspectors, safeguarding the sanctity of class and sex segregation.[7]

Reflecting on these blatant differences in working conditions, some 50 years later many black women expressed anger at the injustice. Annie Barbee recalled: "You're over here doing all the nasty dirty work. And over there on the cigarette side white women over there wore white uniforms. . . . You're over here handling all the old sweaty tobacco. There is a large difference. It ain't right!" Rosetta Branch spoke of her experience with anger. "They did not treat us Black folks right. They worked us like dogs. Put us in separate buildings . . . thinking maybe we were going to hurt those white women. Dirty work, dirty work we had to do. Them white women think they something working doing the lighter jobs."[8] These comments reflect both the effectiveness of management policies to aggravate racial and sexual differences in order to preclude any possible bonds of gender, but also illustrate the unhealthy working conditions to which black women were exposed.

In fact, the interviews indicate that the health of some black women suffered in the factories. Pansy Cheatham, another daughter of Necoda Mack, maintained that the Georgia leaf tobacco "was so dusty that I had to go to the tub every night after work. There was only one window and it got so hot that some women just fainted. The heat and smell was quite potent." Mary Dove recounted one of her fainting spells. "You know on the floor there was a salt dispenser, because it would get so hot. I did not feel so well when I came to work but I had to work. After about two hours standing on my feet, I got so dizzy—I fell out. My clothes was soaking wet from my head to my feet. When I woke up I was in the dispensary."[9]

Blanche Scott and another worker were forced to quit for health reasons. Scott, who began working for Liggett & Myers in 1919, quit four years later. "When I left the factory, it became difficult for me to breathe. The dust and fumes of the burly tobacco made me cough. The burly tobacco from Georgia had chicken feathers and even manure in it. Sometimes I would put an orange in my mouth to keep from throwing up. I knew some women who died of TB." The other worker had miscarried twice. Pregnant again, she decided not to return to the American Tobacco Company. "I felt that all that standing while I stemmed tobacco," she stated, "was the reason I lost my two children." Some women found momentary relief from the dust by retreating outside the confines of the factory complex to breathe the fresh air while sitting under trees or on the sidewalk during lunch.[10]

These comments on the poor, unhealthy working conditions were verified by research on Durham's death records between 1911 and 1930. In many instances, the records were imprecise and failed to provide information about race and occupation. Of the 105 certificates that identified black women as tobacco workers who died between 1911 and 1920, 48 (about 46 percent) died of tuberculosis, sometimes listed as phthisis and consumption. Of the 134 recorded deaths of black female tobacco workers between 1920 and 1930, 86 (64.5 percent) died of tuberculosis. Because tuberculosis is caused by a bacillus that can be transmitted by a tubercular person through the cough, it is likely that poorly ventilated rooms and incessant coughing by workers, possibly by a carrier, made some workers susceptible to the disease, although deplorable living conditions for workers cannot be dismissed as a contributing factor.[11]

As studies have found in other cities, black females in Durham were more likely to work than white females.[12] Black females also earned lower wages than white females. In the early 1900s, wages for black tobacco workers, both female and male, ranked the lowest in the nation. In 1930, 45.5 percent of native-born white women in Durham were gainfully employed—27.7 percent in tobacco. While 44 percent of black women were working, 36.2 percent were employed in tobacco. From 1920 to 1930, Durham's white female tobacco workers averaged about 29 cents per hour, while black female hand stemmers earned about 11.9 cents an hour. However, black men, as well as black women who stemmed tobacco by machine, averaged about 27 cents an hour, still less than white women.[13]

Wage differentials continued and worsened throughout the 1930s. By the eve of the New Deal, a Women's Bureau survey reported figures for North Carolina which revealed an even higher wage discrepancy. White women working in the making and packing departments reported a median weekly wage of $15.35. Wages ranged from $14.10 earned as catchers to $20.50 on older packing machines. On the newest packing machines, the median wage was $18.15. Black women, working in the leaf department, reported a median weekly wage of $7.95. Hand stemmers earned a median wage of $6.50.[14]

The low wage was itself demeaning to black female workers. But the inadequate wages also forced many into the labor force at an early age. Black women thus worked for a longer part of their lives, and henceforth were more vulnerable to diseases and other health problems. Blanche Scott, for example, began working at the age of twelve. "Since my mother stayed so sick, I had to go to work. I worked at Liggett Myers after school got out. I attended West End School. I'd normally get out at 1:30 and worked from two o'clock to 6 P.M. I was just twelve years old. In the summer, they're let children come and work all day until four o'clock." Pansy Cheatham began working at age thirteen. "My father talked to the foreman," she stated. "I worked because my sisters Mae and Annie worked; I stemmed tobacco by hand. But Papa did collect the money and use it for food and clothing." Cheatham's statement would indicate that at the top of the gender hierarchy of the black family was the father, who controlled the daughter's wages.[15]

Many women saw their employment as a means of "helping out the family." Better stated in the words of Margaret Turner, "that's what a family is all about, when we—the children—can help out our parents."[16] Out of the fifteen interviewees, the ten women who entered the work force at an early age all conceptualized the central meaning of their work in relation to their families.

By the late 1920s and early 1930s, the enforcement of the Child Labor Law of 1917 arrested the practice of employing children under the age of sixteen. "They began to ask for your birth certificate," one worker stated. A study done by Hugh Penn Brinton substantiated the decrease of child labor employment in Durham's factories. Brinton found that from 1919 to 1930 the percentage of black laboring-class households sending children into the labor force had decreased from 35 to 14 percent.[17]

However, the legislation against child labor did not force the wages up for black tobacco workers, and the constant low earning power of both female and male breadwinners continued to affect the lives of black female workers psychologically. Many women submitted to the demands of the foreman and other company officials. Viewed as short-term cheap labor, some females submitted to physical and verbal harassment, because in many instances defiance would have certainly resulted in the loss of jobs. Dora Miller asserted that "since the foreman knew you needed the job, you obeyed all of his demands without question. He called you dirty names and used foul language but you took it." Mary Dove recalled what it was like to work under one "of the toughest bosses." "Our foreman was a one-eyed fella named George Hill. He was tight! He was out of South Carolina, and he was tight. I mean tight! He'd get on top of them machines—they had a machine that altered the tobacco—he'd get on top of that machine and watch you, see if you was working all right and holler down and curse. Holler down and say, "GD . . . get to work! GD . . . go to work there you ain't doin' nothing." Janie Mae Lyons remembered one who walked in on her while she "was in the sitting position on the stool" and told her "that if you ain't finished then you can pack up and leave. I was so embarrassed and that's what I did."[18]

Lyons's departure from the factory represented a form of militancy—a definitive stance against further harassment. Other women resisted verbally. Annie Barbee publicly castigated "women who allowed the foreman to fumble their behind" and further stated that if "one did that to me he would be six feet under." She indicated no one ever did. One worker resisted "by playing the fool." "The foreman thought I was crazy and left me alone."[19]

Constantly resisting physical and verbal abuse and trying to maintain their jobs, the workers were further threatened by increased mechanization. "I don't think it is right," one woman stated, "to put them machines to take away from us poor people." "Because of the strain we work under," another maintained, "they don't care nothing for us." One woman recalled crying at the machines because she could not quit in the face of high unemployment. "With them machines you have to thread the tobacco in. Them machines run so fast that after you put in one leaf you got to be ready to thread the other. If you can't keep pace the foreman will fire you right on the spot. Sometimes I get so nervous but I keep on going'."[20]

The increased mechanization of the tobacco factories resulting in physical hardships of female workers can to some degree be attributed to Franklin D. Roosevelt's National Industrial Recovery Acts of 1933 and 1934. On the one hand, President Roosevelt's New Deal measures fostered economic stability for many black families by establishing standard minimum wages and maximum hours. On the other hand, this standardization exacerbated the job insecurity of black workers by indirectly catalyzing many companies to maximize profits by replacing hand labor with technology. During the latter part of the 1930s, Liggett & Myers closed its green leaf department, which had employed the majority of black women.[21]

The long-term insecurities of their jobs led black female stemmers to organize Local 194. The limited success of the union was reflected in the decline of its membership of two thousand in January 1935 to less than two hundred by May 1935. Black female union members found little support from either Local 208, black controlled, or Local 176, white controlled. In the eyes of the male unionists, the temporary nature of women's jobs excluded them from any serious consideration by the locals.[22] Conscious of their auxiliary position and the lack of support from male-led unions, black females chose not to support the April 16, 1939, strike at Liggett & Myers. Reporting for work on that day, they were turned away as management had no other recourse but to close the factory. Dora Miller recalled that the black stemmery workers "were never involved in the strike because demands for wage increases did not include us."[23] On April 26, 1939, the

company capitulated. The contract indeed reaffirmed Miller's assessment because the stemmery workers were not mentioned.[24]

The factory policies of hiring, wages, working conditions, and spatial segregation, inherently reinforced by racism, the "cult of true white womanhood," and the inadvertent effect of New Deal governmental measures, all came together to touch the lives of black women tobacco workers with sex, race, and class exploitation. These practices further dissipated any possible gender bonds between black women and white women workers. As a race, black female tobacco workers were confined to unhealthy segregated areas either in separate buildings or on separate floors. As a working class, they were paid inadequate wages. As a sex, they were relegated to the worst, lowest paid, black women's jobs.

Black females conceptualized work as a means of "helping out the family." Denied self-respect and dignity in the factory, black female tobacco workers felt a need to validate themselves in other spheres. Victimized by their working conditions, female tobacco workers looked to the home as a preferred if not powerful arena. The home became the inner world that countered the factory control over their physical well-being. The duality of their lives—workers of production and nurturers of the family—could be assessed as a form of double jeopardy. But it was their role as nurturers, despite the hardship of work, that provided them with a sense of purpose and "joy." As Pansy Cheatham described her daily routine, "I get up at 5:30 A.M. I feed, clothe, and kiss my children. They stay with my sister while I work. At 7 A.M. I am on the job. A half-hour for lunch at about 12 noon. At 4 P.M. I quit work. At home about 4:30, then I cook, sometimes mend and wash clothes before I retire. About 11:30 I go to bed with joy in my heart for my children are safe and I love them so."[25]

Black females who worked together in the tobacco factories also had the positive experience of creating networks of solidarity. Viewing their plight as one, black females referred to one another as "sisters." This sisterhood was displayed in the collection of money during sickness and death and celebration of birthdays. The networks established in the factory overlapped into the community and church. Many of these workers belonged to the same churches—Mount Vernon, Mount Gilead, and White Rock Baptist churches—and functioned as leaders of the usher boards, missionary circles, and Sunday School programs. These bonds were enhanced in the community by the development of clubs. These church groups and females' clubs overlapped the factory support networks and functioned in similar ways.

Finally, the resistance to the physical and verbal abuse that was a constant in the work lives of black women fostered among some a sense of autonomy, strength, and self-respect. Annie Barbee was one of those women. The assertiveness, dignity, and strength she developed through work became an intricate part of her private life. At age 40 and pregnant, she decided to obtain private medical assistance despite her husband's resistance. "When you know things ain't right God gave you a head and some sense. That's my body. I knew I wasn't going to Duke Clinic. And I was working and making my own money, I went where I

wanted to go. You see, being married don't mean that your husband controls your life. That was my life and I was carrying his child, it's true, but I was going to look after myself."[26]

Although the work experience of black women tobacco workers was one of racial, sex, and class oppression, the early entrance into the labor force, the resistance to exploitation, and the longevity of work created a consciousness that fostered a sense of strength and dignity among some women in this working class. Management tactics of wage inequity, hiring practices, and racial-sexual division of labor pitted black women against white women economically as workers, and made the formation of gender bonds across race lines all but impossible. Yet among black women, the linkages of sisterhood engendered a consciousness of female strength, if not feminism.

ACKNOWLEDGMENTS

I am deeply grateful to North Carolina Central University for a Faculty Research Grant and for the excellent editorial comments of the *Feminist Studies* editors.

NOTES

1. For discussion of the historical involvement of black labor in tobacco manufacturing, see Joseph C. Robert, *The Tobacco Kingdom* (Durham, N.C.: Duke University Press, 1938).

2. Author's interviews with Charlie Necoda Mack, 22 May 1979; Dora Miller, 6 June 1979; Mary Dove, 7 July 1979; Rosetta Branch, 15 August 1981; all on file in the Southern Oral History Program, University of North Carolina, Chapel Hill, hereafter cited as SOHP/UNC.

3. The 1940 labor force figures do not include information for Durham County. U.S. Bureau of the Census, *Population: 1930* (Washington, D.C.: GPO, 1930), 3:341. In 1900, the major tobacco industries in the South were the American Tobacco Company and Liggett & Myers in Durham; R. J. Reynolds in Winston-Salem; and P. Lorillard in Richmond, Virginia.

4. Annie Barbee, interview, 28 May 1979, SOHP/UNC.

5. Mary Dove, interviews, 7 July 1971 and 30 May 1981.

6. Women's Bureau, *The Effects of Changing Conditions in the Cigar and Cigarette Industries,* Bulletin no. 110 (Washington, D.C.: GPO, 1932), 774–75. The Women's Bureau was established by Congress in 1920 under the aegis of the United States Department of Labor. Its purpose was to gather information and to provide advice to working women.

7. Mary Dove, interviews, 7 July 1971, 15 and 28 August 1981.

8. Annie Barbee and Rosetta Branch, interviews.

9. Pansy Cheatham, interview, 9 July 1979, SOHP/ UNC; Mary Dove, interview, 7 July 1971.

10. Blanche Scott, interviews, 11 July 1979 (SOHP/ UNC), 8 and 15 June, 1981; Mary Dove, Annie Barbee interviews.

11. Death certificates, 1911–1930, Durham County Health Department, Vital Records, Durham, North Carolina. I was also interested in the correlation of working conditions and female-related maladies such as stillbirths, miscarriages, and uterine disorders. Further perusal of death

certificates of stillbirths was less valuable for there were no indications of mothers' occupations. Even hospital statistics lacked occupational data. This area of inquiry as it relates to the health of black female workers and working conditions needs further research. Further questions that will have to be explored include: Was there a higher percentage of female tobacco workers dying of tuberculosis than non-female tobacco workers? How long were stricken female workers employed in the factory? How much weight must be given to the working environment over that of home environs? Despite the lack of solid data on these questions, the interviews and death records clearly indicate that racial division of labor negatively impacted upon the health of many black female tobacco workers.

12. Elizabeth H. Pleck, "A Mother's Wage: Income Earning among Married Italian and Black Women, 1896–1911," in *The American Family in Social-Historical Perspective,* 2d ed, ed. Michael Gordon (New York: St. Martin's Press, 1978), 490–510; "Culture, Class, and Family Life among Low-Income Urban Negroes," in *Employment, Race, and Poverty,* ed. Arthur M. Ross and Herbert Hill (New York: Harcourt Brace & World, 1967), 149–72; "The Kindred of Veola Jackson: Residence and Family Organization of an Urban Black American Family," in *Afro-American Anthropology: Contemporary Perspectives,* ed. Norman E. Whitten, Jr., and John F. Szwed (New York: Free Press, 1970), chap. 16.

13. U.S. Bureau of the Census, *Population: 1930,* vols. 3 and 4; U.S. Department of Labor, Women's Bureau, *Hours and Earning in Tobacco Stemmeries,* Bulletin no. 127 (Washington, D.C.: GPO, 1934).

14. Women's Bureau, *Effects of Changing Conditions,* 172–75.

15. Blanche Scott and Pansy Cheatham, interviews.

16. Margaret Turner, interview with author, 25 September 1979, SOHP/UNC.

17. Interview, 8 June 1981; Hugh Penn Brinton, "The Negro in Durham: A Study in Adjustment to Town Life" (Ph.D. diss., University of North Carolina, Chapel Hill, 1930).

18. Dora Miller and Mary Dove, interviews; Janie Mae Lyons, interview with author, 4 August 1981.

19. Annie Barbee, interviews 28 May 1979, 10 July 1981.

20. Interviews, 4 and 15 June 1981.

21. For the best discussions of the National Industrial Recovery Act's impact on blacks, see Raymond Wolters, *Negroes and the Great Depression: The Problem of Economic Recovery,* ed. Stanley E. Kutler (Westport, Conn.: Greenwood, 1970); and Bernard Sternsher, ed., *The Negro in the Depression and War: Prelude to Revolution, 1930–45* (Chicago: Quadrangle, 1969). Also see Dolores Janiewski, "From Field to Factory: Race, Class, and Sex and the Woman Worker in Durham, 1880–1940" (Ph.D. diss., Duke University, 1979).

22. *Durham* (N.C.) *Morning Herald,* 17, 18 April 1939, p. 1; Janiewski.

23. Dora Miller, interview.

24. For terms of contract, see *Durham Morning Herald* and *Durham Sun,* 27 April 1939, pp. 1, 2; Janiewski.

25. Pansy Cheatham, interview.

26. Annie Barbee, interview.

R E A D I N G   2 3

Occupation/Steelworker: Sex/Female

MARY MARGARET FONOW

Occupations in the United States fall into two categories: the *primary sector,* which is characterized by higher pay, union protection, fringe benefits, high rates

Reprinted, with changes, from Mary Margaret Fonow, "Women in Steel: A Case Study of the Participation of Women in a Trade Union," Ohio State University, 1977 (Ph.D. diss.), by permission of the author.

of employment, high profits, and good chances for advancement, and the *secondary sector,* which is characterized by low pay, lack of union protection, few fringe benefits, higher rates of unemployment, few promotional opportunities, and lower profits. Women in the United States have been employed in the secondary sector, and consequently have received lower salaries and few benefits (Acker, 1980). Recent efforts to initiate affirmative action programs in the steel, communications, auto, mining, rubber, electrical, and other basic industries may represent an opportunity for women to break with the traditional pattern of female employment and substantially alter their socio-economic status.

This article will examine the specific experiences of women steelworkers in their attempt to enter a male-dominated occupation. Although the primary method of data collection for this study was participant observation, a combination of methods was employed. First, I conducted an in-depth field study of one steel union local in a major steel-producing region of the Midwest. This local represented approximately 5,000 workers, 60 of whom were women. During the summer of 1977, I was able to make observations of the routine day-to-day activities of the union local and interview union officials. Using the snowball sampling technique, I also conducted a total of 27 in-depth interviews with women steelworkers. Each interview lasted between one and one-half to two hours and all were tape-recorded. I did my own transcribing. In addition, I observed the 18th Constitutional Convention of the United Steelworkers of America, August 30–September 3, 1976, in Las Vegas, Nevada. At this event I conducted formal and informal interviews with 23 women participants (delegates, organizers, and observers). I also observed informal caucus meetings and strategy sessions on women's issues.

JOB ENTRY

On April 15, 1974, in the United States District Court in Birmingham, Alabama, an industry-wide consent decree was signed by nine of the "big ten" steel companies and the union, the United Steelworkers of America. The decree required an entire restructuring of the seniority system and an affirmative action plan for the hiring and promotion of women and minorities. Except for a brief period during World War II, women had been relegated to a sex-segregated unit in the plant, "tin inspection."

The flow of information about the new policy reflected the hierarchy of the work environment. News about the hiring of women in the mill traveled downward from management and its staff to union officials and finally to workers. Few women read about the

openings in the newspaper; most relied on informal sources or "talk around town." Some of the women applied for jobs despite negative publicity about the new hiring policy. A waitress applied for a job after she overheard some of the supervisors from the mill discussing the new policy in her restaurant over breakfast. "I heard them talking about it. This one was saying, ' . . . we are going to hire broads down there. The government is forcing us." Another woman, who had applied for a nontraditional job at the phone company, was told by the personnel director, "The steel mill is being forced to do this too." A third woman had heard about the new policy from a friend employed as a secretary by the mill. "When my friend told me about it, we all laughed. We thought it was ridiculous. Later, I had second thoughts and put my application on file." To apply for a job in a climate of negative or hostile public opinion indicates that these women were little influenced by the normative proscriptions concerning women's work roles.

Initially, management did not believe that women would be interested in jobs as steelworkers. One supervisor remarked, "We never expected them to even apply." Another said, "I was shocked that women would even want to work in the mill. I know this might sound like prejudice, but my idea of a woman is a step above a steelworker." Many of the women steelworkers believed that management deliberately tried to discourage their employment. During the intake interviews, personnel officials repeatedly emphasized the negative aspects of the job, particularly their perception of potential harassment from male co-workers. Typical were such remarks: "They kept stressing that men didn't want the women in there and they would be rough on me," "They kept emphasizing the harassment from men," "You are going to be working around some very vicious people." One woman reported that she was given her first assignment on a nonexistent work crew.

> I went in on a Sunday and was put on a labor gang. There is no labor gang on weekends. I didn't know what to do. It was very discouraging. At the interview I was told that I would be lifting 100-pound bags. He wanted you to say, I can't.

I asked union officials how the men in the mill first responded to the news that women were being hired. I received a variety of responses. One category of responses reflected the idea held by some, that women would expect special privileges because of their status as females. One official told me:

> You heard things like, we are getting those broads on the gang now; broads are coming to work in the mill and they are going to have preference over us; maybe I can get a good-looking helper.

According to union officials, there was widespread fear that women would not be able to do the job and that the men would have to work twice as hard. Some of the men resented a perceived threat to a territory they had exclusively staked out for themselves. One union official said, "Some of those who are hollering the most about women are the same ones who don't appreciate the blacks and other minorities achieving goals greater than theirs." Another male official said:

> Wow, at first there was a lot of resentment. Why don't they go home where they belong; they can't do a man's work; they are taking a man's job; they can't lift . . . a lot of them can't . . . A man is often threatened by a woman who holds her own as an individual.

Finally there was some concern that as good-paying jobs in the region were scarce, the men would no longer be able to secure jobs in the mills for their sons. It was not uncommon for two or even three generations of males from the same family to be employed in the mill. One official said the following about the hiring of women:

> I have mixed emotions about it. Given the employment picture in this country, I feel jobs should go first to heads of the family rather than to movements [women and blacks]. The society is based on the family.

THE JOB

The early years of employment in the mill are characterized by periodic cycles of unemployment and little choice in job assignments. Nearly all mill recruits are initially assigned to the "labor gang." These jobs involve general maintenance work, such as sweeping, shoveling, painting, washing walls, cleaning track, and some semiskilled work such as breaking up cement

and laying concrete. Workers from the labor gang are also chosen on the basis of seniority, to fill in for vacationing or disabled workers in other departments. Most workers consider their stint on the labor gang as temporary, and once they have accumulated enough seniority, the workers may bid on more permanent positions. Women, particularly heads of households, are often limited in their choices of permanent jobs because child-care responsibilities may preclude changing shifts or working weekends. Many trade promotional opportunities for steady daylight work and weekends off. In addition, affirmative action requires that women be admitted to apprenticeship programs that lead to the skilled crafts within the industry. While some of the women qualify for training, very few skilled jobs have opened up in recent years.

Some women deliberately requested jobs that isolated them from other workers as a way to minimize hostile contacts with those male workers who do not approve of their presence. One woman reported, "I like it best when I work by myself or just one other person. It cuts down on all the hassles." Another woman preferred a particular department because it afforded her the opportunity to work alone and because the nature of the work minimized status distinctions.

> You see, everybody over there is in the same class. Everybody is dirty and nobody is clean . . . so nobody really looks down on you. Everybody on the job over there mainly works by himself or else has one helper but you don't get a conglomeration of a lot of people in one department. In other departments there are people who never get dirty and they frown on people who do. You see those kind of people are in a different class from us.

Many women, in part because of low seniority, are assigned jobs in the coke plant or blast furnace. In general, these are the hardest, dirtiest, lowest-paying, and least safe jobs in the mill. However, some women cannot take advantage of transfers because of child-care responsibilities.

Work is also social and can be conceived as a network of interpersonal relationships (Richardson, 1981). How comfortable do the women feel about interaction with the other workers in such a male-dominated environment? Some felt it was difficult to communicate. Understanding the rules that govern conversation became problematic.

If the guys talk to me, I talk to them. But I never go out of my way to talk to the men. If you don't talk to the guys, they say you are stuck up, conceited, a bitch. If you do talk to them, they say you are a whore, so you can't win.

Others simply were not interested in the kinds of things men talk about at work: cars, sports, sex, etc. . . . However, another woman felt that sharing in the same work experience increased understanding between the sexes.

Everybody acts like men and women have never worked together until women came into the steel mills. All of a sudden it's a big deal . . . it's not new. The more we work together on this basic level, sweatin' and workin' the horrible shifts and going through all the suffering you go through, you really begin to understand each other.

Black workers do not always feel that they can be honest in their social relations with white workers in the mill. Attempting to converse across sex and race lines poses special problems for black women. One woman said:

I prefer to work with another black person 'cause it is hard to talk to a white person all day. You are afraid to say what you are doing . . . like fixing up your house or buying a new car. If it looks like you are getting on your feet, the white resents it. They think you are getting too far ahead of yourself. Black and white workers get along fine as long as the black person lets a white person feel as though they are still on top. There are times you would like to say something but you don't. The mill is not as bad as other places I've worked.

Although over time the relationship between men and women and black and white becomes easier to establish, for the most part getting along meant the absence of any overt hostility or conflict. Although they seldom had the opportunity, women preferred working with other women in the mill.

Sexism took a variety of forms within the plant. Job placement, job training, and promotional opportunities were cited as features of sex discrimination. One woman believed that the company deliberately tried to ensure the failure of women, by placing unqualified women in difficult positions.

They pick women for certain jobs that they know in advance will wash out. Placement is not done according to ability or aptitude. In order to fill the quotas, they pick women off the street rather than a woman already in the mill who has a little experience. They build in failure.

Another woman believed that the testing procedure for apprenticeships was biased and successfully argued the case with her employer.

I placed a bid for an apprenticeship program. I failed the mechanical aspect of the aptitude test that would qualify me for the job. I had to convince the company that failure on the aptitude test did not necessarily disqualify me for the apprenticeship. I explained that women are not given the opportunity to become familiar with mechanical principles. I threatened that I felt I was being discriminated against. They let me into the program. My work on the job was termed "above average" by my supervisors and my average in my school work is 89 [70 is passing].

Job evaluation also drew criticism from some of the women. Some believed that women were fired more quickly for mistakes or that the rules governing the performance of tasks were more strictly applied. When the rules were more narrowly interpreted, the men became more hostile and resentful of the presence of women. One woman related the following:

The rules were tightened specifically for women and the men lost some of the informal privileges won over the years. There was an informal agreement between the men working the blast furnace that they could exchange assignments if they didn't want to work a specific job that day. They traded jobs and took turns. In the rush to prove that women can't do the job, the company came down hard and stopped allowing the workers to take turns. They showed us the rules from the book. This caused a lot of resentment toward the women. I think the company knew it would.

Some women even felt that they were assigned to departments where the men were particularly hostile and that men were assigned women helpers as punishment for work infractions.

In addition to the structural features of sexism,

there is the tension and psychological strain associated with being the first women to cross occupational barriers. Because of their high visibility as "groundbreakers," the women faced incredible pressures to do an exemplary job. A sampling of comments: "I put in two parts to their one," "You have to prove yourself over and over," "You are constantly being watched." Sometimes they feel the pressure to be the standard bearer for the entire population of women. One woman explained:

> While I was working on the lids [coke ovens] I was told to move these 100-pound lead boxes. I wanted to prove that I could do it. That all women could do it. After the third lift, I ripped open my intestines and had to be rushed to the hospital. It took surgery and a three-month recovery period. What I didn't know at the time was that no man would have lifted that much weight. They would have asked for a helper or simply refused.

There is also the constant pressure of interpreting male reaction to your presence. Women often hear the men say, "The mill is no place for a woman," "You are taking a job away from a man who needs the money to raise a family," "Women don't do their share," "Women get the easy jobs because they flirt with the foreman." Sometimes their sexuality is called into question. One woman remarked, "If you are too nice, you are a whore, if you aren't nice enough, you're a bitch." Even accepting help from male co-workers becomes problematic.

> You are under so much pressure. If you walk out of the shanty and you are carrying this heavy bucket, the other workers come along and say, how come you let her carry all that? You should be carrying that for her. But if you let them help you, someone else says, see that, you're doing all her work.

One dimension of sexism in the mill is sexual harassment. According to Farley, sexual harassment is unsolicited nonreciprocal male behavior that values a woman's sex role over her function as worker and can include a wide range of behavior, from propositions for dates to touching to actual rape (1979: 33). The practice of sexual harassment is not limited to steel mills or to male-dominated occupations in general. Rather it occurs across the lines of age, marital status, physical appearance, race, class, occupation, pay range

(MacKinnon, 1979: 28). Sexual harassment is rarely about sex. According to Farley (1978) the issue is power or dominance, and sexual harassment is one form of general dominance aimed at keeping women subordinate at work. Steel mill supervisors, who hold the power to reward or punish, are more likely to be perpetrators of sexual harassment. More often than not it is the implicit or explicit promise of a better job assignment or the threat of a worse one. One woman explained, "One foreman used to say, come work for my crew. You can sit in the office all day. Sure, I thought, but what would I have to give in return?" Another woman believed that she was given a particularly hard job because she refused to go out with her supervisor. In addition, the job was deliberately left for her to finish after her days off.

> Last summer this foreman kept bugging me to go out with him. I refused. He stuck me in some of the dirtiest jobs. He put me in the oil pits. They had to lower me in this narrow hole. I was scared to death. I was new in the mill and I was petrified. I had to remove the oil with buckets. It must have been 110° down there. I came up crying; I was really scared. I was off the next two days but when I came back, he put me on the same job. Usually when you start a job the next crew on the next shift finishes it. You see, he saved it for me to finish after my days off.

Direct physical contact of a sexual nature was not prevalent but such incidents did happen.

> Once a foreman grabbed my boob, under eight layers of thermal underwear. It scared the shit out of me 'cause the doors on the trailers aren't locked. What do you do? When it happens, it's a strange thing. At first you think, he doesn't know he is doing it or he didn't mean it . . . but he knew.

Sexual coercion or harassment was not limited solely to supervisory personnel. Some cases were reported between women workers and their male co-workers. However, this type of harassment most often took the form of gossip, verbal remarks, graffiti, or persistent requests for dates.

Despite the hassles, women steelworkers were satisfied with their jobs because the alternatives were less desirable. During the interviews I asked women to compare their present job with previous jobs. Working in the mill is substantially more attractive than jobs that have been traditionally available to women, such as clerical, waitress, and sales jobs. Better pay, greater job security, health-care benefits, degree of supervision, union protection, pace of work were cited again and again as the difference between working in steel and previous jobs. Caught between strict supervision and customer demand, former sales clerks were the most dissatisfied with previous jobs.

It was tougher being a salesgirl. The stores have a strict dress code and for the money they pay, it's just not worth it. There is all this pressure to get a quota of sales. The customers don't understand this. Some would boss you around . . . "get me this, get me that." They feel as if you are their servant. I am the same as the person that comes in and I don't want to be treated like I am below them.

Another former sales clerk responded:

It sounds funny but sales was more difficult. I was hassled constantly, if not by my employer, then by the customers. We had to attack them when they come in and this makes some people belligerent. They treated you like you weren't there.

A factory worker from a nonunion shop compared her old work with her job in the mill.

On my old job, I had to stand on one foot all day. We worked a constant eight-hour day. It was like production but we got a straight hourly wage, no incentive rate. In the mill you can work at your own speed. At the factory they pushed you and pushed you. They didn't care if you lost your fingers in the press; they just wanted that production. I am now making double what I used to and the pressure is a lot less.

Overall the majority of women were much more satisfied with their jobs in the mill than with previous jobs. It seemed nobody wanted to return to the "pink-collar ghetto."

THE UNION

One way to cope with the problems associated with entering a traditional male occupation is union partic-

ipation. The women in the mill, while often critical of union performance, were overwhelmingly in favor of unions. I asked one woman employed in the mill since 1934 to tell me what the mill was like before the union was established.

Before the union came, they worked you harder and they treated you like you weren't human. They never called you by name, they just sissed at you like you were a cat.

She also reported that you never knew from one day to the next if you would even have a job. Workers were often forced to bribe mill supervisors in order to keep their jobs.

At that time the ladies bought gifts so they could hold their jobs and the forelady treats them good. I did not go for that. At $2.44 a day I couldn't afford it.

Most of the women in the mill did not have to reach back in their memories to 1934 in order to recall what life was like without a union. Most had been employed in the nonunionized sector of the labor market prior to their employment in steel and most could make comparisons between the two. In fact, the number one response to the question "What surprised you the most about your new job?" was union protection and union benefits.

Although the number of women who are unionized and the percentage who participate in union affairs is small, their potential influence is far greater than their numbers suggest. In the case of women steelworkers, women are 8 percent of the union members covered by the basic steel agreement and 15 percent of the total membership, yet their impact can be felt on all levels. On the local level women are a source of new ideas and energy needed to revitalize the labor movement. In fact, their participation on the local level exceeds their proportion of the steel work force. At the district level women have formed networks, some publishing newsletters that lobby for the concerns of women steelworkers, the same concerns facing all working women. Their efforts to include child care, maternity leave, and other health and safety issues in the collective bargaining agreement can become a model for other unions. In fact, the steel contract in general is often the model for other industries. On the national level women in the United Steelworkers of America can place pressure on the AFL-CIO to organize the vast number of unorganized women workers. The potential to shape national policy on such work issues as flextime, job sharing, affirmative action, job training, CETA, insurance benefits, and retirement is unprecedented.

Another avenue for change is the Coalition of Labor Union Women (CLUW), a national organization of women trade unionists. Working women from a variety of industries have formed their own network to lobby the unions to promote the rights of women in the workplace and to help to organize the vast number of unorganized women workers in the United States. CLUW is also training women for leadership roles in the trade union movement. The efforts of women to make their unions more responsive to the concerns of working women are very likely to have an impact on the quality of work life for both men and women in the workplace.

REFERENCES

Acker, J. 1980. "Women and stratification: A review of recent literature." *Contemporary Sociology* 9:25–35.

Farley, L. 1979. *Sexual shakedown: The sexual harassment of women on the job.* New York: Warner.

MacKinnon, C. A. 1979. *Sexual harassment of working women.* New Haven: Yale University Press.

Richardson, L. W. 1981. *The dynamics of sex and gender: A sociological perspective.* Boston: Houghton Mifflin.

R E A D I N G   2 4

Peril and Promise: Lesbians' Workplace Participation

BETH SCHNEIDER

Lesbians must work. Put most simply, few lesbians will ever have, however briefly, the economic support of another person (man or woman); lesbians are dependent on themselves for subsistence. Thus, a significant portion of the time and energies of most lesbians is devoted to working. Working as a central feature of lesbian existence is, however, rarely acknowledged. As with any significant primary commitment by a woman to job or career, a lesbian's relationship to work is obscured, denied, or trivialized by cultural assumptions concerning heterosexuality.[1]

Moreover, the concept "lesbian" is so identified with sexual behavior and ideas of deviance, particularly in social science literature,[2] that it has been easy to ignore the fact that lesbians spend their time at other than sexual activities; for a lesbian, working is much more likely to be a preoccupation than her sexual or affectional relations. Given the limited research on the sexual behavior of lesbians over the course of their lives, it is no surprise that there is decidedly less known about the working lives and commitments of lesbians.

In asserting the centrality, if not the primacy, of a working life to lesbians, we assume that work provides both a means of economic survival and a source of personal integrity, identity, and strength. While lesbians are certainly not the only women whose identities are at least partially formed by their relationship to work, in a culture defined for women in terms of heterosexual relations and limited control over the conditions of motherhood, most lesbians are likely to have fewer of the commitments and relations considered appropriate and necessary to the prevailing conceptions of women.

On the other hand, work and one's relationship to it is considered a major source of economic and social status, personal validation, and life purpose—certainly for men—in this society.[3] For lesbians then, whose lives will not necessarily provide or include the constraints or the comforts that other women receive ("heterosexual privileges"), working may well take on additional and special meaning. Thus, lesbians' workplace participation is shaped by the possibility of a unique commitment to working, an outsider status by dint of sexual identity, and the set of conditions common to all women workers. The conflicting aspects of these forces define the problematic and often paradoxical context within which lesbians work.

Being a woman worker has many implications for lesbians' material, social, and emotional well-being. Compared to their male counterparts, women employed full-time continue to receive significantly less pay.[4] Most do not have college degrees and enter occupations of traditional female employment where unionization is rare, benefits meager, and prestige lacking.[5] Continued employment in female-dominated occupations maintains women's disadvantage relative to men, since it is associated with lower wages; typically, lower wages keep women dependent on men—their husbands (when they have them) or their bosses.[6] In those situations in which women and men are peers at work, status distinctions remain, reflecting the realities of sexism in the workplace and the society.[7] In general, then, women are on the lower end of job and authority hierarchies. In addition, basic to the economic realities of all working women is the need to appear (through dress and demeanor) sexually attractive to men, who tend to hold the economic position and power to enforce heterosexual standards and desires.[8]

Thus, as one portion of the female labor force, lesbians are in a relatively powerless and devalued position, located in workplaces occupied but not controlled by women. Herein lies one paradox of a great many lesbians' working lives. The world of women's labor—with its entrenched occupational and job segregation—creates a homosocial female environment, a milieu potentially quite comfortable for lesbians.

But lesbians must also manage their sexual identity difference at work.[9] As women whose sexual, political, and social activities are primarily with other women, lesbians are daily confronted with heterosexual assumptions at work. The nature and extent of heterosexual pressures (over and above those experienced by all women) condition the nature of their social relationships. Two markedly different dynamics simultaneously affect lesbians in their daily interactions at work.

Negative attitudes toward homosexuality are still widespread in the society. The statements and activities of New Right leaders and organizations and the research results of a number of studies on less politicized populations indicate that lesbians and male homosexuals must continue to be cautious in their dealings with the heterosexual world and to be wary of being open about their sexual identity in certain occupations—especially teaching.[10]

Directly related to these public attitudes, employment-related issues and articles tend to predominate in the lesbian and gay press. Either legislative and political efforts toward an end to discrimination are detailed and progress assessed, or some person or persons who have lost their jobs or personal credibility when their sexual identity has become known or suspected are written up. For example, recently readers of both the alternative press and mass media have seen accounts of the anticipated disastrous financial consequences of a publicly revealed lesbian relationship on the women's tennis tour, community censure of public officials who spoke in favor of antidiscrimination laws, lesbian feminists fired or not rehired at academic jobs, and a purge of suspected lesbians aboard a Navy missile ship, among others.[11]

Nevertheless, there is little systematic evidence that indicates how particular heterosexuals react to lesbians in concrete situations. It is these daily encounters and interactions with heterosexuals that are of crucial concern to lesbians; at work, the disclosure of one's sexual identity might have serious consequences. In a recent study of job discrimination against lesbians, fully 50 percent anticipated discrimination at work and 22 percent reported losing a job when their sexual identity became known.[12] But in addition, lesbians fear harassment and isolation from interpersonal networks; often they live under pressure or demands to prove they are as good or better workers than their coworkers.[13]

Whether anyone is fired or legislation is won or lost, the world of work is perceived and experienced by lesbians as troublesome, ambiguous, problematic. And while it is generally assumed that lesbians are more tolerated than gay men and therefore safer at work and elsewhere, a climate of ambivalence and disapproval pervades the world within which lesbians work; most are not likely to feel immediately comfortable about their relationships to coworkers.

Despite these significant disadvantages and potential troubles, a number of studies consistently show that lesbians have stable work histories, are higher achievers than comparable heterosexual women,[14] and have a serious commitment to work, giving it priority because they must support themselves.[15] These findings suggest, but do not describe or document, that lesbians' workplace survival results from a complicated calculation of the degree to which a particular work setting allows them freedom to be open and allows for the negotiation and development of a support network.

At work and elsewhere, lesbians want and have friendships and relationships with other women; while some research suggests that lesbians are no different than single heterosexuals in the extent of their friendship networks, others describe much greater social contacts for lesbians since they must negotiate two possibly overlapping worlds (work and social life) and most are free of familial constraints that pull other women away from work relationships.[16] Whatever the extent of their networks, it is these friendships and relationships that are a major source of workplace support—and complication—for lesbians, as well as an important facet of their emotional well-being and job satisfaction.

However, there is virtually no research that systematically explores lesbian work sociability, the creation of a support mechanism there, or the conditions under which lesbians are willing to make their sexual identity known. Most of what is known about these problems is based on findings from research on male homosexuals, and therefore does not take into account the greater importance women as a group, and lesbians specifically, attach to emotional support and relationships.[17] Nevertheless, this research indicates that the more a male is known as a homosexual, the less stressful are his relationships with heterosexuals because he does not anticipate and defend against rejection.[18] But economic success frequently requires denying one's sexual identity: research findings over the last decade are consistent in showing that high-status males are less open than low-status males.[19] A combination of avoidance, information control, and role distance are strategies used by homosexuals to preserve secrecy; the result is often the appearance of being boring, unfriendly, sexless, or heterosexual.[20]

In addition to focusing on men, many of these studies were completed prior to, or at the onset of, the gay liberation movement, which has continued to encourage and emphasize "coming out" for reasons of either political principle and obligation or personal health.[21] Certainly, in the last decade many lesbians have taken extraordinary risks in affirming their sexual identities and defending their political and social communities.[22]

In sum, lesbians' relationship to the world of work is both ordinary and unique. Based on findings from a recent study of 228 lesbian workers, a number of previously unexamined aspects of the conditions of lesbian participation at the workplace are explored here. Following a brief description of the research project from which these data are taken and a discussion of the sample generation and characteristics, four aspects of lesbian existence at work are discussed: (1) making friends, (2) finding a partner, (3) coming out, and (4) being harassed.

RESEARCH METHODS AND SAMPLE

The findings are part of a larger research project on working women (both lesbian and heterosexual) and their perspectives and experiences concerning sociability, sexual relationships, and sexual harassment at the workplace.[23] The project was not explicitly designed to directly examine instances of discrimination against lesbians and cannot adequately address that problem. It was designed to explore some of the more subtle interpersonal terrain that all women are likely to encounter at work, as well as those situations of particular concern to lesbians.

The lesbian sample was gathered with the assistance of twenty-eight contacts who provided me with the names, addresses, and approximate ages of women who they thought were lesbians. The contacts provided 476 names. A self-administered questionnaire with 316 items was mailed to 307 of these contacts during the period between January and March 1980. The letter that accompanied the questionnaire did not assume any knowledge of a particular woman's sexual identity. Eighty-one percent of these women returned the questionnaire, a very high rate of return that seems to reflect significant interest in all the topics covered.

There were 228 women who identified themselves as either lesbian or homosexual or gay in the question asking for current sexual identity. This sample of lesbians ranged in age from 21 to 58 (median = 29.4); 10 percent were women of color (most Afro-American).[24] The sample was unique in that it was not a San Francisco– or New York City–based population; 55 percent were from New England, 33 percent from Middle Atlantic states, and the rest from other locations east of the Mississippi River.

The lesbians in this study were employed in all kinds of workplaces.[25] More than half (57 percent) were in professional or technical occupational categories (in such jobs as teaching and social work), with the remaining distributed as follows: administrative and managerial (10 percent), clerical (11 percent), craft (7 percent), service (7 percent), operative (5 percent), and sales (2 percent). Sixty-nine percent worked full-time, 20 percent part-time, and the rest were unemployed at the time of the survey. Fifty-two percent were employed in predominantly (55 to 100 percent) female workplaces, 25 percent in workplaces with 80 percent or more females; 10 percent worked in units with 80 percent or more males. While the educational attainment of this group of lesbians was very high for a population of adult women (82 percent were at least college graduates), their median income was $8,800 (in 1979). The low income of the total group reflects a combination of its relative youth and the proportion with less than full-time or full-year employment.

Two questions were asked to determine lesbians' openness about themselves at work, a matter of crucial concern to any understanding of daily workplace experiences. The first asked: "How open would you say you are about your lesbianism at your *present* job?" The choices were: "Totally," "Mostly," "Somewhat," "Not at all." The participants varied widely in the extent to which they felt they were open at work: Only 16 percent felt they were totally open, while 55 percent tended to be and 29 percent were closed about who they were at work.

The second question asked the proportion of each

woman's coworkers who knew she was a lesbian. Twenty-five percent estimated that *all* their coworkers knew about their sexual identity,[26] half estimated that at least one or "some" knew, and 14 percent stated that "none knew." The remainder simply "didn't know" if anyone knew they were lesbians, a difficult and often anxiety-provoking situation.

MAKING FRIENDS

Most lesbians sampled believed it desirable to integrate their work and social lives in some ways.[27] Thus the distinction between public and private life is not terribly useful in describing their lives, despite its persistence as ideology throughout the culture.[28] For example, only one-third maintained that they kept their social life completely separate from their work life, and 39 percent tried not to discuss personal matters with persons from work. Alternatively, 43 percent believed that doing things socially with coworkers makes relationships run more smoothly.

There obviously was variability in beliefs. Lesbians who most consistently and strongly held the view that work and social life should be integrated fell into two categories: those who had to—that is, lesbians in professional employment whose jobs required a certain level of sociability and collegiality; and those who had nothing to lose—women in dead-end jobs with no promise of advancement, those with few or no supervisory responsibilities, and those who were already open with persons from work about their sexual identity.

On the other hand, women who could not or did not believe these spheres could be easily or truly integrated were constrained by powerful forces that limited and denied the possibility of such integration: lesbians in male-dominated workplaces and those in worksites with male supervisors and bosses, in which males bond with each other, often to the exclusion and detriment of the females.

The beliefs of the lesbians in the sample were quite consistent with the actual extent of their social contacts with persons from work. Most lesbians (in fact, most women) maintained social ties with at least some persons from work—at the job and outside it. Not surprisingly, 84 percent ate lunch with coworkers, but fewer engaged in social activities outside the work setting. For example, 9 percent visited frequently, 55 percent visited occasionally at each other's homes, 8 percent frequently and 47 percent occasionally went out socially with persons from work.

Two aspects of these findings merit further comment. First, the figures for the lesbians differ by less than 1 percent from those of the heterosexual women workers in the larger research project; if lesbians curtail contact or make certain judgments about coworkers as acquaintances or friends, they may do so for different reasons, but they do so to an extent similar to heterosexual women.

Second, certain conditions determine both lesbians' beliefs about and the extensiveness of their social contacts. Those in professional employment have more social ties with persons from work than lesbians in working-class jobs (which as a rule require less sociability); lesbians who are older, who have come to be familiar with a particular job setting over a length of time, and those who are open about their sexual identity are much more likely to maintain social contacts with coworkers than their younger or more closeted counterparts. In this particular study, there were no differences of any significance between lesbians of color and whites with regard to sociability; in fact, the lesbians of color had, as a group, more contact with coworkers. This is not surprising in that the networking that produced the original sample reached only as far as a particular group of lesbians of color, who were disproportionately employed in feminist workplaces such as women's centers and women's studies programs, locations that facilitate, however imperfectly, such sociability. Those conditions in which a female culture can develop (granted, often within the limits of a male work world) allow lesbians greater possibilities for being open about their sexual identity with at least some coworkers. Familiar and supportive conditions tend to foster friendships and, as will become clear in the next section, provide the basis upon which more intimate relationships may also develop.

When there is a need to be social, lesbians are; professional jobs require sociability, but very many also require some degree of secrecy as well. This is particularly true for work in traditionally male occupations. In addition, and more important given women's location in the occupational structure, working with children (as teachers, nurses, social workers) can be cause for a relatively closeted existence. In this research, working with children did not seem to influence the extent of lesbian sociability, but it did affect how open they were about themselves at their workplaces. Here lies a classic instance of a highly contradictory situation, one common to many persons in human services and educational institutions. An ideology prevails that encourages (often demands) honesty, trust, and congenial nonalienating working relationships, but a lesbian's ability to actively involve herself in the prescribed ways is often limited or contorted. Frye's description of her experience in a women's studies program captures the essence of the difficulties:

> But in my dealings with my heterosexual women's studies colleagues, I do not take my own advice: I have routinely and habitually muffled or stifled myself on the subject of Lesbianism and heterosexualism ... out of some sort of concern about alienating them.... Much more important to me is a smaller number who are my dependable political coworkers in the university, ... the ones with some commitment to not being homophobic and to trying to be comprehending and supportive of Lesbians and Lesbianism. If I estrange these women, I will lose the only footing I have, politically and personally, in my long-term work-a-day survival in academia. They are important, valuable and respected allies. I am very careful, over-careful, when I talk about heterosexuality with them.[29]

More traditional workplaces provide even fewer possibilities for support than the one described above.

FINDING A PARTNER

In the last section, brief reference is made to lesbians' sexual relationships at work. The typical story of the office affair seems to have little to do with lesbians. It centers on a boss (the powerful person, the man) and his secretary (the powerless person, the woman); the consequences of this double-edged inequality of occupational status and gender are of prime concern. As the story would have it, the powerful one influences the other's (the woman's) career in such a way that she is highly successful ("She slept her way to the top") or her work and career are permanently ruined. It is rarely acknowledged that relationships at work occur between coworkers or between persons of the same gender, or that the consequences may be close to irrelevant—at least with regard to the job. When acknowl-edged it seems that heterosexual affairs are more tol-erated than are lesbian or homosexual relations.[30]

But the facts tell another story.[31] Twenty-one per-cent of the lesbians in this study met their current part-ners at work; overall, 52 percent of the lesbians had had at least one sexual relationship with a person from work during their working lives. This amazingly high proportion makes sense when it is remembered that the vast majority of women (and lesbians) are em-ployed in female-dominated workplaces. Such a work setting is a good location for a lesbian to find a poten-tial lover. But in addition, there have traditionally been few places—other than bars—for lesbians to meet each other socially; most met, and still meet, through friendship networks (44 percent). While re-cently the women's and lesbians' communities have provided some alternatives—restaurants, clubs, polit-ical activities—employment plays such a significant part in lesbians' lives (and takes such a significant part of their time) that the workplace becomes an impor-tant, almost obvious, site for creating and having friendships and more intimate relationships.

Nineteen percent of the currently self-identified les-bians were heterosexual and 9 percent were married at the time of the sexual relationship they reported. This means that 81 percent were lesbians when they entered into at least a somewhat committed (and potentially risky) relationship with a person from work.

The chances that a lesbian will have a relationship with someone at work increase with age. To illustrate, while 79 percent of the sampled lesbians over forty had had a relationship with someone at work some-time in their lifetime, 59 percent in their thirties and 42 percent in their twenties had had such an involve-ment. In addition, the longer a woman has identified herself as a lesbian (whatever her age), the more likely she is to have an intimate relationship with a person at work. This certainly suggests that some part of the freedom to pursue an involvement in the work setting is an easiness with oneself as a lesbian and a flexibility and wisdom gained from years of managing the com-plexities of sexual identity difference at work.

Most of the relationships reported were not brief af-fairs; 60 percent of the lesbians had been or were cur-rently in a relationship of a year or more duration. Having such a relationship can have many effects, many small and predictable, others large and less con-trollable. Perhaps most obviously, the longer a rela-

tionship lasts, the more likely are some people at work (in addition to friends outside work) to know of the involvement. (In contrast to the heterosexuals in the larger study, lesbians tended to be more secretive about the relationship with people from work.)

Since the "office affair" mythology assumes a het-erosexual relationship and the dynamic of superior-subordinate, it is useful to examine who in fact the les-bian workers were involved with. Eighteen percent of the lesbians were involved with a man (most, but not all, were heterosexual at the time); the few self-identi-fied lesbians who were nevertheless involved with a man were almost exclusively involved with their boss in relatively brief affairs. Overall, 75 percent were in-volved with coworkers, 14 percent with boss or super-visor, 6 percent with subordinates, and 5 percent with customers, clients, and the like. With the female boss still very much a rarity, lesbians are less likely to have the option of a relationship with a woman with insti-tutionalized authority over their working lives. This is in contrast to heterosexual women, whose relation-ships at work tend to be unequal as a result of the mix of gender and status inequality.

There were only a few consistent and predictable patterns in the effects and consequences of these rela-tionships for the lesbians as a group. Seventy-two per-cent enjoyed their work more than usual. Some in-volvements improved relationships with other coworkers (25 percent) while others caused problems with coworkers (35 percent) or trouble with a boss or supervisor (20 percent). Much of the difficulty during the course of the relationship seemed to stem from jealousies, irritation at undone work, or in attention on the part of one or both of the parties to others. Also, the involvements often highlighted the lesbians' sex-ual identity, forcing them to be less closeted. The data suggest that one of the conflicts a lesbian must face in having a relationship at work is a willingness to either engage in massive secrecy and denial of the situation or become more clear about who she is. Many lesbians (30 percent) reported relief at the end of their involve-ments in part because hostility or gossip was lessened, in part because the pressures of enforced secrecy were removed.

The effects of being and becoming open about one's sexual identity as a consequence of the relationship are mixed and complicated, and often contradictory. For example, 62 percent of the more open lesbians com-pared to 19 percent of the more closed ones reported significantly greater friction with coworkers and some (22 percent) felt their chances for advancement were diminished. On the other hand, 31 percent of the more open lesbians reported improvement in workplace relations and improved advancement possibilities (10 percent); they enjoyed their work more than the closed lesbians. It is interesting to note that not one lesbian who was closed about her sexual identity at work believed that her chances for promotion were affected one way or the other by her involvement.

Almost everyone reported suffering the usual kinds of emotional problems at the termination of the relationship, obviously the longer the relationship the more so. The work-related consequences of lesbian involvements with women of similar job status are much simpler and less harmful than those with a superior. Thirteen percent of the lesbians resigned or quit because of the breakup; most of the lesbians who resigned were involved with a boss, rather than a coworker, some few of whom were women. A very few lesbians (4 percent) reported losing out on some career-related opportunity, such as a promotion or pay increase; none reported gaining any work benefit. In 15 percent of the instances, the other person left the job at the termination of the relationship; in all these cases, these were female coworkers.

In general, involvements at work are an integral part of a lesbian's emotional commitments to women. This extension of the prescribed limits of relationships beyond friendship is consistent with most other research on lesbians that similarly shows fluid boundaries between friends and lovers and friendship networks of former lovers.[32]

COMING OUT

Most lesbians are acutely aware that their openness about their lesbianism is not an all-or-nothing phenomenon at work or elsewhere but that it varies depending at the very least on the context and on the particular individuals involved. The lesbians in this study clearly varied in their own sense of how open they *felt* they were at work. As we already saw, being open allowed lesbians greater contact with coworkers, facilitating network-building and support as well as being a basis for (and a possible result of) having a sexual relationship with someone at work.

This study indicates that lesbians tend to be open about their sexual identity when their workplace has a predominance of women and most of their work friends are women, when they have a female boss or supervisor, when they are employed in small workplaces, when they have few supervisory responsibilities, when they have relatively low incomes, and when they are not dealing with children as either students, clients, or patients.

Two aspects of these findings require special comment. First, as noted earlier, the situation of professionally employed lesbians is terribly contradictory. Since the jobs require socializing and contacts with others either at work or in the business or professional communities, lesbians maintain those social contacts; on the other hand, high-income professional lesbians are likely to be closeted. The result of this predicament is a well-managed, manicured lie delivered to people with whom one is spending a great deal of time.

Second, the influence of gender proportions is crucial. For example, in workplaces that were heavily female-dominated (80 percent or more women as employees), 55 percent of the lesbians were totally or mostly open about their sexual identity. It is worth noting that this still means that 45 percent tended to be somewhat closeted even in these settings. In contrast, in heavily male-dominated workplaces (80 percent or more men as employees), only 10 percent of the lesbians were open.

A workplace with a predominance of women may include other lesbians to whom a lesbian can be open; they may also become friends or lovers. Of the lesbians who met another lesbian at work, almost all (94 percent) did in fact become friends. But even when there are not other lesbians at work, lesbians take certain risks, trusting at least one heterosexual woman not to react negatively to knowledge of her sexual identity. Moreover, most women are not in a structurally powerful position to affect the conditions under which lesbians work. When lesbians do have a female supervisor or boss, they are more often open about their sexual identity than with a male boss. For example, only 21 percent of lesbians with a male boss were open, compared to 47 percent who were open with a female boss. When lesbians were themselves the boss or were self-employed, 88 percent were open about their sexual identity.

How open a lesbian is at her current job is not related to her age or race or the length of time she has been at that position. However, if she has lost a previous job because she is a lesbian, she is less sociable with people from work at her current job and tends to be more cautious about "coming out" at work. In this study 8 percent of the lesbians reported losing a job when their sexual identity became known and another 2 percent believed (but did not know for certain) they lost a job for this reason. The relatively young age of this sample may account for the lower proportion of job loss than in other studies. Whatever the extent of their openness, 75 percent of all lesbians were concerned that their lesbianism might cause damage to their job or career.

In summary, openness is most likely under conditions that are intimate and safe, free of potentially serious consequences for a lesbian's working life. That is, lesbians are most likely to be open in a small workplace, with a female boss, in a job with relatively little financial or social reward (and possibly few career risks).

The consequences of being open are substantial. Open lesbians have more friends and more social contact at work than closed lesbians; they are more willing to have, and do have, sexual relationships with women from their workplace. In contrast, and almost by definition, lesbians who are closed about their sexual identity at work are more likely to avoid certain situations with coworkers and feel reluctant to talk about their personal life.

While cause and effect is admittedly difficult to disentangle here, open and closed lesbians differ in the extent to which they feel that their sexual identity causes problems in many areas of their life. This research indicates that lesbians who remain closeted at work are obviously more concerned and afraid than open lesbians about losing their jobs. But in addition, closeted lesbians are much more concerned than open ones about losing their friends, harming their relationship with their parents, and where applicable, harming their lovers' careers or child custody situations. Consistent with this is the finding that openness at work is related to a general freedom to be open elsewhere as well: lesbians who are open at work are more likely to be open with parents and with both female and male heterosexual friends.

Not surprisingly, closed and open lesbians have uniquely different feelings about their positions at work. Closeted lesbians suffer from a sense of powerlessness and significant strain and anxiety at work, while open lesbians have greater emotional freedom. Eighty-four percent of the closed lesbians in the study felt they had no choice about being closeted; two-thirds felt uncomfortable about that decision, and 39 percent felt that the anxiety about being found out was "paralyzing." A significant 35 percent devoted time and emotion to maintaining a heterosexual front at work.

On the other hand, 94 percent of the open lesbians felt better since coming out, and while the strength of their feelings varied, most felt they were treated with respect because of their candor. Forty percent reported that their work relationships were a lot better than they were before coming out. Disclosure of one's sexual identity at work allows for the possibility of integrating into the workplace with less anxiety about who one is and how one is perceived. But there are some negative consequences to coming out. Twenty-nine percent of the open lesbians sensed that some coworkers avoided them and 25 percent admitted to working harder to keep the respect they had from their peers. While these consequences seem insignificant in contrast to the benefits of disclosure, it is good to remember that coming out often can be a quite limited communication to a quite limited number of persons; thus, protection is built into the very choice of context and relationship.

BEING HARASSED

Eighty-two percent of the lesbians studied experienced sexual approaches at work in the year of the study; that is, 33 percent were sexually propositioned, 34 percent were pinched or grabbed, 54 percent were asked for a date, and 67 percent were joked with about their body or appearance by someone at the workplace.[33] These figures are high for one year; they are, however, comparable to those for the heterosexual women in the larger research project who were of similar race and age. Relatively young, unmarried women (this fits the description of most of the lesbians in the study) and those who worked in male-dominated work settings were most often the recipients of these sexual approaches. Ironically enough, the lesbians who tended to be secretive about their sexual identity (therefore presumed to be heterosexual) were more often sexually approached in these particular ways than the more open lesbians. For example, while 32 percent of the more closed lesbians were pinched or grabbed, only 12 percent of the more open were; likewise, 26 percent of the more closed in contrast to 13 percent of the more open were sexually propositioned.

In comments written to the researcher, it became evident that some lesbians were occasionally referring to both women and men in reporting on date requests and jokes, the more prevalent types of interactions. Unfortunately, the data for these experiences did not specify the gender of the initiator, thus making impossible a true profile of all interpersonal dynamics of this sort.

When asked their emotional response to these experiences ("like," "mixed," "dislike"), the great majority (more than 90 percent) reported disliking pinching or grabbing and sexual propositions—whoever initiated them; few lesbians in fact ever reported liking any such incident. The one exception was being asked for a date by a coworker, and even here only 9 percent said they liked this interaction, with 46 percent "mixed." Toleration (mixed feelings) was the main response to jokes and date requests. And in all cases, coworkers were the most tolerated group of initiators; some of these coworkers may well be women. Typically, coworkers do not have the institutionalized authority to affect each other's job or career standing though they may nevertheless make life more difficult in these kinds of ways.

We cannot directly infer from these data the meaning of these experiences to lesbian workers. Unwanted sexual approaches can be seen as harassment explicitly targeted at a lesbian because she is a lesbian or as harassment typically experienced by most working women. These sexual approaches highlight the disadvantages of lesbians in a working environment by emphasizing heterosexual norms of intimacy and behavior and accenting further the outsider position many lesbians feel at work. Research that compares lesbian workers with heterosexual women workers indicates that while lesbians and heterosexuals have a quite similar number of such approaches in their daily lives, these interactions are experienced quite differently. Lesbians are more sensitive to the problem of unwanted sexual approaches and are much more willing than heterosexuals to label behaviors of this type as sexual harassment.[34]

CONCLUSION

This research was an effort using quantitative data to describe the context of daily life at work for lesbians and to understand the sources of lesbian survival at work. It was not a definitive study of the prevalence of lesbian job loss or harassment.

The findings showed fewer difficulties at work than other studies seem to indicate, but like that research, it insufficiently explored the meanings lesbians attach to particular situations. One obvious question that remains is the extent to which a problem or harassment situation at work is attributed specifically to discrimination on the basis of sexual identity rather than understood as a reflection of the general condition of women. In this research (in which all but one of the lesbians indicated that she was a feminist), the interpretation of events is complicated and complex.

Applying a feminist interpretation to certain workplace situations could diminish or exaggerate the extent to which lesbians perceive those instances as resulting from, or in reaction to, their lesbianism. Sexual harassment is a particularly clear case. A lesbian may well wonder why she was hugged by a male coworker: was it a gesture of friendship, harassment specifically directed to her as a lesbian, or harassment similar to that most women encounter at work? If most lesbians considered the variety of harassing experiences at work discrimination against them as lesbians, the proportion reporting workplace problems would surely increase.

While a more complete picture of workplace problems awaits additional research, these findings underscore some important dimensions of lesbians' workplace participation. First, the experience of lesbians is both similar and different from that of heterosexual women workers. It is similar in (1) the creation of a supportive environment of work friends, (2) the experience of unwanted sexual approaches from various parties with whom they interact, and (3) the use of the workplace to meet sexual partners. It is different in (1) the necessity of strategizing in the face of fear of disclosure and possible job loss, and (2) the meanings attached to interactions and events in the workplace.

While the fear of job or career loss or damage is often uppermost in a recitation of workplace problems, most lesbians do not lose their jobs. Two mutually reinforcing aspects of a strategy seem to account for this general lack of this most serious and negative sanction. First, lesbians tend to remain closeted, keeping their sexual identity secret from most persons at work; at the same time, they create an environment that protects them, emotional ties with a few people who contribute to a sense of a less hostile and alienating work world.

Coming out is clearly a process; within any particular institutional context, such as work, an assessment is made as to the degree to which a lesbian can be open about who she is. The extent of disclosure varies, dependent on the particulars of personnel and place; it changes over time. Certainly few are the lesbians and fewer still the workplaces that can manage or tolerate complete disclosure. At the minimum, lesbians come out when they are ready and conditions are good, meaning in some workplaces and with some people. While the exact process is not detailed here, it is clear that coming out occurs when a woman believes that a person is trustworthy, sensitive, or politically aware. This is an assessment over which a lesbian has some control. When a lesbian is known as such at work, a congenial and supportive relationship has typically preceded disclosure.

The ease with which a lesbian is disclosing about her sexual identity reflects historically specific conditions as well. In this sample of highly politicized lesbian women workers in late 1979, 40 percent felt they were totally or most open about being lesbians; 75 percent were concerned that their lesbianism might affect their employment situation. In the current climate of conservatism reflected in recent efforts to defend and preserve the "sanctity of the family,"[35] lesbians are forced constantly to weigh the costs of disclosure. Thus, a combination of forces—personal choice, workplace characteristics, and political concerns—continues to define the options and limitations of the workplace environment.

Finally, female support systems at work—allies and networks—can be seen as an integral part of lesbians' emotional commitments to women. While it is certainly ironic and contradictory to proclaim the virtues of "women's work," with its devalued economic and social worth, those workplaces do provide an easier, more congenial atmosphere than is immediately available in more highly paid, male-segregated locations. Many lesbians know these facts and in decisions regarding work may well take them into account.

While the fear and peril of lesbians' workplace situation cannot be denied or diminished, neither can the challenge. Lesbians' participation and relationship to work is similar to the kind of "double vision" shared by other groups who are outsiders:[36] an acute awareness of the strength and force of an oppressive ideology of heterosexuality and its structural manifestations, coupled with an active accommodation and creation of a livable working environment.

NOTES

1. The socioemotional climate of work is based on strong cultural assumptions of heterosexuality. An ideology of heterosexuality includes the following beliefs: (1) All persons are heterosexual. (2) All intimate relationships occur between persons of opposite gender. (3) Heterosexual relationships are better—healthier, more normal—than homosexual relations. With regard to employment, the ideology assumes that every woman is defined by, and in some way is the property of, a man (father, husband, boss); thus a woman's work is secondary, since she is, will be, or ought to be supported by a man. See the following for statements concerning the cultural and structural dimensions of heterosexuality: Charlotte Bunch, "Not for Lesbians Only," reading 49 in this vol-

ume; Gayle Rubin, "The Traffic in Women: Notes on the 'Political Economy' of Sex," in Rayna Rapp, ed. *Toward an Anthropology of Women* (New York: Monthly Review Press, 1975), pp. 157–210; Catharine A. MacKinnon, *Sexual Harassment of Working Women: A Case of Sex Discrimination* (New Haven: Yale University Press, 1979); Adrienne Rich, "Compulsory Heterosexuality and Lesbian Existence," reading 14 in this volume; Lisa Leghorn and Katherine Parker, *Woman's Worth: Sexual Economics and the World of Women* (Boston: Routledge & Kegan Paul, 1981).

2. See Anabel Faraday, "Liberating Lesbian Research," and Kenneth Plummer, "Homosexual Categories: Some Research Problems in the Labelling Perspective of Homosexu-

ality," in Kenneth Plummer, ed., *The Making of the Modern Homosexual* (Totowa, N.J.: Barnes & Noble, 1981).

3. For a review of the literature on the relationship of work to individual well-being, see Rosabeth Moss Kanter, *Work and Family in the United States: A Critical Review and Agenda for Research and Policy* (New York: Russell Sage, 1977).

4. U.S. Bureau of Labor Statistics, *Perspectives on Working Women: A Databook,* Bulletin 2080 (Washington, D.C.: U.S. Government Printing Office, 1980).

5. Louise Kapp Howe, *Pink-Collar Workers: Inside the World of Women's Work* (New York: G. P. Putnam, 1977).

6. Heidi Hartman, "Capitalism, Patriarchy, and Job Segregation by Sex," in Zillah Eisenstein, ed., *Capitalist Patriarchy and the Case for Socialist Feminism* (New York: Monthly Review Press, 1979), pp. 206–47.

7. Neal Gross and Anne Trask, *The Sex Factor and Management of Schools* (New York: Wiley, 1976); and Rosabeth Moss Kanter, *Men and Women of the Corporation* (New York: Basic Books, 1977).

8. MacKinnon (see n. 1 above).

9. Throughout this article, sexual identity, rather than sexual orientation or sexual preference, is the term used to describe and distinguish heterosexual and lesbian women. As a construct, sexual identity most adequately describes the process of creating and maintaining an identity as a sexual being. In contrast to sexual orientation, it does not assume an identity determined by the end of childhood; in contrast to sexual preference, it does not narrow the focus to the gender of one's partner or to particular sexual practices. See Plummer (n. 2 above) for a recent discussion of the issues and problems of homosexual categorization in the social sciences.

10. Amber Hollibaugh, "Sexuality and the State: The Defeat of the Briggs Initiative," *Socialist Review* 45 (May–June 1979): 55–72; Linda Gordon and Alan Hunter, "Sex, Family and the New Right," *Radical America* 11 November 1977–February 1978); George Gallup, "Report on the Summer 1977 Survey of Attitudes Toward Homosexuality," *Boston Globe,* September 10, 1977; Albert Klassen, Jr., and Eugene Levitt, "Public Attitudes Toward Homosexuality," *Journal of Homosexuality* 1 (1974): 29–43.

11. See any issue of *Gay Community News* and any newsletter of the National Gay Task Force for a more complete sampling of these types of stories; also see Judith McDaniel, "We Were Fired: Lesbian Experiences in Academe," *Sinister Wisdom* 20 (Spring 1982): 30–43; and J. R. Roberts, *Black Lesbians* (Tallahassee, Florida: Naiad Press, 1981), pp. 74–76.

12. Martin P. Levine and Robin Leonard, "Discrimination Against Lesbians in the Workforce," paper presented at Annual Meetings of the American Sociological Association, September 1982.

13. Sasha Gregory Lewis, *Sunday's Women: A Report on Lesbian Life Today* (Boston: Beacon Press, 1979); Laud Humphreys, *Out of the Closets: The Sociology of Homosexual Liberation* (Englewood Cliffs, N.J.: Prentice-Hall, 1972).

14. Jack Hedblom, "The Female Homosexual: Social and Attitudinal Dimensions," in Joseph McCaffrey, ed., *The Homosexual Dialectic* (Englewood Cliffs, N.J.: Prentice-Hall, 1972); William Simon and John Gagnon, "The Lesbians: A Preliminary Overview," in W. Simon and J. Gagnon, eds., *Sexual Deviance* (New York: Harper & Row, 1967), pp. 247–82.

15. Fred A Minnegerode and Marcy Adelman, "Adaptations of Aging Homosexual Men and Women," paper presented at Convention of the Gerontological Society, October 1976.

16. For an analysis that suggests a similarity of friendship networks between lesbians and single heterosexual women, see Andrea Oberstone and Harriet Sukoneck, "Psychological Adjustment and Lifestyles of Single Lesbians and Single Heterosexual Women," *Psychology of Women Quarterly* 1 (Winter 1976): 172–88; for one that suggests differences between these two groups, see Alan Bell and Martin Weinberg, *Homosexualities: A Study of Diversity Among Men and Women.*

17. E. M. Ettorre, *Lesbians, Women, and Society* (New York: Methuen, 1980).

18. Martin Weinberg and Colin Williams, *Male Homosexuals: Their Problems and Adaptations* (New York: Oxford University Press, 1975).

19. Joseph Harry, "Costs and Correlates of the Closet," paper presented at annual meeting of the American Sociological Association, September 1982; also, Humphreys (n. 13 above).

20. Kenneth Plummer, *Sexual Stigma: An Interactionist Account* (London: Routledge & Kegan Paul, 1977).

21. Karla Jay and Allen Young, eds., *Out of the Closets: Voices of Gay Liberation* (New York: Pyramid Books, 1972); Karla Jay and Allen Young, eds., *Lavender Culture* (New York: Jove, 1978). See particularly Barbara Grier, "Neither Profit Nor Salvation," in *Lavender Culture,* pp. 412–20.

22. William Paul et al., eds., *Homosexuality: Social, Psychological, and Biological Issues* (Beverly Hills, Calif.: Sage, 1972).

23. For those interested in more detailed statistical and analytical discussion of the findings of this research, see Beth E. Schneider, "Consciousness about Sexual Harassment Among Heterosexual and Lesbian Women Workers," *Journal of Social Issues* 38 (December 1982): 75–97; and Beth E. Schneider, "The Sexualization of the Workplace" (Ph.D. dissertation, University of Massachusetts, 1981).

24. It is difficult to assess the accuracy of the proportion of lesbians of color in this sample since the population is unknown. Moreover, because of racism in the feminist and lesbian communities as well as the varying extent to which sex-

ual identity rather than race or class identity is most salient to lesbians of color, many may not be part of lesbian community networks. Thus, the sampling procedures used here—working through contacts (only two of whom were lesbians of color)—likely proved inadequate to reach them.

25. The only concern of this article is with lesbians in paid employment. Necessarily excluded are volunteer labor in political activities and unpaid labor of household maintenance and child care responsibilities. While there are 17 lesbians who are working for wages in consciously organized feminist workplaces, and they are included in the discussion, no effort is made to talk about the particular challenges of working in such locations.

26. Ninety-four percent of the lesbians who reported that *all* coworkers knew they were lesbians also reported being "totally" or "mostly open" about their sexual identity. They were employed in all occupations, but a disproportionate number were in human service jobs (40 percent), and 27 percent were in explicitly feminist work organizations. Thirty-one percent were self-employed, in a collective, or were the boss or owner of a workplace; of those who worked for someone else, almost all had a woman supervisor.

27. Women workers' beliefs about the integration of their public and private lives were measured using an index composed of four statements. These were: "The best policy to follow is to keep work separate from friendship," "You try to keep your social life completely separate from your work life," "Doing things socially with coworkers makes work relationships run more smoothly," and "You follow the general rule of not discussing personal matters with people from work." The sociability index combined four behaviors to measure the extent of social contact the women had with people at their current jobs. These four were eating lunch together, talking on the phone after work hours, visiting at each other's home, and going out socially.

28. For a discussion of these issues, see Kanter (n. 3 above) and Lydia Sargent, ed., *Women and Revolution: A Discussion of the Unhappy Marriage of Marxism and Feminism* (Boston: South End Press, 1981).

29. Marilyn Frye, "Assignment: NWSA-Bloomington-1980: Lesbian Perspectives on Women's Studies," *Sinister*

Wisdom 14 (1980): 3–7, esp. 3.

30. For one effort to discuss this distinction, see Richard Zoglin, "The Homosexual Executive," in Martin P. Levine, ed., *Gay Men: The Sociology of Male Homosexuality* (New York: Harper & Row, 1979), pp. 68–77.

31. The results described here are in response to a series of questions about involvement in a sexual relationship at the workplace. The initial item—"Have you *ever* been involved in an intimate sexual relationship with someone from your workplace?"—was followed by a series of descriptive questions about the relationship.

32. Ettorre (n. 17 above); Lewis (n. 13 above); Sidney Abbott and Barbara Love, *Sappho Was a Right-On Woman: A Liberated View of Lesbianism* (New York: Stein & Day, 1972); Del Martin and Phyllis Lyon, *Lesbian/Woman* (San Francisco: Glide, 1972).

33. Sixteen questions measured the frequency of experiences in the last year of requests for dates, jokes about body or appearance, pinches or grabs, and sexual propositions by four initiators (boss, coworker, subordinate, and recipient of service). Sixteen additional questions measured levels of dislike of these experiences. In the larger study, there were also questions concerning the general problem of unwanted sexual approaches at work and those behaviors that women most likely define as sexual harassment.

34. Schneider (n. 23 above).

35. Zillah Eisenstein, "Antifeminism in the Politics and Election of 1980," *Feminist Studies* 7 (Summer 1981): 187–205; Susan Harding, "Family Reform Movements," *Feminist Studies* 7 (Spring 1981): 57–75; Rosalind Pollack Petchesky, "Antiabortion, Antifeminism, and the Rise of the New Right," *Feminist Studies* 7 (Summer 1981): 206–246.

36. See Barry Adam, *The Survival of Domination: Inferiorization and Everyday Life* (New York: Elsevier, 1978); Dorothy E. Smith, "A Sociology for Women," in Julia A. Sherman and Evelyn Torton Beck, eds., *The Prism of Sex: Essays in the Sociology of Knowledge* (Madison: University of Wisconsin Press, 1977); Albert Memmi, *Dominated Man: Notes Toward a Portrait* (Boston: Beacon Press, 1968); Erving Goffman, *Stigma: Notes on the Management of Spoiled Identity* (Englewood Cliffs, N.J.: Prentice-Hall, 1963).

Sexuality and Intimate Relationships

Both our sexual behavior and our construction of intimate relationships are culturally produced. Although we like to think of love and even liking as spontaneous, free feelings that simply erupt and take their course, the truth is that even these feelings are culturally conditioned, reflecting ideas and behavior we have incorporated in respect to gender as well as the structured inequality of the sexes.

The importance of understanding the historical and cultural contexts in which intimacy is constructed is seen in Carroll Smith-Rosenberg's article "The Female World of Love and Ritual: Relations between Women in Nineteenth-Century America." Letters exchanged by women, Smith-Rosenberg notes, reveal that in the 19th century women routinely formed strong emotional ties to each other, that same-sex relationships were accepted in America, and that these friendships were an essential aspect of American society. Men made but a shadowy appearance in this female world. Smith-Rosenberg analyzes this world and discusses the spectrum of human emotions that existed between the women who lived in it.

In the world that Smith-Rosenberg describes, a "romantic friendship" between women was not a relationship between women who identified themselves as lesbians; indeed, there was no such public

identity. In the United States the idea of "lesbian" as a *public* identity did not develop until after World War II. In "Oral History and the Study of Sexuality in the Lesbian Community: Buffalo, New York, 1940–1960," Madeline Davis and Elizabeth Lapovsky Kennedy document the sexual, social, and political evolution of a lesbian community. In the construction of that community, lesbians created sexual roles that validated women's sexuality, thus serving as a precursor of feminism and gay liberation.

How peers socialize each other in terms of views about sexuality and gender is explored in Judith Dilorio's "Sex, Glorious Sex: The Social Construction of Masculine Sexuality in a Youth Group." Dilorio uses her experience as a participant observer in a vanning club to document the sexual and gender socialization of young men. Through her elaborate descriptions of van culture—the vans, talk, jokes, play, and fantasies—Dilorio shows us how the "guys" socialize each other.

In "Men, Inexpressiveness, and Power," Jack W. Sattel argues that men's tendency to mask such emotions as tenderness and affection is not just a matter of socialized inability to respond to the needs of others. Rather, he argues, it is an intentional strategy selectively used by men to gain control and advantage in both private and public

227

spheres. Pursuing the effects of masculinity on sexual attitudes and behavior, Clyde W. Franklin II, in "The Male Sex Drive," looks at how the hazards of traditional masculinity, particularly dominance, influence men's intimate relations. Considering both black and white men, Franklin discusses six levels of men's sexual involvement with women and suggests that notions of masculinity have to change.

The Female World of Love and Ritual: Relations Between Women in Nineteenth-Century America

CARROLL SMITH-ROSENBERG

The female friendship of the nineteenth century, the long-lived, intimate, loving friendship between two women, is an excellent example of the type of historical phenomena which most historians know something about, which few have thought much about, and which virtually no one has written about.[1] It is one aspect of the female experience which consciously or unconsciously we have chosen to ignore. Yet an abundance of manuscript evidence suggests that eighteenth- and nineteenth-century women routinely formed emotional ties with other women. Such deeply felt, same-sex friendships were casually accepted in American society. Indeed, from at least the late eighteenth through the mid-nineteenth century, a female world of varied and yet highly structured relationships appears to have been an essential aspect of American society. These relationships ranged from the supportive love of sisters, through the enthusiasms of adolescent girls, to sensual avowals of love by mature women. It was a world in which men made but a shadowy appearance.[2]

Defining and analyzing same-sex relationships involves the historian in deeply problematical questions of method and interpretation. This is especially true since historians, influenced by Freud's libidinal theory, have discussed these relationships almost exclusively within the context of individual psychosexual developments or, to be more explicit, psychopathology.[3] Seeing same-sex relationships in terms of a dichotomy between normal and abnormal, they have sought the origins of such apparent deviance in childhood or adolescent trauma and detected the symptoms of "latent" homosexuality in the lives of both those who later became "overtly" homosexual and those who did not. Yet theories concerning the nature and origins of same-sex relationships are frequently contradictory or based on questionable or arbitrary data. In recent years such hypotheses have been subjected to criticism from both within and without the psychological professions. Historians who seek to work within a psychological framework, therefore, are faced with two hard questions: Do sound psychodynamic theories concerning the nature and origins of same-sex relationships exist? If so, does the historical datum exist which would permit the use of such dynamic models?

I would like to suggest an alternative approach to female friendships—one which would view them within a cultural and social setting rather than from an exclusively individual psychosexual perspective. Only by thus altering our approach will we be in the position to evaluate the appropriateness of particular dynamic interpretations. Intimate friendships between men and men and women and women existed in a larger world of social relations and social values. To interpret such friendships more fully they must be related to the structure of the American family and to the nature of sex-role divisions and of male–female relations both within the family and in society generally. The female friendship must not be seen in isolation; it must be analyzed as one aspect of women's overall relations with one another. The ties between mothers and daughters, sisters, female cousins, and friends at all stages of the female life cycle constitute the most suggestive framework for the historian to begin an analysis of intimacy and affection between women. Such an analysis would not only emphasize general cultural patterns rather than the internal dynamics of a particular family or childhood; it would shift the focus of the study from a concern with deviance to that of defining configurations of legitimate behavioral norms and options.[4]

This analysis will be based upon the correspondence and diaries of women and men in thirty-five families between the 1760s and the 1880s. These families, though limited in number, represented a broad range of the American middle class, from hard-pressed pioneer families and orphaned girls to daughters of the intellectual and social elite. It includes families from most geographic regions, rural and urban, and a spectrum of Protestant denominations ranging from Mormon to orthodox Quaker. Although scarcely a comprehensive sample of America's increasingly heterogeneous population, it does, I believe, reflect accurately the literate middle class to which the historian working with letters and diaries is necessarily bound. It has involved an analysis of many thousands of letters written to women friends, kin, husbands, brothers, and children at every period of life from adolescence to old age. Some collections encompass virtually entire life spans; one contains over 100,000 letters as well as diaries and account books. It is my contention that an analysis of women's private letters and diaries which were never intended to be published permits the historian to explore a very private world of emotional realities central both to women's lives and to the middle-class family in nineteenth-century America.[5]

The question of female friendships is peculiarly elusive; we know so little or perhaps have forgotten so much. An intriguing and almost alien form of human relationship, they flourished in a different social structure and amidst different sexual norms. Before attempting to reconstruct their social setting, therefore, it might be best first to describe two not atypical friendships. These two friendships, intense, loving, and openly avowed, began during the women's adolescence and, despite subsequent marriages and geographic separation, continued throughout their lives. For nearly half a century these women played a central emotional role in each other's lives, writing time and again of their love and of the pain of separation. Paradoxically to twentieth-century minds, their love appears to have been both sensual and platonic.

Sarah Butler Wister first met Jeannie Field Musgrove while vacationing with her family at Stockbridge, Massachusetts, in the summer of 1849.[6] Jeannie was then sixteen, Sarah fourteen. During two subsequent years spent together in boarding school, they formed a deep and intimate friendship. Sarah began to keep a bouquet of flowers before Jeannie's portrait and wrote complaining of the intensity and anguish of her affection.[7] Both young women assumed nom de plumes, Jeannie a female name, Sarah a male one; they would use these secret names into old age.[8] They frequently commented on the nature of their affection: "If the day should come," Sarah wrote Jeannie in the spring of 1861, "when you failed me either through your fault or my own, I would forswear all human friendship, thenceforth." A few months later Jeannie commented: "Gratitude is a word I should never use toward you. It is perhaps a misfortune of such intimacy and love that it makes one regard all kindness as a matter of course, as one has always found it, as natural as the embrace in meeting."[9]

Sarah's marriage altered neither the frequency of their correspondence nor their desire to be together. In 1864, when twenty-nine, married, and a mother, Sarah wrote to Jeannie: "I shall be entirely alone [this coming week]. I can give you no idea how desperately I shall want you. . . . " After one such visit Jeannie, then a spinster in New York, echoed Sarah's longing: "Dear darling Sarah! How I love you & how happy I have been! You are the joy of my life. . . . I cannot tell you how much happiness you gave me, nor how constantly it is all in my thoughts. . . . My darling how I long for the time when I shall see you. . . . " After another visit Jeannie wrote: "I want you to tell me in your next letter, to assure me, that I am your dearest. . . . I do not doubt you, & I am not jealous but I long to hear you say it once more & it seems already a long time since your voice fell on my ear. So just fill a quarter page with caresses & expressions of endearment. Your silly Angelina." Jeannie ended one letter: "Goodbye my dearest, dearest lover—ever your own Angelina." And another, "I will go to bed . . . [though] I could write all night—A thousand kisses—I love you with my whole soul—your Angelina."

When Jeannie finally married in 1870 at the age of thirty-seven, Sarah underwent a period of extreme anxiety. Two days before Jeannie's marriage, Sarah, then in London, wrote desperately: "Dearest darling— How incessantly have I thought of you these eight days—all today—the entire uncertainty, the distance, the long silence—are all new features in my separation from you, grevious to be borne. . . . Oh Jeannie. I have thought & thought & yearned over you these two days. Are you married I wonder? My dearest love to you wherever and *who*ever you are."[10] Like many other women in this collection of thirty-five families, marriage brought Sarah and Jeannie physical separation; it did not cause emotional distance. Although at first they may have wondered how marriage would affect their relationship, their affection remained unabated throughout their lives, underscored by their loneliness and their desire to be together.[11]

During the same years that Jeannie and Sarah wrote of their love and need for each other, two slightly younger women began a similar odyssey of love, dependence and—ultimately—physical, though not emotional, separation. Molly and Helena met in 1868 while both attended the Cooper Institute School of Design for Women in New York City. For several years these young women studied and explored the city together, visited each other's families, and formed part of a social network of other artistic young women. Gradually, over the years, their initial friendship deepened into a close intimate bond which continued throughout their lives. The tone in the letters which Molly wrote to Helena changed over these years from "My dear Helena," and signed "your attached friend," to "My dearest Helena," "My Dearest," "My Beloved," and signed "Thine always" or "thine Molly."[12]

The letters they wrote to each other during these first five years permit us to reconstruct something of their relationship together. As Molly wrote in one early letter:

I have not said to you in so many or so few words that I was happy with you during those few so incredibly short weeks but surely you do not need words to tell you what you must know. Those two or three days so dark without, so bright with firelight and contentment within I shall always remember as proof that, for a time, at least—I fancy for quite a long time—we might be sufficient for each other. We know that we can amuse each other for many idle hours together and now we know that we can also work together. And that means much, don't you think so?

She ended: "I shall return in a few days. Imagine yourself kissed many times by one who loved you so dearly."

The intensity and even physical nature of Molly's love was echoed in many of the letters she wrote during the next few years, as, for instance in this short thank-you note for a small present: "Imagine yourself kissed a dozen times my darling. Perhaps it is well for you that we are far apart. You might find my thanks so expressed rather overpowering. I have that delightful feeling that it doesn't matter much what I say or how I say it, since we shall meet so soon and forget in that moment that we were ever separated. . . . I shall see you soon and be content."[13]

At the end of the fifth year, however, several crises occurred. The relationship, at least in its intense form, ended, though Molly and Helena continued an intimate and complex relationship for the next half-century. The exact nature of these crises is not completely clear, but it seems to have involved Molly's decision not to live with Helena, as they had originally planned, but to remain at home because of parental insistence. Molly was now in her late twenties. Helena responded with anger and Molly became frantic at the thought that Helena would break off their relationship. Though she wrote distraught letters and made despairing attempts to see Helena, the relationship never regained its former ardor—possibly because Molly had a male suitor.[14] Within six months Helena had decided to marry a man who was, coincidentally, Molly's friend and publisher. Two years later Molly herself finally married. The letters toward the end of this period discuss the transition both women made to having male lovers—Molly spending much time reassuring Helena, who seemed depressed about the end of their relationship and with her forthcoming marriage.[15]

It is clearly difficult from a distance of 100 years and from a post-Freudian cultural perspective to decipher the complexities of Molly and Helena's relationship. Certainly Molly and Helena were lovers—emotionally if not physically. The emotional intensity and pathos of their love becomes apparent in several letters Molly wrote Helena during their crisis: "I wanted so to put my arms round my girl of all the girls in the world and tell her . . . I love her as wives do love their husbands, as *friends* who have taken each other for life—and believe in her as I believe in my God. . . . If I didn't love you do you suppose I'd care about anything or have ridiculous notions and panics and behave like an old fool who ought to know better. I'm going to hang on to your skirts. . . . You can't get away from [my] love." Or as she wrote after Helena's decision to marry: "You know dear Helena, I really was in love with you. It was a passion such as I had never known until I saw you. I don't think it was the noblest way to love you." The theme of intense female love was one Molly again expressed in a letter she wrote to the man Helena was to marry: "Do you know sir, that until you came along I believe that she loved me almost as girls love their lovers. *I know I loved her so.* Don't you wonder that I can stand the sight of you." This was in a letter congratulating them on their forthcoming marriage.[16]

The essential question is not whether these women had genital contact and can therefore be defined as heterosexual or homosexual. The twentieth-century tendency to view human love and sexuality within a dichotomized universe of deviance and normality, genitality and platonic love, is alien to the emotions and attitudes of the nineteenth century and fundamentally distorts the nature of these women's emotional interaction. These letters are significant because they force us to place such female love in a particular historical context. There is every indication that these four women, their husbands and families—all eminently respectable and socially conservative—considered such love both socially acceptable and fully compatible with heterosexual marriage. Emotionally and cognitively, their heterosocial and their homosocial worlds were complementary.

One could argue, on the other hand, that these letters were but an example of the romantic rhetoric with which the nineteenth century surrounded the concept of friendship. Yet they possess an emotional intensity and a sensual and physical explicitness that is difficult to dismiss. Jeannie longed to hold Sarah in her arms; Molly mourned her physical isolation from Helena. Molly's love and devotion to Helena, the emotions that bound Jeannie and Sarah together, while perhaps a phenomenon of nineteenth-century society, were not the less real for their Victorian origins. A survey of the correspondence and diaries of eighteenth- and nineteenth-century women indicates that Molly, Jeannie, and Sarah represented one very real behavioral and emotional option socially available to nineteenth-century women.

This is not to argue that individual needs, personalities, and family dynamics did not have a significant role in determining the nature of particular relationships. But the scholar must ask if it is historically possible and, if possible, important to study the intensely individual aspects of psychosexual dynamics. Is it not the historian's first task to explore the social structure and the world view which made intense and sometimes sensual female love both a possible and an acceptable emotional option? From such a social perspective a new and quite different series of questions suggests itself. What emotional function did such female love serve? What was its place within the hetero- and homosocial worlds which women jointly inhabited? Did a spectrum of love-object choices exist in the nineteenth century across which some individuals, at least, were capable of moving? Without attempting to answer these questions it will be difficult to understand either nineteenth-century sexuality or the nineteenth-century family.

Several factors in American society between the mid-eighteenth and the mid-nineteenth centuries may well have permitted women to form a variety of close emotional relationships with other women. American society was characterized in large part by rigid gender-role differentiation within the family and within society as a whole, leading to the emotional segregation of women and men. The roles of daughter and mother shaded imperceptibly and ineluctably into each other, while the biological realities of frequent pregnancies, childbirth, nursing, and menopause bound women together in physical and emotional intimacy. It was within just such a social framework, I would argue, that a specifically female world did indeed develop, a world built around a generic and unself-conscious pattern of single-sex or homosocial networks. These supportive networks were institutionalized in social conventions or rituals which accompanied virtually every important event in a woman's life, from birth to death. Such female relationships were frequently supported and paralleled by severe social restrictions on intimacy between young men and women. Within such a world of emotional richness and complexity, devotion to and love of other women became a plausible and socially accepted form of human interaction.

An abundance of printed and manuscript sources exists to support such a hypothesis. Etiquette books, advice books on child rearing, religious sermons, guides to young men and young women, medical texts, and school curricula all suggest that late eighteenth- and most nineteenth-century Americans assumed the existence of a world composed of distinctly male and female spheres, spheres determined by the immutable laws of God and nature.[17] The unpublished letters and diaries of Americans during this same period concur, detailing the existence of sexually segregated worlds inhabited by human beings with different values, expectations, and personalities. Contacts between men and women frequently partook of a formality and stiffness quite alien to twentieth-century America and which today we tend to define as "Victorian." Women, however, did not form an isolated and oppressed subcategory in male society. Their letters and diaries indicate that women's sphere had an essential integrity and dignity that grew out of women's shared experiences and mutual affection and that, despite the profound changes which affected American social structure and institutions between the 1760s and the 1870s, retained a constancy and predictability. The ways in which women thought of and interacted with each other remained unchanged. Continuity, not discontinuity, characterized this female world. Molly Hallock's and Jeannie Field's words, emotions, and experiences have direct parallels in the 1760s and the 1790s.[18] There are indications in contemporary sociological and psychological literature that female closeness and support networks have continued into the twentieth century—not only among ethnic and working-class groups but even among the middle class.[19]

Most eighteenth- and nineteenth-century women lived within a world bounded by home, church, and the institution of visiting—that endless trooping of women to each other's homes for social purposes. It was a world inhabited by children and by other women.[20] Women helped each other with domestic chores and in times of sickness, sorrow, or trouble. Entire days, even weeks, might be spent almost exclusively with other women.[21] Urban and town women could devote virtually every day to visits, teas, or shopping trips with other women. Rural women developed a pattern of more extended visits that lasted weeks and sometimes months, at times even dislodging husbands from their beds and bedrooms so that dear friends might spend every hour of every day together.[22] When husbands traveled, wives routinely moved in with other women, invited women friends to teas and suppers, sat together sharing and comparing the letters they had received from other close women friends. Secrets were exchanged and cherished, and the husband's return at times viewed with some ambivalence.[23]

Summer vacations were frequently organized to permit old friends to meet at water spas or share a country home. In 1848, for example, a young matron wrote cheerfully to her husband about the delightful time she was having with five close women friends whom she had invited to spend the summer with her; he remained at home alone to face the heat of Philadelphia and a cholera epidemic.[24] Some ninety years earlier, two young Quaker girls commented upon the vacation their aunt had taken alone with another woman; their remarks were openly envious and tell us something of the emotional quality of these friendships: "I hear Aunt is gone with the Friend and wont be back for two weeks, fine times indeed I think the old friends had, taking their pleasure about the country . . . and have the advantage of that fine woman's conversation and instruction, while we poor young girls must spend all spring at home. . . . What a disappointment that we are not together. . . ."[25]

Friends did not form isolated dyads but were normally part of highly integrated networks. Knowing each other, perhaps related to each other, they played a central role in holding communities and kin systems together. Especially when families became geographically mobile women's long visits to each other and their frequent letters filled with discussions of marriages and births, illness and deaths, descriptions of growing children, and reminiscences of times and people past provided an important sense of continuity in a rapidly changing society.[26] Central to this female world was an inner core of kin. The ties between sisters, first cousins, aunts, and nieces provided the underlying structure upon which groups of friends and their network of female relatives clustered. Although most of the women within this sample would appear to be living within isolated nuclear families, the emotional ties between nonresidential kin were deep and binding and provided one of the fundamental existential realities of women's lives.[27] Twenty years after Parke Lewis Butler moved with her husband to Louisiana, she sent her two daughters back to Virginia to attend school, live with their grandmother and aunt, and be integrated back into Virginia society.[28] The constant letters between Maria Inskeep and Fanny Hampton, sisters separated in their early twenties when Maria moved with her husband from New Jersey to Louisiana, held their families together, making it possible for their daughters to feel a part of their cousins' network of friends and interests.[29] The Ripley daughters, growing up in western Massachusetts in the early 1800s, spent months each year with their moth-

er's sister and her family in distant Boston; these female cousins and their network of friends exchanged
gossip-filled letters and gradually formed deeply loving
and dependent ties.[30]

Women frequently spent their days within the social confines of such extended families. Sisters-in-law
visited each other and, in some families, seemed to
spend more time with each other than with their husbands. First cousins cared for each other's babies—for
weeks or even months in times of sickness or childbirth. Sisters helped each other with housework,
shopped and sewed for each other. Geographic separation was borne with difficulty. A sister's absence for
even a week or two could cause loneliness and depression and would be bridged by frequent letters. Sibling
rivalry was hardly unknown, but with separation or illness the theme of deep affection and dependency
reemerged.[31]

Sisterly bonds continued across a lifetime. In her
old age a rural Quaker matron, Martha Jefferis, wrote
to her daughter Anne concerning her own half-sister,
Phoebe: "In sister Phoebe I have a real friend—she
studies my comfort and waits on me like a child. . . .
She is exceedingly kind and this to all other homes (set
aside yours) I would prefer—it is next to being with a
daughter." Phoebe's own letters confirmed Martha's
evaluation of her feelings. "Thou knowest my dear sister," Phoebe wrote, "there is no one . . . that exactly
feels [for] thee as I do, for I think without boasting I
can truly say that my desire is for thee."[32]

Such women, whether friends or relatives, assumed
an emotional centrality in each other's lives. In their
diaries and letters they wrote of the joy and contentment they felt in each other's company, their sense of
isolation and despair when apart. The regularity of
their correspondence underlines the sincerity of their
words. Women named their daughters after one another and sought to integrate dear friends into their
lives after marriage.[33] As one young bride wrote to an
old friend shortly after her marriage: "I want to see
you and talk with you and feel that we are united by
the same bonds of sympathy and congeniality as
ever."[34] After years of friendship one aging woman
wrote of another: "Time cannot destroy the fascination of her manner . . . her voice is music to the
ear. . . . "[35] Women made elaborate presents for each
other, ranging from the Quakers' frugal pies and
breads to painted velvet bags and phantom bouquets.[36]

When a friend died, their grief was deeply felt. Martha
Jefferis was unable to write to her daughter for three
weeks because of the sorrow she felt at the death of a
dear friend. Such distress was not unusual. A generation earlier a young Massachusetts farm woman filled
pages of her diary with her grief at the death of her
"dearest friend" and transcribed the letters of condolence other women sent her. She marked the anniver-
sary of Rachel's death each year in her diary, contrasting her faithfulness with that of Rachel's husband,
who had soon remarried.[37]

These female friendships served a number of emotional functions. Within this secure and empathetic
world women could share sorrows, anxieties, and joys,
confident that other women had experienced similar
emotions. One mid-nineteenth-century rural matron
in a letter to her daughter discussed this particular aspect of women's friendships: "To have such a friend
as thyself to look to and sympathize with her—and
enter into all her little needs and in whose bosom she
could with freedom pour forth her joys and sorrows—
such a friend would very much relieve the tedium of
many a wearisome hour. . . . " A generation later
Molly more informally underscored the importance of
this same function in a letter to Helena: "Suppose I
come down . . . [and] spend Sunday with you quietly,"
she wrote Helena; " . . . that means talking all the time
until you are relieved of all your latest troubles, and I
of mine. . . . "[38] These were frequently troubles that apparently no man could understand. When Anne Jefferis Sheppard was first married, she and her older sister Edith (who then lived with Anne) wrote in detail
to their mother of the severe depression and anxiety
which they experienced. Moses Sheppard, Anne's husband, added cheerful postscripts to the sisters' letters—which he had clearly not read—remarking on
Anne's and Edith's contentment. Theirs was an emotional world to which he had little access.[39]

This was, as well, a female world in which hostility
and criticism of other women were discouraged, and
thus a milieu in which women could develop a sense
of inner security and self-esteem. As one young
woman wrote to her mother's longtime friend: "I cannot sufficiently thank you for the kind unvaried affection & indulgence you have ever shown and expressed
both by words and actions for me. . . . Happy would it
be did all the world view me as you do, through the
medium of kindness and forbearance."[40] They valued

each other. Women, who had little status or power in the larger world of male concerns, possessed status and power in the lives and worlds of other women.[41]

An intimate mother–daughter relationship lay at the heart of this female world. The diaries and letters of both mothers and daughters attest to their closeness and mutual emotional dependency. Daughters routinely discussed their mother's health and activities with their own friends, expressed anxiety in cases of their mother's ill health and concern for her cares.[42] Expressions of hostility which we would today consider routine on the part of both mothers and daughters seem to have been uncommon indeed. On the contrary, this sample of families indicates that the normal relationship between mother and daughter was one of sympathy and understanding.[43] Only sickness or great geographic distance was allowed to cause extended separation. When marriage did result in such separation, both viewed the distance between them with distress.[44] Something of this sympathy and love between mothers and daughters is evident in a letter Sarah Alden Ripley, at age sixty-nine, wrote her youngest and recently married daughter: "You do not know how much I miss you, not only when I struggle in and out of my mortal envelop and pump my nightly potation and no longer pour into your sympathizing ear my senile gossip, but all the day I muse away, since the sound of your voice no longer rouses me to sympathy with your joys or sorrows. . . . You cannot know how much I miss your affectionate demonstrations."[45] A dozen aging mothers in this sample of over thirty families echoed her sentiments.

Central to these mother–daughter relations is what might be described as an apprenticeship system. In those families where the daughter followed the mother into a life of traditional domesticity, mothers and other older women carefully trained daughters in the arts of housewifery and motherhood. Such training undoubtedly occurred throughout a girl's childhood but became more systematized, almost ritualistic, in the years following the end of her formal education and before her marriage. At this time a girl either returned home from boarding school or no longer divided her time between home and school. Rather, she devoted her energies on two tasks: mastering new domestic skills and participating in the visiting and social activities necessary to finding a husband. Under the careful supervision of their mothers and of older

female relatives, such late-adolescent girls temporarily took over the household management from their mothers, tended their young nieces and nephews, and helped in childbirth, nursing, and weaning. Such experiences tied the generations together in shared skills and emotional interaction.[46]

Daughters were born into a female world. The mother's life expectations and sympathetic network of friends and relations were among the first realities in the life of the developing child. As long as the mother's domestic role remained relatively stable and few viable alternatives competed with it, daughters tended to accept their mothers' world and to turn automatically to other women for support and intimacy. It was within this closed and intimate female world that the young girl grew toward womanhood.

One could speculate at length concerning the absence of that mother–daughter hostility today considered almost inevitable to an adolescent's struggle for autonomy and self-identity. It is possible that taboos against female aggression and hostility were sufficiently strong to repress even that between mothers and their adolescent daughters. Yet these letters seem so alive and the interest of daughters in their mothers' affairs so vital and genuine that it is difficult to interpret their closeness exclusively in terms of repression and denial. The functional bonds that held mothers and daughters together in a world that permitted few alternatives to domesticity might well have created a source of mutuality and trust absent in societies where greater options were available for daughters than for mothers. Furthermore, the extended female network—a daughter's close ties with her own older sisters, cousins, and aunts—may well have permitted a diffusion and a relaxation of mother–daughter identification and so have aided a daughter in her struggle for identity and autonomy. None of these explanations are mutually exclusive; all may well have interacted to produce the degree of empathy evident in those letters and diaries.

At some point in adolescence, the young girl began to move outside the matrix of her mother's support group to develop a network of her own. Among the middle class, at least, this transition toward what was at the same time both a limited autonomy and a repetition of her mother's life seemed to have most frequently coincided with a girl's going to school. Indeed, education appears to have played a crucial role in the

IN PRAISE OF "BEST FRIENDS":
THE REVIVAL OF A FINE OLD INSTITUTION

BARBARA EHRENREICH

All the politicians, these days, are "profamily," but I've never heard of one who was "profriendship." This is too bad and possibly shortsighted. After all, most of us would never survive our families if we didn't have our friends.

I'm especially concerned about the fine old institution of "best friends." I realized that it was on shaky ground a few months ago, when the occasion arose to introduce my own best friend (we'll call her Joan) at a somewhat intimidating gathering. I got as far as saying, "I am very proud to introduce my best friend, Joan ... " when suddenly I wasn't proud at all: I was blushing. "Best friend," I realized as soon as I heard the words out loud, sounds like something left over from sixth-grade cliques: the kind of thing where if Sandy saw you talking to Stephanie at recess, she might tell you after school that she wasn't going to be your best friend anymore, and so forth. Why couldn't I have just said "my good friend Joan" or something *grown-up* like that?

But Joan is not just any friend, or even a "good friend"; she is my best friend. We have celebrated each other's triumphs together, nursed each other through savage breakups with the various men in our lives, discussed the Great Issues of Our Time, and cackled insanely over things that were, objectively speaking, not even funny. We have quarreled and made up; we've lived in the same house and we've lived thousands of miles apart. We've learned to say hard things, like "You really upset me when ... " and even "I love you." Yet, for all this, our relationship has no earthly weight or status. I can't even say the name for it without sounding profoundly silly.

Why is best friendship, particularly between women, so undervalued and unrecognized? Partly, no doubt, because women themselves have always

been so undervalued and unrecognized. In the Western tradition, male best friendships are the stuff of history and high drama. Reread Homer, for example, and you'll realize that Troy did not fall because Paris, that spoiled Trojan prince, loved Helen, but because Achilles so loved Patroclus. It was Patroclus' death, at the hands of the Trojans, that made Achilles snap out of his sulk long enough to slay the Trojans' greatest warrior and guarantee victory to the Greeks. Did Helen have a best friend, or any friend at all? We'll never know, because the only best friendships that have survived in history and legend are man-on-man: Alexander and Hephaestion, Orestes and Pylades, Heracles and Iolas.

Christianity did not improve the status of female friendship. "Every woman ought to be filled with shame at the thought that she is a woman," declaimed one of the early church fathers, Clement of Alexandria, and when two women got together, the shame presumably doubled. Male friendship was still supposed to be a breeding ground for all kinds of upstanding traits—honor, altruism, courage, faith, loyalty. Consider Arthur's friendship with Lancelot, which easily survived the latter's dalliance with Queen Guinevere. But when two women got together, the best you could hope for, apparently, was bitchiness, and the worst was witchcraft.

Yet, without the slightest encouragement from history, women have persisted in finding best friends. According to recent feminist scholarship, the 19th century seems to have been a heyday of female best friendship. In fact, feminism might never have gotten off the ground at all if it hadn't been for the enduring bond between Elizabeth Cady Stanton, the theoretician of the movement, and Susan B. Anthony, the movement's first great pragmatist.

And they are only the most famous best friends. According to Lillian Faderman's book *Surpassing the Love of Men*, there were thousands of anony-

Reprinted from *Ms.* magazine (January 1987) by permission of the author.

mous female couples who wrote passionate letters to each other, exchanged promises and tokens of love, and suffered through the separations occasioned by marriage and migration. Feminist scholars have debated whether these great best friendships were actually lesbian, sexual relationships—a question that I find both deeply fascinating (if these were lesbian relationships, were the women involved conscious of what a bold and subversive step they had taken?) and somewhat beside the point. What matters is that these women honored their friendships, and sought ways to give them the kind of coherence and meaning that the larger society reserved only for marriage.

In the 20th century, female best friendship was largely eclipsed by the new ideal of the "companionate marriage." At least in the middle-class culture that celebrated "togetherness," your *husband* was now supposed to be your best friend, as well, of course, as being your lover, provider, coparent, housemate, and principal heir. My own theory (profamily politicians please take note) is that these expectations have done more damage to the institution of marriage than no-fault divorce and the sexual revolution combined. No man can be all things to even one woman. And the foolish idea that one could has left untold thousands of women not only divorced, but what is in the long run far worse—friendless.

Yet even feminism, when it came back to life in the early seventies, did not rehabilitate the institution of female best friendship. Lesbian relationships took priority, for the good and obvious reason that they had been not only neglected, but driven underground. But in our zeal to bring lesbian relationships safely out of the closet, we sometimes ended up shoving best friendships further out of sight. "Best friends?" a politically ever-so-correct friend once snapped at me, in reference to Joan, "why aren't you lovers?" In the same vein, the radical feminist theoretician Shulamith Firestone wrote that after the gender revolution, there would be no asexual friendships. The coming feminist Utopia, I realized sadly, was going to be a pretty lonely place for some of us.

Then, almost before we could get out of our jeans and into our corporate clone clothes, female friendship came back into fashion—but in the vastly attenuated form of "networking." Suddenly we are supposed to have dozens of women friends, hundreds if time and the phone bill allow, but each with a defined function: mentors, contacts, connections, allies, even pretty ones who might be able to introduce us, now and then, to their leftover boyfriends. The voluminous literature on corporate success for women is full of advice on friends: whom to avoid ("turkeys" and whiners), whom to cultivate (winners and potential clients), and how to tell when a friend is moving from the latter category into the former. This is an advance, because it means we are finally realizing that women are important enough to be valued friends and that friendship among women is valuable enough to write and talk about. But in the pushy new dress-for-success world, there's less room than ever for best friendships that last through thick and thin, through skidding as well as climbing.

Hence my campaign to save the institution of female best friendship. I am not asking you to vote for anyone, to pray to anyone, or even to send me money. I'm just suggesting that we all begin to give a little more space, and a little more respect, to the best friendships in our lives. To this end, I propose three rules:

1. Best friendships should be given social visibility. If you are inviting Pat over for dinner, you would naturally think of inviting her husband, Ed. Why not Pat's best friend, Jill? Well, you may be thinking, how childish! They don't have to go everywhere together. Of course they don't, but neither do Pat and Ed. In many settings, including your next dinner party or potluck, Pat and Jill may be the combination that makes the most sense and has the most fun.

2. Best friendships take time and nurturance, even when that means taking time and nurturance away from other major relationships. Everyone knows that marriages require "work." (A ghastly concept, that. "Working on a marriage" has always sounded to me like something on the order of lawn maintenance.) Friendships require effort, too, and best friendships require our very best efforts. It should be possible to say to husband Ed or whomever, "I'm sorry I can't spend the evening with you

because I need to put in some quality time with Jill." He will be offended only if he is a slave to heterosexual couple-ism—in which case you shouldn't have married him in the first place.

3. Best friendship is more important than any work-related benefit that may accrue from it, and should be treated accordingly. Maybe your best friend will help you get that promotion, transfer, or new contract. That's all well and good, but the real question is: Will that promotion, transfer, or whatever help your best friendship? If it's a transfer to San Diego and your best friend's in Cincinnati, it may not be worth it. For example, as a writer who has collaborated with many friends, including "Joan," I am often accosted by strangers exclaiming, "It's just amazing that you got through that book [article, or other project] together and you're still friends!" The truth is, in nine cases out of ten, that the friendship was always far more important

than the book. If a project isn't going to strengthen my friendship—and might even threaten it—I'd rather not start.

When I was thinking through this column—out loud of course, with a very good friend on the phone—she sniffed, "So what exactly do you want—formal legalized friendships, with best-friend licenses and showers and property settlements in case you get in a fight over the sweaters you've been borrowing from each other for the past ten years?" No, of course not, because the beauty of best friendship, as opposed to, say, marriage, is that it's a totally grass-roots creative effort that requires no help at all from the powers-that-be. Besides, it would be too complicated. In contrast to marriage—and even to sixth-grade cliques—there's no rule that says you can have only one "best" friend.

---

lives of most of the families in this study. Attending school for a few months, for a year, or longer was common even among daughters of relatively poor families, while middle-class girls routinely spent at least a year in boarding school.[47] These school years ordinarily marked a girl's first separation from home. They served to wean the daughter from her home, to train her in the essential social graces, and, ultimately, to help introduce her into the marriage market. It was not infrequently a trying emotional experience for both mother and daughter.[48]

In this process of leaving one home and adjusting to another, the mother's friends and relatives played a key transitional role. Such older women routinely accepted the role of foster mother; they supervised the young girl's deportment, monitored her health, and introduced her to their own network of female friends and kin.[49] Not infrequently women, friends from their own school years, arranged to send their daughters to the same school so that the girls might form bonds paralleling those their mothers had made. For years Molly and Helena wrote of their daughters' meeting and worried over each other's children. When Molly finally brought her daughter east to school, their first act on reaching New York was to meet Helena and her daughters. Elizabeth Bordley Gibson virtually adopted

the daughters of her school chum, Eleanor Custis Lewis. The Lewis daughters soon began to write Elizabeth Gibson letters with the salutation "Dearest Mama." Eleuthera DuPont, attending boarding school in Philadelphia at roughly the same time as the Lewis girls, developed a parallel relationship with her mother's friend Elizabeth McKie Smith. Eleuthera went to the same school and became a close friend of the Smith girls and eventually married their first cousin. During this period she routinely called Mrs. Smith "Mother." Indeed, Eleuthera so internalized the sense of having two mothers that she casually wrote her sisters of her "Mamma's" visits at her "mother's" house—that is, at Mrs. Smith's.[50]

Even more important to this process of maturation than their mothers' friends were the female friends young women made at school. Young girls helped each other overcome homesickness and endure the crises of adolescence. They gossiped about beaux, incorporated each other into their own kinship systems, and attended and gave teas and balls together. Older girls in boarding school "adopted" younger ones, who called them "Mother."[51] Dear friends might indeed continue this pattern of adoption and mothering throughout their lives; one woman might routinely assume the nurturing role of pseudomother, the other the dependency role of daughter. The pseudomother performed for the other woman all the services which we normally associate with mothers; she went to absurd lengths to purchase items her "daughter" could have obtained from other sources, gave advice and functioned as an idealized figure in her "daughter's" imagination. Helena played such a role for Molly, as did Sarah for Jeannie. Elizabeth Bordley Gibson bought almost all Eleanor Parke Custis Lewis's necessities—from shoes and corset covers to bedding and harp strings—and sent them from Philadelphia to Virginia, a procedure that sometimes took months. Eleanor frequently asked Elizabeth to take back her purchases, have them redone, and argue with shopkeepers about prices. These were favors automatically asked and complied with. Anne Jefferis Sheppard made the analogy very explicitly in a letter to her own mother written shortly after Anne's marriage, when she was feeling depressed about their separation: "Mary Paulen is truly kind, almost acts the part of a mother and trys to aid and *comfort me,* and also to *lighten my new cares.*"[52]

A comparison of the references to men and women in these young women's letters is striking. Boys were obviously indispensable to the elaborate courtship ritual girls engaged in. In these teenage letters and diaries, however, boys appear distant and warded off—an effect produced both by the girls' sense of bonding and by a highly developed and deprecatory whimsy. Girls joked among themselves about the conceit, poor looks or affectations of suitors. Rarely, especially in the eighteenth and early nineteenth centuries, were favorable remarks exchanged. Indeed, while hostility and criticism of other women were so rare as to seem almost tabooed, young women permitted themselves to express a great deal of hostility toward peer-group men.[53] When unacceptable suitors appeared, girls might even band together to harass them. When one such unfortunate came to court Sophie DuPont she hid in her room, first sending her sister Eleuthera to entertain him and then dispatching a number of urgent notes to her neighboring sister-in-law, cousins, and a visiting friend, who all came to Sophie's support. A wild female romp ensued, ending only when Sophie banged into a door, lacerated her nose, and retired, with her female cohorts, to bed. Her brother and the presumably disconcerted suitor were left alone. These were not the antics of teenagers but of women in their early and mid-twenties.[54]

Even if young men were acceptable suitors, girls referred to them formally and obliquely: "The last week I received the unexpected intelligence of the arrival of a friend in Boston," Sarah Ripley wrote in her diary of the young man to whom she had been engaged for years and whom she would shortly marry. Harriet Manigault assiduously kept a lively and gossipy diary during the three years preceding her marriage, yet did not once comment upon her own engagement nor indeed make any personal references to her fiancé—who was never identified as such but always referred to as Mr. Wilcox.[55] The point is not that these young women were hostile to young men. Far from it; they sought marriage and domesticity. Yet in these letters and diaries men appear as an other or out group, segregated into different schools, supported by their own male network of friends and kin, socialized to different behavior, and coached to a proper formality in courtship behavior. As a consequence, relations between young women and men frequently lacked the spontaneity and emotional intimacy that characterized the young girls' ties to each other.

Indeed, in sharp contrast to their distant relations with boys, young women's relations with each other were close, often frolicsome, and surprisingly long lasting and devoted. They wrote secret missives to each other, spent long solitary days with each other, curled up together in bed at night to whisper fantasies and secrets.[56] In 1862 one young woman in her early twenties described one such scene to an absent friend: "I have sat up to midnight listening to the confidences of Constance Kinney, whose heart was opened by that most charming of all situations, a seat on a bedside late at night, when all the household are asleep & only oneself & one's confidante survive in wakefulness. So she has told me all her loves and tried to get some confidences in return but being five or six years older than she, I know better. . . . "[57] Elizabeth Bordley and Nelly Parke Custis, teenagers in Philadelphia in the 1790s, routinely secreted themselves until late each night in Nelly's attic, where they each wrote a novel about the other.[58] Quite a few young women kept diaries, and it was a sign of special friendship to show their diaries to each other. The emotional quality of such exchanges emerges from the comments of one young girl who grew up along the Ohio frontier:

Sisters CW and RT keep diaries & allow me the inestimable pleasure of reading them and in turn they see mine—but O shame covers my face when I think of it; theirs is so much better than mine, that every time. Then I think well now I *will* burn mine but upon second thought it would deprive me the pleasure of reading theirs, for I esteem it a very great privilege indeed, as well as very improving, as we lay our hearts open to each other, it heightens our love & helps to cherish & keep alive that sweet soothing friendship and endears us to each other by that soft attraction.[59]

Girls routinely slept together, kissed and hugged each other. Indeed, while waltzing with young men scandalized the otherwise flighty and highly fashionable Harriet Manigault, she considered waltzing with other young women not only acceptable but pleasant.[60] Marriage followed adolescence. With increasing frequency in the nineteenth century, marriage involved a girl's traumatic removal from her mother and her mother's network. It involved, as well, adjustment to a husband, who, because he was male, came to marriage with both a different world view and vastly different experiences. Not surprisingly, marriage was an event surrounded with supportive, almost ritualistic practices. (Weddings are one of the last female rituals remaining in twentieth-century America.) Young women routinely spent the months preceding their marriage almost exclusively with other women—at neighborhood sewing bees and quilting parties or in a round of visits to geographically distant friends and relatives. Ostensibly they went to receive assistance in the practical preparations for their new home—sewing and quilting a trousseau and linen—but of equal importance, they appear to have gained emotional support and reassurance. Sarah Ripley spent over a month with friends and relatives in Boston and Hingham before her wedding; Parke Custis Lewis exchanged visits with her aunts and first cousins throughout Virginia.[61] Anne Jefferis, who married with some hesitation, spent virtually half a year in endless visiting with cousins, aunts, and friends. Despite their reassurance and support, however, she would not marry Moses Sheppard until her sister Edith and her cousin Rebecca moved into the groom's home, met his friends, and explored his personality.[62] The wedding did not take place until Edith wrote to Anne: "I can say in truth I am entirely willing thou shouldst follow him even away in the Jersey sands believing if

thou are not happy in thy future home it will not be any fault on his part. . . ."[63]

Sisters, cousins, and friends frequently accompanied newlyweds on their wedding night and wedding trip, which often involved additional family visiting. Such extensive visits presumably served to wean the daughter from her family of origin. As such they often contained a note of ambivalence. Nelly Custis, for example, reported homesickness and loneliness on her wedding trip. "I left my Beloved and revered Grandmamma with sincere regret," she wrote Elizabeth Bordley. "It was sometime before I could feel reconciled to traveling without her." Perhaps they also functioned to reassure the young woman herself, and her friends and kin, that though marriage might alter it would not destroy old bonds of intimacy and familiarity.[64]

Married life, too, was structured about a host of female rituals. Childbirth, especially the birth of the first child, became virtually a *rite de passage,* with a lengthy seclusion of the woman before and after delivery, severe restrictions on her activities, and finally a dramatic reemergence.[65] This seclusion was supervised by mothers, sisters, and loving friends. Nursing and weaning involved the advice and assistance of female friends and relatives. So did miscarriage.[66] Death, like birth, was structured around elaborate unisexed rituals. When Nelly Parke Custis Lewis rushed to nurse her daughter, who was critically ill while away at school, Nelly received support not from her husband, who remained on their plantation, but from her old school friend Elizabeth Bordley. Elizabeth aided Nelly in caring for her dying daughter, cared for Nelly's other children, played a major role in the elaborate funeral arrangements (which the father did not attend), and frequently visited the girl's grave at the mother's request. For years Elizabeth continued to be the confidante of Nelly's anguished recollections of her lost daughter. These memories, Nelly's letters make clear, were for Elizabeth alone. "Mr. L. knows nothing of this" was a frequent comment.[67] Virtually every collection of letters and diaries in my sample contained evidence of women turning to each other for comfort when facing the frequent and unavoidable deaths of the eighteenth and nineteenth centuries.[68] While mourning for her father's death, Sophie DuPont received elaborate letters and visits of condolence—all from women. No man wrote or visited Sophie to offer sympathy at her father's death.[69] Among rural Pennsylvania Quakers, death and mourning rituals assumed an even more extreme same-sex form, with men or women largely barred from the deathbeds of the other sex. Women relatives and friends slept with the dying woman, nursed her, and prepared her body for burial.[70]

Eighteenth- and nineteenth-century women thus lived in emotional proximity to each other. Friendships and intimacies followed the biological ebb and flow of women's lives. Marriage and pregnancy, childbirth and weaning, sickness and death involved physical and psychic trauma which comfort and sympathy made easier to bear. Intense bonds of love and intimacy bound together those women who, offering each other aid and sympathy, shared such stressful moments.

These bonds were often physical as well as emotional. An undeniably romantic and even sensual note frequently marked female relationships. This theme, significant throughout the stages of a woman's life, surfaced first during adolescence. As one teenager from a struggling pioneer family in the Ohio Valley wrote in her diary in 1808: "I laid with my dear R[ebecca] and a glorious good talk we had until about 4[A.M.]—O how hard I do *love* her. . . . "[71] Only a few years later Bostonian Eunice Callender carved her initials and Sarah Ripley's into a favorite tree, along with a pledge of eternal love, and then waited breathlessly for Sarah to discover and respond to her declaration of affection. The response appears to have been affirmative.[72] A half-century later urbane and sophisticated Katherine Wharton commented upon meeting an old school chum: "She was a great pet of mine at school & I thought as I watched her light figure how often I had held her in my arms—how dear she had once been to me." Katie maintained a long intimate friendship with another girl. When a young man began to court this friend seriously, Katie commented in her dairy that she had never realized "how deeply I loved Eng and how fully." She wrote over and over again in that entry: "Indeed I love her!" and only with great reluctance left the city that summer since it meant also leaving Eng with Eng's new suitor.[73]

Peggy Emlen, a Quaker adolescent in Philadelphia in the 1760s, expressed similar feelings about her first cousin, Sally Logan. The girls sent love poems to each other (not unlike the ones Elizabeth Bordley wrote to Nellie Custis a generation later), took long solitary walks together, and even haunted the empty house of the other when one was out of town. Indeed, Sally's absences from Philadelphia caused Peggy acute unhappiness. So strong were Peggy's feelings that her brothers began to tease her about her affection for Sally and threatened to steal Sally's letters, much to both girls' alarm. In one letter that Peggy wrote the absent Sally she elaborately described the depth and nature of her feelings: "I have not words to express my impatience to see My Dear Cousin, what would I not give just now for an hours sweet conversation with her, it seems as if I had a thousand things to say to thee, yet when I see thee, everything will be forgot thro' joy. . . . I have a very great friendship for several Girls yet it dont give me so much uneasiness at being absent from them as from thee. . . . [Let us] go and spend a day down at our place together and there unmolested enjoy each others company."[74]

Sarah Alden Ripley, a young, highly educated woman, formed a similar intense relationship, in this instance with a woman somewhat older than herself. The immediate bond of friendship rested on their atypically intense scholarly interests, but it soon involved strong emotions, at least on Sarah's part. "Friendship," she wrote Mary Emerson, "is fast twining about her willing captive the silken hands of dependence, a dependence so sweet who would renounce it for the apathy of self-sufficiency?" Subsequent letters became far more emotional, almost conspiratorial. Mary visited Sarah secretly in her room, or the two women crept away from family and friends to meet in a nearby woods. Sarah became jealous of Mary's other young woman friends. Mary's trips away from Boston also thrust Sarah into periods of anguished depression. Interestingly, the letters detailing their love were not destroyed but were preserved and even reprinted in a eulogistic biography of Sarah Alden Ripley.[75]

Tender letters between adolescent women, confessions of loneliness and emotional dependency, were not peculiar to Sarah Alden, Peggy Emlen, or Katie Wharton. They are found throughout the letters of the thirty-five families studied. They have, of course, their parallel today in the musings of many female adolescents. Yet these eighteenth- and nineteenth-century friendships lasted with undiminished, indeed often increased, intensity throughout the women's lives. Sarah

Alden Ripley's first child was named after Mary Emerson. Nelly Custis Lewis's love for and dependence on Elizabeth Bordley Gibson only increased after her marriage. Eunice Callender remained enamored of her cousin Sarah Ripley for years and rejected as impossible the suggestion by another woman that their love might someday fade away.[76] Sophie DuPont and her childhood friend Clementina Smith exchanged letters filled with love and dependency for forty years while another dear friend, Mary Black Couper, wrote of dreaming that she, Sophie, and her husband were all united in one marriage. Mary's letters to Sophie are filled with avowals of love and indications of ambivalence toward her own husband. Eliza Schlatter, another of Sophie's intimate friends, wrote to her at a time of crisis: "I wish I could be with you present in the body as well as the mind & heart—I would turn your *good husband out of bed*—and snuggle into you and we would have a long talk like old times in Pine St.—I want to tell you so many things that are not *writable*. . . . "[77]

Such mutual dependency and deep affection is a central existential reality coloring the world of supportive networks and rituals. In the cases of Katie, Sophie, and Eunice—as with Molly, Jeannie, and Sarah—their need for closeness and support merged with more intense demands for a love which was at the same time both emotional and sensual. Perhaps the most explicit statement concerning women's lifelong friendships appeared in the letter abolitionist and reformer Mary Grew wrote about the same time, referring to her own love for her dear friend and lifelong companion, Margaret Burleigh. Grew wrote, in response to a letter of condolence from another woman on Burleigh's death: "Your words respecting my beloved friend touch me deeply. Evidently . . . you comprehend and appreciate, as few persons do . . . the nature of the relation which existed, which exists, between her and myself. Her only surviving niece . . . also does. To me it seems to have been a closer union than that of most marriages. We know there have been other such between two men and also between two women. And why should there not be. Love is spiritual, only passion is sexual."[78]

How then can we ultimately interpret these long-lived intimate female relationships and integrate them into our understanding of Victorian sexuality? Their ambivalent and romantic rhetoric presents us with an ultimate puzzle: the relationship along the spectrum of human emotions between love, sensuality, and sexuality.

One is tempted, as I have remarked, to compare Molly, Peggy, and Sophie's relationships with the friendships adolescent girls in the twentieth century routinely form—close friendships of great emotional intensity. Helena Deutsch and Clara Thompson have both described these friendships as emotionally necessary to a girl's psychosexual development. But, they warn, such friendships might shade into adolescent and postadolescent homosexuality.[79]

It is possible to speculate that in the twentieth century a number of cultural taboos evolved to cut short the homosocial ties of girlhood and to impel the emerging women of thirteen or fourteen toward heterosexual relationships. In contrast, nineteenth-century American society did not taboo close female relationships but rather recognized them as a socially viable form of human contact—and, as such, acceptable throughout a woman's life. Indeed, it was not these homosocial ties that were inhibited but rather heterosexual leanings. While closeness, freedom of emotional expression, and uninhibited physical contact characterized women's relationships with each other, the opposite was frequently true of male–female relationships. One could thus argue that within such a world of female support, intimacy, and ritual it was, only to be expected that adult women would turn trustingly and lovingly to each other. It was a behavior they had observed and learned since childhood. A different type of emotional landscape existed in the nineteenth century, one in which Molly and Helena's love became a natural development.

Of perhaps equal significance are the implications we can garner from this framework for the understanding of heterosexual marriages in the nineteenth century. If men and women grew up as they did in relatively homogeneous and segregated sexual groups, then marriage represented a major problem in adjustment. From this perspective we could interpret much of the emotional stiffness and distance that we associate with Victorian marriage as a structural consequence of contemporary sex-role differentiation and gender-role socialization. With marriage both women and men had to adjust to life with a person who was, in essence, a member of an alien group.

I have thus far substituted a cultural or psychosocial for a psychosexual interpretation of women's emotional bonding. But there are psychosexual implications in this model which I think it only fair to make more explicit. Despite Sigmund Freud's insistence on the bisexuality of us all and the recent American Psychiatric Association decision on homosexuality, many psychiatrists today tend explicitly or implicitly to view homosexuality as a totally alien or pathological behavior—as totally unlike heterosexuality. I suspect that in essence they may have adopted an explanatory model similar to the one used in discussing schizophrenia. As psychiatrists can speak of schizophrenia and of a borderline schizophrenic personality as both ultimately and fundamentally different from a normal or neurotic personality, so they also think of both homosexuality and latent homosexuality as states totally different from heterosexuality. With this rapidly dichotomous model of assumption, "latent homosexuality" becomes the indication of a disease in progress—seeds of a pathology which belie the reality of an individual's heterosexuality.

Yet at the same time we are well aware that cultural values can affect choices in the gender of a person's sexual partner. We, for instance, do not necessarily consider homosexual object choice among men in prison, on shipboard, or in boarding schools a necessary indication of pathology. I would urge that we expand this relativistic model and hypothesize that a number of cultures might well tolerate or even encourage diversity in sexual and nonsexual relations. Based on my research into this nineteenth-century world of female intimacy, I would further suggest that rather than seeing a gulf between the normal and the abnormal we view sexual and emotional impulses as part of a continuum or spectrum of affect gradations strongly effected by cultural norms and arrangements, a continuum influenced in part by observed and thus learned behavior. At one end of the continuum lies committed heterosexuality, at the other uncompromising homosexuality; between, a wide latitude of emotions and sexual feelings. Certain cultures and environments permit individuals a great deal of freedom in moving across this spectrum. I would like to suggest that the nineteenth century was such a cultural environment. That is, the supposedly repressive and destructive Victorian sexual ethos may have been more flexible and responsive to the needs of particular individuals than those of the twentieth century.

ACKNOWLEDGMENTS

Research for this paper was supported in part by a grant from the Grant Foundation, New York, and by National Institutes of Health trainee grant 5 FO3 HD48800-03. I would like to thank several scholars for their assistance and criticism in preparing this paper: Erving Goffman, Roy Schafer, Charles E. Rosenberg, Cynthia Secor, Anthony Wallace. Judy Breault, who has just completed a biography of an important and introspective nineteenth-century feminist, Emily Howland, served as a research assistant for this paper, and her knowledge of nineteenth-century family structure and religious history proved invaluable.

NOTES

1. The most notable exception to this rule is William R. Taylor and Christopher Lasch, "Two 'Kindred Spirits': Sorority and Family in New England, 1839–1846," *New England Quarterly* 36 (1963): 25–41. Taylor has made a valuable contribution to the history of women and the history of the family with his concept of "sororial" relations. I do not, however, accept the Taylor-Lasch thesis that female friendships developed in the mid-nineteenth century because of geographic mobility and the breakup of the colonial family. I have found these friendships as frequently in the eighteenth

century as in the nineteenth and would hypothesize that the geographic mobility of the mid-nineteenth century eroded them as it did so many other traditional social institutions. Helen Vendler (review of *Notable American Women, 1607–1950,* ed. Edward James and Janet James, *New York Times,* November 5, 1972, sec. 7, points out the significance of these friendships.

2. I do not wish to deny the importance of women's relations with particular men. Obviously, women were close to brothers, husbands, fathers, and sons. However, there is evidence that despite such closeness, relationships between men and women differed in both emotional texture and frequency from those between women. Women's relations with each other, although they played a central role in the American family and American society, have been so seldom examined either by general social historians or by historians of the family that I wish in this article simply to examine their nature and analyze their implications for our understanding of social relations and social structure. I have discussed some aspects of male–female relationships in two articles: "Puberty to Menopause: The Cycle of Femininity in Nineteenth-Century America," *Feminist Studies* 1 (1973): 58–72, and, with Charles Rosenberg, "The Female Animal: Medical and Biological Views of Women in 19th Century America," *Journal of American History* 59 (1973): 331–56.

3. See Freud's classic paper on homosexuality, "Three Essays on the Theory of Sexuality," in *The Standard Edition of the Complete Psychological Works of Sigmund Freud,* trans. James Strachey (London: Hogarth Press, 1953), 7:135–72. The essays originally appeared in 1905. Prof. Roy Shafer, Department of Psychiatry, Yale University, has pointed out that Freud's view of sexual behavior was strongly influenced by nineteenth-century evolutionary thought. Within Freud's schema, genital heterosexuality marked the height of human development (Schafer, "Problems in Freud's Psychology of Women," *Journal of the American Psychoanalytic Association* 22 [1974]: 459–85).

4. For a novel and most important exposition of one theory of behavioral norms and options and its application to the study of human sexuality, see Charles Rosenberg, "Sexuality, Class and Role," *American Quarterly* 25 (1973): 131–53.

5. See, e.g., the letters of Peggy Emlen to Sally Logan, 1768–72, Wells Morris Collection, Box 1, Historical Society of Pennsylvania; and the Eleanor Parke Custis Lewis Letters, Historical Society of Pennsylvania, Philadelphia.

6. Sarah Butler Wister was the daughter of Fanny Kemble and Pierce Butler. In 1859 she married a Philadelphia physician, Owen Wister. The novelist Owen Wister is her son. Jeannie Field Musgrove was the half-orphaned daughter of constitutional lawyer and New York Republican politician David Dudley Field. Their correspondence (1855–98) is in the Sarah Butler Wister Papers, Wister Family Papers, Historical Society of Pennsylvania.

7. Sarah Butler, Butler Place, S.C., to Jeannie Field, New York, September 14, 1855.

8. See, e.g., Sarah Butler Wister, Germantown, Pa., to Jeannie Field, New York, September 25, 1862, October 21, 1863; or Jeannie Field, New York, to Sarah Butler Wister, Germantown, July 3, 1861, January 23 and July 12, 1863.

9. Sarah Butler Wister, Germantown, to Jeannie Field, New York, June 5, 1861, February 29, 1864; Jeannie Field to Sarah Butler Wister November 22, 1861, January 4 and June 14, 1863.

10. Sarah Butler Wister, London, to Jeannie Field Musgrove, New York, June 18 and August 3, 1870.

11. See, e.g., two of Sarah's letters to Jeannie: December 21, 1873, July 16, 1878.

12. This is the 1868–1920 correspondence between Mary Hallock Foote and Helena, a New York friend (the Mary Hallock Foote Papers are in the Manuscript Division, Stanford University). Wallace E. Stegner has written a fictionalized biography of Mary Hallock Foote (*Angle of Repose* [Garden City, N.Y.: Doubleday, 1971]). See, as well, her autobiography: Mary Hallock Foote, *A Victorian Gentlewoman in the Far West: The Reminiscences of Mary Hallock Foote,* ed. Rodman W. Paul (San Marino, Calif.: Huntington Library, 1972). In many ways these letters are typical of those women wrote to other women. Women frequently began letters to each other with salutations such as "Dearest," "My Most Beloved," "You Darling Girl," and signed them "tenderly" or "to my dear dear sweet friend, good-bye." Without the least self-consciousness, one woman in her frequent letters to a female friend referred to her husband as "my other love." She was by no means unique. See, e.g., Annie to Charlene Van Vleck Anderson, Appleton, Wis., June 10, 1871, Anderson Family Papers, Manuscript Division, Stanford University; Maggie to Emily Howland, Philadelphia, July 12, 1851, Howland Family Papers, Phoebe King Collection, Friends Historical Library, Swarthmore College; Mary Jane Burleigh to Emily Howland, Sherwood, N.Y., March 27, 1872, Howland Family Papers, Sophia Smith Collection, Smith College; Mary Black Couper to Sophia Madeleine DuPont, Wilmington, Del., n.d. [1834] (two letters), Samuel Francis DuPont Papers, Eleutherian Mills Foundation, Wilmington, Del.; Phoebe Middleton, Concordville, Pa., to Martha Jefferis, Chester County, Pa., February 22, 1848; and see in general the correspondence (1838–49) between Rebecca Biddle of Philadelphia and Martha Jefferis, Chester County, Pa., Jefferis Family Correspondence, Chester County Historical Society, West Chester, Pa.; Phoebe Bradford Diary, June 7 and July 13, 1832, Historical Society of Pennsylvania; Sarah Alden Ripley to Abba Allyn, Boston, n.d. [1818–20], and Sarah Alden Ripley to Sophia Bradford, November 30, 1854, in the Sarah Alden Ripley Correspondence, Schlesinger Library, Radcliffe College; Fanny Canby Ferris to Anne Biddle, Philadelphia, October 11 and November 19, 1811, December 26, 1813; Fanny Canby to Mary Canby, May 27, 1801; Mary

R. Garrigues to Mary Canby, five letters, n.d. [1802–8]; Anne Biddle to Mary Canby, two letters n.d., May 16, July 13, and November 24, 1806, June 14, 1807, June 5, 1808, all in Anne Sterling Biddle Family Papers, Friends Historical Society, Swarthmore College; Harriet Manigault Wilcox Diary, August 7, 1814, Historical Society of Pennsylvania. See as well the correspondence between Harriet Manigault Wilcox's mother, Mrs. Gabriel Manigault, Philadelphia, and Mrs. Henry Middleton, Charleston, S.C., between 1810 and 1830, Cadwalader Collection, J. Francis Fisher Section, Historical Society of Pennsylvania. The basis and nature of such friendships can be seen in the comments of Sarah Alden Ripley to her sister-in-law and long-time friend, Sophia Bradford: "Hearing that you are not well reminds me of what it would be to lose your loving society. We have kept step together through a long piece of road in the weary journey of life. We have loved the same beings and wept together over their graves" (Mrs. O. J. Wister and Miss Agnes Irwin, eds., *Worthy Women of Our First Century* [Philadelphia: Lippincott, 1877] p. 195).

13. Mary Hallock [Foote] to Helena, n.d. [1869–70], n.d. [1871–72], Folder 1, Mary Hallock Foote Letters, Manuscript Division, Stanford University.

14. Mary Hallock [Foote] to Helena, September 15 and 23, 1873, n.d. [October 1873], October 12, 1873.

15. Mary Hallock [Foote] to Helena, n.d. [January 1874], n.d. [Spring 1874].

16. Mary Hallock [Foote] to Helena, September 23, 1873; Mary Hallock [Foote] to Richard, December 13, 1873. Molly's and Helena's relationship continued for the rest of their lives. Molly's letters are filled with tender and intimate references, as when she wrote, twenty years later and from 2,000 miles away: "It isn't because you are good that I love you—but for the essence of you which is like perfume" (n.d. [1890s?]).

17. I am in the midst of a larger study of adult gender-roles and gender-role socialization in America, 1785–1895. For a discussion of social attitudes toward appropriate male and female roles, see Barbara Welter, "The Cult of True Womanhood: 1820–1860," *American Quarterly* 18 (Summer 1966): 151–74; Ann Firor Scott, *The Southern Lady: From Pedestal to Politics, 1830–1930* (Chicago: University of Chicago Press, 1970), chaps. 1–2; Smith-Rosenberg and Rosenberg.

18. See, e.g., the letters of Peggy Emlen to Sally Logan, 1768–72, Wells Morris Collection, Box 1, Historical Society of Pennsylvania; and the Eleanor Parke Custis Lewis Letters, Historical Society of Pennsylvania.

19. See esp. Elizabeth Botts, *Family and Social Network* (London: Tavistock, 1957); Michael Young and Peter Willmott, *Family and Kinship in East London,* rev. ed. (Baltimore: Penguin, 1964).

20. This pattern seemed to cross class barriers. A letter that an Irish domestic wrote in the 1830s contains seventeen separate references to women and only seven to men, most of whom were relatives and two of whom were infant brothers living with her mother and mentioned in relation to her mother (Ann McGrann, Philadelphia, to Sophie M. DuPont, Philadelphia, July 3, 1834, Sophie Madeleine DuPont Letters, Eleutherian Mills Foundation).

21. Harriett Manigault Diary, June 28, 1814, and passim; Jeannie Field, New York, to Sarah Butler Wister, Germantown, April 19, 1863; Phoebe Bradford Diary, January 30, February 19, March 4, August 11, and October 14, 1832, Historical Society of Pennsylvania; Sophie M. DuPont, Brandywine, to Henry DuPont, Germantown, July 9, 1827, Eleutherian Mills Foundation.

22. Martha Jefferis to Anne Jefferis Sheppard, July 9, 1843; Anne Jefferis Sheppard to Martha Jefferis, June 28, 1846; Anne Sterling Biddle Papers, passim, Biddle Family Papers, Friends Historical Society, Swarthmore College; Eleanor Parke Custis Lewis, Virginia, to Elizabeth Bordley Gibson, Philadelphia, November 24 and December 4, 1820, November 6, 1821.

23. Phoebe Bradford Diary, January 13, November 16–19, 1832, April 26 and May 7, 1833; Abigail Brackett Lyman to Mrs. Catling, Litchfield, Conn., May 3, 1801, collection in private hands; Martha Jefferis to Anne Jefferis Sheppard, August 28, 1845.

24. Lisa Mitchell Diary, 1860s, passim, Manuscript Division, Tulane University; Eleanor Parke Custis Lewis to Elizabeth Bordley [Gibson], February 5, 1822; Jeannie McCall, Cedar Park, to Peter McCall, Philadelphia, June 30, 1849, McCall Section, Cadwalader Collection, Historical Society of Pennsylvania.

25. Peggy Emlen to Sally Logan, May 3, 1769.

26. For a prime example of this type of letter, see Eleanor Parke Custis Lewis to Elizabeth Cordley Gibson, passim, or Fanny Canby to Mary Canby, Philadelphia, May 27, 1801; or Sophie M. DuPont, Brandywine, to Henry DuPont, Germantown, February 4, 1832.

27. Place of residence is not the only variable significant in characterizing family structure. Strong emotional ties and frequent visiting and correspondence can unite families that do not live under one roof. Demographic studies based on household structure alone fail to reflect such emotional and even economic ties between families.

28. Eleanor Parke Custis Lewis to Elizabeth Bordley Gibson, April 20 and September 25, 1848.

29. Maria Inskeep to Fanny Hampton, Correspondence, 1823–60, Inskeep Collection, Tulane University Library.

30. Eunice Callender, Boston, to Sarah Ripley [Stearns], September 24 and October 29, 1803, February 16, 1805, April 29 and October 9, 1806, May 26, 1810.

31. Sophie DuPont filled her letters to her younger brother Henry (with whom she had been assigned to correspond while he was at boarding school) with accounts of family visiting (see, e.g., December 13, 1827, January 10 and

March 9, 1828, February 4 and March 10, 1832; also Sophie M. DuPont to Victorine DuPont Bauday, September 26 and December 4, 1827, February 22, 1828; Sophie M. DuPont, Brandywine, to Clementina B. Smith, Philadelphia, January 15, 1830; Eleuthera DuPont, Brandywine, to Victorine DuPont Bauday, Philadelphia, April 17, 1821, October 20, 1826; Evelina DuPont [Biderman] to Victorine DuPont Bauday, October 18, 1816). Other examples, from the Historical Society of Pennsylvania, are Harriet Manigault [Wilcox] Diary, August 17, September 8, October 19 and 22, December 22, 1814; Jane Zook, Westtown School, Chester County, Pa., to Mary Zook, November 13, December 7 and 11, 1870, February 26, 1871; Eleanor Parke Custis [Lewis] to Elizabeth Bordley [Gibson], March 30, 1796, February 7 and March 20, 1798; Jeannie McCall to Peter McCall, Philadelphia, November 12, 1847; Mary B. Ashew Diary, July 11 and 13, August 17, Summer and October 1858, and, from a private collection, Edith Jefferis to Anne Jefferis Sheppard, November 1841, April 5, 1842; Abigail Brackett Lyman, Northampton, Mass., to Mrs. Catling, Litchfield, Conn., May 13, 1801; Abigail Brackett Lyman, Northampton, to Mary Lord, August 11, 1800. Mary Hallock Foote vacationed with her sister, her sister's children, her aunt, and a female cousin in the summer of 1874; cousins frequently visited the Hallock farm in Milton, N.Y. In later years Molly and her sister Bessie set up a joint household in Boise, Idaho (Mary Hallock Foote to Helena, July [1874?] and passim). Jeannie Field, after initially disliking her sister-in-law, Laura, became very close to her, calling her "my little sister" and at times spending virtually every day with her (Jeannie Field [Musgrove] New York, to Sarah Butler Wister, Germantown, March 1, 8, and 15, and May 9, 1863).

32. Martha Jefferis to Anne Jefferis Sheppard, January 12, 1845; Phoebe Middleton to Martha Jefferis, February 22, 1848. A number of other women remained close to sisters and sisters-in-law across a long lifetime (Phoebe Bradford Diary, June 7, 1832, and Sarah Alden Ripley to Sophia Bradford, cited in Wister and Irwin, p. 195).

33. Rebecca Biddle to Martha Jefferis, 1838–49, passim; Martha Jefferis to Anne Jefferis Sheppard, July 6, 1846; Anne Jefferis Sheppard to Rachael Jefferis, January 16, 1865; Sarah Foulke Farquhar [Emlen] Diary, September 22, 1813, Friends Historical Library, Swarthmore College; Mary Garrigues to Mary Canby [Biddle], 1802–8, passim; Anne Biddle to Mary Canby [Biddle], May 16, July 13, and November 24, 1806, June 14, 1807, June 5, 1808.

34. Sarah Alden Ripley to Abba Allyn, n.d., Schlesinger Library.

35. Phoebe Bradford Diary, July 13, 1832.

36. Mary Hallock [Foote] to Helena, December 23 [1868 or 1869]; Phoebe Bradford Diary, December 8, 1832; Martha Jefferis and Anne Jefferis Sheppard letters, passim.

37. Martha Jefferis to Anne Jefferis Sheppard, August 3, 1849; Sarah Ripley [Stearns] Diary, November 12, 1808, Jan-uary 8, 1811. An interesting note of hostility or rivalry is present in Sarah Ripley's diary entry. Sarah evidently deeply resented the husband's rapid remarriage.

38. Martha Jefferis to Edith Jefferis, March 15, 1841; Mary Hallock Foote to Helena, n.d. [1874–75?]; see also Jeannie Field, New York, to Sarah Butler Wister, Germantown, May 5, 1863; Emily Howland Diary, December 1879, Howland Family Papers.

39. Anne Jefferis Sheppard to Martha Jefferis, September 29, 1841.

40. Frances Parke Lewis to Elizabeth Bordley Gibson, April 29, 1821.

41. Mary Jane Burleigh, Mount Pleasant, S.C., to Emily Howland, Sherwood N.Y., March 27, 1872, Howland Family Papers; Emily Howland Diary, September 16, 1879, January 21 and 23, 1880; Mary Black Couper, New Castle, Del., to Sophie M. DuPont, Brandywine, April 7, 1834.

42. Harriet Manigault Diary, August 15, 21, and 23, 1814, Historical Society of Pennsylvania; Polly [Simmons] to Sophie Madeleine DuPont, February 1822; Sophie Madeleine DuPont to Victorine Bauday, December 4, 1827; Sophie Madeleine DuPont to Clementina Beach Smith, July 24, 1828, August 19, 1829; Clementina Beach Smith to Sophie Madeleine DuPont, April 29, 1831; Mary Black Couper to Sophie Madeleine DuPont, December 24, 1828, July 21, 1834. This pattern appears to have crossed class lines. When a former Sunday school student of Sophie DuPont's (and the daughter of a worker in her father's factory) wrote to Sophie, she discussed her mother's health and activities quite naturally (Ann McGrann to Sophie Madeleine DuPont, August 25, 1832; see also Elizabeth Bordley to Martha, n.d. [1797]; Eleanor Parke Custis [Lewis] to Elizabeth Bordley [Gibson], May 13, 1796, July 1, 1798; Peggy Emlen to Sally Logan, January 8, 1786. All but the Emlen/Logan letters are in the Eleanor Parke Custis Lewis Correspondence, Historical Society of Pennsylvania.

43. Mrs. S. S. Dalton, "Autobiography" (Circle Valley, Utah, 1876), pp. 21–22, Bancroft Library, University of California, Berkeley; Sarah Foulke Emlen Diary, April 1809; Louisa G. Van Vleck, Appleton, Wis., to Charlena Van Vleck Anderson, Göttingen, n.d. [1875]; Harriet Manigault Diary, August 16, 1814, July 14, 1815; Sarah Alden Ripley to Sophy Fisher [early 1860s], quoted in Wister and Irwin (n. 12 above), p. 212. The Jefferis family papers are filled with empathetic letters between Martha and her daughters, Anne and Edith. See, e.g., Martha Jefferis to Edith Jefferis, December 26, 1836, March 11, 1837, March 15, 1841; Anne Jefferis Sheppard to Martha Jefferis, March 17, 1841, January 7, 1847; Martha Jefferis to Anne Jefferis Sheppard, April 17, 1848, April 30, 1849. A representative letter is this of March 9, 1837, from Edith to Martha: "My heart can fully respond to the language of my own precious Mother, that absence has not diminished our affection for each other, but has, if possible, strengthened the bonds that have united us together &

I have had to remark how we had been permitted to mingle in sweet fellowship and have been strengthened to bear one another's burdens. . . . "

44. Abigail Brackett Lyman, Boston, to Mrs. Abigail Brackett (daughter to mother), n.d. [1797], June 3, 1800; Sarah Alden Ripley wrote weekly to her daughter, Sophy Ripley Fisher, after the latter's marriage (Sarah Alden Ripley Correspondence, passim); Phoebe Bradford Diary, February 25, 1833, passim, 1832–33; Louisa G. Van Vleck to Charlena Van Vleck Anderson, December 15, 1873, July 4, August 15 and 29, September 19, and November 9, 1875. Eleanor Parke Custis Lewis's long correspondence with Elizabeth Bordley Gibson contains evidence of her anxiety at leaving her foster mother's home at various times during her adolescence and at her marriage, and her own longing for her daughters, both of whom had married and moved to Louisiana (Eleanor Parke Custis [Lewis] to Elizabeth Bordley [Gibson], October 13, 1795, November 4, 1799, passim, 1820s and 1830s). Anne Jefferis Sheppard experienced a great deal of anxiety on moving two days' journey from her mother at the time of her marriage. This loneliness and sense of isolation persisted through her marriage until, finally a widow, she returned to live with her mother (Anne Jefferis Sheppard to Martha Jefferis, April 1841, October 16, 1842, April 2, May 22, and October 12, 1844, September 3, 1845, January 17, 1847, May 16, June 3, and October 31, 1849; Anne Jefferis Sheppard to Susanna Lightfoot, March 23, 1845, and to Joshua Jefferis, May 14, 1854). Daughters evidently frequently slept with their mothers into adulthood (Harriet Manigault [Wilcox] Diary, February 19, 1815; Eleanor Parke Custis Lewis to Elizabeth Bordley Gibson, October 10, 1832). Daughters also frequently asked mothers to live with them and professed delight when they did so. See, e.g., Sarah Alden Ripley's comments to George Simmons, October 6, 1844, in Wister and Irwin, p. 185: "It is no longer 'Mother and Charles came out one day and returned the next,' for mother is one of us: she has entered the penetratice, been initiated into the mystery of the household gods. . . . Her divertissement is to mend the stockings . . . whiten sheets and napkins, . . . and take a stroll at evening with me to talk of our children, to compare our experiences, what we have learned and what we have suffered, and, last of all, to complete with pears and melons the cheerful circle about the solar lamp. . . . " We did find a few exceptions to this mother–daughter felicity (M. B. Ashew Diary, November 19, 1857, April 10 and May 17, 1858). Sarah Foulke Emlen was at first very hostile to her stepmother (Sarah Foulke Emlen Diary, August 9, 1807), but they later developed a warm supportive relationship.

45. Sarah Alden Ripley to Sophy Thayer, n.d. [1861].

46. Mary Hallock Foote to Helena [winter 1873] (no. 52); Jossie, Stevens Point, Wis., to Charlena Van Vleck [Anderson], Appleton, Wis., October 24, 1870; Pollie Chandler, Green Bay, Wis., to Charlena Van Vleck [Anderson], Appleton, n.d. [1870]; Eleuthera DuPont to Sophie DuPont,

September 5, 1829; Sophie DuPont to Eleuthera DuPont, December 1827; Sophie DuPont to Victorine Bauday, December 4, 1827; Mary Gilpin to Sophie DuPont, September 26, 1827; Sarah Ripley Stearns Diary, April 2, 1809; Jeannie McCall to Peter McCall, October 27 [late 1840s]. Eleanor Parke Custis Lewis's correspondence with Elizabeth Bordley Gibson describes such an apprenticeship system over two generations—that of her childhood and that of her daughters. Indeed, Eleanor Lewis's own apprenticeship was quite formal. She was deliberately separated from her foster mother in order to spend a winter of domesticity with her married sisters and her remarried mother. It was clearly felt that her foster mother's (Martha Washington) home at the nation's capital was not an appropriate place to develop domestic talents (October 13, 1795, March 30, May 13, and [summer] 1796, March 18 and April 27, 1797, October 1827).

47. Education was not limited to the daughters of the well-to-do. Sarah Foulke Emlen, the daughter of an Ohio Valley frontier farmer, for instance, attended day school for several years during the early 1800s. Sarah Ripley Stearns, the daughter of a shopkeeper in Greenfield, Mass., attended a boarding school for but three months, yet the experience seemed very important to her. Mrs. S. S. Dalton, a Mormon woman from Utah, attended a series of poor country schools and greatly valued her opportunity, though she also expressed a great deal of guilt for the sacrifices her mother made to make her education possible (Sarah Foulke Emlen Journal, Sarah Ripley Stearns Diary, Mrs. S. S. Dalton, "Autobiography").

48. Maria Revere to her mother [Mrs. Paul Revere], June 13, 1801, Paul Revere Papers, Massachusetts Historical Society. In a letter to Elizabeth Bordley Gibson, March 28, 1847, Eleanor Parke Custis Lewis from Virginia discussed the anxiety her daughter felt when her granddaughters left home to go to boarding school. Eleuthera DuPont was very homesick when away at school in Philadelphia in the early 1820s (Eleuthera DuPont, Philadelphia, to Victorine Bauday, Wilmington, Del., April 7, 1821; Eleuthera DuPont to Sophie Madeleine DuPont, Wilmington Del., February and April 3, 1821).

49. Elizabeth Bordley Gibson, a Philadelphia matron, played such a role for the daughters and nieces of her lifelong friend, Eleanor Parke Custis Lewis, a Virginia planter's wife (Eleanor Parke Custis Lewis to Elizabeth Bordley Gibson, January 29, 1833, March 19, 1826, and passim through the collection). The wife of Thomas Gurney Smith played a similar role for Sophie and Eleuthera DuPont (see, e.g., Eleuthera DuPont to Sophie Madeleine DuPont, May 22, 1825; Rest Cope to Philema P. Swayne [niece], West Town School, Chester County, Pa., April 8, 1829, Friends Historical Library, Swarthmore College). For a view of such a social pattern over three generations, see the letters and diaries of three generations of Manigault women in Philadelphia: Mrs. Gabrielle Manigault, her daughter, Harriet Manigault Wilcox,

and granddaughter, Charlotte Wilcox McCall. Unfortunately the papers of the three women are not in one family collection (Mrs. Henry Middleton, Charleston, S.C., to Mrs. Gabrielle Manigault, n.d. [mid 1800s]; Harriet Manigault Diary, vol. 1, December 1, 1813, June 28, 1814; Charlotte Wilcox McCall Diary, vol. 1, 1842, passim; all in Historical Society of Philadelphia).

50. Frances Parke Lewis, Woodlawn, Va., to Elizabeth Bordley Gibson, Philadelphia, April 11, 1821, Lewis Correspondence; Eleuthera DuPont, Philadelphia, to Victorine DuPont Bauday, Brandywine, December 8, 1821, January 31, 1822; Eleuthera DuPont, Brandywine, to Margaretta Lammont [DuPont], Philadelphia, May 1823.

51. Sarah Ripley Stearns Diary, March 9 and 25, 1810; Peggy Emlen to Sally Logan, March and July 4, 1769; Harriet Manigault [Wilcox] Diary, vol. 1, December 1, 1813, June 28 and September 18, 1814, August 10, 1815; Charlotte Wilcox McCall Diary, 1842, passim; Fanny Canby to Mary Canby, May 27, 1801, March 17, 1804; Deborah Cope, West Town School, to Rest Cope, Philadelphia, July 9, 1828, Chester County Historical Society, West Chester, Pa.; Anne Zook, West Town School, to Mary Zook, Philadelphia, January 30, 1866, Chester County Historical Society, West Chester, Pa.; Mary Gilpin to Sophie Madeleine DuPont, February 25, 1829; Eleanor Parke Custis [Lewis] to Elizabeth Bordley [Gibson], April 27, July 2, and September 8, 1797, June 30, 1799, December 29, 1820; Frances Parke Lewis to Elizabeth Bordley Gibson, December 20, 1820.

52. Anne Jefferis Sheppard to Martha Jefferis, March 17, 1841.

53. Peggy Emlen to Sally Logan, March 1769, Mount Vernon, Va.; Eleanor Parke Custis [Lewis] to Elizabeth Bordley [Gibson], Philadelphia, April 27, 1797, June 30, 1799; Jeannie Field, New York, to Sarah Butler Wister, Germantown, July 3, 1861, January 16, 1863; Harriet Manigault Diary, August 3 and 11–13, 1814; Eunice Callender, Boston, to Sarah Ripley [Stearns], Greenfield, May 4, 1809. I found one exception to this inhibition of female hostility. This was the diary of Charlotte Wilcox McCall, Philadelphia (see, e.g., her March 23, 1842, entry).

54. Sophie M. DuPont and Eleuthera DuPont, Brandywine, to Victorine DuPont Bauday, Philadelphia, January 25, 1832.

55. Sarah Ripley [Stearns] Diary and Harriet Manigault Diary, passim.

56. Sophie Madeleine DuPont to Eleuthera DuPont, December 1827; Clementina Beach Smith to Sophie Madeleine DuPont, December 26, 1828; Sarah Faulke Emlen Diary, July 21, 1808, March 30, 1809; Annie Hethroe, Ellington, Wis., to Charlena Van Vleck [Anderson], Appleton, Wis., April 23, 1865; Frances Parke Lewis, Woodlawn, Va., to Elizabeth Bordley [Gibson], Philadelphia, December 20, 1820; Fanny Ferris to Debby Ferris, West Town School, Chester County, Pa., May 29, 1826. An excellent example of the

warmth of women's comments about each other and the reserved nature of their references to men are seen in two entries in Sarah Ripley Stearn's diary. On January 8, 1811, she commented about a young woman friend: "The amiable Mrs. White of Princeton . . . one of the loveliest most interesting creatures I ever knew, young fair and blooming . . . beloved by everyone . . . formed to please & to charm. . . . " She referred to the man she ultimately married always as "my friend" or "a friend" (February 2 or April 23, 1810).

57. Jeannie Field, New York, to Sarah Butler Wister, Germantown, April 6, 1862.

58. Elizabeth Bordley Gibson, introductory statement to the Eleanor Parke Custis Lewis Letters [1850s], Historical Society of Pennsylvania.

59. Sarah Foulke [Emlen] Diary, March 30, 1809.

60. Harriet Manigault Diary, May 26, 1815.

61. Sarah Ripley [Stearns] Diary, May 17 and October 2, 1812; Eleanor Parke Custis Lewis to Elizabeth Bordley Gibson, April 23, 1826; Rebecca Ralston, Philadelphia, to Victorine DuPont [Bauday], Brandywine, September 27, 1813.

62. Anne Jefferis to Martha Jefferis, November 22 and 27, 1840, January 13 and March 17, 1841; Edith Jefferis, Greenwich, N.J., to Anne Jefferis, Philadelphia, January 31, February 6 and February 1841.

63. Edith Jefferis to Anne Jefferis, January 31, 1841.

64. Eleanor Parke Custis Lewis to Elizabeth Bordley, November 4, 1799. Eleanor and her daughter Parke experienced similar sorrow and anxiety when Parke married and moved to Cincinnati (Eleanor Parke Custis Lewis to Elizabeth Bordley Gibson, April 23, 1826). Helena DeKay visited Mary Hallock the month before her marriage; Mary Hallock was an attendant at the wedding; Helena again visited Molly about three weeks after her marriage; and then Molly went with Helena and spent a week with Helena and Richard in their new apartment (Mary Hallock [Foote] to Helena DeKay Gilder [Spring 1874] (no. 61), May 10, 1874 [May 1874], June 14, 1874 [Summer 1874]. See also Anne Biddle, Philadelphia, to Clement Biddle (brother), Wilmington, March 12 and May 27, 1827; Eunice Callender, Boston, to Sarah Ripley [Stearns], Greenfield, Mass., August 3, 1807, January 26, 1808; Victorine DuPont Bauday, Philadelphia, to Evelina DuPont [Biderman], Brandywine, November 25 and 26, December 1, 1813; Peggy Emlen to Sally Logan, n.d. [1769–70?]; Jeannie Field, New York, to Sarah Butler Wister, Germantown, July 3, 1861.

65. Mary Hallock to Helena DeKay Gilder [1876] (no. 81); n.d. (no. 83), March 3, 1884; Mary Ashew Diary, vol. 2, September–January, 1860; Louisa Van Vleck to Charlena Van Vleck Anderson, n.d. [1875]; Sophie DuPont to Henry DuPont, July 24, 1827; Benjamin Ferris to William Canby, February 13, 1805; Benjamin Ferris to Mary Canby Biddle, December 20, 1825; Anne Jefferis Sheppard to Martha Jefferis, September 15, 1884; Martha Jefferis to Anne Jefferis Sheppard, July 4, 1843, May 5, 1844, May 3, 1847, July 17,

1849; Jeannie McCall to Peter McCall, November 26, 1847, n.d. [late 1840s]. A graphic description of the ritual surrounding a first birth is found in Abigail Lyman's letter to her husband, Erastus Lyman, October 18, 1810.

66. Fanny Ferris to Anne Biddle, November 19, 1811; Eleanor Parke Custis Lewis to Elizabeth Bordley Gibson, November 4, 1799, April 27, 1827; Martha Jefferis to Anne Jefferis Sheppard, January 31, 1843, April 4, 1844; Martha Jefferis to Phoebe Sharpless Middleton, June 4, 1846; Anne Jefferis Sheppard to Martha Jefferis, August 20, 1843, February 12, 1844; Maria Inskeep, New Orleans, to Mrs. Fanny G. Hampton, Bridgeton, N.J., September 22, 1848; Benjamin Ferris to Mary Canby, February 14, 1805; Fanny Ferris to Mary Canby [Biddle], December 2, 1816.

67. Eleanor Parke Custis Lewis to Elizabeth Bordley Gibson, October–November 1820, passim.

68. Emily Howland to Hannah, September 30, 1866; Emily Howland Diary, February 8, 11, and 27, 1880; Phoebe Brandford Diary, April 12 and 13 and August 4, 1833; Eunice Callender, Boston, to Sarah Ripley [Stearns], Greenwich, Mass., September 11, 1802, August 26, 1810; Mrs. H. Middleton, Charleston, to Mrs. Gabrielle Manigault, Philadelphia, n.d. [mid 1800s]; Mrs. H. C. Paul to Mrs. Jeannie McCall, Philadelphia, n.d. [1840s]; Sarah Butler Wister, Germantown, to Jeannie Field [Musgrove], New York, April 22, 1864; Jeannie Field [Musgrove] to Sarah Butler Wister, August 25, 1861, July 6, 1862; S. B. Raudolph to Elizabeth Bordley [Gibson], n.d. [1790s]. For an example of similar letters between men, see Henry Wright to Peter McCall, December 10, 1852; Charles McCall to Peter McCall, January 4, 1860, March 22, 1864; R. Mercer to Peter McCall, Novwember 29, 1872.

69. Mary Black [Couper] to Sophie Madeleine DuPont, February 1827 [November 1, 1834], November 12, 1834, two letters [late November 1834]; Eliza Schlatter to Sophie Madeleine DuPont, November 2, 1834.

70. For a few of the references to death rituals in the Jefferis papers, see Martha Jefferis to Anne Jefferis Sheppard, September 28, 1843, August 21 and September 25, 1844, January 11, 1846, summer 1848, passim; Anne Jefferis Sheppard to Martha Jefferis, August 20, 1843; Anne Jefferis Sheppard to Rachel Jefferis, March 17, 1863, February 9, 1868. For other Quaker families, see Rachel Biddle to Anne Biddle, July 23, 1854; Sarah Foulke Farquhar [Emlen] Diary, April 30, 1811. February 14, 1812; Fanny Ferris to Mary Canby,

August 31, 1810. This is not to argue that men and women did not mourn together. Yet in many families women aided and comforted women and men, men. The same-sex death ritual was one emotional option available to nineteenth-century Americans.

71. Sarah Foulke [Emlen] Diary, December 29, 1808.

72. Eunice Callender, Boston, to Sarah Ripley [Stearns] Greenfield, Mass., May 24, 1803.

73. Katherine Johnstone Brinley [Wharton] Journal, April 26, May 30, and May 29, 1856, Historical Society of Pennsylvania.

74. A series of roughly fourteen letters written by Peggy Emlen to Sally Logan (1768–71) has been preserved in the Wells Morris Collection, Box 1, Historical Society of Pennsylvania (see esp. May 3 and July 4, 1769, January 8, 1768).

75. The Sarah Alden Ripley Collection, the Arthur M. Schlesinger, Sr., Library, Radcliffe College, contains a number of Sarah Alden Ripley's letters to Mary Emerson. Most of these are undated, but they extend over a number of years and contain letters written both before and after Sarah's marriage. The eulogistic biographical sketch appeared in Wister and Irwin (n. 12 above). It should be noted that Sarah Butler Wister was one of the editors who sensitively selected Sarah's letters.

76. See Sarah Alden Ripley to Mary Emerson, November 19, 1823. Sarah Alden Ripley routinely, and one must assume ritualistically, read Mary Emerson's letters to her infant daughter, Mary. Eleanor Parke Custis Lewis reported doing the same with Elizabeth Bordley Gibson's letters, passim. Eunice Callender, Boston, to Sarah Ripley [Stearns], October 19, 1808.

77. Mary Black Couper to Sophie M. DuPont, March 5, 1832. The Clementina Smith–Sophie DuPont correspondence of 1,678 letters is in the Sophie DuPont Correspondence. The quotation is from Eliza Schlatter, Mount Holly, N.J., to Sophie DuPont, Brandywine, August 24, 1834. I am indebted to Anthony Wallace for informing me about this collection.

78. Mary Grew, Providence, R.I., to Isabel Howland, Sherwood, N.Y., April 27, 1892, Howland Correspondence, Sophia Smith Collection, Smith College.

79. Helena Deutsch, *Psychology of Women* (New York: Grune & Stratton, 1944), vol. 1, chaps. 1–3; Clara Thompson, *On Women,* ed. Maurice Green (New York: New American Library, 1971).

Oral History and the Study of Sexuality in the Lesbian Community: Buffalo, New York, 1940–1960

MADELINE DAVIS AND ELIZABETH LAPOVSKY KENNEDY

We began a study of the history of the Buffalo lesbian community, 1940–1960, to determine that community's contribution to the emergence of the gay liberation movement of the 1960s.[1] Because this community centered around bars and was highly role defined, its members often have been stereotyped as low-life societal discards and pathetic imitators of heterosexuality. We suspected instead that these women were heroines who had shaped the development of gay pride in the twentieth century by forging a culture for survival and resistance under prejudicial conditions and by passing this sense of community on to newcomers; in our minds, these are indications of a movement in its pre-political stages.[2] Our original research plan assumed the conceptual division between the public (social life and politics) and the private (intimate life and sex), which is deeply rooted in modern consciousness and which feminism has only begun to question. Thus we began our study by looking at gay and lesbian bars—the public manifestations of gay life at the time—and relegated sex to a position of less importance, viewing it as only incidentally relevant. As our research progressed we came to question the accuracy of this division. This article records the transformation in our thinking and explores the role of sexuality in the cultural and political development of the Buffalo lesbian community.

At first, our use of the traditional framework that separates the public and private spheres was fruitful.[3] Because the women who patronized the lesbian and gay bars of the past were predominantly working class and left no written records, we chose oral history as our method of study. Through the life stories of over forty narrators, we found that there were more bars in Buffalo during the forties and fifties than there are in that city today. Lesbians living all over the city came to socialize in these bars, which were located primarily in the downtown area. Some of these women were born and raised in Buffalo; others had migrated there in search of their kind. In addition, women from nearby cities, Rochester and Toronto, came to Buffalo bars on weekends. Most of the women who frequented these bars had full-time jobs. Many were factory workers, taxi drivers, bartenders, clerical workers, hospital technicians; a few were teachers or women who owned their own businesses.[4]

Our narrators documented, beyond our greatest expectations, the truth of our original hypothesis that this public bar community was a formative predecessor to the modern gay liberation movement. These bars not only were essential meeting places with distinctive cultures and mores, but they were also the central arena for the lesbian confrontation with a hostile world. Participants in bar life were engaged in constant, often violent, struggle for public space. Their dress code announced them as lesbians to their neighbors, to strangers on the streets, and of course to all who entered the bars. Although confrontation with the straight world was a constant during this period, its nature changed over time. In the forties, women braved ridicule and verbal abuse, but rarely physical conflict. One narrator of the forties conveys the tone: "There was a great difference in looks between a lesbian and her girl. You had to take a streetcar—very few people had cars. And people would stare and such."[5] In the fifties, with the increased visibility of the established gay community, the concomitant postwar rigidification of sex roles, and the political repression

Reprinted from *Feminist Studies* 12, no. 1 (Spring 1986):7–26 by permission of the publisher, Feminist Studies, Inc., c/o Women's Studies Program, University of Maryland, College Park, MD 20742.

of the McCarthy era, the street dyke emerged. She was a full-time "queer," who frequented the bars even on week nights and was ready at any time to fight for her space and dignity. Many of our fifties' narrators were both aware and proud that their fighting contributed to a safer, more comfortable environment for lesbians today.

> Things back then were horrible, and I think that because I fought like a man to survive I made it somehow easier for the kids coming out today. I did all their fighting for them. I'm not a rich person; I don't even have a lot of money; I don't even have a little money. I would have nothing to leave anybody in this world, but I have that that I can leave to the kids who are coming out now, who will come out into the future, that I left them a better place to come out into. And that's all I have to offer, to leave them. But I wouldn't deny it; even though I was getting my brains beaten up I would never stand up and say, "No, don't hit me, I'm not gay, I'm not gay." I wouldn't do that.

When we initially gathered this material on the growth and development of community life, we placed little emphasis on sexuality. In part we were swept away by the excitement of the material on bars, dress, and the creation of public space for lesbians. In addition, we were part of a lesbian feminist movement that opposed a definition of lesbianism based primarily on sex. Moreover, we were influenced by the popular assumption that sexuality is natural and unchanging and the related sexist assumption of women's sexual passivity—both of which imply that sexuality is not a valid subject for historical study. Only recently have historians turned their attention to sexuality, a topic that used to be of interest mainly to psychologists and the medical profession. Feminists have added impetus to this study by suggesting that women can desire and shape sexual experience. Finally, we were inhibited by the widespread social reluctance to converse frankly about sexual matters. Thus for various reasons, all stemming, at least indirectly, from modern society's powerful ideological division between the public and the private, we were indisposed to consider how important sexuality might have been to the women we were studying.

The strength of the oral history method is that it enables narrators to shape their history, even when their views contradict the assumptions of historians. As our work progressed, narrators volunteered information about their sexual and emotional lives, and often a shyly asked question would inspire lengthy, absorbing discourse. By proceeding in the direction in which these women steered us, we came to realize that sexuality and sexual identity were not incidental but were central to their lives and their community. Our narrators taught us that although securing public space was indeed important, it was strongly motivated by the need to provide a setting for the formation of intimate relationships. It is the nature of this community that it created public space for lesbians and gay men, while at the same time it organized sexuality and emotional relationships. Appreciation of this dynamic interconnection requires new ways of thinking about lesbian history.

What is an appropriate framework for studying the sexual component of a lesbian community's history and for revealing the role of sexuality in the evolution of twentieth-century lesbian and gay politics? So little research has been done in this area that our work is still exploratory and tentative. At present, we seek primarily to understand forms of lesbian sexual expression and to identify changes in sexual norms, experiences, and ideas during the 1940s and 1950s. We also look for the forces behind these changes in the evolving culture and politics of the lesbian community. Our goal has been to ascertain what part, if any, sexuality played in the developing politics of gay liberation. As an introduction to this discussion, we shall present our method of research because it has been crucial in our move to study sexuality, and so little has been written on the use of oral history for research on this topic.

USING ORAL HISTORY TO CONSTRUCT THE HISTORY OF THE BUFFALO LESBIAN COMMUNITY

The memories of our narrators are colorful, illuminating, and very moving. Our purpose, however, was not only to collect individual life stories, but also to use these as a basis for constructing the history of the community. To create from individual memories a historically valid analysis of this community presented a difficult challenge. The method we developed was slow and painstaking.[6] We treated each oral history as a historical document, taking into account the particular social position of each narrator and how that might affect her memories. We also considered how our own point of view influenced the kind of information we received and the way in which we interpreted a narrator's story. We juxtaposed all interviews with one another to identify patterns and contradictions and checked our developing understanding with other sources, such as newspaper accounts, legal cases, and labor statistics.

As mentioned earlier, we first focused on understanding and documenting lesbian bar life. From the many vibrant and humorous stories about adventures in bars and from the mountains of seemingly unrelated detail about how people spent their time, we began to identify a chronology of bars and to recognize distinctive social mores and forms of lesbian consciousness that were associated with different time periods and even with different bars. We checked and supplemented our analysis by research into newspaper accounts of bar raids and closings and actions of the State Liquor Authority. Contradictions frequently emerged in our material on bars, but, as we pursued them, we found they were rarely due to idiosyncratic or faulty memory on the part of our narrators but to the complexity of bar life. Often the differences could be resolved by taking into account the different social positions of our narrators or the kinds of questions we had asked to elicit the information we received. If conflicting views persisted, we tried to return to our narrators for clarification. Usually we found that we had misunderstood our narrators or that contradictions indeed existed in the community at the time. For instance, narrators consistently told us about the wonderful times in bars as well as how terrible they were. We came to understand that both of these conditions were part of the real experience of bar life.

When we turned our attention to sexuality and romance in this community, we were at first concerned that our method would not be adequate. Using memories to trace the evolution of sexual norms and expression is, at least superficially, more problematic than using them to document social life in bars. There are no concrete public events or institutions to which the memories can be linked. Thus, when a narrator talks about butch–fem sexuality in the forties, we must bear in mind the likelihood that she has modified her view and her practice of butch–fem sexuality in the fifties, sixties, seventies, and eighties. In contrast, when a narrator tells about bars in the forties, even though

social life in bars might have changed over the last forty years, she can tie her memories to a concrete place like Ralph Martin's bar, which existed during a specific time period. Although not enough is known about historical memory to fully evaluate data derived from either type of narrative, our guess is that, at least for lesbian communities, they are equally valid.[7] The vividness of our narrators' stories suggests that the potential of oral history to generate full and rich documents about women's sexuality might be especially rich in the lesbian community. Perhaps lesbian memories about sexual ideals and experiences are not separated from the rest of life because the building of public communities is closely connected with the pursuit of intimate relationships. In addition, during this period, when gay oppression marked most lesbians' lives with fear of punishment and lack of acceptance, sexuality was one of the few areas in which many lesbians found satisfaction and pleasure. This was reinforced by the fact that, for lesbians, sexuality was not directly linked with the pain and/or danger of women's responsibility for childbearing and women's economic dependence on men. Therefore, memories of sexual experience might be more positive and more easily shared. But these ideas are tentative. An understanding of the nature of memory about sexuality must await further research.

The difficulty of tying memories about sexual or emotional life to public events does present special problems. We cannot identify specific dates for changes in sexual and emotional life, such as when sex became a public topic of conversation or when role-appropriate sex became a community concern. We can talk only of trends within the framework of decades. In addition, we are unable to find supplementary material to verify and spark our narrators' memories. There are no government documents or newspaper reports on lesbian sexuality. The best one can find are memoirs or fiction written about or by residents in other cities, and even these don't exist for participants in working-class communities of the forties.[8] In general, we have not found these problems to require significant revision of our method.

Our experience indicates that the number of people interviewed is critical to the success of our method, whether we are concerned with analyzing the history of bar life or of emotional and sexual life. We feel that between five and ten narrators' stories need to be juxtaposed in order to develop an analysis that is not changed dramatically by each new story. At the present time, our analysis of the white lesbian community of the fifties is based on oral histories from over fifteen narrators. In contrast, we have only five narrators who participated in the white community of the forties, four for the black community of the fifties, and one from the black community of the forties. Therefore, we emphasize the fifties in this article and have the greatest confidence in our analysis of that decade. Our discussion of the forties must be viewed as only tentative. Our material on the black community is not yet sufficient for separate treatment; so black and white narrators' memories are interspersed throughout the article. Ultimately, we hope to be able to write a history of each community.

SEXUALITY AS PART OF THE CULTURAL POLITICAL DEVELOPMENT OF THE BUFFALO LESBIAN COMMUNITY

Three features of lesbian sexuality during the forties and fifties suggest its integral connection with the lesbian community's cultural-political development. First, butch–fem roles created an authentic lesbian sexuality appropriate to the flourishing of an independent lesbian culture. Second, lesbians actively pursued rich and fulfilling sexual lives at a time when sexual subjectivity was not the norm for women. This behavior was not only consistent with the creation of a separate lesbian culture, but it also represented the roots of a personal and political feminism that characterized the gay liberation movement of the sixties. Third, although butch–fem roles and the pursuit of sexual autonomy remained constant throughout this period, sexual mores changed in relation to the evolving forms of resistance to oppression.

Most commentators on lesbian bar life in the forties and fifties have noted the prominence of butch–fem roles.[9] Our research corroborates this; we found that roles constituted a powerful code of behavior that shaped the way individuals handled themselves in daily life, including sexual expression. In addition, roles were the primary organizer for the lesbian stance toward the straight world as well as for building love relationships and for making friends.[10] To understand butch–fem roles in their full complexity is a fundamental issue for students of lesbian history; the particular concern of this article is the intricate connection

between roles and sexuality. Members of the community, when explaining how one recognized a person's role, regularly referred to two underlying determinants: image, including dress and mannerism, and sexuality.[11] Some people went so far as to say that one never really knew a woman's role identity until one went to bed with her. "You can't tell butch–fem by people's dress. You couldn't even really tell in the fifties. I knew women with long hair, fem clothes, and found out they were butches. Actually I even knew one who wore men's clothes, haircuts and ties, who was a fem."

Today, butch–fem roles elicit deep emotional reactions from many heterosexuals and lesbians. The former are affronted by women assuming male prerogatives; the latter by lesbians adopting male-defined role models. The hostility is exemplified by the prevalent ugly stereotype of the butch–fem sexual dyad: the butch with her dildo or penis substitute, trying to imitate a man, and the simpering passive fem who is kept in her place by ignorance. This representation evokes pity for lesbians because women who so interact must certainly be sexually unfulfilled; one partner cannot achieve satisfaction because she lacks the "true" organ of pleasure, and the other is cheated because she is denied the complete experience of the "real thing." Our research counters the view that butch–fem roles are solely an imitation of sexist heterosexual society.

Inherent in butch–fem relationships was the presumption that the butch is the physically active partner and the leader in lovemaking. As one butch narrator explains, "I treat a woman as a woman, down to the basic fact it'd have to be my side doin' most of the doin'." Insofar as the butch was the doer and the fem was the desired one, butch–fem roles did indeed parallel the male/female roles in heterosexuality. Yet unlike the dynamics of many heterosexual relationships, the butch's foremost objective was to give sexual pleasure to a fem; it was in satisfying her fem that the butch received fulfillment. "If I could give her satisfaction to the highest, that's what gave me satisfaction." As for the fem, she not only knew what would give her physical pleasure, but she also knew that she was neither object of nor receptacle for someone else's gratification. The essence of this emotional/sexual dynamic is captured by the ideal of the "stone butch," or untouchable butch, that prevailed during this period. A "stone butch" does all the "doin'" and does not ever allow her lover to reciprocate in kind. To be untouchable meant to gain pleasure from giving pleasure. Thus, although these women did draw on models in heterosexual society, they transformed those models into an authentically lesbian interaction. Through role-playing they developed distinctive and fulfilling expressions of women's sexual love for women.

The archetypal lesbian couple of the 1940s and 1950s, the "stone butch" and the fem, poses one of the most tantalizing puzzles of lesbian history and possibly of the history of sexuality in general.[12] In a culture that viewed women as sexually passive, butches developed a position as sexual aggressor, a major component of which was untouchability. However, the active or "masculine" partner was associated with the giving of sexual pleasure, a service usually assumed to be "feminine." Conversely, the fem, although the more passive partner, demanded and received sexual pleasure and in this sense might be considered the more self-concerned or even more "selfish" partner. These attributes of butch–fem sexual identity remove sexuality from the realm of the "natural," challenging the notion that sexual performance is a function of biology and affirming the view that sexual gratification is socially constructed.

Within this framework of butch–fem roles, individual lesbians actively pursued sexual pleasure. On the one hand, butch–fem roles limited sexual expression by imposing a definite structure. On the other hand, this structure ordered and gave a determinant shape to lesbian desire, which allowed individuals to know and find what they wanted. The restrictions of butch–fem sexuality, as well as the pathways it provided for satisfaction, are best captured and explored by examining what it meant for both butch and fem that the butch was the doer; how much leeway was there before the butch became fem, or the fem became butch?

Although there was complete agreement in the community that the butch was the leader in lovemaking, there was a great deal of controversy over the feasibility or necessity of being a "stone butch." In the forties, most butches lived up to the *ideal* of "the untouchable." One fem, who was in a relationship with an untouchable butch at that time, had tried to challenge her partner's behavior but met only with resistance. Her butch's whole group—those who hung out at Ralph Martin's—were the same. "Because I asked her one time, I said, 'Do you think that you might be just the only one?' 'Oh no,' she said. 'I know I'm not, you know, that I've discussed with . . . different people.' [There were] no exceptions, which I thought was ODD, but, I thought, well, you know. This is how it is."

In the fifties, the "stone butch" became a publicly discussed model for appropriate sexual behavior, and it was a standard that young butches felt they had to achieve to be a "real" or "true" butch. In contrast to the forties, a fifties' fem, who was out in the community, would not have had to ask her butch friend why she was untouchable, and if there were others like her. She would have known it was the expected behavior for butches. Today our narrators disagree over whether it was, in fact, possible to maintain the ideal and they are unclear about the degree of latitude allowed in the forties or fifties before a butch harmed her reputation. Some butches claim that they were absolutely untouchable; that was how they were, and that's how they enjoyed sex. When we confronted one of our narrators, who referred to herself as an "untouchable," with the opinion of another narrator, who maintained that "stone butches" had never really existed, she replied, "No, that's not true. I'm an 'untouchable.' I've tried to have my lover make love to me, but I just couldn't stand it. . . . I really think there's something physical about that." Like many of our butch narrators, this woman has always been spontaneously orgasmic; that is, her excitement level peaks to orgasm while making love to another woman. Another "stone butch" explains: "I wanted to satisfy them [women], and I wanted to make love—I love to make love. I still think that's the greatest thing in life. But I don't want them to touch me. I feel like that spoils the whole thing—I am the way I am. And I figure if a girl is attracted to me, she's attracted to me because of what I am."

Other butches who consider themselves, and have the reputation of being, untouchable claim that it is, as a general matter, impossible to be completely untouchable. One, when asked if she were really untouchable, replied, "Of course not. How would any woman stay with me if I was? It doesn't make any sense. . . . I don't believe there was ever such a class—other than what they told each other." This woman preferred not to be touched, but she did allow mutual lovemaking from time to time during her long-term relationships. A first time in bed, however:

There's no way in hell that you would touch me . . . if you mean untouchable like that. But if I'm living with a woman, I'd have to be a liar if I said that she hadn't touched me. But I can say that I don't care for it to happen. And the only reason it does happen is because she wants it. It's not like something I desire or want. But there's no such thing as an untouchable butch—and I'm the finest in Buffalo and I'm telling you straight—and don't let them jive you around it—no way.

This narrator's distinction between her behavior on a first night and her behavior in long-term relationships appeared to be accepted practice. The fact that some—albeit little—mutuality was allowed over the period of a long relationship did not affect one's reputation as an untouchable butch, nor did it counter the presumption of the butch as the doer.

This standard of untouchability was so powerful in shaping the behavior of fifties' butches that many never experienced their fems making love to them. By the seventies, however, when we began our interviewing, norms had changed enough so that our butch narrators had had opportunities to experience various forms of sexual expression. Still, many of them—in fact all of those quoted above on "stone butches"—remained untouchable. It was their personal style long after community standards changed. Today these women offer explanations for their preference that provide valuable clues about both the personal importance and the social "rightness" of untouchability as a community norm in the forties and fifties. Some women, as indicated in one of the above quotes, continue to view their discomfort with being touched as physical or biological. Others feel that if a fem were allowed the physical liberties usually associated with the butch role, distinctions would blur and the relationship would become confusing. "I feel that if we're in bed and she does the same thing to me that I do her, we're the same thing." Another narrator, reflecting on the fact that she always went to bed with her clothes on, suggests that "what it came to was being uncomfortable with the female body. You didn't want people you were with to realize the likeness between the two." Still other butches are hesitant about the vulnerability implicit in mutual lovemaking. "When the first girl wanted to make a mutual exchange sexually, . . . I didn't want to be in the position of being at somebody's disposal, or at their command that much—maybe that's still inside me. Maybe I never let loose enough."

But many untouchables of the fifties did try mutual lovemaking later on, and it came as a pleasant surprise when they found they enjoyed being touched. "For some reason . . . I used to get enough mental satisfaction by satisfying a woman . . . then it got to the point where this one woman said, 'Well, I'm just not gonna accept that,' and she started venturing, and at first I said, 'No, no,' and then I said, 'Well, why not?' and I got to enjoy it." This change was not easy for a woman who had spent many years as an "untouchable." At first she was very nervous and uncomfortable about mutual sex, but "after I started reaching physical climaxes instead of just mental, it went, that little restlessness about it. It just mellowed me right out, y'know." The social pressure of the times prevented some women from experiencing expanded forms of sexual expression they might have enjoyed, and it also put constraints upon some women who had learned mutual sex outside of a structured community. One of our narrators had begun her sex life with mutual relations and enjoyed it immensely, but in order to conform to the community standard for butches, adopted untouchability as her sexual posture. She acceded to this behavioral change willingly and saw it as a logical component of her role during this period.

How was a community able to monitor the sexual activities of its members, and how might people come to know if a butch "rolled over"—the community lingo for a butch who allowed fems to make love to her? The answer was simple: fems talked! A butch's reputation was based on her performance with fems.

Despite the fact that sexual performance could build or destroy a butch's reputation, some butches of the fifties completely ignored the standard of untouchability. Our narrators give two reasons for this. One reason is the opinion that a long-term relationship requires some degree of mutuality to survive. One butch, a respected leader of the community because of her principles, her affability, and her organizational skills, was not only "touchable" but also suspects that most of the butches she knew in the fifties were not "stone butches." "Once you get in bed or in your bedroom and the lights go out, when you get in between those sheets, I don't think there's any male or there's any female or butch or fem, and it's a fifty–fifty thing. And I think that any relationship . . . any true relationship that's gonna survive has got to be that way. You can't be a giver and can't be a taker. You've gotta both be givers and both gotta be takers." The second reason is the pleasure of being touched. Some women experienced this in the fifties and continued to follow the practice.

When it came to sex [in the fifties] butches were un-touchable, so to speak. They did all the lovemak-ing, but love was not made back to them. And after I found out how different it was, and how great it was, I said, "What was I missing?" I remember a friend of mine, that I had, who dressed like a man all her life . . . and I remember talking to [her] and saying to her, you know you've got to stop being an untouchable butch, and she just couldn't agree. And I remember one time reaching over and pinch-ing her and I said, "Did you feel that?" and she said, "Yes," and I said, "It hurt, didn't it? Well, why aren't you willing to feel something that's good?"

We do not know if in the forties, as in the fifties, butches who preferred a degree of mutuality in love-making existed side by side with the ideal of untouch-ability because we have considerably less information on that decade. Therefore, we cannot judge whether there was in fact a development toward mutual sex-uality, the dominant form of lesbian lovemaking of the sixties and seventies, or whether the "stone butch" prescribed ideal and mutual lovemaking couples ex-isted side by side consistently throughout the forties and fifties.

Our information on fem sexuality is not as exten-sive as that on butch sexuality because we have been able to contact fewer fem narrators. Nevertheless, from the fems we have interviewed and from com-ments by butches who sought them out and loved them, we do have an indication that fems were not passive receivers of pleasure, but for the most part knew what they wanted and pursued it.[13] Many butches attributed their knowledge of sex to fems, who educated them by their sexual responsiveness as well as by their explicit directions in lovemaking.

As implied by our discussion of butch sexuality, many fems had difficulty accepting "untouchability." One fem narrator of the forties had a ten-year relation-ship with an untouchable butch, and the sexual restric-tions were a source of discomfort for her. "It was very one-sided, you know, and . . . you never really got a chance to express your love. And I think this kind of suppressed . . . your feelings, your emotions. And I don't know whether that's healthy. I don't think so." But at the same time the majority of these fems appre-ciated being the center of attention; they derived a strong sense of self-fulfillment from seeking their own satisfaction and giving pleasure—by responding to

their butches. "I've had some that I couldn't touch no parts of their bodies. It was all about me. Course I didn't mind! But every once in a while I felt like, well, hey, let me do something to you. I could NEVER un-derstand that. 'Cause I lived with a girl. I couldn't touch any part of her, no part. But boy, did she make me feel good, so I said . . . All right with me . . . I don't mind laying down."

What emerges from our narrators' words is in fact a range of sexual desires that were built into the frame-work of role-defined sexuality. For butches of the pe-riod, we found those who preferred untouchability; those who learned it and liked it; those who learned it and adjusted to it for a time; those who preferred it, but sensed the need for some mutuality; and those who practiced mutuality regularly. For fems, we found those who accepted pleasure, thereby giving pleasure to their lovers; usually such women would aggres-sively seek what they wanted and instruct their lovers with both verbal and nonverbal cues. Some fems ac-tively sought to make love to their butches and were successful. And finally, we found some women who were not consistent in their roles, changing according to their partners. In the varied sex lives of these role-identified women of the past, we can find the roots of "personal-political" feminism. Women's concern with the ultimate satisfaction of other women is part of a strong sense of female and potentially feminist agency and may be the wellspring for the confidence, the goals, and the needs that shaped the later gay and les-bian feminist movement. Thus, when we develop our understanding of this community as a predecessor to the gay liberation movement, our analysis must in-clude sexuality. For these lesbians actively sought, ex-panded, and shaped their sexual experience, a radical undertaking for women in the 1940s and 1950s.

Although butch–fem roles were the consistent framework for sexual expression, sexual mores changed and developed throughout this period; two contradictory trends emerged. First, the community became more open to the acceptance of new sexual practices, the discussion of sexual matters, and the learning about sex from friends as well as lovers. Sec-ond, the rules of butch–fem sexuality became more rigid, in that community concern for the role-appro-priate behavior increased.

In the forties there were at least two social groups, focused in two prominent bars, Ralph Martin's and Winters. According to our narrators, the sexual mores of these two groups differed: the former group was somewhat conservative; the latter group was more experimental, presaging what were to become the accepted norms of the fifties. The lesbian patrons of Ralph Martin's did not discuss sex openly, and oral sex was disdained. "People didn't talk about sex. There was no intimate conversation. It was kind of hush, hush ... I didn't know there were different ways." By way of contrast, this narrator recalls a visit to Winters, where other women were laughing about "sixty-nine." "I didn't get it. I went to [my partner] and said, 'Somebody says "sixty-nine" and everybody gets hysterical.'" Finally her partner learned what the laughter was all about. At that time our narrator would have mentioned such intimacies only with a lover. It wasn't until later that she got into bull sessions about such topics. Not surprisingly, this narrator does not recall having been taught about sex. She remembers being scared during her first lesbian experience, then found that she knew what to do "naturally." She had no early affairs with partners older than herself.

The Winters' patrons had a more open, experimental attitude toward sex; they discussed it unreservedly and accepted the practice of oral sex. These women threw parties in which women tried threesomes and daisy chains. "People would try it and see how it worked out. But nothing really happened. One person would always get angry and leave, and they would end up with two." Even if their sexual adventures did not always turn out as planned, these women were unquestionably innovative for their time. Our narrator from the Winters' crowd reminisced that it was always a contrast to go home to the serene life of her religious family. She also raved about two fems who were her instructors in sexual matters, adding, "I was an apt pupil."

During the fifties the picture changed, and the mores of the Ralph Martin's group virtually disappeared. Sex came to be a conversation topic among all social groups. Oral sex became an accepted form of lovemaking, so that an individual who did not practice it was acting on personal preference rather than on ignorance or social proscription. In addition, most of our fifties' butch narrators recall having been teachers or students of sex. As in the Winters' group in the forties, an important teacher for the butch was the fem. "I had one girl who had been around who told me. I guess I really frustrated the hell out of her. And she took a piece of paper and drew me a picture and she said, 'Now you get this spot right here.' I felt like a jerk. I was embarrassed that she had to tell me this."

According to our narrator, the lesson helped, and she explains that "I went on to greater and better things."

The fifties also saw the advent of a completely new practice—experienced butches teaching novice butches about sex. One narrator remembers that younger women frequently approached her with questions about sex: "There must be an X on my back. They just pick me out.... " She recalls one young butch who "had to know every single detail. She drove me crazy. Jesus Christ, y'know, just get down there and do it—y'get so aggravated." The woman who aggravated her gives the following account of learning about sex:

> And I finally talked to a butch buddy of mine.... She was a real tough one. I asked her "What do you do when you make love to a woman?" And we sat up for hours and hours at a time.... "I feel sexually aroused by this woman, but if I take her to bed, what am I gonna do?" And she says, "Well, what do you feel like doing?" and I says "Well, the only think I can think of doing is ... all I want to do is touch her, but what is the full thing of it ... you know." So when [she] told me I says, "Really," well there was this one thing in there, uh ... I don't know if you want me to state it. Maybe I can ... well, I won't ... I'll put in terms that you can understand. Amongst other things, the oral gratification. Well, that kind of floored me because I never expected something like that and I thought, well, who knows, I might like it.

She later describes her first sexual experience in which she was so scared that her friend had to shove her into the bedroom where the girl was waiting.

At the same time that attitudes toward discussions of and teachings about sexuality relaxed, the fifties' lesbian community became stricter in enforcing role-appropriate sexuality. Those who deviated from the pattern in the forties might have identified themselves as "lavender butch" and might have been labeled by others as "comme ci, comme ça." Although their divergence from the social norm would have been noticed and discussed, such women were not stigmatized. But the community of the fifties left little room to deviate. Those who did not consistently follow one role in bed were considered "ki-ki" (neither–nor), or more infrequently, "AC/DC," both pejorative terms imposed by the community. Such women were viewed as disruptive of the social order and not to be trusted.

They not only elicited negative comments, but they also were often ostracized from social groups. From the perspective of the 1980s, in which mutuality in lovemaking is emphasized as a positive quality, it is important to clarify that "ki-ki" did not refer to an abandonment of role-defined sex but rather to a shifting of sexual posture depending upon one's bed partner. Therefore, it was grounded absolutely in role playing. One of our narrators in fact defined "ki-ki" as "double role playing."[14]

These contradictory trends in attitudes and norms of lesbian sexuality parallel changes in the heterosexual world. Movement toward open discussion of sex, the acceptance of oral sex, and the teaching about sex took place in the society at large, as exemplified by the publication of and the material contained in the Kinsey reports.[15] Similarly, the lesbian community's stringent enforcement of role-defined behavior in the fifties occurred in the context of straight society's postwar move toward a stricter sexual division of labor and the ideology that accompanied it.[16] These parallels indicate a close connection between the evolution of heterosexual and homosexual cultures, a topic that requires further research.[17] At this point, we wish to stress that drawing parallels with heterosexuality can only partially illuminate changes in lesbian sexual mores. As an integral part of lesbian life, lesbian sexuality undergoes transformations that correspond with changing forms of the community's resistance to oppression.

Two developments occurred in this prepolitical period that are fundamental for the later emergence of the lesbian and gay liberation movement of the sixties. The first development was the flourishing of a lesbian culture; the second was the evolving stance of public defiance. The community of the forties was just beginning to support places for public gatherings and socializing, and during this period lesbians were to be found in bars only on weekends. Narrators of the forties do not remember having role models or anyone willing to instruct them in the ways of gay life. The prevalent feeling was that gay life was hard, and if people wanted it, they had to find it for themselves. In the fifties, the number of lesbian bars increased, and lesbians could be found socializing there every night of the week. As bar culture became more elaborate and open, lesbians more freely exchanged information about all aspects of their social lives, including sexuality. Discussion of sex was one of the many dimensions of an increasingly complex culture. The strengthening of lesbian culture and the concomitant repression of gays in the fifties led the community to take a more public stance. This shift toward public confrontation subsequently generated enough sense of pride to counter the acknowledged detriments of gay life so that members of the community were willing to instruct newcomers both socially and sexually. Almost all our narrators who came out in the fifties remember a butch who served as a role model or remember acting as a role model themselves. Instruction about sexuality was part of a general education to community life that developed in the context of expanding community pride.

However, the community's growing public defiance was also related to its increased concern for enforcing role-appropriate behavior in the fifties. Butches were key in this process of fighting back. The butches alone, or the butch–fem couple, were always publicly visible as they walked down the street, announcing themselves to the world. To deal effectively with the hostility of the straight world, and to support one another in physical confrontations, the community developed, for butches in particular, rules of appropriate behavior and forms of organization and exerted pressure on butches to live up to these standards. Because roles organized intimate life, as well as the community's resistance to oppression, sexual performance was a vital part of these fifties' standards.

From the vantage point of the 1980s and twenty more years of lesbian and gay history, we know that just as evolving community politics created this tension between open discussion and teaching about sex and strict enforcement of role-appropriate sexual behavior, it also effected the resolution. Our research suggests that in the late sixties in Buffalo, with the development of the political activities of gay liberation, explicitly political organizations and tactics replaced butch–fem roles in leading the resistance to gay oppression. Because butch–fem roles were no longer the primary means for organizing the community's stance toward the straight world, the community no longer needed to enforce role-appropriate behavior.[18] This did not mean that butch–fem roles disappeared. As part of a long tradition of creating an authentic lesbian culture in an oppressive society, butch–fem roles remain, for many lesbians, an important code of personal behavior in matters of either appearance, sexuality, or both.

ACKNOWLEDGMENTS

This article is a revision of a paper originally presented at the "International Conference on Women's History and Oral History," Columbia University, New York, 18 November 1983. We want to thank Michael Frisch, Ellen DuBois, and Bobbi Prebis for reading the original version and offering us helpful comments. We also want to thank Rayna Rapp and Ronald Grele for their patience throughout the revision process.

NOTES

1. This research is part of the work of the Buffalo Women's Oral History Project, which was founded in 1978 with three goals: (1) to produce a comprehensive, written history of the lesbian community in Buffalo, New York, using as the major source oral histories of lesbians who came out prior to 1970; (2) to create and index an archive of oral history tapes, written interviews, and relevant supplementary materials; and (3) to give this history back to the community from which it derives. Madeline Davis and Elizabeth (Liz) Kennedy are the directors of the project. Avra Michelson was an active member from 1978 to 1981 and had a very important influence on the development of the project. Wanda Edwards has been an active member of the project since 1981, particularly in regard to research on the black lesbian community and on racism in the white lesbian community.

2. This hypothesis was shaped by our personal contact with Buffalo lesbians who came out in the 1940s and 1950s, and by discussion with grass roots gay and lesbian history projects around the country, in particular, the San Francisco Lesbian and Gay History Project, the Boston Area Gay and Lesbian History Project, and the Lesbian Herstory Archives. Our approach is close to and has been influenced by the social constructionist tendency of lesbian and gay history. See in particular, Jonathan Katz, *Gay American History: Lesbians and Gay Men in the U.S.A.* (New York: Crowell, 1976); Gayle Rubin, Introduction to *A Woman Appeared to Me,* by Renée Vivien (Nevada: Naiad Press, 1976), iii–xxxvii; Jeffrey Weeks, *Coming Out: Homosexual Politics in Britain from the Nineteenth Century to the Present* (London: Quartet Books, 1977). We want to thank all these sources which have been inspirational to our work.

3. The Buffalo Women's Oral History Project has written two papers on bar life, both by Madeline Davis, Elizabeth (Liz) Kennedy, and Avra Michelson: "Buffalo Lesbian Bars in the Fifties," presented at the National Women's Studies Association, Bloomington, Indiana, May 1980, and "Buffalo Lesbian Bars: 1930–1960," presented at the Fifth Berkshire

Conference on the History of Women, Vassar College, Poughkeepsie, N.Y., June 1981. Both papers are on file at the Lesbian Herstory Archives, P. O. Box 1258, New York, New York 10116.

4. We think that this community could accurately be designated as a working-class lesbian community, but this is not a concept many members of this community would use; therefore, we have decided to call it a public bar community.

5. All quotes are taken from the interviews conducted for this project between 1978 and 1984. The use of the phrase "lesbian and her girl" in this quote reflects some of our butch narrators' belief that the butch member of a couple was the lesbian and the fem member's identity was less clear.

6. A variety of sources were helpful for learning about issues and problems of oral history research. They include the Special Issue on Women's Oral History, *Frontiers* 2 (Summer 1977); Willa K. Baum, *Oral History for the Local Historical Society* (Nashville, Tenn.: American Association for State and Local History, 1975); Michael Frisch, "Oral History and *Hard Times:* A Review Essay," *Oral History Review* (1979): 70–80; Ronald Grele, ed., *Envelopes of Sound: Six Practitioners Discuss the Method, Theory, and Practice of Oral History and Oral Tradition* (Chicago: Precedent Publishing, 1975); Ronald Grele, "Can Anyone over Thirty Be Trusted: A Friendly Critique of Oral History," *Oral History Review* (1978): 36–44; "Generations: Women in the South," *Southern Exposure* 4 (Winter 1977); "No More Moanin'," *Southern Exposure* 1 (Winter 1974); Peter Friedlander, *The Emergence of a UAW Local, 1936–1939* (Pittsburgh: University of Pittsburgh Press, 1975); William Lynwood Montell, *The Saga of Coe Ridge: A Study in Oral History* (Knoxville: University of Tennessee Press, 1970); Studs Terkel, *Hard Times: An Oral History of the Great Depression* (New York: Pantheon Books, 1970); Martin B. Duberman, *Black Mountain: An Exploration in Community* (Garden City, N.Y.: Doubleday, 1972); Sherna Gluck, ed., *From Parlor to Prison: Five American Suffragists Talk about Their Lives* (New York:

Vintage, 1976); and Kathy Kahn, *Hillbilly Women* (New York: Doubleday, 1972).

7. For a helpful discussion of memory, see John A. Neuenschwander, "Remembrance of Things Past: Oral Historians and Long-Term Memory," *Oral History Review* (1978): 46–53; Many sources cited in the previous note also have relevant discussions of memory; in particular, see Frisch; Grele, *Envelopes of Sound;* Friedlander; and Montell.

8. See for instance, Joan Nestle, "Esther's Story: 1960," *Common Lives/Lesbian Lives* 1 (Fall 1981): 5–9; Joan Nestle, "Butch–Fem Relationships: Sexual Courage in the 1950s," *Heresies* 12 (1981): 21–24; Audre Lorde, "Tar Beach," *Conditions,* no. 5 (1979): 34–47 and Audre Lorde, "The Beginning," in *Lesbian Fiction,* ed. Elly Bulkin (Watertown, Mass.: Persephone Press, 1981), 225–74. Lesbian pulp fiction can also provide insight into the emotional and sexual life of this period; see, for instance, Ann Bannon's *I Am a Woman* (Greenwich, Conn.: Fawcett, 1959) and *Beebo Brinker* (Greenwich, Conn.: Fawcett, 1962).

9. See, for instance, Nestle, "Butch–Fem Relationships"; Lorde, "Tar Beach"; Del Martin and Phyllis Lyon, *Lesbian/Woman* (New York: Bantam, 1972); John D'Emilio, *Sexual Politics, Sexual Communities: The Making of a Homosexual Minority in the United States 1940-1970* (Chicago: University of Chicago Press, 1983).

10. For a full discussion of our research on butch–fem roles, see Madeline Davis and Elizabeth (Liz) Kennedy, "Butch-Fem Roles in the Buffalo Lesbian Community, 1940–1960" (paper presented at the Gay Academic Union Conference, Chicago, October 1982). This paper is on file at the Lesbian Herstory Archives.

11. These two main determinants of roles are quite different from what would usually be considered as indicators of sex roles in straight society; they do not include the sexual division of labor.

12. The origins of the "stone butch" and fem couple are beyond the scope of this paper. For an article that begins to approach these issues, see Esther Newton, "The Mythic Mannish Lesbian: Radclyffe Hall and the New Woman," *Signs* 9 (Summer 1984): 557–75.

13. Our understanding of the fem role has been enhanced by the following: Nestle's "Butch–Fem Relationships" and

"Esther's Story"; Amber Hollibaugh and Cherrie Moraga, "What We're Rolling Around in Bed With: Sexual Silences in Feminism: A Conversation toward Ending Them," *Heresies* 12 (1981): 58–62.

14. For indications that "ki-ki" was used nationally in the lesbian subculture, see Jonathan Katz, *Gay/Lesbian Almanac: A New Documentary* (New York: Harper & Row, 1983), 15, 626.

15. Alfred C. Kinsey, Wardell B. Pomeroy, and Clyde E. Martin, *Sexual Behavior in the Human Male* (Philadelphia: W. B. Saunders, 1948); and Alfred Kinsey et al., *Sexual Behavior in the Human Female* (Philadelphia: W. B. Saunders, 1953). Numerous sources document this trend; see, for instance, Ann Snitow, Christine Stansell, and Sharon Thompson, eds., *Powers of Desire: The Politics of Sexuality* (New York: Monthly Review Press, 1983), in particular, Introduction, sec. 2, "Sexual Revolutions," and sec. 3, "The Institution of Heterosexuality," 9–47, 115–71, 173–275; and Katz, *Gay/Lesbian Almanac.*

16. See Mary P. Ryan, *Womanhood in America: From Colonial Times to the Present* (New York: Franklin Watts, 1975).

17. A logical result of the social constructionist school of gay history is to consider that heterosexuality is also a social construction. Katz, in *Gay/Lesbian Alamanac,* begins to explore this idea.

18. Although national homophile organizations began in the fifties, no such organizations developed in Buffalo until the formation of the Mattachine Society of the Niagara Frontier in 1969. But we do not think that the lack of early homophile organizations in this city made the bar community's use of roles as an organizer of its stance toward the straight world different from that of cities where homophile organizations existed. In general, these organizations, whether mixed or all women, did not draw from or affect bar communities. Martin and Lyon in chap. 8, "Lesbians United," *Lesbian/Woman* (238–79), present Daughters of Bilitis (DOB) as an alternative for those dissatisfied with bar life, not as an organization to coalesce the forces and strengths of the bar community. Gay liberation combined the political organization of DOB and the defiance and pride of bar life and therefore affected and involved both communities.

Sex, Glorious Sex: The Social Construction of Masculine Sexuality in a Youth Group

JUDITH A. DIIORIO

As individuals living in twentieth-century Western society, we feel that no aspect of our selves is so innate, so private, so personal and natural as our sexual desires, fantasies, and behaviors. True, our sexual behaviors are subject to the set of cultural prescriptions and proscriptions that define "normal" sexuality, but even these sexual codes appear to be a reflection of our underlying natural urges and desires. Indeed, if most of us were asked why we do not engage in sex in public places, we would say it was because such behavior would not feel right or natural, not because there are laws prohibiting it. And most of us define people who fail to follow our sexual norms as "sick" or "unnatural," not as mere nonconformists.

Recently, however, historians, anthropologists, and sociologists researching human sexuality have rejected such biological or naturalistic assumptions, well entrenched though they may be, and are creating an alternative view known as social constructionism. As the name implies, this theoretical perspective maintains that the sexuality of individuals, far from being the outward manifestation of innate biological drives and desires, is the creation of complex social and cultural processes (Gagnon & Simon, 1973; Padgug, 1979; Foucault, 1979; Weeks, 1977, 1981, 1985). Furthermore, as feminist theorists have made clear, in most if not all societies, the processes by which human sexuality is constructed are gender-differentiated and patriarchal. The meanings, moralities, learned behaviors, and acquired desires that comprise the sexualities of women and men are distinct and unequal, typically giving men the license to exploit women while denying women sexual autonomy and in some cases sexual pleasure (Barry, 1979; Rich, 1980; MacKinnon, 1982).

Reprinted by permission of the author.

Social constructionism has sparked much discourse and debate but unfortunately too little research. The social processes that mold the sexuality of individuals remain poorly understood and research has focused almost exclusively on the family context—and, I would add, on women's sexual socialization rather than men's.[1] Questions concerning the relationship between sexuality and masculinity and the sexual socialization process in contexts beyond childhood and the family remain poorly investigated.[2]

The research discussed here was designed to fill in some of these gaps by examining the sexual ideologies and sexual identities collectively created by a group of young working-class males. Although this was a case study and the findings are therefore not generalizable beyond the social boundaries of the particular subculture studied, I nevertheless think the substantive realities and identity-creating processes at work in this group are highly suggestive of the meanings given to masculine sexuality by young males in this society at present and of the ways they socialize each other to be sexual.

THE WORLD OF THE VANNERS

During the 1970s a subculture emerged in the United States and Canada as thousands of people—mostly but not exclusively men—bought automotive vans and made them into the symbol of an alternative lifestyle and values. Vanners and lady vanners,[3] as the members of this subculture called themselves, essentially wanted to have fun, to eschew the ethic of work and soberness they associated with the nonvanning "straight" world, and to seek meaning instead in communal pleasure and leisure. Their vans became homes on wheels, mobility with comfort; they provided them with a ready escape from the responsibilities and pressures of work and family. And they escaped not to be alone but to be with others who had similar needs and sought similar pleasures. The most spectacular collective events of this subculture were "van-ins," regional or national gatherings at which vanners spent two to four days camping, partying, playing games, lying in the sun, getting "messed up" on beer, wine, and dope, listening to rock music, and trying to have sex.

Nomad Vans was one small part of this subculture.[4] The club was organized in August 1978 in a midwestern city by a veteran vanner called Wizard, who had recently come to town. Wizard drove through public parks and other areas where young people hung out, asking anyone he saw in a van if he or she wanted to be part of a club. He eventually succeeded in bringing together seventeen vanners, thirteen "guys" and four "girls." Three of the guys remained fairly marginal members. They paid their dues and attended meetings but seldom participated in other club activities and demonstrated little interest in socializing with the other members. For the remainder of the vanners and lady vanners, however, the club, while it existed, was the focal point of their lives. They spent most of their free time together in parks and parking lots during the warm days, in bars and restaurants during the cold months and at night. To enliven most club activities and events, especially parties, they recruited a fairly constant number of friends and acquaintances.

The vanners and their friends were young both objectively and subjectively. Although their chronological age ranged from 17 to 30, the modal age (accounting for approximately 60 percent of the vanners) was 19, and most of them referred to and thought of themselves as "kids," as belonging to a category of persons not yet adult or fully mature. They were predominantly working-class kids, sons and daughters of truck drivers, utility workers, and factory workers who had decided not to attend college after graduating from high school and were working at low-paying service and blue-collar jobs. The lady vanners were employed at various times as waitresses, cashiers, keypunch operators, and receptionists. The male vanners worked as parts runners for auto dealers, gas station attendents, and orderlies, in warehouses and auto body shops. The highest-paid vanner was Free Bird, whose job as a $6-an-hour meter reader for the local gas company made him the envy of the club. In general, the vanners earned too little to be self-supporting and all

but five still lived with their parents. All struggled to meet their expenses, and for all, the biggest expense was the van itself. Most of what they earned went toward payments on their vans, accessories for the vans, and insurance. As a result, the freedom that their vans supposedly afforded them was purchased at the cost of any possibility of real autonomy. The vans certainly gave them a place away from home and work that they could call their own and use as they wished fairly free of adult supervision or surveillance.[5] The vans provided their owners with physical mobility, the ability to get away for weekend camping trips and van-ins, but they also kept them economically dependent on their menial jobs and their parents, unable to save for college and so to hope for social mobility.

My involvement with Nomad Vans began when the club was formed. Through my acquaintance with Wizard, I was invited to attend the first organizational meeting and several of the early social gatherings. I was not a vanner myself and all I knew or thought I knew about vanners was their public reputation as sexual heathens and potential troublemakers. I was intrigued by them and knew that I wanted to explore in depth the social realities they created and the salience of sex and gender in this youthful world outside of home and work. Therefore, at one of their early meetings I asked for permission to study them and they unanimously consented, making me an honorary member of the club at the same time.

For the next eleven months, from August 1978 until July 1979, when the club formally disbanded, I remained with them as a friend and a researcher. By listening to their talk, observing their activities, and reflecting on my own experiences, I learned all I could about their lives, identities, relationships, and values. I also learned that gender and sexuality were critical dimensions of their lives, identities, and relationships.

THE GLORIFICATION OF SEX

What I want to know is did everybody have a good time, hmmmmm? That's all that matters.

Vandura

Hey, we are here to have fun! That's what this club is all about!

Free Bird

To be a vanner was to be in search of good times. Having fun was what vanning was all about; the pursuit of pleasure through and with other vanners was the primary reason for the club's existence. Of course, what constitutes a good time and sets good times apart from other kinds of times is socially variable, meaning different things in different cultural contexts.

For the vanners, having fun was associated not merely with festive social occasions, such as parties and get-togethers, but with particular behaviors that might be provoked at these gatherings—behaviors that aroused exhilaration and raucous humor among the guys present. The vanners referred to such behaviors as "getting messed up" and "getting rowdy," both of which involved some infraction of the customs and etiquette of polite public discourse. To get messed up was to get drunk or stoned to the point where one presumably lost control over one's actions and would willingly do something silly and mildly deviant, such as "shooting the moon" or dancing wildly, which they would have been too self-conscious to do when they were sober. Getting rowdy was a more collective form of rule-breaking: the group of guys would attempt to disrupt the ongoing order in such public places as bars, restaurants, and streets by making loud noises, yelling at passers-by to smile, sticking popcorn up their noses, and feigning incomprehension at the reactions of strangers. Their rule-breaking activities never resulted in harm to the property or persons of others. The intent was to entertain others, not to offend them, and temporarily to dissolve the social barriers that keep strangers aloof and distant. The guys reveled in the sense of community, however fleeting, that such occasions generated.

Yet in this world of pleasure-seeking, no pleasure could quite compare with the joys of sex. Sex—coitus and the physical intimacies associated with it—was in the vanners' estimation not just a good time, it was the best time. A guy could have fun without it, but if he got it, that was all he needed. Whatever else might be happening, if a guy managed to "make it" or "get it on" with a girl, then it was taken for granted that he had had a great time. So exalted were the pleasures of sex that, although club members were expected to want to be with the club, any opportunity to be with a girl instead was considered a legitimate reason for failure to attend a club function.

One Friday evening when the members had arranged to meet at a bar, Travelin' Man failed to ap-pear. He showed up the next afternoon, though, as the guys were hanging out at a community park, and they immediately demanded an explanation for his absence the previous evening.

WIZARD: Hey, Travelin' Man, where were you last night? I thought you said you were gonna be there.

TRAVELIN' MAN: I . . . w-e-e-ll, I was. But I had a date with Marie and I picked her up and we got as far as the parking lot but we never went inside. She said she didn't want to go in.

WIZARD: Why not?

TRAVELIN' MAN: I don't know.

WIZARD: So whatcha do?

TRAVELIN' MAN: *(laughing)* We just stayed in the parking lot, man!

WIZARD: Well, that's cool. There sure as hell wasn't anything better going on inside.

ZOOKEEPER: Are you kiddin'? There ain't nuthin' better!

WIZARD: No argument there, man!

The vanners glorified sex and they talked and joked about it more than anything else, with the possible exception of their vans. They talked little about work, parents, or family and little about their past or future except insofar as vans and sex were involved in their recent past or immediate future. What they had done, were going to do, or hoped to do to their vans; what girls were sexually desirable, who was interested in whom, and sexual jokes—these were the major themes of all their conversations. And through this talk and joking the male vanners collectively expressed and reinforced their beliefs about the nature of masculinity and sexuality.

MASCULINITY AND HETEROSEXUAL VIRILITY

The vanners believed that to be a male was to want, need, and enjoy sex. They saw sex as a biologically based drive so strong that a man sometimes had no control over it, a drive that increased in force with the time that elapsed since it had last been satisfied. Indeed, they referred to their condition after a period of time without sexual encounters as being "hard up." The term had several interesting connotations but its primary implication was that a guy's need for sexual release was becoming so great that even "dogs" (undesirable, ugly females) were beginning to look good to him. "Great guys" and "nice guys" were guys who could joke about their sexual appetites and tease each other about their sexual exploits or lack thereof.

A real man's sex drive, of course, was directed exclusively toward women. The guys believed that the only natural desires and real pleasures came from sex with girls, and gay men were the targets of derisive jokes and pejorative remarks.

Other than this heterosexual imperative, the vanners recognized few moral limitations on their sexual activities. They believed that a girl should never be forced to have sex; although she might have to be coaxed, persuasion should never extend to physical coercion. And they believed a guy should not lie to a girl about his true feelings. If he did not love her, then he should not tell her he did just to get her to submit to his advances. Otherwise, the vanners believed it was equally legitimate for a guy to engage in casual sex with any number of willing, desirable girls without any emotional involvement (sex as consumption) and to engage in sex solely with one girl as an expression of love (sex as commitment). Which mode of sexual activity a vanner adopted was viewed as a matter of either necessity (he could not find a girlfriend) or personal choice, not as a matter of right versus wrong or good versus bad. One evening, for example, Quickdraw, Travelin' Man, Wizard, Free Bird, Vandura, Zookeeper, and I had gathered at a pizza parlor to have a few beers. At one point Wizard asked the guys if they would like to go to a lake and camp next weekend. Travelin' Man replied that he couldn't because he worked on Saturday and had a date with his girlfriend for Saturday evening. Free Bird cautioned Travelin' Man against being in love: "Love is no good, really. It ties you down and I can't afford it 'cause someone always gets hurt." Free Bird claimed to prefer the freedom to pursue sexual activity with a number of girls, any time he wanted to; a sexual commitment was nothing he wanted to pursue. Several of the other vanners argued that casual sex had costs, too.

WIZARD: I don't agree. Man, there's something really special about being in love. I'm serious. You find yourself a good woman and you've got it made. Sometimes I get so tired of playin' all the little games.

ZOOKEEPER: Yeah, you just want someone who's right there when you need 'em.

WIZARD: And you don't have to worry about what to do and everything. You know what I'm sayin'?

FREE BIRD: I know what you're sayin' but I don't agree. As soon as you say you're in love, it's like you're not supposed to do anything else or even look at anybody else. It drives me crazy.

WIZARD: Well, yeah, there's that part of it, too. Course you can always try to get a little piece on the side. *(laughs)*

So while the vanners did see value in heterosexual relationships based on love and monogamy, those guys who were willing and able to have sex with a wide variety of women suffered no loss of esteem or respect.

Girls were not so fortunate. The vanners' sexual beliefs, like those of so many other social groups and of our society in general, incorporated a double standard. Women or girls were defined as sexual objects (the "it" and "any" of "getting it" and "getting any") and evaluated on the basis of their sexual desirability *to* men and their sexual conduct *with* men. The vanners acknowledged that girls enjoy sex, and they did not hold that girls should abstain from sexual intercourse until marriage. But they saw it as natural and right for girls to want to have sex only as an expression of love and commitment. Girls worthy of respect as "nice girls" or "ladies" were not supposed to engage either in casual sex simply for pleasure or in any actions that might be interpreted as sexually suggestive in public settings or around guys other than their boyfriends. Since getting messed up and getting rowdy frequently involved sexual jokes and actions, this code restricted far more than the girls' sexual behavior: it affected all their behaviors, seriously limiting the kinds of social activities any girl could engage in without fear of jeopardizing her reputation or her heterosexual relationship if she had one.

The sexual double standard therefore ensured that the club activities were fairly well dominated by the guys, but it also contributed to a rather fascinating social irony: for all their talk about being hypersexual males, the sexual activities with which the vanners created and validated such identities remained largely just that—talk.

THE COLLECTIVE COCK

Despite the constant talk about the voraciousness of their sexual appetites and despite their public reputations as sexual heathens, most vanners in fact lived lives of involuntary celibacy. Only four of the vanners had girlfriends during at least some of the period of the club's existence, and the same four were also the ones most likely to have casual sexual encounters either during their committed relationships or following a breakup. The remainder seldom had dates, much less regular coitus on either a casual or a committed basis. How, then, I wondered, were these kids able to validate to themselves and to the world their identities as virile males?

Once I had asked myself this question, many aspects of the vanners' activities and relationships began to make sense, as did the process by which they socialized each other as sexual beings. For these young men, sexuality, supposedly the most private and natural of human properties, was neither. Their sense of themselves as sexual beings rested not on their actual behaviors and accomplishments but on the collective, public expression of their desires and drives. The vanners created their sexual identities through four major devices: the vans, collective fantasies, public celebrations of each other's sexual exploits, and the blaming of women for their apparent failures.

The van was the core symbol of this subculture. It was a material object given symbolic meaning through a vanner's relationship with it. Originally marketed as work-related vehicles designed to haul small cargoes, vans were transformed into leisure- and pleasure-related expressions of their owners' creativity and individuality. The process was referred to as "doing a van," and it was the desire and ability to undertake such a project that distinguished the true vanner from a person who merely owned a van. Individuals who bought vans primarily for work or who purchased vans converted by the auto manufacturers or by other professionals were not real vanners. Real vanners did their vans themselves, and although they might need the assistance of more highly skilled artists or craftsmen for particularly difficult and intricate creations, the ideas and basic work of reconstruction had to be their own. Hence the van became an expression of the self, a symbol of its owner's identity.

Although each van differed in some way from every other, identifiable themes related to the vanners' conceptions of masculinity nonetheless wove their way through the van conversion process. The vans were almost always converted so as to portray a sexually active self. The interiors were designed to be romantic environments conducive to seduction, and were always equipped with materials the guys defined as erotic. At a bare minimum, the interiors always included carpeting on the floor, ceiling, and walls, a stereo system to play the appropriate music, and a double bed with a velour or velveteen spread, all in shades of red, royal blue, or black. If money permitted, the owner would add a sink and refrigerator for food and alcohol. And for the public at large who would never be able to see the inside of the van, many vanners added exterior embellishments that sexualized their vehicles. Those with sufficient funds would have elaborate murals painted on the sides of their vans; a typical mural was a mythological scene depicting a young, tall, very muscular Apollo epitomizing strength, emotional restraint, and virility being clung to by one or more adoring, large-busted, scantily clad Daphnes. Vanners who could not afford a mural had a far cheaper way of publicly portraying their sexual psyches: they affixed bumper stickers with such messages as "If this van's rockin', don't come knockin'" and "Don't laugh, mister, it may be your daughter in here."

The guys reinforced the masculine sexuality symbolized by their vans through a type of talk that Julian Wood (1984:65) refers to as "collective fantasizing"—talk that is only tenuously related to real life. I would add that, like individual fantasies, such talk inspires an emotional or physiological response. Collective fantasies sexually arouse the participants and thereby serve to socialize them as to what is arousing or erotic. Among the vanners, such talk was inspired by some unusually attractive girl, referred to as a "fox," who became the erotic object that fed their desires and libidos. One evening while several of the vanners waited in a shopping-center parking lot for a few others to arrive, a well-dressed, large-breasted young woman with long blond hair drove up, got out of her car, and walked toward one of the stores. Her retreating figure inspired the following exchange:

ZOOKEEPER: Damn, would you look at that!

FREE BIRD: *(looking down at his crotch)* Down, boy, down!

TRAVELIN' MAN: She can't be for real, can she?

WIZARD: *(laughing)* Which one of you little dicks is going to get up the nerve to go talk to her?
FREE BIRD: I will. *(laughing)* Just ten minutes with her. That's all I ask and I'd die a happy man.
ZOOKEEPER: Ten! I'd settle for two!
TRAVELIN' MAN: *(laughing)* Yeah, I'd settle for two!

Every van-in featured as part of an evening's entertainment a contest in which women were paraded up onto a stage and then coaxed into stripping by the overwhelmingly male audience of howling, yelling vanners. Through such emotionally charged episodes of sexual arousal the vanners validated their heterosexuality, taught each other what images of women were erotic ideals, objectified the women involved as things to be consumed, glorified the pleasures of sex with such objects ("ten minutes with that and I'd die a happy man"), and attested to their existence as sexually charged beings. They became a collective cock in a perpetual state of arousal.

In addition to these collective fantasies, the vanners engaged in certain ritualized interactions in which they publicly celebrated even the most minor sexual encounter and in the process typically exaggerated its significance. Vandura brought a date to one party the club was giving, something he had never done before, and as far as anyone knew, this was the first time he had dated the girl. They sat together a long time, she on his lap, kissing or "making out." The other club members made note of the occasion and laughed about it among themselves ("Did you see Vandura? God, the two of them are really goin' at it!") but otherwise left him alone. After a few hours, when the party was at its peak, Vandura and his date left, and everyone assumed they were going off to have sex. The following afternoon, at the club's Sunday meeting, Wizard asked if everyone had had a good time at the party.

FREE BIRD: Well, we all know Vandura did, right, Vandura?
WIZARD: Well, I'm not sure. I'm not sure if he even knew where he was last night.

Vandura then joined in the joke, acting as though he had indeed been oblivious of everything and everyone during the party.

VANDURA: Party? What party?
WIZARD: Why, I'm amazed he can talk after goin' at

it like that. I figured his lips would be all worn out. Hell, I should of poured some beer over 'em to put out the fire.
JAY BIRD: That's OK, Vandura. You just go back to wherever you were, man, and we won't bother you again.

In this way the vanners not only made public reference to Vandura's activities of the previous evening but exalted what had occurred as an experience that could make a man forget everything and everyone else.

Several outsiders came to another party the club gave, strangers to all but two of the club members. Free Bird spent an hour talking exclusively to one of the strangers, a girl named Terry, and left with her before the party was over. Again everyone assumed they had gone off to have sex, and the next afternoon Free Bird was kidded about it.

JAY BIRD: Hey, Free Bird, where'd ya go last night, man?
FREE BIRD: Say what?
JAY BIRD: Where'd ya go last night when you left the party?
FREE BIRD: Oh, Terry wanted to see my van so I showed it to her.
WIZARD: Did she like it?
FREE BIRD: I guess so. She seemed to. Anyway, I sure as hell liked showing it to her.
ZOOKEEPER: Shit, how come nobody ever wants to see my van?
WIZARD: Probably cause it's too small for 'em to get into. *(giggles)*

In this brief interaction, "showing the van" became a metaphor for having sexual intercourse—indeed, as Wizard's joking disparagement of Zookeeper indicates, a virtual symbol of the penis. It also represented a rather typical event in which the sexual accomplishment of one of the vanners was publicly attested to and celebrated.

Another ritual through which the vanners collectively celebrated sexual occasions was a ritualized practical joke known as "van-rocking." Within the vanning subculture, a rocking van—a van moving from side to side on its axle—was a metaphor for sexual intercourse (recall the bumper sticker: "When this van's rockin', don't come knockin'"). Furthermore, given the importance the vanners attached to sexual activity and their view of women as objects that existed primarily for men's sexual pleasure, whenever a vanner was alone with a girl in his van he was assumed to be having, about to have, or trying to have sex with her. In many such instances, guys not themselves preoccupied by something or someone else would deliberately rock the target's van from side to side, ostensibly to interrupt or foil his attempted conquest. One or more of the vanners would get on one side of the van, grab it underneath the lower edge of the chassis, and pull up a few times, causing the van to rock vigorously from side to side. They would continue the rocking until the target cursed at them from his window or door.

While the overt and immediate effect of this act was to disrupt the vanner's sexual activity, its symbolic significance was more complex. The vanner who was the brunt of this practical joke was never really angry, nor was he expected to be. Furthermore, I never witnessed a van-rocking when the vanner was with a girl for the first time or when it could have interfered with what was perhaps a delicate situation. In any case, if a guy was really concerned that the other guys might interrupt his sexual activities, it was a simple matter for him to drive the van away somewhere. For both the target and the perpetrators, the van-rocking was experienced as fun, as a means of collectively celebrating the otherwise private pleasure of sexual intercourse. The van-rocking was a mock disruption that called attention to the sexual accomplishments of the vanner and represented a public validation of his sexualized self, whether or not sexual activity had actually been taking place. Through it the vanners attested to each other's heterosexuality and masculinity.

EXPLAINING FAILURES/BLAMING WOMEN

Despite the public and playful ways the guys in the club mutually supported and validated their masculine sexuality, laying claim to a potency and promiscuity seldom tested by real sexual encounters, they did recognize certain threats to their identities and self-esteem. These were events involving some type of rejection of them by a girl in whom they were interested: asking a girl for a date and being refused; having several dates with a girl who would never "put out" sexually; wanting a sexual commitment from a girl who refused to give it.

The vanners had two major ways of minimizing the costs to the self, the possible nicks in their masculine armor, that such situations threatened to inflict. One way was simply to avoid talking about them. This group of friends—these guys who would talk with such frankness and frequency about their overactive libidos and the girls who inspired them—seldom talked about the actual sexual events or experiences of their lives. Sexual talk that was public was impersonal—separated, distanced from the realities of their existence. Intimate talk may have occurred more privately, between guys who were particularly close, but I was not privy to such conversations. I do know that I never observed an occasion when any vanner initiated a conversation about another vanner's love life in such a way as to probe for actual details, to ridicule him, or to elicit public confession of failure. What a vanner actually did or did not do on a date, whom he had asked for a date and been rejected by, why he stopped seeing a girl he had been dating—such topics were off limits unless the guy involved brought them up. It was as if they had an unspoken or informal agreement that there were too many glass houses to risk throwing stones, no matter how innocently or unintentionally.

When a guy had been in some way rejected by a girl and did talk about it, he could employ a second strategy for saving face: blaming the girl. The responsibility for the failure lay not with any inadequacies of his but with her character flaws. The girl was a "bitch," a "tease," or a "slut."

The label that had the broadest, most variable application was "bitch," but judging from the numerous occasions on which it was used, a "bitch" was any girl who hurt a guy, acted aloof or disinterested, or overtly rejected an overture made to her. One evening when the club members had gathered at a park and were sitting around watching people drive by, Travelin' Man came by and told us he had just come from a bar where he had seen Lisa, a girl in whom Quickdraw had at one time expressed some interest:

VANDURA: Who's that?
TRAVELIN' MAN: You know. That's the girl that drives the blue Camaro with the white interior.
JAY BIRD: The one with the long blond hair and the big . . . *(cups his hand to signify large breasts)*
QUICKDRAW: Yeah, she's a bitch.
ME: Why? What's wrong with her?
QUICKDRAW: She thinks she's hot shit.

JAY BIRD: I'll say.

ME: What do you mean?

QUICKDRAW: Oh, she just thinks she's the best thing walkin'. That every guy who sees her wants to get into her pants.

JAY BIRD: Which they do.

QUICKDRAW: And that she's too good for any of 'em.

Lisa became a bitch because she interpreted interactions initiated with her as sexual overtures and rejected them on that basis.

The meaning of "tease" was more precise: a tease was any girl who accepted a date with a guy or an offer to see his van and then refused to have sex. A slut was a girl who was perfectly willing to accept a date and have sex with a vanner but was unwilling to commit herself to him, insisting on retaining the freedom to flirt with or have sex with other guys. Armed with this artillery of misogynistic labels, a vanner had the means to avoid responsibility for a rejection and to shift the blame to the girl. Should he be interested in her and she not in him, she was a bitch. Should he get a date with her and have a nice time and spend a lot of money and get no sex in return, she was a tease. And should he fall for a girl who refused to make a commitment to be monogamous, she became a slut. I cannot be sure whether the other vanners privately agreed with such attacks on a girl's character, but I know of no occasion when a vanner publicly disagreed with the denigration of a girl—even a lady vanner— by a guy. The other vanners were, indeed, quite likely to commiserate with him or even on occasion to initiate an attack on his behalf. When Jay Bird first began to associate with Nomad Vans, for instance, he had a girlfriend named Heidi. They split up shortly after he joined the club, but Heidi continued to participate in club activities. Although Jay Bird continued to speak well of Heidi when he spoke of her at all, it was commonly believed that she had hurt him by initiating the split, and in numerous conversations when Jay Bird was not present she became "the bitch" or "Hairy Heidi."

THE SOCIAL CONSTRUCTION OF SEXUALITY

"Sexuality," writes Jeffrey Weeks (1985:3), "is as much about words, images, rituals and fantasy as it is about the body; the way we think about sex fashions the way we live it." And the way we think about sex is fashioned by the definitions, categories, and meanings transmitted to us by family, church, peers, and the media. As the behavior of the vanners shows, sexuality, far from being a private, natural manifestation of an innate biological drive, was for this group of males a socially constructed and publicly expressed part of their identities. Through their vans, jokes, talk, play, and fantasies they socialized each other into a view of sexuality and gender that glorified sexual intercourse as the most pleasurable of acts, defined men as hypersexual actors, reserved for males the right to seek sexual pleasure for its own sake, reduced women to sexual objects to be consumed symbolically if not in reality for men's pleasure, eroticized certain images of the female body, and imposed on women who were worthy of men's respect the innate desire to confine their sexual activities to relationships based on love.

While the presentation of a hyper-heterosexual self was a vital dimension of the vanner's definition of masculinity, he achieved this self only symbolically. Acceptance as a real guy or nice guy did not require that one actually have sexual intercourse with any frequency or regularity; it depended simply on acting as if one wanted it, needed it, and was seeking it with the appropriate objects.

The lady vanners generally accepted the double standard of sexuality as legitimate and right. Together with the heterosexual imperative of this subculture, the double standard helps to account for the ironic disparity between the vanners' expressed desires and their actual accomplishments. If the guys were ever to achieve the sexual experience and have the sexual pleasures they glorified, they would have to live in a world where women had the same sexual freedom as men and/or where men were free to have sex with each other. Neither of these freedoms did they see as natural or right. The sexual restrictions imposed on women as the price of respect and value established an inherent sex-based conflict of interests and lent to heterosexual encounters and relationships an air of contest, competition, manipulation, and distrust. The guys retained social superiority, but for most of them the price they paid was the forfeiture of the sexual relationships—casual or love-based—that they so highly valued. Their virility and potency became a facade, a mask/ulinity.

NOTES

1. Among the numerous anthologies devoted to exploration of female sexuality from a sociological, if not explicitly social constructionist, perspective are those edited by Carol Smart and Garry Smart (1978), Catharine R. Stimpson and Ethel Spector Person (1980). Researchers investigating male sexuality have been concerned primarily with the social construction of male homosexuality; they include Jeffrey Weeks (1977) and Barry M. Dank (1978).

2. One significant exception is a study by Barrie Thorne and Zella Luria (1986), examining sex and gender in the social worlds of nine-year-olds.

3. In keeping with the linguistic practices of the vanners, I will refer to male vanners simply as "vanners" or "guys" and to female vanners as "lady vanners" or "girls." Needless to say, the use of the modifier "lady" in reference to female vanners symbolizes their secondary or auxiliary status in this subculture and suggests the behaviors expected of them.

4. The name of the club and the names of individual vanners are pseudonyms. The former was a club name proposed but rejected by the members at their initial meeting. The latter were the members' "handles"—names chosen for use on the citizen-band radios with which all of the vans were equipped.

5. The vanners did feel vulnerable to surveillance by the police and were constantly on the lookout for them.

REFERENCES

Barry, K. 1979. *Female sexual slavery.* New York: New York University Press.

Dank, B. M. 1978. "Social construction and deconstruction of the homosexual." Paper presented at the annual meeting of the Society for the Study of Social Problems, San Francisco.

Foucault, M. 1979. *The history of sexuality.* Vol. 1: *An introduction.* London: Allen Lane.

Gagnon, J. H., & Simon, W. 1973. *Sexual conduct.* Chicago: Aldine.

MacKinnon, C. 1982. "Feminism, marxism, method, and the state: An agenda for theory." *Signs* 7:515–44.

Padgug, R. 1979. "Sexual matters: On conceptualizing sexuality in history." *Radical History Review* 20:3–23.

Rich, A. 1980. "Compulsory heterosexuality and lesbian existence." *Signs* 5:62–91 (reading 14 in this volume).

Smart, C., & Smart, B., eds. 1978. *Women: Sex and sexuality.* Chicago: University of Chicago Press.

Stimpson, C. R., & Person, E. S., eds. 1980. *Women, sexuality, and social control.* London: Routledge & Kegan Paul.

Thorne, B., & Luria, Z. 1986. "Sexuality and gender in children's daily worlds." *Social Problems* 33:176–90.

Weeks, J. 1977. *Coming out: Homosexual politics in Britain from the nineteenth century to the present.* London: Quartet Books.

Weeks, J. 1981. *Sex, politics and society: The regulation of sexuality since 1800.* London: Longmans.

Weeks, J. 1985. *Sexuality and its discontents: Meanings, myths, and modern sexualities.* London: Routledge & Kegan Paul.

Wood, J. 1984. "Groping towards sexism: Boys' sex talk." In A. McRobbie & M. Niva, eds., *Gender and generation,* pp. 54–84. London: Macmillan.

Men, Inexpressiveness, and Power

JACK W. SATTEL

Another thing I learned—if you cry, the audience won't. A man can cry for his horse, for his dog, for another man, but he cannot cry for a woman. A strange thing. He can cry at the death of a friend or a pet. But where he's supposed to be boss, with his child or wife, something like that, he better hold 'em back and let them cry.

—*John Wayne,*
in one of his last interviews

Much of the recent commentary on men and sex roles in this society has focused on the inability of males to show affection, tenderness or vulnerability in their dealings with both other men and women. John Wayne may be dead but the masculine style stressing silent strength and the masking of emotions is still very much alive. What are the origins and dynamics of such "male inexpressiveness"? How do the strictures against masculine self-disclosure connect to the other roles men and women play in this society?

In their initial thinking about American sex-roles, sociologists didn't question the social processes which gave rise to the expectations that men would be relatively unemotional and constrained in the amount of intimacy they displayed and expected from others. For example, in an influential early theoretical statement, Talcott Parsons (1951) assumed the existence of a sexual division of labor in this society whereby men largely do the work of the public sphere (the economy) and women perform the socio-emotional work of the private sphere (the family). Parsons fastened on the

Reprinted, with changes, from Jack W. Sattel, "The Inexpressive Male: Tragedy or Sexual Politics?" *Social Problems* 23, no. 4 (April 1976): 469–77, by permission of the publisher and the author. Copyright© 1976 by the Society for the Study of Social Problems.

fact that the economy demands that action be based upon deliberative, calculated premises which are as free as possible from "contaminating" personal or emotional considerations. Simultaneously, in Parsons' theory, the family—women's specialized domain—serves as respite and haven from the harsh coldness of the economy. For Parsons, learning experiences which shaped men into inexpressive ways of relating to others, while reserving for women nurturant and expressive modes of relating, serve nicely to reproduce and perpetuate American institutions.

Only relatively recently, spurred by the insights of the women's and gay people's movements for change in American institutions, have sociologists begun to rethink the neat link Parsons postulated between what men (and women) are and do in this society. Unfortunately, much of the analysis thus far has focused so narrowly on inexpressiveness as a personality trait of men that one is left with the impression the problem's solution lies with merely re-educating individual adult men toward their (human) capacity to feel deeply or authentically. In this essay I want to criticize such analyses as fundamentally shallow—the problem, I want to argue, lies not in men's inexpressiveness *per se,* but in the power and investment men hold *as a group* in the existing institutional and social framework. I am not denying the fact of male inexpressiveness; neither would I deny the destructive consequences inexpressiveness has for individual men and for the tenor of their social relationships (Balswick & Peek, 1971; Jourard, 1971; Farrell, 1974). However, I would deny or certainly argue against an interpretation which fails to connect inexpressiveness to the social and sexual division of labor.

A 1971 article, "The Inexpressive Male: A Tragedy of American Society," typifies a line of argument which has become widespread. The authors, Balswick and Peek, conceptualize male inexpressiveness as a culturally produced personality trait which is simply learned by boys as the major characteristic of their anticipated adult masculinity. Such inexpressiveness is evidenced in two ways: first, in adult male behavior which does not indicate affection, tenderness, or emotion, and second, in men's tendency not to support the affective expectations of others, especially their wives. Balswick and Peek imply that both boys and men *devalue* expressive behavior in others as non-masculine; the taunts and "put-downs" of expressive or sensitive adolescents are a ready example of how such devaluation enforces a masculine style among men. For Balswick and Peek, the "tragedy" of inexpressiveness lies in the inability of the American male to relate effectively to women in the context of the increasingly intimate American style of marriage; that is, the victim of this tragedy is the American male and the traditional American family.

I think this conceptualization of inexpressiveness has two important weaknesses. First, Balswick and Peek assume that inexpressiveness originates in and is the simple result of two parallel and basically equal sex-role stereotypes into which male and female children are differentially socialized:

Children, from the time they are born, both explicitly and implicitly are taught how to be a man or how to be a woman. While the girl is taught to act "feminine", . . . the boy is taught to be a man. In learning to be a man, the boy in American society comes to value expressions of masculinity . . . [such as] toughness, competitiveness, and aggressiveness. [Balswick & Peek, 1971, pp. 353–54]

Such an attempt to ground inexpressiveness in socialization overlooks the fact that masculinity is not the opposite of femininity. The starting point for understanding masculinity lies not in its contrast with femininity but in the asymmetrical dominance and prestige which accrue to males in this society. Male dominance takes shape in the positions of formal and informal *power* men hold in the social division of labor; greater male prestige includes and is evidenced by the greater *reward* which attaches to male than to female activities, as well as the codification of differential prestige in our language and customs (cf. Henley, 1977). What our culture embodies, in other words, is not simply two stereotypes—one masculine, one feminine—but a set of power and prestige arrange-

ments attached to gender. That is what is meant when we talk of this society as being "sexist."

My argument is that one reason little boys become inexpressive is not simply because our culture expects boys to be that way—but because our culture expects little boys to grow up to hold positions of power and prestige. What better way is there to exercise power than *to make it* appear—to dissemble a style—in which *all* one's behavior seems to be the result of unemotional rationality. Being impersonal and inexpressive lends to one's decisions and position an apparent autonomy and "rightness." This is a style we quickly recognize in the recent history of American politics: Nixon guarded the assault to his position by "stonewalling" it; Gerald Ford asked us to "hang tough and bite the bullet"; while Edmund Muskie was perceived as unfit for the presidency because he cried in public.[1]

Keeping cool, keeping distant as others challenge you or make demands upon you is a strategy for keeping the upper hand. This same norm of political office—an image of strength and fitness to rule conveyed through inexpressiveness—is not limited to the public sphere; all men in this culture have recourse to this stye by virtue of their gender. The structural link usually overlooked in discussions of male inexpressiveness is between gender and *power* rather than gender and inexpressiveness.

There is a second problem with the way Balswick and Peek conceptualize male inexpressiveness. They regard inexpressiveness as the source of communicative barriers between men and women. Balswick has particularly focused on this as *the* problem in contemporary marriages: "men who care, often very deeply, for their wives . . . cannot communicate what is really going on in their hearts" (Balswick, 1979). Perhaps, but one of the repeated insights of my students—particularly older women students—is that male inexpressiveness in interpersonal situations has been *used against women* in a fashion Balswick's description fails to capture. Let me share a page of dialogue from Erica Jong's sketch of upper-middle-class sexual etiquette, *Fear of Flying,* to suggest the use of male inexpressiveness to control a situation. The scene is the couple's honeymoon, just after they have returned from a movie:

She: "Why do you always have to do this to me? You make me feel so lonely."
He: "That comes from you."

"What do you mean it comes from me? Tonight I wanted to be happy. It's Christmas Eve. Why do you turn on me? What did I do?"

Silence.

"What did I do?"

He looks at her as if her not knowing were another injury.

"Look, let's just go to sleep now. Let's just forget it."

"Forget what?"

He says nothing.

"Forget the fact that you turned on me? Forget the fact that you're punishing me for nothing? Forget the fact that I'm lonely and cold, that it's Christmas Eve and again you've ruined it for me? Is that what you want me to forget?"

"I won't discuss it."

"Discuss what? What won't you discuss?"

"Shut up! I won't have you screaming in the hotel."

"I don't give a fuck what you won't have me do. I'd like to be treated civilly. I'd like you to at least do me the courtesy of telling me why you're in such a funk. And don't look at me that way . . . "

"What way?"

"As if my not being able to read your mind were my greatest sin. I can't read your mind. I *don't* know why you're so mad. I can't intuit your every wish. If that's what you want in a wife you don't have it in me."

"I certainly don't."

"Then what is it? Please tell me."

"I shouldn't have to."

"Good God! Do you mean to tell me I'm expected to be a mind reader? Is that the kind of mothering you want?"

"If you had any empathy for me . . . "

"But I *do.* My God, you don't give me a chance."

"You tune me out. You don't listen."

"It was something in the movie, wasn't it?"

"What, in the movie?"

"The quiz again. Do you have to quiz me like some kind of criminal? Do you have to cross-examine me? . . . It was the funeral scene . . . The little boy looking at his dead mother. Something got you there. That was when you got depressed."

Silence.

"Well, wasn't it? Oh, come on, Bennett, you're making me *furious.* Please tell me. Please."

(He gives the words singly like little gifts. Like hard little turds.) "What was it about that scene that got me?"

"Don't quiz me. Tell me!" (She puts her arms around him. He pulls away—she falls to the floor holding onto his pajama leg. It looks less like an embrace than a rescue scene, she's sinking, he reluctantly allowing her to cling to his leg for support.)

"Get up!"

(Crying) "Only if you tell me."

(He jerks his leg away.) "I'm going to bed."

[Jong, 1973:108–9]

The dialogue clearly indicates that inexpressiveness on the part of the male is *not* just a matter of inarticulateness or even a deeply socialized inability to respond to the needs of others—the male here is *using* inexpression to guard his own position. To not say anything in this situation is to say something very important indeed; that the battle we are engaged in is to be *fought* by my rules and when I choose to fight. Inexpressiveness signals the limits of the discussion and the tactical alignments of the participants.[2] In general, male inexpressiveness emerges as an intentional manipulation of a situation when threats to the male position occur.

I would extend this point to include the expressive quality of men's interaction with other men. In a perceptive article, "Why Men Aren't Talking," Fasteau (in Pleck & Sawyer, 1974) observes that when men talk, they almost inevitably talk of large problems—politics or art; cars or fishing—but never of anything personal. Even among equal-status peers, men seldom make themselves vulnerable to each other, for to do so may be interpreted as a sign of weakness, an opportunity for the other to secure advantage. As Fasteau puts it: men talk, but they always need a reason—and that reason often amounts to another effort at establishing who *really* is best, stronger, smarter, or ultimately more powerful.

Those priorities run deep and are established early. In Pleck & Sawyer's (1974) collection on masculinity, there is a section dealing with men and sports. Sport activity is important because it is often held out as one area of both authentic and expressive interaction among men. I wonder. Here is an adult male reminiscing about his fourteenth year:

I take off at full speed not knowing whether I would reach it but knowing very clearly that this is my chance. My cap flies off my head . . . and a second later I one-hand it as cool as can be . . . I hear the applause . . . I hear voices congratulating my mother for having such a good athlete for a son . . . Everybody on the team pounds my back as they come in from the field, letting me know that I've MADE IT. [Candell in Pleck & Sawyer, 1974:16]

This is a good picture of boys being drawn together in sport, of sharing almost total experience. But is it? The same person continues in the next paragraph:

> But I know enough not to blow my cool so all I do is mumble thanks under a slightly trembling upper lip which is fighting the rest of my face, the rest of my being, from exploding with laughter and tears of joy. [Candell in Pleck & Sawyer, 1974:16]

Why this silence? Again, I don't think it is just because our culture demands inexpression; silence and inexpression are the ways men learn to consolidate power, to make the effort appear as effortless, to guard against showing the real limits on one's potential and power by making it all seem easy. Even among males, one maintains control over a situation by revealing only strategic proportions of oneself.

Much of what is called "men's liberation" takes as its task the "rescuing" of expressive capacity for men, restoring to men their emotional wholeness and authenticity. To the extent such changes do not simultaneously confront the issue of power and inexpressiveness, I see such changes as a continuation rather than a repudiation of sexism. Again, let me offer a literary example. In Alan Lelchuk's (1974) novel about academic life in Cambridge, *American Mischief,* there is a male character who has gleaned something from the women's movement. The "John Wayne" equivalent of the academic male may be passé, but if one is still concerned with "scoring" sexually with as many women as possible—which this character is—male expressiveness is a good way of coming on. Lelchuk's character, in fact, tells women fifteen minutes after he meets them that he is sexually impotent, but with the clear insinuation that "maybe with you it would be different . . . " In this situation the man's skill at dissembling has less to do with handing a woman a "line" than in displaying his weakness or confidences as signs of authentic, nonexploitative male interest. Again, in a society as thoroughly sexist as ours, men may use

expressiveness to continue to control a situation and to maintain their position of dominance.

I've tried to raise these points in my discussion thus far: that inexpressiveness is related to men's position of dominance, that inexpressiveness works as a method for achieving control both in male–female and in male–male interaction; and that male *expressiveness* in the context of this society might also be used as a strategy to maintain power rather than to move toward non-sexist equality. I think my last point is most important. In 1979 Balswick wrote an article based on the conceptualization of inexpressiveness which I've criticized here. Entitled "How to Get Your Husband to Say 'I Love You,'" the article was published in *Family Circle,* a mass-distribution women's magazine. Predictably, the article suggests *to the wife* some techniques she might develop for drawing her husband out of his inexpressive shell. I think that kind of article—at this point in the struggle of women to define themselves—is facile and wrong-headed. Such advice burdens the wife with additional "emotional work" while simultaneously creating a new arena in which she can—and most likely will—fail.

Sexism is not significantly challenged by simply changing men's capacity to feel or express themselves. Gender relationships in this society are constructed in terms of social power and to forget that fact, as Andrew Tolson's book *The Limits of Masculinity* (1977) so nicely points out, is to assume that men can somehow unproblematically experience "men's liberation"—as if there existed for men some directly analogous experience to the politics created by feminist and gay struggles. Men are not oppressed *as men,* and hence not in a position to be liberated *as men.* This dilemma has prevented—thus far—the creation of a theory (and a language) of liberation which speaks specifically to men. Everyday language, with its false dichotomies of masculinity–feminity/male–female, obscures the bonds of dominance of men over women; feminist theory illuminates those bonds and the experience of women within patriarchy but has little need to comprehend the experience of being male. In the absence of such formulations, masculinity seems often to be a mere negative quality, oppressive in its exercise to both women and men, indistinguishable from oppression *per se.* What would a theory look like which accounts for the many forms being a man can take? An answer to that question poses not a "tragedy" but an opportunity.

NOTES

1. This link is reflected in the peculiarly asymmetrical rules of socialization in our society which make it more "dangerous" for a boy than for a girl to be incompletely socialized to gender expectations (compare the greater stigma which attaches to the label "sissy" than to "tomboy"). The connection of gender to power is also apparent in data which suggest parents, as well as other adults in the child's world, exert greater social control over boys to "grow up male" than girls to "grow up female" (Parsons & Bales, 1955).

2. It would be beside the point to argue that women sometimes will also use inexpressiveness in this manner; when they do so, they are by definition acting "unwomanly." A man acting in this fashion is *within* the culturally acceptable framework.

REFERENCES

Balswick, J. 1979. "How to get your husband to say 'I love you.'" *Family Circle.* August.

Balswick, J., & Peek, C. 1971. "The inexpressive male: A tragedy of American society." *Family Coordinator* 20:363–68.

Farrell, W. 1974. *The liberated man.* New York: Random House.

Henley, N. 1977. *Body politics.* Englewood Cliffs, N.J.: Prentice-Hall.

Jong, E. 1973. *Fear of flying.* New York: New American Library.

Jourard, S. M. 1971. *Self-disclosure.* New York: Wiley-Interscience.

Lelchuk, A. 1974. *American mischief.* New York: New American Library.

Parsons, T. 1951. *The social system,* chaps. 6–7. Glencoe, Ill.: Free Press.

Parsons, T., & Bales, R. 1955. "The American family: Its relation to personality and the social structure." In *Family socialization and interaction process.* Glencoe, Ill.: Free Press.

Pleck, J., & Sawyer, J. 1974. *Men and masculinity.* Englewood Cliffs, N.J.: Prentice-Hall.

Tolson, A. 1977. *The limits of masculinity.* New York: Harper & Row.

R E A D I N G   2 9

The Male Sex Drive

CLYDE W. FRANKLIN II

In the movie *48 Hours,* Eddie Murphy plays a convict who is obsessed with "getting some." He and his co-star, Nick Nolte, depict men as having a "wham-bam-thank-you-ma'am" sex drive, a kind of inborn impulse

Reprinted by permission from Clyde W. Franklin, *The Changing Definition of Masculinity* (New York: Plenum Press, 1984).

to conquer that requires only minimal involvement with a woman in order to score the goal of another ejaculation in another vagina. That's an image of male sexuality that many woman *and* men find insulting. But unfortunately, it's not a distorted picture; it looks a lot like the sexual attitudes and behaviors many men in this country actually act out.

Why are men driven by sex? Men themselves believe the popular notion that the male sex drive is absolutely overwhelming—whether or not they're feeling especially horny at the time. Male sexuality is very complex—and it causes a lot of confusion and misunderstanding in relationships. Individual men vary enormously in their sexual responses, attitudes and relationships, but both men and women tend to share set ideas about "how men are supposed to act sexually." Yet rarely do either men or women really examine what this so-called male sex drive is all about.

Men grow up believing in an ideal of masculinity—a model for male attitudes and behaviors—that sociologists call the male sex role. According to the male sex role in America, it is *normal* to become a conquerer, a subduer, a forcer in sex. This male sex role prepares men psychologically to be dominant over women and other men. And this idea of the male sex role also comes coupled with an idea of the normal *female* sex role: to be a submissive and passive receptor.

Male sexuality is much more than any particular act of sex or any particular fact of anatomy; it's a whole complex of emotional, mental, behavioral and physical components that interact, become defined and are experienced by men as sexual events. And there's a growing body of research to suggest that almost all sexual attitudes and behaviors come more from social and cultural conditions than from inborn tendencies. So-called male sexuality is something boys and men *learn,* not something they're born with.

The sexuality of Black men in America is also burdened with a history of being envied, feared and hated. As a result, the sex role that Black men must learn has distinctive characteristics.

MEN AND SEX

To understand the male sex drive, it's important to understand a key aspect of masculinity in this society: the sexualization of men's relationships with others. Not only are men's relationships with *women* sexualized, but their relationships—or lack of relationships—with *other men* are also sexualized. How a man relates sexually with women is profoundly influenced by his reaction to homophobia—good ol' American fear and loathing of homosexuals. Sexual dynamics between men are always in the background of men's relationships with women, and male–female relation-

ships will remain a mystery so long as there is unexamined homophobia between men.

There are very few names an American male can be called that will result in more emotionally violent responses in him than "faggot," "queer," "sissy" and "fruit." This is true whether a man is heterosexual or homosexual. In general, gay men respond to such slurs the way women and other minority group members feel about racial, ethnic or sexual epithets. But why is it that a "straight" male who is aggressive, dominant and sexually active with women can be so traumatized by being called a "fag"?

To be perceived as a "fag" is to have no power in the eyes of other men. It is to be perceived as being associated too closely with the powerlessness of femininity—which men are taught to shun. In the case of Black men, these ideas take on even more intense—and complex—meaning because of the Black community's historical relationship to the idea and reality of white male dominance and power. To be a "fag" has meant, symbolically, to become what powerful white males want Black men to be: weak and conquered, *unmanned.*

On top of this meaning for Black men, the general perception of "fags" as feminine and powerless leads men to internalize the message that it would be shameful and deviant to be erotically attracted to other men. They simultaneously receive society's message that they *must* be erotically attracted to women. Consequently, expression of affection with men is totally throttled—the only time men are supposed to touch one another is on the football field. And chasing and conquering women sexually is made virtually mandatory.

Social critic Julius Lester recalls how, when he reached adolescence, the pressure to prove himself on the athletic field lessened but the overall situation worsened, "because now I had to prove myself with girls." Intense peer pressure on teenage men directs them toward sexual "accomplishment," as Bill Cosby has recounted in his adolescent memories of the girls in his neighborhood and the pleasure he imagined he could get from their bodies. Such pressures and fantasizing among young American males are commonplace, and to a great extent society requires them. In fact, if boys do not display "appropriate" sexual drives by the time they reach adolescence, parents (especially fathers) are likely to get extremely bent out of shape.

To understand the male sex drive, it's also important to understand how men's relationships with their own body are sexualized. Sexuality becomes a central part of masculine identity early in boyhood because of *both* social and anatomical forces. Physiologically, boys' easy access to their own genitals plus frequent and surprising erections result, for most boys, in their early masturbation activity, which tends to establish a link between sexual desires on the one hand and their penis on the other. As a result, boys develop quite early a genital focus, which is encouraged and reinforced by their buddies' emphasis on "getting over" and by adult society's (especially adult men's) explicit approval. Through such common activities as "proving-yourself-with-girls" banter and "circle-jerk" games (standing in a circle and masturbating together), boys become increasingly preoccupied with sexual climax and the idea that sexual climax is an indicator of sexual accomplishment.

An obsession with achievement pervades men's sexual lives, leading men to strive for the payoff of orgasm and ejaculation while ignoring the pleasures that can accompany leisurely lovemaking. To accommodate men's achievement orientation, women become objects to be manipulated and men stay preoccupied with the *end* of the sexual act, the climax. This aspect of many men's sexuality suggests that not only may a particular man not be interested in a particular woman during sex; he really may not even be very interested in the sex itself. Rather, he may simply be interested in releasing sexual tension.

In a sense, men grow up to become self-contained sexual systems. They equate having a penis and getting an erection with maleness and ego, so anything that causes erections helps a man keep hold on his identity. Females do not even have to be physically present for this to occur. But when they *are* physically present, men will tend to act out the standard sexual script in hopes of affirming and reestablishing (one more time) their masculinity through sexual climax. While it may be true that quick sexual gratification has become more accessible for men as women's sexual "freedom" has increased, men have not become any less goal-oriented in their sexual behavior. In fact one might say that men are having sex *more* but enjoying it *less,* especially with the greater emphasis now being placed on their "performances" but with no accompanying increase in the depth of their sexual involvements.

MEN AND INTIMACY

Obviously, the ability to experience sexual feelings in real intimacy requires more than a close relationship between a man and his own penis—assuming he does not consider his hand his "main squeeze." Yet great numbers of American men need only minimal involvement with a sex partner in order to successfully perform a sexual act: The man doesn't *need* to be extensively involved with a woman in order to climax; he can do that easily enough by himself. In general, men's preoccupations with their penis and sexual climax and men's compartmentalizing of sex preclude their having a specifically chosen sexual relationship that is characterized by deep involvement. Instead, men learn sexual attitudes and strategies that are effective only for casual, relatively indiscriminate sexual encounters—which can be "casual" over and over again even with the same partner.

Because of the way men's sexuality is socialized, many men are driven toward a kind of sexual noninvolvement that is often at odds with women's needs and expectations. Once a man and a woman are together in bed, for instance, the male sex role frequently becomes a third party—a sort of sentinel interfering with the man's sexual involvement and keeping it from becoming any deeper. After all, men learn not to place themselves in vulnerable positions—they are to be strong, in command, powerful and dominant. For many men, to become any more deeply involved in a sexual connection would mean to give up a key to their masculinity. Most men involved in sexual relationships feel they must remain psychologically in control. To go further would mean giving up the male dominance in their sexuality, a step few men today seem capable of taking.

At the deepest level of sexual involvement, there is a feeling of complete oneness, with no boundaries around each separate person. The man's "self" becomes transformed and transported. His involvement with the woman goes beyond the past and the present, goes beyond the two people's egos, goes beyond concern with their appearances and individual personalities. At this depth of involvement between a man and a woman in a sexual encounter, maleness and femaleness become unimportant so that full absorption in this special sexual union may occur. In a very real sense, as the man becomes united with the woman, he experiences that aspect of the union that is "feminine" as well as the aspect that is "masculine." In this loving merger, the barrier between "self" and "other" is transcended. The union itself becomes paramount.

The male sex role is a barrier to such complete acceptance between lovers. That depth of acceptance is more often possible between men and women in *romantic* relationships. But as so many broken hearts can attest, when romantic relationships become primarily sexual, they change. That's when the male sex role steps in to inhibit sexual involvement at the depth to which the romance had gone. Regrettably, the vision of sexual involvement is unattainable for many men and women, because the more that men internalize traditional definitions of masculinity, the more likely they are to adopt patterns of shallow involvement in sexual activities and the less able they are to become deeply involved in sexual relationships. Sex-role socialization of men in our society usually renders them terrified and incapable of deep sexual involvement with a woman. And no wonder. For a man to feel complete oneness with her in sex would require his complete empathy and identification with her sexuality too—which is in direct opposition to society's expectation of how men should be men.

MEN AND DOMINANCE

The advent of the birth-control pill for women in the early sixties and the subsequent "sexual revolution" of the late sixties and early seventies did not result in any real alteration in male sexuality—or in female sexuality either, for that matter. While the sexual revolution might have changed some women's sexual behavior, it did *not* rewrite the sexual script, which basically says that men assume dominant and powerful roles in sexual relationships and women assume passive and submissive ones. Men in America remain in charge of the sexual arena, and as long as male dominance in sexual matters persists, male sexuality and female sexuality will be unalterable.

Male dominance is one of the definitions of masculinity that American men bring with them into sexual encounters—and it is a primary reason that their deep involvement in sexual relationships is impeded. Dominance is so firmly established in most men's identities that it is nearly impossible for them to engage in sex unless the episode follows the traditional sexual script. How do men get to be this way?

The answer seems to be that men in the United States are socialized to become dominant in order to be real men. Dominance—together with competitiveness, the "work ethic" and violence—is a key ingredient in the masculine role.

There are actually two general masculine roles assumed in America: the white masculine role and the Black masculine role. Each of these models has a long history of influences behind it, and they are as significant in the ways that they differ as in the ways they are the same.

White males have a long and complex legacy with respect to the meanings of masculinity. Their white masculine model defines relationships between men and women, men and other men, and men and their "selfhoods." If a white male is to be considered masculine in our society, he must learn to be dominant in each of those three kinds of relationships. White males' dominance over females begins during mixed-sex play in childhood and continues during adolescence, when they learn a sexual language that puts women down—and the acts and attitudes that go with it. Young white males also learn the art of dominating other males—through sports, for instance, but also through ridicule: When boys hurl the words "sissy" or "wimp" at one another, they are both bullying "less masculine" boys and reminding one another that females are deemed even more inferior. The idea of male dominance also involves, for white males, a rather complicated effort to dominate themselves: By valuing only "masculine" qualities such as self-control, logical thought and intellect and by eschewing "feminine" qualities such as emotion, intuition and equivocation, the white masculine role socializes men to cut off a very important part of their personality in order to dominate and control any situation that they're in. In the *Black* masculine role, Black men typically express dominance toward Black women and toward other Black men, but only rarely do Black men express dominance with "self" or with others outside the Black community.

In the words of novelist John O. Killens, "The only thing they [white society] will not stand for is for a Black man to be a man. And everything else is worthless if a man can't be a man." Psychologist Alvin Poussaint says that adult Black males have been recognized as *men* by most of society only since the 1960's, when "a fresh, virile, sexually potent image appeared, bolstered by an assertive, more confident Black man. The Negro male became the Black male— a transformation that henceforth would never be completely safe for White society"—and not safe for Black men either. That's why Black male youth have historically been forced to learn that society does not permit Black males to express dominance in the larger society. And therefore the dominance Black men learn— and we men believe we must learn it if we are to survive—is directed primarily toward other Black people.

Yet, Black male socialization includes a range of very positive results that young white men do not typically experience. From peers, for instance, young Black men learn the concepts "brother" and "blood"—a deep sense of identification with other Black men that cuts across age, class and geography. From adult men, young Black men often learn the nuances of Black masculinity—how you can be a man and still have your soul shine through. From the women who raise us, Black men learn firsthand to respect the strength of so-called feminine qualities—intuition, warmth, cooperation and empathy. At the same time, however, the very negative message is transmitted (from peers, from older men, from the women who are raising us) that passivity and submissiveness are expected of us outside our Black society. The ultimate price for dominant behavior in that outside world, we know, has been castration and death.

It becomes a perilous and precarious double bind: Black males are expected to exhibit "masculine" dominance among Blacks, but we're also expected to exhibit "feminine" submissiveness, passivity and cooperativeness in the larger white society. Many Black youth, confronted with these contradictory messages and also influenced by the remnants of the Black male–led "Black power" movement of the late sixties, develop a masculine role that tries to honor the expectations of both Black culture and the larger society. But American society is based on a white masculine sex-role model. This means that success, achievement, security and, in general, *the good life* go to those who subscribe to and act according to the white masculine sex role—which means, essentially, to be both able and always entitled to dominate women, other men and oneself.

MEN AND CHANGE

Clearly many of us men are very damaged sexually as a result of our sex-role socialization, which insists on the isolation of our feelings and the sacrifice of emotions in our pursuit of a dominant masculine identity. And clearly, in our everyday lives, we men resist changes in our behavior toward women. When we do not encourage women to be independent, when we lapse into traditional masculine ways of thinking about women, when we behave toward female acquaintances, friends, lovers, wives and even strangers in condescending and sexist ways, we resist changing our behavior. But we do not need to resist. We should instead be alert to the idea that traditional masculinity—the masculine role we all admire so much—is hazardous to our relationships, to our health, to our communities and to those we love.

To say that changes in the male sex role are needed is an understatement. It stands between women and men like a barricade. There can be no real intimacy between us until we men stop living emotionally and sexually behind our fortress of traditional masculinity. It's a false front—and it's got us all fooled.

Medicine and Science

Traditional androcentric views of the sexes have found their way into the assumptions that form the foundation of most of our knowledge systems. Science is no exception. Despite claims to objectivity and value neutrality, science is, after all, a human creation. It is not surprising, then, that the norms and structure of science are ideologically consistent with patriarchal values and serve traditionally masculine interests. And this "way of knowing" has consequences for the profession of medicine. In this section we examine medicine and science as social institutions that perpetuate gender inequality.

The depth and rigidity of gender assumptions are illustrated in the selection "Sex Change Operations: The Last Bulwark of the Double Standard," by Margrit Eichler. She argues that the desire for sex change operations is not located in the physiology or even the psychology of the transsexual but in the *social* practices that inculcate such rigid definitions of appropriate behavior for males and females that individuals choose to mutilate their bodies, to change their sex, rather than behave in ways they view as inappropriate for their gender; and medical doctors choose to view these operations as "right" and "moral."

In the 1970s a feminist health movement emerged in the United States as an outgrowth of the women's and the consumer health movements. Women's health advocates criticized and challenged the tendency of the existing medical establishment to view women as abnormal and inher-

ently diseased simply because the female reproductive life cycle deviates from the male's. Women are today asserting a wide number of demands, including the right to control their own bodies, to have safe health care available, and to have access to alternatives to the dangerous and invasive drugs prescribed primarily for women and to unnecessary and risky surgical procedures performed frequently on women. The articles in this section illustrate some of the specific issues raised by feminist researchers concerned about women's health.

In "Hormonal Hurricanes: Menstruation, Menopause, and Female Behavior," Anne Fausto-Sterling examines traditional research on menstruation and menopause and finds that it reflects a deep bias against women; it advances the view that women are "slaves of their reproductive physiologies." Reviewing recent studies on premenstrual syndrome and menopause conducted by feminists, Sterling finds that these researchers, working outside of the mainstream of medical and psychological research, ask different questions about women's health which force us to recognize how social context affects the female reproductive cycle and our interpretation of it.

Barry Adams's article, "The AIDS Crisis," illustrates how a disease can be invisible to scientific scrutiny when the persons who contract it are considered sexually deviant. Adams also tells us how people with an illness can influence the way others respond to it.

An issue that has propelled the women's movement is the right of women to control their own bodies. In "Racism, Birth Control, and Reproductive Rights," Angela Y. Davis discusses the history of the birth control movement and the contemporary abortion rights movement, pointing out that white women in these movements have failed to understand the different experiences and interests of women of color and frequently have used blatantly racist premises to advance their cause. While white women have been struggling for an individual right to birth control, black and Puerto Rican women have confronted forced sterilization as a means of reducing "less desirable" sectors of the population. Davis makes clear the reasons why women of all races and classes have failed to unify around the issue of reproductive rights, even though birth control, as she argues, is a fundamental necessity if women are to achieve equality.

The feminist attack on the medical establishment has focused on the fact that, despite the entry of women into medical schools in growing numbers, the institution of medicine is still dominated by men. Even when women have been allowed into the profession of medicine, they have been socialized into a way of thinking and practice that generally conforms to the canons of Western science. The body is viewed as a machine that can be regulated, controlled, and managed, and the doctor-patient relationship is governed by objectivity, nonemotionality, and impersonality. Medical sociologists refer to this distinctively modern Western conception of medical treatment as "scientific medicine." In "Mothers or MD's: Women Physicians and the Doctor–Patient Relationship," Judith Lorber compares the behaviors and styles of male and female physicians, finds few differences between them, and analyzes the factors that account for the similarities and the few differences that do exist.

Barbara Katz Rothman, in "Midwives in Transition: The Structure of a Clinical Revolution," discusses another issue that is central to the women's health movement, the impact on women of the medicalization of childbirth. Rothman finds that medical timetables commonly used in hospital births structure the experience of childbirth in ways that are unrelated to the process itself. Nurse-midwives who attend home births operate in accordance with a different social construction of the birth process, one that allows the birth to progress at a tempo over which the mother retains some control.

Sex Change Operations: The Last Bulwark of the Double Standard

MARGRIT EICHLER

Sex change operations have become increasingly frequent over the past decade. The fact that modern societies are willing to allocate a portion of their scarce resource of highly trained medical personnel and highly sophisticated and expensive medical instruments for such operations suggests a complete acceptance of sex role ideology and therefore an extreme intolerance of sexual ambiguity.

In conventional psychology, people distinguish between people who have a "sex-appropriate gender identity" and those who have a confused gender identity, or exhibit a "gender dysphoria syndrome" (Meyer, 1974). Within the past decade, the treatment of people with gender dysphoria, that is, people who believe that they have the wrong-sexed body for their "real" self, has increasingly been through sex change operations, more commonly referred to in the literature as "sex reassignment surgery."

Sex reassignment surgery has as its goal to make a man as much as is anatomically possible similar to a woman, although it can never make a woman out of a man. The intention of the surgery is to make it possible for the erstwhile male to live as much as possible like a woman, and to be accepted as a woman by his (now her) friends and acquaintances. Vice versa, the surgery aims to make a woman as much as is anatomically possible similar to a man, although, again, it can never make a man out of a woman. Again, the surgery is considered successful if the erstwhile woman is accepted and treated as a man by her (now his) friends and acquaintances. In general, sex reassignment surgery is a costly and long process, and the final surgery

which gives it its name is only, if responsibly done, the last step in a several years' process of "changing one's sex"—namely, living in the mode of a member of the opposite sex.

As a rule, transsexualism for a man who wants to become a woman involves, first, hormone treatment, which increases his breast development, effectively sterilizes him, and decreases his facial hair growth. A second step would be electrolysis of his facial hair, of his breast hair and, if necessary, of other parts. After the second hair removal, the hair is usually permanently removed. Sometimes a hair transplant to alter his hair line at the forehead and/or a nose operation are performed. Sometimes breast implants are made to increase his breast size beyond the increase that is due to the hormonal treatment. At this point the patient is often expected to live as a woman for a minimum of six months, and, if possible, for several years. Physicians seem to vary greatly in this requirement, but most seem to be more willing to perform the ultimate sex reassignment surgery the longer the patient has already lived as a member of the sex which he wishes to join. The next step, then, is the removal of the penis and the testes and, lastly, the construction of an artificial vagina (vaginoplasty), with which the person is actually capable of having sexual intercourse, assuming the role of the woman, sometimes to such a degree that her partner is unaware of the fact that the person used to be an anatomical male.

For female-to-male transsexuals, the process is even more complicated. As with male-to-female transsexuals, the first medical step is usually hormone treatments. The androgens tend to lower the voice and to stimulate facial hair growth. After a prolonged period of time, they also effectively sterilize the erstwhile woman, and periods cease, just as the man with a great influx of estrogens becomes incapable of ejaculation. The next step would be the surgical removal of the breasts, and preceding or succeeding it a hysterectomy (removal of the uterus). This is about as far as many female-to-male transsexuals can go, although there is, by now, a technology which allows the construction of a penis (phalloplasty). The construction of a penis by surgical means is more complicated than the removal of the male sex organs and the construction of an artificial vagina: female-to-male transsexuals can receive a penile construction and an implant of simulated testes which look like male genitals, but the penis cannot get erect, and, of course, cannot ejaculate since there are no functioning testes, and often it cannot even be used for urination. For sexual intercourse it seems to be useless (with the exception of one case that has been reported). The surgical changes are, therefore, of an even more cosmetic nature (since still less functional than the artificial vagina) than those of the male-to-female transsexual.

As can be seen, the whole process is by necessity painful, physically as well as emotionally, and expensive. Persons undergoing sex reassignment surgery need to possess a great deal of determination in order to obtain the desired treatments and operations. Nevertheless, there is no doubt that the incidence of these sex reassignment surgeries has greatly increased over the past few years. Money and Wolff (1973) estimated that in 1971 there were around 300 postoperative transsexuals in the United States, and in 1976 Feinbloom estimated that there were about 2,000 postoperative transsexuals in the United States. Overall, Pauly (1974a: 493) estimates the prevalence of male transsexualism as 1:100,000 and of female transsexualism as 1:130,000 of the general population. The lower female transsexualism rate may simply be a function of the fact that female-to-male sex reassignment surgery is even more complicated and expensive than male-to-female sex reassignment surgery, and that male transsexualism has received more publicity through some famous cases such as Christine Jorgenson and Jan Morris. Were the possibility of female-to-male surgery better known, more people might request it.

The generic term that is utilized to describe a person who wishes to live as a member of the other sex is "transsexual." In the past years, the term has been utilized to designate all those people who seek (but do not

necessarily obtain) a sex change operation. The ratio of patients receiving surgery and those requesting it has been estimated as 1:9 (Bentler, 1976: 577). The usage of calling all patients requesting surgery transsexual has been criticised by Meyer (1974) as being too vague, and he proposes to call transsexual only those people who have actually managed to live as members of the other sex. It is common to distinguish between postoperative and preoperative transsexuals. This, to me, seems a very questionable custom, since it assumes that all "preoperative" transsexuals will, some day, become postoperative, which is not the case. More important, it stresses the surgical aspect of transsexualism rather than the cultural aspect by implying that transsexualism culminates in sex reassignment surgery, and that a form of transsexualism which involves living as a member of the opposite sex without surgery is simply a step to having surgery performed. If nothing else, it indicates the mechanical nature of the way in which gender dysphoria is regarded among the clinical experts.

Related to, but not synonymous with, transsexualism are transvestism and homosexuality. Transvestism involves an acceptance of oneself as a man, but the overwhelming urge occasionally to dress as and behave like a woman. (There are also female transvestites, but they are less frequently written about and commented upon, except when their transvestism is a prelude to transsexualism, probably because it is vastly more socially acceptable for a woman to dress as a man than it is for a man to dress as a woman. A female transvestite is, therefore, less of a deviant than a male transvestite.) Transvestites may achieve such proficiency in cross-dressing that people do not notice anything strange when they pass them dressed as women.

Transsexuals tend to be homosexual insofar as they tend to prefer sexual contacts with a member of the sex to which they belong physically. Since they believe themselves to be people trapped in an anatomically wrong body, this desire is not subjectively experienced as homosexuality but as heterosexuality, and consequently, a male-to-female transsexual is likely to prefer a man who is not a self-defined homosexual and a female-to-male transsexual is likely to prefer a woman who is not a self-defined lesbian as sexual partners.

This is a brief description of the background information on sex change operations and related phenomena, such as transvestism. What is so very interesting in these phenomena is the underlying, overwhelming sexual dimorphism that becomes obvious when reading the literature. My major thesis here is that transsexual patients have an excessively narrow image of what constitutes "sex-appropriate" behavior, which is reflected in the attitudes of the attending clinicians (psychologists, therapists and medical doctors) and the family of origin of the patient. Were the notions of masculinity and femininity less rigid, sex change operations should be unnecessary. Rather than identify somebody with a "gender identity problem" as sick, we could define a society which insists on raising boys and girls in a clearly differentiated manner as sick. What should be treated as *social* pathology is treated as if it were normal and when it manifests its effect in individuals it is treated as an *individual* pathology and is "corrected," rather than any attempts being made to combat the issue at its root: the oppressive (nonhuman) definition of sex roles, and the lack of recognition of intermediate sexes in Western society and, apparently, Westernized Eastern society, if one can make such a statement on the basis of a few isolated cases.

SEXUAL DIMORPHISM IN TRANSSEXUALITY

Masculinity-Femininity in the Transsexual Patient

Anatomically, contrary to the prevailing notion, the sexes are not "opposites." In many ways we are biologically similar; for example, both males and females have so-called male and female hormones, but the proportions are different for the sexes. Besides the external and internal accessory sexual organs all else is shared between the sexes, although the distributions are, statistically speaking, different.

As far as physical traits are concerned, it is possible to differentiate between different physical characteristics, for example, pitch of voice—at the statistical level—between males and females, but the difference is one of range rather than an absolute difference. As far as character traits are concerned (e.g., gentleness, dependence, emotionality for women; roughness, independence, and nonemotionality for men) we can identify sex stereotypes (as Bem has done for the con-

struction of the Bem Sex-Role Inventory [hereafter BSRI]) and we can observe statistical distributions which point toward differences in the distribution of behavior traits (e.g., greater verbal ability of girls and greater physical aggressiveness of boys). All people encompass in themselves some elements that are stereotypically ascribed to the other sex, and most people seem not to worry about that. However, when we read the accounts of transvestites and transsexuals, we are struck by the very rigid and sharp distinction that is drawn between so-called feminine and masculine attributes and, more significantly, by the perceived inappropriateness of engaging in behaviors that are seen as being fitting for the other sex.

Jan Morris (1975), for example, in her description of the years of her changeover from male to "female," makes very clear statements as to what she expects a man and a woman to be. She notes that " . . . my own notion of the female principle was one of gentleness as against force, forgiveness rather than punishment, give more than take, helping more than leading" (p. 12); ". . . though my body often yearned to give, to yield, to open itself, the machine was wrong" (p. 24). Contrast this with her description of a journalist colleague while Jan was still James Morris.

> Though I never heard evil spoken of him by a living soul, still we were antipathetic from the start. "How marvelous it must be," I once remarked to him by way of small talk, *apropos* of his great height, "to be able to command every room you enter." "I do not want," he replied in his most reproving liberal style, "to command anything at all"—an unfortunate response, though he could not know it, to *one whose ideals of manhood had been molded by military patterns, and who liked a man to be in charge of things.* (p. 75, second emphasis added)

Rather, therefore, than permit it to be legitimate for a man to be gentle, give rather than take, help rather than lead or command, Morris perceives of these character traits as only legitimate for a woman (instead of clearly human)—these yearnings that he himself had were, therefore, for himself illegitimate. He accepts a sexual dimorphism which strictly separates the sexes in terms of character traits, thus trying to live up to an inhuman masculine image, which, after a while, proves to be too much for him. A similar picture emerges from other descriptions (e.g., in Meyer, 1974) and is particularly obvious, also, in transvestites.

In one transvestite club which has recently been studied, the men come for one evening a week to dress up as females, and they go, cross-dressed, to outings. Typically, a man would have selected a female name for himself that would be used exclusively while he was dressed as a female, and that is referred to as his "sister." For reasons of keeping their everyday identity secret, only first names are used, and members would know each other by both names, the "brother" and "sister" names. If a person did not bring his suitcase with clothes, he might say that he did not bring his sister along but that he might do so next week. Reading the accounts of these transvestites who appear in ultrafeminine apparel, with makeup, typically feminine clothes (rather than, for instance, blue jeans and a shirt), wigs, nylons, and so on, it becomes apparent that they uphold a likewise ultramasculine appearance when they are not "dressed" (as females). Feinbloom (1976:126) comments:

> These men are visually perfect examples of "compartmentalized" deviance. For the most part, their cross-dressing is carefully delimited in time and place and hidden from the rest of their lives. Their appearance, occupations, avocations, etc., outside their dressing, are strictly masculine. For example, most are balding or keep their hair very short. They dress conservatively and appropriately. They walk and talk in a masculine way, from the way they cross their legs to the way they hold their cigarettes. Their jobs and hobbies are "accounts" insofar as they are frequently very "masculine" in quality. The reinforced message, as I said before, is that any man who races sportcars, parachute jumps, looks so much like a man, is an army sergeant or a top-level computer analyst could not possibly be a "pansy" or a "deviant."

If it were personally and socially acceptable for these men to wear clothes with ruffles, bright colors and soft materials (as was, for instance, customary in the Middle Ages) and to show their softer and gentler and more dependent side in everyday life, it is an open question whether they would still feel the need to assume, temporarily but regularly, the outer appearance of a member of the other sex.

Sexual Dimorphism in the Family of Origin of Transsexuals

The etiology of transsexualism has not been determined. The only thing that seems clear is that social factors play an extremely important role, and that biological factors are, at the very most, contributing towards predisposing a person to become a transsexual, and that possibly they play no role at all.

Bentler (1976) has recently attempted to isolate the possible developmental basis of male (male-to-female) transsexualism. Of 22 possible causes for male transsexualism which he enumerates, two are clearly biological in character (prenatal feminization of the brain and inborn temperament to fussiness and unresponsiveness), one may be either biological or socially determined (low activity and energy level) and the rest are all social variables (presence of weak and nonnurturant father, learning of negative attitudes toward sexual organs, absence of consistent, effective rewards for sex-role-stereotyped behaviors and interests, learning not to look at females as sex objects, perceived difficulties with masculine work roles, development of a self-concept as different from other boys, etc.).

Clearly, possible explanations of transsexualism are at an early stage. Just as clearly, if people would delineate less sharply between males and females than they do at present, many of the suspected causes would simply cease to exist. The desire to be a member of the opposite sex presupposes very clear and mutually exclusive notions as to what each sex is like.

It is impressive to read some of the accounts of the manner in which parents distinguish between what is proper for a boy and what is proper for a girl. In one reported instance a family had two male-to-female transsexuals. During one of the interviews, the mother was asked:

DR S: When you would buy them gifts for Christmas or birthdays, what would you get them when they were 2 or 3 years old?

MOTHER: I liked to buy them dolls. I like dolls. You know, *dressing* dolls I like. But I buy a little car.

T: Oh yeah, She used to buy us cars. She said she liked dolls. She wanted to buy us dolls but she bought us cars.

DR S: Where did you get the dolls from?

T: My cousin's.

DR S: When they were little, you would buy them
         boys' toys?

MOTHER: Yes. Sometimes they would play, but they
         would play with dolls. They like to play with
         dolls, and I say, "NO!" (Stoller and Baker,
         1973: 327; emphases in the original)

On the other hand, it seems impossible at this point
of time to weigh the familial influences against other
social pressures. Since these transsexuals are from a
culture which is highly sex-stereotyped and very conscious of "sex-appropriate" behavior, some children
who had yearnings to behave in a "sex-inappropriate"
manner may have simply found it impossible to overcome the feeling of inappropriateness and may have
thereby been pushed to imagine themselves as members of the other sex who happen to be endowed with
the wrong body.

Whatever the role of the family may be, one thing
seems certain: clinicians who are attending transsexuals need to believe strongly in "gender differentiation" in order to be willing to offer their services to
transsexuals who request them.

Sexual Dimorphism in Attending Clinicians

The prevailing clinical view of transsexuals, transvestites, and homosexuals is that they have a gender identity problem, that they have chosen improper sex objects (homosexuality), and that they behave, in a
general way, in a gender-inappropriate manner. Indeed, a diagnosis of a gender identity problem is a prerequisite for obtaining sex reassignment surgery. The
factor on which surgery seems to hinge is whether or
not the patient is judged to have a primary identification as a member of the opposite sex.

It warrants a moment's reflection that the reason
for which sex reassignment surgery is performed is
gender confusion, and not sex confusion. In other
words, the patients are all clearly aware what their anatomical sex is. There is absolutely no "confusion" on
this issue. The only "confusion" is their refusal to behave in the manner that is socially prescribed for their
sex.

Clinicians need to believe fairly strongly in the appropriateness of "sex-appropriate behavior" and a
"proper gender identity" in order to be able to justify,
to themselves and others, the removal of physiologically perfectly normal and healthy sex organs in sub-

stantial numbers of patients. Clinicians involved with
transsexuals—at least those who perform sex reassignment surgery—must not only accept the present sex
structure but must passionately believe in its essential
rightness.

There are different ways in which accounts can be
read. So far, we have used accounts of transsexuals in
order to extract information about the femininity-
masculinity attitudes of the patients and their families.
However, the same reports (when written by clinicians) can be used to extract not the problems of the
patients but the prejudices of clinicians. One example
is particularly striking which is reported by Money,
since it reveals at least as much about the clinician's
concern with sex-role behavior and gender identity
(and the malleability of the human character) as about
any problems that the patient may have. It is especially interesting to examine this example because
Money is one of the earliest authors who previously
had advanced the thesis that humans are psychosexually undifferentiated at birth (Money, 1963: 39). According to Money, Hampson, and Hampson (1955:
316), ". . . sexuality is undifferentiated at birth and . . .
becomes differentiated as masculine or feminine in the
course of the various experiences of growing up."
These conclusions are based on studies of people with
inconsistent sex attributes (hermaphrodites) and, in
general, the investigators found that infants can be
successfully raised—irrespective of their biological
sex—in either sex. In this particular example, the raising of a genetic male as a female is reported.

The case is one of identical male twin brothers, one
of whom lost his penis through an accident at the age
of seven months. Consequently, Money advised the
parents to raise the child as a female:

I gave them advice and counseling on the future
prognosis and management of their new daughter,
based on experiences with similar reassignments in
hermaphroditic babies. In particular, they were
given confidence that their child can be expected to
differentiate a female gender identity, in agreement
with her sex of rearing. (Money, 1975: 67)

By the age of nine years (the age when this case was
reported), the two identical (genetically male) twins
showed two clearly differentiated personalities, with
different dress preferences, different attitudes towards
cleanliness, very different toy preferences, different du-

ties around the house which were willingly performed, and generally a sharply differentiated behavior structure. Money is very laudatory of the successful efforts of the mother to raise this child as a girl and reports in positive terms on the mother's activities in these regards, for example, "in pointing out the specifics of the female and male adult reproductive roles," and "their other different roles, such as wife and husband or financial supporter of the family and caretaker of children and house"(p. 69).

> Regarding domestic activities, such as work in the kitchen and house traditionally seen as part of the female's role, the mother reported that her daughter copies her in trying to help her tidying and cleaning up the kitchen, while the boy could not care less about it. She encourages her daughter when she helps her in the housework. (Money, 1975: 69–70)

Through systematically applying a double standard (by differentially rewarding identical behavior—e.g., the mother encourages the daughter when she helps her in the housework, but presumably she does not encourage the son) and with the expert guidance of the clinician two different sex identities of anatomically identical people are constructed. The result of the process is likely to be two more adults who will consider it fitting for the "nature" of a woman to take care of house and children, and fitting for the "nature" of a man to be the breadwinner of a family. The assisting clinician obviously perceives this as the appropriate role division and actively furthers this outcome. Considering that the girl is anatomically a boy, this case graphically illustrates—perhaps clearer than other cases of transsexualism, because we are here dealing with an involuntary transsexual—the completely arbitrary nature of our sex identity which is thereby shown not to be related to the presence of internal and/or external sex organs, counter to the claims of many psychologists.

In another study, Green (1976) compares 60 boys characterized by "extensive cross-gender behavior" who are seen as potential future transsexuals and therefore of a pathological inclination. They were so identified if on a "never, occasionally, or frequently trichotomy" they "at least occasionally cross-dressed, role-played as a female, preferred girls' toys and games, related better to girls, avoided rough-and-tum-

ble play, and were called 'sissy' by their peer group." Instead of viewing a situation in which games are rigidly divided by sex, in which boys and girls are supposed not to like to play with each other, and so on, as a case of social pathology, children who refuse to participate in this form of social sickness are seen as being individually pathological. It is striking that the discussion of transsexual pathology concerns almost exclusively gender identity rather than sex identity. Patients do not have a confused image about their sexual organs, although they display a strongly negative view of their own sex organs since these symbolize to them at the anatomical level the restrictions that they think they must accept at the personality level. Clinicians further this interpretation by themselves subscribing to a sexual dimorphism at the psychic level.

An alternative route would be not to attempt to convince these people to behave in a "gender-appropriate manner" but to try to get them to accept themselves as men or women, boys or girls who happen to have tastes that are similar to those of many (but not all) members of the other sex rather than to those of many (but not all) members of their own sex. Such an effort may possibly be too late for patients who seek sex reassignment surgery, and in that sense one cannot fault clinicians if they do not succeed in fostering a more positive self-image which includes an acceptance of one's sex organs without any attempt to conform to rigid sex roles. However, this does not alter the fact that individual transsexuals are casualties of an overly rigid sex-role differentiation, and that clinicians who perform sex reassignment surgery help to maintain this overly rigid sexual dimorphism which is restrictive to every human being, whether female, male, or transsexual.

There is also some evidence of a scientific double standard on the part of clinicians, that is, a differential interpretation of data according to the sex of the actor. Stoller and Baker (1973: 326), for example, when discussing the background of a male-to-female transsexual, note that he took some pride in getting away from his overly protective mother. "When she [previously he] left the house, it was not to express masculine independence but was simply a rebellion against her mother's demands for housekeeping and for just staying in the house. "The action reported upon is asexual, but the interpretation offered is sexual.

Sexual dimorphism implies that one does not socially accept the presence of persons who are neither unambiguously male nor female, although in nature such people do exist, and in previous times at least some limited recognition was accorded to them.

EUNUCHS AND INTERSEXES

Biological sex is determined in different ways: chromosomal sex, gonadal sex, internal accessory organs, external genital appearance. In addition, the assigned sex and gender role may be consistent or inconsistent with the other determinants of sex (Rosenberg & Sutton-Smith, 1972: 31). In most people, all four biological determinants of sex and the assigned sex and rearing coincide, so that we have persons who are both in anatomy and in behavior unambiguously male or female. However, sometimes the determinants of sex are inconsistent with each other, and then we have cases of hermaphrodism, or mixed sex. The occurrence of different types of hermaphrodism has been estimated to be for true hermaphrodites (with both male and female sex organs) very rare, for pseudomales 1 out of every 2,000, for pseudofemales also 1 out of every 2,000, for male pseudohermaphrodites 1 out of every 2,000 and for female pseudohermaphrodites 1 out of every 50,000 (*Encyclopaedia Britannica,* 1973, vol. 11: 432). Inconsistent sex, therefore, is in any given population not a very frequent phenomenon; but at a world level, it is not an uncommon condition, either. In Western societies we regard these people with inconsistent sex variables as abnormal and we attempt to rear them unambiguously as either male or female, although this is inconsistent with their true "intersex," since contemporary Western society has no social category for intersexes.

This has not always been the case. In some primitive societies, we find a social category for people who are neither female nor male but something else, for example, men who behave like women, or women who behave like men, and the like. (Other primitive societies, however, would kill infants if they seemed somehow "abnormal.") A fair bit has been written about people with an intersex status (for a discussion, see Martin & Voorhies, 1975: 84–107), especially about the berdache, but Stoller (1976: 537–8) suggests that

although the subject has caught the attention of anthropologists and psychiatrists, this may be more for its oddity than frequency. Reviewing the anthropological literature, one cannot judge how many people like this existed at any time. My impression is that it was rare, so much so that whenever an anthropologist heard of such a person, a report was filed. The whole subject is mushy. And now it is too late to know.

Whatever the frequency—or rarity—of social intersexes may have been, it seems certain that quite a number of people recognize more than two sexes, and that these cultures were not threatened by men who wanted to live like women and women who wanted to live like men. For instance, Evans-Pritchard (1945) describes the case of Nyaluthni, a woman among the Nuer (a seminomadic nilotic tribe) who was rich and barren and purchased for herself two wives. The wives bore two children by Dinka men who did not live in Nyaluthni's homestead but frequently visited it, stayed there for one or several nights, and hoed her gardens. She chose them as the genitors of her children because they were known to be hard-working gardeners. Her children

address her as *gwa,* "father," and not as *ma,* "mother." She is a woman of outstanding character, with fine features, and always well-dressed. She is very competent and runs her homestead like a man. If her wives are lazy or disobedient she beats them. They treat her with the respect due to a husband and place meals before her with the same ceremony as they would employ to a male husband. She speaks of them as "my wives." She directs the business of the Kraal and homestead with the skill of an experienced herdsman and householder and stands no interference in matters pertaining to cattle, even from her initiated son. (Evans-Pritchard, 1945: 31–2).

This is the case of a woman who has been socially defined as a man. There are two contemporary reported instances in which nonoperative transsexuals are apparently fully accepted within their own culture: among contemporary American Indians and in Vietnam. In spite of being socially accepted within their own culture, these people expressed the wish for sex reassignment surgery, which is probably due to the influence of Westernized America on their own culture.

In the first of these instances, Stoller (1976) reports on two contemporary male Indians who desired surgery. Neither one reported any ridicule from his peers or parents for his propensity to live as a female, and at least one of them had obtained a very high status within his tribe as the best basketweaver and dressmaker of the tribe. The other case is about "Mimi," another male-to-female (nonoperative) transsexual in Vietnam. Mimi had been arrested as a prostitute by the police and was discovered to be a man only at the time of the routine gynecological examination, at which point he was suspected to be a draft dodger and was sent to the army induction center. He wanted to go to the United States for a sex change operation, but was apparently doing well in Vietnam as he was, and seemed to be relatively well-to-do. The authors reporting on this latter case distinguish between three distinct cultural attitudes towards transsexuals in contemporary Vietnam:

> First, it provides an institutionalized transsexual role with high status and power in the society, perhaps in some ways similar to the Koniag culture and the Chuckchee shaman. Second, there is a tolerant attitude with low prestige but not social ostracism, perhaps similar to the Zuni "la-mana." This tolerance is extended to pre-pubertal children but appears to be considerably less for adults. Finally, westernized Vietnam appears similar to the United States in its strong societal disapproval of the marginal role for the transsexual. (Heiman & Le, 1975: 93–4)

Not only does Western society not award an official—and even less a high and powerful—status to people who behave in a "sex-inappropriate" manner, we also socially deny the existence of people who—since birth or later in life—have changed in some aspect of their sexuality, such as through castration. It used to be the case that in a number of societies, being a eunuch (castrated male) was a recognized sexual status, which was often combined with a powerful political status. Eunuchs tended to be considered as good political advisers, since they were thought to be more likely to be loyal to the ruling dynasty because of their incapacity to sire children. Accordingly, eunuchs were used as political advisers in a number of empires, such as in China during the Chou period and under the Han, T'ang, Ming, and Sung emperors. The Achaeminid Persians employed political eunuchs, as did some Roman emperors and most of the emperors of Byzantium. Many of the patriarchs of Constantinople

were eunuchs (*Encyclopaedia Britannica,* 1973, vol. 8: 822). The Italians used to castrate boys in order to train them as adult sopranos. Without wishing to suggest that it is a recommendable practice to castrate boys (for whatever reason), I simply wish to point out that castrated males were in the past socially recognized as castrated males, whereas today they are likely to be treated as females, as was the twin who lost his penis as reported by Money (1975).

As a little side observation, it is interesting to note that while we have a historical name for castrated males (namely eunuch), we have no corresponding name for castrated females (women with hysterectomies), possibly because the changes in appearance are not as observable.

THE LAST BULWARK OF THE DOUBLE STANDARD

At present, the prevailing sex roles are under attack. At the social level, this manifests itself in collective movements, such as the women's liberation movement and the total-woman movement as a backlash, the men's liberation movement and the National Organization for Men as a backlash, the gay liberation movement and the antihomosexual movement (in the United States spearheaded by Anita Bryant) as a backlash. At the individual level, this is likely to result in more problems for some individuals who feel threatened by the gradual change in sex roles that is occurring. For others, it opens up options which have not been previously available to the same degree. Although changes in sex roles tend to be discussed in terms of female liberation, a change in the role of one sex necessitates a change in the role of the other. Widening of options—for members of both sexes—is as frightening to some as it is exhilarating to others.

While sex roles have been increasingly under attack, sex change operations have also become increasingly popular during the past few years. Historical reviews (e.g., Pauly, 1974a, 1974b; Bullough, 1975) report only sparse information on older transsexuals. According to Pauly (1974b: 520), the "legitimization of sex reassignment surgery is vastly superior to that which existed only a few years ago." The increase in numbers and medical legitimization of sex reassignment surgery is partially a reflection of the increase in technological expertise for performing such operations and the fact that only when the availability of such operations is known will people request it. On the other hand, sex change operations seem to have achieved some modicum of respectability which would indicate a change in the attitudes among physicians.

From a strictly physiological viewpoint, we must designate sex change operations as bodily mutilation—the willful destruction of physically healthy portions of the body for purely social reasons. What is absolutely stunning to me is the fact that, when asked, transsexuals do not seek this form of bodily mutilation primarily for sexual reasons (which seems to me the only conceivable justification) but for social reasons, as the completion of a process of transformation into a member of the other sex. And yet, the transformation can never truly take place, even if phalloplasty and vaginoplasty were vastly improved.

In the follow-up study of 42 male-to-female postoperative transsexuals, the transsexuals were asked to rank nine possible alternatives for "your basic motivations for getting your sex changed." The primary reason that was given was "to make my body more like my mind, as a woman," over such alternatives as the wearing of pretty clothing, being less aggressive, avoiding masculine expectations, having sex with a male, eliminating the male self through amputation of the penis, competing with another female, and winning the love of a parent. When the transsexuals were asked, after surgery, "Which have you found to be more important and satisfying, your life as a female (able to have sex with males) or your social role as a woman in society?" the averages clearly showed that for the subjects surgery was important for nonsexual reasons (Bentler, 1976: 569).

Seeking a sex change operation presupposes that the individual concerned considers him/herself incapable of achieving the goals that he or she has within the given body. This implies a mechanical identification of certain behavior and character traits with one's anatomy which is so strong that people are willing to have their bodies mutilated in order to decrease the differential between their preferred behavior and the restriction that they see as being set on this behavior through their bodies. Performing the operation implies that the physicians agree that the perceived discrepancy is a real discrepancy—that indeed the behaviors and traits displayed are appropriate for a member of the other sex only. Patient and doctor thus jointly reinforce the idea that behavior and character traits are legitimately determined by one's body, in the face of the evidence that suggests that our sex identity is imposed on a sexually largely or entirely undifferentiated character structure and that, therefore, sex identity is a social rather than a biological product.

The rationale for sex reassignment surgery seems to be based on a circular logic which goes like this. Sex determines character. This is natural. Therefore, cases in which biological sex does not result in the expected sex identities are unnatural. Consequently, we need to change the biological sex (i.e., nature) in order to uphold the principle that biological sex determines one's character.

Transsexuals are people who suffer so deeply from the sex structure that they are willing to endure terrible pain and loneliness in order to reduce their suffering. This group of people would—potentially—be the most potent group of people pressing for changes in the sex structure, because their aversion to their "sex-appropriate" roles is apparently insurmountable. By declaring them, by surgical fiat, as members of the other sex, this change potential is diverted and becomes as conservative as it could have been revolutionary. Each situation is individualized, rather than being recognized as the result of a social pathology, and the social pathology has overcome one more threat to its continued well-being.

Jan Morris (1975: 192), who underwent sex reassignment surgery, addressed this issue as follows:

> Is mine only a transient phenomenon, between the dogmatism of the last century, when men were men and women were ladies, and the eclecticism of the next, when citizens will be free to live in the gender role they prefer? Will people read of our pilgrimage to Casablanca, a hundred years hence, as we might read of the search for the philosopher's Stone, or Simeon Stylites on his pillar?
>
> I hope so. For every transsexual who grasps that prize, identity, ten, perhaps a hundred discover it to be only a mirage in the end, so that their latter quandary is hardly less terrible than their first.

Once we recognize the social pathology which creates the discussed individual pathologies, we must recognize the call of clinicians such as Pauly's (1974b: 522) that "Parents ought to be more aware of the need to positively reinforce all infants for those gender characteristics which are consistent with their biological identity" as an attempt to ensure the continuing existence of the preconditions from which the problems with which these clinicians are concerned arise.

REFERENCES

Bem, S. 1974. "The measurement of psychological androgyny." *Journal of Clinical Psychology,* 42 (no. 2): 155–62.

Bem, S. 1977. "On the utility of alternative procedures for assessing psychological androgyny." *Journal of Consulting and Clinical Psychology* 45 (no. 2): 166–205.

Bentler, P. 1976. "A typology of transsexualism: Gender identity theory and data." *Archives of Sexual Behavior* 5 (no. 6): 567–83.

Bullough, V. 1975. "Transsexualism in history." *Archives of Sexual Behavior* 4 (no. 5): 561–71.

Decision Marketing Research Ltd. 1976. *Women in Canada.* 2nd ed. Ottawa: Office of the Coordinator, Status of Women.

Eichler, M. No date. "Power dependency, love and the sexual division of labour. A critique of the decision-making approach." Unpublished paper.

Encyclopaedia Britannica, vols. 8 and 11 (1973 ed.).

Evans-Pritchard, E.E. 1945. *Some aspects of marriage and the family among the Nuer.* The Rhodes-Livingstone Papers no. 11. Livingstone, Northern Rhodesia: The Rhodes Livingstone Institute.

Feinbloom, D. 1976. *Transvestites and transsexuals.* New York: Delacorte Press/Seymour Lawrence.

Green, R. 1976. "One-hundred ten feminine and masculine boys: Behavioral contrasts and demographic similarities." *Archives of Sexual Behavior* 5 (no. 5): 425–46.

Heiman, E., & Van Le, C. 1975. "Transsexualism in Vietnam." *Archives of Sexual Behavior* 4 (no. 1): 89–95.

Holter, H. 1970. *Sex roles and social structure.* Oslo, Bergen, Tromso: Universitetsforlaget.

Hore, B., Nicolle, F., & Calnan, J. "Male transsexualism: Two cases in a single family." *Archives of Sexual Behavior,* pp. 317–31.

Laurie, B. 1977. "An assessment of sex-role learning in kindergarten children: Experimental application of a toy test with direct reinforcement of sex-typed and of androgenous behavior." Unpublished master's thesis, Department of Educational Theory, University of Toronto.

Martin, M., & Voorhies B. 1975. *Female of the species.* Toronto: Methuen.

Meyer, J. 1974. "Clinical variants among applicants for sex reassignment." *Archives of Sexual Behavior* 3 (no. 6): 527–58.

Money, J. 1963. "Development differentiation of femininity and masculinity compared." In *Man and civilization: The potential of women,* pp. 51–65. New York: McGraw-Hill.

Money, J. 1975. "Ablatio penis: Normal male infant sex-reassigned as a girl." *Archives of Sexual Behavior* 4 (no. 1): 65–71.

Money, J., & Ehrhardt, A. 1974. *Man and woman, boy and girl.* New York: New American Library.

Money, J., Hampson, J., & Hampson J. 1955. "An examination of some basic sexual concepts: The evidence of human hermaphroditism." *Bulletin of the Johns Hopkins Hospital* 97: 301–19.

Money, J., & Wolff, G. 1973. "Sex reassignment: Male to female to male." *Archives of Sexual Behavior* 2 (no. 3): 245–50.

Morris, J. 1975. *Conundrum.* New York: Signet Books.

Pauly, I. 1974a. "Female transsexualism: Part I." *Archives of Sexual Behavior* 3 (no. 5): 487–507.

Pauly, I. 1974b. "Female transsexualism: Part II." *Archives of Sexual Behavior* 3 (no. 6): 509–26.

Rosenberg, B. G., & Sutton-Smith, B. 1972. *Sex and identity.* New York: Holt, Rinehart and Winston.

Sawyer, J. 1976. "On male liberation." In D. David & R. Brannon, eds., *The forty-nine percent majority: The male sex role,* pp. 287–90. Reading, Mass.: Addison-Wesley.

Stoller, R. 1972. "Etiological factors in female transsexualism: A first approximation." *Archives of Sexual Behavior* 2 (no. 1): 47–64.

Stoller, R. 1976. "Two feminized male American Indians." *Archives of Sexual Behavior* 5 (no. 6): 529–38.

Stoller, R., & Baker, H. 1973. "Two male transsexuals in one family." *Archives of Sexual Behavior* 2 (no. 4): 323–8.

Swift, J. 1963. *Gulliver's travels.* New York: Airmont Books.

R E A D I N G   3 1

Hormonal Hurricanes: Menstruation, Menopause, and Female Behavior

ANNE FAUSTO-STERLING

Woman is a pair of ovaries with a human being attached, whereas man is a human being furnished with a pair of testes.

—*Rudolf Virchow, M.D. (1821–1902)*

Estrogen is responsible for that strange mystical phenomenon, the feminine state of mind.

—*David Reuben, M.D., 1969*

In 1900, the president of the American Gynecological Association eloquently accounted for the female life cycle:

> Many a young life is battered and forever crippled in the breakers of puberty; if it crosses these unharmed and is not dashed to pieces on the rock of childbirth, it may still ground on the ever-recurring shadows of menstruation and lastly upon the final bar of the menopause ere protection is found in the unruffled waters of the harbor beyond the reach of the sexual storms.[1]

Since then we have amassed an encyclopedia's worth of information about the existence of hormones, the function of menstruation, the regulation of ovulation, and the physiology of menopause. Yet many people, scientists and nonscientists alike, still believe that women function at the beck and call of their hormonal physiology. In 1970, for example, Dr. Edgar Berman, the personal physician of former Vice President Hu-

bert Humphrey, responded to a female member of Congress:

> Even a Congresswoman must defer to scientific truths ... there just are physical and psychological inhibitants that limit a female's potential. ... I would still rather have a male John F. Kennedy make the Cuban missile crisis decisions than a female of the same age who could possibly be subject to the curious mental aberrations of that age group.[2]

In a more grandiose mode, Professor Steven Goldberg, a university sociologist, writes that "men and women differ in their hormonal systems ... every society demonstrates patriarchy, male dominance and male attainment. The thesis put forth here is that the hormonal renders the social inevitable."[3]

At the broadest political level, writers such as Berman and Goldberg raise questions about the competency of *any and all* females to work successfully in positions of leadership, while for women working in other types of jobs, the question is, Should they receive less pay or more restricted job opportunities simply because they menstruate or experience menopause? And further, do women in the throes of premenstrual frenzy frequently try to commit suicide? Do they really suffer from a "diminished responsibility" that should exempt them from legal sanctions when they beat their children or murder their boyfriends?[4] Is the health of large numbers of women threatened by inappropriate and even ignorant medical attention—medical diagnoses that miss real health problems, while resulting instead in the prescription of dangerous medication destined to create future disease?

The idea that women's reproductive systems direct their lives is ancient. But whether it was Plato, writing about the disruption caused by barren uteri wandering about the body,[5] Pliny, writing that a look from a menstruating woman will "dim the brightness of mirrors, blunt the edge of steel and take away the polish from ivory,"[6] or modern scientists writing about the changing levels of estrogen and progesterone, certain messages emerge quite clearly. Women, by nature emotionally erratic, cannot be trusted in positions of responsibility. Their dangerous, unpredictable furies warrant control by the medical profession,* while ironically, the same "dangerous" females also need protection because their reproductive systems, so necessary for the procreation of the race, are vulnerable to stress and hard work.

"The breakers of puberty," in fact, played a key role in a debate about higher education for women, a controversy that began in the last quarter of the nineteenth century and still echoes today in the halls of academe. Scientists of the late 1800s argued on physiological grounds that women and men should receive different types of education. Women, they believed, could not survive intact the rigors of higher education. Their reasons were threefold: first, the education of young women might cause serious damage to their reproductive systems. Energy devoted to scholastic work would deprive the reproductive organs of the necessary "flow of power," presenting particular problems for pubescent women, for whom the establishment of regular menstruation was of paramount importance. Physicians cited cases of women unable to bear children because they pursued a course of education designed for the more resilient young man.[7] In an interesting parallel to modern nature-nurture debates, proponents of higher education for women countered biological arguments with environmental ones. One anonymous author argued that, denied the privilege afforded their brothers of romping actively through the woods, women became fragile and nervous.[8]

*In the nineteenth century, control took the form of sexual surgery such as ovariectomies and hysterectomies, while twentieth-century medicine prefers the use of hormone pills. The science of the 1980s has a more sophisticated approach to human physiology, but its political motives of control and management have changed little. For an account of medicine's attitudes toward women, see Barbara Ehrenreich and 350Deidre English, *For Her Own Good: 150 Years of Experts' Advice to Women* (New York: Doubleday, 1979); and G. J. Barker-Benfield, *The Horrors of the Half-Known Life* (New York: Harper & Row, 1977).

Opponents of higher education for women also claimed that females were less intelligent than males, an assertion based partly on brain size itself but also on the overall size differences between men and women. They held that women cannot "consume so much food as men . . . [because] their average size remains so much smaller; so that the sum total of food converted into thought by women can never equal the sum total of food converted to thought by men. It follows, therefore, that *men will always think more than women*."[9] One respondent to this bit of scientific reasoning asked the thinking reader to examine the data: Aristotle and Napoleon were short, Newton, Spinoza, Shakespeare, and Comte delicate and of medium height, Descartes and Bacon sickly, "while unfortunately for a theory based upon superior digestion, Goethe and Carlyle were confirmed dyspeptics."[10] Finally, as if pubertal vulnerability and lower intelligence were not enough, it seemed to nineteenth-century scientists that menstruation rendered women "more or less sick and unfit for hard work" "for one quarter of each month during the best years of life."[11]

Although dated in some of the particulars, the turn-of-the-century scientific belief that women's reproductive functions make them unsuitable for higher education remains with us today. Some industries bar fertile women from certain positions because of workplace hazards that might cause birth defects, while simultaneously deeming equally vulnerable men fit for the job.* Some modern psychologists and biologists suggest that women perform more poorly than do men on mathematics tests because hormonal sex differences alter male and female brain structures; and many people believe women to be unfit for certain professions because they menstruate. Others argue that premenstrual changes cause schoolgirls to do poorly in their studies, to become slovenly and disobedient, and even to develop a "nymphomaniac urge [that] may be responsible for young girls running away from home . . . only to be found wandering in the park or following boys."[12]

If menstruation really casts such a dark shadow on women's lives, we ought certainly to know more about it—how it works, whether it can be controlled, and whether it indeed warrants the high level of concern expressed by some. Do women undergo emotional

*The prohibited work usually carries a higher wage.

changes as they progress through the monthly ovulatory cycle? And if so, do hormonal fluctuations bring on these ups and downs? If not—if a model of biological causation is appropriate—how else might we conceptualize what happens?

THE SHADOWS OF MENSTRUATION: A READER'S LITERATURE GUIDE

The Premenstrual Syndrome

SCIENCE UPDATE: PREMENSTRUAL STRAIN LINKED TO CRIME

—*Providence Journal*

ERRATIC FEMALE BEHAVIOR TIED TO PREMENSTRUAL SYNDROME

—*Providence Journal*

VIOLENCE BY WOMEN IS LINKED TO MENSTRUATION

—*National Enquirer*

Menstruation makes news, and the headlines summarize the message. According to Dr. Katharina Dalton, Premenstrual Syndrome (PMS) is a medical problem of enormous dimensions. Under the influence of the tidal hormonal flow, women batter their children and husbands, miss work, commit crimes, attempt suicide, and suffer from up to 150 different symptoms, including headaches, epilepsy, dizziness, asthma, hoarseness, nausea, constipation, bloating, increased appetite, low blood sugar, joint and muscle pains, heart palpitations, skin disorders, breast tenderness, glaucoma, and conjunctivitis.[13] Although the great concern expressed in the newspaper headlines just quoted may come from a single public relations source,[14] members of the medical profession seem eager to accept at face value the idea that "70 to 90% of the female population will admit to recurrent premenstrual symptoms and that 20 to 40% report some degree of mental or physical incapacitation."[15]

If all this is true, then we have on our hands nothing less than an overwhelming public health problem, one that deserves a considerable investment of na-

tional resources in order to develop understanding and treatment. If, on the other hand, the claims about premenstrual tension are cut from whole cloth, then the consequences are equally serious. Are there women in need of proper medical treatment who do not receive it? Do some receive dangerous medication to treat nonexistent physiological problems? How often are women refused work, given lower salaries, taken less seriously because of beliefs about hormonally induced erratic behavior? In the game of PMS the stakes are high.

The key issues surrounding PMS are so complex and interrelated that it is hard to know where to begin. There is, as always, the question of evidence. To begin with we can look, in vain, for credible research that defines and analyzes PMS. Despite the publication of thousands of pages of allegedly scientific analyses, the most recent literature reviews simultaneously lament the lack of properly done studies and call for a consistent and acceptable research definition and methodology.[16] Intimately related to the question of evidence is that of conceptualization. Currently held theoretical views about the reproductive cycle are inadequate to the task of understanding the emotional ups and downs of people functioning in a complex world. Finally, lurking beneath all of the difficulties of research design, poor methods, and muddy thinking is the medical world's view of the naturally abnormal woman. Let's look at this last point first.

If you're a woman you can't win. Historically, females who complained to physicians about menstrual difficulties, pain during the menstrual flow, or physical or emotional changes associated with the premenstruum heard that they were neurotic. They imagined the pain and made up the tension because they recognized menstruation as a failure to become pregnant, to fulfill their true role as a woman.[17] With the advent of the women's health movement, however, women began to speak for themselves.[18] The pain is real, they said; our bodies change each month. The medical profession responded by finding biological/hormonal causes, proposing the need for doctor-supervised cures. A third voice, however, entered in: that of feminists worried about repercussions from the idea that women's natural functions represent a medical problem capable of preventing women from competing in the world outside the home. Although this multisided discussion continues, I currently operate on the premise that some women probably do require medical at-

IF MEN COULD MENSTRUATE—

GLORIA STEINEM

A white minority of the world has spent centuries conning us into thinking that a white skin makes people superior—even though the only thing it really does is make them more subject to ultraviolet rays and to wrinkles. Male human beings have built whole cultures around the idea that penis-envy is "natural" to women—though having such an unprotected organ might be said to make men vulnerable, and the power to give birth makes womb-envy at least as logical.

In short, the characteristics of the powerful, whatever they may be, are thought to be better than the characteristics of the powerless—and logic has nothing to do with it.

What would happen, for instance, if suddenly, magically, men could menstruate and women could not?

The answer is clear—menstruation would become an enviable, boast-worthy, masculine event:

Men would brag about how long and how much.

Boys would mark the onset of menses, that

longed-for proof of manhood, with religious ritual and stag parties.

Congress would fund a National Institute of Dysmenorrhea to help stamp out monthly discomforts.

Sanitary supplies would be federally funded and free. (Of course, some men would still pay for the prestige of commercial brands such as John Wayne Tampons, Muhammad Ali's Rope-a-dope Pads, Joe Namath Jock Shields—"For Those Light Bachelor Days," and Robert "Barretta" Blake Maxi-Pads.)

Military men, right-wing politicians, and religious fundamentalists would cite menstruation ("*men*-struation") as proof that only men could serve in the Army ("you have to give blood to take blood"), occupy political office ("can women be aggressive without that steadfast cycle governed by the planet Mars?"), be priests and ministers ("how could a woman give her blood for our sins?"), or rabbis ("without the monthly loss of impurities, women remain unclean").

Male radicals, left-wing politicians, and mystics, however, would insist that women are equal, just different; and that any woman could enter their

tention for incapacitating physical changes that occur in synchrony with their menstrual cycle. Yet in the absence of any reliable medical research into the problem it is impossible to diagnose true disease or to develop rational treatment. To start with, we must decide what is normal.

The tip-off to the medical viewpoint lies in its choice of language. What does it mean to say "70 to 90% of the female population will admit to recurrent premenstrual symptoms"?[19] The word *symptom* carries two rather different meanings. The first suggests a disease or an abnormality, a condition to be cured or rendered normal. Applying this connotation to a statistic suggesting 70 to 90 percent symptom formation leads one to conclude that the large majority of women are by their very nature diseased. The second meaning of *symptom* is that of a sign or signal. If the

figure of 70 to 90 percent means nothing more than that most women recognize signs in their own bodies of an oncoming menstrual flow, the statistics are unremarkable. Consider then the following, written in 1974 by three scientists:

It is estimated that from 25% to 100% of women experience some form of premenstrual or menstrual emotional disturbance.... Eichner makes the discerning point that the few women who do not admit to premenstrual tension are basically unaware of it but one only has to talk to their husbands or co-workers to confirm its existence.[20]

Is it possible that up to 100 percent of all menstruating women regularly experience emotional disturbance? Compared to whom? Are males the unstated standard ranks if only she were willing to self-inflict a major wound every month ("you *must* give blood for the revolution"), recognize the preeminence of menstrual issues, or subordinate her selfness to all men in their Cycle of Enlightenment.

Street guys would brag ("I'm a three-pad man") or answer praise from a buddy ("Man, you lookin' *good!*") by giving fives and saying, "Yeah, man, I'm on the rag!"

TV shows would treat the subject at length. ("Happy Days": Richie and Potsie try to convince Fonzie that he is still "The Fonz," though he has missed two periods in a row.) So would newspapers. (SHARK SCARE THREATENS MENSTRUATING MEN. JUDGE CITES MONTHLY STRESS IN PARDONING RAPIST.) And movies. (Newman and Redford in "Blood Brothers"!)

Men would convince women that intercourse was *more* pleasurable at "that time of the month." Lesbians would be said to fear blood and therefore life itself—though probably only because they needed a good menstruating man.

Of course, male intellectuals would offer the most moral and logical arguments. How could a woman master any discipline that demanded a sense of time, space, mathematics, or measurement, for instance, without that in-built gift for measuring the cycles of the moon and planets—and thus for measuring anything at all? In the rarefied fields of philosophy and religion, could women compensate for missing the rhythm of the universe? Or for their lack of symbolic death-and-resurrection every month?

Liberal males in every field would try to be kind: the fact that "these people" have no gift for measuring life or connecting to the universe, the liberals would explain, should be punishment enough.

And how would women be trained to react? One can imagine traditional women agreeing to all these arguments with a staunch and smiling masochism. (The ERA would force housewives to wound themselves every month": Phyllis Schlafly. "Your husband's blood is as sacred as that of Jesus—and so sexy, too!": Marabel Morgan.) Reformers and Queen Bees would try to imitate men, and *pretend* to have a monthly cycle. All feminists would explain endlessly that men, too, needed to be liberated from the false idea of Martian aggressiveness, just as women needed to escape the bonds of menses-envy. Radical feminists would add that the oppression of the nonmenstrual was the pattern for all other oppressions. ("Vampires were our first freedom fighters!") Cultural feminists would develop a bloodless imagery in art and literature. Socialist feminists would insist that only under capitalism would men be able to monopolize menstrual blood. . . .

In fact, if men could menstruate, the power justifications could probably go on forever.

If we let them.

of emotional stability? If there is but a single definition of what is normal and men fit that definition, then women with "female complaints" must by definition be either crazy or in need of medical attention. A double bind indeed.

Some scientists explicitly articulate the idea of the naturally abnormal female. Professor Frank Beach, a pioneer in the field of animal psychology and its relationship to sexuality, suggests the following evolutionary account of menstruation. In primitive hunter-gatherer societies adult women were either pregnant or lactating, and since life spans were so short they died well before menopause; low-fat diets made it likely that they did not ovulate every month; they thus experienced no more than ten menstrual cycles. Given current life expectancies as well as the widespread use of birth control, modern women may experience a total of four hundred menstrual cycles. He concludes from this reasoning that "civilization has given women *a physiologically abnormal status* which may have important implications for the interpretation of psychological responses to periodic fluctuations in the secretion of ovarian hormones"—that is, to menstruation (emphasis added).[21] Thus the first problem we face in evaluating the literature on the premenstrual syndrome is figuring out how to deal with the underlying assumption that women have "a physiologically abnormal status."

Researchers who believe in PMS hold a wide variety of viewpoints (none of them supported by scientific data) about the basis of the problem. For example, Dr. Katharina Dalton, the most militant promoter of PMS, says that it results from a relative end-of-the-cycle deficiency in the hormone progesterone. Others

TABLE I   ALLEGED CAUSES AND PROPOSED TREATMENTS OF PMS

Hypothesized Causes of Premenstrual Syndrome	Various PMS Treatments (used but not validated)
Estrogen excess	Oral contraceptives (combination estrogen and progesterone pills)
Progesterone deficiency	
Vitamin B deficiency	Estrogen alone
Vitamin A deficiency	Natural progesterone
Hypoglycemia	Synthetic progestins
Endogenous hormone allergy	Valium or other tranquilizers
	Nutritional supplements
Psychosomatic	Minerals
Fluid retention	Lithium
Dysfunction of the neurointermediate lobe of the pituitary	Diuretics
	A prolactin inhibitor/ dopamine agonist
Prolactin metabolism	Exercise
	Psychotherapy, relaxation, education, reassurance

SOURCES: Robert L. Reid and S. S. Yen, "Premenstrual Syndrome," *American Journal of Obstetrics and Gynecology* 139 (1981): 85–104; and Judith Abplanalp, "Premenstrual Syndrome: A Selective Review," *Women and Health* 8 (1983): 107–24.

cite deficiencies in vitamin B-6, fluid retention, and low blood sugar as possible causes. Suggested treatments range from hormone injection to the use of lithium, diuretics, megadoses of vitamins, and control of sugar in the diet[22] (see Table 1 for a complete list). Although some of these treatments are harmless, others are not. Progesterone injection causes cancer in animals. What will it do to humans? And a recent issue of *The New England Journal of Medicine* contains a report that large doses of vitamin B-6 damage the nerves, causing a loss of feeling in one's fingers and toes.[23] The wide variety of PMS "causes" and "cures" offered by the experts is confusing, to put it mildly. Just what *is* this syndrome that causes such controversy? How can a woman know if she has it?

With a case of the measles it's really quite simple. A fever and then spots serve as diagnostic signs. A woman said to have PMS, however, may or may not have any of a very large number of symptoms. Furthermore, PMS indicators such as headaches, depression, dizziness, loss or gain of appetite show up in everyone from time to time. Their mere presence cannot (as would measle spots) help one to diagnose the syndrome. In addition, whether any of these signals con-

note disease depends upon their severity. A slight headache may reflect nothing more than a lack of sleep, but repeated, severe headaches could indicate high blood pressure. As one researcher, Dr. Judith Abplanalp, succinctly put it: "There is no one set of symptoms which is considered to be the hallmark of or standard criterion for defining the premenstrual syndrome."[24] Dr. Katharina Dalton agrees but feels one can diagnose PMS quite simply by applying the term to "any symptoms or complaints which regularly come just before or during early menstruation but are absent at other times of the cycle."[25] Dalton contrasts this with men suffering from potential PMS "symptoms," because, she says, they experience them randomly during the month while women with the same physical indications acknowledge them only during the premenstruum.

PMS research usually bases itself on an ideal, regular, twenty-eight-day menstrual cycle. Researchers eliminate as subjects for study women with infrequent, shorter, or longer cycles. As a result, published investigations look at a skewed segment of the overall population. Even for those women with a regular cycle, however, a methodological problem remains because few researchers define the premenstrual period in the same way. Some studies look only at the day or two preceding the menstrual flow, others look at the week preceding, while workers such as Dalton cite cases that begin two weeks before menstruation and continue for one week after. Since so few investigations use exactly the same definition, research publications on PMS are difficult to compare with one another.[26] On this score if no other, the literature offers little useful insight, extensive as it is.

Although rarely stated, the assumption is that there is but *one* PMS. Dalton defines the problem so broadly that she and others may well lump together several phenomena of very different origins, a possibility heightened by the fact that investigators rarely assess the severity of the symptoms. Two women, one suffering from a few low days and the other from suicidal depression, may both be diagnosed as having PMS. Yet their difficulties could easily have different origins and ought certainly to receive different treatments. When investigators try carefully to define PMS, the number of people qualifying for study decreases dramatically. In one case a group used ten criteria (listed in Table 2) to define PMS only to find that no more than 20 percent of those who had volunteered for their

TABLE 2   TOWARD A DEFINITION OF PREMENSTRUAL SYNDROME

Experimental criteria (rarely met in PMS studies)
  Premenstrual symptoms for at least six preceding cycles
  Moderate to severe physical and psychological symptoms
  Symptoms *only* during the premenstrual period with marked relief at onset of menses
  Age between 18 and 45 years
  Not pregnant
  No hormonal contraception
  Regular menses for six previous cycles
  No psychiatric disorder; normal physical examination and laboratory test profile
  No drugs for preceding four weeks
  Will not receive anxiolitics, diuretics, hormones, or neuroleptic drugs during the study

Minimal descriptive information to be offered in published studies of PMS (rarely offered in the current literature)
  Specification of the ways in which subjects were recruited
  Age limitations
  Contraception and medication information
  Marital status
  Parity
  Race
  Menstrual history data
  Assessment instruments
  Operational definition of PMS
  Psychiatric history data
  Assessment of current psychological state
  Criteria for assessment of severity of symptoms
  Criteria for defining ovulatory status of cycle
  Cut-off criteria for "unacceptable" subjects

SOURCE: Judith Abplanalp, "Premenstrual Syndrome: A Selective Review," *Women and Health* 8 (1983): 107–24.

research project met them.[27] In the absence of any clearly agreed-upon definition(s) of PMS, examinations of the topic should at least state clearly the methodology used; this would enable comparison between publications, and allow us to begin to accumulate some knowledge about the issues at hand (Table 2 lists suggested baseline information). At the moment the literature is filled with individual studies that permit neither replication nor comparison with one another—an appropriate state, perhaps, for an art gallery but not for a field with pretensions to the scientific.

Despite the problems of method and definition, the conviction remains that PMS constitutes a widespread disorder, a conviction that fortifies and is fortified by the idea that women's reproductive function, so different from that of "normal" men, places them in a naturally diseased state. For those who believe that 90 percent of all women suffer from a disease called PMS, it becomes a reasonable research strategy to look at the normally functioning menstrual cycle for clues about

the cause and possible treatment. There are, in fact, many theories but no credible evidence about the origins of PMS. In Table 1 I've listed the most frequently cited hypotheses, most of which involve in some manner the hormonal system that regulates menstruation. Some of the theories are ingenious and require a sophisticated knowledge of human physiology to comprehend. Nevertheless, the authors of one recent review quietly offer the following summary: "To date no one hypothesis has adequately explained the constellation of symptoms composing PMS."[28] In short, PMS is a disease in search of a definition and cause.

PMS also remains on the lookout for a treatment. That many have been tried is attested to in Table 1. The problem is that only rarely has the efficacy of these treatments been tested with the commonly accepted standard of a large-scale, double-blind study that includes placebos. In the few properly done studies "there is usually (1) a high placebo response and (2) the active agent is usually no better than a placebo."[29] In other words, women under treatment for PMS respond just as well to sugar pills as to medication containing hormones or other drugs. Since it is probable that some women experience severe distress caused by malfunctions of their menstrual system, the genuinely concerned physician faces a dilemma. Should he or she offer treatment until the patient says she feels better even though the drug used may have dangerous side effects; or should a doctor refuse help for as long as we know of no scientifically validated treatment for the patient's symptoms? I have no satisfactory answer. But the crying need for some scientifically acceptable research on the subject stands out above all. If we continue to assume that menstruation is itself pathological, we cannot establish a baseline of health against which to define disease. If, instead, we accept in theory that a range of menstrual normality exists, we can then set about designing studies that define the healthy female reproductive cycle. Only when we have some feeling for *that* can we begin to help women who suffer from diseases of menstruation.

Many of those who reject the alarmist nature of the publicity surrounding PMS believe nevertheless that women undergo mood changes during their menstrual cycle. Indeed, most Western women would agree. But do studies of large segments of our population support this generality? And if so, what causes these ups and downs? In trying to answer these questions we confront another piece of the medical model of human behavior, the belief that biology is primary, that hormonal changes cause behavioral ones, but not vice versa. Most researchers use such a linear, unicausal model without thinking about it. Their framework is so much a part of their belief system that they forget to question it. Nevertheless it is the model from which they work, and failure to recognize and work skeptically with it often results in poorly conceived research combined with implausible interpretations of data. Although the paradigm of biological causation has until very recently dominated menstrual cycle research, it now faces serious and intellectually stimulating challenge from feminist experts in the field. . . .

MENOPAUSE: THE STORM BEFORE THE CALM

An unlikely specter haunts the world. It is the ghost of former womanhood (see Figure 1), "unfortunate

FIGURE I   ONE MEDICAL VIEW OF THE POSTMENOPAUSAL WOMAN

NOTE: Robert A. Wilson and Thelma A. Wilson, "The Fate of the Nontreated Postmenopausal Woman: A Plea for the Maintenance of Adequate Estrogen from Puberty to the Grave," *Journal of the American Geriatric Society* II (1963): 351, 356. Reprinted with permission from the W. B. Saunders Co. According to Wilson and Wilson, the woman on the left shows "some of the stigmata of 'Nature's defeminization.' The general stiffness of muscles and ligaments, the 'dowager's hump,' and the 'negativistic' expression are part of a picture usually attributed to age alone. Some of these women exhibit signs and symptoms similar to those in the early stages of Parkinson's disease. They exist rather than live." The woman on the right shows the "typical appearance of the desexed woman found on our streets today. They pass unnoticed and, in turn, notice little."

women abounding in the streets walking stiffly in twos and threes, seeing little and observing less. . . . The world appears [to them] as through a grey veil, and they live as docile, harmless creatures missing most of life's values." According to Dr. Robert Wilson and Thelma Wilson, though, one should not be fooled by their "vapid cow-like negative state" because "there is ample evidence that the course of history has been changed not only by the presence of estrogen, but by its absence. The untold misery of alcoholism, drug addiction, divorce and broken homes caused by these unstable estrogen-starved women cannot be presented in statistical form."[30]

Rather than releasing women from their monthly emotional slavery to the sex hormones, menopause involves them in new horrors. At the individual level one encounters the specter of sexual degeneration, described so vividly by Dr. David Reuben: "The vagina begins to shrivel, the breasts atrophy, sexual desire disappears. . . . Increased facial hair, deepening voice, obesity . . . coarsened features, enlargement of the clitoris, and gradual baldness complete the tragic picture. Not really a man but no longer a functional woman, these individuals live in the world of intersex."[31] At the demographic level writers express foreboding about women of the baby-boom generation, whose life span has increased from an average forty-eight years at the turn of the century to a projected eighty years in the year 2000.[32] Modern medicine, it seems, has played a cruel trick on women. One hundred years ago they didn't live long enough to face the hardships of menopause but today their increased longevity means they will live for twenty-five to thirty years beyond the time when they lose all possibility of reproducing. To quote Dr. Wilson again: "The unpalatable truth must be faced that all postmenopausal women are castrates."[33]

But what medicine has wrought, it can also rend asunder. Few publications have had so great an effect on the lives of so many women as have those of Dr. Robert A. Wilson, who pronounced menopause to be a disease of estrogen deficiency. At the same time in an influential popular form, in his book *Feminine Forever,* he offered a treatment: estrogen replacement therapy (ERT).[34] During the first seven months following publication in 1966, Wilson's book sold one hundred thousand copies and was excerpted in *Vogue* and *Look* magazines. It influenced thousands of physicians to prescribe estrogen to millions of women, many of whom had no clinical "symptoms" other than cessation of the menses. As one of his credentials Wilson lists himself as head of the Wilson Research Foundation, an outfit funded by Ayerst Labs, Searle, and Upjohn, all pharmaceutical giants interested in the large potential market for estrogen. (After all, no woman who lives long enough can avoid menopause.) As late as 1976 Ayerst also supported the Information Center on the Mature Woman, a public relations firm that promoted estrogen replacement therapy. By 1975 some six million women had started long-term treatment with Premarin (Ayerst Labs' brand name for estrogen), making it the fourth or fifth most popular drug in the United States. Even today, two million of the forty million postmenopausal women in the United States contribute to the $70 million grossed each year from the sale of Premarin-brand estrogen.[35] The "disease of menopause" is not only a social problem: it's big business.[36]

The high sales of Premarin continue despite the publication in 1975 of an article linking estrogen treatment to uterine cancer.[37] Although in the wake of that publication many women stopped taking estrogen and many physicians became more cautious about prescribing it, the idea of hormone replacement therapy remains with us. At least three recent publications in medical journals seriously consider whether the benefits of estrogen might not outweigh the dangers.[38] The continuing flap over treatment for this so-called deficiency disease of the aging female forces one to ask just what *is* this terrible state called menopause? Are its effects so unbearable that one might prefer to increase, even ever so slightly, the risk of cancer rather than suffer the daily discomforts encountered during "the change of life"?

Ours is a culture that fears the elderly. Rather than venerate their years and listen to their wisdom, we segregate them in housing built for "their special needs," separated from the younger generations from which we draw hope for the future. At the same time we allow millions of old people to live on inadequate incomes, in fear that serious illness will leave them destitute. The happy, productive elderly remain invisible in our midst. (One must look to feminist publications such as *Our Bodies, Ourselves* to find women who express pleasure in their postmenopausal state.) Television ads portray only the arthritic, the toothless, the wrinkled, and the constipated. If estrogen really is the hormone of youth and its decline suggests the coming of old age, then its loss is a part of biology that our culture ill equips us to handle.

There is, of course, a history to our cultural attitudes toward the elderly woman and our views about menopause. In the nineteenth century physicans believed that at menopause a woman entered a period of depression and increased susceptibility to disease. The postmenopausal body might be racked with "dyspepsia, diarrhea . . . rheumatic pains, paralysis, apoplexy . . . hemorrhaging . . . tuberculosis . . . and diabetes," while emotionally the aging female risked becoming irritable, depressed, hysterical, melancholic, or even insane. The more a woman violated social laws (such as using birth control or promoting female suffrage), the more likely she would be to suffer a disease-ridden menopause.[39] In the twentieth century, psychologist Helene Deutsch wrote that at menopause "woman has ended her existence as a bearer of future life and has reached her natural end—her partial death—as a servant of the species."[40] Deutsch believed that during the postmenopausal years a woman's main psychological task was to accept the progressive biological withering she experienced. Other well-known psychologists have also accepted the idea that a woman's life purpose is mainly reproductive and that her postreproductive years are ones of inevitable decline. Even in recent times postmenopausal women have been "treated" with tranquilizers, hormones, electroshock, and lithium.[41]

But should women accept what many see as an inevitable emotional and biological decline? Should they believe, as Wilson does, that "from a practical point of view a man remains a man until the end," but that after menopause "we no longer have the 'whole woman'—only the 'part woman'"?[42] What is the real story of menopause?

The Change: Its Definition and Physiology

In 1976 under the auspices of the American Geriatric Society and the medical faculty of the University of Montpellier, the First International Congress on the Menopause convened in the south of France. In the volume that emerged from that conference, scientists and clinicians from around the world agreed on a standard definition of the words *menopause* and *climacteric*. "Menopause," they wrote, "indicates the final menstrual period and occurs during the climacteric. The climacteric is that phase in the aging process of women marking the transition from the reproductive stage of life to the non-reproductive stage."[43] By consensus, then, the word *menopause* has come to mean a specific event, the last menstruation, while *climacteric* implies a process occurring over a period of years.*

During the menstrual cycle the blood levels of a number of hormones rise and fall on a regular basis.

At the end of one monthly cycle, the low levels of estrogen and progesterone trigger the pituitary gland to make follicle stimulating hormone (FSH) and luteinizing hormone (LH). The FSH influences the cells of the ovary to make large amounts of estrogen, and induces the growth and maturation of an oocyte. The LH, at just the right moment, induces ovulation and stimulates certain ovarian cells to form a progesterone-secreting structure called a corpus luteum. When no pregnancy occurs the life of the corpus luteum is limited and, as it degenerates, the lowered level of steroid hormones calls forth a new round of follicle stimulating and luteinizing hormone synthesis, beginning the cycle once again. Although the ovary produces the lion's share of these steroid hormones, the cells of the adrenal gland also contribute and this contribution increases in significance after menopause.

What happens to the intricately balanced hormone cycle during the several years preceding menopause is little understood, although it seems likely that gradual changes occur in the balance between pituitary activity (FSH and LH production) and estrogen synthesis.[45] One thing, however, is clear: menopause does not mean the *absence* of estrogen, but rather a gradual lowering in the availability of *ovarian* estrogen. Table 3 summarizes some salient information about changes in steroid hormone levels during the menstrual cycle and after menopause. In looking at the high point of cycle synthesis and then comparing it to women who no longer menstruate, the most dramatic change is seen in the estrogenic hormone estradiol.* The other estrogenic hormones, as well as progesterone and testosterone, drop off to some extent but continue to be synthesized at a level comparable to that observed during the early phases of the menstrual cycle. Instead of concentrating on the notion of estrogen deficiency, however, it is more important to point out that (1) postmenopausally the body makes different kinds of estrogen; (2) the ovaries synthesize less and the adrenals more of these hormones; and (3) the monthly ups and downs of these hormones even out following menopause.

While estrogen levels begin to decline, the levels of FSH and LH start to increase. Changes in these hormones appear as early as eight years before meno-

---

*There is also a male climacteric, which entails a gradual reduction in production of the hormone testosterone over the years as part of the male aging process. What part it plays in that process is poorly understood and seems frequently to be ignored by researchers, who prefer to contrast continuing male reproductive potency with the loss of childbearing ability in women.[44]

*Estrogens are really a family of structurally similar molecules. Their possibly different biological roles are not clearly delineated.

TABLE 3   HORMONE LEVELS AS A PERCENTAGE OF MID-MENSTRUAL-CYCLE HIGH POINT

Stage of Menstrual Cycle	TYPE OF ESTROGEN			Progesterone	Testosterone	Androstenedione
	Estrone	Estradiol	Estriol			
Premenopausal stage						
Early (menses)	20%	13%	67%	100%	55%	87%
Mid (ovulation)	100	100	—	—	100	100
Late (premenstrual)	49	50	100	—	82	—
Postmenopausal stage	17	3	50	50	23	39

SOURCE: Wulf H. Utian, *Menopause in Modern Perspectives* (New York: Appleton-Century-Crofts, 1980), 32.

pause.[46] At the time of menopause and for several years afterward, these two hormones are found in very high concentrations compared to menstrual levels (FSH as many as fourteen times more concentrated than premenopausally, and LH more than three times more). Over a period of years such high levels are reduced to about half their peak value, leaving the postmenopausal woman with one-and-one-half times more LH and seven times more FSH circulating in her blood than when she menstruated regularly.

It is to all of these changes in hormone levels that the words *climacteric* and *menopause* refer. From these alterations Wilson and others have chosen to blame estrogen for the emotional deterioration they believe appears in postmenopausal women. Why they have focused on only one hormone from a complex system of hormonal changes is anybody's guess. I suspect, however, that the reasons are (at least) twofold. First, the normative biomedical disease model of female physiology looks for simple cause and effect. Most researchers, then, have simply assumed estrogen to be a "cause" and set out to measure its "effect." The model or framework out of which such investigators work precludes an interrelated analysis of all the different (and closely connected) hormonal changes going on during the climacteric. But why single out estrogen? Possibly because this hormone plays an important role in the menstrual cycle as well as in the development of "feminine" characteristics such as breasts and overall body contours. It is seen as the quintessential female hormone. So where could one better direct one's attention if, to begin with, one views menopause as the loss of true womanhood?

Physical changes do occur following menopause. Which, if any, of these are caused by changing hormone levels is another question. Menopause research comes equipped with its own unique experimental

traps.[47] The most obvious is that a postmenopausal population is also an aging population. Do physical and emotional differences found in groups of postmenopausal women have to do with hormonal changes or with other aspects of aging? It is a difficult matter to sort out. Furthermore, many of the studies on menopause have been done on preselected populations, using women who volunteer because they experience classic menopausal "symptoms" such as the hot flash. Such investigations tell us nothing about average changes within the population as a whole. In the language of the social scientist, we have no baseline data, nothing to which we can compare menopausal women, no way to tell whether the complaint of a particular woman is typical, a cause for medical concern, or simply idiosyncratic.

Since the late 1970s feminist researchers have begun to provide us with much-needed information. Although their results confirm some beliefs long held by physicians, these newer investigators present them in a more sophisticated context. Dr. Madeleine Goodman and her colleagues designed a study in which they drew information from a large population of women ranging in age from thirty-five to sixty. All had undergone routine multiphasic screening at a health maintenance clinic, but none had come for problems concerning menopause. From the complete clinic records they selected a population of women who had not menstruated for at least one year and compared their health records with those who still menstruated, looking at thirty-five different variables, such as cramps, blood glucose levels, blood calcium, and hot flashes, to see if any of these symptoms correlated with those seen in postmenopausal women. The results are startling. They found that only 28 percent of Caucasian women and 24 percent of Japanese women identified as postmenopausal "reported traditional menopausal symptoms such as hot flashes, sweats, etc., while in nonmenopausal controls, 16% in Caucasians and 10% in Japanese also reported these same symptoms."[48] In other words, 75 percent of menopausal women in their sample reported no remarkable menopausal symptoms, a result in sharp contrast to earlier studies using women who identified themselves as menopausal.

In a similar exploration, researcher Karen Frey found evidence to support Goodman's results. She wrote that menopausal women "did not report significantly greater frequency of physical symptoms or concern about these symptoms than did pre- or postmenopausal women."[49] The studies of Goodman, Frey, and others[50] draw into serious question the notion that menopause is generally or necessarily associated with a set of disease symptoms. Yet at least three physical changes—hot flashes, vaginal dryness and irritation, and osteoporosis—and one emotional one—depression—remain associated in the minds of many with the decreased estrogen levels of the climacteric. Goodman's work indicates that such changes may be far less widespread than previously believed, but if they are troublesome to 26 percent of all menopausal women they remain an appropriate subject for analysis.

We know only the immediate cause of hot flashes: a sudden expansion of the blood flow to the skin. The technical term to describe them, *vasomotor instability*, means only that nerve cells signal the widening of blood vessels allowing more blood into the body's periphery. A consensus has emerged on two things: (1) the high concentration of FSH and LH in blood probably causes hot flashes, although exactly how this happens remains unknown; and (2) estrogen treatment is the only currently available way to suppress the hot flashes. One hypothesis is that by means of a feedback mechanism, artificially raised blood levels of estrogen signal the brain to tell the pituitary to call off the FSH and LH. Although estrogen does stop the hot flashes, its effects are only temporary; remove the estrogen and the flashes return. Left alone, the body eventually adjusts to the changing levels of FSH and LH. Thus a premenopausal woman has two choices in dealing with hot flashes: she can either take estrogen as a permanent medication, a course Wilson refers to as embarking "on the great adventure of preserving or regaining your full femininity,"[51] or suffer some discomfort while nature takes its course. Since the longer one takes estrogen, the greater the danger of estrogen-linked cancer, many health-care workers recommend the latter.[52]

Some women experience postmenopausal vaginal dryness and irritation that can make sexual intercourse painful. Since the cells of the vaginal wall contain estrogen receptors, it is not surprising that estrogen applied locally or taken in pill form helps with this difficulty. Even locally applied, however, the estrogen enters into the bloodstream, presenting the same dangers as when taken in pill form. There are alternative treatments, though, for vaginal dryness. The Boston Women's Health Collective, for example, recommends the use of nonestrogen vaginal creams or jellies, which seem to be effective and are certainly safer. Continued sexual activity also helps—yet another example of the interaction between behavior and physiology.

Hot flashes and vaginal dryness are the *only* climacteric-associated changes for which estrogen unambiguously offers relief. Since significant numbers of women do not experience these changes and since for many of those that do the effects are relatively mild, the wisdom of ERT must be examined carefully and on an individual basis. Both men and women undergo certain changes as they age, but Wilson's catastrophic vision of postmenopausal women—those ghosts gliding by "unnoticed and, in turn, notic[ing] little"[53]—is such a far cry from reality that it is a source of amazement that serious medical writers continue to quote his work.

In contrast to hot flashes and vaginal dryness, osteoporosis, a brittleness of the bone which can in severe cases cripple, has a complex origin. Since this potentially life-threatening condition appears more frequently in older women than in older men, the hypothesis of a relationship with estrogen levels seemed plausible to many. But as one medical worker has said, a unified theory of the disease "is still non-existent, although sedentary life styles, genetic predisposition, hormonal imbalance, vitamin deficiencies, high-protein diets, and cigarette smoking all have been implicated."[54] Estrogen treatment seems to arrest the disease for a while, but may lose effectiveness after a few years.[55]

Even more than in connection with any physical changes, women have hit up against a medical double bind whenever they have complained of emotional problems during the years of climacteric. On the one hand physicians dismissed these complaints as the imagined ills of a hormone-deficient brain, while on the other they generalized the problem, arguing that middle-aged women are emotionally unreliable, unfit for positions of leadership and responsibility. Women had two choices: to complain and experience ridicule and/or improper medical treatment, or to suffer in silence. Hormonal changes during menopause were presumed to be the cause of psychiatric symptoms ranging from fatigue, dizziness, irritability, apprehension, and insomnia to severe headaches and psychotic depression. In recent years, however, these earlier accounts have been supplanted by a rather different consensus now emerging among responsible medical researchers.

To begin with, there are no data to support the idea that menopause has any relationship to serious depression in women. Postmenopausal women who experience psychosis have almost always had similar episodes premenopausally.[56] The notion of the hormonally depressed woman is a shibboleth that must be laid permanently to rest. Some studies have related irritability and insomnia to loss of sleep from nighttime hot flashes. Thus, for women who experience hot flashes, these emotional difficulties might, indirectly, relate to menopause. But the social, life history, and family contexts in which middle-aged women find themselves are more important links to emotional changes occurring during the years of the climacteric. And these, of course, have nothing whatsoever to do with hormones. Quite a number of studies suggest that the majority of women do not consider menopause a time of crisis. Nor do most women suffer from the so-called "empty nest syndrome" supposedly experienced when children leave home. On the contrary, investigation suggests that women without small children are less depressed and have higher incomes and an increased sense of well-being.[57] Such positive reactions depend upon work histories, individual upbringing, cultural background, and general state of health, among other things.

In a survey conducted for *Our Bodies, Ourselves,* one which in no sense represents a balanced cross section of U.S. women, the Boston Women's Health Collective recorded the reactions of more than two hundred menopausal or postmenopausal women, most of whom were suburban, married, and employed, to a series of questions about menopause. About two-thirds of them felt either positively or neutrally about a variety of changes they had undergone,

while a whopping 90 percent felt okay or happy about the loss of childbearing ability![58] This result probably comes as no surprise to most women, but it flies in the face of the long-standing belief that women's lives and emotions are driven in greater part by their reproductive systems.

No good account of adult female development in the middle years exists. Levinson,[59] who studied adult men, presents a linear model of male development designed primarily around work experiences. In his analysis, the male climacteric plays only a secondary role. Feminist scholars Rosalind Barnett and Grace Baruch have described the difficulty of fitting women into Levinson's scheme: "It is hard to know how to think of women within this theory—a woman may not enter the world of work until her late thirties, she seldom has a mentor, and even women with life-long career commitments rarely are in a position to reassess their commitment pattern by age 40," as do the men in Levinson's study.[60]

Baruch and Barnett call for the development of a theory of women in their middle years, pointing out that an adequate one can emerge only when researchers set aside preconceived ideas about the central role of biology in adult female development and listen to what women themselves say. Paradoxically, in some sense we will remain unable to understand more about the role of biology in women's middle years until we have a more realistic *social* analysis of women's postadolescent psychological development. Such an analysis must, of course, take into account ethnic, racial, regional, and class differences among women, since once biology is jettisoned as a universal cause of female behavior, it no longer makes sense to lump all women into a single category.

Much remains to be understood about menopause. Which biological changes, for instance, result from ovarian degeneration and which from other aspects of aging? How does the aging process compare in men and women? What causes hot flashes and can we find safe ways to alleviate the discomfort they cause? Do other aspects of a woman's life affect the number and severity of menopausally related physical symptoms? What can we learn from studying the experience of menopause in other, especially non-Western cultures? A number of researchers have proposed effective ways of finding answers to these questions.[61] We need only time, research dollars, and an open mind to move forward.

CONCLUSION

The premise that women are by nature abnormal and inherently diseased dominates past research on menstruation and menopause. While appointing the male reproductive system as normal, this viewpoint calls abnormal any aspect of the female reproductive life cycle that deviates from the male's. At the same time such an analytical framework places the essence of a woman's existence in her reproductive system. Caught in her hormonal windstorm, she strives to attain normality but can do so only by rejecting her biological uniqueness, for that too is essentially deformed: a double bind indeed. Within such an intellectual structure no medical research of any worth to women's health can be done, for it is the blueprint itself that leads investigators to ask the wrong questions, look in the wrong places for answers, and then distort the interpretation of their results.

Reading through the morass of poorly done studies on menstruation and menopause, many of which express deep hatred and fear of women, can be a discouraging experience. One begins to wonder how it can be that within so vast a quantity of material so little quality exists. But at this very moment the field of menstrual-cycle research (including menopause) offers a powerful antidote to that disheartenment in the form of feminist researchers (both male and female) with excellent training and skills, working within a new analytical framework. Rejecting a strict medical model of female development, they understand that men and women have different reproductive cycles, both of which are normal. Not binary opposites, male and female physiologies have differences and similarities. These research pioneers know too that the human body functions in a social milieu and that it changes in response to that context. Biology is not a one-way determinant but a dynamic component of our existence. And, equally important, these new investigators have learned not only to *listen* to what women say about themselves but to *hear* as well. By and large, these researchers are not in the mainstream of medical and psychological research, but we can look forward to a time when the impact of their work will affect the field of menstrual-cycle research for the better and for many years to come.

NOTES

1. Carroll Smith-Rosenberg and Charles Rosenberg, "The Female Animal: Medical and Biological Views of Woman and Her Role in 19th Century America," *Journal of American History* 60(1973):336.

2. Edgar Berman, Letter to the Editor, *New York Times,* 26 July 1970.

3. Steven Goldberg, *The Inevitability of Patriarchy* (New York: William Morrow, 1973), 93.

4. Herbert Wray, "Premenstrual Changes," *Science News* 122(1982):380–81.

5. Ilza Veith, *Hysteria: The History of a Disease* (Chicago: University of Chicago Press, 1965).

6. Pliny the Elder, quoted in M. E. Ashley-Montagu, "Physiology and Origins of the Menstrual Prohibitions," *Quarterly Review of Biology* 15(1940):211.

7. Smith-Rosenberg and Rosenberg, "The Female Animal"; Henry Maudsley, "Sex in Mind and in Education," *Popular Science Monthly* 5(1874):200; and Joan Burstyn, "Education and Sex: The Medical Case Against Higher Education for Women in England 1870–1900," *Proceeds of the American Philosophical Society* 177(1973):7989.

8. Carroll Smith-Rosenberg, "The Hysterical Woman: Sex Roles and Role Conflict in 19th Century America," *Social Research* 39(1972):652–78.

9. M. A. Hardaker, "Science and the Woman Question," *Popular Science Monthly* 20(1881):583.

10. Nina Morais, "A Reply to Ms. Hardaker on: The Woman Question," *Popular Science Monthly* 21(1882):74–75.

11. Maudsley, "Sex in Mind and in Education," 211.

12. Katharina Dalton, *Once a Month* (Claremont, Calif.: Hunter House, 1983), 78.

13. Ibid.; Katharina Dalton, *The Premenstrual Syndrome* (London: William Heinemann Medical Books, 1972).

14. Andrea Eagan, "The Selling of Premenstrual Syndrome," *Ms.* Oct. 1983, 26–31.

15. Robert L. Reid and S. S. Yen, "Premenstrual Syndrome," *American Journal of Obstetrics and Gynecology* 139(1981):86.

16. J. Abplanalp, R. F. Haskett, and R. M. Rose, "The Premenstrual Syndrome," *Advances in Psychoneuroendocrinology* 3(1980):327–47.

17. Dalton, *Once a Month.*

18. Boston Women's Health Collective, *Our Bodies, Ourselves* (New York: Simon and Schuster, 1979).

19. Reid and Yen, "Premenstrual Syndrome," 86.

20. John O'Connor, M. Shelley Edward, and Lenore O. Stern, "Behavioral Rhythms Related to the Menstrual Cycle," in *Biorhythms and Human Reproduction,* ed. M. Fern et al. (New York: Wiley, 1974), 312.

21. Frank A. Beach, Preface to chapter 10, in *Human Sexuality in Four Perspectives* (Baltimore: Johns Hopkins University Press, 1977), 271.

22. M. B. Rosenthal, "Insights into the Premenstrual Syndrome," *Physician and Patient* (April 1983): 46–53.

23. Herbert Schaumberg et al., "Sensory Neuropathy from Pyridoxine Abuse," *New England Journal of Medicine* 309(1983):446–48.

24. Judith Abplanalp, "Premenstrual Syndrome: A Selective Review," *Women and Health* 8(1983):110.

25. Dalton, *Once a Month,* 12.

26. Abplanalp, Haskett, and Rose, "The Premenstrual Syndrome"; and Abplanalp, "Premenstrual Syndrome: A Selective Review."

27. Abplanalp, "Premenstrual Syndrome: A Selective Review."

28. Reid and Yen, "Premenstrual Syndrome," 97.

29. G. A. Sampson, "An Appraisal of the Role of Progesterone in the Therapy of Premenstrual Syndrome," in *The Premenstrual Syndrome,* ed. P. A. vanKeep and W. H. Utian (Lancaster, England: MTP Press Ltd. International Medical Publishers, 1981), 51–69; and Sampson, "Premenstrual Syndrome: A Double-Bind Controlled Trial of Progesterone and Placebo," *British Journal of Psychiatry* 135(1979):209–15.

30. Robert A. Wilson and Thelma A. Wilson, "The Fate of the Nontreated Postmenopausal Woman: A Plea for the Maintenance of Adequate Estrogen from Puberty to the Grave," *Journal of the American Geriatric Society* 11(1963):352–56.

31. David Reuben, *Everything You Always Wanted to Know about Sex but Were Afraid to Ask* (New York: McKay, 1969), 292.

32. Wulf H. Utian *Menopause in Modern Perspectives* (New York: Appleton-Century-Crofts, 1980).

33. Wilson and Wilson, "The Fate of the Nontreated Postmenopausal Woman," 347.

34. Robert A. Wilson, *Feminine Forever* (New York: M. Evans, 1966).

35. Marilyn Grossman and Pauline Bart, "The Politics of Menopause," in *The Menstrual Cycle,* vol. 1, ed. Dan, Graham, and Beecher.

36. Kathleen MacPherson, "Menopause as Disease: The Social Construction of a Metaphor," *Advances in Nursing Science* 3(1981):95–113; A. Johnson, "The Risks of Sex Hormones as Drugs," *Women and Health* 2(1977):8–11.

37. D. Smith et al., "Association of Exogenous Estrogen and Endometrial Cancer," *New England Journal of Medicine* 293(1975):1164–67.

38. H. Judd et al., "Estrogen Replacement Therapy," *Obstetrics and Gynecology* 58(1981):267–75; M. Quigley, "Postmenopausal Hormone Replacement Therapy: Back to Estrogen Forever?" *Geriatric Medicine Today* 1(1982):78–85; and Thomas Skillman, "Estrogen Replacement: Its Risks and Benefits," *Consultant* (1982):115–27.

39. C. Smith-Rosenberg, "Puberty to Menopause: The Cycle of Femininity in 19th Century America," *Feminist Studies* 1(1973):65.

40. Helene Deutsch, *The Psychology of Women* (New York: Grune and Stratton, 1945), 458.

41. J. H. Osofsky and R. Seidenberg, "Is Female Menopausal Depression Inevitable?," *Obsterics and Gynecology* 36(1970):611.

42. Wilson and Wilson, "The Fate of the Nontreated Postmenopausal Woman," 348.

43. P. A. vanKeep, R. B. Greenblatt, and M. Albeaux-Fernet, eds., *Consensus on Menopause Research* (Baltimore: University Park Press, 1976), 134.

44. Marcha Flint, "Male and Female Menopause: A Cultural Put-on," in *Changing Perspectives on Menopause,* ed. A. M. Voda, M. Dinnerstein, and S. O'Donnell (Austin: University of Texas Press, 1982).

45. Utian, *Menopause in Modern Perspectives.*

46. Ibid.

47. Madeleine Goodman, "Toward a Biology of Menopause," *Signs* 5(1980): 739–53.

48. Madeleine Goodman, C. J. Stewart, and F. Gilbert, "Patterns of Menopause: A Study of Certain Medical and Physiological Variables among Caucasian and Japanese Women Living in Hawaii," *Journal of Gerontology* 32(1977):297.

49. Karen Frey, "Middle-Aged Women's Experience and Perceptions of Menopause," *Women and Health* 6(1981):31.

50. Eve Kahana, A. Kiyak, and J. Liang, "Menopause in the Context of Other Life Events," in *The Menstrual Cycle,* vol. 1, ed. Dan, Graham, and Beecher, 167–78.

51. Wilson, *Feminine Forever,* 134.

52. A. Voda and M. Eliasson, "Menopause: The Closure of Menstrual Life," *Women and Health* 8(1983):137–56.

53. Wilson and Wilson, "The Fate of the Nontreated Postmenopausal Woman," 356.

54. Louis Avioli, "Postmenopausal Osteoporosis: Prevention vs. Cure," *Federation Proceedings* 40(1981):2418.

55. Voda and Eliasson, "Menopause: The Closure of Menstrual Life."

56. G. Winokur and R. Cadoret, "The Irrelevance of the Menopause to Depressive Disease," in *Topics in Psychoendocrinology,* ed. E. J. Sachar (New York: Grune and Stratton, 1975).

57. Rosalind Barnett and Grace Baruch, "Women in the Middle Years: A Critique of Research and Theory," *Psychology of Women Quarterly* 3(1978):187–97.

58. Boston Women's Health Collective, *Our Bodies, Ourselves.*

59. D. Levinson et al., "Periods in the Adult Development of Men: Ages 18–45," *The Counseling Psychologist* 6(1976):21–25.

60. Barnett and Baruch, "Women in the Middle Years," 189.

61. Ibid.; Goodman, "Toward a Biology of Menopause"; and Voda, Dinnerstein, and O'Donnell, eds., *Changing Perspectives on Menopause.*

R E A D I N G   3 2

The AIDS Crisis

BARRY D ADAM

The primary crisis facing the gay movement in the 1980s came from an entirely unexpected source with the discovery of a hitherto unknown fatal virus, which by 1985 claimed more than seven thousand lives, three-quarters of whom were gay men. Lesbians, who were swept along in the discriminatory tide that afflicted gay men following identification of the syndrome, were nevertheless spared from the disease itself. That a disease should apparently pick out certain social groups and not others is no surprise to epidemiologists. Despite the lack of public awareness, many groups defined by social class, age, and ethnic characteristics have their particular disease profiles. Jews are especially vulnerable to Tay-Sachs syndrome, blacks to sickle-cell anemia, women to toxic shock syndrome and breast cancer, and, indeed, middle-aged white men to diseases of the heart and the digestive, respiratory, and genitourinary systems. The virus apparently responsible for acquired immune deficiency syndrome (AIDS) flourishes in blood and semen, leaving gay men uniquely vulnerable to it through semen transmission from man to man. These transmission routes also expose intravenous drug users (through direct blood contact in sharing hypodermic needles), hemophiliacs (through massive blood transfusions), and women who are the sex partners of men carrying the virus. Thus lesbians remain uniquely free. The incidence of AIDS among certain tropical peoples such as heterosexual men and women from central Africa and Haiti was still not well understood in 1985, and, indeed, most of the AIDS cases in Belgium and half in Quebec were counted among these groups.

The first indication of the existence of the new disease was a note in the medical press published in 1981. By 1982, 471 cases of AIDS had been identified in the United States, and by 1985, more than 15,000. Awareness of this new syndrome, which so damages the immune system that normally minor illnesses become fatal, spread through the gay community through 1982, and support groups formed to offer assistance to people with AIDS and to lobby for treatment and research funding. For a year, while gay people watched their friends and lovers dying around them, neither governments nor the media would respond with interest to the pleas of movement groups. Only when the American Broadcasting Company (ABC) ran a news story in the spring of 1983 on *children* with AIDS (typically acquired congenitally from mothers with the disease) did media interest rise, and then media attention focused primarily on the 1 to 2 percent of cases considered to be "innocent victims" of AIDS—female partners of men with AIDS, people with AIDS transmitted through blood transfusions, and children (see Baker, 1985). After several months of coverage, national media and governmental attention waned until the announcement in the summer of 1985 that popular Hollywood actor Rock Hudson was seriously ill with AIDS.

From the beginning, AIDS was socially constructed along a series of moral oppositions that defined gay men as disease carriers polluting an innocent population. Homosexuality, which had only recently been delabeled as an illness, became quickly remedicalized, with gay men labeled as responsible for their own plight and thus undeserving of sympathy. In reviewing the press coverage Edward Albert notes, "Not only is the disease construed as self-caused but, in its presentation on the page, cannot but be read as brought upon us all by 'those' same persons in a causally witnessable way" (1985). AIDS had become the leprosy of the modern age. As Susan Sontag remarks, "In the Middle Ages, the leper was a social text in which corruption was made visible; an exemplar, an emblem of decay" (Sontag, 1978:58). The syndrome was replayed through the moral drama of nineteenth-century cholera, where "disease in the poor retained the power of moral stigma—the slothful poor attracted their diseases—while the . . . same disease in the wealthy was caused by microbes unleashed by *others*" (Patton, 1985:57).

The Christian right was quick to exploit the new opportunity. Jerry Falwell, promoted as an instant expert on the topic by an obliging television network, announced that AIDS was God's punishment upon homosexuals, called upon people with AIDS to be quarantined (or imprisoned if they had sex with anyone), demanded mandatory blood tests for AIDS antibodies and a central file of those testing positive, and urged the closing of gay bathhouses.[1] Fred Niles, on his Sydney television show, demanded that gay Australians traveling to the United States be quarantined on their return.[2] And Republican congressman William Dannemeyer hired professional homophobe Paul Cameron (a psychologist expelled from the American Psychological Association for unethical conduct) as an "AIDS consultant" to advise on how best to exploit the

AIDS issue. Little wonder that rumors began circulating in the gay press that AIDS was a virus developed as a biological weapon by the CIA from the swine fever virus that the CIA had already used to damage hog production in Cuba (Chomsky & Herman, 1979:69).

The result of media exposure was the beginning of research funding and the development of a public panic. With very little understanding of the specific means of transmission, Tulsa city officials drained a municipal swimming pool following its rental to a gay group in 1983, a New York co–op attempted to expel a physician treating people with AIDS, a Florida hospital dumped a person with AIDS on an airplane with a one-way ticket to San Francisco, some medical personnel refused to work with AIDS patients, some police and ambulance workers would not assist people who "looked gay," and a number of funeral directors declined to accept the bodies of people who had died of AIDS.[3]

With national attention focused on the problem of protecting the blood supply, the first research result was the identification in France and the United States of the AIDS virus (LAV/HTLV-3) and the development of a test for antibodies occurring from exposure to the virus. Although the AIDS-antibody test substantially reduced the risk of transmission through blood transfusions, it did not distinguish among people with AIDS, people who carried the virus, people in early stages of AIDS, and people who had recovered from exposure to the virus without developing the disease itself. As with many other diseases, apparently only a minority of those exposed to the virus, in fact, suffered from the disease; many others testing positive remained healthy. Nevertheless, the AIDS antibody offered a new and more effective weapon in identifying large numbers of traditionally stigmatized classes of people, initiating a new round of discriminatory practices. The U.S. military led the way with the announcement that all military personnel would have to take the test and those testing positive would be expelled without benefits. Life insurance companies and employers of food handlers began to press for compulsory blood tests the better to discriminate against (for the most part) gay clients and employees. AIDS-antibody tests were becoming the pink triangles of the 1980s as public labeling procedures setting up gay men and other risk categories as targets for public abuse. In 1985, only San Francisco, Los Angeles, and West Hollywood had legislated against discrimination against people with AIDS. Though some courts elsewhere ruled that the disability category already covered them, the U.S. Justice Department stated publicly that it did not.

In 1983, a national Federation of AIDS-Related Organizations formed in the United States to coordinate public education and support services for people with AIDS. Amid the earlier confusion of the epidemic, even many gay movement organizations accepted the medicoreligious definition of "the" problem, leading to publicity campaigns against promiscuity, arguing that gay men should cut down on the number of their sex partners. Many nongay "experts" did not hesitate to echo the pope in demanding complete celibacy, denying gay men their sexuality altogether. In New York, a sexual compulsion program aimed to convince gay men to get over the sexual freedom of the 1970s, and many were counseled to get a lover—something many would have gladly done long ago if the opportunity had arisen! In San Francisco and then in other cities, public health officials suppressed bathhouses and sex clubs in the belief that AIDS was being spread there (see Levine, 1985; Murray & Payne, 1985; Altman, 1986). But the sex-control policies owed more to entrenched Western mythologies than to scientific logic.

There are some lessons of history to be gained from the study of control measures adopted against sexually transmitted diseases, as Allan Brandt's recent work, *No Magic Bullet,* shows. Sexually transmitted diseases have been wrapped so long in moral reasoning that dispassionate analyses of truly effective means of control have often been pushed aside in the past. As Brandt demonstrates, the control of sexually transmitted diseases has very often been confused with the control of sexuality itself, a conceptualization which overlooks more pragmatic means of prophylaxis, and has led to the unintentional increase of the problem. During the 1910s and 1920s, public health authorities expended a great deal of energy and money attempting to counsel men (especially soldiers) to remain chaste and in closing down "red light" districts across the United States. The results were ever-increasing rates of syphilis and gonorrhea. Infection rates were not brought down until the implementation of quite another policy by the federal government in the 1930s—and this was accomplished in the days before penicillin. The new policy abandoned the daunting task of trying to make sex unpopular in favor of a more prac-

tical approach of making condoms readily available and instructing men in their use. By separating the issue of infection (basically a question of placing a barrier between oneself and the infective agent) from the question of sexuality, significant headway was made in controlling disease.

Bathhouses have existed for more than a century in the United States and have evolved as one of the central institutions of gay male culture. They have offered sexual meeting places, but more important, have also served as places for talk, play, and intimacy—in short, for courtship. In societies traditionally antagonistic to male bonding, bathhouses, along with bars and voluntary associations, have had a significant role to play in providing relatively secure and positive locations for courtship and sociability. From a public health viewpoint, they offer a unique opportunity for encouraging unsensational education about AIDS and other sexually transmitted diseases.

Yet even as the AIDS-related movement consolidated around the safe-sex message, the antigay opposition mobilized to obstruct its efforts. With speech by gay people about their sexuality still targeted by censors, police, and preachers as obscene, safe-sex literature encountered obstacles across the United States and Canada, as a number of local and national jurisdictions confiscated or cut public information fliers intended to limit the spread of AIDS. And the greatest tragedy of all is the approximately five years in which the AIDS virus proliferated with almost no one knowing of its existence.

It is a story in which only the opening chapter has been written. Unrecognized by the larger public are hundreds of stories of individual heroism both of people with AIDS and their supporters—such as the Gay Men's Health Collective in New York, the Shanti Project in San Francisco, and the National Gay Task Force crisis line—who have struggled to make the idea of gay *community* a reality and have ministered to the needs of the beleaguered. In another era, AIDS may have been the occasion for yet another deadly campaign against gay people. In the 1980s, thousands rallied to demand research funding and health care, spoke out to bring the safe-sex message to all, and set up AIDS support committees in every sizeable city. Movement groups often developed their first regular contacts with government agencies to work in common toward containing the virus.

NOTES

1. *Body Politic* 96 (1983):21; *Gay Community News* 13 (no. 3) (1985):2.

2. *Gay Community News* 9 (no. 24) (1983):3.

3. The best coverage of the AIDS crisis is in the *New York Native.* See also the *Advocate, Gay Community News,* and publications of AIDS support groups.

REFERENCES

Albert, E. 1985. "Learning to live with it . . . the routinization of AIDS coverage." Paper presented to the American Sociological Association, Washington, D.C.

Altman, D. 1971. *Homosexual oppression and liberation.* New York: Outerbridge & Dienstfrey.

————.1986, *AIDS in the mind of America.* Garden City, N.Y.: Doubleday.

Baker, A. 1985. "AIDS and the news." Paper presented to the American Sociological Association, Washington, D.C.

Brandt, A. 1985. *No magic bullet.* New York: Oxford University Press.

Chomsky, N., & Herman, E. 1979. *The Washington connection and third world fascism.* Boston: South End Press.

Levine, M. 1985. "The new moral crusade." Paper presented to the Society for the Study of Social Problems, Washington, D.C.

Murray, S. 1984. *Social theory, homosexual realities.* New York: Gai Saber.

Murray, S., & Payne, K. 1985. "The remedicalization of homophobia." Paper presented to the Society for the Study of Social Problems, Washington, D.C.

Patton, C. 1985. *Sex and germs.* Boston: South End Press.

Sontag, S. 1978. *Illness as metaphor.* New York: Farrar, Straus & Giroux.

R E A D I N G 3 3

Racism, Birth Control, and Reproductive Rights

ANGELA Y. DAVIS

When nineteenth-century feminists raised the demand for "voluntary motherhood," the campaign for birth control was born. Its proponents were called radicals and they were subjected to the same mockery as had befallen the initial advocates of woman suffrage. "Vol-

Reprinted from Angela Y. Davis, *Women, Race, and Class* (New York: Random House, 1981), by permission of Random House, Inc. Copyright © 1981 by Angela Davis.

untary motherhood" was considered audacious, outrageous and outlandish by those who insisted that wives had no right to refuse to satisfy their husbands' sexual urges. Eventually, of course, the right to birth control, like women's right to vote, would be more or less taken for granted by U.S. public opinion. Yet in 1970, a full century later, the call for legal and easily accessible abortions was no less controversial than the issue of "voluntary motherhood" which had originally launched the birth control movement in the United States.

Birth control—individual choice, safe contraceptive methods, as well as abortions when necessary—is a fundamental prerequisite for the emancipation of women. Since the right of birth control is obviously advantageous to women of all classes and races, it would appear that even vastly dissimilar women's groups would have attempted to unite around this issue. In reality, however, the birth control movement has seldom succeeded in uniting women of different social backgrounds, and rarely have the movement's leaders popularized the genuine concerns of working-class women. Moreover, arguments advanced by birth control advocates have sometimes been based on blatantly racist premises. The progressive potential of birth control remains indisputable. But in actuality, the historical record of this movement leaves much to be desired in the realm of challenges to racism and class exploitation.

The most important victory of the contemporary birth control movement was won during the early 1970s when abortions were at last declared legal. Having emerged during the infancy of the new Women's Liberation movement, the struggle to legalize abortions incorporated all the enthusiasm and the militancy of the young movement. By January, 1973, the abortion rights campaign had reached a triumphant culmination. In *Roe* v. *Wade* (410 U.S.) and *Doe* v. *Bolton* (410 U.S.), the U.S. Supreme Court ruled that a woman's right to personal privacy implied her right to decide whether or not to have an abortion.

The ranks of the abortion rights campaign did not include substantial numbers of women of color. Given the racial composition of the larger Women's Liberation movement, this was not at all surprising. When questions were raised about the absence of racially oppressed women in both the larger movement and the abortion rights campaign, two explanations were commonly proposed in the discussions and literature of the period: women of color were overburdened by their people's fight against racism; and/or they had not yet become conscious of the centrality of sexism. But the real meaning of the almost lily-white complexion of the abortion rights campaign was not to be found in an ostensibly myopic or underdeveloped consciousness among women of color. The truth lay buried in

the ideological underpinnings of the birth control movement itself.

The failure of the abortion rights campaign to conduct a historical self-evaluation led to a dangerously superficial appraisal of Black people's suspicious attitudes toward birth control in general. Granted, when some Black people unhesitatingly equated birth control with genocide, it did appear to be an exaggerated—even paranoiac—reaction. Yet white abortion rights activists missed a profound message, for underlying these cries of genocide were important clues about the history of the birth control movement. This movement, for example, had been known to advocate involuntary sterilization—a racist form of mass "birth control." If ever women would enjoy the right to plan their pregnancies, legal and easily accessible birth control measures and abortions would have to be complemented by an end to sterilization abuse.

As for the abortion rights campaign itself, how could women of color fail to grasp its urgency? They were far more familiar than their white sisters with the murderously clumsy scalpels of inept abortionists seeking profit in illegality. In New York, for instance, during the several years preceding the decriminalization of abortions in that state, some 80 percent of the deaths caused by illegal abortions involved Black and Puerto Rican women.[1] Immediately afterward, women of color received close to half of all the legal abortions. If the abortion rights campaign of the early 1970s needed to be reminded that women of color wanted desperately to escape the back-room quack abortionists, they should have also realized that these same women were not about to express pro-abortion sentiments. They were in favor of *abortion rights,* which did not mean that they were proponents of abortion. When Black and Latina women resort to abortions in such large numbers, the stories they tell are not so much about their desire to be free of their pregnancy, but rather about the miserable social conditions which dissuade them from bringing new lives into the world.

Black women have been aborting themselves since the earliest days of slavery. Many slave women refused to bring children into a world of interminable forced labor, where chains and floggings and sexual abuse for women were the everyday conditions of life. A doctor practicing in Georgia around the middle of the last century noticed that abortions and miscarriages were far more common among his slave patients than among the white women he treated. According to the physician, either Black women worked too hard or

> as the planters believe, the blacks are possessed of a secret by which they destroy the fetus at an early stage of gestation. . . . All country practitioners are aware of the frequent complaints of planters [about the] . . . unnatural tendency in the African female to destroy her offspring.[2]

Expressing shock that "whole families of women fail to have any children,"[3] this doctor never considered how "unnatural" it was to raise children under the slave system. The episode of Margaret Garner, a fugitive slave who killed her own daughter and attempted suicide herself when she was captured by slavecatchers, is a case in point.

> She rejoiced that the girl was dead—"now she would never know what a woman suffers as a slave"—and pleaded to be tried for murder. "I will go singing to the gallows rather than be returned to slavery!"[4]

Why were self-imposed abortions and reluctant acts of infanticide such common occurrences during slavery? Not because Black women had discovered solutions to their predicament, but rather because they were desperate. Abortions and infanticides were acts of desperation, motivated not by the biological birth process but by the oppressive conditions of slavery. Most of these women, no doubt, would have expressed their deepest resentment had someone hailed their abortions as a stepping-stone toward freedom.

During the early abortion rights campaign it was too frequently assumed that legal abortions provided a viable alternative to the myriad problems posed by poverty. As if having fewer children could create more jobs, higher wages, better schools, etc., etc. This assumption reflected the tendency to blur the distinction between *abortion rights* and the general advocacy of *abortions*. The campaign often failed to provide a voice for women who wanted the *right* to legal abortions while deploring the social conditions that prohibited them from bearing more children.

The renewed offensive against abortion rights that erupted during the latter half of the 1970s has made it absolutely necessary to focus more sharply on the needs of poor and racially oppressed women. By 1977 the passage of the Hyde Amendment in Congress had mandated the withdrawal of federal funding for abortions, causing many state legislatures to follow suit. Black, Puerto Rican, Chicana and Native American Indian women, together with their impoverished white sisters, were thus effectively divested of the right to legal abortions. Since surgical sterilizations, funded by the Department of Health, Education and Welfare, remained free on demand, more and more poor women have been forced to opt for permanent infertility. What is urgently required is a broad campaign to defend the reproductive rights of all women—and especially those women whose economic circumstances often compel them to relinquish the right to reproduction itself.

Women's desire to control their reproductive system is probably as old as human history itself. As early as 1844 the *United States Practical Receipt Book* contained, among its many recipes for food, household chemicals and medicines, "receipts" for "birth preventive lotions." To make "Hannay's Preventive Lotion," for example,

> take pearlash, 1 part; water, 6 parts. Mix and filter. Keep it in closed bottles, and use it, with or without soap, immediately after connexion.[5]

For "Abernethy's Preventive Lotion,"

> take bichloride of mercury, 25 parts; milk of almonds, 400 parts; alcohol, 100 parts; rosewater, 1000 parts. Immerse the glands in a little of the mixture. . . . Infallible, if used in proper time.[6]

While women have probably always dreamed of infallible methods of birth control, it was not until the issue of women's rights in general became the focus of an organized movement that reproductive rights could emerge as a legitimate demand. In an essay entitled "Marriage," written during the 1850s, Sarah Grimke argued for a "right on the part of woman to decide *when* she shall become a mother, how often and under what circumstances."[7] Alluding to one physician's humorous observation, Grimke agreed that if wives and

RIGHT TO LIFE

MARGE PIERCY

Saille

A woman is not a pear tree
thrusting her fruit in mindless fecundity
into the world. Even pear trees bear
heavily one year and rest and grow the next.
An orchard gone wild drops few warm rotting
fruit in the grass but the trees stretch
high and wiry gifting the birds forty
feet up among inch long thorns
broken atavistically from the smooth wood.

A woman is not a basket you place
your buns in to keep them warm. Not a brood
hen you can slip duck eggs under.
Not the purse holding the coins of your
descendants till you spend them in wars.
Not a bank where your genes gather interest
and interesting mutations in the tainted
rain, any more than you are.

You plant corn and you harvest
it to eat or sell. You put the lamb
in the pasture to fatten and haul it in
to butcher for chops. You slice
the mountain in two for a road and gouge
the high plains for coal and the waters
run muddy for miles and years.
Fish die but you do not call them yours
unless you wished to eat them.

Now you legislate mineral rights in a woman.
You lay claim to her pastures for grazing,
fields for growing babies like iceberg
lettuce. You value children so dearly
that none ever go hungry, none weep
with no one to tend them when mothers
work, none lack fresh fruit,
none chew lead or cough to death and your
orphanages are empty. Every noon the best
restaurants serve poor children steaks.

At this moment at nine o'clock a partera
is performing a table top abortion on an
unwed mother in Texas who can't get Medicaid
any longer. In five days she will die
of tetanus and her little daughter will cry
and be taken away. Next door a husband
and wife are sticking pins in the son
they did not want. They will explain
for hours how wicked he is,
how he wants discipline.

We are all born of woman, in the rose
of the womb we suckled our mother's blood
and every baby born has a right to love
like a seedling to sun. Every baby born
unloved, unwanted is a bill that will come
due in twenty years with interest, an anger
that must find a target, a pain that will
beget pain. A decade downstream a child
screams, a woman falls, a synagogue is torched,
a firing squad is summoned, a button
is pushed and the world burns.

I will choose what enters me, what becomes
flesh of my flesh. Without choice, no politics,
no ethics lives. I am not your cornfield,
not your uranium mine, not your calf
for fattening, not your cow for milking.
You may not use me as your factory.
Priests and legislators do not hold
shares in my womb or my mind.
This is my body. If I give it to you
I want it back. My life
is a non-negotiable demand.

husbands alternatively gave birth to their children, "no family would ever have more than three, the husband bearing one and the wife two."[8] But, as she insists, "the *right* to decide this matter has been almost wholly denied to woman."[9]

Sarah Grimke advocated women's right to sexual abstinence. Around the same time the well-known "emancipated marriage" of Lucy Stone and Henry Blackwell took place. These abolitionists and women's rights activists were married in a ceremony that protested women's traditional relinquishment of their rights to their persons, names and property. In agreeing that as husband, he had no right to the "custody of the wife's person,"[10] Henry Blackwell promised that he would not attempt to impose the dictates of his sexual desires upon his wife.

The notion that women could refuse to submit to their husband's sexual demands eventually became the central idea of the call for "voluntary motherhood." By the 1870s, when the woman suffrage movement had reached its peak, feminists were publicly advocating voluntary motherhood. In a speech delivered in 1873, Virginia Woodhull claimed that

> the wife who submits to sexual intercourse against her wishes or desires, virtually commits suicide; while the husband who compels it, commits murder, and ought just as much to be punished for it, as though he strangled her to death for refusing him.[11]

Woodhull, of course, was quite notorious as a proponent of "free love." Her defense of a woman's right to abstain from sexual intercourse within marriage as a means of controlling her pregnancies was associated with Woodhull's overall attack on the institution of marriage.

It was not a coincidence that women's consciousness of their reproductive rights was born within the organized movement for women's political equality. Indeed, if women remained forever burdened by incessant childbirths and frequent miscarriages, they would hardly be able to exercise the political rights they might win. Moreover, women's new dreams of pursuing careers and other paths of self-development outside marriage and motherhood could be realized only if they could limit and plan their pregnancies. In this sense, the slogan "voluntary motherhood" contained a new and genuinely progressive vision of womanhood. At the same time, however, this vision was rigidly bound to the lifestyle enjoyed by the middle classes and the bourgeoisie. The aspirations underlying the demand for "voluntary motherhood" did not reflect the conditions of working-class women, engaged as they were in a far more fundamental fight for economic survival. Since this first call for birth control was associated with goals which could be achieved only by women possessing material wealth, vast numbers of poor and working-class women would find it rather difficult to identify with the embryonic birth control movement.

Toward the end of the nineteenth century the white birth rate in the United States suffered a significant decline. Since no contraceptive innovations had been publicly introduced, the drop in the birth rate implied that women were substantially curtailing their sexual activity. By 1890 the typical native-born white woman was bearing no more than four children.[12] Since U.S. society was becoming increasingly urban, this new birth pattern should not have been a surprise. While farm life demanded large families, they became dysfunctional within the context of city life. Yet this phenomenon was publicly interpreted in a racist and anti-working-class fashion by the ideologues of rising monopoly capitalism. Since native-born white women were bearing fewer children, the specter of "race suicide" was raised in official circles.

In 1905 President Theodore Roosevelt concluded his Lincoln Day Dinner speech with the proclamation that "race purity must be maintained."[13] By 1906 he blatantly equated the falling birth rate among native-born whites with the impending threat of "race suicide." In his State of the Union message that year Roosevelt admonished the well-born white women who engaged in "willful sterility—the one sin for which the penalty is national death, race suicide."[14] These comments were made during a period of accelerating racist ideology and of great waves of race riots and lynchings on the domestic scene. Moreover, President Roosevelt himself was attempting to muster support for the U.S. seizure of the Philippines, the country's most recent imperialist venture.

How did the birth control movement respond to Roosevelt's accusation that their cause was promoting race suicide? The President's propagandistic ploy was a failure, according to a leading historian of the birth control movement, for, ironically, it led to greater support for its advocates. Yet, as Linda Gordon maintains, this controversy "also brought to the forefront those issues that most separated feminists from the working class and the poor."[15]

This happened in two ways. First, the feminists were increasingly emphasizing birth control as a route to careers and higher education—goals out of reach of the poor with or without birth control. In the context of the whole feminist movement, the race-suicide episode was an additional factor identifying feminism almost exclusively with the aspirations of the more privileged women of the society. Second, the pro-birth control feminists began to popularize the idea that poor people had a moral obligation to restrict the size of their families, because large families create a drain on the taxes and charity expenditures of the wealthy and because poor children were less likely to be "superior."[16]

The acceptance of the race-suicide thesis, to a greater or lesser extent, by women such as Julia Ward Howe and Ida Husted Harper reflected the suffrage movement's capitulation to the racist posture of Southern women. If the suffragists acquiesced to arguments invoking the extension of the ballot to women as the saving grace of white supremacy, then birth control advocates either acquiesced to or supported the new arguments invoking birth control as a means of preventing the proliferation of the "lower classes" and as an antidote to race suicide. Race suicide could be prevented by the introduction of birth control among Black people, immigrants and the poor in general. In this way, the prosperous whites of solid Yankee stock could maintain their superior numbers within the population. Thus class bias and racism crept into the birth control movement when it was still in its infancy. More and more, it was assumed within birth control circles that poor women, Black and immigrant alike, had a "moral obligation to restrict the size of their families."[17] What was demanded as a "right" for the privileged came to be interpreted as a "duty" for the poor.

When Margaret Sanger embarked upon her lifelong crusade for birth control—a term she coined and popularized—it appeared as though the racist and anti-

working-class overtones of the previous period might possibly be overcome. For Margaret Higgens Sanger came from a working-class background herself and was well acquainted with the devastating pressures of poverty. When her mother died, at the age of forty-eight, she had borne no less than eleven children. Sanger's later memories of her own family's troubles would confirm her belief that working-class women had a special need for the right to plan and space their pregnancies autonomously. Her affiliation, as an adult, with the Socialist movement was a further cause for hope that the birth control campaign would move in a more progressive direction.

When Margaret Sanger joined the Socialist party in 1912, she assumed the responsibility of recruiting women from New York's working women's clubs into the party.[18] *The Call*—the party's paper—carried her articles on the women's page. She wrote a series entitled "What Every Mother Should Know," another called "What Every Girl Should Know," and she did on-the-spot coverage of strikes involving women. Sanger's familiarity with New York's working-class districts was a result of her numerous visits as a trained nurse to the poor sections of the city. During these visits, she points out in her autobiography, she met countless numbers of women who desperately desired knowledge about birth control.

According to Sanger's autobiographical reflections, one of the many visits she made as a nurse to New York's Lower East Side convinced her to undertake a personal crusade for birth control. Answering one of her routine calls, she discovered that twenty-eight-year-old Sadie Sachs had attempted to abort herself. Once the crisis had passed, the young woman asked the attending physician to give her advice on birth prevention. As Sanger relates the story, the doctor recommended that she "tell [her husband] Jake to sleep on the roof."[19]

I glanced quickly to Mrs. Sachs. Even through my sudden tears I could see stamped on her face an expression of absolute despair. We simply looked at each other, saying no word until the door had closed behind the doctor. Then she lifted her thin, blue-veined hands and clasped them beseechingly. "He can't understand. He's only a man. But you do, don't you? Please tell me the secret, and I'll never breathe it to a soul. Please!"[20]

Three months later Sadie Sachs died from another self-induced abortion. That night, Margaret Sanger says, she vowed to devote all her energy toward the acquisition and dissemination of contraceptive measures.

> I went to bed knowing that no matter what it might cost, I was finished with palliatives and superficial cures; I resolved to seek out the root of evil, to do something to change the destiny of mothers whose miseries were as vast as the sky.[21]

During the first phase of Sanger's birth control crusade, she maintained her affiliation with the Socialist party—and the campaign itself was closely associated with the rising militancy of the working class. Her staunch supporters included Eugene Debs, Elizabeth Gurley Flynn and Emma Goldman, who respectively represented the Socialist party, the International Workers of the World and the anarchist movement. Margaret Sanger, in turn, expressed the anti-capitalist commitment of her own movement within the pages of its journal, *Woman Rebel,* which was "dedicated to the interests of working women."[22] Personally, she continued to march on picket lines with striking workers and publicly condemned the outrageous assaults on striking workers. In 1914, for example, when the National Guard massacred scores of Chicano miners in Ludlow, Colorado, Sanger joined the labor movement in exposing John D. Rockefeller's role in this attack.[23]

Unfortunately, the alliance between the birth control campaign and the radical labor movement did not enjoy a long life. While Socialists and other working-class activists continued to support the demand for birth control, it did not occupy a central place in their overall strategy. And Sanger herself began to underestimate the centrality of capitalist exploitation in her analysis of poverty, arguing that too many children caused workers to fall into their miserable predicament. Moreover, "women were inadvertently perpetuating the exploitation of the working class," she believed, "by continually flooding the labor market with new workers."[24] Ironically, Sanger may have been encouraged to adopt this position by the neo-Malthusian ideas embraced in some socialist circles. Such outstanding figures of the European socialist movement as Anatole France and Rosa Luxemburg had proposed

a "birth strike" to prevent the continued flow of labor into the capitalist market.[25]

When Margaret Sanger severed her ties with the Socialist party for the purpose of building an independent birth control campaign, she and her followers became more susceptible than ever before to the anti-Black and anti-immigrant propaganda of the times. Like their predecessors, who had been deceived by the "race suicide" propaganda, the advocates of birth control began to embrace the prevailing racist ideology. The fatal influence of the eugenics movement would soon destroy the progressive potential of the birth control campaign.

During the first decades of the twentieth century the rising popularity of the eugenics movement was hardly a fortuitous development. Eugenic ideas were perfectly suited to the ideological needs of the young monopoly capitalists. Imperialist incursions in Latin America and in the Pacific needed to be justified, as did the intensified exploitation of Black workers in the South and immigrant workers in the North and West. The pseudoscientific racial theories associated with the eugenics campaign furnished dramatic apologies for the conduct of the young monopolies. As a result, this movement won the unhesitating support of such leading capitalists as the Carnegies, the Harrimans and the Kelloggs.[26]

By 1919 the eugenic influence on the birth control movement was unmistakably clear. In an article published by Margaret Sanger in the American Birth Control League's journal, she defined "the chief issue of birth control" as "more children from the fit, less from the unfit."[27] Around this time the ABCL heartily welcomed the author of *The Rising Tide of Color Against White World Supremacy* into its inner sanctum.[28] Lothrop Stoddard, Harvard professor and theoretician of the eugenics movement, was offered a seat on the board of directors. In the pages of the ABCL's journal, articles by Guy Irving Birch, director of the American Eugenics Society, began to appear. Birch advocated birth control as a weapon to

> prevent the American people from being replaced by alien or Negro stock, whether it be by immigration or by overly high birth rates among others in this country.[29]

By 1932 the Eugenics Society could boast that at least twenty-six states had passed compulsory sterilization laws and that thousands of "unfit" persons had already been surgically prevented from reproducing.[30] Margaret Sanger offered her public approval of this development. "Morons, mental defectives, epileptics, illiterates, paupers, unemployables, criminals, prostitutes and dope fiends" ought to be surgically sterilized, she argued in a radio talk.[31] She did not wish to be so intransigent as to leave them with no choice in the matter; if they wished, she said, they should be able to choose a lifelong segregated existence in labor camps.

Within the American Birth Control League, the call for birth control among Black people acquired the same racist edge as the call for compulsory sterilization. In 1939 its successor, the Birth Control Federation of America, planned a "Negro Project." In the Federation's words,

the mass of Negroes, particularly in the South, still breed carelessly and disastrously, with the result that the increase among Negroes, even more than among whites, is from that portion of the population least fit, and least able to rear children properly.[32]

Calling for the recruitment of Black ministers to lead local birth control committees, the Federation's proposal suggested that Black people should be rendered as vulnerable as possible to their birth control propaganda. "We do not want word to get out," wrote Margaret Sanger in a letter to a colleague,

that we want to exterminate the Negro population and the minister is the man who can straighten out that idea if it ever occurs to any of their more rebellious members.[33]

This episode in the birth control movement confirmed the ideological victory of the racism associated with eugenic ideas. It had been robbed of its progressive potential, advocating for people of color not the individual right to *birth control*, but rather the racist strategy of *population control*. The birth control campaign would be called upon to serve in an essential capacity in the execution of the U.S. government's imperialist and racist population policy.

The abortion rights activists of the early 1970s should have examined the history of their movement.

Had they done so, they might have understood why so many of their Black sisters adopted a posture of suspicion toward their cause. They might have understood how important it was to undo the racist deeds of their predecessors, who had advocated birth control as well as compulsory sterilization as a means of eliminating the "unfit" sectors of the population. Consequently, the young white feminists might have been more receptive to the suggestion that their campaign for abortion rights include a vigorous condemnation of sterilization abuse, which had become more widespread than ever.

It was not until the media decided that the casual sterilization of two Black girls in Montgomery, Alabama, was a scandal worth reporting that the Pandora's box of sterilization abuse was finally flung open. But by the time the case of the Relf sisters broke, it was practically too late to influence the politics of the abortion rights movement. It was the summer of 1973 and the Supreme Court decision legalizing abortions had already been announced in January. Nevertheless, the urgent need for mass opposition to sterilization abuse became tragically clear. The facts surrounding the Relf sisters' story were horrifyingly simple. Minnie Lee, who was twelve years old, and Mary Alice, who was fourteen, had been unsuspectingly carted into an operating room, where surgeons irrevocably robbed them of their capacity to bear children.[34] The surgery had been ordered by the HEW-funded Montgomery Community Action Committee after it was discovered that Depo-Provera, a drug previously administered to the girls as a birth prevention measure, caused cancer in test animals.[35]

After the Southern Poverty Law Center filed suit on behalf of the Relf sisters, the girls' mother revealed that she had unknowingly "consented" to the operation, having been deceived by the social workers who handled her daughters' case. They had asked Mrs. Relf, who was unable to read, to put her "X" on a document, the contents of which were not described to her. She assumed, she said, that it authorized the continued Depo-Provera injections. As she subsequently learned, she had authorized the surgical sterilization of her daughters.[36]

In the aftermath of the publicity exposing the Relf sisters' case, similar episodes were brought to light. In Montgomery alone, eleven girls, also in their teens, had been similarly sterilized. HEW-funded birth control clinics in other states, as it turned out, had also subjected young girls to sterilization abuse. Moreover, individual women came forth with equally outrageous stories. Nial Ruth Cox, for example, filed suit against the state of North Carolina. At the age of eighteen— eight years before the suit—officials had threatened to discontinue her family's welfare payments if she refused to submit to surgical sterilization.[37] Before she assented to the operation, she was assured that her infertility would be temporary.[38]

Nial Ruth Cox's lawsuit was aimed at a state which had diligently practiced the theory of eugenics. Under the auspices of the Eugenics Commission of North Carolina, so it was learned, 7,686 sterilizations had been carried out since 1933. Although the operations were justified as measures to prevent the reproduction of "mentally deficient persons," about 5,000 of the sterilized persons had been Black.[39] According to Brenda Feigen Fasteau, the ACLU attorney representing Nial Ruth Cox, North Carolina's recent record was not much better.

> As far as I can determine, the statistics reveal that since 1964, approximately 65% of the women sterilized in North Carolina were Black and approximately 35% were white.[40]

As the flurry of publicity exposing sterilization abuse revealed, the neighboring state of South Carolina had been the site of further atrocities. Eighteen women from Aiken, South Carolina, charged that they had been sterilized by a Dr. Clovis Pierce during the early 1970s. The sole obstetrician in that small town, Pierce had consistently sterilized Medicaid recipients with two or more children. According to a nurse in his office, Dr. Pierce insisted that pregnant welfare women "will have to submit [sic!] to voluntary sterilization" if they wanted him to deliver their babies.[41] While he was "tired of people running around and having babies and paying for them with my taxes,"[42] Dr. Pierce received some $60,000 in taxpayers' money for the sterilizations he performed. During his trial he was supported by the South Carolina Medical Association, whose members declared that doctors "have a moral and legal right to insist on sterilization permission before accepting a patient, if it is done on the initial visit."[43]

Revelations of sterilization abuse during that time exposed the complicity of the federal government. At first the Department of Health, Education and Welfare claimed that approximately 16,000 women and 8,000 men had been sterilized in 1972 under the auspices of federal programs.[44] Later, however, these figures underwent a drastic revision. Carl Shultz, director of HEW's Population Affairs Office, estimated that between 100,000 and 200,000 sterilizations had actually been funded that year by the federal government.[45] During Hitler's Germany, incidentally, 250,000 sterilizations were carried out under the Nazis' Hereditary Health Law.[46] Is it possible that the record of the Nazis, throughout the years of their reign, may have been almost equaled by U.S. government-funded sterilization in the space of a single year?

Given the historical genocide inflicted on the native population of the United States, one would assume that Native American Indians would be exempted from the government's sterilization campaign. But according to Dr. Connie Uri's testimony in a Senate committee hearing, by 1976 some 24 percent of all Indian women of childbearing age had been sterilized.[47] "Our blood lines are being stopped," the Choctaw physician told the Senate committee. "Our unborn will not be born. . . . This is genocidal to our people."[48] According to Dr. Uri, the Indian Health Services Hospital in Claremore, Oklahoma, had been sterilizing one out of every four women giving birth in that federal facility.[49]

Native American Indians are special targets of government propaganda on sterilization. In one of the HEW pamphlets aimed at Indian people, there is a sketch of a family with *ten children* and *one horse* and another sketch of a family with *one child* and *ten horses.* The drawings are supposed to imply that more children mean more poverty and fewer children mean wealth. As if the ten horses owned by the one-child family had been magically conjured up by birth control and sterilization surgery.

The domestic population policy of the U.S. government has an undeniably racist edge. Native American, Chicana, Puerto Rican and Black women continue to be sterilized in disproportionate numbers. According to a National Fertility Study conducted in 1970 by Princeton University's Office of Population Control, 20 percent of all married Black women have been permanently sterilized.[50] Approximately the same percentage of Chicana women had been rendered surgically infertile.[51] Moreover, 43 percent of the women sterilized through federally subsidized programs were Black.[52]

The astonishing number of Puerto Rican women who have been sterilized reflects a special government policy that can be traced back to 1939. In that year President Roosevelt's Interdepartmental Committee on Puerto Rico issued a statement attributing the island's economic problems to the phenomenon of overpopulation.[53] This committee proposed that efforts be undertaken to reduce the birth rate to no more than the level of the death rate.[54] Soon afterward an experimental sterilization campaign was undertaken in Puerto Rico. Although the Catholic Church initially opposed this experiment and forced the cessation of the program in 1946, it was converted during the early 1950s to the teachings and practice of population control.[55] In this period over 150 birth control clinics were opened, resulting in a 20 percent decline in population growth by the mid-1960s.[56] By the 1970s over 35 percent of all Puerto Rican women of childbearing age had been surgically sterilized.[57] According to Bonnie Mass, a serious critic of the U.S. government's population policy,

> if purely mathematical projections are to be taken seriously, if the present rate of sterilization of 19,000 monthly were to continue, then the island's population of workers and peasants could be extinguished within the next 10 or 20 years . . . [establishing] for the first time in world history a systematic use of population control capable of eliminating an entire generation of people.[58]

During the 1970s the devastating implications of the Puerto Rican experiment began to emerge with unmistakable clarity. In Puerto Rico the presence of corporations in the highly automated metallurgical and pharmaceutical industries had exacerbated the problem of unemployment. The prospect of an ever-larger army of unemployed workers was one of the main incentives for the mass sterilization program. Inside the United States today, enormous numbers of people of color—and especially racially oppressed youth—have become part of a pool of permanently unemployed workers. It is hardly coincidental, considering the Puerto Rican example, that the increasing incidence of sterilization has kept pace with the high rates of un-

employment. As growing numbers of white people suffer the brutal consequences of unemployment, they can also expect to become targets of the official sterilization propaganda.

The prevalence of sterilization abuse during the latter 1970s may have been greater than ever before. Although the Department of Health, Education and Welfare issued guidelines in 1974, which were ostensibly designed to prevent involuntary sterilizations, the situation nonetheless deteriorated. When the American Civil Liberties Union's Reproductive Freedom Project conducted a survey of teaching hospitals in 1975, they discovered that 40 percent of those institutions were not even aware of the regulations issued by HEW.[59] Only 30 percent of the hospitals examined by the ACLU were even attempting to comply with the guidelines.[60]

The 1977 Hyde Amendment has added yet another dimension to coercive sterilization practices. As a result of this law passed by Congress, federal funds for abortions were eliminated in all cases but those involving rape and the risk of death or severe illness. According to Sandra Salazar of the California Department of Public Health, the first victim of the Hyde Amendment was a twenty-seven-year-old Chicana woman from Texas. She died as a result of an illegal abortion in Mexico shortly after Texas discontinued government-funded abortions. There have been many more victims—women for whom sterilization has become the only alternative to the abortions which are currently beyond their reach. Sterilizations continue to be federally funded and free, to poor women, on demand.

The struggle against sterilization abuse has continued to be waged primarily by Puerto Rican, Black, Chicana and Native American women. Their cause has not yet been embraced by the women's movement as a whole. Within organizations representing the interests of middle-class white women, there has been a certain reluctance to support the demands of the campaign against sterilization abuse, for these women are often denied their individual rights to be sterilized when they desire to take this step. While women of color are urged, at every turn, to become permanently infertile, white women enjoying prosperous economic conditions are urged, by the same forces, to reproduce themselves. They therefore sometimes consider the "waiting period" and other details of the demand for "informed consent" to sterilization as further inconveniences for women like themselves. Yet whatever the inconveniences for white middle-class women, a fundamental reproductive right of racially oppressed and poor women is at stake. Sterilization abuse must be ended.

NOTES

1. Edwin M. Gold et al., "Therapeutic Abortions in New York City: A Twenty-Year Review," in *American Journal of Public Health* 55 (July 1965): 964–72, quoted in Lucinda Cisla, "Unfinished Business: Birth Control and Women's Liberation," in Robin Morgan, ed., *Sisterhood Is Powerful: An Anthology of Writings from the Women's Liberation Movement* (New York: Vintage Books, 1970), p. 261. Also quoted in Robert Staples, *The Black Woman in America* (Chicago: Nelson Hall, 1974), p. 146.

2. Herbert Gutman, *The Black Family in Slavery and Freedom, 1750–1925* (New York: Pantheon, 1976), pp. 80–81 (note).

3. Ibid.

4. Herbert Aptheker, "The Negro Woman," *Masses and Mainstream* 11 (no. 2) (February 1948): 12.

5. Quoted in Rosalyn Baxandall, Linda Gordon, & Susan Reverby, eds., *America's Working Women: A Documentary History—1600 to the Present* (New York: Random House, 1976), p. 17.

6. Ibid.

7. Gerda Lerner, *The Female Experience: An American Documentary* (Indianapolis: Bobbs-Merrill, 1977), p. 91.

8. Ibid.

9. Ibid.

10. "Marriage of Lucy Stone under Protest" appeared in *History of Woman Suffrage*, vol. 1, quoted in Miriam Schneir, ed., *Feminism: The Essential Historical Writings* (New York: Vintage, 1972), p. 104.

11. Speech by Virginia Woodhull, "The Elixir of Life," quoted in Schneir, p. 153.

12. Mary P. Ryan, *Womanhood in America from Colonial Times to the Present* (New York: Franklin Watts, 1975), p. 162.

13. Melvin Steinfeld, *Our Racist Presidents* (San Ramon, Calif.: Consensus Publishers, 1972), p. 212.

14. Bonnie Mass, *Population Target: The Political Economy of Population Control in Latin America* (Toronto: Women's Educational Press, 1977), p. 20.

15. Linda Gordon, *Woman's Body, Woman's Right: Birth Control in America* (New York: Penguin, 1976), p. 157.

16. Ibid., p. 158.

17. Ibid.

18. Margaret Sanger, *An Autobiography* (New York: Dover Press, 1971), p. 75.

19. Ibid., p. 90.

20. Ibid., p. 91.

21. Ibid., p. 92.

22. Ibid., p. 106.

23. Mass, *Population Target*, p. 27.

24. Bruce Dancis, "Socialism and Women in the United States, 1900–1912," *Socialist Revolution*, No. 27, vol vi, No. 1 (January–March, 1976), p. 96.

25. David M. Kennedy, *Birth Control in America: The Career of Margaret Sanger* (New Haven and London: Yale University Press, 1976), pp. 21–22.

26. Mass, *Population Target*, p. 20.

27. Gordon, *Woman's Body*, p. 281.

28. Mass, *Population Target*, p. 20.

29. Gordon, *Woman's Body*, p. 283.

30. Herbert Aptheker, "Sterilization, Experimentation and Imperialism," *Political Affairs* 53 (no. 1) (January 1974): 44.

31. Gena Corea, *The Hidden Malpractice* (New York: Jove, 1977), p. 149.

32. Gordon, *Woman's Body*, p. 332.

33. Ibid, pp. 332–333.

34. Aptheker, "Sterilization," p. 38. See also Anne Braden, "Forced Sterilization: Now Women Can Fight Back," *Southern Patriot*, September 1973.

35. Ibid.

36. Jack Slater, "Sterilization, Newest Threat to the Poor," *Ebony* 28 (no. 12) (October 1973): 150.

37. Braden, "Forced Sterilization."

38. Les Payne, "Forced Sterilization for the Poor?" *San Francisco Chronicle*, February 26, 1974.

39. Harold X., "Forced Sterilization Pervades South," *Muhammed Speaks*, October 10, 1975.

40. Slater, "Sterilization."

41. Payne, "Forced Sterilization."

42. Ibid.

43. Ibid.

44. Aptheker, "Sterilization," p. 40.

45. Payne, "Forced Sterilization."

46. Aptheker, "Sterilization," p. 48.

47. Arlene Eisen, "They're Trying to Take Our Future—Native American Women and Sterilization," *The Guardian,* March 23, 1972.

48. Ibid.

49. Ibid.

50. Quoted in a pamphlet issued by the Committee to End Sterilization Abuse, Box A244, Cooper Station, New York 10003.

51. Ibid.

52. Ibid.

53. Gordon, *Woman's Body,* p. 338.

54. Ibid.

55. Mass, *Population Target,* p. 92.

56. Ibid., p. 91.

57. Gordon, *Woman's Body,* p. 401.

58. Mass, *Population Target,* p. 108.

59. Rahemah Aman, "Forced Sterilization," *Union Wage,* March 4, 1978.

60. Ibid.

R E A D I N G   3 4

Mothers or MD's? Women Physicians and the Doctor–Patient Relationship

JUDITH LORBER

The recent influx of women into formerly male-dominated prestigious professions, such as medicine, has been expected to make a difference in perspectives and priorities, relationships with colleagues and clients, and the structure and services of the institutions in which they work. The theory behind such predictions assumes that the increase in numbers gives a formerly token or minority group a "critical mass," that women and men have different attitudes and relationships, that these differences are maintained throughout coeducational training and will become manifest when men and women are located in similar work situations and have similar opportunities for professional behavior.

The strategy of emphasizing women's special qualities as a way of enhancing their social status was prominent in the nineteenth century (Freedman, 1979; Rothman, 1978) but fell out of favor with feminists in the early twentieth century (Rosenberg, 1982). Its recurrence as a feminist political tactic has been

Reproduced by permission from a paper presented at the meetings of the Eastern Sociological Society, Philadelphia, March 1985. Copyright © 1985 by the Social Policy Corp.

useful to combat the cooptation of a small elite and the subtle denigration of women as a group (Lorber, 1981). Yet the emphasis on difference rather than on the similarity of women and men is disturbing to those who feel women do not have a priority on sensitivity, sympathy, and care-giving behavior (Epstein, 1984; Jagger, 1983; Merton, 1972; Stacey, 1983).

In medicine, nineteenth-century women physicians successfully used claims of gender congruity in the cutthroat competition for patients, but male physicians countered by challenging their capacity for mastering the new scientific medical curriculum (Drachman, 1976; Morantz, 1978; Walsh, 1977). With the help of wealthy women who served as trustees, women physicians were able to establish and run their own clinics and dispensaries (Walsh, 1977:76–105; Drachman, 1984). Though the women physicians' medical knowledge differed not at all from that of male physicians, Marie Zakrzewska's New England Hospital for Women kept more careful records, varied the length of stay by social need, and designed the layout of the wards to minimize the spread of infection (Morantz & Zschoche, 1980).

In the first part of the twentieth century, women

physicians helped set up and staff state and federally funded prenatal and child health centers throughout the United States. As called for by the Sheppard-Towner Act of 1921, these women-dominated centers offered preventive care, education in hygiene, and low-cost medical services (Rothman, 1978:136–53; Starr, 1982:260–61). Under pressure from private physicians, their federal funding was withdrawn, and they were closed in 1930 (Costin, 1983). In the ensuing years, low numbers, geographical isolation, and competition from client-hungry male physicians made women physicians in the United States a virtually invisible part of their professional communities (Lorber, 1984).

Now that the proportion of women has risen to approximately one-quarter of the total of U.S. medical school graduates, we must ask again if they do differ from male students, and if so, whether these differences will affect their behavior as doctors; and finally, whether the actions of the substantially increased numbers of women physicians in this country will significantly affect the structure of medical institutions and the delivery of medical services. In the Soviet Union, where medicine is a female-dominated profession, male physicians hold the majority of the positions of prestige and power (Dodge, 1971:218). Women physicians' relations with their patients in primary care settings are maternal and solicitous, but since they lack significant structural power, their work reflects government policies, not their own (Haug, 1976).

In the United States there is little evidence that women medical students are particularly nurturant (McGrath & Zimet, 1977), nor do they have more patient-oriented or altruistic attitudes when they graduate (Leserman, 1981). Yet women physicians seem to find it easier to communicate with dying patients and their families (Dickerson & Pearson, 1979). Women physicians are less frequently sued for malpractice, which may be a consequence of their concentration in low-risk specialties (Holder, 1979).

GENDER CONGRUITY IN THE DOCTOR–PATIENT RELATIONSHIP

Patients who choose physicians tend to prefer physicians of their own religion and ethnic background, and white patients in the United States are very reluctant to consult black physicians, but women patients do not strongly or consistently prefer physicians of their own gender (Ackerman-Ross & Sochat, 1980; Levinson et al., 1984). The issue of gender incongruity may be one of default. More women than men visit physicians, but since most physicians in the United States are men, unless women deliberately seek out women physicians, they are likely to be referred to male doctors. Since the physician is an authority figure and the patient often feels like a "passive object," it may go against the cultural grain for men to submit to women "for problems involving extensive handling, probing, and undressing," but not for women to submit to male physicians (Ackerman-Ross & Sochat, 1980:64).

In the Soviet Union, where the majority of physicians are women, male patients are routinely examined by women physicians. Like women patients in the United States, they have little choice but to consult physicians of the opposite sex. As women physicians become more numerous in the United States, women patients who prefer them will have more of a choice, and those who are neutral will have greater exposure to the experience. When the presence of women physicians is common, as it is getting to be on hospital house staffs and in clinics and group practices, patients with negative attitudes will be more reluctant to express them openly.

In a turnabout, one male physician I interviewed, a dermatologist, felt he was discriminated against because patients preferred to see one of his sisters, who was in practice in the same community. He said, "Ladies like to see ladies. There are even men who prefer to see lady doctors; they think they're more sympathetic." A woman general practitioner in her seventies similarly felt that "men go to women doctors when they are in trouble—for a mother image." A woman internist, however, felt that men who sought out female physicians were "unsavory." She described two experiences with men who got her name from a hospital directory who she felt were psychosexually abnormal, and she now refuses any male patients who are not referred by someone she knows. Another internist felt she frequently got referrals of "crocks" or difficult patients because she was a woman and supposedly could handle these patients better than a male physician. In general, the gender composition of most practices depends on the specialty. Those with general practices have more women than men patients whether they themselves are male or female.

RELATIONSHIPS WITH PATIENTS—ARE WOMEN DOCTORS DIFFERENT?

Patients' choices of women or men physicians raises the perennial question of whether women doctors actually relate to patients differently from male physicians. Only one physician I interviewed, a patient-oriented general practitioner, felt women and men physicians handled patients differently. She said, "Women in medicine by and large pay attention to small things. Most patients do not have major diseases—they have little annoying things. And also there's always a psychological component."

To see whether, from the physicians' point of view, men and women relate to patients differently, I asked what kinds of patients they liked most and least. The responses from male and female physicians in office-based practice were monotonously similar. The women's best-liked patients were "young, basically healthy, pleasant, and easy to get along with," "cooperative," "successful, self-assured, interested in knowing," "intelligent," "normal, straightforward," "very educated and very achieved." The men's best-liked patients were those who were "medically compliant, understanding, well-paying," "appreciate what you're trying to do," "were middle-class, moderately educated," "my kind, my level of education, easy to get on with and don't question your expertise," "a person where there's some kind of intervention that can help," "bright, successful, creative."

Male and female physicians were equally similar in their descriptions of the patients they liked least. The women disliked patients who were "demanding," "had chronic pain," "lunatic of the month," "worrywort, completely dissatisfied," "neurotic and demanding," "narcissistic," "very garrulous, very demanding, very manipulative," "tells you what to do." The men disliked patients who were "nitpicking," "show an obvious suspicion, lack of confidence from the outset, hostile and aggressive," "question without good reason," "argue with you about every medical decision," "call up several times a day about minor problems."

In short, women and men physicians, like most medical workers, prefer patients who allow them to carry out their tasks with a minimum of fuss and make little trouble; are cooperative, trusting, and appreciative of their care; and are likely to benefit from their treatment. Problem patients for both male and female physicians are those with intractable physical problems, who complain a great deal, are very emotional and anxious, and need a lot of reassurance, encouragement, and attention. They are especially disliked when they are not very sick (Lorber, 1975). Although many patients come to doctors' offices with minor complaints and just need someone to talk to, physicians are trained to deal with serious illnesses and life-threatening pathologies, and they often consider many of their consultations to be "trivial, unnecessary, or inappropriate" (Cartwright & Anderson, 1981). There is little indication that women physicians are more feeling-oriented than their male colleagues, and patients who seek sympathy from them and do not get it may turn hostile.

Both the differences and similarities between men and women physicians may be situational and interactional. Women physicians may be perceived by patients as more empathic (Davidson, 1975; Heins et al., 1979) or they may cultivate a more expressive style of interaction. If women physicians are sought out by potential patients for their sympathetic qualities, they may respond in ways that are likely to keep their patients coming to them. If affectively neutral behavior is the norm, as in medical school or in the care of hospital patients, and their behavior is under scrutiny by teachers and colleagues, men and women may display less affect than they feel (Daniels, 1960; Klass, 1984). Overt behavior is probably not a reflection of feelings but a response to what is seen as situationally appropriate by the people—clients or faculty or colleagues—whose opinions must necessarily be attended to.

An important contingency in the behavior of physicians, as with members of other professions, is the extent of their control over their work situation. In order to be able to dominate a work situation, a professional needs to have exclusive training, valued expertise, control of resources to carry out the work, decisive powers of authority, and the belief and trust of the recipients of services (Freidson, 1970a, 1970b). If a woman physician is in a position of authority or is offering scarce and valued services, then we might expect that she would be freer to behave in ways that *she* felt were appropriate, which may be more detached than patients would like or more concerned than her colleagues would like.

WOMEN PHYSICIANS' EFFECT ON MEDICAL PRACTICE

Rosabeth Moss Kanter contended that placement in a work situation has greater salience than gender in predicting behavior (1975, 1977a), and that as the number of men and women in a workplace becomes more balanced, gender differences are minimized (1977a, 1977b). One of Kanter's predictions made the structure of organizations the most important factor in predicting the behavior of those differentially positioned; the other, the well-known "Kanter hypothesis," predicted that the numerical aggregate of like and unlike individuals was crucial in effects on behavior. The two hypotheses should be combined. With command of resources, decision-making powers, and prestigious status, an individual can exert enough control within a work situation to express his or her differences from the dominant group, but only when enough of the minority group with similar perspectives, priorities, and new ways of behaving gain positions of control will the organizational structure be changed in significant ways (cf. Kanter, 1983).

If women are more nurturant, empathic, and sensitive to others' needs, and if enough women with these characteristics become physicians with authority, resources, and high professional status, then the routine delivery of health care in the United States might exhibit more sensitivity to patients' psychological and social needs. In that case, the burden of change is on women, who would be expected, if given enough resources and power, to reform the system. The feminist message of difference is that they can do so and should be given the authority to do so, although feminists committed to this point of view have also recognized the dilemmas and pitfalls of the double task of feminist reform and professional work (Howell, 1977; Ruzek, 1978).

At this point, we do not know if the small number of women physicians with a high degree of control over their work lives do relate to their patients in ways that are different from those of similarly situated men. If they do, and these differences improve the quality of care, then increasing the resources and authority of more women physicians would be sound policy. If they do not, fairness would encourage the increase of women in medicine, but the area of change would have to lie in medical school curricula, postgraduate

medical training, and the attitudes of those who are in a position to advance the careers of novice physicians. The burden of change would then be on the system as a whole, with the goal of producing men and women physicians with patient-oriented perspectives. Those who claim that women and men are more alike than different would argue that reforming the system and changing both men and women physicians is a sounder policy than making the whole project of improving the quality of care the responsibility of women physicians (Hubbard, 1977; Marieskind, 1975). In neither instance would just increasing the numbers of women physicians make much difference in the quality of care, for if the project is to be women's, they must also have the authority and prestige to carry out their policies.

The crucial issue is whether the status and power of women physicians will rise commensurately with their increase in numbers. Like women physicians in England and the Soviet Union, women physicians in the United States may increasingly find themselves doing mainly primary and preventive care. These are vital areas of medical work, but they bring women doctors into competition with other women health workers, particularly nurse-practitioners, who claim expertise in the same areas of health care (Lurie, 1981). If nurse-practitioners also offer diagnoses and treatment of routine illnesses and preventive care, and offer it at lower cost, women physicians will be hard-pressed to claim superior status or payment. And yet it is as primary care practitioners that the new women physicians are being "welcomed" into the profession (Geyman, 1980; Relman, 1980; Wallace, 1980). A typical statement is the following:

> The women's groups in the United States now trying to take steps to improve women's health care are the consumer, nurse midwives, and nurse practitioners. One would expect women physicians to be in the vanguard of this movement, but this is not the case. Similarly, one would hope that the care of women of childbearing age and the care of infants and children would be delivered together. This would be the beginning of family health care. Thus, women physicians have a unique opportunity and role to play in improving the system by delivery of health care in the United States. This should be one

of the top priorities for women physicians for today and tomorrow. [Wallace, 1980:211]

Would such a mandate give women physicians a powerful position in medicine? Only if family health care had top priority in funding and women doctors were given the authority to organize and direct these services. In the United States, under entrepreneurial practice, when services become lucrative, they are taken over by male physicians (Pawluch, 1983). In England, under the National Health Service, this sector of medical care is underfunded (Elston, 1977). In the Soviet Union, where extensive primary and preventive care is mandated by the state, women physicians have authority over patients but not over state medical policy (Lapidus, 1978; Haug, 1976).

In the United States, as medical practice becomes more bureaucratized under government and corporate control (Freidson, 1983; Starr, 1982:235–49; Mechanic, 1976), women physicians will probably be overrepresented in the rank-and-file of provider institutions. Rather than forming the vanguard of a consumer-oriented, open-access medical system, women physicians are likely to find themselves in open competition for autonomy, status, and even jobs with nurse-practitioners, nurse-midwives, and physicians' assistants. They will all be doing virtually the same work, and professional status will depend on success in political power games (Lorber & Satow, 1977). Such infighting makes the colleague group in the workplace crucial, and it is precisely here that women lose out (Lorber, 1984; Olson & Miller, 1983; Wolf & Fligstein, 1979a, 1979b). With increasing numbers of doctors and growing competition from non-MD licensed health workers, male physicians are not likely to forgo the chance to point to women's family commitments or unsuitability for leadership in an effort to retain a competitive edge and administrative control of health care delivery institutions and academic medicine. Under pressure from outside, the colleague group can be expected to close ranks against competitors, and for male physicians, these competitors may very well be women physicians.

In the near future, women physicians in the United States are likely to split into two groups: those who align with other physicians in the fight to maintain professional dominance and those who align with other women health-care workers and consumers in the fight for a health-care system with a flatter hierarchy and a holistic and self-help perspective (Howell, 1977; Kleiber & Light, 1978; Ruzek, 1978; Shapiro & Jones, 1979). As with so much else about women physicians, their opportunities and dilemmas mirror the structured choices and political strategies of other women workers in their respective societies.

REFERENCES

Ackerman-Ross, S., & Sochat, N. 1980. "Close encounters of the medical kind: Attitudes toward male and female physicians." *Social Science and Medicine* 14A:60–64.

Cartwright, A., & Anderson, R. 1981. *General practice revisited.* New York: Methuen.

Costin, L. B. 1983. "Women and physicians: The 1930 White House Conference on Children." *Social Work,* March–April, pp. 108–14.

Daniels, M. J. 1960. "Affect and its control in the medical intern." *American Journal of Sociology* 66:259–67.

Davidson, L. R. 1975. "Sex roles, affect, and the woman physician: A study of the impact of latent social identity upon the role of the professional." Ph.D. dissertation, New York University.

Dickerson, G. R., & Pearson, A. A. 1979. "Sex differences of physicians in relating to dying patients." *Journal of the American Medical Women's Association* 34:45–47.

Dodge, N. 1971. "Women in the Soviet economy." In A. Theodore, ed., *The professional woman,* pp. 207–23. Cambridge, Mass.: Schenckman.

Drachman, V. G. 1976. "Women doctors and the women's medical movement: Feminism and medicine, 1850–1895." Ph.D. dissertation, State University of New York.

Drachman, V. G. 1984. *Hospital with a heart.* Ithaca, N.Y.: Cornell University Press.

Elston, M. A. 1977. "Women in the medical professional: Whose problem?" In M. Stacey, M. Reid, C. Heath, & R. Dingwall, eds., *Health and the division of labour,* pp. 115–38. London: Croom Helm.

Epstein, C. 1984. "Ideal images and real roles." *Dissent,* Fall, pp. 441–47.

Freedman, E. 1979. "Separatism as strategy: Female institution building and American feminism, 1970–1930." *Feminist Studies* 5:512–29.

Freidson, E. 1970a. *Professional dominance.* New York: Atherton

Freidson, E. 1970b. *Profession of medicine.* New York: Dodd, Mead.

Freidson, E. 1983. "The reorganization of the profession by regulation." *Law and Human Behavior* 7:279–90.

Geyman, J. P. 1980. "Increasing number of women in family practice: An overdue trend." *Journal of Family Practice* 10:207–08.

Haug, M. R. 1976. "The erosion of professional authority: A cross-cultural inquiry in the case of physicians." *Health and Society,* Winter, pp. 83–106.

Heins, M.; Hendricks, J.; & Martindale, L. 1979. "Attitudes of women and men physicians." *American Journal of Public Health* 69:1132–39.

Holder, A. R. 1979. "Women physicians and malpractice suits." *Journal of the American Medical Women's Association* 34:239–40.

Howell, M. C. 1977. "Guest editorial: Can we be feminist physicians? Mirages, dilemmas, and traps." *Journal of Health Politics, Policy, and Law* 2:168–72.

Hubbard, R. 1977. "On constructing a non-sexist medical school curriculum." American Medical Women's Association Workshop for Women in Medical Academia, Tucson, May.

Jagger, A. M. 1983. *Feminist politics and human nature.* Totowa, N.J.: Rowman & Allenheld.

Kanter, R. M. 1975. "Women and the structure of organizations: Explorations in theory and behavior." In R. M. Kanter & M. Millman, eds., *Another voice: Feminist perspectives on social life and social science,* pp. 34–74. Garden City, N.Y.:Doubleday/Anchor.

Kanter, R. M. 1977a. *Men and women of the corporation.* New York: Basic Books.

Kanter, R. M. 1977b. "Some effects of proportions on group life: Skewed sex ratios and responses to token women." *American Journal of Sociology* 82:965–90.

Kanter, R. M. 1983. *The change masters.* New York: Simon & Schuster.

Klass, P. 1984. "Doctors cry, too, although they may not like to admit it." *New York Times,* September 27.

Kleiber, N., & Light, L. 1978. *Caring for ourselves: An alternative structure for health care.* Vancouver: University of British Columbia School of Nursing.

Lapidus, G. W. 1978. *Women in Soviet society.* Berkeley: University of California Press.

Leserman, J. 1981. *Men and women in medical school.* New York: Praeger.

Levinson, R. M.; McCollum, K. T.; & Kutner, W. G. 1984. "Gender homophily in preferences for physicians." *Sex Roles* 10:315–25.

Lorber, J. 1975. "Good patients and problem patients: Conformity and deviance in a general hospital." *Journal of Health and Social Behavior* 16:213–25.

Lorber, J. 1981. "Minimalist and maximalist feminist ideologies and strategies for change." *Quarterly Journal of Ideology* 5:61–66.

Lorber, J. 1984. *Women physicians: Careers, status, and power.* London & New York: Tavistock.

Lorber, J., & Satow, R. 1977. "Creating a company of unequals: Sources of occupational stratification in a ghetto community mental health center." *Sociology of Work and Occupations* 4:281–302.

Lurie, E. 1981. "Nurse practitioners: Issues in professional socialization." *Journal of Health and Social Behavior* 22:31–48.

McGrath, E., & Zimet, C. N. 1977. "Female and male medical students: Differences in specialty choice selection and personality." *Journal of Medical Education* 52:293–300.

Marieskind, H. I. 1975. "Restructuring ob-gyn." *Social Policy,* September–October, pp. 48–49.

Mechanic, D. 1976. *The growth of bureaucratic medicine.* New York: Wiley.

Merton, R. K. 1972. "Insiders and outsiders: A chapter in the sociology of knowledge." *American Journal of Sociology* 78:9–47.

Morantz, R. M. 1978. "The 'connecting link': The case for the woman doctor in nineteenth-century America." In J. W. Leavitt & R. L. Numbers, eds., *Sickness and health in America,* pp. 117–28. Madison: University of Wisconsin Press.

Morantz, R. M., & Zschoche, S. 1980. "Professionalism, feminism and gender roles: A comparative study of nineteenth-century medical therapeutics." *Journal of American History* 68:568–88.

Olson, J., & Miller, J. 1983. "Gender and interaction in the workplace." In H. Lopata & J. H. Pleck, eds., *Research in the interweave of social roles: Jobs and families,* 3:35–58. Greenwich: JAI Press.

Pawluch, D. 1983. "Transitions in pediatrics: A segmental analysis." *Social Problems* 30:449–65.

Relman, A. S. 1980. "Here come the women" (editorial). *New England Journal of Medicine* 302:1252–53.

Rosenberg, R. 1982. *Beyond separate spheres.* New Haven: Yale University Press.

Rothman, B. K. 1978. *Woman's proper place.* New York: Basic Books.

Ruzek, S. B. 1978. *The women's health movement.* New York: Praeger.

Shapiro, E. C., & Jones, A. B. 1979. "Women physicians and the exercise of power and authority in health care."In E. Shapiro & L. M. Lowenstein, eds., *Becoming a physician: Development of values and attitudes in medicine,* pp. 237–45. Cambridge, Mass.: Ballinger.

Stacey, J. 1983. "The new conservative feminism." *Feminist Studies* 9:559–83.

Starr, P. 1982. *The social transformation of American medicine.* New York: Basic Books.

Wallace, H. M. 1980. "Women in medicine." *Journal of the American Medical Women's Association* 35:201–11.

Walsh, M. R. 1977. *"Doctors wanted: No women need apply": Sexual barriers in the medical profession, 1835–1975.* New Haven: Yale University Press.

Wolf, W. C., & Fligstein, N. D. 1979a. "Sex and authority in the workplace: The causes of sexual inequality." *American Sociological Review* 44:235–52.

Wolf, W. C., & Fligstein, N. D. 1979b. "Sexual stratification: Differences in power in the work setting." *Social Forces* 58:94–107.

R E A D I N G   3 5

Midwives in Transition: The Structure of a Clinical Revolution

BARBARA KATZ ROTHMAN

There has been considerable interest in the United States in recent years in the medical management of the reproductive processes in healthy women. Much of this interest represents a growing recognition by many mothers that hospital births impose structures upon the birth process unrelated to and in many cases disruptive of the process itself.

This paper contends that changing the setting of birth from hospital to home alters the timing of the birth process, a result of the social redefinition of birth. Through an analysis of the medical literature on birth, I compare the social construction of timetables for childbirth—how long normal labor and birth takes—by hospital and home-birth practitioners. I argue that, like all knowledge, this knowledge is socially determined and socially constructed, influenced both by ideology and social setting.

This paper is based on interviews I conducted in 1978 with one subgroup of the home-birth movement: nurse-midwives certified by the State of New York to attend births. I located 12 nurse-midwives in the New York metropolitan area who were attending births in homes and at an out-of-hospital birth center. Nurse-

midwives in the United States are trained in medical institutions one to two years beyond nursing training and obtain their formative experience in hospitals. They differ from lay midwives, who receive their training outside of medical institutions and hospitals. Once nurse-midwives are qualified, most of them continue to practice in hospitals. I use the term *nurse-midwives* to distinguish them from lay midwives. I discuss those parts of the interviews with these nurse-midwives which focus on their reconceptualization of birth timetables as they moved from hospital to home settings.

This sample was selected for two reasons: first, because of the position that nurse-midwives hold in relation to mothers compared with that held by physicians; while physicians in hospital settings control the birth process, nurse-midwives in home settings permit the birth process to transpire under the mother's control. Second, because nurse-midwives have been both formally trained within the medical model and extensively exposed to the home-birth model, data gathered in monitoring their adjustment to and reaction to the home-birth model provide a cross-contextual source for comparing the two birth settings.

Observation of the reactions of nurse-midwives to the home-birth setting demonstrates the degree to which their medical training was based on social con-

Reprinted by permission from *Social Problems* 30, no. 3 (February 1983): 262–71. Copyright © 1983 by the Society for the Study of Social Problems.

vention rather than biological constants. The nurse-midwives did not embrace their non-medical childbirth work as ideological enthusiasts; rather, they were drawn into it, often against what they perceived as their better medical judgment. The nurse-midwives were firmly grounded in the medical model. Their ideas of what a home birth should and would be like, when they first began doing them, were based on their extensive experience with hospital births. While they believed that home birth would provide a more pleasant, caring, and warm environment than that ordinarily found in hospital birth, they did not expect it to challenge medical knowledge. And at first, home births did not. What the nurse-midwives saw in the home setting was screened through their expectations based on the hospital setting. The medical model was challenged only with repeated exposures to the anomalies of the home-birth experience.

The nurse-midwives' transition from one model to another is comparable to scientists' switch from one paradigm to another—a "scientific revolution," in Kuhn's (1970) words. Clinical models, like paradigms, are not discarded lightly by those who have invested time in learning and following them. The nurse-midwives were frequently not prepared for the anomalies in the timetable that they encountered at home. These involved unexpected divergences from times for birthing stages as "scheduled" by hospitals. Breaking these timetable norms without the expected ensuing "complications" provided the nurse-midwives attending home births with anomalies in the medical model. With repeated exposure to such anomalies, the nurse-midwives began to challenge the basis of medical knowledge regarding childbirth.

The medical approach divides the birth process into socially structured stages. Each of these stages is supposed to last a specific period of time. Roth (1963) notes that medical timetables structure physical processes and events, creating sanctioned definitions and medical controls. Miller (1977) has shown how medicine uses timetables to construct its own version of pregnancy. Similarly, medical timetables construct medical births: challenging those timetables challenges the medical model itself.

There are four parts of the birth process subject to medical timetables: (1) term (the end of pregnancy); (2) the first stage of labor; (3) delivery; and (4) expulsion of the placenta. I describe the hospital and home-birth approaches to these four parts and how each

part's timetable issues arise. Then I consider the function of these timetables for doctors, hospitals, and the medical model.

(1) TERM: THE END OF PREGNANCY

The Hospital Approach

In the medical model, a full-term pregnancy is 40 weeks long, though there is a two-week allowance made on either side for "normal" births. Any baby born earlier than 38 weeks is "premature"; after 42 weeks, "postmature." Prematurity does not produce any major conceptual anomalies between the two models. If a woman attempting home birth goes into labor much before the beginning of the 38th week, the nurse-midwives send her to a hospital because they, like physicians, perceive prematurity as abnormal, although they may not agree with the subsequent medical management of prematurity. In fact, few of the nurse-midwives' clients enter labor prematurely.

Postmaturity, however, has become an issue for the nurse-midwives. The medical treatment for postmaturity is to induce labor, either by rupturing the membranes which contain the fetus or by administering hormones to start labor contraction, or both. Rindfuss (1977) has shown that physicians often induce labor without any "medical" justification for mothers' and doctors' convenience.

Induced labor is more difficult for the mother and the baby. Contractions are longer, more frequent, and more intense. The more intense contractions reduce the baby's oxygen supply. The mother may require medication to cope with the more difficult labor, thus further increasing the risk of injury to the baby. In addition, once the induced labor (induction) is attempted, doctors will go on to delivery shortly thereafter, by Cesarian section if necessary.

The Home-Birth Approach

These techniques for inducing labor are conceptualized as "interventionist" and "risky" within the home-birth movement. The home-birth clients of the nurse-midwives do not want to face hospitalization and inductions, and are therefore motivated to ask for more time and, if that is not an option, to seek "safe" and "natural" techniques for starting labor. Some nurse-midwives suggest nipple stimulation, sexual relations, or even castor oil and enemas as means of stimulating uterine contractions. As I interviewed the 12 nurse-midwives about their techniques it was unclear whether their concern was avoiding postmaturity *per se* or avoiding medical treatment for postmaturity.

The nurse-midwives said that the recurring problem of postmaturity has led some home-birth practitioners to re-evaluate the length of pregnancy. Home-birth advocates point out that the medical determination of the length of pregnancy is based on observations of women in medical care. These home-birth advocates argue that women have been systematically malnourished by medically ordered weight-gain limitations. They attribute the high level of premature births experienced by teenage women to malnourishment resulting from overtaxing of their energy reserves by growth as well as fetal needs. The advocates believe that very well-nourished women are capable of maintaining a pregnancy longer than are poorly nourished or borderline women. Thus, the phenomenon of so many healthy women going past term is reconceptualized in this developing model as an indication of even greater health, rather than a pathological condition of "postmaturity."

The first few times a nurse-midwife sees a woman going past term she accepts the medical definition of the situation as pathological. As the problem is seen repeatedly in women who manifest no signs of pathology, and who go on to have healthy babies, the conceptualization of the situation as pathological is shaken. Nurse-midwives who have completed the transition from the medical to home-birth model reject the medical definition and reconceptualize what they see from "postmature" to "fully mature."

(2) THE FIRST STAGE OF LABOR

The Hospital Approach

Childbirth, in the medical model, consists of three "stages" that occur after term. (In this paper I consider term as the first part of the birth process, occurring at the end of pregnancy.) In the first stage of childbirth, the cervix (the opening of the uterus into the vagina) dilates to its fullest to allow for the passage of the baby. In the second stage, the baby moves out of the open cervix, through the vagina, and is born. The third stage

is the expulsion of the placenta. The second example of a point at which anomalies arise is in "going into labor," or entering the first stage.

The medical model of labor is best represented by "Friedman's Curve" (Friedman, 1959). To develop this curve, Friedman observed labors and computed averages for each "phase" of labor. He defined a *latent phase* as beginning with the onset of labor, taken as the onset of regular uterine contractions, to the beginnings of an *active phase*, when cervical dilation is most rapid. The onset of regular contractions can be determined only retroactively. *Williams' Obstetrics* (Hellman & Pritchard, 1971), the classic obstetric text, says that the first stage of labor (which contains the two "phases") "begins with the first true labor pains and ends with the complete dilation of the cervix" (1971:351). "True labor pains" are distinguished from "false labor pains" by what happens next:

> The only way to distinguish between false and true labor pains, however, is to ascertain their effect on the cervix. The labor pains in the course of a few hours produce a demonstrable degree of effacement [thinning of the cervix] and some dilation of the cervix, whereas the effect of false labor pains on the cervix is minimal. [1971:387]

The concept of "false" labor serves as a buffer for the medical model of "true" labor. Labors which display an unusually long "latent phase," or labors which simply stop, can be diagnosed as "false labors" and thus not affect the conceptualization of true labor. Friedman (1959:97) says:

> The latent phase may occasionally be found to be greater than the limit noted, and yet the remaining portion of the labor, the active phase of dilatation, may evolve completely normally. These unusual cases may be explained on the basis of the difficulty of determining the onset of labor. The transition from some forms of false labor into the latent phase of true labor may be completely undetectable and unnoticed. This may indeed be an explanation for the quite wide variation seen among patients of the actual duration of the latent phase.

In creating his model, Friedman obtained average values for each phase of labor, both for women with first pregnancies and for women with previous births.

Then he computed the statistical limits and equated statistical normality with physiological normality:

> It is clear that cases where the phase-durations fall outside of these [statistical] limits are probably abnormal in some way. . . . We can see now how, with very little effort, we have been able to define average labor and to describe, with proper degree of certainty, the limits of normal. [1959:97]

Once the equation is made between statistical abnormality and physiological abnormality, the door is opened for medical intervention. Thus, statistically abnormal labors are medically treated. The medical treatments are the same as those for induction of labor: rupture of membranes, hormones, and Cesarian section.

"Doing something" is the cornerstone of medical management. Every labor which takes "too long" and which cannot be stimulated by hormones or by breaking the membranes will go on to the next level of medical management, the Cesarian section. Breaking the membranes is an interesting induction technique in this regard: physicians believe that if too many hours pass after the membranes have been ruptured, naturally or artificially, a Cesarian section is necessary in order to prevent infection. Since physicians within the hospital always go on from one intervention to the next, there is no place for feedback; that is, one does not get to see what happens when a woman stays in first stage for a long time without her membranes being ruptured.

Hospital labors are shorter than home-birth labors. A study by Mehl (1977) of 1,046 matched, planned home and hospital births found that the average length of first-stage labor for first births was 14.5 hours in the home and 10.4 hours in the hospital. *Williams' Obstetrics* reports the average length of labor for first births was 12.5 hours in 1948 (Hellman & Pritchard, 1971:396). For subsequent births, Mehl found first-stage labor took an average of 7.7 hours in the home and 6.6 hours in the hospital. Hellman and Pritchard reported 7.3 hours for the same stage. Because 1948 hospital births are comparable to contemporary home births, and because contemporary hospital births are shorter, it is probable that there has been an increase in "interventionist obstetrics," as home-birth advocates claim. These data are summarized in Table 1.

TABLE 1   LABOR TIMETABLES FOR THE FIRST AND SECOND STAGES OF BIRTH, FOR FIRST AND SUBSEQUENT BIRTHS

Birth	LENGTH OF FIRST STAGE OF LABOR (hours)		
	Home 1970s	Hospital 1948	Hospital 1970s
First	14.5	12.5	10.4
Subsequent	7.7/8.5[a]	7.3[b]	6.6/5.9[a]
	LENGTH OF SECOND STAGE OF LABOR (minutes)		
First	94.7	80	63.9
Subsequent	48.7/21.7[a]	30[b]	19/15.9[a]

[a]Second births and third births.
[b]Second and all subsequent births.

The Home-Birth Approach

Home-birth advocates see each labor as unique. While statistical norms may be interesting, they are of no value in managing a particular labor. When the nurse-midwives have a woman at home, or in the out-of-hospital birth-center, both the nurse-midwife and the woman giving birth to complete birth without disruption. Rather than using arbitrary time limits, nurse-midwives look for progress, defined as continual change in the direction of birthing. A more medically oriented nurse-midwife expressed her ambivalence this way: "They don't have to look like a Friedman graph walking around, but I think they should make some kind of reasonable progress." Unable to specify times for "reasonable" progress, she nonetheless emphasized the word "reasonable," distinguishing it from "unreasonable" waiting.

A nurse-midwife with more home-birth experience expressed more concern for the laboring woman's subjective experience: "There is no absolute limit—it would depend on what part of the labor was the longest and how she was handling that. Was she tired? Could she handle that?" A labor at home can be long but "light," uncomfortable but not painful. A woman at home may spend those long hours going for a walk, napping, listening to music, even gardening or going to a movie. This light labor can to on for quite some time. Another nurse-midwife described how she dealt with a long labor:

> Even though she was slow, she kept moving. I have learned to discriminate now, and if it's long I let them do it at home on their own and I try to listen carefully and when I get there it's toward the end of labor. This girl was going all Saturday and all Sunday, so that's 48 hours worth of labor. It wasn't forceful labor, but she was uncomfortable for two days. So if I'd have gone and stayed there the first time, I'd have been there a whole long time, then when you get there you have to do something.

(3) DELIVERY: PUSHING TIME LIMITS

The Hospital Approach

The medical literature defines the second stage of labor, the delivery, as the period from the complete dilatation of the cervix to the birth of the fetus. Hellman and Pritchard (1971) found this second stage took an average of 80 minutes for first births and 30 minutes for all subsequent births in 1948. Mehl (1977) found home births took an average of 94.7 minutes for first births and, for second and third births, 48.7 to 21.7 minutes. Contemporary medical procedures shorten the second stage in the hospital to 63.9 minutes for first births and 19 to 15.9 minutes for second and third births (Mehl, 1977).

The modern medical management of labor and delivery hastens the delivery process, primarily by the use of forceps and fundal pressure (pressing on the top of the uterus through the abdomen) to pull or push a fetus out. Friedman (1959) found the second stage of birth took an average of 54 minutes for first births and 18 minutes for all subsequent births. He defined the "limits of normal" as 2.5 hours for first births and 48 minutes for subsequent births. Contemporary hospitals usually apply even stricter limits, and allow a maximum of two hours for first births and one hour for second births. Time limits vary somewhat within U.S. hospitals, but physicians and nurse-midwives in training usually do not get to see a three-hour second stage, much less anything longer. "Prolonged" second stages are medically managed to effect immediate delivery.

Mehl (1977) found low forceps were 54 times more common and mid-forceps 21 times more common for prolonged second-stage and/or protracted descent in the hospital than in planned home births. This does not include the elective use of forceps (without "medical" indication), a procedure which was used in none of the home births and 10 percent of the hospital births (4 percent low forceps and 6 percent mid-forceps). Any birth which began at home but was hospitalized for any reason, including protracted descent or prolonged second stage (10 percent of the sample), was included in Mehl's home-birth statistics.

The Home-Birth Approach

Nurse-midwives and their out-of-hospital clients were even more highly motivated to avoid hospitalization for prolonged delivery than for prolonged labor. There is a sense of having come so far, through the most difficult and trying part. Once a mother is fully dilated she may be so close to birth that moving her could result in giving birth on the way to the hospital. Contrary to the popular image, the mother is usually working hard but not in pain during the delivery, and as tired as she may be, is quite reluctant to leave home.

Compare the situation at home with what the nurse-midwives saw in their training. In a hospital birth the mother is moved to a delivery table at or near the end of cervical dilation. She is usually strapped into leg stirrups and heavily draped. The physician is scrubbed and gowned. The anesthetist is at the ready. The pediatric staff is in the room. It is difficult to imagine that situation continuing for three, four, or more hours. The position of the mother alone makes that impossible. In the medical model, second stage begins with complete cervical dilation. Cervical dilation is an "objective" measure, determined by the birth attendant. By defining the end of the first stage, the birth attendant controls the time of formal entry into second stage. One of the ways nurse-midwives quickly learn to "buy time" for their clients is in measuring cervical dilation: "If she's honestly fully dilated I do count it as second stage. If she has a rim of cervix left, I don't count it because I don't think it's fair. A lot of what I do is to look good on paper."

Looking good on paper is a serious concern. Nurse-midwives expressed their concern about legal liability if they allow the second stage to go on for more than the one- or two-hour hospital limit, and then want to hospitalize the woman. One told of allowing a woman to stay at home in second stage for three hours and then hospitalizing her for lack of progress. The mother, in her confusion and exhaustion, told the hospital staff that she had been in second stage for five hours. The nurse-midwife risked losing the support of the physician who had agreed to provide emergency and other medical services at that hospital. Even when a nurse-midwife's experiences cause her to question the medical model, the constraints under which she works may thus prevent her from acting on new knowledge. Nurse-midwives talked about the problems of charting second stage:

If I'm doing it for my own use I start counting when the woman begins to push, and push in a directed manner, really bearing down. I have to lie sometimes. I mean I'm prepared to lie if we ever have to go to the hospital because there might be an hour or so between full dilation and when she begins pushing and I don't see—as long as the heart tones are fine and there is some progress being made—but like I don't think—you'd be very careful to take them to the hospital after five hours of pushing—they [hospital staff] would go crazy.

All my second stages, I write them down under two hours: by hospital standards two hours is the upper limit of normal, but I don't have two-hour second stages except that one girl that I happened to examine her. If I had not examined her, I probably would not have had more than an hour and a half written down because it was only an hour and a half that she was voluntarily pushing herself.

Not looking for what you do not want to find is a technique used by many of the nurse-midwives early in their transition away from the medical model. They are careful about examining a woman who might be fully dilated for fear of starting up the clock they work under: "I try to hold off on checking if she doesn't have the urge to push, but if she has the urge to push, then I have to go in and check.

With more home-birth experience, the nurse-midwives reconceptualized the second stage itself. Rather than starting with full dilatation, the "objective" measure, they measured the second stage by the subjective measure of the woman's urge to push. Most women begin to feel a definite urge to push, and begin bearing down, at just about the time of full dilatation. But not all women have this experience. For some, labor contractions ease after they are fully dilated. These are the "second-stage arrests" which medicine treats by the use of forceps or Cesarian section. Some nurse-midwives reconceptualized this from "second-stage arrest" to a naturally occurring rest period at the end of labor, after becoming fully dilated, but before second stage. In the medical model, once labor starts it cannot stop and start again and still be "normal." If it stops, that calls for medical intervention. But a nurse-midwife can reconceptualize "the hour or so between full dilation and when she starts pushing" as other than second stage. This is more than just buying time for clients: this is developing an alternative set of definitions, reconceptualizing the birth process.

Nurse-midwives who did not know each other and who did not work together came to the same conclusions about the inaccuracy of the medical model:

My second stage measurement is when they show signs of being in second stage. That'd be the pushing or the rectum bulging or stuff like that. . . . I usually have short second stages [laughter]. Y'know, if you let nature do it, there's not a hassle.

I would not, and this is really a fine point, encourage a mother to start pushing just because she felt fully dilated to me. I think I tend to wait till the mother gets a natural urge to push. . . . The baby's been in there for nine months.

It may be that buying time is the first concern. In looking for ways to avoid starting the clock, nurse-midwives first realize that they can simply not examine the mother. They then have the experience of "not looking" for an hour, and seeing the mother stir herself out of a rest and begin to have a strong urge to push. The first few times that hour provokes anxiety in the nurse-midwives. Most of the nurse-midwives told of their nervousness in breaking timetable norms. The experience of breaking timetable norms and having a successful outcome challenges the medical model; it is a radicalizing experience. This opportunity for feedback does not often exist in the hospital setting, where medicine's stringent control minimizes anomalies. A woman who has an "arrested" second stage will usually not be permitted to sleep, and therefore the diagnosis remains unchallenged. Forceps and/

or hormonal stimulants are introduced. The resulting birth injuries are seen as inevitable, as if without the forceps the baby would never have gotten out alive.

(4) EXPULSION OF THE PLACENTA

The Hospital Approach

Third stage is the period between the delivery of the baby and the expulsion of the placenta. In hospitals, third stage takes five minutes or less (Hellman & Pritchard, 1971; Mehl, 1977). A combination of massage and pressure on the uterus and gentle pulling on the cord are used routinely. Hellman and Pritchard (1971:417) instruct that if the placenta has not separated within about five minutes after birth it should be removed manually. In Mehl's (1977) data, the average length of the third stage for home births was 20 minutes.

The Home-Birth Approach

For the nurse-midwives, the third stage timetable was occasionally a source of problems. Sometimes the placenta does not slip out, even in the somewhat longer time period that many nurse-midwives have learned to accept. Their usual techniques—the mother putting the baby to suckle, squatting, walking—may not have shown immediate results:

> I don't feel so bad if there's no bleeding. Difficult if it doesn't come, and it's even trickier when there's no hemorrhage because if there's a hemorrhage then there's a definite action you can take; but when it's retained and it isn't coming it's a real question—is it just a bell-shaped curve and that kind of thing—in the hospital if it isn't coming right away you just go in and pull it out.

> I talked with my grandmother—she's still alive, she's 90, she did plenty of deliveries—and she says that if the placenta doesn't come out you just let the mother walk around for a day and have her breastfeed and it'll fall out. And I believe her. Here I would have an hour because I am concerned about what appears on the chart.

> If there was no bleeding, and she was doing fine, I think several hours, you know, or more could elapse, no problem.

WHY THE RUSH? THE FUNCTIONS OF TIMETABLES

The Hospital Approach

There are both medical and institutional reasons for speeding up the birth. The medical reasons are: (1) A prolonged third stage is believed to cause excessive bleeding. (2) The second stage is kept short in order to spare the mother and the baby, because birth is conceptualized as traumatic for both. (3) The anesthetics which are routinely used create conditions encouraging, if not requiring, the use of forceps. The position of the woman also contributes to the use of forceps because the baby must be pushed upwards.

There are several institutional reasons for speeding up birth. Rosengren and DeVault (1963) discussed the importance of timing and tempo in the hospital management of birth. Tempo relates to the number of deliveries in a given period of time. The tempo of individual births is matched to the space and staffing limitations of the institution. If there are too many births, the anesthetist will slow them down. An unusually prolonged delivery will also upset the hospital's tempo, and there is even competition to maintain optimal tempo. One resident said, "Our [the residents'] average length of delivery is about 50 minutes, and the pros' [the private doctors'] is about 40 minutes" (1963:282). That presumably includes delivery of baby and placenta, and probably any surgical repair as well. Rosengren and DeVault further note:

> This "correct tempo" becomes a matter of status competition, and a measure of professional adeptness. The use of forceps is also a means by which the tempo is maintained in the delivery room, and they are so often used that the procedure is regarded as normal. [1963:282]

Rosengren and DeVault, with no out-of-hospital births as a basis for comparison, apparently did not perceive the management of the third stage as serving institutional needs. Once the baby is quickly and efficiently removed, one certainly does not wait 20 minutes or more for the spontaneous expulsion of the placenta.

Hospitals so routinize the various obstetrical interventions that alternative conceptualizations are unthinkable. A woman attached to an intravenous or a machine used to monitor the condition of the fetus cannot very well be told to go out for a walk or to a movie if her contractions are slow and not forceful. A woman strapped to a delivery table cannot take a nap if she does not feel ready to push. She cannot even get up and move around to find a better position for pushing. Once the institutional forces begin, the process is constructed in a manner appropriate to the institutional model. Once a laboring woman is hospitalized, she will have a medically constructed birth.

Therefore, not only the specific rules, but also the overall perspective of the hospital as an institution, operate to proscribe hospital-birth attendants' reconceptualization of birth. Practitioners may "lose even the ability to think of alternatives or to take known alternatives seriously because the routine is so solidly established and embedded in perceived consensus" (Holtzner, 1968:96).

The Home-Birth Approach

In home births the institutional supports and the motivations for maintaining hospital tempo are not present; birth attendants do not move from one laboring woman to the next. Births do not have to be meshed to form an overriding institutional tempo. Functioning without institutional demands or institutional supports, nurse-midwives are presented with situations which are anomalies in the medical model, such as labors stopping and starting, the second stage not following immediately after the first, and a woman taking four hours to push out a baby without any problems—and feeling good about it. Without obstetrical interventions, medically defined "pathologies" may be seen to right themselves, and so the very conceptualization of pathology and normality is challenged.

In home or out-of-hospital births, the routine and perceived consensus is taken away. Each of the nurse-midwives I interviewed stressed the individuality of each out-of-hospital birth, saying that each birth was so much "a part of each mother and family." They described tightly knit extended-kin situations, devoutly religious births, party-like births, intimate and sexual births—an infinite variety. The variety of social contexts seemed to overshadow the physiological constants. That is not to say that constraints are absent, but that at home the constraints are very different than they are within hospitals. At home, the mother as patient must coexist or take second place to the mother as mother, wife, daughter, sister, friend, or lover.

SUMMARY AND CONCLUSIONS

The hospital setting structures the ideology and the practice of hospital-trained nurse-midwives. Home birth, by contrast, provides an ultimately radicalizing experience, in that it challenges the taken-for-granted assumptions of the hospital experience. Timetables provide structure for the hospital experience: structures—statistical constructions, models, or attempts at routinization or standardization—are not necessarily bad in and of themselves. Medical timetables, however, have termed pathological whatever does not conform to statistical norms, which are themselves based on biased samples and distorted by structural restraints imposed in the interests of efficiency. Thus, the range of normal variation does not permeate the model.

One final conclusion to be drawn from this research is a reaffirmation that knowledge, including medical knowledge, is socially situated. Medical reality is a socially constructed reality, and the content of medical knowledge is as legitimate an area of research for medical sociology as are doctor–patient relations, illness behavior, and the other more generally studied areas.

ACKNOWLEDGMENTS

The author thanks Maren Lockwood Carden, Leon Chazanow, Sue Fisher, Betty Leyerle, Judith Lorber, Eileen Moran, and the anonymous *Social Problems* reviewers. Correspondence to: Box 511, Baruch College, New York, New York 10010.

REFERENCES

Friedman, E. 1959. "Graphic analysis of labor." *Bulletin of the American College of Nurse-Midwifery* 4 (3):94–105.

Hellman, L., & Pritchard, J., eds. 1971. *Williams' obstetrics.* 14th ed. New York: Appleton-Century-Croft.

Holtzner, B. 1968. *Reality construction in society.* Cambridge, Mass.: Schenkmann.

Kuhn, T. S. 1970. *The structure of scientific revolutions.* Chicago: University of Chicago Press.

Mehl, L. 1977. "Research on childbirth alternatives: What can it tell us about hospital practices?" In D. Stewart & L. Stewart, eds., *Twenty-first-century obstetrics now,* pp. 171–208. Chapel Hill, N.C.: National Association of Parents and Professionals for Safe Alternatives in Childbirth.

Miller, R. S. 1977. "The social construction and reconstruction of physiological events: Acquiring the pregnant identity." In N. K. Denzin, ed., *Studies in symbolic interaction,* pp. 87–145. Greenwich, Conn.: JAI Press.

Rindfuss, R. R. 1977. "Convenience and the occurrence of births: Induction of labor in the United States and Canada." Paper presented at the 72nd annual meeting of the American Sociological Association, Chicago, August.

Rosengren, W. R., & DeVault, S. 1963. "The sociology of time and space in an obstetric hospital." In Eliot Friedson, ed., *The hospital in modern society,* pp. 284–85. New York: Free Press.

Roth, J. 1963. *Timetables: Structuring the passage of time in hospital treatment and other careers.* Indianapolis: Bobbs Merrill.

Rothman, B. K. 1982. In *Labor: Women and power in the birthplace.* New York: Norton.

Politics

*P*olitics refers to the organized pattern by which power is distributed and exercised within a particular society. Scholars are only just beginning to understand the forces that account for women's minimal participation in political life and the impact that it has had on women's status as well as on politics generally. The selections in this section explore women's political status by looking at women's participation in both institutionalized and revolutionary politics and the impact of political crises and other societal-level changes on women's roles.

In "Women in Political Life: Variations at the Global Level," Shirley Nuss analyzes women's involvement in political life globally. Using data from 60 countries on women's participation in elective and appointive office at both the national and local levels, Nuss concludes that, overall, women are not represented in significant numbers among political elites. Some of the variation of women's access to elite positions in politics is explained by differences among industrialized, centrally planned, and market economies, as well as by regional differences.

Lest we forget that the state has a most awesome kind of power—the power to determine why, when, and who should engage in warfare—the next reading shows that when it serves the interests of the politically powerful, women not only have been allowed to participate in activities ordi-

narily reserved for men but have been pressured to do so. Leila J. Rupp, in "Woman's Place Is in the War: Propaganda and Public Opinion in the United States and Germany, 1939–1945," finds that during World War II both governments appealed for women's participation in the war effort. The campaign for women to take jobs previously held by men appealed, however, to women's traditional roles as wives and mothers rather than to the economic benefits they would realize from holding the jobs. A propaganda campaign in the United States urged women to assume responsibility for supporting the men involved in the war effort. Because the appeal did not challenge fundamental female roles, it was easier for industry to discharge women at the close of the war and send them back to lower-paying, traditionally female jobs.

The final selection focuses on women's participation in political struggles that challenge existing governmental structures. In "Women in Revolution: The Mobilization of Latin American Women in Revolutionary Guerrilla Movements," Linda Lobao Reif discusses major factors that affect women's mobilization in guerrilla struggles and applies them to case studies of movements that have occurred over the last three decades in five Latin American nations. She examines and compares women's participation and roles in revolutionary movements in Cuba, Colombia, Uruguay, Nicaragua, and El Salvador.

READING 36

Women in Political Life: Variations at the Global Level

SHIRLEY NUSS

In 1854, Auguste Comte, the father of sociology, maintained that women were inferior to men because their maturation had been arrested during childhood. He viewed sociology as a powerful method for inhibiting the drift of western nations toward "degrading equality."[1] Overall, Comte justified the oppression of women as for the good of society. Later, in 1876, Herbert Spencer contended that for women to compete for business and political careers would be positively "mischievous."[2] Comte and Spencer thought women should be confined to domestic roles.[3]

More than a century later, as nearly ten thousand women from more than 140 nations gathered to celebrate the United Nations Decade for Women (1976–1985), it was clear that major changes had taken place in the international consensus about the position of women in society. Rather than a result of natural or biological inferiority, inequities between women and men have been increasingly viewed as "rooted in the political, economic, and social structure, the cultural framework and the level of development."[4]

At the end of this historic Decade for Women, equality is increasingly viewed as good for society, rather than being "degrading." Further, the full integration of women into social, political and economic life is increasingly viewed as central to the total development of the individual as well as the nation.[5] The goals of the Decade explicitly recognized the importance of "a greater participation of women in policy-making positions at the local, national and international levels."[6]

It is not only recognized that such participation is associated with human as well as social progress, it is also recognized that the full integration of women as

part of the political elite requires special measures to increase this participation at every level.[7] This recognition led to recommendations of specific measures to facilitate this integration beginning with the World Plan of Action and the United Nations Decade for Women.[8] In an effort to review and evaluate such progress, or the lack thereof, the United Nations began collecting data on political participation from UN member nations.[9]

The review and evaluation documents for the Decade of Women suggest changes in the direction of equality in a number of areas of political participation. For example, important changes in legislation and litigation have facilitated the increased participation of women in political activities.[10] In addition, women have increased their voter participation.[11]

Changes in legislation and voter participation, however, have not been accompanied by changes of similar magnitude in the participation of women in elite decision-making positions.[12] Women have not moved in significant numbers beyond the ballot box into local and national office. Overall, the participation of women as political elites is remarkably similar throughout the world—low.[13] The political arena appears to be an area of access to power where women have made little headway in the contemporary world; politics seems to be one of the last male strongholds.[14]

Research on women as political elites suggests important global variations in the ways women exercise political power.[15] The research also suggests significant variation in the access of women to positions among the political elite.

For example, Nadia Youssef suggests the importance of regional differences for understanding the status of women.[16] In particular, she suggests regional differences in family organization and religion as factors influencing differential access of women in public roles. Audrey Chapman Smock suggests that regional variations associated with religion and purdah are meaningful in explaining the dominance of men as well as the absence of women in political roles.[17] She and Nadia Youssef show that politics is exclusively a male concern where religion confines the sphere of women to the family, e.g., Islam.[18]

Margaret Stacy and Marion Price suggest that development, in particular the development of industrial capitalism, increased both the privatization of women and their removal from power.[19] Janet Zollinger Giele and Audrey Chapman Smock argue that political tradition, not economic development, appears to give women access to high office.[20] They suggest this as an explanation for higher levels of participation in socialist countries, including the countries of Eastern Europe and the USSR as well as the Scandinavian countries, than in nonsocialist western countries.

Magdalena Sokolowska sheds additional light on the high levels of political participation of women in socialist relative to nonsocialist countries.[21] She emphasizes the importance of the role of government in educating people to accept new patterns and different behaviors for women. Similarly, Cynthia Fuchs Epstein emphasizes the importance of an ideology that supports the participation of women along with legislation which facilitates the entry of women into the political elite.[22] She also suggests that this entry is further facilitated in countries with liberal or leftist parties.

The research also suggests that the colonial experience has important consequences for the access of women to positions among the political elite. Nancy Hafkin and Edna Bay, for example, suggest that the colonial experience actually diminished the prerogatives and rights women in Africa formerly enjoyed.[23] Judith Van Allen[24] and Kamena Okonjo[25] suggest that prior to colonialism, politics was traditionally the sphere of women as well as men among the Ibo of Nigeria, for example.

Of particular concern to this investigation are variations between industrialized and industrializing countries, socialist or centrally planned economies and capitalist or market-oriented economies, and countries which have been colonized and those which have been colonizers. Variations are also expected among the regions of Africa, Asia and Latin America due to differences in tradition, culture, religion and level of economic development. More explicitly, significant differences are anticipated between the industrialized and industrializing countries, between market-oriented and centrally planned countries as well as among the industrializing countries in the regions of Africa, Asia and Latin America.

Data made available from United Nations sources as a consequence of the Decade of Women (1976–1985) provide a data set which is more extensive than has heretofore been available for such an investigation. Previous data sets were western in focus. In contrast, the investigation assesses the participation of women as political elites in 60 countries, including significant representation from Africa, Asia and Latin America. As such, this data set provides for an assessment of variations in political inequality at the global level along the lines suggested by the literature reviewed herein.

METHOD

The data analyzed in this paper were collected by the United Nations from member nations for the 1980 World Conference of the United Nations Decade for Women as part of its review and evaluation of progress made by women since 1975, an evaluation that was mandated by the UN General Assembly in 1978.[26]

In 1978, member nations received a 53-page questionnaire designed to assess the implementation of recommendations in the World Plan of Action adopted at the World Conference of the International Women's Year in 1975. Countries were asked to report for 1975 and 1978 the percentages of women out of the total of women and men elected to public office at the local level and at the national level, and holding office at higher levels in the diplomatic service.[27]

Ninety-three United Nations member nations responded to the questionnaire.[28] These responses were used in the preparation of review and evaluation documents for the 1980 World Conference of the UN Decade for Women held in Copenhagen, Denmark.[29] The data as reported by member nations also were published for the conference to facilitate further analyses.[30] The UN data were supplemented by the Secretariat[31] in an effort to maximize the number of countries evaluated herein. The resulting data for 60 countries are used to assess the access of women to elected office at the local and national levels and to appointive office in the diplomatic service.

While these data address the major problem of

such analyses, the scarcity of data,[32] they are not without limitation. A concern may be voiced about their self-reported nature. Simply stated, the countries provided the data with the knowledge that it would be used to evaluate progress in the position of women since the beginning of the Decade for Women in 1975. The concern here is whether the countries inflated the data to improve their image in the international community.

This may have happened with some countries for a variety of reasons. Some of the nations with a more liberal ideology may have inflated the data. What is interesting to note in this regard is the number of countries who reported no change or actual declines in the political participation of women during this period. Hence, it is possible to argue that the data are relatively accurate given the willingness of countries to report such stagnation or progress away from equality during this historic decade.

However, in an effort to take concern about the possible inaccuracies of the data into account, this analysis will utilize the data conservatively by focusing on trends rather than attempting to draw conclusions about individual countries.

An additional concern is variation among countries in the possible definitions used in response to the questionnaire. This is a problem addressed elsewhere by Karen Beckwith.[33] Of concern here are the positions which are included in the figures for national and local office. Similar problems may be associated with the concept of "higher levels" of office in the diplomatic services where the data rely on a national self-definition of "higher office" that may vary by nation.

Despite their limitations, these data are the most comprehensive data available to date on women's political participation cross-nationally and, as a consequence, much can be learned from their analysis. Hence, these data, in the forms of indices, are used to explore whether political, economic, social and cultural factors such as industrialized versus industrializing, experience with colonization, centrally planned versus market-oriented economy and regional considerations explain global variations in the political participation of women.

To accomplish this exploration at the elite level, indices of female participation for the 60 respondent countries are evaluated by highs and lows as well as by variation in participation. Median figures are evaluated for each index. The countries are classified: in-

dustrialized or industrializing nation; centrally planned and market-oriented economy; as well as by the geographic regions of Africa, Asia and Latin America. These data are further evaluated in terms of the statistical significance of differences among these categories.

VARIATION

Indices for 60 countries include 31 industrializing and 29 industrialized countries. The industrializing countries include 11 African, 10 Asian and 10 Latin American countries. The industrialized countries are divided between 11 market-oriented economies, including 1 North American, 17 Western European and the 4 market-oriented economies of Australia, Israel, Japan and New Zealand, and the 7 centrally planned economies, including Eastern European countries and the Soviet Union.[34]

The declines, no change and increases during the 1975–1978 period resulted in the level of female access to political elite positions reported in 1978.[35] Indices for elected office at both the local and national levels and for high appointive office in the diplomatic service are examined for a measure of median participation and variation among countries.

Women comprise 8.3% of those elected to public office at the local level in 29 countries. Levels range from no women elected at the local level in Sri Lanka to 49% women at this level in the Soviet Union (see Table 1). A third of the countries have considerably less than 8% women at the local level (see Table 2). In more than a fourth of the countries, more than one-fifth of all elected officials at the local level are female.

The participation of women is lower at the national level. Women comprise a median of 6% of elected officials for 37 countries. The range, while more narrow at the national than the local level, spans no women elected in Singapore and Sri Lanka to 33.6% in the German Democratic Republic (see Table 1). The lowest participation (see Table 3) is marked in over two-fifths of the countries. In 25% of the countries, women represent over 15% of elected national officials, or two and one-half times the median figure.

The lowest level of political participation is found in appointment to high office in the diplomatic service. A median of 4% of the appointees in 1978 were

TABLE I   HIGH AND LOW INDICES OF FEMALE PARTICIPATION IN POLITICAL LIFE IN 1978

Index	Low	High
Elected		
Local office	No women	49%
Country	Sri Lanka	USSR
National office	No women	33.6%
Country	Singapore	German
	Sri Lanka	Democratic
		Republic
Appointed		
Diplomatic service	No women	30%
	Nepal	Equador
	Papua New	
	Guinea	
	Swaziland	
	Togo	

SOURCE: *Statistical Abstract (A/Conf. 94/25), World Conference of the UN Decade for Women* (New York, 1980); *Women in Socialist Society* (Moscow: Council for Mutual Economic Assistance Secretariat, 1980).

women. Data for 37 countries (see Table 4) demonstrate that less than 3% of high diplomatic service officers were women in nearly 40% of the countries. More than 16% were women in nearly 30% of the countries.

An examination of median indices yields the following pyramid for women elites:

	Median	Range
Elected office, local level	8.3%	49.0
Elected office, national level	6.0	33.6
Appointive office, diplomatic service	4.6	30.0

These data reaffirm that the participation of women in government office remained low during the first half of the UN Decade for Women. However, the wide variation among countries suggests that a great deal may be learned from examination of factors tending to explain these variations. Countries classified as industrializing (Africa, Asia and Latin America), centrally planned (Eastern European countries and the Soviet Union) and market-oriented economies (Western Europe, North America, Australia, Israel, Japan and New Zealand) vary significantly in levels of par-

TABLE 2   INDEX OF FEMALE PARTICIPATION IN ELECTED OFFICE AT THE LOCAL LEVEL, 1978

Participation Level	Country
Low (0.0–6.4%)	Dominican Republic
	Equador
	India
	Iceland
	Israel
	Madagascar
	Mauritius
	Papua New Guinea
	Paraguay
	Sri Lanka
Medium (7.1–17.7%)	Austria
	Belgium
	Botswana
	Colombia
	Cuba
	Denmark
	France
	Jamaica
	Netherlands
	New Zealand
	Swaziland
	United States of America
High (20.0–29.0%)	Bylorussian Soviet
	Socialist Republic
	Kenya
	Mongolia
	Poland
	Romania
	Sweden
	Union of Soviet Socialist
	Republics

SOURCE: *Statistical Abstract (A/Conf. 94/25), World Conference of the UN Decade for Women* (New York, 1980); *Women in Socialist Society* (Moscow: Council for Mutual Economic Assistance Secretariat, 1980).

ticipation by women in local elected office, as demonstrated by Table 2 (chi square $= 18.5$, $p < .001$, Cramer's $V = .56$). Low levels of participation and, to a lesser extent, medium levels are most characteristic of the industrializing countries. Over one-half of the industrializing countries have a low level of female participation and a third may be categorized as having moderate participation. High levels of participation are most characteristic of the centrally planned economies: all of them have more than 20% female partic-

TABLE 3   INDEX OF FEMALE PARTICIPATION IN ELECTED OFFICE AT THE NATIONAL LEVEL, 1978

Participation Level	Country
Low (0.0–5.0%)	Botswana
	France
	India
	Iceland
	Ireland
	Jamaica
	Madagascar
	Mauritius
	New Zealand
	Papua New Guinea
	Paraguay
	Singapore
	Sri Lanka
	Turkey
	United Kingdom
	United States of America
Medium (5.5–13.2%)	Austria
	Belgium
	Colombia
	Dominican Republic
	Germany, Federal Republic of
	Israel
	Kenya
	Netherlands
	Pakistan
	Philippines
	Swaziland
High (15.5–33.6%)	China
	Denmark
	Finland
	German Democratic Republic
	Mongolia
	Norway
	Poland
	Romania
	Sweden
	Vietnam

SOURCE: *Statistical Abstract (A/Conf. 94/25), World Conference of the UN Decade for Women* (New York, 1980); *Women in Socialist Society* (Moscow: Council for Mutual Economic Assistance Secretariat, 1980).

TABLE 4   INDEX OF FEMALE PARTICIPATION IN APPOINTIVE OFFICE IN THE DIPLOMATIC SERVICE, 1978

Participation Level	Country
Low (0.0–3.0%)	Botswana
	Greece
	Iceland
	Libyan Arab Jamehiriya
	Nepal
	Norway
	Pakistan
	Papau New Guinea
	Spain
	Sri Lanka
	Swaziland
	Switzerland
	Togo
	Turkey
Medium (3.8–6.0%)	Argentina
	Australia
	Belgium
	Denmark
	Finland
	Iraq
	Israel
	Kenya
	Paraguay
	Sweden
	United Kingdom
	United States of America
High (8.0–30.0%)	Austria
	Barbados
	Cuba
	Ecuador
	Egypt
	Ireland
	Jamaica
	New Zealand
	Philippines
	Singapore
	Uruguay

SOURCE: *Statistical Abstract (A/Conf. 94-25), World Conference of the UN Decade for Women* (New York, 1980); *Women in Socialist Society* (Moscow: Council for Mutual Economic Assistance Secretariat, 1980).

ipation in local office. Moderate participation is most characteristic of the market-oriented economies: 70% have between 7 and 17.7% female participation at the local level. These significant differences are associated with factors differentiating industrializing countries

from both the market-oriented and centrally planned economies such as differences in ideology, capitalist development, and experience with colonialism.

At the national level there is also a significant difference between female participation in elected office in industrializing, centrally planned and market-oriented economies (chi square $= 9.12$, $p < .05$, Cramer's $V = .35$). Again, the industrializing countries characteristically present low levels of participation. One-half are classified as having low participation and another one-third are categorized as having medium levels. All the centrally planned economies are classified in the high category and the majority of market-oriented economies are classified in the low category. Some market-oriented economies, however, are classified in the median and others in the high category of female access to public office at the national level.

Variation in female participation in the diplomatic service for industrializing countries is best explained by regional differences (chi square $= 3.4$, $p < .04$, Cramer's $V = .57$). Two-thirds of the countries in the African and Asian regions have low levels (below 3%) of female participation in the diplomatic service. Many Latin American countries report levels of participation twice as high. For example, in five of the seven Latin American countries for which data are available, females represent more than 6% of persons in high levels of diplomatic service.

The data suggest developmental factors in contrast to regional variations as important factors for female participation in elected office at both the national and local levels. For these indices, regional differences among developing countries are not significant factors. They were, however, important for suggesting likely variations in female appointments to diplomatic service. Here, developmental factors such as industrializing versus industrialized or centrally planned versus market-oriented economies did not yield statistically significant variations.

CONCLUSION

. . . The data show wide variation between countries with low and high levels of female participation in elected office at the local and national levels and in appointment to the diplomatic service. . . .

The purpose of this paper was to assess the significance of differences in the access of women to elite positions in countries classified by region as well as by industrialized versus industrializing and centrally planned versus market-oriented economies.

Examination of the data suggests that political, economic, social and cultural characteristics underlying these classifications contribute to the global diversity observed in female access to elite positions in politics. Variation in the participation of women in elected office at both the national and local levels may be explained by differences between industrializing, centrally planned and market-oriented economies. Regional differences appear to contribute to an understanding of the variation in female participation as high officials in the diplomatic service of the industrializing countries.

These findings support as well as challenge some of the suggestions in existing literature. Margaret Stacy and Marion Price have contended that the development of industrial capitalism increases women's removal from political power.[36] While this may account for differences in female election to public office observed between centrally planned and market-oriented economies, it does not explain the fact that Latin America has a significantly higher level of female participation than either Asia or Africa. Given their thesis, one would expect the opposite since Latin America is a more industrialized region than are Africa and Asia.

At the same time, it could be argued that centrally planned economies make headway in reversing the removal of women from the public sphere brought about by industrial capital. This factor may account for the significant difference observed between centrally planned and market-oriented economies.

Significant differences between market oriented economies and the industrializing suggest further consideration of the importance of the colonial experience as inhibiting high levels of access of women to public office. Further, differences between centrally planned and market-oriented economies suggested in the literature were supported by this analysis. Such differences, however, were not statistically significant for females appointed to the diplomatic service of their countries.

The data suggest that regions of the industrializing countries have similarly low levels of election of women to public office. For appointed office, however, Latin America, Africa and Asia are significantly different. Cynthia Fuchs Epstein suggests that where governments are pressured to make concessions to women, women often do better as appointees than as elected representatives where other impediments slow their progress.[37] Such pressure appears to be suggested for Latin America for the first half of the Decade for Women in contrast to Asia and Africa. Since appointment to government is often an important spring-board to elected office, it is possible to anticipate a greater increase in female participation in elected office in Latin America than in either Africa or Asia when data for the end of the UN Decade for Women become available for analysis.

NOTES

1. August Comte, *System of Positive Polity* IV (London: Longmans, Green; originally published in 1854).

2. Herbert Spencer, *Principles of Sociology* I (New York: D. Appleton; originally published in 1876).

3. Herman Schwendinger and Julia R. Schwendinger, *The Sociologists of the Chair: A Radical Analysis of the Formative Years of North American Sociology (1883–1922)* (New York: Basic Books, 1974).

4. United Nations, *World Plan of Action for Implementation of the Objectives of the International Women's Year* (New York, 1980), p. 2.

5. Ibid.

6. Ibid., p. 11.

7. Helvi Sipila, "Women in the Developing Regions of the World," *Journal of International Affairs* 30 (Fall 1976–1977): 183–90.

8. See, for example, United Nations, *World Plan of Action;* United Nations, *Review and Evaluation of Progress Achieved in the Implementation of the World Plan of Action: Political Participation, International Cooperation and the Strengthening of International Peace,* A/CONF. 94/13 and CORR. 1 (New York: World Conference of the United Nations Decade for Women, 1980); and United Nations, *Report of the World Conference of the United Nations Decade for Women: Equality, Development and Peace,* Copenhagen, 14 to 30 July 1980 (New York: World Conference of the United Nations Decade for Women, 1980).

9. See, for example, United Nations, *Questionnaire on the Implementation during the Period 1975–1978 of the World Plan of Action Adopted at the World Conference of the International Women's Year,* 79-41341 (New York, 1978); and United Nations, *Questionnaire to Governments for World Conference to Review and Appraise the Achievements of the United Nations Decade for Women: Equality, Development and Peace, 1978–1985,* V. 83-61554 (Vienna, Branch for the Advancement of Women, August 1983).

10. United Nations Report of the Secretary-General, *Review and Appraisal of Progress Achieved and Obstacles Encountered at the National Level in the Realization of the Goals and Objectives of the United Nations Decade for Women: Equality, Development and Peace, Overview,* A/CONF. 116/5 (Nairobi, 1985).

11. United Nations, *Review and Evaluation of Progress,* A/CONF. 94/14 and CORR. 1.

12. United Nations, *World Plan of Action;* United Nations, *Review and Appraisal,* A/CONF. 116/5; and United Nations, *Review and Evaluation,* A/CONF. 94/13 and CORR. 1.

13. Maurice Duverger, *The Political Role of Women* (Paris: Educational, Scientific and Cultural Organizations, 1955); United Nations, *Review and Evaluation,* A/CONF. 94/13 and CORR. 1; and United Nations, *Review and Appraisal, Overview,* A/CONF. 116/5.

14. See, for example, Elsa M. Chaney, "Women in Latin American Politics: The Case of Peru and Chile," in *Female and Male in Latin America, Essays,* ed. Ann Pescatello (Pittsburgh: University of Pittsburgh Press, 1973), pp. 103–40; Janet Zollinger Giele, *Women and the Future: Changing Sex Roles in Modern America* (New York: Free Press, 1978); Walter S. G. Kohn, *Women in National Legislatures: A Comparative Study of Six Countries* (New York: Praeger, 1980); Kathleen Newland, *The Sisterhood of Man* (New York: Norton, 1979); Donna S. Sanzone, "Women in Politics: A Study of Political Leadership in the United Kingdom, France and the Federal Republic of Germany," in *Access to Power: Cross-National Studies of Women and Elites,* ed. Cynthia Fuchs Epstein and Rose Laub Coser (London: George Allen & Unwin, 1981); Jessie Bernard, *The Female World* (New York: Free Press, 1981).

15. See, for example, Jane Jaquette, "Women in Revolutionary Movements in Latin America," *Journal of Marriage and the Family* 35 (2) (1973): 344–54; Judith Van Allen, "Memsahib, Militante, Femme Libre: Political and Apolitical," in *Women in Politics,* ed. Jane Jaquette (New York: Wiley, 1974), pp. 304–21; Carol MacCormack, "Sande Women and Political Power in Sierra Leone," *West African Journal of Sociology and Political Science* 1 (1975): 42–50; Jean F. O'Barr, "Making the Invisible Visible: African

Women in Politics and Policy," *African Studies Review,* December 1975, pp. 19–25; Elise Boulding, *Women in the Twentieth Century World* (New York: Wiley, 1977).

16. Nadia Youssef, *Women and Work in Developing Societies* (Westport, Conn.: Greenwood Press, 1974).

17. Audrey Chapman Smock, "Bangladesh: A Struggle with Tradition and Poverty," in *Women: Roles and Status in Eight Countries,* ed. Janet Zollinger Giele and Audrey Chapman Smock (New York: Wiley, 1977), pp. 81–126.

18. Audrey Chapman Smock and Nadia Haggag Youssef, "Egypt: From Seclusion to Limited Participation," in *Women: Roles and Status,* ed. Giele and Smock, pp. 33–80.

19. Margaret Stacy and Marion Price, "Women and Power," *Feminist Review* 5 (Summer 1980): 33–52.

20. Giele and Smock, *Women: Roles and Status.*

21. Magdalena Sokolowska, "Poland: Women's Experience Under Socialism," in *Women: Roles and Status,* ed. Giele and Smock, pp. 347–82.

22. Cynthia Fuchs Epstein, "Women and Elites: A Cross-National Perspective," in *Access to Power,* ed. Epstein and Coser, pp. 3–15.

23. Nancy J. Hafkin and Edna G. Bay, eds., *Women in Africa: Studies in Social and Economic Change* (Stanford: Stanford University Press, 1976).

24. Judith Van Allen, "Aba Riots or Igbo Women's War? Ideology, Stratification, and the Invisibility of Women," in *Women in Africa,* ed. Hafkin and Bay, pp. 59–86.

25. Kamena Okonjo, "The Dual-Sex Political System in Operation: Igbo Women and Community Politics in Midwestern Nigeria," in *Women in Africa,* ed. Hafkin and Bay, pp. 45–58.

26. United Nations, *Review and Evaluation of Press Achieved in the Implementation of the World Plan of Action* (New York, 1978).

27. United Nations, *Questionnaire on the Implementation,* 79-41341.

28. United Nations, *Report on the World Conference.*

29. United Nations, *Review and Evaluation,* A/CONF. 94/13 and CORR. 1.

30. United Nations, *Statistical Abstract,* A/CONF. 94/25 (New York, 1980).

31. *Women in Socialist Society* (Moscow: Council for Mutual Economic Assistance Secretariat, 1980).

32. Karen Beckwith, "The Cross-Cultural Study of Women and Politics: Methodological Problems," *Women & Politics* 1 (Summer 1980): 7–28.

33. Ibid.

34. United Nations, *Statistical Abstract,* A/CONF. 94/25.

35. United Nations, *Review and Evaluation,* A/CONF. 94-13 and CORR. 1.

36. Stacy and Price, "Women and Power."

37. Cynthia Epstein, "Women and Elites," in *Access to Power,* ed. Epstein and Coser.

R E A D I N G 3 7

Woman's Place Is in the War: Propaganda and Public Opinion in the U.S. and Germany, 1939–1945

LEILA J. RUPP

" . . . [M]en are apt to wake up some day and stop wars on the ground that women win them," editor Anne O'Hare McCormick wrote optimistically in 1943.[1] She

expressed a conviction as widely held in our time as in hers, that women benefit from wars because they are drawn into areas of activity previously closed to them. The Second World War, in particular, brought an unprecedented number of women into such areas, including heavy industry and the armed forces.

But the temporary lowering of barriers made no permanent impact on women's opportunities or status in society. In both the United States and Nazi Germany, recruitment propaganda urged women to participate in the war effort but did not challenge traditional conceptions of women's nature and roles. The appeals addressed to women in both countries reveal an insistence that women function primarily as wives and mothers. Despite the fact that both governments collected information on public opinion suggesting that women responded in greater numbers to economic motivation, recruitment campaigns seldom appealed to women on this basis. Instead, propaganda urged women to protect and care for their sons and husbands by taking up war work. An examination of the content of propaganda directed at women and of women's attitudes toward employment indicates that women could be and were mobilized in wartime without challenging traditional ideas or bringing about permanent changes in the status of women. This essay concentrates on the American experience during the war and considers briefly the similarities of the German case in order to suggest that women do not necessarily "win" modern wars regardless of the political or economic system under which they live.

AMERICAN AND GERMAN PROPAGANDA FOR THE MOBILIZATION OF WOMEN

The government of Franklin Roosevelt and the Nazi regime of Adolf Hitler differed in ideological foundations, ultimate objectives, and methods of social control.[2] Nevertheless, both handled the problem of mobilizing women in similar ways, a fact that suggests that women have been assigned similar roles in modern Western societies and that these roles are subject to manipulation in response to the needs of highly industrialized economies in wartime. Women constituted the largest available labor reserve in both countries. The American government debated but did not institute labor conscription, choosing to rely instead on intensive propaganda campaigns designed to "sell" war work to women. The Nazis, hampered by a chaotic bureaucratic structure and Hitler's conviction until mid-war that Germany could win in a state of partial mobilization, passed but did not systematically enforce the registration of women for civilian labor. In lieu of effective conscription, Nazi propaganda urged women to participate in the war effort. Although the Nazi effort pales beside the massive American campaigns, both governments relied on propaganda rather than conscription to mobilize women for war.

The United States succeeded in mobilizing women, but Germany did not. The American female labor force increased by 32 percent from 1941 to 1945; the German increased by only 1 percent from 1939 to 1944. In spite of the fact that preparations for war began in Germany before 1939, the insignificant increase in the German female labor force does not reflect an advanced stage of mobilization. American women assumed the places of men called into military service, but German women did not respond to the increasingly serious labor shortages that even the importation of foreign workers and prisoners of war could not solve.

The Office of War Information (OWI), in conjunction with the War Manpower Commission, designed the American campaigns responsible for, in its own words, "selling" the war to women. Even after a Congressional attack on the Domestic Branch of the OWI in 1943 resulted in a severe budget cut, the Office continued to act as a coordinating agency for promotional campaigns. It issued monthly guides to magazine and newspaper writers, editors, and radio commentators, suggesting approaches to war topics and recommending allocation of time and space so that the various media would emphasize the same themes at the same time; supervised and distributed films; maintained a close relationship with the advertising industry through the War Advertising Council; and planned major national campaigns designed to recruit women for war work. Four campaigns, launched in December 1942, March 1943, September 1943, and March 1944, combined national information efforts with intensive local campaigns in areas of labor shortage.[3]

All of these campaigns used similar media techniques. Newspapers and magazines publicized the need for women workers and featured stories about women who were already at work. The OWI urged magazines to picture women workers on their front covers in September 1943 and arranged a competition for the best cover, with prizes awarded during a special exhibition at the Museum of Modern Art in New York. Posters and billboards appealed to women to take war jobs. The OWI distributed announcements and recordings prepared by famous radio personalities in order to encourage stations to devote spot announcements, special features, and entire shows to the campaigns. Theaters across the country showed special womanpower shorts such as *Glamour Girls of 1943*. A retailers War Campaign Committee published a calendar that suggested advertising techniques such as displays of work clothes and included a schedule to coordinate war advertising. The War Advertising Council encouraged advertisers of all kinds of products to tie in war themes with their ads. The War Manpower Commission prompted Boy Scouts to paint recruitment slogans on sidewalks and suggested that officials in labor shortage areas ceremoniously inscribe the names of new women war workers on a roster in the city hall.

In contrast to American campaigns, the German propaganda effort seems minor.[4] Propaganda emanating from both a Nazi Party and a state propaganda agency spread throughout Germany by means of regional and local offices. Newspapers, pamphlets, posters, films, slide shows, exhibitions, and community bulletin boards reached the most isolated areas. But such propaganda was never a top priority for the Nazis. Responsibility for much of it devolved upon the Nazi women's organization, indicating the relative unimportance of the propaganda, for the organization was neither important nor powerful in the Nazi hierarchy. Only one major campaign, launched in 1941, matched the American ones in planning and intensity. Despite the lack of concerted campaigns, however, German propaganda continued to call for sacrifice for the good of the state, a theme much in evidence in prewar propaganda aimed at both women and men.

THE PATRIOTIC APPROACH

The appeals to American women recommended by the OWI campaign plans and those actually used in the recruitment efforts reveal a great deal about attitudes toward women in the United States. Although some of the campaign plans suggested an appeal to women on the basis of high wages—"There's a good job, at war wages, that are the same as men's wages, waiting"—this was never the major emphasis of a campaign plan and was rarely mentioned in actual recruitment. Even as the government recommended such an appeal, it cautioned that wages should not be stressed too much or increased spending and inflation might result. But more complex, although perhaps not entirely conscious, reasons underlay American reluctance to appeal to women as economic beings interested in earning good money. Most of the campaign plans emphasized the importance of reaching women

through emotion rather than reason: "The copy should be pitched on a *highly emotional, patriotic appeal.*" The cherished notion that women are ruled by their emotions set the tone and determined the content of most of the recruitment efforts.

American propaganda developed a special form of emotional appeal in addressing women. Assuming that women responded to personalized patriotism rather than any abstract ideal, the government noted: "The 'shorten-the-war' theme is obviously the one which appeals most deeply to women. Mothers, grandmothers, sisters, wives, sweethearts—there isn't one who doesn't want her man back as fast as possible. Working will speed the day—and will help make the waiting easier."

Such personalized patriotism took two forms. Women were promised that their contributions could help to bring their men back sooner, or were threatened with responsibility for the death of a soldier if they refused to cooperate. One plan stated: "It should be made clear that by working on a war job (war production or civilian) a woman is protecting her own loved ones from death on the battlefield. . . ." An announcer in one radio spot told women: "You *can* do something—you can shorten the war, make your son or husband's chances of coming home better!" A second spot illustrates the guilt approach: "Certain women in [city] are unintentionally prolonging the war. They have *not* taken war jobs. The need for them is critical. *Are you one?*" Likewise, a special booklet for critical labor shortage areas warned: "Unless local women like yourself apply for war jobs now, our soldiers on the war fronts may die needlessly."

This appeal to personalized patriotism dominated actual mobilization propaganda. A War Manpower Commission recruitment poster pictured an obviously nonemployed woman sadly clutching a letter from her husband in the service. The caption read: "Longing won't bring him back sooner . . . GET A WAR JOB!" Another poster, taking up the government's suggestion that men needed to be persuaded to let their wives take jobs, showed a woman worker and her husband in front of an American flag, and proclaimed: "I'm proud . . . my husband *wants* me to do my part." An advertisement for DuBarry Beauty Preparations promised that "One woman can shorten this war!" Making perfectly explicit the personalized appeal, a newspaperwoman wrote of the "deep satisfaction which a woman of today knows who has made a rub-

Longing won't bring him back sooner...
GET A WAR JOB!
SEE YOUR U. S. EMPLOYMENT SERVICE

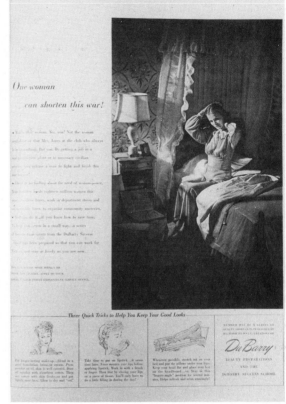

ber boat which may save the life of her aviator husband, or helped to fashion a bullet which may avenge her son!"[5]

These selected examples of personalized patriotism are typical of the primary appeal used in propaganda addressed to women, although recruitment efforts used other approaches as well, including the glamorization and the domestication of factory work.

Glamour became an integral part of much of the propaganda. One woman newspaper-reporter-turned-factory-worker complained that there were "too many pictures of beautiful girls posed on the wings of planes with a glowing caption to make you think that war is glamorous."[6] *Life* featured a two-page spread of models in work clothes entitled "Flying Fortress Fashions." *Woman's Home Companion* proved that women war workers could be beautiful by taking four of them to Hollywood to be dressed and made up as

starlets. An advertisement for Woodbury Facial Soap enticed women with the caption: "She turned her back on the Social Scene and is finding Romance at work!" Such propaganda promised women that they could be glamorous and desirable as war workers in industry, despite overalls and smudged noses.

The appeal to glamour revealed an underlying assumption that women are frivolous and concerned with their appearance above all else. Another secondary appeal assumed that women were naturally suited to housework but not other types of work. Campaign plans constantly recommended that recruitment liken war work to "women's work": "Millions of women find war work pleasant and as easy as running a sewing machine, or using a vacuum cleaner." Following this suggestion, one writer reported that women took to industrial machines "as easily as to electric cake-mixers and vacuum cleaners."[7] A top official at the Aberdeen

Proving Ground found that women workers "justified his hunch that a determined gal can be just as handy on a firing range as over the kitchen stove."[8]

Similarities in German propaganda make clear that the concept of woman as wife and mother is pervasive in Western culture. Because Nazi ideology had called on women as well as men to sacrifice their individual interests to the good of the state even before the war, the Nazi image of women (as opposed to Nazi policy toward women) had to change less than the American image. But in spite of the emphasis on abstract patriotism, the Nazi propagandists utilized a concept of extended motherhood similar to that of the Americans.

The American woman who avenged her son by producing a bullet had her counterpart in the German factory worker who reportedly spoke of her devotion to her soldier son in this way: "Earlier I buttered bread for him, now I paint grenades and think, this is for him."[9] Nazi propaganda did not glamorize war work, but at least one writer used an approach identical to the American domestication of factory work, arguing that women could master industrial jobs because they were experienced at running sewing machines and using typewriters.

These various appeals reveal the way in which propaganda in both countries exhorted women to take up jobs in areas previously reserved for men without challenging traditional ideas about women's nature and roles. War work for women threatened to upset the social order by breaking down sex roles, a threat symbolized by the furor, especially in the United States, over women appearing in public in pants. But the danger could be neutralized by presenting war work as an extension of a woman's traditional role as wife and mother. The concept of personalized patriotism assumed that women took war jobs in order to bring their men home sooner. The glamorization of war work and women workers in the United States assured the public that the wearing of overalls wrought no permanent changes, while the domestication of factory work, intended to persuade women that they could handle industrial jobs, also assured the public that such jobs would not transform women.

In the United States and Germany, contrary to the intentions of its disseminators, propaganda was more important in adapting public images to the wartime situation without disrupting the social order than it was in mobilizing women.

The relationship between propaganda and the success or failure of mobilization is a complex one. Propaganda may operate in conjunction with a number of objective factors, such as financial incentive, by stressing or ignoring appeals that touch on women's actual concerns. This relationship does not assume that women are simply manipulated into and out of the labor force. Although it would be difficult to recover women's motivations in seeking or not seeking employment during the war, even with exhaustive interview data, the information on public attitudes toward employment of women collected by both the American and German governments sheds some light on the question of women's motives and sets in perspective the propaganda campaigns in both countries.

GOVERNMENTAL NEGLECT OF PUBLIC ATTITUDES

Propagandists in both countries assumed that patriotism would be the strongest factor motivating women to take war jobs and, at a more basic level, that women accepted the current idea of their "place." The information on public attitudes collected by the governments suggests that both assumptions were wrong. While the German material is somewhat sketchy on these points, the information gathered by the United States government gives a good indication of public attitudes.

The idea that woman's "place" was in the home except in the war emergency maintained a strong following in the United States during the war, but among men more than women. Real obstacles such as childcare and domestic responsibilities, rather than their own attitudes, kept most nonemployed American women from seeking employment. Despite the lack of conclusive material on the motives of women who did work during the war years, evidence indicates that the women to whom the propaganda was addressed believed financial incentive, rather than patriotism, brought women into the labor force. The American and German governments collected information on public opinion in order to improve the effectiveness of their recruitment efforts, but they failed to act on their knowledge. This seeming paradox strengthens the argument that a major function of propaganda was the adaptation of public images of women in a nonthreatening way.

In the United States, the Office of War Information collected two basic types of information. The first included surveys of representative samples of the population, undertaken in conjunction with the National Opinion Research Center at the University of Denver, and weekly intelligence reports on public attitudes.[10] The second, more interesting, type of information consists of letters solicited from volunteer correspondents.[11]

The OWI compiled lists of possible "able and unbiased observers" in several major categories: editors, labor editors, clergymen, businessmen, social workers, and housewives. The head of the Correspondence Panels Section asked these individuals to write a confidential monthly report on public opinion among the people with whom they came into contact. The records of the Correspondence Panels Section include the letters of hundreds of individuals from urban and rural locations throughout the country, recruited throughout the war years. While the panels are by no means representative of the population as a whole, they do consist of a fairly wide range of mostly middle-class respondents in the selected occupational categories. The choice of categories precluded women war workers; most of the 139 women correspondents were housewives (51.8 percent) or social workers (36.7 percent). This material cannot reconstruct the motivations of women who chose to take up war work, but the letters of the women correspondents, and especially their responses to a March 1944 questionnaire on the employment of women, provide valuable evidence on the attitudes of women toward mobilization and propaganda. After all, these women, especially the housewives, were the ones at whom the recruitment propaganda was aimed.

The OWI surveys and reports, designed to guide the officials in charge of the recruitment campaigns, tended to stress the reluctance of nonemployed women to take up war work. A report dated May 6, 1942, noted that two-thirds of the country's women had "given little thought as yet to undertaking such employment." In August of the same year, a special report indicated that the most important obstacle to the employment of women was their reluctance to enter the labor market. Asked in January 1943 how they felt they could best contribute to the war effort, a large majority (77 percent) of nonemployed women replied that they could continue to do just what they were doing. By June 1943, the OWI still reported widespread resistance among nonemployed women to taking up war work. A survey undertaken late in 1943 showed that a majority of American women were aware of the need for labor and thought more women

should enter the labor force, but that 73 percent of the nonemployed women were unwilling to take a full-time war job. The OWI continued to report resistance among nonemployed women into 1944.

Such results spurred the OWI to investigate the reasons why women avoided employment. Most women, when asked, expressed concern over home responsibilities. A June 1943 survey reported that women with children overwhelmingly opposed the idea of employment, and noted that this fact had serious consequences for the recruitment effort, since five out of six nonemployed young women were mothers.

Women with young children often faced real problems in taking a job, and many of the intelligence reports took seriously the obstacles women felt prevented them from participating in the war effort. While some of these reports called for the provision of services, especially childcare, which would make possible the employment of women, the OWI concluded that the attitudes of the women themselves were extremely important in keeping women out of the labor force. One report commented: "Not all of these reasons [i.e., domestic responsibilities] are to be taken at face value. . . . There are strong prejudices in some social groups against married women working, and the feeling that woman's place is in the home has a deep appeal for most women." This statement, however, reflects attitudes of government officials more fathfully than those of women themselves.

A poll taken in 1944 on attitudes toward the registration of women found that of the 36 percent of the women surveyed who opposed registration, only 27 percent gave as a reason their belief that "woman's place is in the home." Despite the fact that this was the reason women gave most often, it still represents less than 10 percent of all the women surveyed, hardly the basis for the statement that most women believed that their place is in the home. Another 1944 survey reported that only 1 percent of the women and men who thought that the demand for women workers had decreased in the last months believed that women should stay at home and take care of their children.

MALE FEARS AND FEMALE ATTITUDES

If attitudes did in fact stop women from seeking employment, the OWI's information suggests that men's attitudes, rather than women's, were responsible. Men often expressed fears that women might replace them in the labor force or depress wages or that the employ-ment of women might destroy family life. Such fears prompted the OWI to address men specifically in the campaigns designed to recruit women. One survey in-vestigated the attitudes of both women and men and reported: "Women are more prone than men to favor the use of married women in war industries; and, as might be expected, women who are now working ap-prove the idea more frequently than housewives and unemployed women."

The letters of male correspondents strengthen the impression created by the surveys and polls that men, rather than women, believed in the old adage about woman's place. An OWI report based on letters writ-ten in September and October 1943 expressed fear that women would want to remain in the labor force after the war. One man summed up this attitude well: "We should immediately start planning to get these women back where they belong, amid the environment of homelife, where they can raise their children in nor-mal, healthy, happy conditions, free from demoraliz-ing influences." Women correspondents, too, reported male fears that women would not be satisfied to return to housekeeping after the war. An Ohio farm woman warned: "And be very careful about how many women you men push into industry. Post-war days will come bye and bye and women in industry will be a head-ache for someone." Several women reported that husbands prevented their wives from taking jobs.

A social worker with personal experience saw the problem as more subtle than overcoming the objec-tions of men who flatly refused to permit their wives to work:

Here is the difference between a man working & a woman as seen in our home—while I prepare the evening meal, my husband reads the evening paper. We then do the dishes together after which he reads his medical journals or cogitates over some lecture he is to give or some problem at his lab. I have to make up grocery lists, mend, straighten up a drawer, clean out the ice box, press clothes, put away anything strewn about the house, wash bric a brac, or do several hundreds of small "woman's work is never done stuff." . . . All this while my husband is relaxing & resting. When I worked full time, we tried doing the housecleaning together but it just didn't click.

This woman put into words a classic problem: how can women manage paid employment and the domes-tic responsibilities society assigns them at the same time? Her dismissal of full sharing of household duties with her husband as an attempt that "just didn't click" indicates the difficulties of changing long-established patterns in the sexual division of labor.

Significantly, the women correspondents, and even the housewives, did not express the conviction that women belonged at home. Yet of all the housewife correspondents, not one seems to have taken a job in the course of the war. Only two women even noticed the irony of their reporting on the effectiveness of re-cruitment campaigns. An Indiana housewife wrote: "My own personal suggestion is that woman power (especially me) be drafted before breaking up any more families." Yet she appeared to be waiting to be drafted rather than voluntarily taking a war job. A woman from Iowa apologetically noted that the care of her two young children kept her from taking em-ployment. Her comment prompted a marginal note penned by an OWI staff member to the effect that she was "about the only HW [housewife] who seems to have considered taking a job." That seems to be true.

In fact, a number of correspondents actually quit jobs, or reported that women were leaving employ-ment, because of increased household responsibilities. A Philadelphia woman with the Amalgamated Cloth-ing Workers Union, recruited as a member of the labor editors panel in 1943, married and quit her job, resulting in a transfer to the housewives panel. She noted:

Too bad you didn't want a comment on manpower this week because I am a victim of the m-p-short-age, and have had to give up my own job in order to come home and keep house for lack of an ade-quate housekeeper at any price. I think I detect a trend in this direction with a majority of my mar-ried friends caught in the same predicament.

Other correspondents complained about the "servant problem" or reported that many women were doing their own housework for the first time. Statistics show that most women did not leave their jobs for lack of domestic help, but the letters indicate the social con-fusion that must have resulted as women employed in domestic service responded to the opportunity of bet-ter employment.

The letters of the correspondents show that the

OWI was wrong in assuming that women avoided employment out of a belief that they belonged at home. The Office was also wrong in believing that women sought jobs out of personalized patriotism. The attitudes of the women correspondents on the issue of women's motives in taking up war work are extremely interesting in light of the government's insistence on using an emotional patriotic approach in recruitment propaganda. Although many correspondents mentioned patriotism as a factor influencing women to seek employment, most believed that money was the primary motive. One housewife summed up what many others expressed:

The main inducement is money! So-called patriotism plays a minor part. It's only in newsreels and in write-ups or on propaganda radio programs that a noble femme takes over a grease-monkey's job, or rivets or welds because her husband or sweetheart is a Jap prisoner—or something! I've never met up with any such noble motive. It's more apt to be a fur coat.

Only one correspondent supported the government's interpretation of why women worked, reporting that women took jobs out of a "feeling of identification with beloved member of family attached to fighting forces and personal stake in each additional shell manufactured."

More surprising than the correspondents' reports that women, like men, took employment for the income is the frequent expression of the belief that women sought jobs out of dissatisfaction with housewifery. A social worker in Utah wrote: "Many women thoroughly enjoy working & getting away from the home. They seem to get much more satisfaction out of it than out of housework or bringing up children." A Baltimore housewife agreed: "Women like to be out taking a part in the world. They feel a grateful sense of freedom, an aliveness, a personal satisfaction. They forget their own small lives." One unusually articulate correspondent, a social worker from Houston, summed up the feelings of several of the women:

To many, it affords an opportunity to escape the responsibilities of housekeeping and caring for children which was never really accepted in the first place. Employment, particularly at a job ordinarily filled by a man, is to some a legitimate channel for the expression of aggressive drives in women. I have talked with quite a number of women who seemed to me to be rather obviously competing with their husbands and at least one who was watching her husband who was employed in the same plant.

Such opinions suggest that the war may have provided an eagerly awaited opportunity for some women to take up paid employment in a socially approved fashion. One letter makes this point explicitly: "For some women the war situation has made work acceptable whereas heretofore they were inhibited against paid employment." A glimpse of the women the government ignored, women who had worked before the war, is provided in the comments of a Pittsburgh housewife:

I have talked to women that are working in big plants doing men's work that say "Boy, have the men been getting away with murder all these years. Why I worked twice as hard selling in a department store and got half the pay." Grandmothers are working out in the real heavy stuff and are jolly and like it.

Thus, the letters of the women correspondents offer an extraordinary opportunity to examine the views of ordinary—if mostly white middle-class—women on the issue of wartime employment. These letters provide the first indication in the OWI records that women might enjoy the economic independence and satisfaction of a job. That the correspondents, most of them housewives, believed that women sought employment for financial gain and often preferred employment to full-time housework suggests that the OWI staff overemphasized the reluctance of women to take employment.

Public opinion generally accepted the wartime employment of women, yet fears that women might want to linger on in the labor force after the war indicate little change in basic attitudes. Home responsibilities and lack of institutional arrangements to lighten women's load kept some women out of the labor force, but the government failed to act on this information in order to make possible the employment of more women. The OWI continued to attempt to persuade women that their place was in the war, despite indications that men's attitudes were more significant in erecting barriers to women's participation.

WOMEN IN THE LABOR FORCE

Despite the obstacles, however, millions of American women moved into war industry or took jobs for the first time. Germany presents a sharp contrast, even though the Nazi government, like the American, anxiously kept an eye on public opinion. The Security Service of the SS collected and compiled reports on the attitudes of the population, circulating these reports to government agencies every few days.[12] But the Nazi regime failed to make use of this information to improve the recruitment effort. As the war continued, German women complained about low wages, suggesting that they too were interested in working for money. Their complaints about receiving less pay than men doing the same work led the Security Service to recommend an equal pay policy to encourage women to seek employment, but the policy was never implemented. And so, as in the United States, heavy household responsibilities and lack of institutional arrangements to alleviate the burden combined to keep women out of the labor force.

The German government, like the American, viewed women's participation in the labor force as a temporary arrangement. One report stressed that "the main task of every woman lies in the performance of her domestic and maternal duties, and that if in exceptional times the woman must to a great extent be brought into industry for reasons of state, her nature should be taken into account as much as possible." It then went on to emphasize the importance of suiting the conditions of work to woman's nature and of convincing "the woman through propaganda of the necessity of her voluntary participation in the labor force."

One important factor in explaining the reluctance of German women to take employment was unique to the Nazi state. The Security Service reports make clear that German women feared the imposition of controls by the regime should they take jobs. This led to enormous resentment on the part of employed women, who were subject to such controls, against nonemployed women who avoided registering with the employment offices. Women often criticized the "so-called better circles" and the wives and daughters of Nazi Party leaders for avoiding employment. Employed women could not understand why the government did not conscript the nonemployed for war work. Since women already in the labor force could be punished by law for infractions of work discipline, they believed that other women too should be subject

to legal sanctions. A February 1942 report noted that employed women were willing to make sacrifices but could not understand why the burden of war should be so unequally distributed. In particular, workers in armaments industries favored the conscription of women in the interests of social justice.

When a registration decree ordering women to report to the employment offices went into effect in January 1943, the working population greeted it enthusiastically, wondering only why it had not been passed earlier. In the weeks that followed, the Security Service noted first that women were reporting to employment offices that were often unprepared to place them, later that the willingness of women to take war work had not increased. The working class believed that not all women covered by the order had registered, a conviction that the statistics bear out. The complaint that leading personalities used their influence to keep women out of the labor force surfaced in a December 1943 report. In April 1944, women were still complaining that many had not registered, that those who had registered had not been employed, and that middle- and upper-class women were not cooperating.

The fear of German women that employment would subject them to greater control by the government indicates that women were not the fanatical supporters of the regime pictured in Nazi propaganda. Although the Security Service reported that women stood resolutely behind Hitler, they in fact avoided registering with the employment offices, complained about wages and working conditions, and criticized Party measures and even Party leaders. For purposes of comparison, however, the indications that women were not moved by appeals to patriotism are most important. The German government, like the American, paid little attention to its own information about public opinion when designing recruitment campaigns.

CONCLUSION

The divergence between Nazi propaganda and the realities of the Third Reich is clear. Although the American case was less extreme, it also shows propaganda diverging from reality. Nazi propaganda portrayed the German woman joyfully sacrificing her personal interests for the good of the people, but in reality German women avoided employment. The American woman, according to propaganda, took a war job in order to bring her man home sooner, but the OWI's own survey material suggested that women in fact responded predominantly to the high wages offered in war industry.

In light of the OWI's information on the importance of financial incentive to American women, one would expect propaganda that emphasized wages to succeed in encouraging women to enter the labor force. The Nazi government, in a situation of low wages for women, could not use such an appeal and would not raise wages, but the United States faced no such difficulties. American wages were attractively high, and the OWI's correspondents indicated that they believed that women took employment because of high wages.

Early on in the propaganda effort, the OWI recommended an appeal based on high wages, but only hesitantly, fearful of encouraging inflation. But the appeal based on wages was never central or even prominent in the campaign plans, and rarely if ever appeared at all in actual mobilization propaganda. The OWI concentrated on an emotional patriotic appeal in disregard of both women's motives and the very real obstacles preventing women from seeking employment. The lack of appeals to women's needs or desires to earn money, in spite of information suggesting that women would respond to such appeals, strengthens the impression that wartime propaganda avoided challenging traditional assumptions about women. By ignoring or downplaying economic motivation, women could be viewed as wives and mothers responding to the needs of the country rather than as workers.

An examination of propaganda and public opinion shows that both the United States and Germany urged women to move into new areas of activity without changing basic attitudes about women. The wartime changes expanded the options of women in a way intended by the propagandists and understood by the population as temporary. The way in which public images of women adapted to the needs of recruitment propaganda—by presenting women's participation in the war effort as an extension of traditional maternal roles, particularly in the American case—helped to assure that the wartime range of options would contract once again in peacetime. The German experience was complicated by defeat and occupation, but the postwar situation in the United States shows that the image of women did not have to make tremendous adjustments after the war. The American public perceived the war as an extraordinary situation and accepted many temporary changes it would not tolerate in peacetime.

The OWI material on public opinion suggests that the public accepted the employment of women in war industry without revising traditional attitudes. Many men feared permanent changes, but the postwar situation assured them that little had changed. The proportion of employed women in the female population continued to increase after the immediate postwar layoffs, as it had throughout the twentieth century, but the war itself had no permanent impact on this trend. Women who had found their first opportunity to work during the war and women who moved from poorly paying jobs into more desirable factory jobs were no doubt affected by the experience, yet the impact of the war on public attitudes toward women was negligible. The seeming paradox of the intensely domestic 1950s following on the heels of a supposedly liberating war dissolves if one considers the form in which war participation was presented to the public.

Thus, in two very different but highly industrialized societies women were recruited for war work without challenging traditional attitudes or bringing about permanent changes. The form of recruitment propaganda reveals how tenacious the image of woman as wife and mother is, even in crisis situations. Such evidence indicates that modern war is a factor of dubious value in the struggle of women for status and power in society. Despite the fact that millions of women experienced the male world of heavy industry and high wages for the first time, Anne O'Hare McCormick was wrong. The case of the Second World War suggests that in wartime women are not necessarily the winners.

NOTES

1. *New York Times,* March 8, 1943, p. 8.

2. Much of this essay is based on my book *Mobilizing Women for War: German and American Propaganda, 1939–*

1945 (Princeton: Princeton University Press, 1978). Full documentation is available in the book.

3. Copies of OWI publications and information about

its activities can be found in the Records of the OWI (RG 208), Washington National Records Center, Suitland, Maryland.

4. Information on the dissemination of propaganda urging women to participate in the war effort can be found in the Records of the NSDAP (T-81), National Archives Microcopy, Washington, D.C. T-81 includes directives from the Propaganda Ministry (roll 24), the Party propaganda agency (roll 117), and the women's organization (roll 75).

5. Mrs. William Brown Meloney, "Foreward," in *American Women at War,* by 7 Newspaper Women (New York: National Association of Manufacturers, 1942), p. 6.

6. Nell Giles, *Punch In, Susie! A Woman's War Factory Diary* (New York: Harper, 1943), pp. 1–2.

7. Mary Hornaday, "Factory Housekeeping," in *American Women at War,* p. 35.

8. Quoted in Peggy McEvoy, "Gun Molls," *Reader's Digest,* March 1943, p. 48.

9. "Munition für die Söhne," in Magda Menzerath, *Kampffeld Heimat: Deutsche Frauenleistung im Kriege* (Stuttgart: Allemannen Verlag Albert Jauss, 1944), p. 49.

10. The OWI reports of poll data and weekly intelligence reports can be found in the Records of the Office of Government Reports (RG 44), boxes 1798, 1802, 1803, 1805, 1806, Washington National Records Center, Suitland, Maryland.

11. The Correspondence Panels materials can be found in the Records of the Office of Government Reports (RG 44), boxes 1733–1761, WNRC, Suitland, Maryland.

12. The Security Service reports on the German population can be found in the Records of the Reich Leader of the SS and Chief of the German Police (T-175), rolls 258–266, National Archives Microcopy, Washington, D.C.

R E A D I N G   3 8

Women in Revolution: The Mobilization of Latin American Women in Revolutionary Guerrilla Movements

LINDA LOBAO REIF

Guerrilla movements have long been considered a male domain of political contest. Latin American women have historically participated in guerrilla movements, but not in extensive numbers until recently (Chinchilla, 1982; Vitale, 1981; Jaquette, 1973; Rowbotham, 1972). The influx of women into modern revolutionary movements in Nicaragua, El Salvador, and Guatemala has forced analysts to acknowledge and reconsider women's contributions to armed struggle.

Guerrillas are members of political organizations

This paper is drawn from Linda Lobao Reif, "Women in Latin American Guerrilla Movements: A Comparative Perspective," *Comparative Politics* 18 (January 1986). Reprinted by permission of the author.

operating in both rural and urban areas which use armed warfare for the purpose of changing societal structure (Kohl & Litt, 1974; Jaquette, 1973; Gilio, 1970; Guevara, 1969). In contrast to the regular warfare employed by large armies, guerrillas possess "a much smaller number of arms for use in defense against oppression" (Guevara, 1969:4). Rather than try to outfight government forces, guerrillas concentrate on breaking down the legitimacy of the regime by morally isolating it from popular support (Chailand, 1982:240). Past revolutionary struggles in Latin America have been directed at colonial regimes as well as at internal political elites. These struggles have arisen from each nation's pattern of "dependent" development—development shaped by the domination of the United States, Britain, France, and earlier colonial powers (Cardoso & Faletto, 1979).

BARRIERS TO POLITICAL PARTICIPATION

Latin American women are limited in their involvement in nondomestic spheres of national life (Vitale, 1981; Chaney, 1979; Schmidt, 1976). The subordinate position of women in Latin American society is a major barrier to women's participation in nondomestic activities, including revolutionary struggle. Recent Marxian and feminist theory argue that the sphere of reproduction must be taken into account in order to explain women's roles, relegation to domestic activites, and historical subordination (Brenner & Ramas, 1984; Chodorow, 1979). Women are the primary directors of the household reproductive activities that are necessary for the reproduction of labor power. Such activities include childbearing, socialization of children, and the care of family members. Women are thus first located in the private sphere of the home by the sexual division of labor, while men are first located in the public sphere outside the home (Chodorow, 1979; López de Piza, 1977).

The sexual division of labor in production builds upon women's subordination in the sphere of reproduction (Deere & León de Leal, 1982). Women are socialized not to perform or to become expert at tasks that are incompatible with their reproductive roles. Further, in the occupational sphere, as well as in all areas of social organization, the energy, time, and freedom of movement available to most women is greatly limited by their role in reproductive activities (Chaney, 1979; Schlegel, 1977). Most men do not face the double burden of participating in nondomestic areas while taking primary responsibility for the domestic area.

In Latin America, patriarchal attitudes reflect and reinforce the subordination of women. These attitudes, which represent "ideal" configurations held by both sexes, include beliefs that women are "childlike" and "apolitical," and achieve "their highest fulfillment as wives and mothers" (Schmidt, 1976:244). While traditional patriarchal ideals are undermined by women who head households or who are professionals in charge of men, at the national level the formal pattern of male dominance still prevails. The legal status of women in most Latin American civil codes is based on *patria potestas,* the patriarchal right of the father to control his family. Women are legally "equated with idiots and children" (Kinzer, 1973:304).

In addition to the subordinate roles that limit women's political involvement, class differences affect women's ability to participate. The classes that support revolutionary movements depend on the specific historical conditions experienced by each nation. Urban and rural workers, potentially the most radical classes, face the greatest barriers toward political involvement. Historically they have been marginalized from formal political participation. They are vulnerable to employer threats, and political participation can take away from paid work time (Nash, 1977). Working-class women in the labor force face even greater obstacles as a result of their role in the reproductive activities of the household. Their work is exhausting and pays little, and is likely to restrict them to domestic areas (two out of five Latin American women in the labor force are domestic servants) where class and gender consciousness are not likely to arise (Safa, 1977). Working-class women who do not work outside the home still share the disadvantages of their class and gender—low education, low income, few marketable skills, and major domestic responsibilities.

Should the middle classes (or, in some cases, segments of the elite) also support a revolutionary movement, such women would have greater ability to participate than working-class women. Although patriarchal ideology pervades the middle class (Chaney, 1979), these women have been less marginalized from formal political processes, education, and other important areas of national life. Political involvement is more feasible for middle-class women, as they are not burdened by the basic problems of family survival faced by working-class women. While middle-class women still face major domestic responsibility, they are able to escape much of the drudgery of housework and child care through their exploitation of lower-class women as domestic servants (Chaney, 1973). Thus, although middle-class women face gender barriers to participation, working-class women are doubly burdened by class and gender.

MOBILIZING WOMEN: REVOLUTIONARY STRATEGY AND IDEOLOGY

While women confront greater barriers than men and lower-class women face particular difficulties, certain factors can mitigate them and facilitate women's participation. Since the early 1970s, revolutionary strategy and ideology have undergone changes that have particularly encouraged women's involvement (Chinchilla, 1982). Before this period, a small group of revolutionaries relying on military action, in contrast to mass-based political organization, formed the center of struggle (Chinchilla, 1982). By the early 1970s, the failure of this strategy became apparent and pointed to the increased necessity for popular support in the face of greater repression from the right. According to Chinchilla (1982:20), women's mobilization is an important component of the "prolonged people's war" (gradual organization of all mass sectors) which has been adopted as current revolutionary strategy in Central America.

Increasing awareness of feminist issues and their incorporation into movement ideology have also encouraged participation (Chinchilla, 1982). The women's liberation movement that began in the late 1960s, primarily in developed nations, sensitized activists to feminist issues (Chinchilla, 1982; Flynn, 1980). From the 1970s onward, the "problems of gender oppression" were integrated with those of class oppression in leftist ideology (Flora, 1984:71). Women's liberation issues diffused not only to the socialist left but also to emergent feminist movements (Flora, 1984; Molyneux, 1985) and to the mass media (Chinchilla, 1982). Thus changes in guerrilla strategy and the diffusion of feminist thought have encouraged recent efforts to recruit women at a time when Latin American women have become receptive to the idea of their own liberation.

Socioeconomic and political conditions related to family survival can also mobilize women (Molyneux, 1985; Flora, 1984; Chinchilla, 1982). Because large numbers of men are unemployed or work only sporadically as agricultural migrants, large numbers of Central American households are dependent on female breadwinners (Chinchilla, 1982:9–11). Such women may join guerrilla movements when they perceive government as threatening and guerrilla movements as bolstering their joint roles of mother and wage earner.

Internal organizational characteristics, such as the way revolutionary goals are formulated, and male–female relationships within guerrilla groups, can foster women's participation (Chinchilla, 1982). Maxine Molyneux (1985) defines two major ways—strategic and practical—in which women's interests may be articulated by movements seeking their support. Strategic gender interests involve long-term, essentially feminist objectives toward ending women's subordination, such as abolishing the sexual division of labor and institutionalized forms of gender discrimination. Practical gender interests arise in response to an immediate need, such as domestic provision and public welfare, and "do not generally entail a strategic goal such as women's emancipation or gender equality" (Molyneux, 1985:233). Practical gender interests are closely intertwined with class and family interests, as economic necessity most directly motivates poorer women. According to Molyneux (1985), movements must be perceived as supporting women's short-term practical interests first, before they will gain the mass support of women for longer-term strategic objectives.

Male–female relations within the guerrilla movements can also encourage women's participation, when egalitarian relationships in the division of labor and in the opportunity for leadership are promoted. An indication that earlier guerrillas held patriarchal attitudes, despite their otherwise radical orientations, is found in Che Guevara's handbook on guerrilla warfare (1969:87):

> But also in this stage [of the guerrilla struggle] a woman can perform her habitual tasks of peacetime; it is very pleasing to a soldier subjected to the extremely hard conditions of life to be able to look forward to a seasoned meal which tastes like something. . . . The woman as cook can greatly improve the diet and, furthermore, it is easier to keep her in these domestic tasks; . . . [such duties] are scorned by those [males] who perform them; they are constantly trying to get out of those tasks in order to enter into forces that are actively in combat.

WOMEN IN GUERRILLA MOVEMENTS: CASE STUDIES

Data about women in guerrilla movements are inherently limited by the nature of the subject. This is an area outside conventional politics where censorship and political reprisals may silence reports. Latin America is such a highly gender-stratified society that literature on women is sparse. Information about earlier guerrilla movements is impressionistic and fragmentary. Only one study presents a systematic comparative investigation of women's participation in the movements of several Latin American nations (see Jaquette, 1973).

Cuba

Armed struggle in Cuba was first aimed at overthrowing the regime of Fulgencio Batista, who had seized power in 1952 (Blasier, 1967). Cubans' outrage over the corruption and repressiveness of the regime, inequalities of wealth and living conditions, high unemployment, and Batista's policies toward U.S. investment in Cuba contributed to the dictator's downfall (Laquer, 1977; Blassier, 1967). The Cuban Revolution succeeded through the efforts of a core group of revolutionaries rather than through mass-based struggle.

The Cuban government under Fidel Castro has been lauded for the mobilization it achieved among women (Jaquette, 1973:347). They were mobilized generally after the insurgent period, however, and do not appear to have been extensively involved in the armed struggle itself. Jane S. Jaquette (1973:346–47) mentions only three women, all linked to male leaders, who participated in the guerrilla struggle in the Sierra Maestra: Celia Sánchez (Fidel's secretary), Vilma Espín (wife of Rául Castro), and Haydee Santamaría (wife of a party leader). Sheila Rowbotham (1972:223) notes that although a women's Red Army battalion was formed, "the conditions of guerrilla fighting did not encourage the emergence of women." Men took control of the revolution. They "were not accustomed to taking orders from a woman," according to Che Guevara (quoted in Rowbotham, 1972:224). Dickey Chapelle (1962:327) estimates that by December 1958, one in twenty revolutionary troops was a woman.

While there is disagreement over the social origins of those who participated in the insurgency, analysts acknowledge the important contributions made by the middle class and the peasantry (Blasier, 1967:45–46). Evidence that middle-class women participated is suggested by the backgrounds of the women who have been named and the existence of student guerrilla organizations, which sometimes included women (Franqui, 1980:186, 526–27, 532; López, 1976:111). Peasant women were generally not organizationally active until they were mobilized after the insurgency period (Purcell, 1973:263).

Through letters and interviews with Cuban revolutionaries, Carlos Franqui (1980:215, 219, 229) indicates that women performed mainly support rather than combat duties. Women were "mobilized" to obtain a guerrilla's corpse from the police, delivered secret correspondence, and were active in street demonstrations. According to Olga López (1976:112), women were combatants, nurses, messengers, scouts, and teachers, and withstood battle conditions "to perform domestic tasks on guerrilla fronts." Che Guevara (1969) noted, however, that women were not routinely combatants, but sometimes substituted for relief purposes in these positions. Chapelle (1962:327) observed that with the exception of one sniper platoon, women in the guerrilla army did housekeeping and supply assignments. Celia, Haydee, and Vilma are exceptional in that they held actual combat positions. Fidel Castro "commended" Celia's work in a letter: "Even when a woman goes around the mountains with a rifle in hand, she always makes our men tidier, more decent, more gentlemanly" (Franqui, 1980:192).

While the Castro government early recognized the incompatibility between gender inequality and commitment to a classless, egalitarian society, women do not appear to have been actively recruited during the insurgency itself. Widespread mobilization of women came after revolutionary victory, with the establishment of the Federation of Cuban Women in 1960. Vilma Espín's comments reveal the initial lack of awareness of women's issues. When asked by Fidel Castro to organize the Federation, she responded: "Precisely why do we have to have a women's organization? I had never been discriminated against. I had my career as a chemical engineer. I never suffered, I never had any difficulty" (quoted in Azicri, 1979:29).

Colombia

Revolutionary struggle in Colombia during the mid-1960s was directed against an oligarchic regime that allowed political competition only between two indistinguishable parties serving elite interests (Gott, 1971). Few women appear to have participated in two important guerrilla organizations of the mid-1960s: the Army of National Liberation (ELN) of Camilo Torres and the People's Liberation Army (EPL) (Jaquette, 1973; Gott, 1971; Gómez, 1967). The goals of both groups included an end to oligarchic rule and imperialism and institution of agrarian reform (Gott, 1971:525–34). Jaquette (1973:348) notes that "progressively educated" women in Torres' movement researched conditions of women in various areas of Colombia so that policies could be developed toward these groups. When Torres was killed by the army in 1966, a female comrade was presumed to be firing at the troops (Jaquette, 1973:348). The EPL, which was formed after Torres' death, encouraged women to join an auxiliary, but there is no evidence of women's involvement in this unit.

The women who participated in Torres' group were most likely middle-class, if we may judge by the support Torres received from students in general and the reference to "progressively educated" women (Broderick, 1975). Peasants also comprised part of Torres' organization, but in somewhat lesser numbers than students (Gott, 1971:227). The EPL purportedly had "real peasant support," though its organizers seem to have been educated and middle-class (Gott, 1971:303–4). The role women may have performed in the two movements is unclear. Participation in combat activities is alluded to only in the "presumed" account of an armed *guerrillera* at Torres' death.

Both Torres and the EPL seem to have made no real attempt to mobilize women (Broderick, 1975; Jaquette, 1973; Gott, 1971). Torres' platform (Gott, 1971:528) stated that "protection for women and children [would] be provided by the law by means of effective sanction," and that both men and women would be drafted into civic rather than military service. The EPL offered women branches to join but presented little rationale as to why they should join them (Gott, 1971:533). Platforms and policies thus addressed few of women's concerns and, correspondingly, women were not highly involved in the movements.

Uruguay

The Tupamaros arose as a response to a national economic crisis that resulted in stagnating production and rising unemployment and inflation. Uruguayans protested with strikes and riots in full stride during the late 1960s. The government responded by declaring states of seize and engaging in repression (Kohl & Litt, 1974; Porzencanski, 1973). The Tupamaros, founded in 1962, advocated an end to foreign hegemony, oligarchic rule, and government repression, and called for the establishment of socialism (Movimiento de Liberación Nacional, 1974:293–96).

A higher proportion of women were members of the Tupamaros than of the Cuban and Colombian guerrilla movements. A study of Tupamaro arrest records indicates that at the onset of the movement, in 1966, women composed approximately 10 percent of the group (Porzencanski, 1973:31). By 1972 they were over one-quarter of all Tupamaro members. A variety of other sources have also noted the importance of women to the movement (Wilson, 1974; Madruga, 1974; Jaquette, 1973).

The Tupamaros recruited members from all classes of society, but primarily from the middle class. Arrest records reveal that middle-class professionals and students outnumbered working-class members by about 2 to 1 (Porzencanski, 1973:28–31). Uruguay is a middle-class and highly urbanized nation, and the movement reflected this fact (Kohl & Litt, 1974:191).

Women seem to have filled both support and combat roles. All active Tupamaro squads had one or two female members, but emphasis was placed on such support activities as liaison, logistics, and operation of safe houses (Halperin, 1976:45). Women guarded prisoners and passed out leaflets (Gilio, 1970). Tupamaro reports indicated large numbers of women involved in robberies and kidnappings, often as decoys (Jaquette, 1973; Gilio, 1970). To distract government troops, women would strike a provocative pose and feign accidents and helplessness. The Tupamaros thus used women in important tactical roles that often capitalized on the patriarchal attitudes of government troops.

According to Jane Jaquette (1973:351), the Tupamaros were the only group (as of 1973) to have developed a detailed position on "revolutionary women." This position stressed an end to cultural and educational discrimination against women and advocated complementary rather than differential performance of guerrilla tasks. The Tupamaros also developed a program for revolutionary government which would seem to appeal to women. They called for, among other things, free education, equitable distribution of income, and state control of the health industry and wholesale food enterprises (Movimiento de Liberación Nacional, 1974). As the proportion of women in the Tupamaro movement was substantial and continually increasing, Tupamaro strategies appear to have been effective in recruiting women. Though this movement never achieved a mass base of support, it arose at a period when educated, middle-class Uruguayans had increased exposure to gender issues. Tupamaro women soon filled both combat and support positions, in contrast with women in Cuba and Colombia, where their low rates of participation were associated with basically noncombatant performance.

Nicaragua

Revolution in Nicaragua followed the pattern of a protracted people's war, with mass-based mobilization (Chinchilla, 1982). The immediate aim of the revolution was to overthrow Anastasio Somoza and his National Guard, who brutally repressed the population in an attempt to maintain the privileges of a small elite (FSLN, 1983:139). The process of dependent "development" in Nicargua meant the dispossession of small farmers, the creation of a landless proletariat, high unemployment, a low standard of living, and a short life expectancy (Ramirez-Horton, 1982). It also meant the destabilization of family life, as men abandoned families and migrated in search of seasonal or other employment (Ramirez-Horton, 1982; Chinchilla, 1982). The number of female-headed households has thus been high, an estimated one-third of all families in 1978 (Chinchilla, 1982:11). Women have also participated in large numbers in the labor force (in comparison with women in other Latin American nations), as so many of them have had to work to support their families (AMNLAE, 1982:24). Thus, according to Norma Stoltz Chinchilla, "capitalist development in Nicaragua made impossible the realization of bourgeois ideals of the nuclear family and economically dependent women" (1982:14).

Female membership in the Sandinista movement during the final offensive in mid-1979 has been estimated at 30 percent (Flynn, 1980:29). A central factor in the large proportion of women in the Sandinista movement was active recruitment by AMPRONAC, the Association of Women Confronting the National Problem, founded in 1977 by FSLN cadres (Chinchilla, 1982:24). The earliest organizers of AMPRONAC had been mainly middle- and upper-class women, such as lawyers, journalists, and bureaucrats (Ramirez-Horton, 1982:151; Flynn, 1980:29). Susan E. Ramirez-Horton (1982:147) interviewed one woman, for example, who "decided to use her university education and leave her daughter with the maid, over the strong protests of her husband, to begin organizing women in the urban areas in defense of human rights." By 1978 the organization had achieved mass support, incorporating women of all social classes opposed to the dictatorship: peasants, workers, students, as well as the middle class and segments of the upper class (AMPRONAC, 1982; Booth, 1982; Randall, 1978).

Women initially participated in the Sandinista struggle in support operations, but later took combat roles. They secured positions of leadership in combat operations, commanding "everything from small units to full battalions" (Flynn, 1980:29). At the major battle at León, four of the seven Sandinista commanders were women (Schultz, 1980:38).

The organizational conditions created by the Sandinistas are an important reason that so many women participated in the movement. As Chinchilla (1982:14) notes, women's commitment to their families, which had been a traditional barrier to their participation in revolutionary movements, actually facilitated participation under the Sandinistas. The FSLN responded to the immediate problems faced by women under Somoza. First, it attempted to counter the repression felt sharply and uniquely by women: women were expected to protect their children, but their children had increasingly become targets of repression; and many women needed to work outside the home, but they, too, were subjected to harassment from Somoza's troops (Chinchilla, 1982:11). Second, the FSLN incorporated in its formal platform longer-term objectives important to women. It called for a "struggle to end discrimination against women," particularly in the forms of prostitution and domestic servitude, and encouraged women to organize "in defense of their rights" under the dictatorship (FSLN, 1979:112). AMRPONAC's (1982:4–5) 1978 platform included among its major demands: "Better living conditions, improved housing, education. Equal salary for equal work. . . . An end to prostitution and the usage of women as economic commodities. . . . Abolishment of all laws that discriminate against women." FSLN goals were thus oriented toward more immediate, social-welfare issues as well as the long-term end to discrimination. Such goals bolstered rather than undercut the familial roles of many women and tended to promote family survival, especially for lower-class and female-headed households.

The FSLN also created internal organizational conditions conducive to female participation. According to Chinchilla (1982:17), it stressed "correct relationships" among members, based advancement on merit and skill, and cultivated respect and support for women—all of which sharply contrasted with the sexism outside the movement. This organizational climate was not easily achieved. The first women recruited into the FSLN during the 1960s encountered isolation and an undervaluing of their achievements. As more women entered the movement, however, sexism began to break down. The opportunity for respect based on merit provided important motivation for women to join the movement (Chinchilla, 1982).

Nicaragua clearly demonstrates the possibility of women's mass mobilization despite class and gender barriers. The FSLN gained extensive support and ultimate victory by focusing on issues relevant throughout the society, on the overthrow of a repressive regime, and on gender issues that specifically addressed the role of working-class women. It created an organization, AMPRONAC, to mobilize women and the internal organizational conditions conducive to their participation.

El Salvador

El Salvador has had a history of military rule and corrupt and repressive regimes supported by the oligarchy, big business, and right-wing military officials. Recent government by the moderate Christian Democrats has not succeeded in curbing the power of the oligarchy and its allies, and repression by the right continues (NACLA, 1984). The major opposition to right-wing forces now consists of the joint opposition fronts of the FMLN/FDR (Martí Front for National Liberation/Democratic Revolutionary Front). Their present platform includes demands for direct power sharing, extensive agrarian reform, reform of the financial system and foreign trade, a mixed economy, and a pluralistic polity (NACLA, 1984:16). At this time, the position of women is not specifically mentioned among the principal objectives of the struggle (NACLA, 1984:16; Balyora, 1982:165).

Women make up a great part of the popular organizations that comprise the FMLN/FDR (Thomson, 1986; Herrera, 1983; Montgomery, 1982). The FMLN is a coalition of four political-military organizations and the Communist Party of El Salvador. Two of the organizations within the FMLN have high-ranking female *commandantes* (Armstrong, 1982:28) and female participation has been estimated to be as high as 40 percent (Armstrong & Shenk, 1980:20). The FDR is an umbrella organization for socialist, social democratic, student, and worker parties. Women are prominent among its leadership, with 40 percent of the Revolu-

tionary Council composed of women (Central American Information Office, 1982:57).

The FMLN/FDR has a broad base of support and includes individuals from the middle and working classes: students, union members, and professionals (WIRE, 1982a; Armstrong & Shenk, 1980). In rural areas, local peasants play a key part in guerrilla operations (NACLA, 1981). Middle-class women, particularly teachers and students, were the first to be drawn into political/military organizations in the late 1960s. Rural and then urban working-class women followed (Castillo, 1982:8).

Women are involved in both support and combat operations (AMES, 1982; Castillo, 1982; WIRE, 1982b, 1982c). Interviews with guerrilla troops suggest a strong attempt to promote egalitarian relations between men and women. One guerrilla notes that women are encouraged to assume nontraditional roles: "We have some peasant women who join us as cooks but they soon realize that they have opportunities to do other things. They become combatants, medics, or leaders" (NACLA, 1981:13). Another (Montgomery, 1982:151) states that fighting beside women, he and his fellow guerrillas learned "to see women as *compañeras* and not as sex objects." Two-thirds of the combatants in his unit were women, and there was great concern "to destroy *machismo*." A female guerrilla, however, states that despite the great organizational commitment to equality, "even now, a woman has to be triply brave, triply astute on missions to win the recognition a man would receive" (Thomson, 1986:127).

The FMLN/FDR has no unified mass organization for women on the scale of the Sandinista AMPRONAC. Rather various smaller organizations affiliated with the FMLN/FDR deal with gender-related issues, such as AMES (Association of Salvadoran Women), which incorporates housewives, professionals, teachers, students, and previously unorganized groups; organizations of peasant women in the zones of FMLN Control; the Committee of Mothers and Relatives of the Disappeared, Assassinated, and Political Prisoners; and women's trade and professional associations (Latin American Working Group, 1983; WIRE, 1982a; Castillo, 1982).

The FMLN/FDR tacitly supports women's issues and encourages women to share tasks and leadership with men. While it has no formal platform on women's issues comparable to that of Nicaragua's FSLN, it does advocate goals important to women, such as the development of social services, literacy programs, and low-cost housing programs (Armstrong & Shenk, 1980:31–33). The Association of Salvadoran Women (AMES, 1982:19) has noted that the movements of the left have "not dealt with the problems of women with the same consistency with which they confront other social problems. Their pronouncements in this regard are limited to the realm of class struggle . . . they do not make reference to the specific condition of women." The various women's organizations affiliated with the FMLN/FDR therefore have the major task of organizing women around gender- as well as class-based issues. The AMES platform, for example, includes an end to forced sterilization; safe family planning; free child care; and the right to education and training (WIRE, 1982c:3). As in Nicaragua, the number of female-headed households is high (because of employment patterns), so that issues of family support are critical.

In sum, the FMLN/FDR has formally tended to focus on class-based issues, which appeal to women as well as men, and has created internal organizational conditions conducive to women's participation on an egalitarian basis. Women's organizations in the FMLN/FDR have the major task of addressing gender-based issues.

DISCUSSION AND CONCLUSIONS

The conclusions drawn from these case studies must be regarded as tentative because of the paucity of information about the *guerrillera*. The structural constraints of women's roles in reproductive activities and the patriarchal nature of Latin American society are barriers against women's participation in political movements. While it is impossible to ascertain directly to what extent these factors constrained women's participation, a statement by the Association of Salvadoran Women (AMES, 1982:18–19) acknowledges women's structural role in reproductive activities and the attitudes associated with this role as major limiting factors:

If men have, for centuries, devoted themselves to political work . . . it is because they have always had the support of one or several women who have provided them with children, with affection, with

domestic services; to these women are diverted all psychological tensions, thereby freeing men from the small and large problems of domestic life.

We women, on the other hand, do not have such support systems available to us, and in order to utilize our intellectual potential we must organize ourselves in such a way that the private sphere does not interfere with our specific political work. It is indeed dramatic to organize ourselves physically and psychologically to exercise this role without experiencing guilt vis-à-vis the "neglected" roles of mother and wife which relegate us to the domestic sphere. . . . This situation is aggravated by the fact that until now it has not appeared that men have the intention of truly assuming some of the responsibility which for centuries has been delegated to women. It is not easy for men, even with good intentions, to raise their consciousness concerning the privileges conveyed by masculinity and to relinquish their role as the star members of the cast, becoming instead comrades who share daily life and struggle.

The analysis of the five movements indicates that middle-class women probably face fewer barriers to participation than working-class women do. Middle-class women are more likely to have been earlier participants in political struggles. Such activities may be linked to their higher education and perhaps greater awareness of political issues. Even *campesino* and working-class women who recognized the benefits of involvement, however, still faced the burdens of class as well as gender. As these women pay the highest costs for political participation, it is not surprising that they would enter movements later, when they have become conscious of fundamental interests, such as those related to household survival, and when revolutionary groups have provided the means to address these interests. The Nicaraguan and Salvadoran movements, for example, mobilized working-class and *campesino* women through attention to their specific class and gender interests. Practical gender interests, such as social welfare and child care, are critical because of the many female-headed households in both nations.

The historical location of a movement, social-structural impacts on women's roles, and the movement's internal organizational characteristics to a great extent determine the extent of women's participation. The Colombian and Cuban struggles, occurring before the 1970s, did not follow the mass-based mobilization strategy or prolonged "people's war" of Nicaragua and El Salvador. These movements also occurred before feminist thought had begun to diffuse throughout Latin America. The two earlier groups thus did not develop special platforms for women, nor did they direct efforts to their recruitment. They likewise overlooked gender egalitarianism as an essential component of internal organizational relations. There was, correspondingly, only a small degree of female involvement in the Cuban and Colombian movements.

In contrast, the three later movements with high female participation occurred during a period of increasing awareness of feminist issues and of women's contributions to other national struggles, which encouraged women's recruitment. The Sandinista and Salvadoran movements were also based on the current revolutionary strategy of protracted, mass-based struggle, which increases the possibility that women (as well as men) from all segments of society will participate.

Social-structural characteristics related to women's roles in Uruguay, Nicaragua, and El Salvador seem to have fostered women's participation. All three nations have high rates of female labor force participation (Wilkie & Haber, 1982:174), and Nicaragua and El Salvador also had many female-headed households. In the latter two nations, issues of family sustenance and government repression seemed particularly threatening to women's roles as family nurturers and protectors.

The Tupamaros, Sandinistas, and Salvadorans promoted routine policies of egalitarian relations between men and women. They also employed platforms attractive to women which seemed to be of two types. First, in opposition to patriarchalism, women were offered some feminist objectives, in line with long-term, strategic gender interests—an end to discrimination in such areas as the work force, the polity, and education. Second, they advocated programs stressing shorter-term, practical gender interests, such as child care, health care, and literacy, which maximized social welfare and facilitated women's roles in the workplace and household. The Tupamaros and Sandinistas formally offered women both types of platforms. In the Salvadoran case, the FMLN/FDR offers social welfare policies in conjunction with the feminist planks offered by its affiliated women's organization. According to Molyneux (1985), the latitude that revolutionary movements possess in addressing gender issues depends in part on the severity of the struggle and the need for popular support. Advocacy of feminist or strategic gender interests in patriarchal societies becomes more problematic when the need for mass support is great. This may explain why the Salvadorans have formally made little reference to women, except through their affiliated women's organizations.

As women's revolutionary participation increased, the division of labor by gender became less rigid and women began to occupy combat as well as support positions. The diffusion of feminist thought and examples of women's previous successes in combat undoubtedly contributed to the broadening of women's roles. The sheer numbers of women in the three later movements also made them a visible force that served to break down patriarchal attitudes and the division of labor by gender.

While women have historically faced enormous obstacles to participation in revolutionary activity, the Tupamaro, Sandinista, and Salvadoran movements reveal how a number of interrelated factors fostered women's involvement. The mass-based mobilization of women and their greater role in combat indicate new patterns of Latin American revolutionary struggle. Women will continue to play important roles in future struggles, particularly since the Sandinista victory and other guerrilla successes can be attributed directly to their involvement. The critical task facing Sandinista and future revolutionary women is to expand and institutionalize the gender egalitarianism created in the context of struggle to the new revolutionary society.

ACKNOWLEDGMENTS

The author gratefully acknowledges the helpful comments made on a previous draft of this paper by Maxine Atkinson, Norma Chinchilla, Barbara Risman, Michael Schulman, and Richard Slatta.

REFERENCES

AMES (Association of Salvadoran Women). 1982. "Participation of Latin American women in social and political organizations: Reflections of Salvadoran women." *Monthly Review* 34 (June): 11–23.

AMNLAE (Luisa Amanda Espinoza Association of Nicaraguan Women). 1982. "Our participation in the economy." In Women's International Resource Exchange, ed., *Nicaraguan woman and the revolution*, pp. 23–25. New York.

AMPRONAC (Association of Women Confronting the National Problem). 1982. "Nicaraguan women: Struggle for a free homeland." In Women's International Resource Exchange, ed., *Nicaraguan women and the revolution*, pp. 3–4. New York.

Armstrong, R. 1982. "The revolution stumbles." *NACLA Report on the Americas* 16 (March–April): 23–30.

Armstrong, R., & Shenk, J. 1980. "There's a war going on." *NACLA Report on the Americas* 14 (July–August): 20–30.

Azicri, M. 1979. "Women's development through revolutionary mobilization: A study of the Federation of Cuban Women." *International Journal of Women's Studies* 2 (January–February): 27–30.

Balyora, E. 1982. *El Salvador in transition*. Chapel Hill: University of North Carolina Press.

Blasier, C. 1967. "Studies of social revolution: Origins in Mexico, Bolivia, and Cuba." *Latin American Research Review* 2 (3): 28–62.

Booth, J. A. 1982. *The end and the beginning: The Nicaraguan revolution*. Boulder: Westview.

Brenner, J., & Ramas, M. 1984. "Rethinking women's oppression." *New Left Review* 144 (March–April): 33–71.

Broderick, W. J. 1975. *Camilo Torres: A biography of the priest-guerrillero*. New York: Doubleday.

Cardoso, F. H., & Faletto, E. 1979. *Dependency and development in Latin America*. Berkeley: University of California Press.

Castillo, C. 1982. "The situation of women in El Salvador." In Women's International Resource Exchange, ed., *Women and war: El Salvador*, pp. 5–9. New York.

Central American Information Office. 1982. *El Salvador: Background to the crisis*. Cambridge, Mass.: Central America Information Office.

Chailand. G. 1982. *Guerrilla strategies*. Berkeley: University of California Press.

Chaney, E. M. 1973. "Old and new feminists in Latin America." *Journal of Marriage and the Family* 35 (May): 331–43.

Chaney, E. M. 1979. *Supermadre: Women in politics in Latin America*. Austin: University of Texas Press.

Chapelle, D. 1962. "How Castro won." In F. M. Osand, ed., *Modern guerrilla warfare*, pp. 325–35. New York: Free Press.

Chinchilla, N. S. 1982. "Women in revolutionary movements: The case of Nicaragua." Paper presented at the annual meetings of the American Sociological Society, San Francisco.

Chodorow, N. 1979. "Mothering, male dominance, and capitalism." In Z. R. Eisenstein, ed., *Capitalist patriarchy and the case for socialist feminism*, pp. 83–106. New York: Monthly Review Press.

Deere, C. D., & León de Leal, M. 1982. "Peasant production, proletarianization, and the sexual division of labor in the Andes." In L. Beneria, ed., *Woman and development*, pp. 65–93. New York: Praeger.

Flora, C. B. 1984. "Socialist feminism in Latin America." *Women and Politics* 4 (Spring): 69–93.

Flynn, P. 1980. "Women challenge the myth." *NACLA Report on the Americas* 14 (September–October): 20–32.

Franqui, C. 1980. *Diary of the Cuban revolution*. New York: Viking.

FSLN (Frente Sandinista de Liberación Nacional). 1979. "Why the FSLN struggles in unity with the people." *Latin American Perspectives* 6 (Winter): 108–13.

FSLN. 1983. "The historic program of the FSLN." In P. Rosset & J. Vandermeer, eds., *The Nicaragua reader*, pp. 139–47. New York: Grove Press.

Gilio, M. E. 1970. *La guerrilla tupamara*. Havana: Casas de las Américas.

Gómez, A. 1967. "The revolutionary forces of Colombia and their perspectives." *World Marxist Review* 10 (April): 59–67.

Gott, R. 1971. *Guerrilla movements in Latin America*. Garden City, N.Y.: Doubleday.

Guevara, Che. 1969. *Guerrilla warfare*. New York: Vintage.

Halperin, E. 1976. *Terrorism in Latin America*. Beverly Hills, Calif.: Sage.

Herrera, N. 1983. *La mujer en la revolución salvadoreña*. Morelos, Mexico: CCOPEC/CECOPE.

Jaquette, J. S. 1973. "Women in revolutionary movements in Latin America." *Journal of Marriage and the Family* 35 (May): 344–54.

Jaquette, J. S. 1976. "Female political participation in Latin America." In J. Nash & H. Safa, eds., *Sex and class in Latin America*, pp. 221–44. New York: Praeger.

Kinzer, N. S. 1973. "Priests, machos, and babies." *Journal of Marriage and the Family* 35 (May): 300–311.

Kohl, J., & Litt, J. 1974. "Urban guerrilla warfare: Uruguay." In J. Kohn & J. Litt, eds., *Urban guerrilla warfare in Latin America*, pp. 173–95. Cambridge: MIT Press.

Laquer, W. 1977. *Guerrilla: A historical and critical study*. London: Weidenfeld & Nicolson.

Latin American Working Group. 1983. "El Salvador." In *Central American women speak for themselves*, pp. 35–55. Toronto.

López, O. 1976. "Las guerrilleras cubanas." In M. Flouret, ed., *La guerrilla en Hispano America*. Paris: Masson.

López de Piza, E. 1977. "La labor doméstica como fuente importante de valor de plusvalía en los paises dependientes." *Revista de Ciencias Sociales* 14 (October): 19–29.

Madruga, L. 1974. "Interview with Urbano." In J. Kohl & J. Litt, eds., *Urban guerrilla warfare in Latin America*, pp. 266–92. Cambridge: MIT Press.

Molyneux, M. 1985. "Mobilization without emancipation? Women's interests, the state, and revolution in Nicaragua." *Feminist Studies* 11 (Summer): 227–54.

Montgomery, T. S. 1982. *Revolution in El Salvador*. Boulder: Westview.

Movimiento de Liberación Nacional. 1974. "The Tupamaros' program for revolutionary government." In J. Kohl & J. Litt, eds., *Urban guerrilla warfare in Latin America*, pp. 293–96. Cambridge: MIT Press.

NACLA (North American Congress on Latin America). 1981. "No easy victory." *NACLA Report on the Americas* 15 (May–June): 8–17.

NACLA. 1984. "El Salvador 1984: Locked in battle." *NACLA Report on the Americas* 18 (March–April): 14–17.

Nash, J. 1977. "Women in development: Dependency and exploitation." *Development and Change* 8 (2): 161–82.

Porzencanski, A. C. 1973. *Uruguay's Tupamaros: The urban guerrilla*. New York: Praeger.

Purcell, S. K. 1973. "Modernizing women for a modern society: The Cuban case." In Ann Pescatello, ed., *Female and male in Latin America*, pp. 257–71. Pittsburgh: University of Pittsburgh Press.

Ramirez-Horton, S. E. 1982. "The role of women in the Nicaraguan revolution." In T. W. Walker, ed., *Nicaragua in revolution*, pp. 147–59. New York: Praeger.

Randall, M. 1978. *Doris Tijerino: Inside the Nicaraguan revolution*. Vancouver: New Star.

Rowbotham, S. 1972. *Women, resistance, and revolution*. New York: Random House.

Safa, H. I. 1977. "The changing class composition of the female labor force in Latin America." *Latin American Perspectives* 4 (Fall): 126–36.

Schlegel, A. 1977. "Toward a theory of sexual stratification." In A. Schlegel, ed., *Sexual stratification*, pp. 1–40. New York: Columbia University Press.

Schmidt, S. W. 1976. "Political participation and development: The role of women in Latin America." *Journal of International Affairs* 30 (Fall–Winter): 243–60.

Schultz, V. 1980. "Organizer! Women in Nicaragua." *NACLA Report on the Americas* 14 (March–April): 36–39.

Thomson, M. 1986. *Women of El Salvador: The price of freedom*. Philadelphia: Institute for the Study of Human Issues.

Vitale, L. 1981. *Historia y sociología de la mujer latinoamericana*. Barcelona: Fontamara.

Wilkie, J. W., & Haber, S., eds. 1982. *Statistical abstract of Latin America*, vol. 22. Los Angeles: UCLA Latin American Center for Publications.

Wilson, C. 1974. *The Tupamaros*. Boston: Branden Press.

WIRE (Women's International Resource Exchange). 1982a. "An interview with Sister Margarita Navarro, member of Human Rights Commission for El Salvador." In Women's International Resource Exchange, ed., *Women and War: El Salvador*, pp. 34–35. New York.

WIRE. 1982b. "Reconciliation is no longer possible: An interview with Ana Guadalupe Martínez, member of FMLN and FDR." In Women's International Resource Exchange, ed., *Women and war: El Salvador*, pp. 23–24. New York.

WIRE. 1982c. "Women's lives in El Salvador: An interview with Miriam Galdeméz, an El Salvadoran refugee." In Women's International Resource Exchange, ed., *Women and war: El Salvador*, pp. 1–3. New York.

Institutionalized Violence Against Women

Violence against women in the form of rape, battering, and sexual harassment is prevalent in many societies. The extent of these practices, combined with the fact that the threat of violence is pervasive and affects all women, supports the view that such practices form a system by which males frighten and therefore control and dominate women. Sexual harassment is a form of sexual coercion that affects women's ability to function appropriately in work and academic settings. In "The Lecherous Professor: A Portrait of the Artist," Billie Wright Dziech and Linda Weiner describe the problem of sexual harassment on college campuses. This article does more than simply provide an analysis of the problem; it offers practical information, such as how to recognize early warning signs of the harasser and how to differentiate harassers from their more benign colleagues. The second article in this section, " 'The Man in the Street': Why He Harasses," by Cheryl Bernard and Edit Schlaffer, points out just how common these daily assaults on women are; they occur not only at work but in many public places—in coffee shops, at bus stops, in laundromats, on the street. Bernard and Schlaffer interviewed men on the streets who harassed them and found that what feminists have suggested is indeed accurate. Street harassment is not a means of flattering women but a form of male bonding through which men aggrandize their egos. Although the street harasser may be consid-

ered only a minor offender, this article suggests that he is nevertheless "an accomplice in the more massive forms of violence against women."

In her classic article "Rape: The All-American Crime," Susan Griffin examines the relationship between sexuality and violence. She argues that in many ways the "normal" heterosexual script for dating and sexual relationships within the context of a structurally unequal power relationship—men as active and women as passive—has created a world in which rape is but one end of the continuum of sexual relationships between men and women. In "A Rapist Gets Caught in the Act," James K. Skipper and William L. McWhorter interview a rapist who uses the common rape stereotype that women want and ask to be raped to justify his behavior. The next article explores the impact that one American myth—that the rapist is most often a black man—has on all black men and suggests that men who rape exercise control not only over women but over less powerful men as well. "Just Walk on By," by Brent Staples, is a revealing account of a black man's perceptions of his ability to alter public space because of women's fear of rape. The "language of fear"—car doors locking, women breaking into a run when they see him behind them on the street—quickly translates for Staples into the recognition that he is perceived as a threat because he is a black man.

Feminist activists have focused considerable attention over the past ten years on developing strategies to avoid rape. In "Stopping Rape: Effective Avoidance Strategies," Pauline B. Bart and Patricia H. O'Brien report the results of a study of women who have been raped and of others who have avoided rape. Their findings confirm and explain the importance of multiple defense strategies and shatter the myth that lack of resistance mitigates the harm suffered by rapists' victims. Bart and O'Brien's study is a good example of feminist research that aims to benefit women by offering a tool that women can use to reduce the likelihood of sexual assault.

Among the worst forms of sexual violence is wife battering. Many people wonder why a bat-tered woman remains in such a dangerous relationship. Kathleen J. Ferraro and John M. Johnson address this question in their article "How Women Experience Battering: The Process of Victimization." From interviews with battered women, Ferraro and Johnson report six types of rationalization women use to accommodate to battering situations. They also identify six potential catalysts that led women to redefine themselves as victims and to seek an end to their victimization.

Finally, Mary Daly's "Indian Suttee: The Ultimate Consummation of Marriage," from her book Gyn/Ecology, describes the now illegal Indian practice of burning a widow alive on her husband's funeral pyre.

READING 39

The Lecherous Professor: A Portrait of the Artist

BILLIE WRIGHT DZIECH AND LINDA WEINER

"When I use a word," Humpty Dumpty said, in a rather scornful tone, "it means just what I choose it to mean—neither more nor less." "The question is," said Alice, "whether you can make words mean so many different things." "The question is," said Humpty Dumpty, "which is to be the master—that's all."

Lewis Carroll, *Alice in Wonderland*

In a recent *Cosmopolitan* article on sexual harassment, Adrian L., a student at a large Midwestern state university, described Tom, one of her professors:

[He's] like a rabid wolf hovering at the edge of a sheep pack—the incoming class of freshmen.

When he's selected a girl who's unusually attractive, intelligent, and naive, he moves right in. Believe me, he's *predatory*—I've seen him in action. First, he'll "rap and relate" with the freshman over drinks at the college bar. In a couple of weeks, he has her dizzy with the "existential nihilism of Sartre" or "archetypal patterns of Jung." All this may sound exciting, but the results are tragicomic. Two years ago, he "shared" a girl with a friend of his, another faculty member. The three of them made it while watching a particularly beautiful sunrise—very aesthetic, you know. His current ploy is backgammon. You see him shaking those dice at a table in the rathskeller with this hazy-eyed kid. Several dormitory assistants have seen him leaving her room at six in the morning, and the campus security guard once caught him with a student in the stacks of the library. You can guess what he found.

Is Tom exploiting his pupils? You bet he is. Does he know what he's doing? Of course. Is the administration aware of what he's up to? Sure they are, but these days, to get fired for what they used to call "moral turpitude," you'd have to rape an entire cheerleading squad at half time. Tom's like a pothead turned loose in a Twinkies factory.[1]

Although there is limited evidence of the number of harassers who may be "loose" on the nation's campuses, one point is clear. They are tolerated because society doubts that men are capable of sexual restraint. Sexual harassers are often defended with the shrugged observation, "After all, they're only human." A middle-aged professor, notorious for pursuing sexual relations with female students, offered a variation on this view. "If you put me at a table with food (with coeds), I eat."

The appeal to "human nature" is a reminder that even in an era of ostensible sexual liberalism and freedom, both men and women suffer and stereotypes die hard. Even in the 1980s, society has not freed itself of the Victorian notion that men are creatures barely capable of controlling their bestial appetites and aggressions. All the contemporary rhetoric about liberating the sexes from stereotypes has done little to change the popular view of the male as a kind of eternal tumescence, forever searching and forever unsatisfied.

Such an attitude demeans the notion of "human." To be human does not mean that a man is at the mercy of his genitalia. Whatever it is that constitutes "humanness" is located in the mind and heart, not the libido. "Human" implies reason, compassion, control—all the qualities that distinguish college professors from their cats and dogs. Without these, they are "only animal," a defense few find appealing. Sexual harassment unquestionably harms females, but men are equally debased when it is allowed to flourish. On

367

the college campus, a very small number of men damage the reputations of colleagues who perform difficult tasks for relatively low wages without "succumbing" to the "irresistible" temptations of women students.

The professor-as-lecher is so much a part of the folklore of higher education that it appears consistently in popular writing. One of the most telling examples is Anna Sequoia's *The Official J.A.P. Handbook.* The work is intended as a parody of the Jewish American Princess stereotype, but in order to accomplish the parody, the author relies on the universally familiar stereotype of the lecherous professor. According to Sequoia, Marsha Lynn, the typical J.A.P., "looks for love in all the wrong places." One of the most predictable is college:

Marsha Lynn and the Professor. Marsha Lynn often meets her professor during the first term of her freshman year. Usually, Professor Maisel is teaching an art-survey course or a freshman English course. He may be a painter or a poet: probably the first real painter or poet Marsha Lynn's met. Professor Maisel, of course, won't put the touch on Marsha Lynn that term: he'll wait until she has her (well-deserved) A, but they'll become friends. Perhaps they'll have long, passionate conversations about Faulkner. Perhaps Professor Maisel will introduce Marsha Lynn to *Roethke: Collected Poems,* or *The Selected Poems of Margaret Atwood.* Maybe when Adrienne Rich or David Ignatow come to read on campus, Professor Maisel will invite Marsha Lynn to the party afterward and get her as drunk on the proximity to Real Poets as on the cheap white wine. Little by little, Marsha Lynn will become incorporated into Professor Maisel's world, visiting him in the afternoons in his office, perhaps stopping by on occasion—usually with two or three other bright students—for a dinner of homemade pasta and intelligent conversation.

And coming from what Marsha Lynn will perceive as her intellectually limited suburb, in (temporary) rebellion against her parents' milieu of conspicuous (even if tasteful) consumption, hungry for the stimulation and surface glamour of the Literary Life, Marsha Lynn will fall into Professor Maisel's carefully laid trap. Poor Marsha Lynn really has no adequate defense. Professor Maisel is an old hand at seducing students and makes a regular, if moderately discreet, practice of it.

JAP parents have few resources against the Predatory Professor. If they withdraw Marsha Lynn from that college, she may refuse to leave and move in with her Older Man. If Daddy goes to talk to the professor, he'll embarrass himself and have no effect. Usually, the dean or chairman of the department or even the president of the college will do nothing: they know that every campus has its share of Professor Maisels, and they choose to do nothing about it. Usually, the only resource is to have a powerful friend on the college's board of trustees: sometimes that works.

But generally it's just a question of time. Sooner or later, Marsha Lynn will realize that Professor Maisel drinks too much, or sleeps with other students, or is just too old for her (even though he may be in his late thirties or early to middle forties), or too condescending.[2]

Popular fiction also perpetuates the lecherous stereotypes. Jacob Horner, John Barth's protagonist in *The End of the Road,* described his opening day of classes:

Indeed! One hundred spelling words dictated rapidly enough to keep their heads down, and I, perched high on my desk, could diagnose to my heart's content every bump of femininity in the room (praised be American grade schools, where little girls learn to sit up front!). Then, perhaps, having ogled my fill, I could get on with the business of the course. For as a man must grow used to the furniture before he can settle down to read in his room, this plentitude of girlish appurtenances had first to be assimilated before anyone could concentrate attention on the sober prescriptions of English grammar.

Four times I repeated the ritual pronouncements—at eight and nine in the morning and at two and three in the afternoon. Between the two sessions I lounged in my office with a magnificent erection, wallowing in my position, and watched with proprietary eye the parade of young things passing my door. I had nothing at all to do but spin indolent daydreams of absolute authority—neurotic, Caligular authority of the sort that summons up officefuls of undergraduate girls, hot and submissive—leering professorial dreams![3]

Horner's adventures may sell books, but they miss the point about everyday life in higher education. The truth is that most faculty probably lack the time and energy required for "leering professorial dreams." Literary characters can afford the luxury of "magnificent erection[s]," whereas real-life college professors spend their working hours juggling time between classes, meetings, research, writing, and professional conferences. Those who fit the Jacob Horner stereotype are the exception, not the rule, but lecherous professors repeat their offenses on multiple victims and do so much damage that they claim more attention than professors who simply do their jobs.

A crucial concern for both students and academicians is learning to recognize the characteristics that differentiate the lecherous professor from his colleagues. There are no infallible predictors for recognizing sexual harassment. The most pernicious behavior can occur exclusive of "giveaways," or isolated actions can be misinterpreted as sinister when they are simply examples of clumsy professional or social style. However, a tentative list of warning signs might include the following:

- *Staring, leering, ogling* These behaviors may be surreptitious or very obvious. In any case, college faculty should possess knowledge of social decorum, and must avoid such activities.
- *Frequently commenting on personal appearance of the student* In the academic setting, most professors refrain from discussing the apparel and physical traits of their students.
- *Touching out of context* Every physical gesture should be appropriate to the occasion, setting, and need and character of the individual student. Professional educators may legitimately be expected to possess the ability to make such determinations.
- *Excessive flattery and praise of the student* This behavior, exhibited with others present, is especially seductive to students with low self-esteem *or* high aspirations. By convincing a student that she is intellectually and/or physically exceptional, the lecherous professor gains psychological access to her.
- *Deliberately avoiding or seeking encounters with the student in front of colleagues* Depending on the type of harasser, he may either attempt to hide from or to perform for colleagues in interactions with the student. The key is that in either case his behavior with the student changes when he is being observed.
- *Injecting a "male versus female" tone into discussions with the students or colleagues* A frequent behavior of verbal harassers, this conduct signals a generally disparaging attitude toward women. Its initial effect is to make them feel outsiders in the academic environment, but it may also be an indicator of other potential forms of abuse.
- *Persistently emphasizing sexuality in all contexts* Pervasive, inordinate emphasis on sex can occur in class or outside. For the lecherous professor, sexuality becomes, in effect, the prism through which all topics are focused. Students, male and female, can usually detect this behavior readily, and such professors often acquire a reputation for "being fixated on sex" in papers, tests, and discussions.

Such behaviors can serve as signals to the student. Another key to understanding the lecherous professor is assessing the setting or context in which he works. There are both public and private harassers, and they act in very different fashions. The public harasser engages in observable, flagrant posturing toward women. He is the most likely to intimidate or seek control through sexist remarks and advances that may be offensive but are essentially free from sanctions. Students sometimes refer to him as "hands," "touchy-feely," or "mouth." Colleagues describe him as "patronizing," "always performing," "convinced of his own cuteness." He frequently costumes himself by extreme dressing up or down and seldom employs standard academic vocabulary—except to punctuate a witticism. He is articulate, glib, sarcastic and/or funny. His general image is that of a casual "good guy" or an imposing man of the world.

The public harasser appears always available, always approachable. He spends enormous amounts of time with students—in his office, in the halls during breaks, in the student union or at a nearby bar when the day or week ends. His informality is a welcome contrast to the authoritarian style of most of his colleagues. The more perceptive of them detect but hesitate to question his intentions. This was the position of a male philosophy professor:

I'm really not particularly comfortable with ————'s style. Perhaps because it's so different from mine and so unlike what we were taught to emulate in graduate school. I do feel a sense of unease when I see him several times a week huddled with a group of young women over coffee in the Union. I have other colleagues who are just as concerned about students and spend equal amounts of time with them, but they don't seem to need to flaunt those relationships before others.

The high profile of the public harasser is his defense. It deters observers or victims from protesting when he touches too often or cracks one joke too many. Even male students hesitate to criticize public harassers. A sophomore at a college in Michigan explained:

Sure, I was afraid to say anything to anyone about Mr. ———. They all laughed every time he made some stupid remark. You would have thought he was a burlesque comedian or something. What I really couldn't get, what really floored me was why the girls laughed at him too. He was supposed to be teaching psychology, and there he was making these gross remarks that should have embarrassed them half to death (they sure as hell embarrassed me) and they just kept on laughing all year.

When an individual's remarks to and about women or his physical contact with them appears open, he can easily contend, "I have nothing to hide. There's nothing malevolent in my intentions. Everything I say or do is right out there for everyone to see." The difficulty is that an institution's ability to restrain a public harasser depends upon the level of awareness of those within the environment. Some "see" malevolent intentions and others do not, but the harasser's reputation as communicative, friendly, and open provides a sure defense. Thus he is free to perform and be observed but not challenged or chastized for his behavior.

The style and intent of the private harasser are directly opposite. He may be the more genuinely "lecherous" of the two, for he uses his authority to gain private access to the student. Unlike his counterpart, he deliberately avoids notoriety. He not only seeks but depends upon privacy because he requires a domain in which there are no witnesses to his behavior. He is the harasser of greatest interest to the public and the media, the one who demands sexual favors of students, the one most readily cast in the image of despoiler of innocence and molester of youth.

His personal and professional styles lend credence to the epithets. The private harasser often adheres to academic stereotypes. He usually dresses conservatively. His language and demeanor are generally formal, perhaps even intimidating, to the student. Be-

cause he appears so circumspect, he is the last to be suspected by colleagues. The Levi-clad professor who sits casually before the class seems more culpable than the imposing man with the resonant voice who stands behind the lectern.

The lectern symbolizes the private harasser's teaching style. Characteristically removed and aloof, he lectures while the class listens. Just as the public harasser uses his openness to move the student to compliance, the private offender employs authority to lure her into acquiescence. The ability to control the setting gives him special access to the women under his power. He can seduce them into his private domain with a simple oral or written directive. "Please see me" or "I would like a conference with you" are familiar demands.

But, few are prepared for the deception that occurs when the professor closes the office door and sheds the professorial for the male role. Whether he begins with overt sexual advances or the more subtle verbal approach ("My wife doesn't love me anymore," "Young women like you are so lovely"), his sudden role change causes the student surprise and confusion. Her role submissiveness, female self-doubt, and shock combine with the privacy of the interaction to provide a cover for the harasser. When there are no witnesses and the student experiences extreme disorientation, there are seldom sexual harassment grievances.

Another way of understanding sexual harassers is to describe the roles they most commonly assume:

- *The Counselor-Helper* This type of professor uses the guise of nurturer and caretaker to gain access to the student. If she feels lonely and anonymous on campus, she may be flattered or consoled by his interest. He invites her confidence and uses information about her private life to discover her vulnerabilities, commitments, and attitudes about men and sex. Then he can tailor his "line" to her specific need. One professor, after encouraging a student's anguished account of rejection by a boyfriend, replied earnestly, "I'd never treat you like that." To her, it was a terribly moving assertion. To the witness to the incident, it was far less compelling because she had observed the professor making the statement to at least three other female students from whom he later sought sexual favors.

  The counselor-helper may act as a go-between in male–female relationships of students. This behavior, described by one ombudsman as "pimping," encourages the student to see the professor as a broker or gatekeeper in her relationship with a significant male. The professor's intent can be to derive vicarious sexual pleasure from thus involving himself or to use the male as a foil to increase his own stature in the eyes of the female. One administrator describes this as "seduction with an agent." An accomplished harasser in one university was fond of acting as go-between and then reporting to the female that he had advised her boyfriend, "She's a real woman. Are you prepared to satisfy her?" The motive was to win the seduction when the student became attracted to the professor's image of her as experienced and voluptuous.

- *The Confidant* This individual approaches the student not as a superior who can help her but as an equal and friend. Sharing is an essential element in their interaction. He may invite her confidences, but he also offers his own. In an attempt to impress or win sympathy from the student, he may relate or invent stories about his private and professional life. Placed in this role, the student often feels that he values and trusts her, so she becomes an involuntary confidante. Without genuine mutual agreement, the relationship is moved to an intimate domain from which she may find it difficult to extricate herself.

   Another method a harasser may employ is creating indebtedness through gestures of friendship. Offers from a professor to lend the student books, money, notes, a place to study or providing her with free tickets or rides may signal an attempt to make her feel obligated.

- *The Intellectual Seducer* Called "mind fucking" or "intellectual intercourse" by some, this kind of seduction results from the professor's ability to impress students with his skill and knowledge. He may use class content to gain access to personal information about the student. Self-disclosure on the part of the student is often invited in disciplines like psychology, sociology, philosophy, and literature where personal values, beliefs, and experiences are easily related to course content. At one college, students told of being required to write about their sex fantasies. Such information may be used to identify areas of vulnerability and/or accessibility in the student. A psychology professor bragged to a colleague about requiring students to take personality inventories. He told them the demonstrated uses of the test, but his real motivation was to gain personal information about respondents in whom he was interested.

A professor's avocations may also be engaging or dangerous. A common example is the faculty member who uses his knowledge of books or movies to move the student into discussions of erotic topics. Another is that of the professor who hypnotizes students outside the classroom. While some use hypnosis appropriately, it can be dangerous when done by a sexual harasser. Finally, there is the case of the art professor who employs female students as nude models for private studio work.

- *The Opportunist* This person takes advantage of the physical setting and unusual or occasional circumstances to obscure his inappropriate behavior and to gain intimacy with students. He may rely on equipment or subject matter to gain physical access to the student. A serious problem in clinical, laboratory, counseling, performance, and vocational-technical settings, this behavior is often described by students as stealing "cheap feels." The lecherous professor discovers ways to touch the student by using proximity to equipment as an excuse or by employing parts of her body in class demonstrations. One student complained that her woodwind professor persisted in touching her breasts while telling her he was illustrating the movements of her diaphragm; another that her nursing instructor "felt [her] up" while using her body to demonstrate physical disabilities in patients.

   The opportunist may also use field trips, meetings, and conventions as occasions to escape institutional restraints. The problem for the student is that these are often described as scholastic or professional honors and/or necessities, and she feels compelled to attend.

- *The Power Broker* The most familiar type of harasser, the power broker, trades on his ability to control grades, credentials, recommendations, or jobs. The assumption that he works only through crude and raw assertions of power is inaccurate. Direct promises of rewards or threats of punishment can exert enormous influence on students, but they feel equally victimized by promises and threats that are implied rather than stated openly. Because so much may be at stake, the student is unlikely to risk a complaint unless the harasser has been very overt about his intentions.

Regardless of the role he assumes or the type of harassment in which he engages, the lecherous professor always controls the circumstances surrounding the student victim. Sexual harassment is a power issue, and the power of the professoriate is enormous. It is easy for some college professors to deceive themselves about the relationship between their power and students' responses to them. Reviewing a number of studies on sexual harassment, Marilyn B. Brewer commented in "Further Beyond Nine to Five: An Integration and Future Directions":

> In general, the participant in a high power position is likely to perceive an interaction—especially one involving positive expressions—as motivated by interpersonal attraction, and to assume that flattering remarks, compliance, and agreement are sincere and attributable to internal causes. The lower-power participant, on the other hand, is more likely to be aware of the external constraints imposed by the threat of abuse of power and consciously to use flattery and compliance as strategies to win approval and/or to avoid the displeasures of persons in high power positions. The low-power participant is also likely to *assume* that the high-power individual is aware of these external causes to a greater extent than is actually the case.[4]

In *Power and Innocence,* Rollo May commented on the environment of higher education:

> If we take the university as the setting, we need only ask any graduate student whether his professors have power over him, and he will laugh at our naiveté. Of course professors have power; the perpetual anxiety of some graduate students as to whether they will be passed or not is proof enough. The professor's power is even more effective because it is clothed in scholarly garb. It is the power of prestige, status, and the subtle coercion of others that follow from these. This is not due to the professor's conscious aims; it has more to do with the organization of the university and the teacher's unconscious motivations for being part of it.[5]

Sexual harassers are people who misuse the power of their positions to abuse members of the opposite sex. Higher education tends to discuss their behavior in the abstract—as if it were unrelated to real-life human beings. But sexual harassment cannot be understood or curtailed until professors are subjected to the same scrutiny as students. What motivates a man with so much education and power over others to act abusively toward women?

Obviously, there are no simple cause–effect relationships to explain so complex a behavior. There is an infinite number of variables that may intervene in the experiences of individuals to influence their actions, and there is little reliable, verifiable information on the psychology of sexual harassers or college professors in general. There is also no means to gather from individual faculty the enormous retrospective data necessary to establish an image of a prototypic sexual harasser.

What *can* be examined are some relevant questions about contemporary male professors: What traits are generally associated with male academics? Are there knowable similarities in the developmental cycles of a significant number of men who choose the academic profession? How might one or a combination of these contribute to the aberrant professor's decision to harass women students? Although there is currently little information to aid in analyzing the sexual harasser's motivations, this speculation may be valuable in raising the consciousness of the academic community and encouraging new perspectives on the issue. To anyone attempting to understand the problem of professors who harass women, analyses of the developmental cycles of human beings are particularly interesting. Perhaps most worth consideration at this point are unresolved adolescent crisis, professional crisis, and midlife crisis.

ADOLESCENT CRISIS

The socialization that underlies sexual harassment by men is easy to recognize and understand. It would be heartening and convenient to find that the harassers of academe are freaks and outcasts, true outlaws in society where men value equality, compassion, intimacy, and authenticity in relation to women. But the reality, however painful, is that the code of sexual ethics that harassers follow is simply a crude extension of the norms some consider acceptable for males.

By the time the average male reaches school age, he already believes that "real boys" must be assertive, aggressive, competitive, and physically strong. Peers, parents, and society in general influence boys to behave in traditionally masculine ways. The elementary school setting presents them with a serious dilemma, which Herb Goldberg described in *The Hazards of Being Male:*

> While there is great peer pressure to act like a boy, the teacher's coveted classroom values are traditionally "feminine" ones. The emphasis is on politeness, neatness, docility, and cleanliness, with not much approved room being given for the boy to flex his muscles. Teacher's greatest efforts often go into keeping the boys quiet and in their seats.
>
> A recent study of 12,000 students produced some interesting findings along this line. The researcher correlated masculinity scores of boys on the California Psychological Inventory with their school grades. She found that the higher the boy scored on the masculine scale, the lower his report card average tended to be.
>
> Of the 277 students with a D or F average, 60 percent were boys. Of the two boys with the most distinguished scholastic records, one was noted to be markedly effeminate in speech and gesture while the other "gave the strong impression of being more feminine than effeminate." Both boys had very low scores in physical fitness.[6]

The male experience may become especially traumatic during adolescence, which is the period when the masculine stereotype exerts its greatest influence. Adolescence is the bridge between childhood and adulthood, the period during which biological, sociological, and psychological forces converge to produce self-concept and identity. Psychologists like Robert Havighurst and Erik Erikson used various terms to describe the tasks essential to healthy transition into adulthood. Whatever the language, almost all developmental theories stress the importance of adolescence as the time during which one crystallizes a sex role, develops satisfying relationships with peers of the same sex, forms adequate heterosexual relationships, and lays the foundation for a career choice. Asserting that an identity crisis occurs in its purest form in adolescence, Erikson maintained that if the crisis was not resolved during this period, the conflicts of adulthood would be greater and more difficult.[7]

Although many have studied adolescence in the abstract, few have examined the real-life arena in which it takes place. The American high school is the most significant setting in which the developmental tasks of adolescence are carried out or left uncompleted. Whether it works through formal or informal mechanisms, the high school experience influences adults. Oddly, or perhaps predictably, college professors who study adolescence often limit their observations to issues such as "socioeconomic influences on achievement" and "intellectual-cognitive development." But high school graduates usually recall that the primary effect of the high school is not educational but social. Long after the last geometry theorem has been forgotten, graduates remember the captain of the football team, the prom queen, and their own positions in the status quo of adolescence.

In *Is There Life after High School?* Ralph Keyes stated colloquially a concept similar to more erudite theories about ego-identity formation during adolescence. Arguing that adult values grow directly out of high school, Keyes contended that the imprinting of adolescent peer acceptance remains with Americans throughout life. In other words, people go through life seeing themselves socially as they did in high school— as "innies" or "outies." High school "innies" and "outies" differ from one another solely on the basis of status or power. Keyes reported surprise at discovering, "Power is central to innie status. . . . I always thought status in high school had to do with being well-liked, and liking yourself. . . . That isn't what status is all about. What it's about is power."[8] And lack of power can leave indelible marks on the self-images of those unfortunate enough to be among the outies.

What constitutes the power and status for which adolescent American males strive? *The Adolescent Society,* James Coleman's classic 1957–1958 study of this subject, provided impressive empirical data to prove what most Americans already knew. Coleman contended that desire for status was the controlling force in the adolescent society and that for males athletic stardom was the highest symbol of success, the surest guarantee of entry into the leading crowd, and the most reliable means of gaining popularity with females.[9]

The masculine myth rests in large part upon equating athletic achievement and physical prowess with masculinity and success. Early in American history frontiersmen and farm and factory workers defined manliness as having the strength and stamina to endure the rigors of physical labor. As conditions changed during the twentieth century and intellectual achievement became more important, the value system incorporated the new without discarding the old. The playing field became the testing ground for masculinity, and American faith in the importance of physical superiority remained so unwavering that no one raised an eyebrow when Robert F. Kennedy, Attorney General of the United States, declared in the early 1960s, "Except for war, there is nothing in American life—nothing—which trains a boy better for life than football."[10]

Males learn very early what Marc Feigen Fasteau in *The Male Machine* described as

> a skewing of values which tends to make sports a compulsion for many boys, the mandated center of their lives. Some boys can live with this. . . . Boys who can't conform easily to the athletic ideal are made to feel inadequate. They either quit completely, developing a compensatory disdain for sports as a result, or they keep trying, setting standards for themselves that have nothing to do with their own talents or desires.[11]

Burt Avedon in *Ah, Men* expressed a similar point:

> The pressure on boys is most intense during their teens. . . . The demands of rapidly budding masculinity reach their heights for the boy in high school (perhaps earlier now), where the laurels of success adorn the competitive athlete, the masculine ideal. (Schools often seem geared toward elevation of athletic endeavor over all activities, including academic achievement.)[12]

James Coleman's findings corroborated this. In his studies, scholastic achievement was ambiguously regarded by adolescents. In some institutions it was respected; in others, it was a source of embarrassment. However, it was never in any of his research settings ranked above athletic ability, the primary determinant of recognition and respect.

The recognition awarded athletes over scholars comes not only from other males. Coleman and his colleagues found that adolescent girls overwhelmingly preferred athletes. Avedon supported this view: "In high school, boys find that only those who fit the ideal male image, principally through sports, are able to achieve another conquest of growing importance for adolescents reaching adulthood: the attraction of beautiful, desirable females."[13]

To the adolescent, physical attractiveness in males means looking "athletic," and Coleman found "good looks" to be another key to status and power within the adolescent society. Very early, but reaching a culmination in adolescence, the body becomes a primary symbol of self. A recent poll of sixty thousand *Psychology Today* readers found that "adults who thought they were unattractive teenagers currently have lower self-esteem than those who felt beautiful, even adults who blossomed in maturity."[14] The relationship between physical appearance and self-image is clear. The male who sees himself as unattractive in adolescence does not often acquire physical self-confidence as an adult and may never forget his failure to achieve the masculine ideal in the difficult world of high school and youth. It is, after all, as Keyes quoted one female, a time when "nothing didn't matter."[15]

Keyes, a self-acknowledged "outie," is firm in his view of the placement of college professors in the adolescent status system:

> Here is how the sides break down: we give the innies all of pro sports and its cheerleaders; we concede them the military, insurance agencies, PE departments, and heavy equipment. Politics and show business are divided zones, but we write everybody's lines because outies control America's means of communication. We write the speeches, publish the books, produce the movies, make the music, do the research, report for the paper and comment on reports. . . .
>
> Teaching is a field shared by innies, but we tell them how to do it. Our strategy here is to take over the colleges of education [i.e., higher education], control research, and write all the books about how to teach high school. In these books we never take seriously any of the values innies used to keep us down. "Popularity" is a topic we're very condescending about and brush under the heading of "Peer Relations." Sports generally get ridiculed, and activities such as cheerleading and homecoming are reduced to "Student Culture: Ceremony and Ritual."[16]

The future professor might easily be recognized in *Fear of Flying,* when Erica Jong described the "brainy boys" at Columbia:

> [They wore] flannel shirts with twenty-five leaky ballpoint pens in their breast pockets, [and had] flesh-colored frames on their thick glasses, black-

heads in their ears, pustules on their necks, pleated trousers, greasy hair. . . . They commuted by subway from their mothers' [kitchens] in the Bronx to the classrooms of Moses Hadas and Gilbert Highet on Morningside Heights, where they learned enough literature and philosophy to get straight A's, but never seemed to lose their gawkiness, their schoolboy defensiveness, their total lack of appeal.[17]

Jong is not the only one to notice the phenomenon. Students, alumni, staff, and women faculty often recognize it too. They hesitate to say that they, like men, observe and evaluate the appearance of the opposite sex; they are also uncomfortable because the idea of characterizing an entire profession as "plain" seems so outlandish. Yet two women professors and a university secretary were among a number of women who admitted to finding male professors physically unappealing:

I'm embarrassed to say this but I really do find most of my colleagues unattractive physically. When I began teaching eight years ago, I thought my standards were probably adolescent or too demanding; but after all this time, I'm still not impressed. If I had to depend on the university for attractive male companionship, I might never have married.

The assumptions that college professors who are women are sexless is absurd. Of course, I look at men; and what I see here is not what you'd call encouraging. There are more short men, more men with glasses, more men with bad skin, more unkempt men here than in any single place I've ever been. Don't ask me to explain. I just know it's true.

When I first became a secretary at the college, my husband was upset because he knew I would be around men so much of the time. If I ever thought it would cause a strain, I know now how silly I was. There isn't a man here anyone would want to look at once—let alone twice. There are days when I honestly wonder where these people come from. I probably sound like a sex fiend, but you can't help noticing things like that. I've had three secretarial jobs, and I've never worked anywhere else where there were so many sexless men.

A woman dean explained the situation more graphically:

You're asking me what I think of the way these guys look? I *don't*. You work with the same types. You must understand why.

It is difficult to determine how the media developed the image of the sexy college professor with the corduroy jacket and the ever-present pipe. He may be alive and well on the silver screen and in the pages of best sellers, but he is not in abundance at the Faculty Club or meetings of the American Association of University Professors. The typical professor does not resemble Fred MacMurray, Elliott Gould, Donald Sutherland, or any other of the Hollywood types who have portrayed him over the years. If there is a star who most resembles the typical accounting, art history, or seventeenth-century literature professor, it would have to be Woody Allen.

Some college professors have been critical of organized team sports on the campus. This faculty hostility probably results from a conviction that sports receive excessive emphasis and financial support from institutions and seem at odds with academic priorities. But sometimes the fervor appears personal as well as political. Is it possible that student athletes can become surrogates for former classmates who captured attention denied the future college professor? One college coach, countering criticism of the athletic program, inadvertently touched on this possibility. While hardly unbiased, his point of view is a reminder that faculty criticism of athletic programs may be motivated by many factors.

You want to know the truth? I don't think these guys [faculty] are upset about these boys' grades at all. I don't think they know or care what happens to them. I think what bothers them, what really makes them come down on these kids is they're jealous. You take a look at them—most of them almost pass out once a week on the racquetball court. You think they like seeing these younger men in top physical condition when they probably couldn't even make manager for the high school team? I don't think they ever forgot that or forgive it, and all the rest of the talk about standards is just that—talk.

A woman professor also noticed how male members of her department raised dubious objections to the football program:

> I have to admit when I sit in faculty meetings and listen to the assault on the football program, I detect a certain adolescent hysteria. It's as if the skeletons have come out of the closet, and some of these men are foolish enough to believe they can clothe them with flesh and make them pay for the defeats of the past. If you listen carefully, the debate hinges as much on the perceived ills of athletic types as it does on the economics of football. If I could be certain their opposition to the football program was really based on academic and economic concerns rather than on some perverse need to resurrect and redo the past, my own position would be easier to decide.

There are women professors who are quick to maintain that adolescent attitudes and behaviors color their colleagues' interactions with them. Sometimes they are frustrated and angry for themselves as well as for their students. Jackie T., an instructor in a community college, exclaimed:

> There are days when I just want to scream! If I'm late to a faculty meeting, it's like running the goddamned gauntlet or something. There are maybe a hundred people in the room, but all the men in business and math sit together, and having to squeeze past them is a nightmare. These are forty- and fifty-year-old men and they're saying things like, "Hey, you can sit on my lap" or "We've got room for you here, if you don't mind a tight fit." I feel like I'm a sophomore in high school having to pass the greased-up motorcycle gang that used to stand outside until the last bell rang. I really dislike the way they all chuckle and guffaw after one of these remarks—as if to imply that they have some secret bond. They're no different with the students. They make the same kind of disgusting remarks to them in front of other people; and when they talk about some of the attractive ones, it's even worse. Back to sophomorics. I've seen them stand in a group and do everything but whistle when an attractive student walks by. Two weeks ago I walked into a conversation three of my educated colleagues were having, and it turned out to be a discussion

about "what a piece of ass" a student in the economics class of one of them was. The thing that makes me most angry is that I was embarrassed, and they couldn't have cared less.

These are subjective impressions, and there should be caution about opinions unsubstantiated by statistics. In this case, however, there are previously unpublished data to support the thesis that, as adolescents, a majority of male academicians did not fit the masculine stereotype. Coleman's 1957–1958 study, which was replicated several times, included approximately 9,000 male and female students. In 1975, Lloyd Temme, who was then with the Bureau of Social Science Research, composed *The History and Methodology of "The Adolescent Society" Follow-up Study.* Temme was able to locate a remarkably high number of the original participants in the Coleman survey— approximately 85 percent. In his own exhaustive study of these adults, Temme gathered considerable data on their vocational experiences. These records enabled him and his associate Jere Cohen to isolate from the original Coleman sample those individuals who became college professors. They found 120 males who were actively working in the profession.

The results of their findings are significant. One of the questions asked of Coleman's male adolescents was "What do you and the fellows you go around with here at school have most in common? What are the things you do together?" Out of several choices, the most relevant here was "Organized outdoor sports— including football, basketball, tennis, etc." Of those who became college professors, 94.2 percent replied they did not share with friends participation in organized athletics.[18]

Coleman provided five responses to the query "Suppose you had an extra hour in school and could either take some course of your own choosing, or use it for athletics or some other activity, or use it for study hall. How would you use it?" The choices were (1) course, (2) athletics, (3) club or activity, (4) study hall, to study, (5) study hall, to do something else. Future college professors differed most significantly from their peers on the first two items. Most, 41 percent, preferred to use the extra time for a course; only 17.2 percent of the general population selected this item. While 42.6 percent of the total group indicated they would spend the time in athletic activity, 31.6 percent of the subgroup chose this option.

Another item in the Coleman survey read, "Suppose the circle below represented the activities that go on here at school. How far out from the center of things are you?" The number 1 was the center, and 6 the periphery. As adolescents, most academicians viewed themselves on the fringes of the "innie" group: 9.4 percent saw themselves at the center (1), 31.6 percent at point 2, 41.0 percent at point 3, and the remainder in the outer three categories. Keyes and Temme had interesting observations on adolescents who were just beyond the center of status in high school. Keyes reported:

Temme says it's important to distinguish between those who were at the bottom of the social ladder and those who stood on the "second tier," one rung below the top. Those lower in the pecking order get used to being dumped on over time, he speculates, and are less resentful of it. But those on the second tier aren't accustomed to being excluded and resent it bitterly. Adults from the second rung don't lose this resentment after graduation.[19]

Another set of statistics from the sample was college professors' responses to the question "If you could be remembered here at school for one of three things below, which one would you want it to be? Brilliant student, athletic star, most popular." Their responses were the following: brilliant student, 51.0 percent; athletic star, 22.3 percent; most popular, 25.0 percent. These are considerably different from the aggregate responses of 3,696 adolescent boys of whom they are a part: brilliant student, 31.3 percent; athletic star, 43.6 percent; and most popular, 25.0 percent.

Although the future college professors very early defined themselves as different from their male peers, their attitudes toward females were quite typical. Asked whether they would prefer dating a cheerleader, the best-looking girl in class, or the best student in class, their interest in intellectual pursuits lessened considerably. By a majority of 54.5 percent, they preferred the best-looking girl; the cheerleader received the next highest vote, 32.7 percent; and only 12.7 percent were enthusiastic about dating the best female student. The aggregate responses were very similar: best-looking girl, 63.1 percent; cheerleader, 26.1 percent; best female student, 10.8 percent.

When they have been fully analyzed, the Coleman-Temme materials provide fascinating insights into the relationships between adolescence and adult choices, behaviors, and opinions. They serve as a reminder that adults—even the aberrant ones—may not be as mysterious as most choose to believe. Some sexually harassing behavior may logically have roots in adolescence if Temme's assertion is valid: "I think the rest of our lives are spent making up for what we did or didn't do in high school."[20]

This is not to suggest that all college professors were adolescent failures or that high school stereotypes are necessarily desirable. On the contrary, achievement of status in the adolescent society can be seriously detrimental to those who cannot adjust to the demands of the adult world. Emotionally healthy adults translate the superficial standards of adolescence into mature values. But there are some people who never recover from its trauma, and some sexual harassers may be among them.

If physical attractiveness and athletic achievement are the access to status with adolescent females, what is the long-term effect upon the individual outside the high school mainstream? Education is one of the few vocations in which adult males are exposed for extended periods to large groups of very young women at the height of physical desirability. For the few who have never resolved the ego problems developed in adolescent society, this may become a serious difficulty. How do a professor's recollections of adolescence influence his behaviors and attitudes toward the women over whom he exercises power? If he has painful memories of adolescent females, what are his behaviors when the tables are turned and scholarship is finally a symbol of prestige and authority? Is it likely that the past will trigger misuse of power in the present?

Unresolved adolescent conflict may contribute to the motivation of the harasser seeking sex from students. For him, as for other promiscuous men, young women can represent a means of remaking the past. To the professor denied status in high school, the prospect of a relationship with an attractive, desirable student may be especially enticing. It offers not only sexual gratification but also an opportunity to prove, if only to himself, that he can "score" as successfully as any musclebound jock.

A 1980 *Glamour* article paraphrased the statement of a psychiatrist who refused to use her name because "so many of [her] patients [were] involved in [student–professor] relationship[s], and not happily."[21]

She believed that such relationships "arise because of the professor's need to take advantage of a younger person who looks for his approval and is probably quite vulnerable. Consciously or not, he is bolstering his ego by choosing from a crop of 'subjects' who are readily attracted to him—thanks to the showmanship of teaching—and readily available to him." In the same article, Dr. Maj-Britt Rosenbaum, associate clinical professor of psychiatry at Albert Einstein College of Medicine, stated, "The male-teacher is the dominant man on campus and . . . has the chance to preen and show off because of the nature of his position."[22]

Arrested adolescent development may also influence the verbal or gender harasser. In high school, football heroes dominate the spotlight and the fantasies of females, but the academic harasser learns that when the setting changes his image can be altered. In *Ah, Men* Burt Avedon emphasized the male's concern about image:

> The desire for an image of sexual prowess inheres in almost all males no matter what their income or social position. . . . Sexual conquest is an essential part of the masculine persona. Sexual prowess, or at least the image of sexual prowess, is the goal. Sex is part of a game men play, much like the games they played as boys. The aim is to score. Once they won on the field of play; now they score and win in the great pastures of prurience.[23]

Those denied the recognition that comes from victory "on the field of play" may discover later in life that power is an aphrodisiac and that words aimed at the right audience can be as much of an ego trip as scoring a touchdown. Some professors use sarcasm and repartee about gender and sex to demonstrate that despite their bookishness, they are nevertheless virile and exciting. Others employ words as a way of asserting control and putting women in their place.

Sue W., a senior at a college in Texas, saw both motivations in the verbal harassment of a psychology professor who was "fixated on the parts of girls' bodies":

> He was always saying these dumb, off-color things he thought were real cute. I don't know if he thought they were going to make us like him or if he just wanted to watch us squirm. I *do* know I've heard funnier remarks and seen more grown-up behavior from my fourteen-year-old brother.

A botany major at a large university described the behavior of a verbal harasser even more explicitly:

> I was standing in the hall just outside of the student lounge carrying on a discussion with a senior botany major when Dr. ———— walked past, stood by the window and called out my name. He motioned for me to come over and I did. He had a roll of lifesavers. He took a green lifesaver from the pack, placed it in the palm of my hand and said, "The green ones make you want to screw." He then gave me a red lifesaver and said, "The red ones make you want to fuck." I tried to put both lifesavers back into his hand; however, he was laughing and refused them, so I put them on his briefcase and said, "That's okay, you can have your lifesavers." He acted surprised and somewhat taken aback, but I walked away and continued to talk with my friend.

Verbal harassment can also be related to insecurities about male bonding. The adolescent boy whose interests are intellectual rather than athletic has a more difficult time feeling a part of the peer group. In adulthood, he may assume that the way to gain peer acceptance is to "be cool" with the women. Whistles, insistence on eye contact, nonreciprocal touching, jokes, and off-color remarks are standard tactics that unsophisticated men suppose to be masculine behaviors. A well-known professor at a large Midwestern university was fond of beginning his first class with a sweeping glance at the women and an injunction to them to "cross your legs and close the gates to hell." It was his way of declaring to the male community his place in the order of things, and he was said to take pride in his reputation. A similar motivation inspired the language of a business instructor whose department head described him as having "locker-room humor." The department head claimed that the professor needed to "feel himself one of the boys" and mistakenly assumed that salacious remarks to and about women were a way of "making the grade with the group."

Bonding can assume more ominous tones, however. Sometimes protection of turf and preservation of conventions and the status quo are the primary forces underlying harassment. This is the reason that women who enter nontraditional fields suffer so much verbal abuse. Consciously or subconsciously, instructors may try to punish females for invading their ranks, for entering the locker room uninvited. The perpetrators of such offenses claim a standard defense. A law professor stated matter-of-factly:

> Lawyers must learn the element of give and take. Women are no exception to the rule. If they're not prepared to withstand classroom pressure, they don't belong in the courtroom.

A similar view was expressed by an engineering professor:

> If you're going to enter a man's profession, you had better be prepared to take harassment and learn to defend yourself. Engineering has been male territory for years, and our job is to teach these young ladies how to live in it with dignity and calm.

PROFESSIONAL CRISIS

Arrested adolescent development is only one concept that can help explain the behaviors of men who harass. Another is the professional crisis contemporary college professors face. The financial crises facing most campuses in the 1980s mean that college professors, especially those who are younger, confront harsh realities over which they have no control. In the foreseeable future, mobility in most disciplines will be limited, promotion and tenure will be harder to achieve, and salaries will not improve significantly. Since the financial rewards of higher education have never been good, such bleak forecasts only add to the professor's dilemma. Because society sees the academic profession as prestigious, rewarding, and influential, there is widespread confusion about the realities of the profession.

College professors pay thousands of dollars for educations that, at best, qualify them economically for inclusion in the middle class. *The Chronicle of Higher Education* reported that in 1982–1983, the average salary for faculty in all types of higher education institutions was $26,063. The survey did not include instructors, who receive the lowest pay. Its breakdown of average pay for the other three ranks demonstrated the limited financial mobility of academics: assistant professors, $20,636; associate professors, $24,876; professors, $32,258.[24]

In a 1980 article in *Academe,* Walter F. Abbot, Associate Professor of Sociology at the University of

Kentucky, presented a painstaking analysis of recent trends in academic salaries. His thesis confirmed the gravity of the college professor's professional crisis:

> The working poor comprise those who are employed but receive incomes that provide a marginal level of existence. An academic career has traditionally been considered a middle-class occupation that will provide neither an upper-level nor a poverty-level income.... [H]owever, if 1970–1977 trends in academic salaries and the poverty-level threshold persist, lower-ranking American academicians may expect to enter the ranks of the working poor in the eighties and faculty in the professor rank will receive an income in 2000 that compares about as well with the poverty threshold as assistant professors at the present time.[25]

In popular myth and movies, college professors live in Victorian houses with wood-burning fireplaces, oak staircases, and paneled, book-lined studies. In reality, many drive secondhand cars, consider themselves fortunate to afford tract housing, and wonder how they will accumulate enough money to send their own children to college. A party of professors often means moving the department or college meeting to someone's basement family room to nibble cheddar cheese and drink wine from Styrofoam cups. This scenario is not all that bleak unless one considers the discrepancy between the ideal and actual worlds of academics. College professors are the people who teach others to appreciate expensive and sophisticated equipment, books, art, theater, and music—all that society recognizes as manifestations of "the good life"—and who cannot readily afford them for themselves or their families.

In *The Male Mid-Life Crisis,* Nancy Mayer pointed out that "in America success has always meant making money and translating it into status or fame,"[26] and the relationship between financial success, power, and sexuality is a frequent topic of psychologists and organization specialists. In their article "The Executive Man and Woman: The Issue of Sexuality," Bradford, Sargent, and Sprague observed:

> An important aspect of the sense of self-identity for both males and females is their masculinity and femininity.... How do males assert their sexuality? Teenagers resort to fistfighting ... playing football, and competing against one another to see who

can consume more beer or have more dates. While this may do for youth, an educated adult must find more discreet and indirect proofs.... For many men, work serves as the major vehicle defining their identity, including sexual identity.... Status and pay of the job also bear an element of sexuality.... [Men] strive to advance, build up their programs, and compete in meetings partially to obtain status and financial records that connote masculine success, but also to affirm their masculinity more directly.[27]

A professor who sees himself in a static or unsuccessful professional and financial position may choose to exert his masculinity in negative ways. Feelings of frustration and defeat can be displaced onto the women students under his control. He can affirm his authority by being openly abusive to them, or he can turn to them for solace and ego-gratification. The dean of students at a very selective liberal arts college considered such displacement significant in some sexual harassment:

I guess you might say that many men consider access to females one of the perks of the profession. If you don't make a lot of money, if you can't go to Europe without scrimping and sacrificing, if publication of your dream book seems less and less a reality and even promotion becomes a vain hope, life looks fairly dim. It's also not hard to see why some of these men turn to students for comfort or excitement or whatever it is their egos need. Sometimes they're abusive to students because that's a way to deal with their own anger and despair. It's not right, but it's one of the realities we have to live with.

MIDLIFE CRISIS

The frustration and confusion inherent in professional crisis are similar to and sometimes synonymous with those of midlife crisis. Not surprisingly, midlife crisis is the most frequently—if not the only—explanation offered for sexually harassing behavior. Peter A., professor at a large Massachusetts university, voiced this common defense:

Another problem, and one not easily dismissed, is the fact that many of us are in our thirties and for-

ties and are watching our youth slip away at the very time we're in extremely close contact with women who are just coming into bloom. Let me tell you, it's not easy to hit the beginning of a midlife crisis when you're surrounded by nubile twenty-year-olds.[28]

If a man is going to follow the traditional pattern for male midlife crisis, academe is the best of all possible worlds in which to be. Mayer described this period in the male's life:

In response to wrenching change, a man at this stage of life is struggling to revise his own self-image and find dignity in the face of undeniable limitations. More than ever, he needs the confirmation of being seen as a powerful and desirable man—a need that the nubile girl is uniquely suited to satisfy. Our culture's most obvious symbol of hot-blooded sexuality, she can meet the aging male's intensified need for reassurance both in public and in private....

Seeking refuge from the harsh assaults of this midlife period and release from heightened anxieties that haunt and perplex them, [some men in middle age] confirm their manhood through the worshipful gaze of a nubile girl—who mirrors back an image of their most potent self. Contrary to popular wisdom, men in their middle years are generally drawn to younger women not because they want to recapture their youth, but because they need to reconfirm their maturity....

This, then, is the single most seductive reason for the appeal of the nubile girl: A yielding innocent on whom a man can project whatever fantasy he craves, she makes him feel not merely potent, but also omnipotent. A soothing balm indeed. Where else, after all, can the aging male find a sexual partner who will offer applause and adulation without demanding reciprocal attentions? Who will satisfy his emotional needs without requiring him to cater to hers? Only the young can afford to be so selfless.[29]

The enormous advantage that college professors have over men in similar situations is that for them, the stage is already set. Not only are there more than enough "nubile girls" from whom to choose, but they are women who have already been conditioned to regard the teacher as intellectually omnipotent. As individual desires and needs change over time, a wife who is a peer may become intellectually, professionally, or emotionally menacing; the attraction to a younger woman may lie in her lack of competition or threat. A person with whom the professor has no shared history is cleaner, less complicated. If she is also a student, she exhibits all of the deference that comes with discrepancies in roles, experience, and sophistication. A male confused about responding to an older woman's demands may find those of female students more manageable and less intense.

The middle-aged professor suffering from sexual insecurity may find college women especially appealing sexually. Older women may pose not only intellectual and professional threats but also—and perhaps more important—very real sexual pressure. Their sexual demands are greater, and they increase the anxiety of the male in crisis. One man explained to Mayer:

> One thing that's true, though, I think you can get a younger woman to respond to you very strongly. She's going to be less appraising than an older woman. She's had less experience. There are fewer men in her life to which she can compare you. You can dominate her more, sort of impose your myth on her. And you can feel you're initiating her into all sorts of things and blowing her mind and enslaving her—or whatever the hell it is that you want to do with a woman.[30]

The professor whose sexual insecurity contributes to his harassment of students can easily delude himself. He has heard that women students today are freer and engage in intercourse earlier, so taboos about despoiling or deflowering the innocent can be rationalized. At the same time, women students are, by and large, young and lacking the sexual experience of older, more demanding women. Thus the student seems "safe," a novice flattered by the attentions of the professor who can introduce her to the mysterious pleasures of adult sexuality. And the harasser can delude himself into believing that he has done no harm and that the student is responding to his sexuality rather than his position.

Even when sexual activity with the student is the end of harassment, it is not the only motivation. Mayer noted that contemporary social scientists, "in contrast to Freud, who said all human actions were shaped by sexual needs . . . now suggest the opposite: that sexual activity is often motivated by other needs. Non sexual needs."[31] At any point in a man's life cycle, but especially during midlife, one such need may be competition with other males. The college professor at forty is in an unusual position: he is surrounded by physically desirable young women, as well as by young men in their physical prime. If he has been reared in traditional fashion, he knows that beyond all the myths about male friendships, the truth is that males are taught to relate to one another in one way—competition. Fasteau was clear on this point:

> Competition is the principal mode by which men relate to each other—at one level because they don't know how else to make contact, but more basically because it is the way to demonstrate, to themselves, and others, the key masculine qualities of unwavering toughness and the ability to dominate and control. The result is that they inject competition into situations which don't call for it.[32]

The classroom may be one such situation. Male students represent youth, virility, vigor, uncircumscribed futures—everything the man in midlife crisis may feel himself lacking. Added to this may be the professor's doubts about the masculinity of his profession. The males he teaches in the 1980s are interested in careers in high technology, business, engineering, law, and medicine. His own profession is not especially popular—not only because it does not pay well but also because many men do not view it as particularly masculine. A study by David F. Aberle and Kaspar Naegele found, for instance, that middle-class fathers rejected academic careers for their sons because they did "not consider the academic role to exemplify appropriate masculine behavior."[33] The exception was a father who replied that such a role would be appropriate for his son, who was shy, bookish, and needed women to care for him.

One way a professor can assert his masculinity in such a situation is to prove himself and other males that he is attractive to and can control women. Dean Z., a basketball player at a small college in the Midwest, seemed aware of this possibility:

> Sometimes I think my English prof is trying to tell us something when he tries to make it with the girls. I could care less if they like him. He's so over the hill he's not really any competition, but he makes a big deal out of trying to show us that he can get our girls.

The harasser in midlife crisis may also be influenced by curiosity about contemporary youth and their life-styles. The young women who populate the nation's campuses in the 1980s may appear terribly exotic to men who began dating in the 1950s. Alison Lurie's *The War Between the Tates* depicted this condition. Brian Tate, the middle-aged political science professor in the novel, temporarily abandoned his family for Wendy, a seductive student who not only bolstered his ego but also introduced him to a new way of life. Wendy's attraction for Brian resulted in part from her membership in a culture that appeared alien to him:

> Brian had known for some time that he and his colleagues were not living in the America they had grown up in; it was only recently though that he had realized they were also not living in present-day America, but in another country or city state with somewhat different characteristics. The important fact about this state, which can for convenience sake be called "University," is that the great majority of its population is aged eighteen to twenty-two. Naturally the physical appearance, interests, activities, preferences and prejudices of this majority are the norm in University. Cultural and political life is geared to their standards, and any deviation from them is a social handicap.
>
> Brian had started life as a member of the dominant class in America, and for years had taken this position for granted. Now, in University, he finally has the experience of being among a depressed minority.[34]

If some sexual harassment is influenced by adolescent, professional, and/or midlife crises, others spring from more disturbing roots that only in-depth analyses of individuals could explain. An undergraduate art student felt that one of her professors was "deeply troubled":

> At first I wasn't so scared of him because I figured his line was just like that of all the other guys I knew, even if he was older. I started to get upset when he started saying crazy things to me—like he would like to smear me with grape jelly and paint me naked. One day he told me that if I was his girl-friend he would tie me up to the bed, and I don't know why but all I could think of was getting the hell out of there. I never went back to his class. And I'm not sorry.

A respondent to the National Advisory Council reported an experience that indicated that harassment is seldom a simple case of "boys will be boys":

> All the incidents with this professor share a pattern: indecent exposure. Although the precise circumstances vary, this faculty member (young, supposedly socially conscious) would initiate the incidents by tucking his shirt in, "fixing his belt," or otherwise rearranging his clothing. He is also known to verbally sexually abuse students by initiating discussion on penis size, how he has overcome his inferiority complex about his small penis size and following this with a verbal offer to expose his penis to view. This faculty member has also exposed himself in his home to at least one other graduate student in another department.[35]

Obviously, in such cases only individuals skilled in the study of psychology and familiar with the histories of individual subjects should analyze such behaviors. But most sexual harassment follows a more familiar pattern and is easier to understand. Higher education needs to use its resources to learn more about common causes for the behavior and the motivations of those who engage in it. When that happens, people will recognize that sexual harassment is more controllable than most realize.

If the problem is to be understood, there are a number of issues that researchers need to consider. If, for example, the physical appearance of a woman student is relevant in a discussion of sexual harassment, that of her professor is no less important. If the culture and socialization of contemporary women students is worthy of discussion, that of their instructors must also be taken into account. If students' motivations and self-concepts warrant consideration, those of their teachers are equally relevant. If sex stereotyping influences women's behavior, it must also affect men and must be considered in attempts to analyze the behaviors of harassers. There also needs to be more research on the relationships between sexual attitudes and vocational choice and experiences. Are there preestablished sexual attitudes, behaviors, and opportunities within specific occupational groups that attract certain types of men? How do work experiences and relationships affect men's perceptions of the opposite sex?

To an extent, of course, the motivations of professors who harass will always be enigmatic. Like their colleagues, most are products of traditional sex stereotyping; they are schooled in similar attitudes toward women and sexual codes of ethics. Yet harassers act on their impulses and assumptions when others do not. Harassers either cannot or will not subordinate personal drives and desires to professional ethics. Nonharassers can and do.

If responsible college professors have anything to fear as a result of students' and the public's learning about sexual harassment, it is not that women will make unjust or capricious accusations. The real fear should be that students will hold the institution and the faculty accountable for transgressions of which they *are* guilty. Sexual harassment is deviant behavior, and while those within the institution probably cannot alter the personal psychologies of individual academicians, they *can* influence the campus environment. Aberrant organizational activity may be impossible to eliminate, but it can be curtailed if colleagues refuse to tolerate improprieties.

The behaviors of harassers and nonharassers have become much easier to differentiate as awareness has grown. Many professors, often grudgingly, now monitor their behaviors and avoid questionable interac-

tions with students. They hesitate before making certain kinds of statements or engaging in physical gestures; they pause before placing themselves in questionable situations. And none of that really is so bad. It may be annoying, but it is not wrong or oppressive. If men and women had treated one another with greater sensitivity in the first place, sexual harassment would not be such a problem today. If teachers had approached students with greater sensitivity in the past, students would not seem such enigmas.

The harasser lives by an outlaw code. Relying upon colleagues' reluctance to intervene in student–faculty relationships and the romantic notion that eccentricity is tolerable in academe, he has failed to read the signs of change. Higher education may accept idiosyncratic dress, manners, speech, and interests, but sexual harassment is different from these—less superficial and more threatening to the profession. Once professors realize that their own reputations suffer with that of the harasser, male college professors are likely to find the "eccentricity" of the lecherous professor less tolerable and less deserving of defense.

NOTES

1. Harry Zehner, "Love and Lust on Faculty Row," *Cosmopolitan,* April 1982, pp. 271–72.

2. Anna Sequoia, *The Official J.A.P. Handbook* (New York: New American Library, 1982), pp. 114–15.

3. John Barth, *The End of the Road* (New York: Doubleday, 1958), p. 98.

4. Marilyn B. Brewer, "Further Beyond Nine to Five: An Integration and Future Directions," *Journal of Social Issues* 38 (1982): 155.

5. Rollo May, *Power and Innocence* (New York: Dell, 1972), p. 102.

6. Herb Goldberg, *The Hazards of Being Male* (New York: New American Library, 1976), p. 175.

7. Erik Erikson, *Identity, Youth and Crisis* (New York: Norton, 1968).

8. Ralph Keyes, *Is There Life After High School?* (Boston: Little, Brown, 1976), pp. 94–95.

9. James S. Coleman, *The Adolescent Society* (New York: The Free Press, 1961).

10. Quoted in Nancy G. Clinch, *The Kennedy Neurosis* (New York: Grosset & Dunlap, 1973), p. 266.

11. Marc Feigen Fasteau, *The Male Machine* (New York: McGraw-Hill, 1974), p. 105.

12. Burt Avedon, *Ah, Men* (New York: A & W Publishers, 1980), p. 72.

13. Avedon, p. 45.

14. Ellen Berscheid, Elaine Walster, and George Behrnstedt, "Body Image," *Psychology Today,* November 1973, p. 250.

15. Keyes, p. 10.

16. Keyes, pp. 97, 98.

17. Erica Jong, *Fear of Flying* (New York: Holt, Rinehart and Winston, 1974), p. 188.

18. The data on college professors are derived from James Coleman's *The Adolescent Society* and Lloyd Temme's *"Adolescent Society" Follow-up Study* (Washington, D.C.: Bureau of Social Science, 1976). Temme and his associate Jere Cohen made this previously unreported information available for use in *The Lecherous Professor.* This particular question was selected for analysis to demonstrate that college professors were not among Coleman's athletic "elite." It should be noted that the responses of the total sample were similar to those of men who became professors; 92 percent of the total gave negative responses to this query.

19. Keyes, p. 56.

20. Keyes, p. 57.

21. Mopsy Strange Kennedy, "'A' for Affairs with the Professor: What Happens When a Student Falls in Love with Her Teacher?," *Glamour,* August, 1980, p. 237.

22. Kennedy, p. 241.

23. Avedon, p. 72.

24. American Association of University Professors, "9-Month Salaries for 1982–83," Fact File, *The Chronicle of Higher Education,* June 22, 1983, p. 20.

25. Walter F. Abbot, "Commentary: When Will Academicians Enter the Ranks of the Working Poor?" *Academe* 66 (October 1980): 349.

26. Nancy Mayer, *The Male Mid-Life Crisis* (New York: New American Library, 1978), p. 164.

27. David Bradford, Alice Sargent, and Melinda Sprague, "The Executive Man and Woman: The Issue of Sexuality," *Bringing Women Into Management,* eds. Francine Gordon and Myra Strober (New York: McGraw-Hill, 1975), pp. 18–19.

28. Zehner, p. 273.

29. Mayer, pp. 107, 111–13.

30. Mayer, p. 108.

31. Mayer, p. 107.

32. Fasteau, p. 11.

33. David F. Aberle and Kaspar Naegele, "Middle-Class Fathers' Occupational Role and Attitudes Toward Children," *American Journal of Orthopsychiatry* 22 (1952): 366.

34. Alison Lurie, *The War Between the Tates* (New York: Warner Books, 1975), p. 40.

35. Frank J. Till, *Sexual Harassment: A Report on the Sexual Harassment of Students,* Report of the National Advisory Council on Women's Education Programs (Washington, D.C.: 1980), p. 23.

R E A D I N G   4 0

"The Man in the Street": Why He Harasses

CHERYL BERNARD AND EDIT SCHLAFFER

It is a violation of my natural external freedom not to be able to go where I please, and to experience other restrictions of this kind. . . . Even though the body and life are something external, just like property, nevertheless my personality is wounded by such experiences, because my most immediate identity rests in my body.

Hegel, *Texte zur philosophischen Propaedeutik*

I am standing at Wittenbergplatz waiting for the light to turn green, in my left hand I am carrying a bag filled with groceries . . . behind me I sense the approach of two men and turn

my head, at that moment the man on my left reaches for my hair which falls to my shoulders colored with henna, he runs his fingers through my hair experimentally and says to his friend: great hair. . . . An ordinary everyday experience for the colonized in a city of the First World.

Verena Stefan, *Haeutungen*

By the time we are in our twenties we have become accustomed to the laws of the street. The abrupt but regular interruptions of our daily movements have become familiar, we have acquired the habit of overhearing comments, we are graceful at dodging straying hands, we have the skill of a general in making rapid strategic evaluations, we can usually tell at a glance whether that group of young men leaning against a car door might use physical intimidation or just jokes, whispered comments, laughter, whether it's worth crossing over to the other side of the street or enough to act nonchalant and cultivate deafness. It's no longer frightening, just annoying, sometimes jolting when one is called abruptly out of a train of thought or a moment of absentmindedness. One gets used to it.

Is all of this normal, inevitable? It was a question I had stopped asking myself by the time I spent a year abroad at the university in Beirut. In the dorm I shared a room with Widad from Bahrein, an 18-year-old who wanted to be a teacher. At home, Widad always wrapped an abaya around her jeans and T-shirt when she went out of the house, and to Widad, the behavior of men on the street was news. Not yet hardened by long experience, Widad spent her first week in Beirut in tears. Sobbing with anger and confusion, she would report on the insulting and unbelievable things that had been said to her, the grabbing, the pushing, the comments, the aggressive looks, the smacking lips, the hissing in her ear. The abaya, she would conclude, has nothing to do with women. In Bahrein we wear it because of the men, someday maybe we won't have to but right now, this is how they are, and who can stand it? The final outcome, I am sorry to report, was not that Widad became hardened and militant, schooled in the martial arts and an example to us all, but that she was instrumental in organizing a group of Bahreini men, so that for the rest of the academic year the women from Bahrein moved through the city like a convoy flanked by a string of guards ready to fight at the sign of a covetous glance.

For the American women, this was an occasion to think again about the kind of world we have learned to accept as normal. On public streets, we plan our routes and our timing as if we were passing through a mine field. We are touched, harassed, commented upon in a stream of constant small-scale assaults, and in a culture which values privacy and anonymity in crowds these intimacies are considered inevitable. Secretly, women like it, popular opinion believes, and posters of men whistling after a woman are thought by advertising agencies to sell their product. Besides, popular opinion goes on to explain, women provoke it, with their fashions, their manner of walking, their behavior. These are familiar arguments; we hear them whenever the subject of violence against women comes up. There are few facts to hold up against them. Stamped as trivial, the harassment of women has received no attention from sociology, and cities that regulate almost everything from bicycles and dogs to the use of roller skates in order to keep the traffic moving have no ordinances or rules to guarantee women the right to free passage.

What kinds of men harass women, what do they think they are doing, how do women feel about it? Diaries and essays by women, and reports from other times and cultures, give some very sketchy information. For a more systematic picture, we observed the behavior of men in four cities (Berlin, Los Angeles, Rome, and Vienna) over the period of a year, allowing for differences in season, time of day, and part of town. Interviews with women provided information on how the victims feel. Some of the results were surprising and some were depressingly predictable.

That the behavior of the "man on the street" has received so little attention is odd, because it captures in quintessential, almost primordial form the combination of the ordinary and the bizarre which we have learned to regard as normal. The "man on the street" is a synonym for everyone, which in our society means every man. The behavior he casually accords to randomly passing women he has never seen before serves to identify him as a member of the ruling group, to whom the streets and the society belong. And at the same time this behavior, looked at with an analytic eye, is very peculiar. The anthropologist from outer space, that popular device for viewing the world with a bit more perspective, would be very astonished to find adult males moaning, jumping, whistling, singing, honking, winking, contorting face and body, hissing obscenities, laughing hysterically, and mumbling hoarse endearments to perfect strangers without apparent provocation. However odd, though, these single and seemingly irrational instances add up to a pattern, and the pattern spells intimidation.

Women are assigned, in this interaction, an inevitably passive part. They have a number of available responses, but their response makes little difference. A woman can ignore what she sees or hears, she can reply, she can curse, keep walking, stop, try for a disarming smile, get angry, start a discussion. What she does has little influence. A friendly answer may stop the man, or it may encourage him to further intimacies; threats and curses may silence him, or they may prompt genuine aggression. The language itself puts us at a permanent disadvantage; it is hard to exchange serious insults without using sexual putdowns that invariably go against women. And passers-by, far from supporting a woman who defends herself, will shed their former indifference to disapprove of feminine vulgarity.

It is commonly supposed that certain countries and cultures display this behavior more than others; the Mediterranean cultures, particularly, are assumed to be swarming with papagallos dedicated to the female foreign tourist. In fact, this form of male behavior is distributed quite evenly across the continents, races, and generations. The nationalist author Qasim Amin deplored the harassment of the heavily veiled Egyptian women at the turn of the century and in fact attributed masculine aggression to the veil. As a sign of women's inferior status, he argued, it encouraged men to treat them with disrespect and take liberties. This interpretation comes very close to the truth. Like other forms of sexual violence, harassment has little to do with the individual woman and nothing to do with sex; the issue is power.

Whether you wear a slit skirt or are covered from head to foot in a black chador, the message is not that you are attractive enough to make a man lose his self-control but that the public realm belongs to him and you are there by his permission as long as you follow his rules and as long as you remember your place. Badr-al-Moluk Bamdad recalls in her book on growing up in Iran that there was no way for a woman to win this game; if, in the opinion of any passing male, one's veil was not wrapped with sufficient modesty, one could be insulted, reprimanded, and threatened, while if obediently covered one would be followed and taunted by boys and young men shouting that one looked like a "black crow or an inkwell."[1]

Harassment of women is timeless, but the notion that women really like it and feel flattered is a refinement that has been added more recently. Women's own accounts have always shown a clear awareness of the essential hostility implied by these male attentions, even when they didn't put that awareness into the context of any more general picture of sexist structures. Descriptions have been handed down to us from many different sources. Evelyn Scott, an American woman who later was to become a successful author, spent the year of 1916 in Brazil with her lover. They were poor, she was pregnant. In her diary, she wrote that, in Rio, "something objectionable always occurred" when she went outdoors unaccompanied. "Perhaps it is because I am only 20 years old," she wrote. "Perhaps it is because I am shabbily dressed. I know perfectly well that I am not particularly pretty.

Inwardly shrinking and cold with an obscure fear, I make it a point to look very directly at all the men who speak to me. I want to shame them by the straightforwardness of my gaze. Perhaps I am ridiculous. If I could consider sex more factually and with less mystical solemnity I might find amusement in the stupidity of these individuals who can't be so sinister after all."[2]

Anger and an "obscure fear" are the most common responses of women, and those feelings are all the greater when the situation seems too intimidating to allow a reply. Pretending to have heard nothing, looking away, hoping the men will get bored and stop or will be too busy with the woman walking in front of you to attend to you are calculations that increase the impact of the experience. A 22-year-old law student remembered one pivotal incident in her life: "I was 17, and just walking around downtown with my friend Marie. Two men started talking to us, making jokes and telling us to come with them. They grabbed our arms and tried to pull us along. Marie got angry and told them to let us go. The men pushed her against a building and started shaking her and saying she was unfriendly and stuck up and should watch out. Finally they left. It was afternoon and there were a lot of people around, but nobody said anything. At the time I learned from that that it was better to ignore men who talked to you like that. If you act like you don't care, they usually let you go without any trouble. I don't think that's a very good conclusion to draw, but I still don't know how to act in situations like that without getting into trouble."

What is going on in the minds of the men who do this? Not much, judging from their difficulties in articulating their intentions. We interviewed 60 men, choosing a range of age groups out of those who addressed us on the street. (Incidentally, this was the only female response we found that genuinely and predictably disarms the harassing male, so if you want to transform a lewdly smirking man into a politely confused one within a matter of seconds you need only pull a mimeographed questionnaire out of your bag and inform him that he is part of a research project. This method, however, is rather time-consuming.) Pressed for an explanation of their behavior, most of the men initially played it down. Boredom and a feeling of youthful camaraderie that came over them when discussing women with other men emerged as the most frequent feelings prompting harassment. The notion that women disliked this and felt infringed upon in their freedom of movement was a novel one for most men, not because they had another image of the woman's response but because they had never given it any thought at all. Only a minority, around 15%, explicitly set out to anger or humiliate their victims. This is the same group that employs graphic sexual commentary and threats. Other forms of antagonism often become mixed up with the sexual. Some migrant laborers or construction workers insult not so much the woman as the snobbish privileged class she symbolizes to them. Another minority of men believes with firm conviction that women enjoy receiving their attention. One 45-year-old construction worker portrayed himself as a kind of benefactor to womanhood and claimed to specialize in older and less attractive women to whom, he was sure, his display of sexual interest was certain to be the highlight in an otherwise drab and joyless existence. A significant group of men, around 20%, said that they would not engage in this behavior when alone, but only in the company of male friends. This supports the explanation that the harassment of women is a form of male bonding, of demonstrating solidarity and joint power.

The symbolic nature of the behavior is its most important attribute. A surprising finding was that harassment declines in the late evening and during the night, and that men are then more likely to display the kind of behavior typical of the avoidance usually shown to strangers in public or crowded situations: averting one's eyes, accelerating the pace of walking to keep a distance, etc. At first glance, this finding is surprising. It would seem that harassment would be even more effective at night, even more intimidating to the woman. Probably, this is precisely the reason it declines during the night; on a deserted street, it would be *too* effective. The woman, not merely annoyed or unnerved but genuinely alarmed, might well be driven to an "extreme" response (such as calling for help) that the good citizen would not like to have to explain. In the daytime, he takes no such risk. The age, education, and income of the man make little difference; in their street behavior, they revert to a primordially uniform condition across the lines of class and generation. Younger men tend to be more aggressive, and older men to lower their voices and whisper hastily as they pass you. Some areas are exempt altogether: small villages, where all the inhabitants know each other, and residential suburban areas.

The genuinely *public* world is the main arena for harassment. The street, as a place where strangers encounter each other, is also the place where societies have always taken care to clearly mark the lines of order and status. It is on the streets that members of subordinate groups have to wear special clothing or identifying marks, that they must salute, take off their hat, or jump down from the sidewalk to make way for the members of the superior group. Harassment is a way of ensuring that women will not feel at ease, that they will remember their role as sexual beings available to men and not consider themselves equal citizens participating in public life. But the ritual of harassment does more than that. By its seeming harmlessness and triviality, it blurs the borders of women's right to personal integrity, and encourages men who would never commit a violent crime against a strange woman to participate in minor transgressions against her right to move freely, to choose which interactions to participate in and which people to communicate with. By making of the "man on the street," the average man, a minor sex offender, it also makes him an accomplice in the more massive forms of violence against women.

NOTES

1. Badr-al-Moluk Bamdad, *Women's Emancipation in Iran* (New York, 1977).

2. Mary Jane Moffat and Charlotte Painter, eds., *Revelations: Diaries of Women* (New York: Vintage, 1974), p. 100.

R E A D I N G   4 1

Rape: The All-American Crime

SUSAN GRIFFIN

I have never been free of the fear of rape. From a very early age I, like most women, have thought of rape as part of my natural environment—something to be feared and prayed against like fire or lightning. I never asked why men raped; I simply thought it one of the many mysteries of human nature.

I was, however, curious enough about the violent side of humanity to read every crime magazine I was able to ferret away from my grandfather. Each issue featured at least one "sex crime," with pictures of a victim, usually in a pearl necklace, and of the ditch or the orchard where her body was found. I was never certain why the victims were always women, nor what the motives of the murderer were, but I did guess that the world was not a safe place for women. I observed that my grandmother was meticulous about locks, and quick to draw the shades before anyone removed so much as a shoe. I sensed that danger lurked outside.

At the age of eight, my suspicions were confirmed. My grandmother took me to the back of the house where the men wouldn't hear, and told me that strange men wanted to do harm to little girls. I learned not to walk on dark streets, not to talk to strangers, or get into strange cars, to lock doors, and to be modest. She never explained why a man would want to harm a little girl, and I never asked.

If I thought for a while that my grandmother's fears were imaginary, the illusion was brief. That year, on the way home from school, a schoolmate a few years older than I tried to rape me. Later, in an obscure aisle of the local library (while I was reading *Freddy the Pig*) I turned to discover a man exposing himself. Then, the friendly man around the corner was arrested for child molesting.

My initiation to sexuality was typical. Every woman has similar stories to tell—the first man who attacked her may have been a neighbor, a family friend, an uncle, her doctor, or perhaps her own father. And women who grow up in New York City always have tales about the subway.

But though rape and the fear of rape are a daily part of every woman's consciousness, the subject is so rarely discussed by that unofficial staff of male intellectuals (who write the books which study seemingly every other form of male activity) that one begins to suspect a conspiracy of silence. And indeed, the obscurity of rape in print exists in marked contrast to the frequency of rape in reality, for *forcible rape is the most frequently committed violent crime in America today.* The Federal Bureau of Investigation classes three crimes as violent: murder, aggravated assault and forcible rape. In 1968, 31,060 rapes were *reported.* According to the FBI and independent criminologists, however, to approach accuracy this figure must be multiplied by at least a factor of ten to compensate for the fact that most rapes are not reported; when these compensatory mathematics are used, there are more rapes committed than aggravated assaults and homicides.

When I asked Berkeley, California's Police Inspector in charge of rape investigation if he knew why men rape women, he replied that he had not spoken with "these people and delved into what really makes them tick, because that really isn't my job. . . ." However, when I asked him how a woman might prevent being raped, he was not so reticent. "I wouldn't advise any female to go walking around alone at night . . . and she should lock her car at all times." The Inspector illustrated his warning with a grisly story about a man who lay in wait for women in the back seats of their cars, while they were shopping in a local supermarket. This man eventually murdered one of his rape victims. "Always lock your car," the Inspector repeated, and then added, without a hint of irony, "Of course, you don't have to be paranoid about this type of thing."

The Inspector wondered why I wanted to write

about rape. Like most men he did not understand the urgency of the topic, for, after all, men are not raped. But like most women I had spent considerable time speculating on the true nature of the rapist. When I was very young, my image of the "sexual offender" was a nightmarish amalgamation of the bogey man and Captain Hook: he wore a black cape, and he cackled. As I matured, so did my image of the rapist. Born into the psychoanalytic age, I tried to "understand" the rapist. Rape, I came to believe, was only one of many unfortunate evils produced by sexual repression. Reasoning by tautology, I concluded that any man who would rape a woman must be out of his mind.

Yet, though the theory that rapists are insane is a popular one, this belief has no basis in fact. According to Professor Menachem Amir's study of 646 rape cases in Philadelphia, *Patterns in Forcible Rape,* men who rape are not abnormal. Amir writes, "Studies indicate that sex offenders do not constitute a unique or psychopathological type; nor are they as a group invariably more disturbed than the control groups to which they are compared." Alan Taylor, a parole officer who has worked with rapists in the prison facilities at San Luis Obispo, California, stated the question in plainer language: "Those men were the most normal men there. They had a lot of hang-ups, but they were the same hang-ups as men walking out on the street."

Another canon in the apologetics of rape is that, if it were not for learned social controls, all men would rape. Rape is held to be natural behavior, and not to rape must be learned. But in truth rape is not universal to the human species. Moreover, studies of rape in our culture reveal that, far from being impulsive behavior, most rape is planned. Professor Amir's study reveals that in cases of group rape (the "gangbang" of masculine slang), 90 percent of the rapes were planned; in pair rapes, 83 percent of the rapes were planned; and in single rapes, 58 percent were planned. These figures should significantly discredit the image of the rapist as a man who is suddenly overcome by sexual needs society does not allow him to fulfill.

Far from the social control of rape being learned, comparisons with other cultures lead one to suspect that, in our society, it is rape itself that is learned. (The fact that rape is against the law should not be considered proof that rape is not in fact encouraged as part of our culture.)

This culture's concept of rape as an illegal, but still understandable, form of behavior is not a universal one. In her study *Sex and Temperament,* Margaret Mead describes a society that does not share our views. The Arapesh do not "have any conception of the male nature that might make rape understandable to them." Indeed, our interpretation of rape is a product of our conception of the nature of male sexuality. A common retort to the question, why don't women rape men, is the myth that men have greater sexual needs, that their sexuality is more urgent than women's. And it is the nature of human beings to want to live up to what is expected of them.

And this same culture which expects aggression from the male expects passivity from the female. Conveniently, the companion myth about the nature of female sexuality is that all women secretly want to be raped. Lurking beneath her modest female exterior is a subconscious desire to be ravished. The following description of a stag movie, written by Brenda Starr in Los Angeles' underground paper *Everywoman,* typifies this male fantasy. The movie "showed a woman in her underclothes reading on her bed. She is interrupted by a rapist with a knife. He immediately wins her over with his charm and they get busy sucking and fucking." An advertisement in the *Berkeley Barb* reads, "Now as all women know from their daydreams, rape has a lot of advantages. Best of all it's so simple. No preparation necessary, no planning ahead of time, no wondering if you should or shouldn't; just whang! bang!" Thanks to Masters and Johnson, even the scientific canon recognizes that for the female, "whang! bang!" can scarcely be described as pleasurable.

Still, the male psyche persists in believing that, protestations and struggles to the contrary, deep inside her mysterious feminine soul, the female victim has wished for her own fate. A young woman who was raped by the husband of a friend said that days after the incident the man returned to her home, pounded on the door and screamed to her, "Jane, Jane. You loved it. You know you loved it."

The theory that women like being raped extends itself by deduction into the proposition that most or much of rape is provoked by the victim. But this too is only myth. Though provocation, considered a mitigating factor in a court of law, may consist of only "a gesture," according to the Federal Commission on Crimes of Violence, only 4 percent of reported rapes involved any precipitative behavior by the woman.

"I MAKE NO APOLOGY"

To Whom It May Concern—Which I'm sure is no one of any importance

I don't believe in petitions.
I don't believe in the feminist movement.
I don't even believe in authority.

Since joining the intramural football team known as THE STATUTORY RAPISTS during

Reprinted from "I Make No Apology," anonymous letter by the Quarterback of the Statutory Rapists, Football Team of the College of Law, The Ohio State University, Columbus, Ohio.

their second year of regular play, I have felt that the name lacked intelligence and creativity. However disgusting I find such a label I do, however, strongly believe in the concept behind it and as a member of the male species I feel that it has been both my prerogative and my pleasure. Recognizing that I can not speak for my team and my team captain, and realizing what little loss there is, I can only say that some of us will play under no other name.

I make no apology.

Quarterback of THE STATUTORY RAPISTS

The notion that rape is enjoyed by the victim is also convenient for the man who, though he would not commit forcible rape, enjoys the idea of its existence, as if rape confirms that enormous sexual potency which he secretly knows to be his own. It is for the pleasure of the armchair rapist that detailed accounts of violent rapes exist in the media. Indeed, many men appear to take sexual pleasure from nearly all forms of violence. Whatever the motivation, male sexuality and violence in our culture seem to be inseparable. James Bond alternately whips out his revolver and his cock, and though there is no known connection between the skills of gun-fighting and lovemaking, pacifism seems suspiciously effeminate.

In a fictional treatment of the Manson case, Frank Conroy writes of his vicarious titillation when describing the murders to his wife:

"Every single person there was killed." She didn't move.

"It sounds like there was torture," I said. As the words left my mouth I knew there was no need to say them to frighten her into believing that she needed me for protection.

The pleasure he feels as his wife's protector is inextricably mixed with pleasure in the violence itself. Conroy writes, "I was excited by the killings, as one is excited by catastrophe on a grand scale, as one is alert to pre-echoes of unknown changes, hints of unrevealed secrets, rumblings of chaos...."

The attraction of the male in our culture to vio-

lence and death is a tradition Manson and his admirers carried on with tireless avidity (he dreamed of the purification of fire and destruction). It was Malraux in his *Anti-Memoirs* who said that, for the male, facing death was *the* illuminating experience analogous to childbirth for the female. Certainly our culture does glorify war and shroud the agonies of the gun-fighter in veils of mystery.

And in the spectrum of male behavior, rape, the perfect combination of sex and violence, is the penultimate act. Erotic pleasure cannot be separated from culture, and in our culture male eroticism is wedded to power. Not only should a man be taller and stronger than a female in the perfect lovematch, but he must also demonstrate his superior strength in gestures of dominance which are perceived as amorous. Though the law attempts to make a clear division between rape and sexual intercourse, in fact the courts find it difficult to distinguish between a case where the decision to copulate was mutual and one where a man forced himself upon his partner.

The scenario is even further complicated by the expectation that not only does a woman mean "yes" when she says "no," but that a really decent woman ought to begin by saying "no," and then be led down the primrose path to acquiescence. Ovid, the author of Western civilization's most celebrated sex manual, makes this expectation perfectly clear:

... and when I beg you to say "yes," say "no." Then let me lie outside your bolted door.... So love grows strong....

That the basic elements of rape are involved in all heterosexual relationships may explain why men often identify with the offender in this crime. But to regard the rapist as the victim, a man driven by his inherent sexual needs to take what will not be given him, reveals a basic ignorance of sexual politics. For in our culture heterosexual love finds an erotic expression through male dominance and female submission. A man who derives pleasure from raping a woman clearly must enjoy force and dominance as much as or more than the simple pleasures of the flesh. Coitus cannot be experienced in isolation. The weather, the state of the nation, the level of sugar in the blood—all will affect a man's ability to achieve orgasm. If a man can achieve sexual pleasure after terrorizing and humiliating the object of his passion, and in fact while inflicting pain upon her, one must assume he derives pleasure directly from terrorizing, humiliating and harming a woman. According to Amir's study of forcible rape, on a statistical average the man who has been convicted of rape was found to have a normal sexual personality, tending to be different from the normal, well-adjusted male only in having a greater tendency to express violence and rage.

And if the professional rapist is to be separated from the average dominant heterosexual, it may be mainly a quantitative difference. For the existence of rape as an index to masculinity is not entirely metaphorical. Though this measure of masculinity seems to be more publicly exhibited among "bad boys" or aging bikers who practice sexual initiation through group rape, in fact, "good boys" engage in the same rites to prove their manhood. In Stockton, a small town in California which epitomizes silent-majority America, a bachelor party was given last summer for a young man about to be married. A woman was hired to dance "topless" for the amusement of the guests. At the high point of the evening the bridegroom-to-be dragged the woman into a bedroom. No move was made by any of his companions to stop what was clearly going to be an attempted rape. Far from it. As the woman described it, "I tried to keep him away— told him of my Herpes Genitalis, et cetera, but he couldn't face the guys if he didn't screw me." After the bridegroom had finished raping the woman and returned with her to the party, far from chastizing him, his friends heckled the woman and covered her with wine.

It was fortunate for the dancer that the bridegroom's friends did not follow him into the bedroom

for, though one might suppose that in group rape, since the victim is outnumbered, less force would be inflicted on her, in fact, Amir's studies indicate, "the most excessive degrees of violence occurred in group rape." Far from discouraging violence, the presence of other men may in fact encourage sadism, and even cause the behavior. In an unpublished study of group rape by Gilbert Geis and Duncan Chappell, the authors refer to a study by W. H. Blanchard which relates, "The leader of the male group ... apparently precipitated and maintained the activity, despite misgivings, because of a need to fulfill the role that the other two men had assigned to him. 'I was scared when it began to happen,' he says. 'I wanted to leave but I didn't want to say it to the other guys—you know—that I was scared.'"

Thus it becomes clear that not only does our culture teach men the rudiments of rape, but society, or more specifically other men, encourages the practice of it.

II

Every man I meet wants to protect me. Can't figure out what from.

Mae West

If a male society rewards aggressive, domineering sexual behavior, it contains within itself a sexual schizophrenia. For the masculine man is also expected to prove his mettle as a protector of women. To the naive eye, this dichotomy implies that men fall into one of two categories: those who rape and those who protect. In fact, life does not prove so simple. In a study euphemistically entitled "Sex Aggression by College Men," it was discovered that men who believe in a double standard of morality for men and women, who in fact believe most fervently in the ultimate value of virginity, are more liable to commit "this aggressive variety of sexual exploitation."

(At this point in our narrative it should come as no surprise that Sir Thomas Malory, creator of that classic tale of chivalry, *The Knights of the Round Table,* was himself arrested and found guilty for repeated incidents of rape.)

In the system of chivalry, men protect women against men. This is not unlike the protection relationship which the Mafia established with small businesses in the early part of this century. Indeed, chivalry is an age-old protection racket which depends for its existence on rape.

According to the male mythology which defines and perpetuates rape, it is an animal instinct inherent in the male. The story goes that sometime in our prehistorical past, the male, more hirsute and burly than today's counterparts, roamed about an uncivilized landscape until he found a desirable female. (Oddly enough, this female is *not* pictured as more muscular than the modern woman.) Her mate does not bother with courtship. He simply grabs her by the hair and drags her to the closest cave. Presumably, one of the major advantages of modern civilization for the female has been the civilizing of the male. We call it chivalry.

But women do not get chivalry for free. According to the logic of sexual politics, we too have to civilize our behavior. (Enter chastity. Enter virginity. Enter monogamy.) For the female, civilized behavior means chastity before marriage and faithfulness within it. Chivalrous behavior in the male is supposed to protect that chastity from involuntary defilement. The fly in the ointment of this otherwise peaceful system is the fallen woman. She does not behave. And therefore she does not deserve protection. Or, to use another argument, a major tenet of the same value system: what has once been defiled cannot again be violated. One begins to suspect that it is the behavior of the fallen woman, and not that of the male, that civilization aims to control.

The assumption that a woman who does not respect the double standard deserves whatever she gets (or at the very least "asks for it") operates in the courts today. While in some states a man's previous rape convictions are not considered admissible evidence, the sexual reputation of the rape victim is considered a crucial element of the facts upon which the court must decide innocence or guilt.

The court's respect for the double standard manifested itself particularly clearly in the case of the *People* v. *Jerry Plotkin.* Mr. Plotkin, a 36-year-old jeweler, was tried for rape in San Francisco. According to the woman who brought the charges, Plotkin, along with three other men, forced her at gunpoint to enter a car one night in October 1970. She was taken to Mr. Plotkin's fashionable apartment, where he and the three other men first raped her and then, in the delicate language of the *San Francisco Chronicle,* "subjected her to perverted sex acts." She was, she said, set free in the morning with the warning that she would be killed if she spoke to anyone about the event. She did report the incident to the police, who then searched Plotkin's apartment and discovered a long list of names of women. Her name was on the list and had been crossed out.

In addition to the woman's account of her abduction and rape, the prosecution submitted four of Plotkin's address books containing the names of hundreds of women. Plotkin claimed he did not know all of the women since some of the names had been given to him by friends and he had not yet called on them. Several women, however, did testify in court that Plotkin had, to cite the *Chronicle,* "lured them up to his apartment under one pretext or another, and forced his sexual attentions on them."

Plotkin's defense rested on two premises. First, through his own testimony Plotkin established a reputation for himself as a sexual libertine who frequently picked up girls in bars and took them to his house, where sexual relations often took place. He was the Playboy. He claimed that the accusation of rape, therefore, was false—this incident had simply been one of many casual sexual relationships, the victim one of many playmates. The second premise of the defense was that his accuser was also a sexual libertine. However, the picture created of the young woman (fully 13 years younger than Plotkin) was not akin to the lighthearted, gay-bachelor image projected by the defendant. On the contrary, the day after the defense cross-examined the woman, the *Chronicle* printed a story headlined, "Grueling Day for Rape Case Victim." (A leaflet passed out by women in front of the courtroom was more succinct: "Rape was committed by four men in a private apartment in October; on Thursday, it was done by a judge and a lawyer in a public courtroom.")

Through skillful questioning fraught with innuendo, Plotkin's defense attorney, James Martin MacInnis, portrayed the young woman as a licentious opportunist and unfit mother. MacInnis began by asking the young woman (then employed as a secretary) whether or not it was true that she was "familiar with liquor" and had worked as a "cocktail waitress." The young woman replied (the *Chronicle* wrote "admitted") that she had worked once or twice as a cocktail waitress. The attorney then asked if she had worked as a secretary in the financial district but had "left that employment after it was discovered that you had sexual intercourse on a couch in the office." The woman replied, "That is a lie. I left because I didn't like working in a one-girl office. It was too lonely." Then the defense asked if, while working as an attendant at a health club, "you were accused of having a sexual affair with a man?" Again the woman denied the story. "I was never accused of that."

Plotkin's attorney then sought to establish that his client's accuser was living with a married man. She responded that the man was separated from his wife. Finally he told the court that she had "spent the night" with another man who lived in the same building.

At this point in the testimony the woman asked Plotkin's defense attorney, "Am I on trial? . . . It is embarrassing and personal to admit these things to all these people. . . . I did not commit a crime. I am a human being." The lawyer, true to the chivalry of his class, apologized and immediately resumed questioning her, turning his attention to her children. (She is divorced, and the children at the time of the trial were in a foster home.) "Isn't it true that your two children have a sex game in which one gets on top of another and they—" "That is a lie!" the young woman interrupted him. She ended her testimony by explaining, "They are wonderful children. They are not perverted."

The jury, divided in favor of acquittal ten to two, asked the court stenographer to read the woman's testimony back to them. After this reading, the court acquitted the defendant of the charges of both rape and kidnapping.

According to the double standard, a woman who has had sexual intercourse out of wedlock cannot be raped. Rape is not only a crime of aggression against the body; it is a transgression against chastity as defined by men. When a woman is forced into a sexual relationship, she has, according to the male ethos, been violated. But she is also defiled if she does not behave according to the double standard, by maintaining her chastity, or confining her sexual activities to a monogamous relationship.

One should not assume, however, that a woman can avoid the possibility of rape simply by behaving. Though myth would have it that mainly "bad girls" are raped, this theory has no basis in fact. Available statistics would lead one to believe that a safer course is promiscuity. In a study of rape done in the District of Columbia, it was found that 82 percent of the rape victims had a "good reputation." Even the Police Inspector's advice to stay off the streets is rather useless, for almost half of reported rapes occur in the home of the victim and are committed by a man she has never before seen. Like indiscriminate terrorism, rape can happen to any woman, and few women are ever without this knowledge.

But the courts and the police, both dominated by white males, continue to suspect the rape victim, *sui generis,* of provoking or asking for her own assault. According to Amir's study, the police tend to believe that a woman without a good reputation cannot be raped. The rape victim is usually submitted to countless questions about her own sexual mores and behavior by the police investigator. This preoccupation is partially justified by the legal requirements for prosecution in a rape case. The rape victim must have been penetrated, and she must have made it clear to her assailant that she did not want penetration (unless of course she is unconscious). A refusal to accompany a man to some isolated place to allow him to touch her does not, in the eyes of the court, constitute rape. She must have said "no" at the crucial genital moment. And the rape victim, to qualify as such, must also have put up a physical struggle—unless she can prove that to do so would have been to endanger her life.

But the zealous interest the police frequently exhibit in the physical details of a rape case is only partially explained by the requirements of the court. A woman who was raped in Berkeley was asked to tell the story of her rape four different times "right out in the street," while her assailant was escaping. She was then required to submit to a pelvic examination to prove that penetration had taken place. Later, she was taken to the police station where she was asked the same questions again: "Were you forced?" "Did he penetrate?" "Are you sure your life was in danger and you had no other choice?" This women had been pulled off the street by a man who held a 10-inch knife at her throat and forcibly raped her. She was raped at midnight and was not able to return to her home until five in the morning. Police contacted her twice again in the next week, once by telephone at two in the morning and once at four in the morning. In her words, "The rape was probably the least traumatic incident of the whole evening. If I'm ever raped again, . . . I wouldn't report it to the police because of all the degradation. . . ."

If white women are subjected to unnecessary and

often hostile questioning after having been raped, third-world women are often not believed at all. According to the white male ethos (which is not only sexist but racist), third-world women are defined from birth as "impure." Thus the white male is provided with a pool of women who are fair game for sexual imperialism. Third-world women frequently do not report rape and for good reason. When blues singer Billie Holliday was 10 years old, she was taken off to a local house by a neighbor and raped. Her mother brought the police to rescue her, and she was taken to the local police station crying and bleeding:

> When we got there, instead of treating me and Mom like somebody who called the cops for help, they treated me like I'd killed somebody.... I guess they had me figured for having enticed this old goat into the whorehouse.... All I know for sure is they threw me into a cell ... a fat white matron ... saw I was still bleeding, she felt sorry for me and gave me a couple glasses of milk. But nobody else did anything for me except give me filthy looks and snicker to themselves.
>
> After a couple of days in a cell they dragged me into a court. Mr. Dick got sentenced to five years. They sentenced me to a Catholic institution.

Clearly the white man's chivalry is aimed only to protect the chastity of "his" women.

As a final irony, that same system of sexual values from which chivalry is derived has also provided womankind with an unwritten code of behavior, called femininity, which makes a feminine woman the perfect victim of sexual aggression. If being chaste does not ward off the possibility of assault, being feminine certainly increases the chances that it will succeed. To be submissive is to defer to masculine strength; is to lack muscular development or any interest in defending oneself; is to let doors be opened, to have one's arm held when crossing the street. To be feminine is to wear shoes which make it difficult to run; skirts which inhibit one's stride; underclothes which inhibit the circulation. Is it not an intriguing observation that those very clothes which are thought to be flattering to the female and attractive to the male are those which make it impossible for a woman to defend herself against aggression?

Each girl as she grows into womanhood is taught fear. Fear is the form in which the female internalizes both chivalry and the double standard. Since, biologically speaking, women in fact have the same potential for sexual expression as do men, if not greater, the woman who is taught that she must behave differently from a man must also learn to distrust her own carnality. She must deny her own feelings and learn not to act from them. She fears herself. This is the essence of passivity, and of course, a woman's passivity is not simply sexual but functions to cripple her from self-expression in every area of her life.

Passivity itself prevents a woman from ever considering her own potential for self-defense and forces her to look to men for protection. The woman is taught fear, but this time fear of the other; and yet her only relief from this fear is to seek out the other. Moreover, the passive woman is taught to regard herself as impotent, unable to act, unable even to perceive, in no way self-sufficient, and, finally, as the object and not the subject of human behavior. It is in this sense that a woman is deprived of the status of a human being. She is not free to be.

III

Since Ibsen's Nora slammed the door on her patriarchal husband, woman's attempt to be free has been more or less fashionable. In this 19th-century portrait of a woman leaving her marriage, Nora tells her husband, "Our home has been nothing but a playroom. I have been your doll-wife just as at home I was papa's doll-child." And, at least on the stage, "The Doll's House" crumbled, leaving audiences with hope for the fate of the modern woman. And today, as in the past, womankind has not lacked examples of liberated women to emulate: Emma Goldman, Greta Garbo and Isadora Duncan all denounced marriage and the double standard, and believed their right to freedom included sexual independence; but still their example has not affected the lives of millions of women who continue to marry, divorce and remarry, living out their lives dependent on the status and economic power of men. Patriarchy still holds the average woman prisoner not because she lacks the courage of an Isadora Duncan, but because the material conditions of her life prevent her from being anything but an object.

In *The Elementary Structures of Kinship,* Claude Lévi-Strauss gives to marriage this universal description: "It is always a system of exchange that we find at the origin of the rules of marriage." In this system of exchange, a woman is the "most precious possession." Lévi-Strauss continues that the custom of including women as booty in the marketplace is still so general that "a whole volume would not be sufficient to enumerate instances of it." Lévi-Strauss makes it clear that he does not exclude Western civilization from his definition of "universal" and cites examples from modern wedding ceremonies. (The marriage ceremony is still one in which the husband and wife become one, and "that one is the husband.")

The legal proscription against rape reflects this possessory view of women. An article in the 1952–53 *Yale Law Journal* describes the legal rationale behind laws against rape: "In our society sexual taboos, often enacted into law, buttress a system of monogamy based upon the law of 'free bargaining' of the potential spouses. Within this process the woman's power to withhold or grant sexual access is an important bargaining weapon." Presumably, then, laws against rape are intended to protect the right of a woman, not for physical self-determination, but for physical "bargaining." The article goes on to explain explicitly why the preservation of the bodies of women is important to men:

> The consent standard in our society does more than protect a significant item of social currency for women; it fosters, and is in turn bolstered by, a masculine pride in the exclusive possession of a sexual object. The consent of a woman to sexual intercourse awards the man a privilege of bodily access, a personal "prize" whose value is enhanced by sole ownership. An additional reason for the man's condemnation of rape may be found in the threat to his status from a decrease in the "value" of his sexual possession which would result from forcible violation.

The passage concludes by making clear whose interest the law is designed to protect. "The man responds to this undercutting of his status as *possessor* of the girl with hostility toward the rapist; no other restitution device is available. The law of rape provides an orderly outlet for his vengeance." Presumably the female victim in any case will have been sufficiently socialized so as not to consciously feel any strong need

JUDGE FACES RECALL

COLUMBUS CITIZEN-JOURNAL

A citizens group in Lancaster, Wis., said Tuesday it will circulate petitions seeking the ouster of a circuit judge who called a 5-year-old sexual assault victim an "unusually sexually promiscuous young lady."

Diane Barton said her ouster group has decided "it was an irresponsible thing to say this child was promiscuous."

Mrs. Barton said she expected the petitions to be ready for distribution next week in the group's quest to force a recall election of Judge William Reinecke. Reinecke contended his remarks were taken out of context.

Reinecke made the remark in sentencing Ralph Snodgrass, 24, to 90 days in a work-release program for sexually assaulting the 5-year-old daughter of the woman with whom he was living.

The judge observed the girl was "an unusually sexually promiscuous young lady" and Snodgrass "did not know enough to refuse. No way do I believe Mr. Snodgrass initiated sexual contact."

The hired hand said he was sleeping and the girl climbed on top of him. The girl later was found to have been sexually assaulted.

The judge said he was simply trying to show that the girl, not really knowing what she was doing, was the aggressor.

Reprinted from the *Columbus Citizen-Journal,* 20 January 1982. Courtesy of Scripps Howard News Service.

for vengeance. If she does feel this need, society does not speak to it.

The laws against rape exist to protect the rights of the male as possessor of the female body, and not the right of the female over her own body. Even without this enlightening passage from the *Yale Law Review,* the laws themselves are clear: In no state can a man be accused of raping his wife. How can any man steal what already belongs to him? It is in the sense of rape as theft of another man's property that Kate Millet writes, "Traditionally rape has been viewed as an offense one male commits against another—a matter of abusing his woman." In raping another man's woman, a man may aggrandize his own manhood and concurrently reduce that of another man. Thus a man's honor is not subject directly to rape, but only indirectly, through "his" woman.

If the basic social unit is the family, in which the woman is a possession of her husband, the superstructure of society is a male hierarchy, in which men dominate other men (or patriarchal families dominate other patriarchal families). And it is no small irony that, while the very social fabric of our male-dominated culture denies women equal access to political, economic and legal power, the literature, myth and humor of our culture depict women not only as the power behind the throne but as the real source of the oppression of men. The religious version of this fairy tale blames Eve for both carnality and eating of the tree of knowledge, at the same time making her gullible to the obvious devices of a serpent. Adam, of course, is merely the trusting victim of love. Certainly this is a biased story. But no more biased than the one television audiences receive today from the latest slick comedians. Through a medium which is owned by men, censored by a state dominated by men, all the evils of this social system which make a man's life unpleasant are blamed upon "the wife." The theory is: were it not for the female who waits and plots to "trap" the male into marriage, modern man would be able to achieve Olympian freedom. She is made the scapegoat for a system which is in fact run by men.

Nowhere is this more clear than in the white racist use of the concept of white womanhood. The white male's open rape of black women, coupled with his overweening concern for the chastity and protection of his wife and daughters, represents an extreme of sexist and racist hypocrisy. While on the one hand she was held up as the standard for purity and virtue, on the other the Southern white woman was never asked if she wanted to be on a pedestal, and in fact any deviance from the male-defined standards for white womanhood was treated severely. (It is a powerful commentary on American racism that the historical role of blacks as slaves, and thus possessions without power, has robbed black women of legal and economic protection through marriage. Thus black women in Southern society and in the ghettoes of the North have long been easy game for white rapists.) The fear that black men would rape white women was, and is, classic paranoia. Quoting from Ann Breen's unpublished study of racism and sexism in the South "The New South: White Man's Country," Frederick Douglass legitimately points out that, had the black man wished to rape white women, he had ample opportunity to do so during the Civil War, when white women, the wives, sisters, daughters and mothers of the rebels, were left in the care of blacks. But yet not a single act of rape was committed during this time. The Ku Klux Klan, who tarred and feathered black men and lynched them in the name of the purity of white womanhood, also applied tar and feathers to a Southern white woman accused of bigamy, which leads one to suspect that Southern white men were not so much outraged at the violation of the woman as a person, in the few instances where rape was actually committed by black men, but at the violation of his property rights. In the situation where a black man was found to be having sexual relations with a white woman, the white woman could exercise skin-privilege, and claim that she had been raped, in which case the black man was lynched. But if she did not claim rape, she herself was subject to lynching.

In constructing the myth of white womanhood so as to justify the lynching and oppression of black men and women, the white male has created a convenient symbol of his own power which has resulted in black hostility toward the white "bitch," accompanied by an unreasonable fear on the part of many white women of the black rapist. Moreover, it is not surprising that after being told for two centuries that he wants to rape white women, occasionally a black man does actually commit that act. But it is crucial to note that the frequency of this practice is outrageously exaggerated in the white mythos. Ninety percent of reported rape is intra- not inter-racial.

In *Soul on Ice,* Eldridge Cleaver has described the mixing of a rage against white power with the internalized sexism of a black man raping a white woman. "Somehow I arrived at the conclusion that, as a matter of principle, it was of paramount importance for me to have an antagonistic, ruthless attitude toward white women. . . . Rape was an insurrectionary act. It delighted me that I was defying and trampling upon the white man's law, upon his system of values, and that I was defiling his women—and this point, I believe, was the most satisfying to me because I was very resentful over the historical fact of how the white man has used the black woman." Thus a black man uses white women to take out his rage against white men. But in fact, whenever a rape of a white woman by a black man does take place, it is again the white man who benefits. First, the act itself terrorizes the white woman and makes her more dependent on the white male for protection. Then, if the woman prosecutes her attacker, the white man is afforded legal opportunity to exercise overt racism. Of course, the knowledge of the rape helps to perpetuate two myths which are beneficial to white male rule—the bestiality of the black man and the desirability of white women. Finally, the white man surely benefits because he himself is not the object of attack—he has been allowed to stay in power.

Indeed, the existence of rape in any form is beneficial to the ruling class of white males. For rape is a kind of terrorism which severely limits the freedom of women and makes women dependent on men. Moreover, in the act of rape, the rage that one man may harbor toward another higher in the male hierarchy can be deflected toward a female scapegoat. For every man there is always someone lower on the social scale on whom he can take out his aggressions. And this is any woman alive.

This oppressive attitude towards women finds its institutionalization in the traditional family. For it is assumed that a man "wears the pants" in his family—he exercises the option of rule whenever he so chooses. Not that he makes all the decisions—clearly women make most of the important day-to-day decisions in a family. But when a conflict of interest arises, it is the man's interest which will prevail. His word, in itself, is more powerful. He lords it over his wife in the same way his boss lords it over him, so that the very process of exercising his power becomes as important an act as obtaining whatever it is his power can get for him. This notion of power is key to the male ego in this culture, for the two acceptable measures of masculinity

are a man's power over women and his power over other men. A man may boast to his friends that "I have 20 men working for me." It is also aggrandizement of his ego if he has the financial power to clothe his wife in furs and jewels. And, if a man lacks the wherewithal to acquire such power, he can always express his rage through equally masculine activities—rape and theft. Since male society defines the female as a possession, it is not surprising that the felony most often committed together with rape is theft. As the following classic tale of rape points out, the elements of theft, violence and forced sexual relations merge into an indistinguishable whole.

The woman who told this story was acquainted with the man who tried to rape her. When the man learned that she was going to be staying alone for the weekend, he began early in the day a polite campaign to get her to go out with him. When she continued to refuse his request, his chivalrous mask dropped away:

I had locked all the doors because I was afraid, and I don't know how he got in; it was probably through the screen door. When I woke up, he was shaking my leg. His eyes were red, and I knew he had been drinking or smoking. I thought I would try to talk my way out of it. He started by saying that he wanted to sleep with me, and then he got angrier and angrier, until he started to say, "I want pussy, I want pussy." Then, I got scared and tried to push him away. That's when he started to force himself on me. It was awful. It was the most humiliating, terrible feeling. He was forcing my legs apart and ripping my clothes off. And it was painful. I did fight him—he was slightly drunk and I was able to keep him away. I had taken judo a few years back, but I was afraid to throw a chop for fear that he'd kill me. I could see he was getting more and more violent. I was thinking wildly of some way to get out of this alive, and then I said to him, "Do you want money. I'll give you money." We had money but I was also thinking that if I got to the back room I could telephone the police—as if the police would have even helped. It was a stupid thing to think of because obviously he would follow me. And he did. When he saw me pick up the phone, he tried to tie the cord around my neck. I screamed at him that I did have the money in another room, that I was going to call the police because I was scared, but that I would never tell anybody what happened. It would be an absolute secret. He said, okay, and I went to get the money. But when he got it, all of a sudden he got this crazy look in his eye and he said to me, "Now I'm going to kill you." Then I started saying my prayers. I knew there was nothing I could do. He started to hit me—I still wasn't sure if he wanted to rape me at this point—or just to kill me. He was hurting me, but hadn't yet gotten me into a strangle-hold because he was still drunk and off balance. Somehow we pushed into the kitchen where I kept looking at this big knife. But I didn't pick it up. Somehow, no matter how much I hated him at that moment, I still couldn't imagine putting the knife in his flesh, and then I was afraid he would grab it and stick it into me. Then he was hitting me again and somehow we pushed through the back door of the kitchen and onto the porch steps. We fell down the steps and that's when he started to strangle me. He was on top of me. He just went on and on until finally I lost consciousness. I did scream, though my screams sounded like whispers to me. But what happened was that a cab driver happened by and frightened him away. The cab driver revived me—I was out only a minute at the most. And then I ran across the street and I grabbed the woman who was our neighbor and screamed at her, "Am I alive? Am I still alive?"

Rape is an act of aggression in which the victim is denied her self-determination. It is an act of violence which, if not actually followed by beatings or murder, nevertheless always carries with it the threat of death. And finally, rape is a form of mass terrorism, for the victims of rape are chosen indiscriminately, but the propagandists for male supremacy broadcast that it is women who cause rape by being unchaste or in the wrong place at the wrong time—in essence, by behaving as though they were free.

The threat of rape is used to deny women employment. (In California, the Berkeley Public Library, until pushed by the Federal Employment Practices Commission, refused to hire female shelvers because of perverted men in the stacks.) The fear of rape keeps women off the streets at night. Keeps women at home. Keeps women passive and modest for fear that they be thought provocative.

It is part of human dignity to be able to defend oneself, and women are learning. Some women have learned karate; some to shoot guns. And yet we will not be free until the threat of rape and the atmosphere of violence is ended, and to end that the nature of male behavior must change.

But rape is not an isolated act that can be rooted out from patriarchy without ending patriarchy itself. The same men and power structure who victimize women engaged in the act of raping Vietnam, raping black people and the very earth we live upon. Rape is a classic act of domination where, in the words of Kate Millett, "the emotions of hatred, contempt, and the desire to break or violate personality" take place. This breaking of the personality characterizes modern life itself. No simple reforms can eliminate rape. As the symbolic expression of the white male hierarchy, rape is the quintessential act of our civilization, one which, Valerie Solanis warns, is in danger of "humping itself to death."

R E A D I N G   4 2

A Rapist Gets Caught in the Act

AS TOLD TO JAMES K. SKIPPER, JR., AND WILLIAM L. MCWHORTER

INTERVIEWER: Can you tell me something about yourself?

RESPONDENT: Sure, why not, I am 32 years old. I am 5 feet 7 inches tall and I weigh 165 pounds. I drive a truck for a living and make pretty good money. I got an old lady and two nice kids. One is 12, a nice girl, and a boy almost 9 now. What else is there to say? Oh, yes, I am not dumb. I got a high school diploma. I never got arrested for nothing before, not even a parking violation. What else do you want to know? Yes, I love my wife and I loved my father and mother. Isn't that what you are supposed to say? Well, in my case it is true except for my father. I did not know him very well because he left my mother when I was about four and we never saw him again. I don't think she cared whether she saw him again or not. She never went looking. I guess she figured he didn't have anything she wanted anyway. She never wanted to talk about him much and there wasn't anything for me to talk about. I didn't know enough about him to miss him.

INTERVIEWER: Do you remember anything else about your father?

RESPONDENT: Not really, I guess he had a lot of odd jobs like store clerk, repair man. I think he worked in a mail room once, but was not what you would call a mailman. I mean he did not deliver mail. Mom said he liked to collect coins. That's all I can remember. Like I said he left when I was about 4, maybe it was 5. It does not matter. Anyway I never

Reprinted from James K. Skipper and William L. Mc-Whorter, "A Rapist Gets Caught in the Act," in *Deviance: Voices from the Margin,* ed. by James K. Skipper, Jr., William L. McWhorter, Charles H. McCaghy, and Mark Lefton (Belmont, Calif.: Wadsworth, 1981), pp. 28–30, by permission of the publisher. Copyright © 1981 by Wadsworth, Inc.

hated the guy if that's what you are trying to get at. How can you hate someone you don't even remember? You can't blame him for what I did.

INTERVIEWER: What was your relationship with your mother?

RESPONDENT: What do you mean what was my relationship with my mother? I never screwed her if that's what you mean. For Christ sake what type of guy do you think I am? Sure I fucked some women in my time whether they liked it or not, but your own mother that is disgusting. My God man, what do you take me for?

INTERVIEWER: I am sorry, you misunderstood me. I meant how did you get along with your mother. Did you have a happy family life?

RESPONDENT: Oh, I see what you mean. Well it is like this. I loved my mother a lot I really did. She was always good to me and gave me all the things she could afford. She was a waitress at a fancy type restaurant. You know the type where you got to have money and class or you don't get in the door. She worked at night and did not get in until late. I was always asleep when she got home. That's after I was in school. I don't remember before that. She used to get up early and see me off to school and then give me an early dinner before she went to work. I was on my own most of the time since I was about 7. But I didn't mind. I could find things to do for myself. We didn't live in a real bad neighborhood and besides she used to give me money. I always had more money than the other kids to do things. We always used to spend Sundays together and do things like going to movies, out to dinner. Things like that. I always liked to have Sundays with her until I was about 15. Then I didn't like to do it any more. I had better things to do by then. You know what I mean? Now I kind of miss them. She died in a car crash about a year after I got married. It really came as a shock. I had not seen her much after I got married. Then I got this phone call at work that she had been killed in a head-on collision. It was right here in town. The police said the cars couldn't been going more than 35, but it was enough to kill both drivers. I really felt bad about it. After all she had done for me, she deserved something better. Anyway, you can't blame her either for what I have done. It couldn't be her. It was all just me.

INTERVIEWER:　What do you think was the cause of your conduct?

RESPONDENT:　Well if you mean my wife you are crazy. I have had a normal sexual life with my wife. We have two kids don't we? I am normal in every respect. I have never beat my wife or my kids. I have fooled around a little in my day but nothing serious. You get me? I take my women one at a time. That way nothing gets serious. It does not interfere with your life. At least not until now it has not. My wife never knew nothing.

INTERVIEWER:　You mean your wife was not aware of your affairs with other women?

RESPONDENT:　Now there you go again. I didn't say I had affairs with other women did I? That's not right. What I meant was sometimes you just have the urge to go out and fuck the living shit out of some broad. You don't have to like them. You don't have to want to ever see them again. You just get the urge to go out and fuck one of them. It does not matter who they are or what they look like. You just want to do it. It has nothing to do with loving your wife. Once it is over it is over. Anyway I suppose it is normal for a guy to want to do that once or twice a year. I think most women expect it.

INTERVIEWER:　You mean women would not consider it a case of rape?

RESPONDENT:　Hell no, Hell no. I mean most women like to get their box battered as much as a man likes to get his balls off. They want to be grabbed and taken hard. It makes them feel like a woman. I know that to be a fact. And

what's more you feel more like a man when you do it that way. This time I just got unlucky and got a cold-hearted bitch. That's the only difference.

INTERVIEWER:　Could you describe the circumstances of your present offense?

RESPONDENT:　OK I guess so. There really is not much to tell though. I got up one morning. It was a hot day in August. I had not got much sleep the night before. I felt kind of mean and ugly. My wife was nagging again. The kids were getting on my nerves even before I got out of the house. I had trouble starting the truck and I was late to work. The boss did not like that much, I could tell he didn't. But he did not yell at me or nothing. He just told me to get going and make up the time as best I could. I tried but I got stuck in traffic and it got later and later. By lunch time I was so far behind I was not going to make all my deliveries by 5:00 no matter what I did. I stopped at this little diner and had a few beers. I did not feel like eating at all. Then I thought by God what you need is a good piece. That ought to fix you up good. Just go out and grab yourself a broad. Hell I was not going to make my deliveries anyway. It was after 2:00 by then. So I got me back in the truck and started cruising around looking. About an hour went by and nothing. I thought oh God don't let this be my unlucky day. Then I saw this woman standing alone at a bus stop. She was not much to look at. Skinny as a rail, about 40 years old I would say. I pulled up and asked her if she could give me directions to County Line Road. She told me the way right off. But I pretended not to understand. After she told me again and I said I still did not get it, I asked her if she would like to get in the truck and show me. I knew she must be going in that general direction because that is the way the bus was going. She hesitated for a moment and looked to see if the bus was coming. It was not. She said, "Well I suppose it would be OK. You look like a nice enough kid, but I am not going quite that far." Right then I figured I had her. So I says, "Hop in." She does and we are on our way. I know a good place just outside of town down a side road where there is an old abandoned barn. It is not far from the road, but you can't see it from the road and sound does not carry from it very well. I have been there before. I figure it is safe. We get to talking real nice. I start thinking about how I am going to grab her. We miss her stop and she doesn't even seem to know. Finally she realizes it and says, "You missed my stop! You missed my stop! You even missed County Line Road." I apologize and play dumb and say I didn't know we had passed them. I stop the truck and start to turn around and then I say, "Wait a minute. We are just a couple of miles from another of my deliveries. Would you mind if we just drove a little farther down this road?" She agrees if it will not take long. I assure her it won't and we are on our way again. Before you know it we are at my safe place. I grab a couple of packages out of the back and start toward the trees to the barn. I stop and say, "Hey I hate to leave you alone in the car. Why don't you walk with me to the house? It is just through the trees." She thinks that is a good idea and we start out. We get about 200 feet from the barn through the trees and she sees it is no farm house and says, "I am going back." I grab her by the arm and she starts fighting and screaming. I figure I got a real loony this time I am never going to make it to the barn. It might as well be right here on the ground. I tell her to be quiet and quit fighting. She won't stop so I slug her one and that takes most of the steam out of her and she falls down and starts groaning. I figure let her groan. Nobody is going to hear that. I plop down on her and start to get her dress off and in the meantime I get my cock out. I may have got my cock close to her, but I sure never got it in let alone come. The last thing I remember is a big crash on my head. It felt like the whole world came down on my head. I remember waking up and thinking lord my God that must have been the biggest come I ever had. I remember them picking me up and taking me to a police car. I can't move my hands they are cuffed. I don't know what the hell happened to me. It was not until much later until I figure it out. You know what happened?

INTERVIEWER: No I do not. Please tell me what happened.

RESPONDENT: Well it was like this. There was some Goddamn 19-year-old kid fucking his broad in the barn. They hear the goings on outside and instead of getting scared and running away the cocksucker sneaks up behind me and crowns me on the head with a quart beer bottle. No wonder I went out like a light. The son of a bitch never gave me a chance to explain. And he had been doing the same thing! If I had caught him in the barn I sure as hell would not have tried to break his head. I would let him alone. Anyway he called the police on his C.B. I never did find out where he had his car hid. I sure never saw it. Well I did not have a leg to stand on. The woman was half naked and had a cut lip and black eye. My cock was out, and there were two witnesses. She claimed rape and I swear I never got in her. But all the evidence looked against me. This is the first time for me. I have pushed a few women around before when I got the urge and fucked them. But I never hurt them and they never said nothing about it. I don't think this woman would have either if that prick had not hit me over the head. What right did he have to do that? I never did nothing to him. I never saw him before. I guess I just got unlucky.

R E A D I N G   4 3

Just Walk on By: A Black Man Ponders His Power to Alter Public Space

BRENT STAPLES

My first victim was a woman—white, well dressed, probably in her early twenties. I came upon her late one evening on a deserted street in Hyde Park, a relatively affluent neighborhood in an otherwise mean, impoverished section of Chicago. As I swung onto the avenue behind her, there seemed to be a discreet, un-inflammatory distance between us. Not so. She cast back a worried glance. To her, the youngish black man—a broad six feet two inches with a beard and billowing hair, both hands shoved into the pockets of a bulky military jacket—seemed menacingly close. After a few more quick glimpses, she picked up her pace and was soon running in earnest. Within seconds she disappeared into a cross street.

That was more than a decade ago. I was 22 years old, a graduate student newly arrived at the University of Chicago. It was in the echo of that terrified woman's footfalls that I first began to know the unwieldy inheritance I'd come into—the ability to alter public space in ugly ways. It was clear that she thought herself the quarry of a mugger, a rapist, or worse. Suffering a bout of insomnia, however, I was stalking sleep, not defenseless wayfarers. As a softy who is scarcely able to take a knife to a raw chicken—let alone hold it to a person's throat—I was surprised, embarrassed, and dismayed all at once. Her flight made me feel like an accomplice in tyranny. It also made it clear that I was indistinguishable from the muggers who occasionally seeped into the area from the surrounding ghetto. That first encounter, and those that followed, signified that a vast, unnerving gulf lay between nighttime pedestrians—particularly women—and me. And I soon gathered that being perceived as dangerous is a hazard in itself. I only needed to turn a corner into a dicey situation, or crowd some frightened, armed person in a foyer somewhere, or make an errant move after being pulled over by a policeman. Where fear and weapons meet—and they often do in urban America—there is always the possibility of death.

In that first year, my first away from my hometown, I was to become thoroughly familiar with the language of fear. At dark, shadowy intersections in Chicago, I could cross in front of a car stopped at a traffic light and elicit the *thunk, thunk, thunk, thunk* of the driver—black, white, male, or female—hammering down the door locks. On less traveled streets after dark, I grew accustomed to but never comfortable with people who crossed to the other side of the street rather than pass me. Then there were the standard unpleasantries with police, doormen, bouncers, cab drivers, and others whose business it is to screen out troublesome individuals *before* there is any nastiness.

I moved to New York nearly two years ago and I have remained an avid night walker. In central Manhattan, the near-constant crowd cover minimizes tense one-on-one street encounters. Elsewhere—visiting friends in SoHo, where sidewalks are narrow and tightly spaced buildings shut out the sky—things can get very taut indeed.

Black men have a firm place in New York mugging literature. Norman Podhoretz in his famed (or infamous) 1963 easay, "My Negro Problem—And Ours," recalls growing up in terror of black males; they "were tougher than we were, more ruthless," he writes—and as an adult on the Upper West Side of Manhattan, he continues, he cannot constrain his nervousness when he meets black men on certain streets. Similarly, a decade later, the essayist and novelist Edward Hoagland extols a New York where once "Negro bitterness bore down mainly on other Negroes." Where some see mere panhandlers, Hoagland sees "a mugger who is clearly screwing up his nerve to do more than just *ask* for money." But Hoagland has "the New Yorker's quick-hunch posture for broken-field maneuvering," and the bad guy swerves away.

I often witness that "hunch posture," from women after dark on the warrenlike streets of Brooklyn where I live. They seem to set their faces on neutral and, with their purse straps strung across their chests bandolier style, they forge ahead as though bracing themselves against being tackled. I understand, of course, that the danger they perceive is not a hallucination. Women are particularly vulnerable to street violence, and young black males are drastically overrepresented among the perpetrators of that violence. Yet these truths are no solace against the kind of alienation that comes of being ever the suspect, against being set apart, a fearsome entity with whom pedestrians avoid making eye contact.

It is not altogether clear to me how I reached the ripe old age of 22 without being conscious of the lethality nighttime pedestrians attributed to me. Perhaps it was because in Chester, Pennsylvania, the small, angry industrial town where I came of age in the 1960s, I was scarcely noticeable against a backdrop of gang warfare, street knifings, and murders. I grew up one of the good boys, had perhaps a half-dozen fist fights. In retrospect, my shyness of combat has clear sources.

Many things go into the making of a young thug. One of those things is the consummation of the male romance with the power to intimidate. An infant discovers that random flailings send the baby bottle flying out of the crib and crashing to the floor. Delighted, the joyful babe repeats those motions again and again, seeking to duplicate the feat. Just so, I recall the points at which some of my boyhood friends were finally seduced by the perception of themselves as tough guys. When a mark cowered and surrendered his money without resistance, myth and reality merged—and paid off. It is, after all, only manly to embrace the power to frighten and intimidate. We, as men, are not supposed to give an inch of our lane on the highway; we are to seize the fighter's edge in work and in play and even in love; we are to be valiant in the face of hostile forces.

Unfortunately, poor and powerless young men seem to take all this nonsense literally. As a boy, I saw countless tough guys locked away; I have since buried several, too. They were babies, really—a teenage cousin, a brother of 22, a childhood friend in his mid-twenties—all gone down in episodes of bravado played out in the streets. I came to doubt the virtues of intimidation early on. I chose, perhaps even uncon-

sciously, to remain a shadow—timid, but a survivor.

The fearsomeness mistakenly attributed to me in public places often has a perilous flavor. The most frightening of these confusions occurred in the late 1970s and early 1980s when I worked as a journalist in Chicago. One day, rushing into the office of a magazine I was writing for with a deadline story in hand, I was mistaken for a burglar. The office manager called security and, with an ad hoc posse, pursued me through the labyrinthine halls, nearly to my editor's door. I had no way of proving who I was. I could only move briskly toward the company of someone who knew me.

Another time I was on assignment for a local paper and killing time before an interview. I entered a jewelry store on the city's affluent Near North Side. The proprietor excused herself and returned with an enormous red Doberman pinscher straining at the end of a leash. She stood, the dog extended toward me, silent to my questions, her eyes bulging nearly out of her head. I took a cursory look around, nodded, and bade her good night. Relatively speaking, however, I never fared as badly as another black male journalist. He went to nearby Waukegan, Illinois, a couple of summers ago to work on a story about a murderer who was born there. Mistaking the reporter for the killer, police hauled him from his car at gunpoint and but for his press credentials would probably have tried to book him. Such episodes are not uncommon. Black men trade tales like this all the time.

In "My Negro Problem—And Ours," Podhoretz writes that the hatred he feels for blacks makes itself known to him through a variety of avenues—one being his discomfort with that "special brand of paranoid touchiness" to which he says blacks are prone. No doubt he is speaking here of black men. In time, I learned to smother the rage I felt at so often being taken for a criminal. Not to do so would surely have led to madness—via that special "paranoid touchiness" that so annoyed Podhoretz at the time he wrote the essay.

I began to take precautions to make myself less threatening. I move about with care, particularly late in the evening. I give a wide berth to nervous people on the subway platforms during the wee hours, particularly when I have exchanged business clothes for jeans. If I happen to be entering a building behind some people who appear skittish, I may walk by, letting them clear the lobby before I return, so as not to seem to be following them. I have been calm and extemely congenial on those rare occasions when I've been pulled over by the police.

And on late-evening constitutionals along streets less traveled by, I employ what has proved to be an excellent tension-reducing measure: I whistle melodies from Beethoven and Vivaldi and the more popular classical composers. Even steely New Yorkers hunching toward nighttime destinations seem to relax, and occasionally they even join in the tune. Virtually everybody seems to sense that a mugger wouldn't be warbling bright, sunny selections from Vivaldi's *Four Seasons*. It is my equivalent of the cowbell that hikers wear when they know they are in bear country.

R E A D I N G   4 4

Stopping Rape: Effective Avoidance Strategies
PAULINE B. BART AND PATRICIA H. O'BRIEN

Try and fight him . . . it's more natural to be angry, if you let yourself feel the anger, maybe that'll give you strength . . . I used to think you could give him some kind of Jesus rap . . . I used to think you could reason 'em out of it, and talk to them like a human being, say "OK you don't want to do this, what are you doing?" . . . He seemed to listen to anger, yelling.

INTERVIEWER: What methods do you think would be ineffective, once a man tries to accost a woman?

INTERVIEWEE: Crying and pleading and begging. [Interview with a raped woman]

Women threatened with rape are in a double bind. On the one hand we are told, "Fighting back will only excite him. Fighting back will only get him angry," advice which assumes that the assailant is not already angry and that immediate retaliation is the most dangerous strategy. We are warned as well that resistance

will result in serious injury, if not mutilation and death; our mangled bodies will turn up in garbage cans and under park benches.

On the other hand, rape has traditionally and legally been defined as an adult man's carnal knowledge of a woman *by force and against her will* (the man must be over fourteen and the woman must not be his wife).[1] According to this definition, it is not enough that a man used or threatened to use force for the act to be considered rape; a man can compel a woman to have sex and still not legally be acting against her will. Therefore, in order to prove legally that what happened was rape, the woman has to prove that it was indeed against her will. The best way to prove that she is not willing to be forced to have sex is *not* by saying "Please don't," or "I have my period." The best way to prove that the act is not mutually consensual is by physically resisting.[2] In this article we describe the strategies that have prevented rape and the conditions under which they were effective. The 1976 Queen's Bench study was the first to show that "acting like a lady" was more likely to result in rape than in rape avoidance.[3] More recently, William Sanders, Jennie McIntyre, and Richard Block and Wesley Skogan— the latter using national victimization data—have come to similar conclusions.[4] All the studies based on interviews with raped women and women who prevented their rapes, as well as Block and Skogan's work, find that active strategies, notably fighting back, are effective in rape avoidance.

Our study also addresses important theoretical issues. For many years the question whether situational or personality factors have most influence in determining behavior has been central in social psychology, with sociologists leaning toward the former and psychologists and psychiatrists toward the latter. In this study, we do not deal with personality per se, partly because we do not think there are valid and reliable ways of measuring personality in interviews. More important, we do not use personality variables because research looking at the association of personality and victimization neglects variables such as autonomy training, independence, and competence.[5]

METHODOLOGY

This report is based on an analysis of 94 interviews with women eighteen or older who had been attacked and who had either avoided being raped ($N = 51$) or been raped ($N = 43$) in the two years prior to the interview. We limited the sample to women who experienced either force or the threat of force. The interview consisted of a self-report dealing with demographic variables, and answers to unstructured and semistructured questions about situational and background factors. Because of the exploratory nature of the research, we added questions when unanticipated patterns emerged—for instance, on incest, sexual assault in childhood, or other violence in the woman's life, or on whether the woman was primarily concerned with being killed or mutilated or primarily concerned with not being raped. The first part of the interview addressed such situational variables as the presence of a weapon, the number of assailants, the response of the woman, the acts that occurred during the assault, the degree of acquaintance with the assailant. The second part dealt with background variables, with questions about a woman's sense of competence and autonomy and about her socialization as a child and an adult into a traditional female role. We asked the raped woman about how her significant others responded to the assault and about interaction with institutions such as the police, hospitals, and therapists. We also examined the negotiation process between the

woman and her assailant(s) if such negotiation took place.

Eighty percent of the interviews were conducted by the principal investigator (Pauline Bart) and 20 percent by a female clinical psychologist (Marlyn Grossman). The interviews lasted from one-and-a-half to six hours, depending on the subject's desire to talk and on the history of violence in her individual life. These interviews were transcribed.

Because of the nature of our major research question, we could not obtain a random sample. Therefore, following a pretest, we launched a campaign to find respondents and recruited 94 women through newspaper ads (including major Black and Hispanic papers), press releases, public service announcements (the radio announcements were in both English and Spanish), appearances on radio and television, flyers, and contacts initiated through friendship networks of the project staff.

The resulting purposive, that is, nonrandom sample, when compared to the female population of the Chicago standard metropolitan statistical area (SMSA), which includes Cook and the surrounding counties, was disproportionately white, young, and unmarried (either single or divorced). Also none of the women who responded was engaged only in domestic labor at the time of the interview; all were either working outside the home or attending school. However, while the sample is not representative of women in the Chicago SMSA, it is not very different from the population of raped women and rape avoiders in national victimization data, except for an overrepresentation of white women (tables 1 and 2).[6] In addition to the demographic bias, the sample is shaped by the fact that the participants were volunteers.[7] A final source of possible bias in our sample was the very high proportion of women who had been raped by strangers or near strangers (approximately 80 percent).[8] An additional 10 percent were attacked by men they had met for the first time just prior to the assault.

Actually, we currently have no way of knowing what the "real" population of women who have been sexually assaulted looks like. On the one hand, rapes reported to the police are known to be gross undercounts of total rapes and to involve a disproportionate number of rapes by strangers.[9] On the other hand, victimization researchers have found that some respondents fail to tell interviewers about rapes actually reported to the police.[10] The problem of defining rape

TABLE I   DEMOGRAPHIC CHARACTERISTICS

	%	N
Race:		
White	81	76
Black	15	14
Hispanic	4	4
Religion:		
Protestant	38	35
Catholic	35	33
Jewish	19	18
No religion	6	...
Other	2	...
Marital status:		
Never married	58	54
Married, living with husband	15	14
Married, not living with husband	6	6
Divorced	19	18
Married, divorcing	1	...
Missing information	1	...
Education:		
High school or less	12	11
Some college	44	41
Four-year degree	19	18
Some graduate work	26	24
Occupation:		
Dependent	2	2
Homemaker	2	2
Blue-collar worker	10	9
Clerical worker	33	32
Professional	31	29
Student	9	8
Interim employment (usually student)	12	11
Missing information	1	...

NOTE: Interviewees ranged in age from 18 to 72. The mean age was 28.14 years.

adds further complications; many women who agree that they have been forced to have sex do not label the act as rape.[11]

We paid the women $25.00 for their time; moreover, all their expenses—including babysitting and travel for those who were from outside Chicago—were reimbursed. When the women telephoned us initially, we told them of the remuneration, and we asked for their own definition of the situation. Specifically, we asked them to tell us whether they had been raped or had been attacked but had avoided being raped. In this way, the women defined themselves into the two parts of the sample: rape avoiders and raped women.

A serendipitous finding was that while there was no problem in differentiating rape from seduction, there was no hard and fast line differentiating rape from rape avoidance.[12] Since we can conceptualize rape as a continuum starting with the first approach, verbal or physical, and ending with the rapist's penetration and intercourse to orgasm, any interruption in the continuum before the rapist's orgasm could theoretically be considered an avoidance.

In order to address this issue, we examined the data in three ways: the woman's perception of herself as either a raped woman or one who had avoided rape, the nature of the acts that occurred, and the legal definition of them.[13] The acts consisted of genital intercourse, sodomy, fellatio, interfemoral penetration (the assailant masturbating himself between the woman's thighs), cunnilingus, digital penetration, fondling and touching, and kissing. The possible legal definitions coded (using Illinois statutes at that time) were rape, attempted rape, and deviant sexual assault. When we examined the relationship between self-perception and the acts that had occurred, we learned that, for the most part, the women define rape by what is done with a man's penis (genital intercourse, sodomy, fellatio), not by what is done to a woman's genitals (digital penetration, fondling and touching, cunnilingus) (see table 3).[14]

FINDINGS

Defense Strategies

When the women described their assaults, distinct types of defense techniques emerged that were classified in the following way. A woman could

1. flee or try to flee.
2. scream, yell, or talk loudly—usually in an effort to attract attention.
3. use "affective verbal" techniques such as begging and pleading with the assailant in order to gain his sympathy.
4. use "cognitive verbal" techniques, which included attempting to reason with the assailant, "conning" him, trying to make him "see her as a person," and stalling.
5. take advantage of environmental intervention—someone or something in the surroundings that in-

TABLE 2 COMPARISON OF DATA ON SEXUALLY ASSAULTED WOMEN

	Bart and O'Brien (N = 94) (%)	McIntyre (N = 32) (%)	Queen's Bench (N = 108) (%)	National Victimization Surveys[a] (N = approx. 22,000) (%)
Age:				
Under 25	36	66[b]	71	59
Over 35	10	. . .	7	15
Race:				
White	81	75	79	69
Nonwhite	19	. . .	21	31
Marital status:				
Single	57	68	80	58
Married	16	. . .	10	22
Separated or divorced	27	. . .	11	17
Widowed	. . .	. . .	. . .	3
Work status:				
Employed full-time	62	46	39	46
Employed part-time	13	. . .	. . .	. . .
Student	12	35	37	15
Unemployed	8	. . .	13	6
Homemaker	4	. . .	1	33
Missing information	1	. . .	. . .	. . .
Attacked by stranger	78[c]	77	81	82
Rape completed	46	60	63	33
Weapon present	46	. . .	33	40
Attacked by multiple assailants	13	14	15	16
Reported attack to police	66	. . .	. . .	56

SOURCES: Jennie J. McIntyre, "Victim Response to Rape: Alternative Outcomes" (final report to National Institute of Mental Health, grant R01MH29045); Queen's Bench Foundation, "Rape: Prevention and Resistance" (Queen's Bench Organization, 1255 Post St., San Francisco, California, 1976); Joan McDermott, "Rape Victimization in 26 American Cities" (Washington, D.C.: Department of Justice, Law Enforcement Assistance Administration, Government Printing Office, 1979).
[a]All percentages (except for the percent attacked by strangers) are calculated for attacks by strangers only.
[b]Percentage calculated for women under 26, not 25.
[c]Includes 71 percent raped by total strangers and 7 percent raped by men known by sight or met on a casual first encounter.

truded on the scene and either caused the assailant to stop the assault or gave her an opportunity to escape.

6. respond with physical force, the possibilities ranging from a simple push to self-defense techniques to use of a weapon.

Avoiders used a substantially greater number of strategies than raped women. All of the five respondents who employed *no* strategies were raped; these made up 11.6 percent of the raped women in the sample. Of the respondents who used only one strategy, 30 percent (13) were raped women and 18 percent (9) were avoiders. Of the respondents who used two kinds

of strategies, 28 percent (12) were raped women and 29 percent (15) were avoiders. The difference between raped women and avoiders sharply increases after this. Twenty-one percent (9) of the raped women and 35 percent (18) of the avoiders used three types of strategies; 9 percent (4) of the raped women and 18 percent (9) of the avoiders used four types of strategies. The modal number of strategies for raped women was one, while for avoiders it was three. The mean number of types of strategies for raped women was 1.86 and for avoiders was 2.53, consistent with the results reported in the Queen's Bench study.[15]

Not only did avoiders use more types of strategies, the strategies they used differed from the strategies of

TABLE 3   SELF-PERCEPTION AS RAPED WOMAN OR RAPE AVOIDER, BY OCCURRENCE OF PHALLIC SEX (%)

	SELF-PERCEPTION	
	Raped Woman	Rape Avoider
Phallic sex occurred[a] .... (N = 45)	93	7
Phallic sex did not occur[b] .... (N = 49)	2	98

NOTE.—This table was constructed by Kim Scheppele.
[a]Phallic sex includes any one or any combination of the following: penile-vaginal penetration, sodomy, fellatio, interfemoral penetration, or female masturbation of assailant.
[b]Phallic sex is considered not to have occurred if only the following took place: digital penetration, cunnilingus, fondling, touching and kissing. It is considered not to have occurred as well in situations where the attack was thwarted before any overt sexual acts took place.

the raped women. Avoiders were more likely to flee or try to flee, to talk loudly or scream, to use physical force, and to be aided by environmental intervention. Raped women were more likely to plead. Both were about equally likely to use cognitive verbal techniques, the strategy most frequently used (see table 4).

Because we have qualitative data, we can also study the sequence of strategies. Our analysis took particular note of women who used physical strategies since most debates revolve around this response. Six women who stopped their rapes first used physical strategies and then yelled or screamed. Another effective sequence of strategies for women who stopped their rapes involved using cognitive verbal strategies, and when those proved ineffective, changing to physical strategies. Such strategies, then, can convince the assailant that the woman is serious, not just feigning resistance.[16] The modal strategy for women who stopped their rapes was a combination of screaming/ yelling and physical resistance. The correlation between the two strategies was +0.42 for avoiders.

Avoiding Death or Avoiding Rape

A woman's primary focus emerged during the interviews as a factor sharply differentiating raped women from rape avoiders: the women whose primary concern lay in avoiding death or mutilation have been less likely to avoid rape than those who had a gut reaction of rage and were primarily determined not to be raped. Because of the exploratory nature of this study, we were able to add a question to the interview schedule addressing this point after the pattern emerged. Twenty-eight women who were raped and 19 women who avoided rape expressed fear of death or mutilation as their foremost concern, while 3 women who were raped and 26 women who avoided rape were primarily determined not to be raped.

For example, the first woman we interviewed, a college student, was able to stop her rape even though her assailant was armed. She said, "We circled for a while; he had a knife. I was wearing some loose clothing . . . he knocked me to the ground, so he managed to get the top half of all of my clothes off and there's sort of a blank. I remember clearly wanting to fight this, not want this . . . not wanting to allow this to happen and

TABLE 4   STRATEGIES OF RAPE AVOIDANCE, BY OUTCOME OF ATTACK (%)

	Raped Women (N = 43)	Rape Avoiders (N = 51)
Fled or tried to flee	9	33
Screamed	35	49
Used physical force	33	59
Used cognitive verbal strategies	72	67
Used affective verbal strategies	33	22
Benefited from environmental intervention	5	20
Used no strategy	12	. . .

I just thought, 'Well, I'm not going to stand for this, you know.' And I didn't. . . . He did have a knife and he did slash my coat. I didn't have any clothes on. I had an acute sense of being vigorous, stronger, and more overpowering in myself and then there was sort of a brief flurry or something . . . or sliding away." (She had, in fact, slid away from her attacker.)

This response was surprising since we had originally thought that if there were a weapon no resistance would be possible. At the same time, the women who feared death should in no way be blamed, since descriptions of rape in the media emphasize the more lurid rape/murders and give scant attention to the women who stopped their rapes.

Psychological and Bodily Consequences of Physical Resistance

The effectiveness of using physical force to resist rape proved to be our most controversial finding, albeit one that is replicated in other studies.[17] We have suggested above that its effectiveness may lie in its communicating a clear message to the assailant, in addition to any physical injury he might receive or be in danger of receiving. Some assailants were not convinced by other strategies, presumably because they subscribed to the ideology prevalent in pornography and other media that women, whatever they might say, really want to be sexually assaulted. But what of the effect of this strategy on the women? We found that raped women who used physical strategies were less likely to be depressed than raped women who did not. The largest number of women who said they were depressed or who had symptoms of depression such as insomnia and weight loss were among those who were raped but did not use physical strategies. There was no difference in frequency of depression among women who avoided rape by fighting back and those who avoided rape without using physical strategies. Thus we can say that one of the most important functions of physical resistance is to keep women from feeling depressed even if they have been raped.[18]

If what we are tapping were merely personality differences between those who physically resisted and those who did not, then we would not find differences in depression only for those women who were raped. We think the results stem from the traditional vocabulary of motives used in our society to account for rape, a vocabulary many women have internalized.[19]

In this vocabulary, rape is provoked by women through their dress, their carelessness, their foolhardiness in going to a "forbidden" place, such as a bar. Women are told, moreover, that they cannot be raped against their will—that, indeed, women really want to be raped and enjoy it. By resisting rape, however, women demonstrate to themselves and to others that this vocabulary does not apply to them. They are less likely to attribute their rape to their "personality defects"—weakness, cowardice, ineffectiveness—and thus less likely to say, "If only I had fought back it wouldn't have happened."[20] They are less likely to blame themselves and to feel depressed, more likely to gain strength from the belief that they did everything they could in that situation.

We are told that if we fight back, if we physically resist, we will pay the price through severe injury or death. This admonition is not supported by our findings or in the studies reported above. Furthermore, advising women to comply or risk injury assumes that rape in itself does not result in injury, physical as well as mental. Several women who talked to us reported serious injury from rape. One woman had a psychotic breakdown which resulted in her hospitalization. Her rapist also tore the area between her vagina and her anus so badly that it required surgical repair. In addition she became pregnant and had an abortion. Since she was not conscious during the attack, the injury did not stem from her resistance. Another contracted venereal disease, which led to pelvic inflammatory disease; she is now permanently sterile. She screamed and tried to reason with her assailant but did not resist physically.

We know that women who resist physically are more likely to avoid rape. We also know that there is little relationship between women's use of physical resistance and rapists' use of additional physical force over and above the attempted rape. True, sexual assault does not usually produce serious physical harm, while physical resistance often results in minor injuries such as bruises and scratches. Some women who used physical force were moderately or seriously injured. One such woman while arguing with her assailant, who was trying to enter her apartment, was punched in the eye and pushed into her apartment where she continued to struggle. Her screams alerted the neighbors who called the police. They arrived in time to stop the rape. A second woman screamed while being attacked in a cornfield and tried to strike her assailant. He pulled a knife, hit her twice with his fist, knocked her unconscious, and raped her. A woman who had decided to submit to rape, rather than be choked to death with a telephone cord, couldn't yield "because he was so dirty." The would-be rapist beat her, but when she yanked at his penis he hurriedly left.

Women who fought back sustained the following kinds of injuries: bruises and bite marks on the neck, soreness for a few days, strained muscles, bruises and minor cuts, more serious cuts, back injury, and aching the next morning. While we asked the women about the assailant's tactics including physical abuse, we did not systematically ask about their own injuries and so there may have been minor injuries not reported. It is likely, however, that all the women who had serious injuries told us of them.

To judge the correlation between injury and physical resistance we must consider the interviews of the 5 women who were brutally beaten or suffered serious injury. Three were raped and 2 avoided being raped. Both avoiders' injuries resulted from their having fought back. However, for one of them, the resistance delayed the rape long enough for a train to pull into the platform where the assault was taking place, and the assailants fled. A third woman who was raped fought back even though her assailant had an ice pick as a weapon. It is unclear whether her beating was in response to her fighting back or to her screams. A

raped virgin, attacked by two armed assailants, fought back and was seriously injured. But the injury was a result not of her struggle but of her seven rapes and her escape method. The last woman became sterile, as we described above.

These experiences suggest that by fighting back a woman significantly increases her chances of rape avoidance and somewhat increases her chance of rough treatment. However, not resisting is no guarantee of humane treatment.

Degree of Acquaintance with Assailant

Do women respond differently when attacked by men they know than when attacked by strangers? If so, is such difference in response associated with whether the outcome of the attack is rape or rape avoidance? Being assaulted by a stranger results in different patterns of response than does being assaulted by an acquaintance (see table 5). Both groups of women were more likely to yell or scream as well as to use both cognitive and affective verbal strategies when the assailant was a stranger than when he was someone they knew. In addition, there was environmental intervention more often among women who were not raped.

Environmental intervention, in general, occurred more frequently for women who avoided rape. In only two instances did raped women experience environmental intervention, and in both of these the assailant

TABLE 5   STRATEGIES OF RAPE AVOIDANCE, BY OUTCOME OF ATTACK AND DEGREE OF ACQUAINTANCE*

	RAPED WOMEN (N = 43)		RAPE AVOIDERS (N = 51)	
	Known Assailant (N = 13) (%)	Stranger (N = 30) (%)	Known Assailant (N = 14) (%)	Stranger (N = 37) (%)
Fled or tried to flee	—	13.3	14.3	40.5
Screamed	23.1	40.0	42.8	51.3
Used physical force	38.5	30.0	57.1	59.5
Used cognitive verbal strategies	46.2	83.3	57.1	75.7
Used affective verbal strategies	30.7	33.3	21.4	21.6
Benefited from environmental intervention	—	6.7	21.4	18.9

ᵃPercentages are based on the number of women in a given category who knew/did not know their assailant(s) and employed a particular strategy.

was a stranger. It should be noted that the mere occurrence of environmental intervention was not always sufficient to thwart attack. Sometimes the assail-
ant(s) fled. But sometimes the woman had to be able
to utilize such an opportunity in order to escape. One
woman, for instance, who had been pinned against an
alley wall, was able to flee when the sudden noise of a
fire engine's siren caused her assailant to loosen his
grip. On another occasion a woman had negotiated
with her assailant to rape her in his van rather than in
the alley where he first attacked her. While walking
with him to the van, she saw a strange man approach
and asked him to help her. Although he never actually
intervened, she used this opportunity to break away
and run to a nearby tavern.

Presence of a Weapon

Conventional wisdom would suggest that the most important variable in a woman's response to attack is the
assailant's possession of a weapon. And indeed, presence of a weapon does influence the outcome.[21] Of the
group of women who were attacked by an unarmed
assailant, 37 percent (19) were raped and 63 percent
(32) avoided rape. Of the group of women who were
attacked when an assailant had a weapon, when a
weapon was presumed to be present, or when the assailant used a weapon to threaten or wound the
woman, 56 percent (24) were raped and 44 percent
(19) stopped the rape. The last point needs emphasis,
however; even where there was some indication of a
weapon, 44 percent of the women avoided being
raped.

When the assailant had a weapon, 2 raped women
fled, and 16 did not; 8 rape avoiders fled, and 6 did
not. When the assailant had a weapon, 6 raped women
screamed, and 12 did not; 4 avoiders screamed and 10
did not. When a weapon was present, 4 raped women
used physical force, and 14 did not; 5 avoiders used
that strategy, and 9 did not. When the assailant was
armed, 13 raped women and 11 avoiders used cognitive verbal strategies. Five raped women and 3
avoiders did not use such strategies. Four raped
women faced with weapons used affective verbal strategies and 12 did not, while 4 avoiders used this strategy and 10 did not. Of the 5 victims who used no strategies, 3 were faced with armed assailants, and in 2
cases the assailant was not armed.

Since much of the debate about rape avoidance focuses on whether women should use physical force, it
is important that one of the most striking differences
between raped women and rape avoiders occurred in
the case where the assailant did not have a weapon. In
such situations, three-quarters (24) of the avoiders
used physical strategies while one-quarter (8) did not;
about half (9) of the raped women used such strategies, and about half (10) did not.

Being Attacked While Asleep

We have already seen that the most obvious situational variable, presence of a weapon, is associated
with victimization rather than with avoidance. But we
have also seen that even under such circumstances
some women avoid rape. We will now turn to another
variable that makes appropriate defense difficult and,
in fact, according to Ann Burgess and Lynda Holmstrum, has particularly long-lasting effects: being attacked while asleep.[22] Two of the 5 women who were
asleep used no strategies. How did the women who
were not raped manage to avoid the assault? None
pleaded, although all used cognitive verbal strategies.
One, whom we call the "Super Negotiator," screamed,
talked, and fought. Another talked, used physical
force, and took advantage of environmental intervention. Their assailants were armed in both cases, and
yet both women physically resisted. A third screamed
and used cognitive verbal strategies, while a fourth
was one of the few women who was able to avoid rape
simply by persuading the man that she was not interested. The latter case is particularly striking because
the assailant was later apprehended on numerous rape
charges. While in prison, he wrote a letter to one of the
women he raped in which he mentioned that, while he
really liked her, he did not like another woman he
tried to assault. We interviewed this second woman
for our study. But he asked the woman to whom he
wrote the letter why he was being charged with assault
when he actually was raping.[23]

Two case histories give a sense of the kinds of strategies that can be employed in difficult situations. One
of them involves the five-foot eight-inch tall Super Negotiator. She awoke to find herself pinned beneath the
covers of her bed by a naked, armed man who was
straddling her. She made an attempt to reach the
phone but agreed to give up this bid for assistance in
return for his removing a knife from her throat. She
told the assailant she was menstruating and feigned

embarrassment at the thought of removing her tampon in his presence. He agreed to allow her to go to the bathroom. However, once there, he would not allow her to close the door and scream for help. After removing her tampon, she refused to return to the bedroom, claiming that the knife, which was still in the room, frightened her. At this point, the assailant removed the knife from the nightstand and threw it down the hallway. She had attempted unsuccessfully to convince him to throw it outdoors, but he claimed that walking through the living room might cause him to be seen. Returning to the bedroom, he began to fondle her breasts and digitally penetrate her vagina. In response she feigned hysteria, in an effort to make him think that she was "going crazy." Finding this strategy unsuccessful, she asked if she could smoke some hash in order to relax. The hash pipe was big and heavy, and initially she planned on using it as a weapon; however, she was unable to work up enough nerve. After pretending to smoke for awhile, she asked if it would be all right if she went to the kitchen for a beer, as the hash had not had the desired effect. He refused and shoved her on her back on the bed. She responded by jumping and throwing him on his back, grabbing his hair and yanking his head as hard as she could over the footboard of the bed. The assailant began to whimper. She reprimanded him for being "pushy" and for hurting her, and once again made her request for a beer and cigarette. The assailant complied, but retrieved his knife and followed her to the kitchen, pressing the knife to her back.

Once in the kitchen, she had hoped to make her escape, but she found that this was not possible. Not having any beer in the refrigerator, she successfully passed off a can of soda as a beer. As they were walking back to the bedroom she feigned anger at their return to the initial scenario—being in the bedroom with an armed man. In order to appease her, he placed the knife on the bookcase in the living room. For the first time since the start of the incident, she knew exactly where the knife was; thus, it would be accessible if she could somehow maneuver away from him. After smoking her cigarette and drinking the "beer," she clutched her stomach, pretending nausea, and ran out of the room. When he realized that she wasn't heading for the bathroom, he began to pursue her, but by this time she had reached the knife. He reached for a nearby lamp, which he intended to use as a weapon, but discovered that it was far too light to be useful. At

this point she was moving toward the door and he said, "All right, that's it, I'm leaving. I was gonna try to be nice, but I'm leaving. Forget it." She ran out the back door and screamed for help. He made a couple of attempts to run out after her, but every time he did, she'd raise the knife to threaten him. Finally, he made a dash out the door, still naked from the waist down, carrying his pants. Less than a week after the attack, he parked his car behind her building after following her home from work. She flagged down a police car and he was apprehended.

Another case in which a woman was faced with seemingly impossible odds against avoiding assault involved a five-foot-ten-inch worker in a drug rehabilitation center. After completing her duties one evening, she crawled into her sleeping bag and fell asleep. Not long afterward, one of the residents came in asking for the time. In her stupor, she yelled at him and he appeared to leave. The next thing she knew "he was on top of" her with a knife pressed to her neck. Initially she froze, but then she fought him. Somehow she managed to get him off and get to the door, all the while screaming at the top of her lungs. After escaping from the room, she ran into a very large fellow female worker. Two women were too much for this assailant and he took off. Returning from the hospital, the avoider and a female companion spotted the assailant on the highway and reported his presence to the police. He was apprehended.

While both of these women were comparatively tall, we do not think it was simply their size that made the difference, although women five feet seven inches and over proved more likely to avoid rape. Rather, we suggest that short and tall women are treated differently in this society. Tall women do not have the option of being "cute" or acting helpless. They are less likely than short women to have a trained incapacity to be competent and assertive. Therefore, they are less likely to have the option of assuming the traditional "feminine" role, which rape analysts such as Susan Brownmiller and Susan Griffin suggest is conducive to being a rape victim.[24]

Much of what occurs in any assault depends on the woman's interaction with her assailant. In our interviews we discovered that women were able to negotiate parts of the scenario. Although it was difficult to avoid genital intercourse itself through negotiation, some of the women whom we interviewed were able to negotiate their way out of other sex acts after intercourse was completed; several through argument avoided sodomy, fellatio, and multiple acts of intercourse. Women also made bargains involving money or credit cards, negotiated regarding the place of assault, and modified some of the conditions of their assaults—arranged to be tied up in a more comfortable position, got assistance in walking from one place to another. The Super Negotiator superbly illustrates the range of individual negotiations.[25]

CONCLUSIONS AND POLICY IMPLICATIONS

Women who avoided rape used more kinds of strategies in response to the assault than women who were raped. They also used different strategies. Strategies associated with avoidance were fleeing or trying to flee, yelling, and using physical force. In cases where rape was avoided, there was also more likely to be environmental intervention. Women who were raped were more likely to use no strategies (no woman who avoided rape fell into this category) or to rely on affective verbal strategies. The most common strategies used were cognitive verbal—reasoning, verbally refusing, threatening, and conning. Use of such tactics, though they are frequently advised, did not differentiate raped women from those who avoided rape, and those strategies alone were rarely effective. The modal response which resulted in avoidance was a combination of yelling and using physical force. While the assailant's having a weapon made rape the more probable outcome, 37 percent of the women who avoided rape did so when the assailant was armed or claimed to be armed.

Because of the exploratory nature of the study and because ours was not a random sample, caution should be used in interpreting these results. Nonetheless, four empirical studies comparing the strategies of raped women and rape avoiders came up with similar findings. It is no accident that these findings, which suggest that women should physically resist their assailants, run counter to official ideology that women can avoid rape by behaving in ways more consonant with traditional socialization. Since rape is, after all, a paradigm of sexism in society,[26] it is not surprising that male advice to women on how to avoid rape also reflects that paradigm.

The tactics that women are usually advised to employ—verbal strategies, feigning insanity, or appealing to the assailant's humanity—are relatively ineffective. One might well conclude not only that the traditional ideology regarding rape is a form of social control over women,[27] but that traditional advice on rape avoidance also functions in this manner. This advice, when not such simple caveats about restricting one's behavior as "don't go out at night," suggests coping strategies consistent with the conventional female role, particularly use of verbal skills to manipulate the situation rather than confrontational behavior and fighting back. One police official is quoted as saying, "We recommend passive resistance, like getting a person's confidence by talking and doing what you were taught to do as girls growing up, to help resist attack."[28]

The importance of the policy implications of our study is augmented by Diana Russell and Nancy Howell's report of an intensive interview survey in San Francisco. They demonstrated the pervasiveness of the problem of sexual assault, contending "that there is at least a 26 percent probability that a woman in that city will become the victim of completed rape at some time in her life, and a 46 percent probability that she will become a victim of rape *or* attempted rape."[29] They conclude that the feminist analysis of rape, which states that sexual violence against women is endemic, is supported by research.

Feminist analysis has succeeded in making the point that rape is not a joke, that it has detrimental effects not only on the particular woman who is assaulted but on all women. For even though not all women are raped, fear of rape causes women generally to constrict their behavior.[30] Thus, it is clearly important to have data-based advice on which strategies are most effective in stopping a sexual assault. Indeed, since the National Institute of Mental Health released our findings, not only have the media been interested in disseminating our results—albeit in simplified form—but rape crisis centers and police departments have asked for our reports and papers so that they could be incorporated into their programs. We thus have the privilege of knowing that the pain our respondents endured not only during their assaults but in anticipation of their interviews, and the stress we experienced while listening to them and while analyzing the data, have not been in vain.

ACKNOWLEDGEMENTS

This paper is based on research funded by the Center for the Prevention and Control of Rape of the National Institute of Mental Health, grant MH 29311-0. An earlier version was presented at the annual meetings of the American Sociological Association, New York, 1980, entitled "How to Say No to Storaska and Survive: Rape Avoidance Strategies." Frederick Storaska is the author of a book that is demeaning to women and is full of misinformation (*How to Say No to a Rapist and Survive* [New York: Random House, 1975]).

NOTES

1. Wallace D. Lok, "What Has Reform of Rape Legislation Wrought?" *Journal of Social Issues* 37, no. 4 (1981): 28–52. The Illinois sexual assault statute that went into effect in July 1984 omits the phrase "against her will." Catharine MacKinnon suggests that consent should be proven by the defense rather than disproven by the prosecution, making consent an "affirmative defense." See "Feminism, Marxism, Method, and the State: Toward Feminist Jurisprudence," *Signs: Journal of Women in Culture and Society* 8, no. 4 (1983): 635–58, esp. 648, n. 29.

2. In fact, the People v. Joel Warren, 446 N.W. 2d 591, 1983, Illinois Appellate Court Fifth District (no. 82-180), reversed an original decision that found an assailant guilty of two counts of deviate sexual assault. The court reasoned that the complainant's "failure to resist when it was within her power to do so conveys the impression of consent regardless of her mental state, amounts to consent and removes from the act performed an essential element of the crime." The defendant maintained "that once complainant became aware that defendant intended to engage in sexual relations, it was incumbent upon her to resist." This decision was rendered even though the woman was five feet two inches and weighed one hundred pounds and the assailant was over six feet and weighed 185 pounds, the attack took place in an isolated area, and the woman was afraid that physically assaulting the man would anger him.

3. Queen's Bench Foundation, "Rape: Prevention and Resistance" (Queen's Bench Organization, 1255 Post St., San Francisco, 1976). See also Greer Litton Fox, "'Nice Girl': Social Control of Women through a Value Construct," *Signs* 2, no. 4 (1977): 805–17.

4. William B. Sanders, *Rape and Woman's Identity* (Beverly Hills, Calif.: Sage, 1980); Jennie J. McIntyre, "Victim Response to Rape: Alternative Outcomes" (final report to National Institute of Mental Health, grant R01MH29045); Richard Block and Wesley G. Skogan, "Resistance and Outcome in Robbery and Rape: Non-fatal, Stranger to Stranger Violence" (Center for Urban Affairs and Policy Research, Northwestern University, 1982).

5. Elsewhere we have addressed childhood and adult socialization as well as background and situational variables: Pauline B. Bart and Ellen Perlmutter, "Socialization and Rape Avoidance" (paper presented at the Association for Women in Psychology, Santa Monica, Calif., 1980); Bart, "A Study of Women Who Both Were Raped and Avoided Rape," *Journal of Social Issues* 37, no. 4 (1981): 123–37; Bart and Patricia H. O'Brien, "Stopping Rape: Strategies for Success" (Department of Psychiatry, University of Illinois at Chicago Health Sciences Center, 1983).

6. Joan McDermott, "Rape Victimization in 26 American Cities" (Washington, D.C.: Government Printing Office, 1979).

7. We attempted to allow for bias through the use of volunteers in two ways: we first asked women why they volunteered (the two primary motives proved to be altruism and catharsis, often in combination); and we then asked them where they had learned about the study. Our inquiries revealed no substantial bias from a single source.

8. While rapes reported to the police and McDermott's secondary analysis of a "representative sample of 10,000 households" also show similarly high rates of rape by strangers, other studies have found that as many as half the rapes involved assailants known to the woman: Pauline B. Bart, "Rape Doesn't End with a Kiss," *Viva*, June 1975, pp. 39–41, 100–101; Joseph J. Peters, *The Philadelphia Rape Victim Project in Forcible Rape: The Crime, the Victim, and the Offender* (New York: Columbia University Press, 1977); Menachem Amir, *Patterns of Forcible Rape* (Chicago: University of Chicago Press, 1971).

9. Bart, "Rape Doesn't End."

10. McDermott (n. 6 above).

11. Irene Hanson Frieze et al., "Psychological Factors in Violent Marriages" (Department of Psychology, University of Pittsburgh, 1979); Frieze, "Investigating the Causes and Consequences of Marital Rape," *Signs* 8, no. 3 (1983): 532–53.

12. It has become increasingly apparent that the concept of seduction is itself a male ideology. We have found that

much, if not all, of what men perceive as seduction is in fact the result of women's having decided "to put up with it" or having planned in advance to "allow" themselves to be seduced. Bart has further refined the continuum as follows: consensual sex/altruistic sex/compliant sex/rape. In consensual sex both partners are sexually aroused. In altruistic sex the man wants sex and the woman goes along with it. When men engage in altruistic sex they use the pejorative term "mercy fucking." In compliant sex one person, usually the female, engages in the act because of the adverse consequences that follow if she doesn't, although there is no threat of force. We define rape as sexual behavior the woman engages in because of force or threat of force.

13. Pauline B. Bart and Kim Scheppele, "There Ought to Be a Law: Self-Definition and Legal Definitions of Sexual Assault" (paper presented at the meetings of the American Sociological Association, New York, 1980).

14. Kim Lane Scheppele and Pauline B. Bart, "Through Women's Eyes: Defining Danger in the Wake of Sexual Assault," *Journal of Social Issues* 39, no. 2 (1983): 63–80.

15. Queen's Bench Foundation (n. 3 above).

16. See Roseann Giarusso et al., "Adolescents' Cues and Signals: Sex and Assault" (paper presented at the annual meeting of the Western Psychological Association, San Diego, California, April 1979) for an analysis of the differences in the way in which males and females perceive the world.

17. Queen's Bench Foundation (n. 3 above); Sanders, McIntyre, and Block and Skogan (all n. 4 above).

18. Pauline B. Bart and Patricia H. O'Brien, "The Aftermath of Rape and Rape Avoidance: Behaviors, Attitudes, Ideologies and Response of Significant Others" (paper presented at the International Sociological Association meeting, Mexico City, August 1982).

19. Pauline B. Bart, "Social Structures and Vocabularies of Discomfort: What Happened to Female Hysteria?" *Journal of Health and Social Behavior* 9 (September 1968):188–93, esp. 189.

20. Ronnie Janoff-Bulman, "Characterological versus Behavioral Self-Blame: Inquiries into Depression and Rape," *Journal of Personality and Social Psychology* 37 (1979):1798–1809.

21. This finding is also reported in McDermott (n. 6 above). According to our study, this relationship does not hold for Black women.

22. Ann Wolbert Burgess and Lynda L. Holmstrum, *Rape: Crisis and Recovery* (Bowie, Md.: Robert J. Brady, 1979).

23. Personal communication with Mary Pennington Anderson, attorney in the case.

24. Susan Brownmiller, *Against Our Will: Men, Women and Rape* (New York: Simon & Schuster, 1975); Susan Griffin, "Rape: The All-American Crime," reading 41 in this volume.

25. While we have been focusing on rape avoidance strategies as a way of coping with assault, there were additional ways in which women coped. Depersonalization—feeling as if it were happening to someone else, as if it were not really happening, as if one were dreaming—was a relatively common response, although, as one might expect, it was more common among raped women. Thus, 44 percent (19) of the raped women mentioned they experienced depersonalization, while 22 percent (11) of the avoiders had this response.

26. Pauline B. Bart, "Rape as a Paradigm of Sexism in Society," *Women's Studies International Quarterly* 2, no. 3 (1979): 347–57.

27. Stephanie Riger and Margaret T. Gordon, "The Fear of Rape: A Study in Social Control," *Journal of Social Issues* 37, no. 4 (1981): 71–92.

28. Quoted in Tacie Dejanikus, "New Studies Support Active Resistance to Rape," *Off Our Backs,* February 1981, pp. 9, 23.

29. Diana E. H. Russell and Nancy Howell, "The Prevalence of Rape in the United States Revisited," *Signs* 8, no. 4 (1983): 688–95, esp. 695.

30. Riger and Gordon (n. 27 above).

R E A D I N G   4 5

How Women Experience Battering: The Process of Victimization

KATHLEEN J. FERRARO AND JOHN M. JOHNSON

On several occasions since 1850, feminists in Britain and the United States have initiated campaigns to end the battering of women by husbands and lovers, but have received little sympathy or support from the public (Dobash & Dobash, 1979). Sociologists systematically ignored the existence of violence against women until 1971, when journal articles and conferences devoted to the topic of domestic violence began to appear (Gelles, 1974; O'Brien, 1971; Steinmetz & Straus, 1974). Through the efforts of grass-roots activists and academics, battering has been recognized as a widespread social problem (Tierney, 1982). In 1975 a random survey of U.S. families found that 3.8 percent of women experienced severe violence in their marriage (Straus et al., 1980). The National Crime Survey of 1976 found that one-fourth of all assaults against women who had ever been married were committed by their husbands or ex-husbands (Gacquin, 1978). Shelters providing services to battered women in the United States have not been able to keep pace with requests for assistance (Colorado Association for Aid to Battered Women, 1978; Ferraro, 1981a; Roberts, 1981; Women's Advocates, 1980).

Although the existence of violence against women is now publicly acknowledged, the experience of being battered is poorly understood. Research aimed at discovering the incidence and related social variables has been based on an operational definition of battering which focuses on the violent act. The Conflict Tactic Scales (CTS) developed by Straus (1979), for example, is based on the techniques used to resolve family conflicts. The Violence Scale of the CTS ranks eight violent behaviors, ranging in severity from throwing something at the other person to using a knife or gun (Straus, 1979). The scale is not designed to explore the

context of violent actions or their meanings for the victim or perpetrator. With notable exceptions (Dobash & Dobash, 1979), the bulk of sociological research on battered women has focused on quantifiable variables (Gelles, 1974, 1976; O'Brien, 1971; Steinmetz, 1978; Straus, 1978).

Interviews with battered women make it apparent that the experience of violence inflicted by a husband or lover is shocking and confusing. Battering is rarely perceived as an unambiguous assault demanding immediate action to ensure future safety. In fact, battered women often remain in violent relationships for years (Pagelow, 1981).

Why do battered women stay in abusive relationships? Some observers answer facilely that they must like it. The masochism thesis was the predominant response of psychiatrists writing about battering in the 1960s (Saul, 1972; Snell et al., 1964). More sympathetic studies of the problem have revealed the difficulties of disentangling oneself from a violent relationship (Hilberman, 1980; Martin, 1976; Walker, 1979). These studies point to the social and cultural expectations of women and their status within the nuclear family as reasons for the reluctance of battered women to flee the relationship. The socialization of women emphasizes the primary value of being a good wife and mother, at the expense of personal achievement in other spheres of life. The patriarchal ordering of society assigns a secondary status to women and provides men with ultimate authority, both within and outside the family unit. Economic conditions contribute to the dependency of women on men; in 1978 U.S. women earned, on the average, 58 percent of what men earned (U.S. Department of Labor, 1980). In sum, the position of women in U.S. society makes it extremely difficult for them to reject the authority of men and develop independent lives free of marital violence (Dobash & Dobash, 1979; Pagelow, 1981).

Material and cultural conditions are the background in which personal interpretations of events are developed. Women who depend on their husbands for practical support also depend on them as sources of self-esteem, emotional support, and continuity. This paper looks at how women make sense of their victimization within the context of these dependencies. Without dismissing the importance of the macro forces of gender politics, we focus on inter- and intrapersonal responses to violence. We first describe six techniques of rationalization used by women who are in relationships where battering has occurred. We then turn to catalysts which may serve as forces to reevaluate rationalizations and to initiate serious attempts at escape. Various physical and emotional responses to battering are described, and finally, we outline the consequences of leaving or attempting to leave a violent relationship.

THE DATA

The data for this study were drawn from diverse sources. From July 1978 to September 1979 we were participant observers at a shelter for battered women located in the southwestern United States. The shelter was located in a suburban city of a major urban center. The shelter served five cities as well as the downtown population, resulting in a service population of 170,000. It was funded primarily by the state through an umbrella agency concerned with drug, mental health, and alcoholism problems. It was initially staffed by paraprofessionals and volunteers, but since this research it has become professionalized and is run by several professional social workers.

During the time of the research, 120 women passed through the shelters; they brought with them 165 children. The women ranged in age from 17 to 68, generally had family incomes below $15,000, and did not work outside the home. The characteristics of shelter residents are summarized in Table 1.

We established personal relationships with each of these women and kept records of their experiences and verbal accounts. We also tape-recorded informal conversations, staff meetings, and crisis phone conversations with battered women. This daily interaction with shelter residents and staff permitted first-hand observation of feelings and thoughts about the battering experience. Finally, we taped interviews with 10 resi-

TABLE 1   DEMOGRAPHIC CHARACTERISTICS OF SHELTER RESIDENTS DURING FIRST YEAR OF OPERATION (N = 120)

AGE		EDUCATION	
–17	2%	Elementary school	2%
18–24	33%	Junior high	8%
25–34	43%	Some high school	28%
35–44	14%	High school graduate	43%
45–54	6%	Some college	14%
55+	1%	College graduate	2%
		Graduate school	1%

ETHNICITY		NUMBER OF CHILDREN	
White	78%	0	19%
Black	3%	1	42%
Mexican-American	10%	2	21%
American Indian	8%	3	15%
Other	1%	4	2%
		5+	1%
		Pregnant	7%

FAMILY INCOME		EMPLOYMENT STATUS	
–$5,000	27%	Full time	23%
$ 6,000–10,000	36%	Part time	8%
$11,000–15,000	10%	Housewife	54%
$16,000+	10%	Student	5%
No response*	17%	Not employed	8%
		Receiving welfare	2%

*Many women had no knowledge of their husband's income.

dents and five battered women who had left their abusers without entering the shelter. All quotes in this paper are taken from our notes and tapes.

In addition to this participant study, both authors have been involved with the problem of domestic violence for more than 10 years. In 1976–77, Ferraro worked as a volunteer at Rainbow Retreat, the oldest shelter still functioning in the United States. In 1977–78, we both helped to found a shelter for battered women in our community. This involvement has led to direct contact with hundreds of women who have experienced battering and many informal talks with people involved in the shelter movement in the United States and Europe.

The term "battered woman" is used in this paper to describe women who are battered repeatedly by men with whom they live as lovers. Marriage is not a prerequisite for being a battered woman. Many of the women who entered the shelter we studied were living with, but were not legally married to, the men who abused them.

RATIONALIZING VIOLENCE

Marriages and their unofficial counterparts develop through the efforts of each partner to maintain feelings of love and intimacy. In modern, Western cultures, the value placed on marriage is high; individuals invest a great amount of emotion in their spouses and expect a return on that investment. The majority of women who marry still adopt the roles of wives and mothers as primary identities, even when they work outside the home, and thus have a strong motivation to succeed in their domestic roles. Married women remain economically dependent on their husbands. In 1978, married men in the United States earned an average of $293 a week, while married women earned $167 a week (U.S. Department of Labor, 1980). Given these high expectations and dependencies, the costs of recognizing failures and dissolving marriages are significant. Divorce is an increasingly common phenomenon in the United States, but it is still labeled a social problem and is seldom undertaken without serious deliberations and emotional upheavals (Bohannan, 1971). Levels of commitment vary widely, but some degree of commitment is implicit in the marriage contract.

When marital conflicts emerge there is usually some effort to negotiate an agreement or bargain, to ensure the continuity of the relationship (Scanzoni, 1972). Couples employ a variety of strategies, depending on the nature and extent of resources available to them, to resolve conflicts without dissolving relationships. It is thus possible for marriages to continue for years, surviving the inevitable conflicts that occur (Sprey, 1971).

In describing conflict management, Spiegel (1968) distinguishes between "role induction" and "role modification." Role induction refers to conflict in which "one or the other parties to the conflict agrees, submits, goes along with, becomes convinced, or is persuaded in some way" (1968:402). Role modification, on the other hand, involves adaptations by both partners. Role induction seems particularly applicable to battered women who accommodate their husbands'

abuse. Rather than seeking help or escaping, as people typically do when attacked by strangers, battered women often rationalize violence from their husbands, at least initially. Although remaining with a violent man does not indicate that a woman views violence as an acceptable aspect of the relationship, the length of time that a woman stays in the marriage after abuse begins is a rough index of her efforts to accommodate the situation. In a U.S. study of 350 battered women, Pagelow (1981) found the median length of stay after violence began was four years; some left in less than one year, others stayed as long as 42 years.

Battered women have good reasons to rationalize violence. There are few institutional, legal, or cultural supports for women fleeing violent marriages. In Roy's (1977:32) survey of 150 battered women, 90 percent said they "thought of leaving and would have done so had the resources been available to them." Eighty percent of Pagelow's (1981) sample indicated previous, failed attempts to leave their husbands. Despite the development of the international shelter movement, changes in police practices, and legislation to protect battered women since 1975, it remains extraordinarily difficult for a battered woman to escape a violent husband determined to maintain his control. At least one woman, Mary Parziale, has been murdered by an abusive husband while residing in a shelter (Beverly, 1978); others have been murdered after leaving shelters to establish new, independent homes (Garcia, 1978). When these practical and social constraints are combined with love for and commitment to an abuser, it is obvious that there is a strong incentive—often a practical necessity—to rationalize violence.

Previous research on the rationalizations of deviant offenders has revealed a typology of "techniques of neutralization," which allow offenders to view their actions as normal, acceptable, or at least justifiable (Sykes & Matza, 1957). A similar typology can be constructed for victims. Extending the concepts developed by Sykes and Matza, we assigned the responses of battered women we interviewed to one of six categories of rationalization: (1) the appeal to the salvation ethic; (2) the denial of the victimizer; (3) the denial of injury; (4) the denial of victimization; (5) the denial of options; and (6) the appeal to higher loyalties. The women usually employed at least one of these techniques to make sense of their situations; often they employed two or more, simultaneously or over time.

1. *The appeal to the salvation ethic:* This rationalization is grounded in a woman's desire to be of service to others. Abusing husbands are viewed as deeply troubled, perhaps "sick," individuals, dependent on their wives' nurturance for survival. Battered women place their own safety and happiness below their commitment to "saving my man" from whatever malady they perceive as the source of their husbands' problems (Ferraro, 1979a). The appeal to the salvation ethic is a common response to an alcoholic or drug-dependent abuser. The battered partners of substance abusers frequently describe the charming, charismatic personality of their sober mates, viewing this appealing personality as the "real man" being destroyed by disease. They then assume responsibility for helping their partners to overcome their problems, viewing the batterings they receive as an index of their partners' pathology. Abuse must be endured while helping the man return to his "normal" self. One woman said:

> I thought I was going to be Florence Nightingale. He had so much potential; I could see how good he really was, and I was going to "save" him. I thought I was the only thing keeping him going, and that if I left he'd lose his job and wind up in jail. I'd make excuses to everybody for him. I'd call work and lie when he was drunk, saying he was sick. I never criticized him, because he needed my approval.

2. *The denial of the victimizer:* This technique is similar to the salvation ethic, except that victims do not assume responsibility for solving their abusers' problems. Women perceive battering as an event beyond the control of both spouses and blame it on some external force. The violence is judged situational and temporary, because it is linked to unusual circumstances or a sickness which can be cured. Pressures at work, the loss of a job, or legal problems are all situations which battered women assume as the causes of their partners' violence. Mental illness, alcoholism, and drug addiction are also viewed as external, uncontrollable afflictions by many battered women who accept the medical perspective on such problems. By focusing on factors beyond the control of their abuser, women deny their husbands' intent to do them harm, and thus rationalize violent episodes.

> He's sick. He didn't used to be this way, but he can't handle alcohol. It's really like a disease, being an alcoholic. . . . I think too that this is what he saw at home, his father is a very violent man, and alcoholic too, so it's really not his fault, because this is all he has ever known.

3. *The denial of injury:* For some women, the experience of being battered by a spouse is so discordant with their expectations that they simply refuse to acknowledge it. When hospitalization is not required—and it seldom is for most cases of battering[1]—routines quickly return to normal. Meals are served, jobs and schools are attended, and daily chores completed. Even with lingering pain, bruises, and cuts, the normality of everyday life overrides the strange, confusing memory of the attack. When husbands refuse to discuss or acknowledge the event, in some cases even accusing their wives of insanity, women sometimes come to believe the violence never occurred. The denial of injury does not mean that women feel no pain. They know they are hurt but define the hurt as tolerable or normal. Just as individuals tolerate a wide range of physical discomfort before seeking medical help, battered women tolerate a wide range of physical abuse before defining it as an injurious assault. One woman explained her disbelief at her first battering:

> I laid in bed and cried all night. I could not believe it had happened, and I didn't want to believe it. We had only been married a year, and I was pregnant and excited about starting a family. Then all of a sudden, this! The next morning he told me he was sorry and it wouldn't happen again, and I gladly kissed and made up. I wanted to forget the whole thing, and wouldn't let myself worry about what it meant for us.

4. *The denial of victimization:* Victims often blame themselves for the violence, thereby neutralizing the responsibility of the spouse. Pagelow (1981)

found that 99.4 percent of battered women felt they did not deserve to be beaten, and 51 percent said they had done nothing to provoke an attack. The battered women in our sample did not believe violence against them was justified, but some felt it could have been avoided if they had been more passive and conciliatory. Both Pagelow's and our samples are biased in this area, because they were made up almost entirely of women who had already left their abusers, and thus would have been unlikely to feel major responsibility for the abuse they received. Retrospective acounts of victimization in our sample, however, did reveal evidence that some women believed their right to leave violent men was restricted by their participation in the conflicts. One subject said:

> Well, I couldn't really do anything about it, because I did ask for it. I knew how to get at him, and I'd keep after it and keep after it until he got fed up and knocked me right out. I can't say I like it, but I shouldn't have nagged him like I did.

As Pagelow (1981) noted, there is a difference between provocation and justification. A battered woman's belief that her actions angered her spouse to the point of violence is not synonymous with the belief that violence was therefore *justified*. But belief in provocation may diminish a woman's capacity for retaliation or self-defense, because it blurs her concept of responsibility. A woman's acceptance of responsibility for the violent incident is encouraged by an abuser who continually denigrates her and makes unrealistic demands. Depending on the social supports available, and the personality of the battered woman, the man's accusations of inadequacy may assume the status of truth. Such beliefs of inferiority inhibit the development of a notion of victimization.

5. *The denial of options:* This technique is composed of two elements: practical options and emotional options. Practical options, including alternative housing, source of income, and protection from an abuser, are clearly limited by the patriarchal structure of Western society. However, there are differences in the ways battered women respond to these obstacles, ranging from determined struggle to acquiescence. For a variety of reasons, some battered women do not take full advantage of the practical opportunities which are available to escape, and some return to abusers voluntarily even after establishing an independent lifestyle. Others ignore the most severe constraints in their efforts to escape their relationships. For example, one resident of the shelter we observed walked 30 miles in her bedroom slippers to get to the shelter and required medical attention for blisters and cuts to her feet. On the other hand, a woman who had a full-time job, had rented an apartment, and had been given by the shelter all the clothes, furniture, and basics necessary to set up housekeeping, returned to her husband two weeks after leaving the shelter. Other women refused to go to job interviews, keep appointments with social workers, or move out of the state for their own protection (Ferraro, 1981b). Such actions are frightening for women who have led relatively isolated or protected lives, but failure to take action leaves few alternatives to a violent marriage. The belief of battered women that they will not be able to make it on their own—a belief often fueled by years of abuse and oppression—is a major impediment to acknowledging that one is a victim and taking action.

The denial of *emotional* options imposes still further restrictions. Battered women may feel that no one else can provide intimacy and companionship. While physical beating is painful and dangerous, the prospect of a lonely, celibate existence is often too frightening to risk. It is not uncommon for battered women to express the belief that their abuser is the only man they could love, thus severely limiting their opportunities to discover new, more supportive relationships. One woman said:

> He's all I've got. My dad's gone, and my mother disowned me when I married him. And he's really special. He understands me, and I understand him. Nobody could take his place.

6. *The appeal to higher loyalties:* This appeal involves enduring battering for the sake of some higher commitment, either religious or traditional. The Christian belief that women should serve their husbands as men serve God is invoked as a rationalization to endure a husband's violence for later rewards in the afterlife. Clergy may support this view by advising women to pray and try harder to please their hus-

bands (Davidson, 1978; McClinchey, 1981). Other women have a strong commitment to the nuclear family and find divorce repugnant. They may believe that for their children's sake, any marriage is better than no marriage. One woman we interviewed divorced her husband of 35 years after her last child left home. More commonly women who have survived violent relationships for that long do not have the desire or strength to divorce and begin a new life. When the appeal to higher loyalties is employed as a strategy to cope with battering, commitment to and involvement with an ideal overshadows the mundane reality of violence.

CATALYSTS FOR CHANGE

Rationalization is a way of coping with a situation in which, for either practical or emotional reasons, or both, a battered woman is stuck. For some women, the situation and the beliefs that rationalize it may continue for a lifetime. For others, changes may occur within the relationship, within individuals, or in available resources which serve as catalysts for redefining the violence. When battered women reject prior rationalizations and begin to view themselves as true victims of abuse, the victimization process begins.[2]

There are a variety of catalysts for redefining abuse; we discuss six: (1) a change in the level of violence; (2) a change in resources; (3) a change in the relationship; (4) despair; (5) a change in the visibility of violence; and (6) external definitions of the relationship.

1. *A change in the level of violence:* Although Gelles (1976) reports that the severity of abuse is an important factor in women's decisions to leave violent situations, Pagelow (1981) found no significant correlation between the number of years spent cohabiting with an abuser and the severity of abuse. On the contrary: the longer women lived with an abuser, the more severe the violence they endured, since violence increased in severity over time. What does seem to serve as a catalyst is a sudden change in the relative level of violence. Women who suddenly realize that battering may be fatal may reject rationalizations in order to save their lives. One woman who had been severely beaten by an alcoholic husband for many years explained her decision to leave on the basis of a direct threat to her life:

> It was like a pendulum. He'd swing to the extremes both ways. He'd get drunk and beat me up, then he'd get sober and treat me like a queen. One day he put a gun to my head and pulled the trigger. It wasn't loaded. But that's when I decided I'd had it. I sued for separation of property. I knew what was coming again, so I got out. I didn't want to. I still loved the guy, but I knew I had to for my own sanity.

There are, of course, many cases of homicide in which women did not escape soon enough. In 1979, 7.6 percent of all murders in the United States where the relationship between the victim and the offender was known were murders of wives by husbands (Flanagan et al., 1982). Increases in severity do not guarantee a reinterpretation of the situation but may play a part in the process.

2. *A change in resources:* Although some women rationalize cohabiting with an abuser by claiming they have no options, others begin reinterpreting violence when the resources necessary for escape become available. The emergence of safe homes or shelters since 1970 has produced a new resource for battered women. While not completely adequate or satisfactory, the mere existence of a place to go alters the situation in which battering is experienced (Johnson, 1981). Public support of shelters is a statement to battered women that abuse need not be tolerated. Conversely, political trends which limit resources available to women, such as cutbacks in government funding to social programs, increase fears that life outside a violent marriage is economically impossible. One 55-year-old woman discussed this catalyst:

> I stayed with him because I didn't want my kids to have the same life I did. My parents were divorced, and I was always so ashamed of that. . . . Yes, they're all on their own now, so there's no reason left to stay.

3. *A change in the relationship:* Walker (1979), in discussing the stages of a battering relationship, notes that violent incidents are usually followed by periods of remorse and solicitude. Such phases deepen

the emotional bonds and make rejection of an abuser more difficult. But as battering progresses, periods of remorse may shorten, or disappear, eliminating the basis for maintaining a positive outlook on the marriage. After a number of episodes of violence, a man may realize that his victim will not retaliate or escape and thus feel no need to express remorse. Extended periods devoid of kindness or love may alter a woman's feelings toward her partner so much so that she eventually begins to define herself as a victim of abuse. One woman recalled:

> At first, you know, we used to have so much fun together. He has kind've, you know, a magnetic personality; he can be really charming. But it isn't fun anymore. Since the baby came, it's changed completely. He just wants me to stay at home, while he goes out with his friends. He doesn't even talk to me, most of the time. . . . No, I don't really love him anymore, not like I did.

4. *Despair:* Changes in the relationship may result in a loss of hope that "things will get better." When hope is destroyed and replaced by despair, rationalizations of violence may give way to the recognition of victimization. Feelings of hopelessness or despair are the basis for some efforts to assist battered women, such as Al-Anon.[3] The director of an Al-Anon organized shelter explained the concept of "hitting bottom":

> Before the Al-Anon program can really be of benefit, a woman has to hit bottom. When you hit bottom, you realize that all of your own efforts to control the situation have failed; you feel helpless and lost and worthless and completely disenchanted with the world. Women can't really be helped unless they're ready for it and want it. Some women come here when things get bad, but they aren't really ready to be committed to Al-Anon. Things haven't gotten bad enough for them, and they go right back. We see this all the time.

5. *A change in the visibility of violence:* Creating a web of rationalizations to overlook violence is accomplished more easily if no intruders are present to question their validity. Since most violence between couples occurs in private, there are seldom conflicting interpretations of the event from outsiders. Only 7 percent of the respondents in Gelles's (1976) study who discussed spatial location of violence indicated events which took place outside the home, but all reported incidents within the home. Others report similar findings (Pittman & Handy, 1964; Pokorny, 1965; Wolfgang, 1958). If violence does occur in the presence of others, it may trigger a reinterpretation process. Battering in private is degrading, but battering in public is humiliating, for it is a statement of subordination and powerlessness. Having others witness abuse may create intolerable feelings of shame which undermine prior rationalizations.

> He never hit me in public before—it was always at home. But the Saturday I got back [returned to husband from shelter], we went Christmas shopping and he slapped me in the store because of some stupid joke I made. People saw it, I know, I felt so stupid, like, they must all think what a jerk I am, what a sick couple, and I thought, "God, I must be crazy to let him do this."

6. *External definitions of the relationship:* A change in visibility is usually accomplished by the interjection of external definitions of abuse. External definitions vary depending on their source and the situation; they either reinforce or undermine rationalizations. Battered women who request help frequently find others—and especially officials—don't believe their story or are unsympathetic (Pagelow, 1981; Pizzey, 1974). Experimental research by Shotland and Straw (1976) supports these reports. Observers usually fail to respond when a woman is attacked by a man, and justify nonintervention on the grounds that they assumed the victim and offender were married. One young woman discussed how lack of support from her family left her without hope:

> It wouldn't be so bad if my own family gave a damn about me. . . . Yeah, they know I'm here, and they don't care. They didn't care about me when I was a kid, so why should they care now? I got raped and beat as a kid, and now I get beat as an adult. Life is a big joke.

Clearly, such responses from family members contribute to the belief among battered women that there are no alternatives and that they must tolerate the abuse. However, when outsiders respond with unqualified support of the victim and condemnation of violent men, their definitions can be a potent catalyst toward victimization. Friends and relatives who show genuine concern for a woman's well-being may initiate an awareness of danger which contradicts previous rationalizations.

> My mother-in-law knew what was going on, but she wouldn't admit it. . . . I said, "Mom, what do you think these bruises are?" and she said "Well, some people just bruise easy. I do it all the time, bumping into things." . . . And he just denied it, pretended like nothing happened, and if I'd said I wanted to talk about it, he'd say, "life goes on, you can't just dwell on things." . . . But this time, my neighbor *knew* what happened, she saw it, and when he denied it, she said, "I can't believe it! You know that's not true!" . . . and I was so happy that finally, somebody else saw what was goin' on, and I just told him then that this time I wasn't gonna' come home!

Shelters for battered women serve not only as material resources but as sources of external definitions which contribute to the victimization process. They offer refuge from a violent situation in which a woman may contemplate her circumstances and what she wants to do about them. Within a shelter, women meet counselors and other battered women who are familiar with rationalizations of violence and the reluctance to give up commitment to a spouse. In counseling sessions and informal conversations with other residents, women hear horror stories from others who have already defined themselves as victims. They are supported for expressing anger and rejecting responsibility for their abuse (Ferraro, 1981a). The goal of many shelters is to overcome feelings of guilt and inadequacy so that women can make choices in their best interests. In this atmosphere, violent incidents are reexamined and redefined as assaults in which the woman was victimized.

How others respond to a battered woman's situation is critical. The closer the relationship of others, the more significant their response is to a woman's perception of the situation. Thus, children can either help or hinder the victim. Pizzey (1974) found adolescent boys at a shelter in Chiswick, England, often assumed the role of the abusing father and themselves abused their mothers, both verbally and physically. On the other hand, children at the shelter we observed often became extremely protective and nurturing toward their mothers. This phenomenon has been thoroughly described elsewhere (Ferraro, 1981a). Children who have been abused by fathers who also beat their mothers experience high levels of anxiety and rarely want to be reunited with their fathers. A 13-year-old, abused daughter of a shelter resident wrote the following message to her stepfather:

> I am going to be honest and not lie. No, I don't want you to come back. It's not that I am jealous because mom loves you. It is [I] am afraid I won't live to see 18. I did care about you a long time ago, but now I can't care, for the simple reason you['re] always calling us names, even my friends. And another reason is, I am tired of seeing mom hurt. She has been hurt enough in her life, and I don't want her to be hurt any more.

No systematic research has been conducted on the influence children exert on their battered mothers, but it seems obvious that the willingness of children to leave a violent father would be an important factor in a woman's own decision to leave.

The relevance of these catalysts to a woman's interpretation of violence varies with her own situation and personality. The process of rejecting rationalizations and becoming a victim is ambiguous, confusing, and emotional. We now turn to the feelings involved in victimization.

THE EMOTIONAL CAREER OF VICTIMIZATION

As rationalizations give way to perceptions of victimization, a woman's feelings about herself, her spouse, and her situation change. These feelings are imbedded in a cultural, political, and interactional structure. Initially, abuse is contrary to a woman's cultural expectations of behavior between intimates and therefore engenders feelings of betrayal. The husband has violated his wife's expectations of love and protection and thus betrayed her confidence in him. The feeling of betrayal, however, is balanced by the husband's efforts to explain his behavior and by the woman's reluctance to abandon faith. Additionally, the political dominance of men within and outside the family mediates women's ability to question the validity of their husbands' actions.

At the interpersonal level, psychological abuse accompanying violence often invokes feelings of guilt and shame in the battered victim. Men define violence as a response to their wives' inadequacies or provocations, which leads battered women to feel that they have failed. Such character assaults are devastating and create long-lasting feelings of inferiority (Ferraro, 1979b):

> I've been verbally abused as well. It takes you a long time to . . . you may say you feel good and you may . . . but inside, you know what's been said to you and it hurts for a long time. You need to build up your self-image and make yourself feel like you're a useful person, that you're valuable, and that you're a good parent. You might think these things, and you may say them. . . . I'm gonna prove it to myself.

Psychologists working with battered women consistently report that self-confidence wanes over years of ridicule and criticism (Hilberman & Munson, 1978; Walker, 1979).

Feelings of guilt and shame are also mixed with a hope that things will get better, at least in the early stages of battering. Even the most violent man is non-violent much of the time, so there is always a basis for believing that violence is exceptional and the "real man" is not a threat. The vacillation between violence and fear on the one hand, and nonviolence and affection on the other, was described by a shelter resident:

> First of all, the first beatings—you can't believe it yourself. I'd go to bed, and I'd cry, and I just couldn't believe this was happening. And I'd wake up the next morning thinking that couldn't of happened, or maybe it was my fault. It's so unbelievable that this person that you're married to and you love would do that to you, but yet you can't leave either because, ya'know, for the other 29 days of the month that person loves you and is with you.

Hope wanes as periods of love and remorse dwindle. Feelings of love and intimacy are gradually replaced with loneliness and pessimism. Battered women who no longer feel love for their husbands but remain in their marriages enter a period of emotional dormancy. They survive each day, performing necessary tasks, with a dull depression and lack of enthusiasm. While some battered women live out their lives in this emotional desert, others are spurred by catalysts to feel either the total despair or mortal fear which leads them to seek help.

Battered women who perceive their husbands' actions as life-threatening experience a penetrating fear that consumes all their thoughts and energies. The awareness of murderous intent by a presumed ally who is a central figure in all aspects of her life destroys all bases for safety. There is a feeling that death is imminent, and that there is nowhere to hide. Prior rationalizations and beliefs about a "good marriage" are exploded, leaving the woman in a crisis of ambiguity (Ridington, 1978).

Feelings of fear are experienced physiologically as well as emotionally. Battered women experience aches and fatigue, stomach pains, diarrhea or constipation, tension headaches, shakes, chills, loss of appetite, and insomnia. Sometimes, fear is expressed as a numbed shock, similar to rape trauma syndrome (Burgess & Holmstrom, 1974), in which little is felt or communicated.

If attempts to seek help succeed, overwhelming feelings of fear subside, and a rush of new emotions are felt: the original sense of betrayal reemerges, creating strong feelings of anger. For women socialized to reject angry feelings as unfeminine, coping with anger is difficult. Unless the expression of anger is encouraged in a supportive environment, such women may suppress anger and feel only depression (Ball & Wyman, 1978). When anger is expressed, it often leads to feelings of strength and exhilaration. Freedom from threats of violence, the possibility of a new life, and the unburdening of anger create feelings of joy. The simple pleasures of going shopping, taking children to the park, or talking with other women without fear of criticism or punishment from a husband, constitute amazing freedoms. One middle-aged woman expressed her joy over her newly acquired freedom this way:

> Boy, tomorrow I'm goin' downtown, and I've got my whole day planned out, and I'm gonna' do what

I wanna' do, and if somebody doesn't like it, to *hell* with them! You know, I'm having so much fun, I should've done this years ago!

Probably the most typical feeling expressed by women in shelters is confusion. They feel both sad and happy, excited and apprehensive, independent, yet in need of love. Most continue to feel attachment to their husbands, and feel ambivalent about divorce. There is grief over the loss of an intimate, which must be acknowledged and mourned. Although shelters usually discourage women from contacting their abusers while staying at the shelter, most women do communicate with their husbands—and most receive desperate pleas for forgiveness and reconciliation. If there is not strong emotional support and potential material support, such encouragement by husbands often rekindles hope for the relationship. Some marriages can be revitalized through counseling, but most experts agree that long-term batterers are unlikely to change (Pagelow, 1981; Walker, 1979). Whether they seek refuge in shelters or with friends, battered women must decide relatively quickly what actions to take. Usually, a tentative commitment is made, either to independence or working on the relationship, but such commitments are usually ambivalent. As one woman wrote to her counselor:

> My feelings are so mixed up sometimes. Right now I feel my husband is really trying to change. But I know that takes time. I still feel for him some. I don't know how much. My mind still doesn't know what it wants. I would really like when I leave here to see him once in a while, get my apartment, and sort of like start over with our relationship for me and my baby and him, to try and make it work. It might. It kind of scares me. I guess I am afraid it won't. . . . I can only hope this works out. There's no telling what could happen. No one knows.

The emotional career of battered women consists of movement from guilt, shame, and depression to fear and despair, to anger, exhilaration, and confusion. Women who escape violent relationships must deal with strong, sometimes conflicting, feelings in attempting to build new lives for themselves free of violence. The kind of response women receive when they seek help largely determines the effects these feelings have on subsequent decisions.

THE AFTERMATH

The consequences of leaving a violent husband vary widely and depend on such situational variables as the atmosphere of a shelter, the availability of new partners, success at employment, and the response of the spouse. Interestingly, most battered women, like most divorcees, are optimistic about future relationships (Scanzoni, 1972). When the opportunity presented itself, battered women at the shelter we observed were happy to date and establish new relationships. The idea that battered women seek out violent men has been refuted by both Pagelow (1981) and Walker (1979). However, entering a new relationship shortly after escaping a violent one does interfere with a woman's opportunity to develop autonomy and overcome problems created by years of abuse. Involvement in a new relationship is, however, appealing, because it cushions the impact of divorce and the prospect of making it alone.

Some battered women, however, develop a feeling of repugnance to romantic involvements. They may feel that "men are no good," or simply enjoy their freedom too much to consider entering a relationship. Most women in shelters reject feminism as a total philosophy but adopt many of its tenets. Living in a shelter operated by and for women changes ideas about the role of women and their ability to run their own lives. It also provides an opportunity to develop female friendships and to overcome the view of other women as "competitors." The rights of women to defend themselves and to make their own decisions are not easily given up once they are found. So, while women who have extricated themselves from violent relationships may not call themselves feminists, or become politically active, they do gain a commitment to certain feminist goals (Ridington, 1978).

Some formerly battered women do join in political activity to help other victims. Many of the grass-roots shelters now in existence in the United States and Europe were created by formerly battered women (Warrior, 1978), and some shelters make a special effort to recruit such women for their staffs. Entry into the battered women's movement provides an opportunity to develop a new support group, as well as build feelings of self-worth by contributing service to others.

Of course, some women return to violent relationships. There is a tendency for observers to view such decisions as failures, but they are often part of the process of gaining independence. Women may leave and return to violent relationships a number of times before making a final break. As Pagelow (1981:219) explains it:

> Women who return home are not "failures" in any sense of the word. If there was only a short history of abuse and their spouses recognize they have a problem and begin to correct it, there is a possibility of no further violence. But these women had the courage to leave the first time; they were exposed to alternatives and new ideas; they found out that other people outside their homes can and do care for their welfare; they learned that they are not ugly "freaks" with a rare, individual problem. They may return to the men that abused them, but they do not return the same women they were when they left.

Most shelters are too overworked and understaffed to conduct systematic follow-ups for more than a month or two after women leave. Because our research was participatory, we were able to develop personal knowledge about each resident of the shelter, allowing for a more complete understanding of their postshelter experiences. If success is defined in terms of life satisfaction (positive relationships with others, self-confidence, and optimism about the future), only 30 of the 120 women we met during the study period could be said to have successfully dealt with their battering. An additional 30 women did not return to their marriages, to anyone's knowledge, but continued to face severe problems, either financially, interpersonally, or emotionally. The other 60 shelter residents (50 percent of the sample) returned to their marriages. Further systematic research on the experiences of battered women who permanently leave violent marriages is needed to expand our knowledge of the battering phenomenon.

CONCLUSION

The process of victimization is not synonymous with experiencing violent attacks from a spouse. Rationalizing the violence inhibits a sense of outrage and efforts to escape abuse. Only after rationalizations are rejected, through the impact of one or more catalysts, does the victimization process begin. When previously rationalized violence is reinterpreted as dangerous, unjustified assault, battered women actively seek al-

ternatives. The success of their efforts to seek help depends on available resources, external supports, reactions of husbands and children, and their own adaptation to the situation. Victimization includes not only cognitive interpretations but feelings and physiological responses. Creating a satisfying, peaceful environment after being battered involves emotional confusion and ambiguity, as well as enormous practical and economic obstacles. It may take years of struggle and aborted attempts before a battered woman is able to establish a safe and stable life style; for some, this goal is never achieved.

The victimization process which we have described refers to the interpretation of a specific set of violent events within a particular relationship. It is important to emphasize that this victimization is limited to those violent events, and does not encompass a more global perspective on the woman's life. Individuals working with battered women have pointed out the importance of helping battered women to distinguish between being a victim of an assault and assuming the identity of a victim (Ridington, 1978; Vaughan, 1979). The first involves rejecting the responsibility for being beaten; the second involves giving up the responsibility for one's life. The role of victim is contradictory to the assertive and creative action necessary to establish a life free of violence. To accomplish the latter goal, women must quickly overcome the feelings of helplessness and self-pity that accompany victimization. They must confidently assume responsibility for making decisions and working towards the goals they set, and reject identification with the role of victim.

Our data and analysis are limited to the victimization experienced by battered women. But this raises questions about similar experiences with other forms of victimization, such as street crime or white-collar crime, or political violence and corruption. The literature on vigilantism and revolution deals with the social and structural variables conducive to the emergence of these forms of collective behavior but largely overlooks subjective factors (Arendt, 1963; Graham & Gurr, 1979; Gurr, 1970). Investigation of how individuals come to view situations as oppressive and in need of redress would enhance our knowledge of social protest, rebellion, and revolution. Information on the subjective experiences of people involved in efforts to eliminate threatening, abusive situations of all kinds would make an important contribution to our understanding of why and how movements of social change emerge.

ACKNOWLEDGMENTS

The authors thank Patti Adler, David Altheide, Jaber Gubrium, Paul Higgins, Danny Jorgensen, Carol Warren, and the anonymous *Social Problems* reviewers for their comments.

NOTES

1. National crime survey data for 1973–76 show that 17 percent of persons who sought medical attention for injuries inflicted by an intimate were hospitalized. Eighty-seven percent of injuries inflicted by a spouse or ex-spouse were bruises, black eyes, cuts, scratches, or swelling (National Crime Survey Report, 1980).

2. Explanation of why and how some women arrive at these feelings is beyond the scope of this paper. Our goal is to describe feelings at various stages of the victimization process.

3. Al-Anon is the spouse's counterpart to Alcoholics Anonymous. It is based on the same self-help, 12-step program that A.A. is founded on.

REFERENCES

Arendt, H. 1963. *On revolution.* New York: Viking.

Ball, P., & Wyman, E. 1978. "Battered wives and powerlessness: What can counselors do?" *Victimology* 2(3–4):545–552.

Beverly. 1978. "Shelter resident murdered by husband." *Aegis,* September/October:13.

Bohannan, P., ed. 1971. *Divorce and after.* Garden City, N.Y.: Anchor.

Burgess, A., & Holmstrom, L. 1974. *Rape: Victims of crisis.* Bowie, Md.: Brady.

Colorado Association for Aid to Battered Women. 1978. *Services to battered women.* Washington, D.C.: Office of Domestic Violence, Department of Health, Education and Welfare.

Davidson, T. 1978. *Conjugal crime.* New York: Hawthorn.

Dobash, R., & Dobash, R. 1979. *Violence against wives.* New York: Free Press.

Ferraro, K. 1979a. "Hard love: Letting go of an abusive husband." *Frontiers* 4(2):16–18.

Ferraro, K. 1979b. "Physical and emotional battering: Aspects of managing hurt." *California Sociologist* 2(2):134–149.

Ferraro, K. 1981a. "Battered women and the shelter movement." Unpublished Ph.D. dissertation, Arizona State University.

Ferraro, K. 1981b. "Processing battered women." *Journal of Family Issues* 2(4):415–438.

Flanagan, T., van Alstyne, D., & Gottfredson, M., eds. 1982. *Sourcebook of criminal justice statistics:1981.* U.S. Department of Justice, Bureau of Justice Statistics. Washington, D.C.: U.S. Government Printing Office.

Gacquin, D. 1978. "Spouse abuse: Data from the National Crime Survey." *Victimology* 2:632–643.

Garcia, D. 1978. "Slain women 'lived in fear.'" *The Times* (Erie, Pa.), June 14:B1.

Gelles, R. 1974. *The violent home.* Beverly Hills: Sage.

Gelles, R. 1976. "Abused wives: Why do they stay?" *Journal of Marriage and the Family* 38(4):659–668.

Graham, H., & Gurr, T., eds. 1979. *Violence in America.* Beverly Hills: Sage.

Gurr, T. 1970. *Why men rebel.* Princeton, N.J.: Princeton University Press.

Hilberman, E. 1980. "Overview: The 'wife-beater's wife' reconsidered." *American Journal of Psychiatry* 137(11):1336–1347.

Hilberman, E., & Munson, K. 1978. "Sixty battered women." *Victimology* 2(3–4):460–470.

Johnson, J. 1981. "Program enterprise and official cooptation of the battered women's shelter movement." *American Behavioral Scientist* 24(6):827–842.

McGlinchey, A. 1981. "Woman battering and the church's response." In A. Roberts, ed., *Sheltering battered women,* pp. 133–140. New York: Springer.

Martin, D. 1976. *Battered wives.* San Francisco: Glide.

National Crime Survey Report. 1980. *Intimate victims.* Washington, D.C.: U.S. Department of Justice.

O'Brien, J. 1971. "Violence in divorce-prone families." *Journal of Marriage and the Family* 33(4):692–698.

Pagelow, M. 1981. *Woman-battering.* Beverly Hills: Sage.

Pittman, D. J., & Handy, W. 1964. "Patterns in criminal aggravated assault." *Journal of Criminal Law, Criminology, and Police Science* 55(4):462–470.

Pizzey, E. 1974. *Scream quietly or the neighbors will hear.* Baltimore: Penguin.

Pokorny, A. 1965. "Human violence: A comparison of homicide, aggravated assault, suicide, and attempted suicide." *Journal of Criminal Law, Criminology, and Police Science* 56 (December):488–497.

Ridington, J. 1978. "The transition process: A feminist environment as reconstitutive milieu." *Victimology* 2(3–4):563–576.

Roberts, A. 1981. *Sheltering battered women.* New York: Springer.

Roy, M. ed. 1977. *Battered women.* New York: Van Nostrand.

Saul, L. 1972. "Personal and social psychopathology and the primary prevention of violence." *American Journal of Psychiatry* 128(12):1578–1581.

Scanzoni, J. 1972. *Sexual bargaining.* Englewood Cliffs, N.J.: Prentice-Hall.

Shotland, R., & Straw, M. 1976. "Bystander response to an assault: When a man attacks a woman." *Journal of Personality and Social Psychology* 34(5):990–999.

Snell, J., Rosenwald, R., & Robey, A. 1964. "The wifebeater's wife: A study of family interaction." *Archives of General Psychiatry* 11(August):107–112.

Spiegel, J. 1968. "The resolution of role conflict within the family." In N. Bell & E. Vogel, eds., *A modern introduction to the family,* pp. 391–411. New York: Free Press.

Sprey, J. 1971. "On the management of conflict in families." *Journal of Marriage and the Family* 33(4):699–706.

Steinmetz, S. 1978. "The battered husband syndrome." *Victimology* 2(3–4):499–509.

Steinmetz, S., & Straus, M., eds. 1974. *Violence in the family.* New York: Harper & Row.

Straus, M. 1978. "Wife beating: How common and why?" *Victimology* 2(3–4):443–458.

Straus, M. 1979. "Measuring intrafamily conflict and violence: The conflict tactics (CT) scales." *Journal of Marriage and the Family* 41(1):75–88.

Straus, M., Gelles, R., & Steinmetz, S. 1980. *Behind closed doors: Violence in the American family.* Garden City, N.Y.: Doubleday.

Sykes, G., & Matza, D. 1957. "Techniques of neutralization: A theory of delinquency." *American Sociological Review* 22(6):667–670.

Tierney, K. 1982. "The battered women movement and the creation of the wife beating problem." *Social Problems* 29(3):207–220.

U.S. Department of Labor. 1980. *Handbook of labor statistics.* Washington, D.C.: U.S. Government Printing Office.

Vaughan, S. 1979. "The last refuge: Shelter for battered women." *Victimology* 4(1):113–150.

Walker, L. 1979. *The battered woman.* New York: Harper & Row.

Warrior, B. 1978. *Working on wife abuse.* Cambridge, Mass.: Betsy Warrior.

Wolfgang, M. 1958. *Patterns in criminal homicide.* New York: Wiley.

Women's Advocates. 1980. *Women's Advocates: The story of a shelter.* St. Paul, Minn.: Women's Advocates.

R E A D I N G   4 6

Indian Suttee: The Ultimate Consummation of Marriage

MARY DALY

"Widow" is a harsh and hurtful word. It comes from the Sanskrit and it means "empty."... I resent what the term has come to mean. I am alive, I am part of the world.

Lynn Caine, *Widow*

The Indian rite of *suttee,* or widow-burning, might at first appear totally alien to contemporary Western society, where widows are not ceremoniously burned alive on the funeral pyres of their husbands.* Closer examination unveils its connectedness with "our" rituals. Moreover, the very attempt to examine the ritual and its social context through the resources of Western scholarship demonstrates this connectedness. For the scholars who produced these resources exhibit by their very language their complicity in the same social order which was/is the radical source of such rites of female sacrifice.

*Although *suttee* was legally banned in 1829, and despite the existence of other legal reforms, it should not be imagined that the lot of most Indian women has changed dramatically since then, or since the publication of Katherine Mayo's *Mother India* in 1927. The situation of most widows is pitiable. An article in an Indian paper, the *Sunday Standard,* May 11, 1975, described the wretched existence of the 7,000 widows of the town of Brindaban, "the living spectres whose life has been eroded by another's death." These poverty-stricken women with shaved heads and with a single white cloth draped over their bare bodies are forced every morning to chant praise (*"Hare Rama, Hare Rama, Rama Rama, Hare Hare, Hare Krishna"*... ad nauseam) for four hours in order to get a small bowl of rice. In mid-afternoon they must chant for four more hours in order to receive the price of a glass of tea. A not unusual case is that of a sixty-nine-year-old widow who was married at the age of nine and widowed at eleven, and has been waiting ever since for the "day of deliverance." Surveys carried out by an Indian Committee on the Status of Women revealed that a large percentage of the Indian population still approves of such oppression of widows.

The Hindu rite of *suttee* spared widows from the temptations of impurity by forcing them to "immolate themselves," that is, to be burned alive, on the funeral pyres of their husbands. This ritual sacrifice must be understood within its social context. Since their religion forbade remarriage and at the same time taught that the husband's death was the fault of the widow (because of her sins in a previous incarnation if not in this one), everyone was free to despise and mistreat her for the rest of her life. Since it was a common practice for men of fifty, sixty, or seventy years of age to marry child-brides, the quantitative surplus of such unmarriageable widows boggles the imagination. Lest we allow our minds to be carried away with astronomic numerical calculations, we should realize that this ritual was largely confined to the upper caste, although there was a tendency to spread downward. We should also realize that in some cases—particularly if the widow was an extremely young child before her husband's unfortunate (for her) death—there was the option of turning to a life of prostitution, which would entail premature death from venereal disease.[1] This, however, would be her only possible escape from persecution by in-laws, sons, and other relatives. As a prostitute, of course, she would be held responsible for the spread of more moral and physical impurity.

If the general situation of widowhood in India was not a sufficient inducement for the woman of higher caste to throw herself gratefully and ceremoniously into the fire, she was often pushed and poked in with long stakes after having been bathed, ritually attired, and drugged out of her mind.[2] In case these facts should interfere with our clear misunderstanding of the situation, Webster's invites us to re-*cover* women's history with the following definition of *suttee:* "the act or custom of a Hindu woman *willingly* cremating herself or being cremated on the funeral pyre of her husband as an indication of her *devotion* to him [emphases mine]." It is thought-provoking to consider the reality behind the term *devotion,* for indeed a wife must have shown signs of extraordinarily slavish devotion during her husband's lifetime, since her very life depended upon her husband's state of health. A thirteen-year-old wife might well be concerned over the health of her sixty-year-old husband.

Joseph Campbell discusses *suttee* as the Hindu form of the widely practiced "custom" of sending the family or part of it "into the other world along with the chief member."[3] The time-honored practice of "human sacrifice," sometimes taking the form of live burial, was common also in other cultures, for example in ancient Egypt. Campbell notes that Professor George Reisner excavated an immense necropolis in Nubia, an Egyptian province, and found, without exception, "a pattern of burial with human sacrifice— specifically, female sacrifice: of the wife and, in the more opulent tombs, the entire harem, together with the attendants."[4] After citing Reisner's descriptions of female skeletons, which indicated that the victims had died hideous deaths from suffocation, Campbell writes:

In spite of these signs of suffering and even panic in the actual moment of the pain of suffocation, we should certainly not think of the mental state and experience of these individuals after any model of our own more or less imaginable reactions to such a fate. For these sacrifices were not properly, in fact, individuals at all; that is to say, they were not particular beings, distinguished from a class or group by virtue of any sense or realization of a personal, individual destiny or responsibility.[5]

I have not [emphasized] any of the words in this citation because it seemed necessary to stress *every* word. It is impossible to make any adequate comment.

At first, *suttee* was restricted to the wives of princes and warriors, but as one scholar (Benjamin Walker) deceptively puts it, "in course of time *the widows* of weavers, masons, barbers and others of lower caste *adopted the practice* [emphases mine]."[6] The use of the active voice here suggests that the widows actively sought out, enforced, and accepted this "practice." Apparently without any sense of inconsistency the same author supplies evidence that relatives forced widows to the pyre. He describes a case reported in 1796, in which a widow escaped from the pyre during the night in the rain. A search was made and she was dragged from her hiding place. Walker concludes the story of this woman who "adopted the practice" as follows:

She pleaded to be spared but her own son insisted that she throw herself on the pile as he would lose caste and suffer everlasting humiliation. When she still refused, the son with the help of some others present bound her hands and feet and hurled her into the blaze.[7]

The same author gives information about the numerical escalation of *suttee:*

Among the Rājputs and other warrior nations of northern India, the observance of suttee took on

---

DOWRY DEMANDS BLAMED IN SLAYINGS

DHAKA, Bangladesh (AP)—Many of the almost 300 Bangladeshi women slain during the last 14 months were killed by their husbands or in-laws for failing to meet dowry demands, police say.

Home Minister Abdul Matin told Parliament on Tuesday that 290 women have been killed and 545 have been kidnapped since January 1986. He gave no further details.

Police sources said yesterday that many of the women died after they were tortured by husbands or in-laws demanding dowry from the brides' families. In some cases, disappointed suitors killed their intended brides by spraying them with acid, they said.

Matin told Parliament the government has made provisions for heavy punishment to deal with crimes against women.

Reprinted from *Columbus Dispatch*, 19 March 1987.

staggering proportions, since wives and concubines *immolated themselves* by the hundred. It became customary not only for wives but for mistresses, sisters, mothers, sisters-in-law and other near female relatives and retainers *to burn themselves* along with their deceased master. With Rājputs it evolved into the terrible rite of *jauhar* which took place in times of war or great peril *in order to save the honour of the womenfolk of the clan* [emphases mine].[8]

Again the victims, through grammatical sleight of hand, are made to appear as the agents of their own destruction.

NOTES

1. See Katherine Mayo, *Mother India* (New York: Blue Ribbon Books, 1927), esp. pp. 81–89, 51–62.

2. See P. Thomas, *Indian Women through the Ages* (New York: Asia Publishing Company, 1964), p. 263. This author describes the situation in Muslim India of widows who tried to escape cremation, writing that "to prevent her escape, she was usually surrounded by men armed with sticks who goaded her on to her destination by physical force."

3. Joseph Campbell, *The Masks of God: Oriental Mythology* (New York: Viking Press, 1962), p. 62.

4. Ibid., p. 60.

5. Ibid., p. 65.

6. Benjamin Walker, *The Hindu World: An Encyclopedic Survey of Hinduism,* 2 vols. (New York: Praeger, 1968), vol. II, p. 461.

7. Ibid., p. 464.

8. Ibid., pp. 462–63.

P A R T   T H R E E

The Feminist Movement

We have seen that socialization and the structure and content of major social institutions converge to produce and maintain a social order in which males and females are differentially valued and differentially rewarded. Those forces are so powerful, pervasive, and intricately interwoven that to effect social change is beyond the power of the individual, no matter how well intentioned that individual may be.

Yet societies can and do change. In democratic and quasi-democratic societies, the most effective avenue to social change is the social movement. Social movements originate in collective discontent, establish linkages between individuals and groups who share common concerns, and mobilize the resources necessary to pursue collective goals. Social movements and the strategies they employ (marches, boycotts, strikes, demonstrations) are a legitimate and regular part of the democratic process—so much so that in American society, today's established social institution is likely to have been yesterday's social movement.

Since we are concerned with social movement activity directed toward altering women's status, most of our attention in Part Three must be addressed to the women's movement, for it is this movement that has been the primary force in altering sex-based inequalities. Although the media have presented the women's movement as a modern phenomenon, its roots are well grounded historically. Indeed, the continuity between the contemporary movement and the suffrage movement, which culminated in the enfranchisement of women in 1920, is remarkable. More than 200 years ago, for example, Abigail Adams gave this warning to her husband, John, when he was fashioning the Constitution of the United States:

> In the new code of laws which I suppose will be necessary for you to make, I desire you would remember the ladies and be more generous and favorable to them than your ancestors. Do not put such unlimited power in the hands of husbands. Remember, all men would be tyrants if they could. If particular care and attention is not paid to the ladies, we are determined to foment a rebellion, and will not hold ourselves bound by any laws in which we have no voice or representation.

John Adams nonetheless failed to take his wife's warning seriously; he urged her to be patient, noting that there were more important issues than "ladies'" rights.

We have, then, a long history in this society of feminist activism. The contemporary women's movement and the backlash against it must be viewed, therefore, in the context of a long progressive struggle to redress inequality and to reduce the impact of masculinist values.

During the 1960s, when the contemporary women's movement emerged, the country was witnessing a spate of social movement activities focused on a variety of issues: civil rights, the Vietnam War, and student rights in higher education. The women's movement of this period grew from the discontent of two distinct groups of women: older, college-educated professional women who experienced intense discrimination in employment and dissatisfaction with traditional family roles; and younger women, enrolled in college and/or immersed in the university community, who found themselves cast into the traditional roles of "chicks," secretaries, dishwashers, and cooks by the male leadership of the antiwar, civil rights, and student movements of the day. Not surprisingly, these two social bases created and built different forms and styles of movement organizations, and developed different goals and strategies. The older professional women moved toward a moderate ideology and traditional organizational form, establishing such groups as the National Organization for Women (NOW), the Women's Equity Action League (WEAL), and the National Women's Political Caucus. The younger women claimed a more radical vision and organized smaller collectivities, based on consciousness-raising and geared toward political activism around a variety of issues: women's health and reproduction; the media portrayal of women; lesbian ideology and activism; racism and other issues affecting women of color; nuclear proliferation; and violence against women in the form of rape, incest, sexual harassment, pornography, and domestic violence. They established alternative structures within which a distinctively feminist women's culture could flourish, such as women's recording companies, bookstores, theater groups, restaurants, poetry groups, spirituality groups, and publishing companies.

The women's movement of today, like all other general social movements, continues to be composed of many separate and diverse movement organizations, each with its own strategies, style, membership base, leadership, and specific goals. Holding ideologies that may be moderate, radical, socialist, or Marxist, these smaller movement organizations are held together by overlapping membership and occasional participation in common political activities around a particular issue, such as violence against women. Disputes over ideology and strategy are sometimes bitter among various branches of the women's movement, but such conflicts are in no way unique to this particular movement. To some extent, all social movements thrive when they are heterogeneous and diverse in their goals and ideologies; any social movement, whatever its focus, needs radicals to define its ultimate political utopia and to demonstrate to society how moderate are the reforms sought by liberals.

The ultimate vision of many women's groups is so broad as to include a fundamental restructuring of all institutions that perpetuate and sustain male dominance. The fact that feminist groups can be found within every major institution—in the professions, in academia, in labor, in religion, in politics, and in the worlds of art, music, and literature—and are mobilized around practically every issue imaginable, from employment issues, pornography, prostitution, abortion, health, disability rights, child care, nuclear power, women's sexuality, to lesbian, black, Native American, Jewish, and Hispanic women's concerns by no means indicates that the movement is about to crumble for lack of unity. Rather, because it permeates every facet of social life, feminist thought is having a major impact not only on the economic and political institutions of society but on the lives of individuals as well.

In Part Three we examine the contemporary feminist movement and its relation to other organized interests, emphasizing the diversity of the movement and the major issues confronting it today. We conclude with a look to the future.

The Diversity of Feminism

Historically the American women's movement has been composed largely of white middle-class married women. It is not surprising, therefore, that the movement's goals, style, and strategies have tended to reflect the interests of such women. A crucial question that has faced the women's movement since the late 1970s has been whether it could build an agenda that would speak to the concerns of the mass of women in American society; that is, not only to white middle-class married women but also to women of color and of a variety of ethnic backgrounds, to lesbians, and to working-class women. In addition, men who were interested in altering the social arrangements between the sexes began to ask what they might do to redress the political wrongs articulated by feminists and what role they might play in the movement. In this section we see the diversity of the women's movement in past eras and in the present and the extent to which this movement, like other general and broad-based social movements, has been made up of organizations with unique, distinctive, and occasionally conflicting ideologies, identities, organizational styles, and memberships.

"The First Feminists," by Judith Hole and Ellen Levine, describes the struggles of American feminists during the suffrage campaign of the 19th century. Describing how the women's rights movement grew out of the abolitionist movement of the 1830s, Hole and Levine reconstruct the events leading to the passage in 1920 of the 19th Amendment,

which accorded women the right to vote. In "Black Women and Feminism," Bell Hooks examines the historical involvement of black women in the struggle for women's rights. She analyzes the tensions and conflicts that emerged between black men and women in the 1950s and 1960s, and examines the racism that permeates the contemporary women's movement, so that the concerns of many women of color are not addressed.

In "Not for Lesbians Only," Charlotte Bunch discusses yet another issue that has divided women in the movement and at times has led lesbians to believe that there is no place for them in the feminist movement: the gay–straight split. Bunch argues that lesbian feminism should be viewed not as a political analysis and struggle "for lesbians only" but as a cause that all women should embrace in an effort to end the domination of heterosexuality as one of the major institutions of all women's oppression.

In the 1970s, violence against women in the form of rape was a major issue unifying the feminist movement. Out of women's grass-roots efforts to define the nature and causes of rape and to develop strategies to stop it emerged a series of crisis centers around the country. Most were organized and run by feminist collectives. Other forms of violence against women—battering, incest, and sexual harassment—have become public issues as well, largely as a result of feminist activism. In confronting the various forms of violence encountered by women, feminists argue that none of these issues

435

can be understood and dealt with as an isolated "social problem." Rather, the very society in which violence against women thrives must be questioned.

In the 1980s, much feminist attention and debate have been directed toward the violence perpetrated against women through pornography. Feminists are divided on the appropriateness of demands for censorship of pornography, in view of the First Amendment's guarantee of freedom of the press, but some see pornography as a form of violence against women. Around the country, these feminists are organizing to confront pornography, using such methods as public education, media presentations, the introduction of antipornography legislation, and civil disobedience. In recent years some groups have conducted raids on adult bookstores, taking special aim at "snuff" films (films in which the woman is actually murdered at the end) and "kiddie porn" (photos and films of young children being used as sexual objects by adult men). In "Pornography and the Women's Liberation Movement," Diana E. H. Russell, a sociologist and one of the founders of Women against Violence in Pornography and the Media, outlines the reasons she believes pornography is a feminist issue and proposes actions to combat it.

We conclude this section by examining an issue that feminists have championed for more than 50 years, the Equal Rights Amendment (ERA). The ERA was first drafted by the National Woman's Party in 1923, only three years after the passage of the suffrage amendment. Although the ERA failed to win massive support among women for several decades, in the 1970s it became a major issue around which a diverse constituency of women mobilized. In "The Cultural Politics of the ERA's Defeat," Jane Dehart-Mathews and Donald Mathews analyze the reasons that the ERA was defeated even though a majority of Americans favored its ratification.

R E A D I N G   4 7

The First Feminists

JUDITH HOLE AND ELLEN LEVINE

The contemporary women's movement is not the first such movement in American history to offer a wide-ranging feminist critique of society. In fact, much of what seems "radical" in contemporary feminist analysis parallels the critique made by the feminists of the nineteenth century. Both the early and the contemporary feminists have engaged in a fundamental reexamination of the role of women in all spheres of life, and of the relationships of men and women in all social, political, economic and cultural institutions. Both have defined women as an oppressed group and have traced the origin of women's subjugation to male-defined and male-dominated social institutions and value systems.

When the early feminist movement emerged in the nineteenth century, the "woman issue" was extensively debated in the national press, in political gatherings, and from church pulpits. The women's groups, their platforms, and their leaders, although not always well received or understood, were extremely well known. Until recently, however, that early feminist movement has been only cursorily discussed in American history textbooks, and then only in terms of the drive for suffrage. Even a brief reading of early feminist writings and of the few histories that have dealt specifically with the woman movement (as it was called then) reveals that the drive for suffrage became the single focus of the movement only after several decades of a more multi-issued campaign for women's equality.

The woman movement emerged during the 1800s. It was a time of geographic expansion, industrial development, growth of social reform movements, and a

general intellectual ferment with a philosophical emphasis on individual freedom, the "rights of man," and universal education. In fact, some of the earliest efforts to extend opportunities to women were made in the field of education. In 1833, Oberlin became the first college to open its doors to both men and women. Although female education at Oberlin was regarded as necessary to ensure the development of good and proper wives and mothers, the open admission policy paved the way for the founding of other schools, some devoted entirely to women's education.[1] Much of the ground-breaking work in education was done by Emma Willard, who had campaigned vigorously for educational facilities for women beginning in the early 1820s. Frances Wright, one of the first women orators, was also a strong advocate of education for women. She viewed women as an oppressed group and argued that "until women assume the place in society which good sense and good feeling alike assign to them, human improvement must advance but feebly."[2] Central to her discussion of the inequalities between the sexes was a particular concern with the need for equal educational training for women.

It was in the abolition movement of the 1830s, however, that the woman's rights movement as such had its political origins. When women began working in earnest for the abolition of slavery, they quickly learned that they could not function as political equals with their male abolitionist friends. Not only were they barred from membership in some organizations, but they had to wage an uphill battle for the right simply to speak in public. Sarah and Angelina Grimke, daughters of a South Carolina slaveholding family, were among the first to fight this battle. Early in their lives the sisters left South Carolina, moved north, and began to speak out publicly on the abolition issue. Within a short time they drew the wrath of different sectors of society. A pastoral letter from the Council of

the Congregationalist Ministers of Massachusetts typ-
ified the attack:

> The appropriate duties and influence of woman are
> clearly stated in the New Testament. . . . The power
> of woman is her dependence, flowing from the con-
> sciousness of that weakness which God has given
> her for her protection. . . . When she assumes the
> place and tone of man as a public reformer . . . she
> yields the power which God has given her . . . and
> her character becomes unnatural.[3]

The brutal and unceasing attacks (sometimes physical)
on the women convinced the Grimkes that the issues
of freedom for slaves and freedom for women were
inextricably linked. The women began to speak about
both issues, but because of the objections from male
abolitionists who were afraid that discussions of woman's rights would "muddy the waters," they often
spoke about the "woman question" as a separate issue.
(In fact, Lucy Stone, an early feminist and abolitionist,
lectured on abolition on Saturdays and Sundays and
on women's rights during the week.)

In an 1837 letter to the president of the Boston Female Anti-Slavery Society—by that time many female
anti-slavery societies had been established in response
to the exclusionary policy of the male abolitionist
groups—Sarah Grimke addressed herself directly to
the question of woman's status:

> All history attests that man has subjugated woman
> to his will, used her as a means to promote his self-
> ish gratification, to minister to his sensual pleasure,
> to be instrumental in promoting his comfort; but
> never has he desired to elevate her to that rank she
> was created to fill. He has done all he could to de-
> base and enslave her mind; and now he looks
> triumphantly on the ruin he has wrought, and says,
> the being he has thus deeply injured is his infe-
> rior. . . . But I ask no favors for my sex. . . . All I ask
> of our brethren is, that they will take their feet from
> off our necks and permit us to stand upright on that
> ground which God designed us to occupy.[4]

The Grimkes challenged both the assumption of the
"natural superiority of man" and the social institutions predicated on that assumption. For example, in
her *Letters on the Equality of the Sexes . . .* Sarah
Grimke argued against both religious dogma and the

institution of marriage. Two brief examples are
indicative:

> . . . Adam's ready acquiescence with his wife's pro-
> posal, does not savor much of that superiority *in
> strength of mind,* which is arrogated by man.[5]

> . . . [M]an has exercised the most unlimited and
> brutal power over woman, in the peculiar character
> of husband—a word in most countries synony-
> mous with tyrant. . . . Woman, instead of being el-
> evated by her union with man, which might be ex-
> pected from an alliance with a superior being, is in
> reality lowered. She generally loses her individual-
> ity, her independent character, her moral being.
> She becomes absorbed into him, and henceforth is
> looked at, and acts through the medium of her
> husband.[6]

They attacked as well the manifestations of "male superiority" in the employment market. In a letter "On
the Condition of Women in the United States" Sarah
Grimke wrote of

> the disproportionate value set on the time and
> labor of men and of women. A man who is engaged
> in teaching, can always, I believe, command a
> higher price for tuition than a woman—even when
> he teaches the same branches, and is not in any re-
> spect superior to the woman. . . . [Or] for example,
> in tailoring, a man has twice, or three times as
> much for making a waistcoat or pantaloons as a
> woman, although the work done by each may be
> equally good.[7]

The abolition movement continued to expand, and
in 1840 a World Anti-Slavery Convention was held in
London. The American delegation included a group of
women, among them Lucretia Mott and Elizabeth
Cady Stanton. In Volume I of the *History of Woman
Suffrage,* written and edited by Stanton, Susan B. Anthony, and Matilda Joslyn Gage, the authors note that
the mere presence of women delegates produced an
"excitement and vehemence of protest and denuncia-
tion [that] could not have been greater, if the news had
come that the French were about to invade England."[8]
The women were relegated to the galleries and prohibited from participating in any of the proceedings. That

society at large frowned upon women participating in political activities was one thing; that the leading male radicals, those most concerned with social inequalities, should also discriminate against women was quite another. The events at the world conference reinforced the women's growing awareness that the battle for the abolition of Negro slavery could never be won without a battle for the abolition of woman's slavery:

> As Lucretia Mott and Elizabeth Cady Stanton wended their way arm in arm down Great Queen Street that night, reviewing the exciting scenes of the day, they agreed to hold a woman's rights convention on their return to America, as the men to whom they had just listened had manifested their great need of some education on that question.[9]

Mott and Stanton returned to America and continued their abolitionist work as well as pressing for state legislative reforms on woman's property and family rights. Although the women had discussed the idea of calling a public meeting on woman's rights, the possibility did not materialize until eight years after the London Convention. On July 14, 1848, they placed a small notice in the *Seneca* (New York) *Country Courier* announcing a "Woman's Rights Convention." Five days later, on July 19 and 20, some three hundred interested women and men, coming from as far as fifty miles, crowded into the small Wesleyan Chapel (now a gas station) and approved a Declaration of Sentiments (modeled on the Declaration of Independence) and twelve resolutions. The delineation of issues in the Declaration bears a startling resemblance to contemporary feminist writings. Some excerpts are illustrative:[10]

> We hold these truths to be self-evident: that all men and women are created equal; that they are endowed by their Creator with certain inalienable rights; that among these are life, liberty, and the pursuit of happiness. . . .
>
> The history of mankind is a history of repeated injuries and usurpations on the part of man toward woman, having in direct object the establishment of an absolute tyranny over her. To prove this, let facts be submitted to a candid world. . . .
>
> He has compelled her to submit to laws, in the formation of which she has no voice. . . .

> He has made her, if married, in the eye of the law, civilly dead. . . .
>
> He has monopolized nearly all the profitable employments, and from those she is permitted to follow, she receives but a scanty remuneration. He closes against her all the avenues to wealth and distinction which he considers most honorable to himself. As a teacher of theology, medicine, or law, she is not known.
>
> He allows her in church, as well as State, but a subordinate position, claiming Apostolic authority for her exclusion from the ministry, and, with some exceptions, from any public participation in the affairs of the Church.
>
> He has created a false public sentiment by giving to the world a different code of morals for men and women, by which moral delinquencies which exclude women from society, are not only tolerated, but deemed of little account in man.
>
> He has usurped the prerogative of Jehovah himself, claiming it as his right to assign for her a sphere of action, when that belongs to her conscience and to her God.
>
> He has endeavored, in every way that he could, to destroy her confidence in her own powers, to lessen her self-respect, and to make her willing to lead a dependent and abject life.

Included in the list of twelve resolutions was one which read: "*Resolved,* That it is the duty of the women of this country to secure to themselves their sacred right to the elective franchise."

Although the Seneca Falls Convention is considered the official beginning of the woman's suffrage movement, it is important to reiterate that the goal of the early woman's rights movement was not limited to the demand for suffrage. In fact, the suffrage resolution was included only after lengthy debate, and was the only resolution not accepted unanimously. Those participants at the Convention who actively opposed the inclusion of the suffrage resolution feared a demand for the right to vote would defeat others they deemed more rational, and make the whole movement ridiculous. But Mrs. Stanton and Frederick Douglass seeing that the power to choose rulers and make laws, was the right by which all others could be secured, persistently advocated the resolution. . . .[11]

Far more important to most of the women at the Convention was their desire to gain control of their property and earnings, guardianship of their children, rights to divorce, etc. Notwithstanding the disagreements at the Convention, the Seneca Falls meeting was of great historical significance. As Flexner has noted:

> [The women] themselves were fully aware of the nature of the step they were taking; today's debt to them has been inadequately acknowledged. . . . Beginning in 1848 it was possible for women who rebelled against the circumstances of their lives, to know that they were not alone—although often the news reached them only through a vitriolic sermon or an abusive newspaper editorial. But a movement had been launched which they could either join, or ignore, that would leave its imprint on the lives of their daughters and of women throughout the world.[12]

From 1848 until the beginning of the Civil War, woman's rights conventions were held nearly every year in different cities in the East and Midwest. The 1850 convention in Salem, Ohio,

> had one peculiar characteristic. It was officered entirely by women; not a man was allowed to sit on the platform, to speak, or vote. *Never did men so suffer.* They implored just to say a word; but no; the President was inflexible—no man should be heard. If one meekly arose to make a suggestion he was at once ruled out of order. For the first time in the world's history, men learned how it felt to sit in silence when questions in which they were interested were under discussion.[13]

As the woman's movement gained in strength, attacks upon it became more vitriolic. In newspaper editorials and church sermons anti-feminists argued vociferously that the public arena was not the proper place for women. In response to such criticism, Stanton wrote in an article in the Rochester, New York, *National Reformer:*

> If God has assigned a sphere to man and one to woman, we claim the right to judge ourselves of His design in reference to *us,* and we accord to man the same privilege. . . . We have all seen a man making

a jackass of himself in the pulpit, at the bar, or in our legislative halls. . . . Now, is it to be wondered at that woman has some doubts about the present position assigned her being the true one, when her every-day experience shows her that man makes such fatal mistakes in regard to himself?[14]

It was abundantly clear to the women that they could not rely on the pulpit or the "establishment" press for either factual or sympathetic reportage; nor could they use the press as a means to disseminate their ideas. As a result they depended on the abolitionist papers of the day, and in addition founded a number of independent women's journals, including *The Lily, The Una, Woman's Advocate, Pittsburgh Visitor* [*sic*], etc.

One of the many issues with which the women activists were concerned was dress reform. Some began to wear the "bloomer" costume (a misnomer since Amelia Bloomer, although an advocate of the loose-fitting dress, was neither its originator not the first to wear it) in protest against the tight-fitting and singularly uncomfortable cinched-waisted stays and layers of petticoats. However, as Flexner has noted, "the attempt at dress reform, although badly needed, was not only unsuccessful but boomeranged and had to be abandoned."[15] Women's rights advocates became known as "bloomers" and the movement for equal rights as well as the individual women were subjected to increasing ridicule. Elizabeth Cady Stanton, one of the earliest to wear the more comfortable outfit, was one of the first to suggest its rejection. In a letter to Susan B. Anthony she wrote:

> We put the dress on for greater freedom, but what is physical freedom compared with mental bondage? . . . It is not wise, Susan, to use up so much energy and feeling that way. You can put them to better use. I speak from experience.[16]

When the Civil War began in 1861, woman's rights advocates were urged to abandon their cause and support the war effort. Although Anthony and Stanton continued arguing that any battle for freedom must include woman's freedom, the woman's movement activities essentially stopped for the duration of the war. After the war and the ratification of the Thirteenth Amendment abolishing slavery (for which the women activists had campaigned vigorously), the abolitionists began to press for passage of a Fourteenth Amendment to secure the rights, privileges, and immunities of citizens (the new freedmen) under the law. In the second section of the proposed amendment, however, the word "male" appeared, introducing a sex distinction into the Constitution for the first time. Shocked and enraged by the introduction of the word "male," the women activists mounted an extensive campaign to eliminate it. They were dismayed to find that no one, neither the Republican administration nor their old abolitionist allies, had any intention of "complicating" the campaign for Negroes' rights by advocating women's rights as well. Over and over again the women were told, "This is the Negroes' hour." The authors of *History of Woman Suffrage* analyzed the women's situation:

> During the six years they held their own claims in abeyance to the slaves of the South, and labored to inspire the people with enthusiasm for the great measures of the Republican party, they were highly honored as "wise, loyal, and clear-sighted." But again when the slaves were emancipated and they asked that women should be recognized in the reconstruction as citizens of the Republic, equal before the law, all these transcendent virtues vanished like dew before the morning sun. And thus it ever is so long as woman labors to second man's endeavors and exalt *his* sex above her own, her virtues pass unquestioned; but when she dares to demand rights and privileges for herself, her motives, manners, dress, personal appearance, character, are subjects for ridicule and detraction.[17]

The women met with the same response when they campaigned to get the word "sex" added to the proposed Fifteenth Amendment, which would prohibit the denial of suffrage on account of race.[18]

As a result of these setbacks, the woman's movement assumed as its first priority the drive for woman's suffrage. It must be noted, however, that while nearly all the women activists agreed on the need for suffrage, in 1869 the movement split over ideological and tactical questions into major factions. In May of that year, Susan B. Anthony and Elizabeth Cady Stanton organized the National Woman Suffrage Association. Six months later, Lucy Stone and others organized the American Woman Suffrage Association. The American, in an attempt to make the idea of woman's

suffrage "respectable," limited its activities to that issue, and refused to address itself to any of the more "controversial" subjects such as marriage or the church. The National, on the other hand, embraced the broad cause of woman's rights; the vote was seen primarily as a *means* of achieving those rights. During this time Anthony and Stanton founded *The Revolution*, which became one of the best known of the independent women's newspapers. The weekly journal began in January, 1868, and took as its motto "Men, their rights and nothing more; women, their rights and nothing less." In addition to discussion of suffrage, *The Revolution* examined the institutions of marriage, the law, organized religion, etc. Moreover, the newspaper touched on "such incendiary topics as the double standard and prostitution."[19] Flexner describes the paper:

> [It] made a contribution to the women's cause out of all proportion to either its size, brief lifespan, or modest circulation. . . . Here was news not to be found elsewhere—of the organization of women typesetters, tailoresses, and laundry workers, of the first women's clubs, of pioneers in the professions, of women abroad. But *The Revolution* did more than just carry news, or set a new standard for professionalism for papers edited by and for women. It gave their movement a forum, focus, and direction. It pointed, it led, and it fought, with vigor and vehemence.[20]

The two suffrage organizations coexisted for over twenty years and used some of the same tactics in their campaigns for suffrage: lecture tours, lobbying activities, petition campaigns, etc. The American, however, focused exclusively on state-by-state action, while the National in addition pushed for a Woman Suffrage Amendment to the Constitution. Susan B. Anthony and others also attempted to gain the vote through court decisions. The Supreme Court, however, held in 1875[21] that suffrage was not necessarily one of the privileges and immunities of citizens protected by the Fourteenth Amendment. Thus, although women were *citizens*, it was nonetheless permissible, according to the Court, to constitutionally limit the right to vote to males.

During this same period, a strong temperance movement had also emerged. Large numbers of women, including some suffragists, became actively involved in the temperance cause. It is important to note that one of the main reasons women became involved in pressing for laws restricting the sale and consumption of alcohol was that their legal status as married women offered them no protection against either physical abuse or abandonment by a drunken husband. It might be added that the reason separate women's temperance organizations were formed was that women were not permitted to participate in the men's groups. In spite of the fact that temperance was in "woman's interests," the growth of the women's temperance movement solidified the liquor and brewing industries' opposition to woman suffrage. As a result, suffrage leaders became convinced of the necessity of keeping the two issues separate.

As the campaign for woman suffrage grew, more and more sympathizers were attracted to the conservative and "respectable" American Association, which, as noted above, deliberately limited its work to the single issue of suffrage. After two decades "respectability" won out, and the broad ranging issues of the earlier movement had been largely subsumed by suffrage. (Even the Stanton-Anthony forces had somewhat redefined their goals and were focusing primarily on suffrage.) By 1890, when the American and the National merged to become the National American Woman Suffrage Association, the woman's movement had, in fact, been transformed into the single-issue suffrage movement. Moreover, although Elizabeth Cady Stanton, NAWSA's first president, was succeeded two years later by Susan B. Anthony, the first women activists, with their catholic range of concerns, were slowly being replaced by a second group far more limited in their political analysis. It should be noted that Stanton herself, after her two-year term as president of the new organization, withdrew from active work in the suffrage campaign. Although [she had been] one of the earliest feminist leaders to understand the need for woman suffrage, by this time Stanton believed that the main obstacle to woman's equality was the church and organized religion.

During the entire development of the woman's movement, perhaps the argument most often used by anti-feminists was that the subjugation of women was divinely ordained as written in the Bible. Stanton attacked the argument head-on. She and a group of twenty-three women, including three ordained ministers, produced The Woman's Bible,[22] which presented a systematic feminist critique of woman's role and

image in the Bible. Some Biblical chapters were presented as proof that the Scripture itself was the source of woman's subjugation; others to show that, if reinterpreted, men and women were indeed equals in the Bible, not superior and inferior beings. "We have made a fetich [sic] of the Bible long enough. The time has come to read it as we do all other books, accepting the good and rejecting the evil it teaches."[23] Dismissing the "rib story" as a "petty surgical operation," Stanton argued further that the entire structure of the Bible was predicated on the notion of Eve's (woman's) corruption:

> Take the snake, the fruit-tree and the woman from the tableau, and we have no fall, nor frowning Judge, no Inferno, no everlasting punishment;— hence no need of a Savior. Thus the bottom falls out of the whole Christian theology. Here is the reason why in all the Biblical researches and higher criticisms, the scholars never touch the position of women.[24]

Not surprisingly, The Woman's Bible was considered scandalous and sacrilegious by most. The Suffrage Association members themselves, with the exception of Anthony and a few others, publicly disavowed Stanton and her work. They feared that the image of the already controversial suffrage movement would be irreparably damaged if the public were to associate it with Stanton's radical tract.

Shortly after the turn of the century, the second generation of woman suffragists came of age and new leaders replaced the old. Carrie Chapman Catt is perhaps the best known; she succeeded Anthony as president of the National American Woman Suffrage Association, which by then had become a large and somewhat unwieldy organization. Although limited gains were achieved (a number of western states had enfranchised women), no major progress was made in the campaign for suffrage until Alice Paul, a young and extremely militant suffragist, became active in the movement. In April, 1913, she formed a small radical group known as the Congressional Union (later reorganized as the Woman's Party) to work exclusively on a campaign for a federal Woman Suffrage Amendment using any tactics necessary, no matter how unorthodox. Her group organized parades, mass demonstrations, hunger strikes, and its members were on several occasions arrested and jailed.[25] Although many suf-

SISTERSONG

GAY HADLEY

If we should turn against each other now
If we should turn
   to little wars of envy
   seizing castoffs
   cutting patterns from old cloths
   satisfied with remnants from the sun

If we should turn against each other now
If we should turn
   from our own stars
   our primal energy
   pale moonbeams vying
   for a sunken light
What will there be left for us if we should turn
Save one more endless, separated night?

fragists rejected both the militant style and tactics of the Congressional Union, they nonetheless did consider Paul and her followers in large part responsible for "shocking" the languishing movement into activity pressuring for the federal amendment. The Woman Suffrage Amendment (known as the "Anthony Amendment"), introduced into every session of Congress from 1878 on, was finally ratified on August 26, 1920.

Nearly three-quarters of a century had passed since the demand for woman suffrage had first been made at the Seneca Falls Convention. By 1920, so much energy had been expended in achieving the right to vote that the woman's movement virtually collapsed from exhaustion. To achieve the vote alone, as Carrie Chapman Catt had computed, took

> fifty-two years of pauseless campaign . . . fifty-six campaigns of referenda to male voters; 480 campaigns to get Legislatures to submit suffrage amendments to votes; 47 campaigns to get State constitutional conventions to write woman suffrage into state constitutions; 277 campaigns to get State party conventions to include woman suffrage planks; 30 campaigns to get presidential party conventions to adopt woman suffrage planks in party platforms, and 19 campaigns with 19 successive Congresses.[26]

With the passage of the Nineteenth Amendment the majority of women activists as well as the public at large assumed that having gained the vote, women had virtually obtained complete equality.

It must be remembered, however, that for most of the period that the woman's movement existed, suffrage had been seen not as an all-inclusive goal but as a means of achieving equality—suffrage was only one element in the wide-ranging feminist critique questioning the fundamental organization of society. Historians, however, have for the most part ignored this radical critique and focused exclusively on the suffrage campaign. By virtue of this omission they have, to all intents and purposes, denied the political significance of the early feminist analysis. Moreover, the summary treatment by historians of the nineteenth- and twentieth-century drive for woman's suffrage has made that campaign almost a footnote to the abolitionist movement and the campaign for Negro suffrage. In addition, the traditional textbook image of the early feminists—if not wild-eyed women waving placards for the vote, then wild-eyed women swinging axes at saloon doors—has further demeaned the importance of their philosophical analysis.

The woman's movement virtually died in 1920 and, with the exception of a few organizations, feminism was to lie dormant for forty years.

NOTES

1. Mount Holyoke opened in 1837; Vassar, 1865; Smith and Wellesley, 1875; Radcliffe, 1879; Bryn Mawr, 1885.

2. Quoted in Eleanor Flexner, *Century of Struggle: The Woman's Rights Movement in the United States* (Cambridge: Belknap Press of Harvard University Press, 1959), p. 27.

3. *History of Woman Suffrage* (republished by Arno Press and *The New York Times,* New York, 1969), vol. I, p. 81. Hereafter cited as *HWS.* Volumes I–III were edited by Elizabeth Cady Stanton, Susan B. Anthony, and Matilda Joslyn Gage. The first two volumes were published in 1881, the third in 1886. Volume IV was edited by Susan B. Anthony and Ida Husted Harper and was published in 1902. Volumes V and VI were edited by Ida Husted Harper and published in 1922.

4. Sarah M. Grimke, *Letters on the Equality of the Sexes and the Condition of Woman* (Boston: Issac Knapp, 1838, reprinted by Source Book Press, New York, 1970), pp. 10ff.

5. Ibid., pp. 9–10.
6. Ibid., pp. 85–86.
7. Ibid., p. 51.
8. *HWS,* p. 54.
9. Ibid., p. 61.
10. Ibid., pp. 70–73.
11. *HWS,* p. 73.
12. Flexner, p. 77.

13. *HWS,* p. 110.
14. Ibid., p. 806.
15. Flexner, p. 83.
16. Ibid., p. 84.
17. *HWS,* vol. II, p. 51.
18. The Thirteenth Amendment was ratified in 1865; the Fourteenth in 1868; the Fifteenth in 1870.
19. Flexner, p. 151.
20. Ibid.
21. Minor v. Happersett, 21 Wall. 162, 22 L. Ed. 627 (1875).
22. (New York: European Publishing Company, 1895 and 1898. Two parts.)
23. Ibid., pt. 2, pp. 7–8.
24. Stanton, letter to the editor of *The Critic* (New York), March 28, 1896, quoted in Aileen S. Kraditor, *The Ideas of the Woman Suffrage Movement, 1890–1920* (New York: Columbia University Press, 1965), n. 11, p. 86.
25. A total of 218 women from 26 states were arrested during the first session of the Sixty-fifth Congress (1917). Ninety-seven went to prison.
26. Carrie Chapman Catt and Nettie Rogers Shuler, *Woman Suffrage and Politics* (New York, 1923), p. 107; quoted in Flexner, p. 173.

R E A D I N G   4 8

Black Women and Feminism

BELL HOOKS

A large number of black women, many who were young, college-educated, and middle class, were seduced in the 60s and 70s by the romanticized concept of idealized womanhood first popularized during the Victorian age. They stressed that woman's role was

Reprinted from Bell Hooks, *Ain't I A Woman: Black Women and Feminism* (Boston: South End Press, 1981), by permission of the publisher.

that of a helpmate to her man. And for the first time in the history of black civil rights movements, black women did not struggle equally with black men. Writing of the 60s black movement in *Black Macho and the Myth of the Superwoman,* Michelle Wallace comments:

Misogyny was an integral part of Black Macho. Its philosophy, which maintained that black men had been more oppressed than black women, that black women had, in fact, contributed to that oppression, that black men were sexually and morally superior and also exempt from most of the responsibilities human beings had to other human beings, could only be detrimental to black women. But black women were determined to believe—even as their own guts were telling them it was not so—that they were finally on the verge of liberation from the spectre of the omnipotent blonde with the rosebud lips and the cheesecake legs. They would no longer have to admire another woman on the pedestal. The pedestal would be theirs. They would no longer have to do their own fighting. They would be fought for. The knight in white armor would ride for them. The beautiful fairy princess would be black.

The women of the Black Movement had little sense of the contradictions in their desire to be models of fragile Victorian womanhood in the midst of revolution. They wanted a house, a picket fence around it, a chicken in the pot, and a man. As they saw it, their only officially designated revolutionary responsibility was to have babies.

Not all black women succumbed to the sexist brainwashing that was so much a part of black liberation rhetoric, but those who did not received no attention. People in the U.S. were fascinated with the image of the black female—strong, fierce, and independent—meekly succumbing to a passive role, in fact longing to be in a passive role.

Although Angela Davis became a female heroine of the 60s movement, she was admired not for her political commitment to the Communist party, not for any of her brilliant analyses of capitalism and racial imperialism, but for her beauty, for her devotion to black men. The American public was not willing to see the "political" Angela Davis; instead they made of her a poster pinup. In general, black people did not approve of her communism and refused to take it seriously. Wallace writes of Angela Davis:

For all her achievements, she was seen as the epitome of the selfless, sacrificing "good woman"—the only kind of black woman the Movement would accept. She did it for her man, they said. A woman in a woman's place. The so-called political issues were irrelevant.

Contemporary black women who supported patriarchal dominance placed their submission to the status quo in the context of racial politics and argued that they were willing to accept a subordinate role in relationship to black men for the good of the race. They were indeed a new generation of black females—a generation that had been brainwashed not by black revolutionaries but by white society, by the media, to believe that woman's place was in the home. They were the first generation of black women to face competition with white women for the attention of black men. Many of them accepted black male sexism solely because they were afraid of being alone, of not having male companions. The fear of being alone, or of being unloved, had caused women of all races to passively accept sexism and sexist oppression. There was nothing unique or new about the black woman's willingness to accept the sexist-defined female role. The 60s black movement simply became a background in which their acceptance of sexism, or patriarchy, could be announced to the white public that was so convinced that black women were more likely to be assertive and domineering than white women.

Contrary to popular opinion, the sexual politics of the 50s socialized black women to conform to sexist-defined role patterns—not the black macho of the 70s. Black mothers of the 50s had taught their daughters that they should not be proud to work, that they should educate themselves in case they did not find that man who would be the most important force in their lives, who would provide for and protect them. With such a legacy it was not surprising that college-educated black women were embracing patriarchy. The 60s black movement simply exposed a support of sexism and patriarchy that already existed in the black community—it did not create it. Writing of the black woman's response to the 60s civil rights struggle, Michelle Wallace comments:

The black woman never really dealt with the primary issues of the Black movement. She stopped straightening her hair. She stopped using lighteners and brighteners. She forced herself to be submissive and passive. She preached to her children about the glories of the black man. But then, suddenly, the Black movement was over. Now she has begun to straighten her hair again, to follow the latest fashions in *Vogue* and *Mademoiselle,* to rouge her cheeks furiously, and to speak, not infrequently, of what a disappointment the black man has been. She has little contact with other black women, and if she does, it is not of a deep sort. The discussion is generally of clothes, makeup, furniture, and men. Privately she does whatever she can to stay out of that surplus of black women (one million) who will never find mates. And if she doesn't find a man, she might just decide to have a baby anyway.

Now that an organized black civil rights movement no longer exists, black women do not find it necessary to place their willingness to assume a sexist-defined role in the context of black liberation; so it is much more obvious that their support of patriarchy was not engendered solely by their concern for the black race but by the fact that they live in a culture in which the majority of women support and accept patriarchy.

When the movement toward feminism began in the late 60s, black women rarely participated as a group. Since the dominant white patriarchy and black male patriarchy conveyed to black women the message that to cast a vote in favor of social equality of the sexes, i.e. women's liberation, was to cast a vote against black liberation, they were initially suspicious of the white woman's call for a feminist movement. Many black women refused to participate in the movement because they had no desire to fight against sexism. Theirs was not an unusual stance. The great majority of women in the U.S. did not participate in the women's movement for the same reason. White men were among the first observers of the women's movement to call attention to the absence of black women participants, but they did so solely to mock and ridicule the efforts of white feminists. They smugly questioned the credibility of a women's liberation movement that could not attract women from the most oppressed female groups in American society. They were among the first critics of feminism to raise the question of white female racism. In response, white women liberationists urged black and other non-white women to join their ranks. Those black women who were most vehemently anti-feminist were the most eager to respond. Their stance came to be depicted as *the* black female position on women's liberation. They expressed their views in essays like Ida Lewis' "Women's Rights, Why the Struggle Still Goes On," Linda LaRue's "Black Liberation and Women's Lib," "Women's Liberation Has No Soul," first published in *Encore* magazine, and Renee Fergueson's "Women's

Liberation Has a Different Meaning for Blacks." Linda LaRue's comments on women's liberation were often quoted as if they were the definitive black female response to women's liberation:

> Let it be stated unequivocally that the American white women has had a better opportunity to live a free and fulfilling life, both mentally and physically, than any other group in the United States, excluding her white husband. Thus any attempt to analogize black oppression with the plight of American white women has all the validity of comparing the neck of a hanging man with the rope-burned hands of an amateur mountain climber.

In their essays, black female anti-feminists revealed hatred and envy of white women. They expended their energy attacking white women liberationists, not by offering any convincing evidence that would support their claim that black women had no need of women's liberation. Black sociologist Joyce Ladner expressed her views on women's liberation in her study of black women, *Tomorrow's Tomorrow:*

> Many black women who have traditionally accepted the white models of femininity are now rejecting them for the same general reasons that we should reject the white middle-class lifestyle. Black women in this society are the only ethnic or radical group which has had the opportunity to be women. By this I simply mean that much of the current focus on being liberated from the constraints and protectiveness of the society which is proposed by women's liberation groups has never applied to Black women, and in that sense, we have always been "free," and able to develop as individuals even under the most harsh circumstances. This freedom, as well as the tremendous hardships from which black women suffered, allowed for the development of a personality that is rarely described in the scholarly journals for its obstinate strength and ability to survive. Neither is its peculiar humanistic character and quiet courage viewed as the epitome of what the American model of femininity should be.

Ladner's assertion that black women were "free" became one of the accepted explanations for black female refusal to participate in a women's liberation movement. But such an assertion merely reveals that black women who were most quick to dismiss women's liberation had not thought seriously about feminist struggle. For while white women may have seen feminism as a way to free themselves from the constraints imposed upon them by idealized concepts of femininity, black women could have seen feminism as a way to free themselves from constraints that sexism clearly imposed on their behavior. Only a very naive unenlightened person could confidently state that black women in the U.S. are a liberated female group. The black women who patted themselves on the back for being "already liberated" were really acknowledging their acceptance of sexism and their contentment with patriarchy.

The concentrated focus on black anti-feminist thought was so pervasive that black women who supported feminism and participated in the effort to establish a feminist movement received little attention, if any. For every black anti-feminist article written and published, there existed a pro-feminist black female position. Essays like Cellestine Ware's "Black Feminism," Shirley Chisholm's "Women Must Rebel," Mary Ann Weather's "An Argument for Black Women's Liberation as a Revolutionary Force," and Pauli Murray's "The Liberation of Black Women" all expressed black female support of feminism.

As a group, black women were not opposed to social equality between the sexes but they were not eager to join with white women to organize a feminist movement. The 1972 Virginia Slims American Women's Opinion Poll showed that more black women supported changes in the status of women in society than white women. Yet their support of feminist issues did not lead them as a collective group to actively participate in the women's liberation movement. Two explanations are usually given for their lack of participation. The first is that the 60s black movement encouraged black women to assume a subservient role and caused them to reject feminism. The second is that black women were, as one white women liberationist put it, "repelled by the racial and class composition of the women's movement." Taken at face value, these reasons seem adequate. Examined in a historical context in which black women have rallied in support of women's rights despite pressure from black men to assume a subordinate position, and despite the fact that white middle and upper class women have dominated every women's movement in

the U.S., they seem inadequate. While they do provide justification for the anti-feminist black female position, they do not explain why black women who support feminist ideology refuse to participate fully in the contemporary women's movement.

Initially, black feminists approached the women's movement white women had organized eager to join the struggle to end sexist oppression. We were disappointed and disillusioned when we discovered that white women in the movement had little knowledge of or concern for the problems of lower class and poor women or the particular problems of non-white women from all classes. Those of us who were active in women's groups found that white feminists lamented the absence of large numbers of non-white participants but were unwilling to change the movement's focus so that it would better address the needs of women from all classes and races. Some white women even argued that groups not represented by a numerical majority could not expect their concerns to be given attention. Such a position reinforced the black female participants' suspicion that white participants wanted the movement to concentrate not on the concerns of women as a collective group, but on the individual concerns of the small minority who had organized the movement.

Black feminists found that sisterhood for most white women did not mean surrendering allegiance to race, class, and sexual preference, to bond on the basis of the shared political belief that a feminist revolution was necessary so that all people, especially women, could reclaim their rightful citizenship in the world. From our peripheral position in the movement we saw that the potential radicalism of feminist ideology was being undermined by women who, while paying lip service to revolutionary goals, were primarily concerned with gaining entrance into the capitalist patriarchal power structure. Although white feminists denounced the white male, calling him an imperialist, capitalist, sexist, racist pig, they made women's liberation synonymous with women obtaining the right to fully participate in the very system they identified as oppressive. Their anger was not merely a response to sexist oppression. It was an expression of their jealousy and envy of white men who held positions of power in the system while they were denied access to those positions.

Individual black feminists despaired as we witnessed the appropriation of feminist ideology by elitist, racist white women. We were unable to usurp leadership positions within the movement so that we could spread an authentic message of feminist revolution. We could not even get a hearing at women's groups because they were organized and controlled by white women. Along with politically aware white women, we, black feminists, began to feel that no organized feminist struggle really existed. We dropped out of groups, weary of hearing talk about women as a force that could change the world when we had not changed ourselves. Some black women formed "black feminist" groups which resembled in almost every way the groups they had left. Others struggled alone. Some of us continued to go to organizations, women's studies classes, or conferences, but were not fully participating.

For ten years now I have been an active feminist. I have been working to destroy the psychology of dominance that permeates Western culture and shapes female/male sex roles and I have advocated reconstruction of U.S. society based on human rather than material values. I have been a student in women's studies classes, a participant in feminist seminars, organizations, and various women's groups. Initially I believed that the women who were active in feminist activities were concerned about sexist oppression and its impact on women as a collective group. But I became disillusioned as I saw various groups of women appropriating feminism to serve their own opportunistic ends. Whether it was women university professors crying sexist oppression (rather than sexist discrimination) to attract attention to their efforts to gain promotion; or women using feminism to mask their sexist attitudes; or women writers superficially exploring feminist themes to advance their own careers, it was evident that eliminating sexist oppression was not the primary concern. While their rallying cry was sexist oppression, they showed little concern about the status of women as a collective group in our society. They were primarily interested in making feminism a forum for the expression of their own self-centered needs and desires. Not once did they entertain the possibility that their concerns might not represent the concerns of oppressed women.

Even as I witnessed the hypocrisy of feminists, I clung to the hope that increased participation of women from different races and classes in feminist activities would lead to a reevaluation of feminism, radical reconstruction of feminist ideology, and the

launching of a new movement that would more adequately address the concerns of both women and men. I was not willing to see white women feminists as "enemies." Yet as I moved from one women's group to another trying to offer a different perspective, I met with hostility and resentment. White women liberationists saw feminism as "their" movement and resisted any efforts by non-white women to critique, challenge, or change its direction.

During this time, I was struck by the fact that the ideology of feminism, with its emphasis on transforming and changing the social structure of the U.S., in no way resembled the actual reality of American feminism. Largely because feminists themselves, as they attempted to take feminism beyond the realm of radical rhetoric into the sphere of American life, revealed that they remained imprisoned in the very structures they hoped to change. Consequently, the sisterhood we talked about has not become a reality. And the women's movement we envisioned would have a transformative effect on U.S. culture has not emerged. Instead, the hierarchical pattern of sex-race relationships already established by white capitalist patriarchy merely assumed a different form under feminism. Women liberationists did not invite a wholistic analysis of woman's status in society that would take into consideration the varied aspects of our experience. In their eagerness to promote the idea of sisterhood, they ignored the complexity of woman's experience. While claiming to liberate women from biological determinism, they denied women an existence outside that determined by our sexuality. It did not serve the interest of upper and middle class white feminists to discuss race and class. Consequently, much feminist literature, while providing meaningful information concerning women's experiences, is both racist and sexist in its content. I say this not to condemn or dismiss. Each time I read a feminist book that is racist and sexist, I feel a sadness and an anguish of spirit. For to know that there thrives in the very movement that has claimed to liberate women endless snares that bind us tighter and tighter to old oppressive ways is to witness the failure of yet another potentially radical, transformative movement in our society.

Although the contemporary feminist movement was initially motivated by the sincere desire of women to eliminate sexist oppression, it takes place within the framework of a larger, more powerful cultural system that encourages women and men to place the fulfillment of individual aspirations above their desire for collective change. Given this framework, it is not surprising that feminism has been undermined by the narcissism, greed, and individual opportunism of its leading exponents. A feminist ideology that mouths radical rhetoric about resistance and revolution while actively seeking to establish itself within the capitalist patriarchal system is essentially corrupt. While the contemporary feminist movement has successfully stimulated an awareness of the impact of sexist discrimination on the social status of women in the U.S., it has done little to eliminate sexist oppression. Teaching women how to defend themselves against male rapists is not the same as working to change society so that men will not rape. Establishing houses for battered women does not change the psyches of the men who batter them, nor does it change the culture that promotes and condones their brutality. Attacking heterosexuality does little to strengthen the self-concept of the masses of women who desire to be with men. Denouncing housework as menial labor does not restore to the woman houseworker the pride and dignity in her labor she is stripped of by patriarchal devaluation. Demanding an end to institutionalized sexism does not ensure an end to sexist oppression.

The rhetoric of feminism with its emphasis on resistance, rebellion, and revolution created an illusion of militancy and radicalism that masked the fact that feminism was in no way a challenge or a threat to capitalist patriarchy. To perpetuate the notion that all men are creatures of privilege with access to a personal fulfillment and a personal liberation denied women, as feminists do, is to lend further credibility to the sexist mystique of male power that proclaims all that is male is inherently superior to that which is female. A feminism so rooted in envy, fear, and idealization of male power cannot expose the de-humanizing effect of sexism on men and women in American society. Today, feminism offers women not liberation but the right to act as surrogate men. It has not provided a blueprint for change that would lead to the elimination of sexist oppression or a transformation of our society. The women's movement has become a kind of ghetto or concentration camp for women who are seeking to attain the kind of power they feel men have. It provides a forum for the expression of their feelings of anger, jealousy, rage, and disappointment with men. It provides an atmosphere where women who have little in common, who may resent or even feel indifferent to

one another, can bond on the basis of shared negative feelings toward men. Finally, it gives women of all races who desire to assume the imperialist, sexist, racist positions of destruction men hold with a platform that allows them to act as if the attainment of their personal aspirations and their lust for power is for the common good of all women.

Right now, women in the U.S. are witnessing the demise of yet another women's rights movement. The future of collective feminist struggle is bleak. The women who appropriated feminism to advance their own opportunistic causes have achieved their desired ends and are no longer interested in feminism as a political ideology. Many women who remain active in women's rights groups and organizations stubbornly refuse to critique the distorted analysis of woman's lot in society popularized by women's liberation. Since these women are not oppressed they can support a feminist movement that is reformist, racist, and classist because they see no urgent need for radical change. Although women in the U.S. have come closer to obtaining social equality with men, the capitalist-patriarchal system is unchanged. It is still imperialist, racist, sexist, and oppressive.

The recent women's movement failed to adequately address the issue of sexist oppression, but that failure does not change the fact that it exists, that we are victimized by it to varying degrees, nor does it free any of us from assuming responsibility for change. Many black women are daily victimized by sexist oppression. More often than not we bear our pain in silence, patiently waiting for a change to come. But neither passive acceptance nor stoic endurance lead to change. Change occurs only when there is action, movement, revolution. The 19th century black female was a woman of action. Her suffering, the harshness of her lot in a racist, sexist world, and her concern for the plight of others motivated her to join feminist struggle. She did not allow the racism of white women's rights advocates or the sexism of black men to deter her from political involvement. She did not rely on any group to provide her with a blueprint for change. She was a maker of blueprints. In an address given before an audience of women in 1892 Anna Cooper proudly voiced the black woman's perspective on feminism:

Let woman's claim be as broad in the concrete as in the abstract. We take our stand on the solidarity of humanity, the oneness of life, and the unnatu-

THE BRIDGE POEM

DONNA KATE RUSHIN

I've had enough
I'm sick of seeing and touching
Both sides of things
Sick of being the damn bridge for everybody

Nobody
Can talk to anybody
Without me
Right?

I explain my mother to my father my father to my
    little sister
My little sister to my brother my brother to the
    white feminists
The white feminists to the Black church folks the
    Black church folks
To the ex-hippies the ex-hippies to the Black
    separatists the
Black separatists to the artists the artists to my
    friends' parents . . .

Then
I've got to explain myself
To everybody

I do more translating
Than the Gawdamn U.N.

Forget it
I'm sick of it

I'm sick of filling in your gaps

Sick of being your insurance against
The isolation of your self-imposed limitations

Sick of being the crazy at your holiday dinners
Sick of being the odd one at your Sunday Brunches
Sick of being the sole Black friend to 34 individual
    white people

Find another connection to the rest of the world
Find something else to make you legitimate
Find some other way to be political and hip

I will not be the bridge to your womanhood
Your manhood
Your human-ness

I'm sick of reminding you not to
Close off too tight for too long

I'm sick of mediating with your worst self
On behalf of your better selves

I am sick
Of having to remind you
To breathe
Before you suffocate
Your own fool self

Forget it
Stretch or drown
Evolve or die

The bridge I must be
Is the bridge to my own power
I must translate

My own fears
Mediate
My own weaknesses

I must be the bridge to nowhere
But my true self
And then
I will be useful

ralness and injustice of all special favoritism, whether of sex, race, country, or condition. If one link of the chain is broken, the chain is broken. A bridge is no stronger than its weakest part, and a cause is not worthier than its weakest element. Least of all can woman's cause afford to decry the weak. We want, then, as toilers for the universal triumph of justice and human rights, to go to our homes from this Congress demanding an entrance not through a gateway for ourselves, our race, our sex, or our sect, but a grand highway for humanity. The colored woman feels that woman's cause is one and universal; and that not till the image of God whether in parian or ebony, is sacred and inviolable; not till race, color, sex, and condition are seen as accidents, and not the substance of life; not till the universal title of humanity to life, liberty, and the pursuit of happiness is conceded to be inalienable to all; not till then is woman's cause won—not the white woman's, nor the black woman's, nor the red woman's, but the cause of every man and of every woman who has writhed silently under a mighty wrong. Woman's wrongs are thus indissolubly linked with all undefended woe, and the acquirement of her "rights" will mean the final triumph of all right over might, the supremacy of the moral forces of reason, and justice, and love in the government of the nations of earth.

Cooper spoke for herself and thousands of other black women who had been born into slavery, who because they had been severely victimized, felt a compassion and a concern for the plight of all oppressed peoples. Had all women's rights advocates shared their sentiments, the feminist movement in the U.S. would be truly radical and transformative.

Feminism is an ideology in the making. According to the Oxford English Dictionary, the term "feminism" was first used in the latter part of the 19th century and it was defined as having the "qualities of females." The meaning of the term has been gradually transformed and the 20th century dictionary definition of feminism is a "theory of the political, economic, and social equality of the sexes." To many women this definition is inadequate. In the introduction to *The Remembered Gate: Origins of American Feminism* Barbara Berg defines feminism as a "broad movement embracing numerous phases of woman's emancipation." She further states:

It is the freedom to decide her own destiny; freedom from sex-determined role; freedom from society's oppressive restrictions; freedom to express her thoughts fully and to convert them freely to actions. Feminism demands the acceptance of woman's right to individual conscience and judgment. It postulates that woman's essential worth stems from her common humanity and does not depend on the other relationships of her life.

Her expanded definition of feminism is useful but limited. Many women have found that neither the struggle for "social equality" nor the focus on an "ideology of woman as an autonomous being" are enough to rid society of sexism and male domination. To me feminism is not simply a struggle to end male chauvinism or a movement to ensure that women will have equal rights with men; it is a commitment to eradicating the ideology of domination that permeates Western culture on various levels—sex, race, and class, to name a few—and a commitment to reorganizing U.S. society so that the self-development of people can take precedence over imperialism, economic expansion, and material desires. Writers of a feminist pamphlet published anonymously in 1976 urged women to develop political consciousness:

In all these struggles we must be assertive and challenging, combating the deep-seated tendency in Americans to be liberal, that is, to evade struggling over questions of principle for fear of creating tensions or becoming unpopular. Instead we must live by the fundamental dialectical principle: that progress comes only from struggling to resolve contradictions.

It is a contradiction that white females have structured a women's liberation movement that is racist and excludes many non-white women. However, the existence of that contradiction should not lead any woman to ignore feminist issues. Oftentimes I am asked by black women to explain why I would call myself a feminist and by using that term ally myself with a movement that is racist. I say, "The question we must ask again and again is how can racist women call themselves feminists." It is obvious that many women have appropriated feminism to serve their own ends, especially those white women who have been at the forefront of the movement; but rather than resigning myself to this appropriation I choose to re-appropriate the term "feminism," to focus on the fact that to be "feminist" in any authentic sense of the term is to want for all people, female and male, liberation from sexist role patterns, domination, and oppression.

Today masses of black women in the U.S. refuse to acknowledge that they have much to gain by feminist struggle. They fear feminism. They have stood in place so long that they are afraid to move. They fear change. They fear losing what little they have. They are afraid to openly confront white feminists with their racism or black males with their sexism, not to mention confronting white men with their racism and sexism. I have sat in many a kitchen and heard black women express a belief in feminism and eloquently critique the women's movement, explaining their refusal to participate. I have witnessed their refusal to express these same views in a public setting. I know their fear exists because they have seen us trampled upon, raped, abused, slaughtered, ridiculed and mocked. Only a few black women have rekindled the spirit of feminist struggle that stirred the hearts and minds of our 19th century sisters. We, black women who advocate feminist ideology, are pioneers. We are clearing a path for ourselves and our sisters. We hope that as they see us reach our goal—no longer victimized, no longer unrecognized, no longer afraid—they will take courage and follow.

REFERENCES

Berg, B. 1979. *The remembered gate: Origins of American feminism.* New York: Oxford University Press.

Chisholm, S. 1970. "Racism and anti-feminism." *The Black Scholar,* pp. 40–45.

Cooper, J. 1892. *A voice from the South.* Xenia, Ohio.

Ladner, J. 1972. *Tomorrow's tomorrow.* New York: Anchor Books.

Wallace, M. 1978. *Black macho and the myth of the super woman.* New York: Dial Press.

Ware, C. 1970. *Woman power.* New York: Tower.

R E A D I N G   4 9

Not for Lesbians Only
CHARLOTTE BUNCH

The following is an expanded and revised version of a speech given at the Socialist Feminist Conference, Antioch College, Yellow Springs, Ohio, July 5, 1975. Many of the ideas expressed here about lesbian feminist politics were first developed several years ago in The Furies. Nevertheless, I am continually discovering that most feminists, including many lesbians, have little idea what lesbian feminist politics is. This speech takes those basic political ideas and develops them further, particularly as they relate to socialist feminism.

I am listed in your program as Charlotte Bunch-Weeks, a rather ominous slip of the tongue (or slip in historical timing) that reflects a subject so far avoided at this conference that I, for one, want to talk about.

Five years ago, when I *was* Charlotte Bunch-Weeks, and straight, and married to a man, I was also a socialist feminist. When I left the man and the marriage, I also left the newly developing socialist feminist movement—because, for one reason, my politics then, as now, were inextricably joined with the way I lived my personal, my daily life. With men, with male politics, I was a socialist; with women, engaged in the articulation of women's politics, I became a lesbian feminist—and, in the gay–straight split, a lesbian feminist separatist.

It's that gay–straight split that no one here seems to want to remember—and I bring it up now, not because I want to relive a past painful to all concerned, but because it is an essential part of our political history which, if ignored, will eventually force lesbians to withdraw again from other political women. There were important political reasons for that split, reasons explicitly related to the survival of lesbians—and those reasons and the problems causing them are still with us. It is important—especially for political groups who wish to give credence and priority to lesbian issues—to remember why separatism happened, why it is not a historical relic but still vital to the ongoing debate over lesbianism and feminism.

In my own personal experience, I, and the other women of The Furies collective, left the women's movement because it had been made clear to us that there was no space to develop a lesbian feminist politics and life style without constant and nonproductive conflict with heterosexual fear, antagonism, and insensitivity. This was essentially the same experience shared by many other lesbian feminists at about the same time around the country. What the women's movement could not accept then—and still finds it difficult to accept—is that lesbianism is political: this is the essence of lesbian feminist politics. Sounds simple. Yet most feminists still view lesbianism as a personal decision or, at best, as a civil rights concern or a cultural phenomenon. Lesbianism is more than a question of civil rights and culture, although the daily discrimination against lesbians is real and its alleviation through civil libertarian reforms is important. Similarly, although lesbianism is a primary force in the emergence of a dynamic women's culture, it is much more. Lesbian feminist politics is a political critique of the institution and ideology of heterosexuality as a cornerstone of male supremacy. It is an extension of the analysis of sexual politics to an analysis of sexuality itself as an institution. It is a commitment to women as a political group, which is the basis of a political/economic strategy leading to power for women, not just an "alternative community."

There are many lesbians still who feel that there is no place in socialist feminist organizations in particular, or the women's movement in general, for them to develop that politics or live that life. Because of this, I am still, in part, a separatist; but I don't want to be a total separatist again; few who have experienced that kind of isolation believe it is the ultimate goal of liberation. Since unity and coalition seem necessary, the question for me is unity on what terms? with whom? and around what politics? For instance, to unify the lesbian feminist politics developed within the past four years with socialist feminism requires more than token reference to queers. It requires an acknowledgement of lesbian feminist analysis as central to understanding and ending woman's oppression.

The heart of lesbian feminist politics, let me repeat, is a recognition that heterosexuality as an institution and an ideology is a cornerstone of male supremacy. Therefore, women interested in destroying male supremacy, patriarchy, and capitalism must, equally with lesbians, fight heterosexual domination—or we will never end female oppression. This is what I call "the heterosexual question"—it is *not* the lesbian question.

Although lesbians have been the quickest to see the challenge to heterosexuality as a necessity for feminists' survival, straight feminists are not precluded from examining and fighting against heterosexuality. The problem is that few have done so. This perpetuates lesbian fears that women remaining tied to men prevents them from seeing the function of heterosexuality and acting to end it. It is not lesbianism (women's ties to women) but heterosexuality (women's ties to men), and thus men themselves, which divides women politically and personally. This is the "divisiveness" of the lesbian issue to the women's movement. We won't get beyond it by demanding that lesbians retreat, politics in hand, back into the closet. We will only get beyond it by struggling over the institutional and ideological analysis of lesbian feminism. We need to discover what lesbian consciousness means for any woman, just as we struggle to understand what class or race consciousness means for women of any race or class. And we must develop strategies that will destroy the political institutions that oppress us.

It is particularly important for those at this conference to understand that heterosexuality—as an ideology and as an institution—upholds all those aspects of female oppression discussed here. For example, heterosexuality is basic to our oppression in the workplace. When we look at how women are defined and exploited as secondary, marginal workers, we recognize that this definition assumes that all women are tied to men. I mention the workplace because it upset me yesterday at the economics panel that no one made that connection; and further, no one recognized that a high percentage of women workers are lesbians and therefore their relationship to, and attitudes toward, work are fundamentally different from those assumed by straight workers. It is obvious that heterosexuality upholds the home, housework, the family as both a personal and economic unit. It is apparently not so obvious that the whole framework of heterosexuality defines our lives, that it is fundamental to the negative self-image and self-hatred of women in this society. Lesbian feminism is based on a rejection of male definitions of our lives and is therefore crucial to the development of a positive woman-identified identity, of redefining who we are supposed to be in every situation, including the workplace.

What is that definition? Basically, heterosexuality means men first. That's what it's all about. It assumes that every woman is heterosexual; that every woman is defined by and is the property of men. Her body, her services, her children belong to men. If you don't accept that definition, you're a queer—no matter who you sleep with; if you do not accept that definition in this society, you're queer. The original imperialist assumption of the right of men to the bodies and services of women has been translated into a whole variety of forms of domination throughout this society. And as long as people accept that initial assumption—and question everything *but* that assumption—it is impossible to challenge the other forms of domination.

What makes heterosexuality work is heterosexual privilege—and if you don't have a sense of what that privilege is, I suggest that you go home and announce to everybody that you know—a roommate, your family, the people you work with—everywhere you go—that you're a queer. Try being a queer for a week. Do not walk out on the street with men; walk only with women, especially at night, for example. For a whole week, experience life as if you were a lesbian, and I think you will know what heterosexual privilege is

very quickly. And, hopefully, you will also learn that heterosexual privilege is the method by which women are given a stake in male supremacy—and that is therefore the method by which women are given a stake in their own oppression. Simply stated, a woman who stays in line—by staying straight or by refusing to resist straight privileges—receives some of the benefits of male privilege indirectly and is thus given a stake in continuing those privileges and maintaining their source—male supremacy.

Heterosexual women must realize—no matter what their personal connection to men—that the benefits they receive from men will always be in diluted form and will ultimately result in their own self-destruction. When a woman's individual survival is tied to men, she is at some intrinsic place separated from other women and from the survival needs of those other women. The question arises not because of rhetorical necessity—whether a woman is personally loyal to other women—but because we must examine what stake each of us has in the continuation of male supremacy. For example, if you are receiving heterosexual benefits through a man (or through his social, cultural, or political systems), are you clear about what those benefits are doing to you, both personally and in terms of other women? I have known women who are very strong in fighting against female job discrimination, but when the battle closes in on their man's job, they desert that position. In universities, specifically, when a husband's job is threatened by feminist hiring demands, I have seen feminists abandon their political positions in order to keep the privileges they receive from their man's job.

This analysis of the function of heterosexuality in women's oppression is available to any woman, lesbian or straight. Lesbian feminism is not a political analysis "for lesbians only." It is a political perspective and fight against one of the major institutions of our oppression—a fight that heterosexual women can engage in. The problem is that few do. Since lesbians are materially oppressed by heterosexuality daily, it is not surprising that we have seen and understood its impact first—not because we are more moral, but because our reality is different—and it is a *materially* different reality. We are trying to convey this fact of our oppression to you because, whether you feel it directly or not, it also oppresses you; and because if we are going to change society and survive, we must all attack heterosexual domination.

R E A D I N G   5 0

Pornography and the Women's Liberation Movement
DIANA E. H. RUSSELL

Why have most women in the Women's Movement shied away from pornography as a woman's issue for so long? This is an important question. Until a greater portion of the Women's Movement is with us on this, we aren't going to get very far. The fact is that an incredible, scary hate campaign against women has been escalating in the last eight years with scarcely a peep of protest from most feminists. Only with the "snuff" movies can we talk of the movement taking action. But after the "snuff" movies left town—temporarily—so did most of the action.

Why?

I believe there are many reasons. First, because we have observed that the anti-pornography forces have almost always been conservative, homophobic, antisex, and pro the traditional family. They have equated nudity and explicit sex with pornography. They are often against abortion, the Equal Rights Amendment, and the Women's Liberation Movement. We have been so put off by the politics of these people that our knee-jerk response is that we must be *for* whatever they are *against.*

But we don't have to ally ourselves with them. We haven't yet. And we won't! The women amongst them can relate to our focus on the abuse of women by pornography better than we can relate to the "sin" approach. They can come to us if they can accept the rest of our politics too.

The second reason why most feminists have so far ignored the issue of pornography is that most of us

bought the male liberal and radical line that being against any aspect of the so-called sexual revolution meant being a reactionary, unliberated prude. Men were seen as the sexually liberated sex, women the sexually repressed sex. To be liberated, women at least had to tolerate and accept male sex trips, including pornography, and sometimes try to imitate them, as in *Playgirl* magazine. But all this assumes that there can be a sexual revolution without a sex-*role* revolution too, and that change means women changing to be more like men. No thank you!

The third reason for neglecting this issue is that most of us have refused to look at pornography ourselves. It is painful to face the hatred of women so evident in it. While we resent what we are *forced* to see in our newspaper ads, in the grocery stores, in the red-light-district posters and neon signs, few of us follow through and say, "My Goddess! This stuff is hateful. I need to check out what is going on *inside* some of these places!" Like some Jews in Germany early on in the Nazi period who didn't want to read the writing on the wall, many women prefer not to know the depth and dangerousness of misogyny. Heterosexual women in particular have a hard time facing this aspect of male culture, since they don't want to see this side of the men they relate to. But most lesbians haven't made an issue out of it either, and a few have even confused male abuse of lesbians in pornography with lesbian pornography. Far more disturbing yet, some actually argue that sadomasochistic sex is fun and healthy for lesbians. Sadly, few of us have been immune to the liberal-radical line on pornography.

A fourth reason is that we have been deceived like everybody else by the male scientists and so-called experts who claim that there is no evidence showing that pornography is harmful. We are told that pornography helped diminish the problem of rape and other sex crimes in Denmark, that this is a fact, and that any feelings we may have to the contrary about pornography are irrational. But new research and a more thor-

Reprinted from Diana E. H. Russell, "Pornography and the Women's Liberation Movement," in *Take Back the Night,* ed. Laura Lederer (New York: William Morrow, 1980), pp. 301–96, by permission of the author.

This article was first presented as the concluding speech at the Feminist Perspectives on Pornography conference in 1978, where Diana E. H. Russell, a founding member of Women against Violence in Pornography and Media, gave her views on how the Women's Movement should proceed to fight pornography.

ough analysis of the existing research has revealed that this was an irresponsible conclusion of the Commission on Obscenity and Pornography, as well as of many other almost exclusively male scientists who have done similar research.

A fifth reason why so few feminists have confronted pornography is that we have often, for practical and strategic reasons, taken a piecemeal approach to problems. We focus on battered women, or rape, or the molestation of female children, or whatever. But all these crimes against women are linked. How can we stop rape and woman-battering by staffing rape-crisis centers and refuges when there are thousands of movie houses, millions of publications, a multibillion-dollar business that promote the idea that violence and the rape of women is sexually exciting to men, and that *we* like it too?

Sixth, as with prostitution, many of us get confused by the argument that it is an issue of survival (money) for some women. This is true, and I think it's important to recognize that women's role in pornography is not the primary problem. It is the men who profit most from it, and who are its consumers, who must be attacked and exposed. But beyond that, we cannot automatically support every institution which happens to provide some money for some women. The German concentration camps did that too. We *have* to consider whether the institution is operating in such a way as to be destructive to women as a *class*. Money aside, many women, including ex-pornography models, have made a strong case for the destructive effect on the women involved.

Seventh, there is a fear that being anti-pornography means we are necessarily pro-censorship. For people who have worked through all the other reasons, this one often still bothers them. So I'd like to spend a little more time on it.

With few exceptions, most feminists, as well as liberal and radical nonfeminists, have been so hung up on the censorship issue that they have refused to allow themselves to recognize pornography as a problem for women, refused to analyze what is going on in pornography and why, and refused even to allow themselves to *feel* outraged by it. We have largely remained silent while this ever more conspicuous and vicious campaign against us has been mounted—even though it is impossible to open our newspapers to the entertainment section and not see something of what is going on, at least in this city.

I wish we could end this short-circuiting in our thinking and feeling. It seems to me there are four distinct and important steps in dealing with a social problem.

1. First, we need to *recognize* it. Many problems are never recognized as such. The murder of women, for example, is still hidden by the word homicide. There are very few murders of women by women—when we are murdered it is almost always by men. We have to recognize *fem*icide before we can consider why the problem exists and what can be done about it.
2. The second step involves *feeling* about the problem once it is recognized. To simply acknowledge rape, woman-battering, woman-hatred in pornography and not *feel* outraged is another kind of unhealthy short-circuiting that goes on.
3. Third, we need to try to understand the *cause* of the problem, to analyze it, before we can take action. If, for example, our analysis of rape is that it happens rarely and a few crazy men are responsible, clearly it has very different implications than if we see rape as an extreme acting out of the socially sanctioned male role.
4. And, finally, there is the question of what to do about it. In the case of pornography it is only at step four that the issue of the pros and cons of censorship or banning comes up, and it is only one of many, many questions. Equally important are questions on the pros and cons of civil disobedience, demonstrations, boycotts, education, petitions, legal suits, or the use of more militant tactics.

In the case of pornography many people, including feminists, don't allow themselves to contemplate the first three steps—is pornography a problem, is it a woman's problem, and if so, what do I *feel* about this problem? Why does this problem exist? They simply say, "I'm against censorship of any kind!" And the meaning of the First Amendment becomes the topic of discussion. In this way the freedom of speech issue has been used, not always consciously, to freeze us into saying and doing nothing against pornography.

I would hope that whatever your particular view is on the First Amendment in relation to pornography, *you* will avoid this short-circuiting process, and you will point out to others when they are doing it. I believe that to act together we have to be in agreement regarding the first steps of recognition, feeling, and analysis. We also have to be able to agree on some actions we think are worth doing. But we don't have to agree on the banning issue.

I personally believe that portraying women being bound, raped, beaten, tortured, and killed for so-called sexual stimulation and pleasure should be banned, because I believe these portrayals encourage and condone these crimes against women in the real world. People seem to have forgotten that many individual liberties are curtailed by all societies for the perceived welfare of the whole society. Examples in the United States are polygamy, marriage or sex with individuals below a certain age, incest, cannibalism, slavery, rape, homicide, assault, and, absurdly, homosexuality. The point is that all societies have found it necessary to outlaw many forms of violent and exploitive behavior, and thereby deny individuals the right to act out certain impulses. Sometimes, of course, prejudice and ignorance are behind these restrictions, as in the case of homosexuality. But it is clear that pornography is not such a case. I do not see myself as unconcerned about free speech and the First Amendment. And I am quite happy to work with other feminists who disagree with my position on banning pornography.

However, working to obtain laws to bar violent pornography does not seem to me to be a *priority* strategy at this time. Not that I believe in any one strategy to the exclusion of others. I think a multi-strategy approach is appropriate, with women choosing tactics in keeping with their politics, their skills, and their circumstances. However, I do believe action is necessary—lots of it—and soon! Change is not brought about by magic spells or ardent wishes.

I want to say more about civil disobedience, a strategy that I believe would be particularly effective for women in this country at this time.

I believe this strategy has lost some of its appeal as an effective tool because its victories for Black people in this country seemed very short-lived and insufficient. But women as a caste are obviously in a very different situation from Blacks as a caste, and I believe some of these differences would make civil disobedience much more effective for women.

The depth of concern about an issue is sometimes measured by willingness to pay a price of some kind, e.g., the inconvenience and indignity of arrest. The suffragettes' fight is a case in point. But if the tactics used scare and threaten the public, as happened with the Weathermen or the SLA (Symbionese Liberation Army), for example, then they are likely to backfire. Civil disobedience shows commitment and concern in a very dramatic way without making people feel so threatened.

When a minority group engages in civil disobedience, it ultimately depends on the often nonexistent goodwill of the majority whether demands are met or not. Women are not only a majority but are so integrated into the male world, particularly in the family, that we cannot be isolated and ghettoized in the same way that members of minority groups have been. If wives and girl friends are being arrested for actions against pornography, husbands and lovers are going to have to deal with it. First, they will have to take care of children and/or the household—itself a consciousness-raiser. They will be *made* to care about pornography, at least in this indirect way, because it will affect them negatively in a way they can recognize.

Another way in which civil disobedience is a particularly suitable tactic is that most of us don't relish being violent. Civil disobedience is therefore much easier for us to practice than for men.

Hence, a factor that is often a *strategic* weakness for us—our integration with the male population—becomes a strength. A factor that is often a *tactical* weakness for us—a common unwillingness to meet violence with violence—becomes a strength. And to the extent that we are badly treated by the police in this situation, we will gain all the more support for our cause. This is not to say that those of us who are less integrated into the male world—particularly lesbians—don't have an important place in this struggle. We have the advantage of not having to deal with male resistance in our homes, which is why we have played and continue to play such a key role in the Women's Movement. This also means we would probably be among the first to take the risks necessary to show how powerful civil disobedience can be as a strategy for women on this and other issues.

Women have been taking life-and-death risks for centuries. Simply by being women, we risk being raped. Many of us are hassled at work or beaten at home because we are women. Some of these risks we cannot avoid. Some risks perhaps we can. Continuing to live with a violent husband or lover, for example, is very, very risky. Indeed, marrying someone we barely know, or even someone we know very well, can be very risky in a society that does not recognize rape within marriage, and in which the interests of males are so entrenched both legally and socially. I would like to urge all of us to examine our lives and see if there isn't a way to take fewer personal risks and more political risks.

The time has surely come for us to face the vi-ciously sexist nature of pornography; to confront this form of the male backlash; and to spread the word to other women that we will have to organize to take action, to stop this dangerous anti-women propaganda. By taking more political risks where necessary, women may need to take fewer personal risks later on.

R E A D I N G   5 I

The Cultural Politics of the ERA's Defeat

JANE DEHART-MATHEWS AND DONALD MATHEWS

The defeat of the Equal Rights Amendment seemed virtually impossible in the spring of 1972. The Senate had joined the House of Representatives to submit the amendment to the states by an impressively lopsided vote of eighty-four to eight, suggesting that ratification would come as the natural product of the explosive egalitarianism of the 1960s. The exhilaration of confrontation with authority and the excitement of what was thought to be rapid change had made the word *revolution* universal currency in the political marketplace. The civil rights revolution, the student revolution, and the cultural revolution telegraphed an impatience with the past and a hope for significant social change shared by some within government (the War on Poverty), as well as by those attacking its policies in Vietnam.

Young women, caught up in the vortex of protest, became self-conscious revolutionaries on their own behalf as they came to understand that personal experience separated them not only from the structure that they defied but also from male comrades whose limited understanding of sexual equality was epitomized by the draft resisters' slogan: "Girls Say Yes to Guys Who Say No." Joining with other women who differed substantially in style and ideology, these new feminists challenged a male-defined "reality." The

mood of giddy optimism and dead seriousness was captured in a pamphlet published by the National Organization for Women entitled *Revolution: The Time Is NOW.* What was not fully appreciated in 1972 was that with revolutions come counterrevolutionaries. That these should have been women as well as men, and that they should have been as assertive as feminists, suggests something of the cultural ramifications of defeat.

Although there is no consensus to explain the ERA's defeat, there are several theories. For the victors, it resulted from an uprising of the people against irresponsible elites who had too long used government to meddle in private concerns. It was also a rejection of the feminist ideal of what women ought to be, an ideal that threatened to destroy the American family and sap the strength of a society already crippled by moral permissiveness and political weakness and indecision. Ratificationists had other explanations. Some—following the political axiom "If you can't defeat your enemies, attack your friends"—charged that Jimmy Carter had not done enough. Others claimed that banks and insurance companies, together with the Church of Jesus Christ of Latter Day Saints, spent great sums of money to defeat the amendment. Conservatives throughout the religious spectrum of Protestant-Catholic-Mormon-Jew had combined to resist subversion of patriarchal supremacy. Traditionalist male legislators had thwarted the public will. Men did

Reprinted by permission from the Organization of American Historians *Newsletter* 10, 4 (November 1982): 13–15.

it (which of course they did). It escaped no one's notice that archconservatives used the ratification fight to enlist otherwise elusive moderates in striking at the heart of liberalism—the commitment to equality. Finally, there was the manner in which anti-ERA women attacked ratification. It was a seemingly alarmist, shrill, hysterical, and perverse assault. Proponents believe that opponents lied and screamed the amendment to death.

In the process of a struggle over ratification, it became clear that, for conservatives as well as young radicals of the sixties, the personal had become political. But it was personal in a manner that did not seem authentic to pro-ERA activists. It did not arise from recognition of oppression and the conviction that sexism could be rooted out of laws, institutions, and customs. Nor did it come from an understanding of complex patterns of behavior and values that had socialized individuals in a male-defined culture. Rather, politicization of the personal came from women whose personal and familial experience made them wary of changes that would transform their way of life. Involved was defense against what was perceived as an attack upon them by feminists, resistance to placing their daughters and themselves in danger, and an assertion of self in a public drama. It is the meaning of this response that is the key to understanding opposition to the ERA and, by implication, the cultural context of its defeat.

Charges against the amendment had ranged over a broad spectrum to warn of "danger!" Ratification presumably would have meant drafting young mothers for combat. It would have meant the sexual integration of public restrooms, decriminalization of rape, legitimation of homosexuality, further entrenchment of abortion as a medical choice, increased opportunities for mischief from an interventionist federal bureaucracy, the loss by women of legal privileges, and the destruction of the American family. Responding to what they believed to be alarmist apocalypticism, ratificationists attempted to show how each objection was exaggerated, irrelevant, highly unlikely, or simply untrue. Taken altogether, the opposition seemed to be irrational and senseless or, at best, the political contrivance of a manipulative right.

Behind what proponents thought was senseless, however, there was and continues to be a pattern that lies within, behind, and beyond expressions of opposition—the elusive subjective experiences that anti-ERA women share with each other. These experiences flow from patterns of behavior and shared ways of talking about self and community. They provide coherence to one's life from the inner, subjective life of the individual, through common, everyday interaction with intimates, and beyond into the public life of work, social role, and frequently politics. Theorist Charles Taylor calls this coherence *intersubjective meanings,* the subjective experience of the social body, the meaning experienced in social practices that lies behind the flawed and incomplete expressions of it in public debate. Anti-ERA women no more doubted the authenticity of their position than did ratificationists, and for the same reason: subjective confirmation that they were right.

Public discourse is the window into the meaning that sustained anti-ratificationists. Take, for example, the draft. One of the most damaging charges was that the ERA would force young women into combat. Children carried signs reading "Please don't send my mommy to war!" When ratification was first debated, Americans had become accustomed to the images of terror and death flashing from their television screens. These images of danger overlay those of young men opposing the war, fleeing the draft, and deserting the army. Eventual withdrawal from Vietnam was part of this pattern of flight from masculine responsibility. The strength of America had been sapped. Somehow the women's movement was part of the degeneracy, the confusion of a society in which the authenticity of behavior and values based on the most basic and elementary fact of human life—sex—had been denied by misguided radicals. America was becoming a unisex society, said Phyllis Schlafly in disgust.

Within this mental context, women in the military meant a flight from responsibility by men and an anomalous intrusion by women into places where they had no reason to be. The facts that women were already in the military and that they had not been treated equitably there were irrelevant to opponents of the ERA. Women stepping out of female roles were women-who-want-to-be-men—anomalous persons who rejected the kind of life that nature (God and sex) had ordained. The implication of punishment for stepping outside of traditional roles was inherent in the dangers awaiting women in uniform. Thus, behind, under, and imminent in the image of women in combat was a cry of danger, the accusation of anomaly, and the implied threat of punishment.

ERA

ED STEIN

Ed Stein. Courtesy of the Rocky Mountain News.

The charge that the amendment would mandate the decriminalization of rape is the kind of alarmist mystification often characterizing right-wing rhetoric. While untrue, it does represent the sense of personal vulnerability that women felt when faced with the jumbled meanings of change associated with gender over the past fifteen years. For women who had so internalized traditional female roles that the very concepts of sexual oppression and emancipation seemed absurd, the temptation to reduce the ERA to an absurdity was irresistible. "If you *really* mean to enforce the law without reference to sex, you would have to wipe out all sex crimes. And, if you deny that, you do so because sex really does make a difference in how people should be treated, and this feminist blabbering about equality is just so much hokum." Beneath the accusation lay a sense of danger, the anomalous treatment of men and women as if "the same," and just punishment (rape) of women so foolish as to believe the sexes really were "the same."

This confusion of equality with sameness, and therefore, with absurdity and danger, was also linked with impurity represented by anomalous men—homosexuals. Identification of gay liberation with women's liberation and the latter with the ERA was not a tortured reading of the contemporary feminist movement or of the sexual revolution, although it had nothing to do with legal equality guaranteed by the proposed Twenty-seventh Amendment. The words of the ERA, "on account of sex," were joined with "sexual preference" or homosexuality to evoke loathing, fear, and anger at the grotesque perversion of masculine responsibility represented by the women's movement. The linkage was a matter not so much of logic as of intuition. It is significant that although lesbians were identified in antifeminist politics as women-who-want-to-be-men, they were not nearly so threatening to antifeminists as homophiles, or men-who-refuse-to-be-men.

Charges that the ERA would entrench abortion, mandate sexual integration of public restrooms, and destroy the family seemed as irrelevant and mistaken to ratificationists as association of the amendment with homosexuality. Yet these indictments revealed the social-subjective reality underlying the opposition. The danger inherent in the cry that abortion was murder and that the ERA was the same as abortion is obvious. "Equality is the right of everyone," wrote a constituent to his senator, "but this ERA is a bad bill. No one, man or woman, has any right to murder babies."

Although ratificationists include pro-life as well as pro-choice partisans, identification of the ERA with abortion is pervasive and persistent. It is made not only for political reasons, but also because the conjunction represents feminists' presumed hatred of the biological function for which their sex has prepared them. The anomalous merges with the dangerous to allow condemnation of sexual irresponsibility—the trivialization of the sacred process by which human reproduction occurs. Women seeking abortion are women-who-refuse-to-be-mothers, which means women-who-refuse-to-be-women: anomalies. Implicit in the accusation that the availability of abortion allows "them" to "get off the hook" is an indignant sense of responsibility evaded and punishment denied.

As for the "potty issue," sexually integrated public restrooms became for pro-ERA activists a cross between comic relief and chronic despair. The image gathers in subconscious connections and anxieties which express more than the niceties implied in the term *ladies' lounge.* Restrooms had been integrated once before, that is, by race. And the word *integration* evokes memories of struggle over racial equality. Linking sexual equality with racial integration, ERA opponents parodied the latter with the "potty parable." Some troublemaker, denied access to the toilet of the opposite sex, would take the matter to the Supreme Court, which once again would order integrated facilities. It is not surprising that opponents of ratification should evoke roars of approval by pleading with state legislators not to "de-sexigrate" us.

Whether or not a serious statement, the idea of "integration" clearly captured the imagination of people who thought that the idea of equality—whether sexual or racial—was ridiculous. The ridicule seemed deserved, because equality was interpreted as sameness. As such, sexual equality implied a utopian, willful attempt to ignore cultural implications of a biological distinction. The sense of anomaly ran like a rich lode through the subterranean ethos of antifeminist argument. Objections to integrated toilets expressed in a different fashion the same diffuse sense of disbelief, frustration, and anxiety that was expressed in the emphatic "We don't want to be men." There was almost a religious intensity about the process, as if by calling attention to the anomalous, antifeminists could cleanse themselves of the defilement of traditional roles perceived to have been heaped upon them by feminists (women-who-want-to-be-men).

NATIONAL ORGANIZATION FOR CHANGING MEN: STATEMENT OF PRINCIPLES

The National Organization for Changing Men is an activist organization supporting positive changes for men today. NOCM advocates a male-positive, pro-feminist and gay-affirmative perspective. Open to men and women, it is committed to a broad goal of personal and social change.

We believe that the new opportunities becoming available to women and men will be beneficial to both. Men can live as happier and more fulfilled human beings by challenging the old-fashioned rules of masculinity that embody the assumption of male superiority.

Traditional masculinity includes many positive characteristics in which we take pride and find strength, but it also contains qualities that have limited and harmed us. Our love of men and our joy in being men move us to protest the ways men are wounded and alienated in this society. Our understanding of how each man is damaged enables us to understand how others are damaged.

As an organization for changing men, we strongly support the continuing struggle of women for full equality. We applaud and support the insights and positive social changes that feminism

has stimulated for both women and men. We oppose such injustices to women as economic and legal discrimination, rape, domestic violence, sexual harassment, and many others. Women and men can and do work together as allies to change the injustices that have so often made them see one another as enemies.

One of the strongest and deepest anxieties of most American men is their fear of homosexuality. This homophobia contributes directly to the many injustices experienced by gay, lesbian and bisexual persons, and is a debilitating restriction for heterosexual men. We call for an end to all forms of discrimination based on sexual-affectional orientation, and for the creation of a gay-affirmative society.

We acknowledge too that many people are oppressed today because of their race, class, age and religion and physical condition. We believe that such injustices are vitally connected to sexism, with its fundamental premise of unequal distribution of power.

Our goal is to change not just ourselves and other men but also the institutions that create inequality. We welcome any person who agrees in substance with these principles to membership in the NATIONAL ORGANIZATION FOR CHANGING MEN.

Reprinted with permission from the By-Laws of the National Organization for Changing Men.

The words *equality* and *integration* were also part of a generalized claim that the ERA would help to undermine the American family. Although vague and all-inclusive, the charge was meaningful for a variety of reasons. Many women understood the amendment to be a part of a feminist agenda to strip women of social roles defined by sex, which would mean that "mother" would be less an ideological or cultural concept than a biological one. The implied danger to the family was clear to nonfeminists; but it was also clear that the issue was not family life but rather its traditional form: father (head and provider), mother (nurturer and manager), and children (replicas of the older genera-

tion). The internal dynamics and quality of relationships independent of form were not so important to anti-ERA, pro-family forces as the ability of the father to stay out of the family, the mother to stay out of the job market, and children to stay out of public child-care facilities.

Changing the form of the family—or even acknowledging that there could be various forms—defied the orthodoxy of social roles defined by sex. The underlying sense beneath this accusation of antifamily engineering was represented in three images: loss of children, attack on homemakers, and the escape of husbands and fathers from financial responsibility.

One of the most striking examples of losing one's children was their being "bused" from their homes into distant neighborhoods to achieve "racial balance." That represents to many parents their helplessness before a bureaucracy not directly responsible to them. Policies of the courts and the Department of Health, Education, and Welfare (now Health and Human Services) represented intrusions by the federal government into family life which would have been broadened by the ERA. If ratificationists argued that fears of such invasion were absurd, their opponents replied that no one had expected the absurdity of busing, either.

These and other responses to ratification suggest that the assault on the ERA was an assault on the ideal of equality. This displaced aggression was made possible by labeling feminism and sexual equality as absurd and dangerous. That was not a sleight-of-hand trick by conservative politicians and businessmen, although there is no doubt that both groups fought the amendment and that ultraright organizations such as the John Birch Society and Eagle Forum exploited the issue to their own advantage. It is also true that conservative religious leaders played upon the fears of traditionalist women to defeat ratification. More significant, however, was resistance expressed in evocative rhetoric that suggested a base of "intersubjective meanings" of womanhood and sex. Whether in New Jersey or New York or Iowa or North Carolina, women repudiated state or federal equal rights amendments because they had become the symbol of feminism, an ideology profoundly alien to their experience of what it meant to be a woman. One did not have to be manipulated by men or become gullible dupes of the patriarchy in order to resist the claims of feminists to speak for women. The process of socialization to which feminists were so sensitive had been as subtle and indelible as theorists said it was, allowing for an interpretation of personal experience that had been

not only meaningful but perhaps even rewarding for women who believed that they were defending themselves in fighting the ERA.

To understand this aspect of the ratification struggle as a conflict over the meaning of womanhood is to place it within a broad context of historical process that has yet to run its course. The great numbers of Americans responsible for the steady drift to the right since the presidential election of 1972 could see in the issue of sexual equality—if successfully identified as absurd and dangerous—a way to achieve political advantage. Anything so engraved in us as experiences of what sex means could create a broad base for conservative recruitment, especially in a postwar climate of conservatism. That was especially true after the identification of sexual behavior with political liberation in the sixties. When the personal became political for the "left," the same thing was quite natural for the right. The result was the fusion of the ERA with both feminism and liberalism.

That does not mean that in the long run either will have lost. Every historian knows that historical and cultural change is rarely abrupt. Changes within a generation are swift; the "intersubjective meanings" passed from generation to generation result from a dialectic of which the defeat of the ERA is only one act among many stretching back in the past. The social base of feminism and protofeminism is much more secure now than in 1920. Although the experiences of women since that time have broadened considerably—the social base required for change—the failure of the ERA in 1982 was not as significant as the fact that a majority of Americans favored ratification. Given this achievement, the ideological concessions made to sexual equality by conservatives may yet provide political capital for a renewed effort to elaborate the insights of feminism and the genius of American egalitarianism and to lessen the weight of cultural baggage.

The Future of Feminism

We have learned from the earlier selections that the feminist movement has had a decided influence on institutions, individual consciousness, and intimate relationships. Yet the movement has still not attained its ultimate objective: the creation of a society in which the double standard in all its forms has been eradicated. The principles on which the movement is based require fundamental and major restructuring of all our established institutions. It is partly because the ultimate goals are based on a *revision* of society and partly because the movement has been relatively successful in mobilizing activists and achieving some of its lesser goals (e.g., changes in rape and battering laws, the establishment of affirmative action programs, an increase in the numbers of women in the professions and in law and medical schools, the passage of credit bills and homemaker bills, the recognition of abortion rights, the establishment of women's studies, and textbook revisions) that the feminist movement continues to meet powerful and sustained opposition.

It is fitting, then, that we end our analysis by examining some of the challenges confronting feminism. Women's struggle for equality is not simply an American one. Indicative of the international scope of the women's movement is the fact that in July 1985, 13,500 women converged in Nairobi, Kenya, to mark the end of the United Nations Decade for Women. Nilüfer Çağatay, Caren Grown, and Aida Santiago, in "The Nairobi Women's Conference: Toward a Global Feminism?" discuss the constructive dialogue that took place in Nairobi between First World and Third World women. Recognizing that women are a potential force at the global level, the delegates came away from the conference with a renewed commitment to pursue equality for all women in the political, social, and economic realms. Verta Taylor's article "The Future of Feminism: A Social Movement Analysis" examines the structure, strategies, ideas, and new directions of the American women's movement since the 1970s.

We conclude, then, not by mourning the passing of the peak of feminist activism in the early 1970s but by celebrating the resiliency of those who continue, even in the face of strong opposition, to build a movement committed to the establishment of a just and nonsexist society. History has taught us that patriarchy will not wither away; it is only through feminist struggle that society will be transformed. Such is the theme of the song "The Rock Will Wear Away," written in 1976 by the feminist composers Meg Christian and Holly Near and sung by women in the movement at protests, feminist celebrations, and other public events throughout the years since then. The theme of its chorus—many small, weak entities joining together to defeat a larger, strong one—still stands as the challenge facing feminists of the future.

The Nairobi Women's Conference: Toward a Global Feminism?

NILÜFER ÇAĞATAY, CAREN GROWN, AND AIDA SANTIAGO

In the end we will find the way to be united, if even to be united in diversity. And all of us will take home with us the richness of this experience, the awareness of the difficulties, and a renewed faith in the justice of our cause.

> Margarita Papandreou,
> Nairobi, Kenya, July 1985

In July 1985, women from all over the globe gathered in Nairobi, Kenya, to mark the culmination of the United Nations Decade for Women. Bringing diverse experiences, concerns, and visions, women engaged in ten days of intense discussions, dialogues, cultural exchange, and celebration. For many of us who had the opportunity to participate in what turned out to be the largest world gathering of women ever, it was a momentous event that will leave its stamp on our future activities and consciousness.

Established in 1975 at the first International Women's Conference in Mexico City, the Decade for Women had as its goals the eradication of underdevelopment, the quest for peace, and the pursuit of equality for women in all forms of political, economic, and social life. Delegates to the Mexico City conference laid out an ambitious World Plan of Action with a series of recommendations for governments to follow during the next ten years. A parallel nongovernmental tribunal took place in which women activists raised and discussed issues similar to those on the U.S. agenda. Five years later in Copenhagen, governmental

Reprinted from *Feminist Studies* 12, no. 2 (Summer 1986): 401–12, by permission of the publisher, Feminist Studies, Inc., c/o Women's Studies Program, University of Maryland, College Park, MD 20742.

delegates and nongovernmental representatives reconvened to assess the progress (or lack of it) made during the first half of the decade and to evaluate a Program of Action for the second half.[1]

Although the Copenhagen meetings represented a step forward for women around the world, they unfolded in a contentious atmosphere that left some participants skeptical about the usefulness of such future world gatherings.[2] For reasons that will be discussed below, we believe that the nature of the discussions in Nairobi were qualitatively different from those that took place in the previous conferences. Indeed, the Nairobi gathering provided an opening for wider reflection on such issues as the nature of development and the meanings of feminism around the globe. In what follows, we would like to address several questions. First, what were the most important aspects of the nongovernmental (NGO) forum? What differentiated it from the earlier meetings? Second, what were the underlying factors that account for these differences? Have there been changes in women's consciousness and organization and, if so, how can we explain them? Third, can we speak of feminism(s) on a global scale? Finally, to answer the question of "What next?" we will point out areas that women agreed need further attention.

The NGO meeting in Nairobi (known as Forum '85) was the site of over 1,000 activities, including panels and workshops; a multitude of cultural events; a film festival; a Tech n' Tools Appropriate Technology Fair; and the Peace Tent, an arena for discussions of feminist alternatives for peace.[3] The attendance figure for Forum '85 was approximately 13,500, much higher than expected and far exceeding the two previous world gatherings. As the majority of those attending came from the Third World, the composition of Forum '85 was more representative of the world population than that of previous conferences in Copenhagen and Mexico City. Approximately 3,000 were Kenyan women, most of whom came from rural areas. The composition of U.S. participants was also noticeably different, for of the 2,500, close to one-half were women of color. In general, delegates included organizers and activists, professional and grass roots, poor, rich, and middle-class women. They represented diverse ethnicities, class backgrounds, sexual preferences, and political perspectives.[4]

One of the strengths of the Nairobi gathering was the recognition and acceptance that women have diverse perspectives, issues, and priorities. In Copenhagen, by contrast, the denial of this reality by many of the most vocal women was manifested in a division among First World and Third World women. A significant number of First World women advocated confining the Copenhagen forum to issues they perceived as common to all women independent of nationality, race, and class. On the other hand, a minority of First World and most Third World women argued that gender oppression cannot be separated from national, class, or racial oppression. These two different approaches to women's oppression were at the core of some of the most heated exchanges at the Copenhagen forum.

There were those among First World women who argued that the focus on "women's issues" got lost within such discussions as the New International Economic Order, the Situation of Women in Palestine, or Women under Apartheid. Thus, they charged that Copenhagen became a "politicized" conference—politicized in the sense that these issues detracted from those "common" to all women. It is worth pointing out the differences among those who held this view. Some arrived at this position because of the limited nature of their definition of feminism. A number of others, who were not conscious of the role played by their governments in the world economy, felt uncomfortable with discussions characterizing imperialism and colonialism as a source of women's problems in the Third World. Although this reaction came more from ignorance than anything else, a third group of people took this view as a result of their identification with official Western governmental positions. In contrast, Third World women, together with a minority of First World women, insisted that political issues are women's issues and that women's issues are not

monolithic. These tensions were left unresolved, and many thus came away from Copenhagen uncertain about the prospects for future international solidarity actions and concerned about moving beyond the divisiveness.

We think that there are several reasons why the tenor of discussions in Nairobi turned out to be so different from those of Copenhagen. First, women's groups, determined not to repeat the outcome of Copenhagen, prepared intensively for Forum '85. Researchers and activists all around the world began to integrate (both analytically and practically) gender, class, and race in more effective ways. This led to the understanding among women's organizations (particularly those in the First World) that feminism must deal with survival issues if it is to be relevant to women's lives throughout the world. At the same time, Third World feminists realized that it is fundamental for national liberation movements to struggle around women's specific issues—however women may define them. Therefore, the greater diversity of views in Nairobi generated a wealth of information on ways in which women's struggles are carried out within different contexts.

The widespread recognition that political issues are women's issues, and that the women's movement is a fundamentally political movement, was an important change from 1980. In this context, it was possible to discuss all issues—global and local—that affect the lives of women, as part of the agendas of women's movements around the globe and the social revolution they have come to be. Thus, no one group of women determined the scope of questions; no one group prevented political and challenging discussion on problems some considered to be outside the realm of feminism.

A second factor that contributed to a qualitatively different conference in Nairobi was the fact that it was held in an African country. As a result of being in a region affected by severe crises (of debt and of food, fuel, and water availability), many women from advanced capitalist countries gained their first direct understanding of the effects of underdevelopment. Observing firsthand the reality of Third World women's lives tempered the arrogance of many First World women. At the same time, Third World women were able to express their positions and concerns in a familiar environment.

Third, world economic, social, and political conditions in 1985 were not as bright as they were ten—or even five—years earlier. Women in particular have borne a greater share of the negative consequences of the world crisis and the accompanying ideological movement toward conservatism and religious fundamentalism evident in the United States and in parts of the Third World.[5] This in turn reinforced the commonality of many women's experiences with gender subordination. The sense of urgency to address problems of poverty, debt, famine, international militarization, and violence from women's perspectives set the stage for wide-ranging and productive dialogue in most Forum '85 workshops.

Between 1980 and 1985, women in the United States experienced severe ideological and economic setbacks. The effects of the economic crisis were manifested in high unemployment rates and the increasing impoverishment of women. The Reagan administration increased military expenditures while slashing welfare programs and those social services that could have helped to alleviate poor people's increasing misery. At the same time, a rising right-wing fundamentalist movement focused its attacks on women's reproductive rights, freedom for sexual expression, struggle for comparable worth and affirmative action, and women's demands for equality in general. Accompanying these domestic antiwomen/antipoor/antiminority policies was the increasingly militaristic posture of the U.S. government abroad. Policies of intervention and foreign domination whipped up sentiments of macho manhood and national chauvinism in the United States. Thus, many U.S. feminists began to see more clearly the connections between the internal and external components of the right's agenda.

In the face of social and economic losses suffered in particular by poorer women and by women of color, it became more apparent that the mainstream feminist movement in the United States did not adequately speak for the needs of the majority of North American women. The proponents of liberal feminism began to realize that the gains of the seventies were both limited and reversible. Also throughout this period, women of color and some white feminists strongly criticized the racism of many white women within the feminist movement and emphasized the need to see gender through the core experiences of race and class. Daily reports on the African famine and the international debt crisis made it impossible to ignore the broader problems of poverty and underdevelopment and con-

tributed to making First World feminists more sensitive to the specific conditions faced by Third World women. Rethinking feminism beyond sexual egalitarianism, therefore, has become a central task for many within the North American feminist movement.

For Third World women, the effects of the crisis since 1980 have been severe and have exacerbated the failure of past development policies.[6] Two of the most pressing issues are the debt crisis and unavailability of food in many parts of the Third World. Both of these crises, the results of long-term structural problems within the world economy, the international financial and monetary system, and skewed patterns of income distribution, have decreased women's access to and control over productive resources and lengthened their working day. Proposed solutions continue to emphasize a growth-centered approach to development and neglect women's central positions as producers and reproducers.

The general economic crisis has also been accompanied by growing violence within the home; attacks on women's civil status, physical mobility, and control over their reproduction. In many parts of the Third World, traditional religion, often with the support of the state, is being used to return women to their "proper" place in the family. Popular fears of the breakdown of the traditional family structure and culture have been played on, often in a carefully organized manner. The proponents of religious fundamentalism have projected these moves as a nationalist reaction to the economic crisis and the role of U.S. imperialism on a world scale and have attracted many young adherents. One important component of these reactions entails a significant glorification of women's roles within the family as wives and mothers. Yet this glorification of traditional values is often at odds with the increasing need for women's income from nonhousehold production as a result of the crisis.[7]

Third World women have confronted this configuration of forces in multifaceted ways. They have amassed a large body of evidence criticizing existing development policies and strategies and proposing alternative directions and methodologies. There has been a proliferation of local and regional efforts to organize women around alternative economic proposals as well as around ideological struggles. During the past several years, Third World feminists began to question the traditional left's subordination of gender issues to class contradictions, demanding a more integrated analysis and program. In Peru, for example, this resulted in the active participation of feminists in the recent electoral campaign under the ticket of the Izquierda Unida (United Left). Two feminists ran as independents on a platform of leftist and explicitly feminist demands. Although they did not win the election, the women's campaign raised many feminist issues throughout the country for the first time. A second example is the campaign of *democracia en el país y en la casa* in Chile, in which feminists have attempted to extend the concept of democracy in the country to democracy within the home. In India, the Self-Employed Women's Association (SEWA) developed out of the trade union movement to organize specifically around the needs of women engaged in informal-sector activities, including handicraft and home-based production, small-scale retail trade, petty food production, and other services. As this type of employment is low-waged and highly unstable, a core element of SEWA's program includes the provision of credit, coupled with other necessary economic and social services, to those who are most marginalized.

Regional feminist research and action networks were created and have now been consolidated in all parts of the Third World. They include the Women and Development Unit of the University of the West Indies in Barbados; the Association of African Women for Research and Development, based in Dakar, Senegal; the Asian Women's Research and Action Network in the Philippines; and the Pacific and Asian Women's Forum. Women's studies centers exist in most Third World countries, including the Centro de Investigación para la Acción Feminina in the Dominican Republic, Anveshi in India, and Flora Tristan in Peru. Women's studies journals are also flourishing in the Third World. Links have grown among women from the "south," as demonstrated by the regional meetings held in Latin America, Africa, Asia, and the Pacific during the past five years. These meetings constituted the basis for sharing analyses and strategies to combat the common denominators of gender subordination within the context of the interrelated crises.

The transformations in First World women's consciousness and the consolidation of feminisms in the Third World thus helped to make constructive dialogue in Nairobi possible. First World and Third World women shared different, but often converging, perspectives on a number of issues without the divisiveness that marked many such exchanges in Copen-

hagen. This can best be illustrated by examples drawn from several panel and workshop discussions.[8]

First, the issue of clitoridectomy was extremely contentious in Copenhagen, partly because a group of women from the North attempted to both define the problem for and impose their own plan of action on Third World women. In Nairobi, the issue was discussed in a very different context. Third World women took the lead in examining the health and related problems of clitoridectomy, and they discussed the issue in ways that are consonant with their cultures.

Second, women from the Third World, with the collaboration of women from the West, passed a major resolution opposing the cutoff of U.S. funds to the United Nations Fund for Population Activities for family planning activities in the Third World. The resolution denounced the activities of the so-called prolife groups and called for safe and accessible methods of family planning that would protect women's health and allow women to control their fertility. Convergence around this resolution is significant in light of exchanges at previous conferences. The failure of orthodox development policies in the postwar period has often been blamed on high population growth. Family planning programs have therefore been designed as a component of development projects with population control objectives. Such programs have aroused strong suspicion and opposition among Third World women. It has been difficult to separate birth control programs from population control policies. The complexity has not been clearly understood by many First World feminists who advocate birth control as a primary feminist objective. Although Third World women desire to control their fertility, the lack of medically safe alternatives and the antinatalism of policy planners has led them to oppose the implementation of many family planning programs. Previous conferences reflected these conflicting perspectives and made it difficult for First World and Third World women to come together.

A third example is the discussion that took place on lesbianism. Prior to Forum '85, rumors circulated that both the Kenyan government and Forum organizers intended to censor discussions, materials, and films on lesbianism. However, Forum organizers took every precaution to ensure that lesbian issues, as women's issues, would be given the space to be freely discussed in as open an atmosphere as possible. Both First and

Third World women expressed and gave support when the issue was in danger of becoming either suppressed or sensationalized.[9] Again, this was possible because the issue had been discussed in the context of feminism in many parts of the Third World, most notably at the three Latin American feminist *encuentros* (encounters) and at informal gatherings in several Asian countries during the latter half of the Decade.

Fourth, there was a noticeable convergence on such issues as international debt and reform of the monetary and financial system. One condition of International Monetary Fund (IMF) loans to Third World governments stipulates wage and price policies that redistribute income from wages to profits, as well as increase unemployment. Women from the West took up the call for a moratorium on debt payments from the most heavily indebted countries and demanded that the IMF and other financial institutions located in the West take the burden off the Third World poor and make structural adjustments of their own. The connections were drawn between the role of the U.S. government and multinational corporations in the current crisis and the impoverished conditions of the poor—particularly women in affected areas.

Finally, we would like to mention the Peace Tent, creatively designed as an arena for the discussion of such issues as international militarization, East–West disarmament, and regional peace initiatives. The enthusiastic participation of women from all over demonstrated that peace is a fundamental concern in every region. Workshops underscored, however, that peace and the struggle against violence cannot be achieved without the alleviation of poverty, economic justice, national liberation, and development oriented to these ends. Perhaps most interestingly, a fundamental purpose of the Peace Tent was to serve as an avenue for the resolution of conflicts and tensions arising from panel and workshop discussions, indicating another aspect of women's determination to engage in productive and peaceful dialogue, even on issues that have historically divided them by nationality, class, or race.

We do not want to convey only an idyllic image of 13,500 women coming to unified positions on "correct" priorities, approaches, or strategies to be pursued. Although the Nairobi meeting affirmed that women are constituting themselves as a potential force on a global scale, we still live in a world divided by profound social, political, and economic inequalities and hierarchies. At times, conflicting views resulted in

vocal clashes. However, we do not think these were the dominant features of Forum '85, even though they were given prominent coverage by the mainstream media.[10] Rather, Nairobi marks a new stage in our understandings about the struggle for social transformation.

The Forum discussions could not generate the blueprints for such global and regional strategies, nor should we have expected them to. What can be achieved in a ten-day conference, especially one that "officially" prohibits final resolutions, platforms, or statements, is limited. Women have only recently begun to identify and discuss ways to tackle problems that are the products of complex historical processes. It would be naive to expect that women alone will or can devise the solutions to world-scale questions. As feminists, we are striving for a fundamental restructuring of the social and economic order, one that does not reproduce the hierarchies under which we presently live. To accomplish this, we need to develop more concrete and powerful strategies at the local, regional, and global levels; to strengthen our links and networks; to be supportive and aware of each other's struggles; and to be in positions to ensure that the implementation of our visions has a longer-lasting impact.

It is now time to organize both formal and informal local and regional gatherings, to "transcreate" what we learned from the diversity of women at Nairobi. By "transcreation" we mean the appropriation of those concepts, experiences, and initiatives developed by diverse women and their reformulation in ways that are relevant to our everyday struggles. For example, in India women's organizations at the grass-roots level have begun to meet to pursue the linkages between the different dimensions of the development process and to consider alternative economic strategies from their own experiences and in their regional languages. In addition, since Nairobi, women have held discussions and workshops recreating the highlights of Forum '85 both to relate what they learned to wider audiences and to inspire new organizing agendas.

We think that smaller, perhaps more issue-specific, international gatherings are crucial in providing a necessary space for the cross-fertilization of ideas and strategies and in allowing us to further strengthen the connections built throughout the Decade for Women. The proposal to hold an international meeting in Madras, India, in 1990 specifically for grass-roots women is an important initiative in this regard. Regional preparatory meetings would allow grass-roots women the opportunity to exchange agendas and tactics.

One important bridge needs to be built between grass-roots women and feminist researchers. It is important for both groups to exchange and benefit from each other's expertise. All too often, feminist research has been of little use to those researched, and the process of education has remained unidirectional. One proposal offering both groups the possibility of working more closely together has come from a group of activists from the United States. They would like to work toward an alternative women's economic summit meeting that would challenge the economic summit held by Western finance ministers. These women envision a series of local and regional women's tribunals that would gather together testimony from grass-roots women as well as empirical data on women's lives, to feed into the larger international gathering.[11]

Despite the lack of concrete, immediate agendas

drawn up to tackle the world's problems, we came away from Forum '85 revitalized by the power of women's visions and potential. The Nairobi meeting therefore marks a fundamental turning point in the development and consolidation of feminisms around the globe, feminisms that are already developing the necessary agendas. It is clear that such a consolidation depends substantially on the basic recognition that feminism is not a monolithic movement. As many feminists in Nairobi recognized

> feminism constitutes the political expression of the concerns and interests of women from different regions, classes, nationalities, and ethnic backgrounds. There is and must be a diversity of feminisms, responsive to the different needs and concerns of different women, and defined by them for themselves. This diversity builds on a common opposition to gender oppression and hierarchy which, however, is only the first step in articulating and acting upon a political agenda.[12]

ACKNOWLEDGMENTS

We wish to thank Lourdes Beneria, Charlotte Bunch, Katharine McKee, and Rayna Rapp for their helpful comments and suggestions on an earlier draft of this article.

NOTES

1. Although each of the three conferences consisted of an official government component as well as a forum for nongovernmental organizations (NGOs), our focus here will mainly be on the nongovernmental conferences, which are widely viewed as the arena where consciousness raising, networking, and strategy formulation for grass-roots feminists has taken place.

2. For a skeptical point of view on the Copenhagen conference, see Irene Tinker, "A Feminist View of Copenhagen," *Signs* 6 (Spring 1981): 531–35. A variety of responses and alternative views were printed in *Signs* 6 (Summer 1981): 771–90.

3. The Peace Tent was one of the most innovative aspects of Forum '85. Organized by forty women from fifteen countries, it provided an open and constructive environment for the discussion of controversial issues, such as the question of Palestinian women and a U.S.–U.S.S.R. women's dialogue. The Tech n' Tools exhibition demonstrated the multiple forms of alternative technology that women use around the world. In many instances the exhibits were safer and cheaper than "modern" technology, and they showed the often simple nature of resources that women have at their disposal.

4. An exact statistical breakdown of the participants by region, occupation, and so forth is unfortunately unavailable.

5. See Gita Sen, with Caren Grown, *Development, Cri-*

sis, and Alternative Visions: Third World Women's Perspectives (Bergen, Norway: Christian Michelsen Institute, 1985), for more elaboration of the various effects of the crisis.

6. See Orlandina de Oliveira and Teresita de Barbarieri, "The Presence of Women in Latin America in a Decade of Crisis" (paper presented at the Nairobi conference, July 1985); papers detailing the "Impact of the World Crisis on Women" gathered from regional Society for International Development (SID) meetings and presented at the SID annual meeting in Rome, Italy, in June 1985; and Marie-Angelique Savane, "Femmes, Production, et Crise Alimentaire en Afrique au Sud du Sahara" (paper presented at the ORSTOM [Institut français de Recherche pour le Developpement en Cooperation] conference on "Women's Role in Food Self-Sufficiency and Food Strategies," Paris, January 1985).

7. This is particularly (but not exclusively) evident in Islamic countries. Iran provides a clear example of the construction of a cultural identity centered around what is argued to be an essential element of Islam, using nationalist, anti-American, antifeminist sentiments. Iran is an extreme example; similar developments on a lesser scale have occurred in Egypt, Pakistan, Tunisia, and Morocco. For discussion of the impact of pentecostals in Central America, see "Salvation Brokers: Conservative Evangelicals in Central America," *NACLA* [*Northern American Congress on Latin America*] *Report on the Americas* 18 (January–February 1984). For a detailed exposition on the impact of increasing religious fundamentalism on women, see Azar Tabari, "The Enigma of Veiled Iranian Women," *Feminist Review* 5 (1980): 19–31; and Mervat Hatem, "The Enduring Alliance of Nationalism and Patriarchy in Muslim Personal Status Laws: The Case of Modern Egypt," *Feminist Issues* 6 (Spring 1986).

8. These are only five of a multiplicity of examples that we can cite. Many important and stimulating exchanges took place in the panels and workshops devoted to other themes. Limitations of space, however, prevent their elaboration here.

9. The Kenyan government's position on homosexuality contrasted with that of the conference organizers. The government attempted to censor parts of the film festival; however, pressure by the participants and Forum '85 convenors prevented this from happening for most films.

10. The press, for example, distorted and exaggerated tensions in discussions between Israeli and Palestinian women, between Iranian and Iraqi women, and in workshops dealing with the Morocco/Polisario situation. In those workshops where these issues were debated calmly and constructively, the results went largely unreported.

11. For more information on this proposed alternative economic summit meeting, contact Joyce Yu, Church Women United, 777 United Nations Plaza, New York, New York 10017.

12. See Sen, p. 13.

R E A D I N G   5 3

The Future of Feminism: A Social Movement Analysis

VERTA TAYLOR

All social movements originate in some contradiction or conflict in the larger social order (Useem, 1975). When a social movement persists throughout modern history, as the American feminist movement has done, we can only assume that the injustices, grievances, and oppression on which it is based are deeply rooted in society. The long and arduous struggle of

women to gain equality and the frequency with which this struggle has risen to become a mass movement compels us to recognize that the more central a social pattern is to the perpetuation of a way of life, the more difficult will be the process of altering that pattern. Feminism owes its existence to the universality of misogyny, androcentrism, gynophobia, and heterosexism. Feminism exists and expresses itself throughout history as a collective struggle to transform society because women are, and have been, everywhere oppressed at every level of social exchange, from the simplest social encounter to the most complex and elaborate traditions and institutional forms on which societies rest. From a social movement perspective, then, the general conditions that create the context for feminist activity were always present in American society. Indeed, instances of collective action on the part of women abound in history, especially if one includes female reform societies, women's church groups, alternative religious societies, and women's clubs. However, it seems that collective activity on the part of women directed specifically toward improving their own status has flourished only in periods of generalized social upheaval, when sensitivity to moral injustice, discrimination, and social inequality has been widespread in the society as a whole (Chafe, 1977).

The first wave of feminism in this country grew out of the abolitionist struggle of the 1930s; the second developed out of the social reform ethos of the 1890s; and the contemporary movement emerged out of the general social discontent of the 1960s. It is significant that of all the manifestations of social activism in the 1960s, feminism is one of the few that continued to flourish in the 1970s and 1980s.

American society still confronts the feminist challenge. Yet the 1980s saw the rise of political and social trends that reflected a turning away from the values of equality, human rights, and social justice. Some people have even argued that the swing toward political and social conservatism that culminated in the election of Ronald Reagan to the presidency was a deliberate backlash against the feminist momentum of the 1970s and the gains women have spent decades inching toward in this country (O'Reilly, 1980; Yankelovich, 1981). Even those recently won rights that, according to major public opinion polls, have been applauded not only by feminist activists but by the majority of Americans—all the way from equal pay for equal work to legal abortion—are now under siege. In response to the growing attack on women's rights on every front, one woman was quoted by syndicated columnist Ellen Goodman (1981) as saying, "All I know is that I am in the same movement for the second time in my life and I'm not even 40." Although this woman was talking specifically about women's rights, she also might have been talking about peace, poverty, civil rights, or the environment. Put bluntly, feminism in

the 1980s confronted a social milieu that was inhospitable to all those who sought fundamental change in society.

CHARACTERISTICS OF THE CONTEMPORARY WOMEN'S MOVEMENT: FEMINISM AS A MOVEMENT OF SOCIAL TRANSFORMATION

The contemporary women's movement, like its predecessor movements in this country, was influenced by women's past efforts to gain equality in American society, and grew out of and remains closely tied to other social movements that seek to alter various aspects of society. However, the feminist movement of today differs from its forerunners in at least three important ways: it has developed a more diverse membership and decentralized organizational base; it is pursuing through multiple strategies a wide range of objectives that strike at the root causes of sex-based inequality; and it has developed an ideology and politics directed at transforming other oppressive social institutions that perpetuate and sustain patriarchy, such as capitalism, racism, and heterosexism (Ferree & Hess, 1985). No other feminist movement over the course of American history has attempted so much (Chafe, 1977).

Ideology

While ideas do not necessarily cause social movements, ideology in large part shapes the dynamics of any social movement. Feminist ideology today is a mix of several orientations that differ in the scope of change sought and the extent to which they link women's inequality to other basic social institutions, such as capitalism, racism, and heterosexism (Jaggar & Struhl, 1978; Eisenstein, 1981). I will not attempt to describe systematically the values and beliefs of the contemporary feminist movement here, but will focus instead on the relationship between two general strands of contemporary feminist thought: liberal feminism and radical feminism.

All feminist politics today is predicated on the belief that women disproportionately occupy *peripheral* positions in society, that is, roles that are subordinate to, deemed less important than, and accorded lesser rewards than those held by men. Men are more frequently found in *core* positions, those that command higher social prestige, power, and wealth (Richardson, 1988). From a feminist perspective, two major strategies for change follow from this analysis, and both historically have been reflected in the ideology and actions of the feminist movement in this country (Giele, 1978). The first strategy for change, what traditionally has been termed the liberal feminist approach, holds that society should make a greater effort to *redistribute persons* (women and men) between the core and the periphery, as through affirmative action. The second and more radical approach is for society to *redistribute rewards* between the core and the periphery, that is, to replace the present hierarchical relations with an egalitarian structure, which ultimately means transforming all the existing forms of hierarchy and stratification that sustain and perpetuate patriarchy, in other words, fundamentally changing the whole social system.

These two strategies of change reflect the difference between what is traditionally conceptualized in the social movement literature as a reform and a revolutionary movement. As far as ideology is concerned, the basic difference between a reform and a revolutionary movement lies in the scope or amount of social change sought, that is, whether its objectives are restricted or comprehensive (Killian, 1973). A reform movement accepts the basic social order and seeks to change only some limited part of it, such as a law or a specific institution. A revolutionary movement, by contrast, has the purpose of introducing an entirely new set of values to replace prevailing ones and thus advocates change in a society's most basic and important institutions. Of course, the line between a reform and a revolutionary movement is not always clear. As we shall see, neither of these conceptualizations characterizes adequately the contemporary feminist movement. Furthermore, if we look more closely at these two strategies for change and the ideology and actions associated with each, the differences between the contemporary women's movement and earlier waves of feminist activism in this country are apparent.

The American women's rights movement of the 19th century was essentially a liberal feminist reform movement. It asked for equality within the existing social structure and, indeed, in many ways can be considered to have been, like all reform movements, a reaffirmation of existing values within the society. Feminists believed that if they obtained the right to an education, the right to own property, the right to vote, employment rights—in other words, equal civil rights under the law—they would attain equality with men.

The basic ideas identified today as liberal feminist have changed very little since their formulation in the 19th century, when they seemed progressive, even radical (Eisenstein, 1981). Today, liberal feminist ideas are best understood as "mainstream" feminism. Liberal feminist ideology holds that women lack power simply because they are not as women allowed equal opportunity to compete and to succeed in the male public world, but instead are relegated to the subordinate private world of home, domestic labor, motherhood, and family. Feminism becomes but one wave of the larger human rights movement, its objective to bring women into the mainstream, that is, into full participation in public life. The major strategy is to gain formal legal equalities for women while at the same time making up for the fact that women's starting place in the "race of life" is unequal to men's (Eisenstein, 1981). This is why liberal feminists often place as much emphasis, if not more, on changing individual women as they do on changing society. To use the popular jargon of the day, women are urged to "dress for success," to "play games mother never taught them," to become more "assertive," and to "open up their own options" by choosing freely whether to work or not to work, to become a mother or to remain childless, to marry or to remain single. Liberal feminists likewise tend to define patriarchy in individualistic rather than structural terms—as a problem of certain men oppressing certain women, for example (Friedan, 1963). In sum, the liberal conception of equality involves equality within government, under the law, and in the economic sphere, or, more generally, in the public arena, and fails to recognize how deeply women's inequality is rooted in their responsibility for the care of children and the home and in their dependence on men in the context of traditional heterosexual marriage. Liberal feminism is, in essence, a reform movement. It asks for equality for women within a structure that is patriarchal.

Contemporary radical feminist ideology began in the early 1950s with Simone de Beauvoir's theory of "sex class," developed further out of women's activism of the late 1960s, and flourished and took root in the feminist movement of the 1970s. Today it is emerging as the dominant, though often implicit, ideology behind organized feminist activism. The radical approach, in contrast to the liberal perspective, recognizes women's identity and subordination as a "sex class," which means that the distribution of all of society's scarce goods, services, and privileges is profoundly related to, if not determined by, whether one is female or male (Beauvoir, 1952; Firestone, 1970; Millett, 1971; Atkinson, 1974; Rubin, 1975; Rich, 1976; Griffin, 1978; Daly, 1978; Eisenstein, 1978; Hartman, 1981; Frye, 1983; Hartsock, 1983; MacKinnon, 1983). Once women view themselves as a "sex class," they cannot simply ignore the structural and social nature of their subordination by treating patriarchy merely in individual terms. Rather, sex-based inequality derives from the fact that all the institutions of society are constructed so as to create and perpetuate a social world in which males are dominant and females are subordinate, and furthermore are linked to one another in such a way that male superiority is dependent upon female subordination (Acker, 1980; Richardson, 1988). In American society, as in most other industrialized societies, power, prestige, and wealth belong to those who control the distribution of resources outside the home, in the extradomestic spheres of work and politics. The assignment of domestic responsibilities to women, or the ideology that woman's place is in the home, is therefore one of the primary ways in which sex-based inequality is maintained not only in the home but in political and economic institutions as well (Huber & Spitze, 1983).

Radical feminism, unlike the liberal position, does not deny that men are privileged as men and that they benefit as a group from their privilege—not just in the public arena but also in relation to housework, reproduction, sexuality, and marriage. Rather, patriarchy is a system of power which structures and sustains male privilege and female subordination in every sphere of life, in the nature and dynamics of the economic, political, and domestic institutions of society as well as in all its authority structures—religion, the law, and the sciences (Richardson, 1988). To unravel the complex structure of sex-based inequality requires, from a radical feminist perspective, a fundamental transformation of all institutions in society and the existing relations among them.

Radical feminism is therefore a transformational politics. Its ultimate vision is revolutionary in its scope: a fundamentally new social order that alters all the established patriarchal ways of seeing, defining, thinking about, structuring, and experiencing the world.

Although contemporary feminist ideology is diverse and complex, the most important trend in feminist ideology today is the increased radicalization of the contemporary movement. This shift is evident at both the individual and the organizational levels.

The feminist movement of the late 1960s and 1970s sought to alter not only the larger society but also its individual participants. Central to the movement was the objective of "raising women's consciousness." Consciousness raising is an identity-altering experience that transforms a woman's world: as her identity changes, her biography, beliefs, behavior, and relationships fundamentally change as well (Cassell, 1977). Particularly interesting is the extent to which participation in liberal feminist reform organizations and in work on such "women's issues" as rape and battered women in the context of established organizations has raised women's consciousness, increased their feminist activism, and contributed to their radicalization (Schlesinger & Bart, 1983; Sparks, 1979). Women have also become radicalized in working through their own personal experiences, such as sexual harassment, divorce, abortion, employment discrimination, incest, and rape; they have become aware of the political rather than the personal nature of these experiences (Huber, 1973; Keuck, 1980; Klein, 1984).

Radicalization is evident at the group level also. By the end of the 1970s, liberal feminist organizations, such as the National Organization for Women (NOW), the Women's Equity Action League, the Women's Legal Defense Fund, the National Abortion Rights Action League, which had been pursuing women's equality within the law, began to adopt objectives and strategies consistent with a more radical stance. Many of these groups do not explicitly identify the radical bases of their actions. NOW, for instance, included among its objectives in 1979 not only the immediate goals of the Equal Rights Amendment (ERA) and reproductive choice but also a variety of issues to be taken up in the future: the threat of nuclear energy to the survival of the species, lesbian and gay rights, homemakers' rights, the exploitation of women in the home, the sexual segregation of women in the workplace, and the influence of corporate, patriarchal, and hierarchical models of organization on the activities and strategies of NOW (Eisenstein, 1981). If there was a single objective of the women's movement that reflected the extent to which the dichotomy between liberal reform and revolutionary change had blurred by the 1980s, it was the Equal Rights Amendment. Although the ERA asked for equality for women within the existing legal and economic structure, it was based on the fact that women are discriminated against as a "sex class" and therefore had radical feminist implications.

Thus, despite the fact that contemporary feminist thought encompasses diverse beliefs and is by no means a monolithic perspective, as an ideology feminism generally is today far more comprehensive in its analysis of the institutions that perpetuate and sustain patriarchy than it has been in any other period of history. As the feminist activist and writer Charlotte Bunch (1987) puts it, the feminism of the 1980s is not, as it has been in past periods, just a "laundry list of women's issues" or areas for social reform—abortion, rape, wife beating, equal pay. Neither is feminism merely a constituency of women; that is, it is not just "what women want." There are and will always be a large number of women organized against feminism (Marshall, 1984). Feminism in its contemporary context is a transformational politics, a comprehensive ideology that addresses nearly every issue in the world, from international peace to the economic policy of the United States. It is precisely because feminist ideology has become a tool for linking various social issues that it has become so threatening to the established patriarchal order. The belief in a woman's right to control her body, for example, raises the questions not only of rape, sexual harassment, and incest but also of job safety, the destruction of life through starvation, poverty, chemical dumping, nuclear proliferation, and the exporting of unsafe drugs banned in this country to the Third World (Bunch, 1981).

In some ways, then, as an ideology feminism has come full circle; it is renewing its alliance with other movements for human rights from which it emerged in this country and around the world. The difference between this wave of feminism and earlier ones is that this time the fundamental analysis of human injustice is a distinctively feminist one that envisions a world guided by feminist egalitarian principles. The feminist sociologist Jessie Bernard (1975) describes "the current restructuring of sex roles as no less epochal than the restructuring of the class system which was one of the first consequences of the industrial revolution." Thus, while the feminists of the 1970s viewed the "woman problem" primarily from the perspective of the wrongs that have been done to women and the discrimination they have borne, feminists now are asking a much larger question: How can American society be changed according to feminist principles so that it is just and fair for all people regardless of sex, race, class, sexual orientation, or any other social characteristic?

Although the contemporary feminist movement appears to be moving toward an increasingly radical ideological position, ideology alone is an incomplete explanation of either the dynamics or the consequences of a social movement (Marx & Wood, 1975; McCarthy & Zald, 1977; Useem, 1975). Much depends on its structure as well.

Structure

There is a tendency to think of social movements as having well-defined membership, clear-cut leadership, and central direction that operates in a hierarchical fashion. This conceptualization is neither a valid nor a useful model with which to depict or to analyze organized feminist activity in the United States today. A more useful conceptualization is the multigroup model, developed by Luther Gerlach and Virginia Hine (1970) and applied to the women's movement by Joan Cassell (1977). It views any general and broad-based social movement as composed of a number of relatively independent organizations that differ in ideology, goals, and tactics, are characterized by decentralized leadership, and are loosely connected by multiple and overlapping memberships, friendship networks, and cooperation in working toward common goals. As Jo Freeman (1975) found in her analysis of the women's movement of the late 1960s, the most recent wave of feminist activism in this country has conformed to this kind of structural model from its beginnings. Freeman further pointed out that it was not so much differing feminist ideologies that accounted for the emergence of multiple, relatively independent, and strategically diverse branches of the movement; to a large extent, the movement actually began without an ideology. Rather, it was the diversity of its membership base (for example, differences in members' prior organizational expertise, experience in other movements, expectations, social status, and relations with different kinds of target groups) that created a decentralized structure (Freeman, 1979). Not surprisingly, the necessity for a decentralized structure found its way into movement ideology, specifically as the belief that large hierarchical organizations were a part of the problem rather than the solution.

The spread of the feminist movement in the United States in the 1970s resulted in the formation of uncounted numbers of independent feminist groups, and the decentralized structure of the movement made possible the expansion of goals associated with increasing radicalization. Independent groups in the 1980s continued to proliferate and work toward such objectives as the reintroduction of the ERA; the provision of services to displaced homemakers; the elimination of pornography; reproductive freedom; the demedicalization of childbirth, including home births; support for women with substance abuse problems; comparable worth; affirmative action in hiring; lesbian rights; the elimination of racism and anti-Semitism; workplace organizing of clerical workers; the rights to pregnancy leave and accessible child care; the elimination of discrimination against women in religion; the eradication of various forms of violence against women; the abolition of apartheid; support for Third World liberation movements; and the halting of nuclear proliferation. Alternative structures guided by a distinctively feminist women's culture also flourished—women's bookstores, theater groups, music collectives, poetry groups, art collectives, publishing and recording companies, women's spirituality groups, women's vacation resorts, and other feminist-run businesses. Many of these segments or branches of the women's movement recruit from different sectors of the population, develop their own organizational styles, and have their own specific goals and means; each, in other words, "does its own thing" (Freeman, 1979).

The women's movement as a whole grew throughout the 1970s—NOW numbered almost 60,000 members in 1977 and small groups formed in cities and towns across the country—but it remained relatively homogeneous. Although individual women of color and working-class women had participated in the founding of NOW and in the early protests against sexism in the civil rights movement, the women's movement continued to attract primarily white middle-class women. It was not that other women experienced no oppression as women. The 1972 Virginia Slims Poll showed clearly that black women as a group

were more likely than white women to support the women's movement. Forty-eight percent of the female population at large favored efforts to strengthen or change women's status in society; the comparable figure for black women was 62 percent. And 67 percent of black women, compared to 39 percent of all women, were sympathetic toward women's liberation. Yet the movement remained predominantly white and middle class, because of the continuation of its tradition of defining its goals with an eye to the concerns of white middle-class women and because black women and other women of color believed it was more important to work with men of their own communities to advance their own collective interests.

The class bias of the women's movement has also made working-class and poor women unlikely to participate in sizable numbers. It should not be forgotten, however, that union women played a significant role in the formation of NOW in 1966. They supported the fledgling organization by providing office space and clerical services until the group's endorsement of the ERA in 1967 forced the women of the United Auto Workers, an organization that at the time opposed the ERA, to withdraw such support. Women committed to both feminism and the union movement eventually formed their own organization, the Coalition of Labor Union Women (CLUE) in 1974. CLUE claimed 16,000 members by 1982 and had made progress in its fight to win AFL-CIO support for feminist issues.

Throughout the 1970s, then, the women's movement grew and expanded its focus. The basic composition of the movement may not have changed, but feminists began to recognize the need to expand the definition of "women's issues" to include problems of central concern to women of color, working-class and poor women, and lesbian women.

To state that the movement as a whole grew increasingly more radical throughout the 1970s is not to suggest that there are no longer any differences among groups on the basis of ideology, structure, goals, and strategies. In fact, the women's movement experienced considerable internal conflict over "ideological purity" during the late 1970s and early 1980s (Ryan, 1986). Ironically, it was during this same period that some groups that identified themselves as part of the radical branch of the movement assumed a more reform-oriented stance and adopted such institutionalized strategies for change as the establishment of rape-prevention workshops and shelters for battered women and the presentation of women's theatrical and musical productions. In one community, in contrast, feminist terrorist groups emerged out of the traditionally more liberal NOW and turned to militant and illegal tactics: they spray-painted slogans, sent pig testicles to a judge who treated defendants in rape cases leniently, and conducted raids on adult bookstores to destroy pornographic materials.

To categorize the diversity of the contemporary movement, Myra Ferree and Beth Hess (1985:41–43) have developed a schema that distinguishes groups on the basis of two dimensions: (1) whether the *means* to produce change is individual transformation or sociopolitical struggle; and (2) whether the *goal* of change is individual freedom or the creation of new societal structures. On the basis of these dimensions, Ferree and Hess propose a typology of four kinds of feminist activists. *Career feminists* see personal empowerment and increased assertiveness as the means by which women can achieve greater freedom to compete and succeed in the traditionally male-dominated world. *Radical feminists* also emphasize personal transformation, but the change is geared toward a woman-centered identity in an effort to create an autonomous female community separate from and beyond the control of men. *Liberal feminists* focus their efforts on social policies—the establishment of affirmative action in hiring, child care, equal pay, increased access to education, and pregnancy leave, among others—in an effort to produce a political world that will guarantee men and women equal treatment as individual people. Finally, *socialist feminists,* like liberal feminists, focus on societal change, but they deny that the transformation can come about simply through changes in individuals. In a patriarchal and capitalist society, they believe, the concept of individual freedom divides women and other disadvantaged groups and masks and perpetuates an economic and political structure that permits some groups (men, capitalists, whites) to control and benefit from others (women, workers, blacks).

Because the structure of the contemporary women's movement is amorphous and its goals and strategies are diverse, it is sometimes easy to be misled into thinking that there is no movement, only a series of unrelated efforts. Its noncentralized structure is, however, a major source of the movement's strength.

Sociologically speaking, the movement can be described as segmentary, that is, made up of many groups of varying sizes and scope; polycephalous, that is, having many and competing leaders among its diverse groups or branches; and reticulate, that is, its various branches are woven together to form a loosely held network (Gerlach & Hine, 1970). Segmentation and proliferation occur within any movement, according to Gerlach and Hine (1970), when the movement's ideology stresses a belief in personal access to power and its members vary in age, class, racial, and ethnic background. The women's movement of course has sought to transform women as much as society. Participants have therefore been encouraged to launch new projects and groups in new directions. Many women involved in the early antirape movement, for instance, later organized child-assault, incest, and antipornography groups. In this type of movement structure, leadership is ephemeral, since it is weakly developed and exists primarily at the local level. But such movements produce multiple leaders who build a name and establish a wide following on the basis of personal qualities and relationships. Nevertheless, despite the fact that separate groups under their own leader tend to "do their own thing," they intersect at both the personal and organizational levels to form a reticulate macrostructure.

Cohesion between segments of the movement is obtained primarily through overlapping friendship networks, including ties between members and group leaders; through shared basic ideological themes (e.g., as Cassell [1977] terms it, the belief in "women's way versus men's way"); through a common culture (e.g., social events, conferences, and publications); through common operations (e.g., national marches, demonstrations, and letter-writing campaigns); and through traveling spokespersons from the movement (often sponsored by local feminist collectives and women's studies programs in major universities). The extent to which feminist gatherings have proliferated can be seen in the annual meetings of the Women and the Law Conference, the National Women's Studies Association, and the Association for Feminist Psychologists; numerous other annual cultural events, such as the Michigan Womyns' Music Festival, attended by more than 5,000 women; and such local events as "Take Back the Night" (antirape) marches, feminist concerts, lesbian writers' workshops, and conferences on topics ranging from substance abuse to feminist spirituality.

The ability of this type of structure to adapt to social change helps a movement to survive in the face of strong opposition. Because such a movement permeates every institution of society, operates in multiple localities, and recruits from different sociocultural and socioeconomic groups, it becomes difficult to suppress. Its flexible structure also encourages innovation in strategy and ideology and is functional in efforts to recruit new members. New feminists are made not by membership drives or official recruitment campaigns but through individual proselytyzing, through women's radicalization by work on reform-oriented issues, through women's studies classes, through survival of rape or incest (Keuck, 1980), and through a method of feminist recruitment that has always been important to the women's movement in this country, the transmission of feminism from mothers to daughters, sometimes even to sons, husbands, and fathers (Rupp & Taylor, 1987). In short, there is no such thing as a "card-carrying" feminist.

The women's movement gains strength also from its extramovement linkages, two especially: its ties to other movements and to organizations and persons in the established order. Many feminists have ties to other social movements—socialist feminists to other progressive movements, feminists working in women's health to the antinuclear movement, women of color to other liberation movements, lesbians to the gay rights movement, liberal feminists to the various established institutions in which they work. A participant in any one movement branch may prevail upon her extramovement friends to aid the women's movement indirectly by, for example, providing funds to support a rape project or produce a feminist play; or even directly by, for example, picketing a pornographic movie or instigating the creation of a sexual harassment policy at work. Thus nonparticipants become influenced to support the movement by word or deed.

Finally, the women's movement has another potential for social change which others do not. Women frequently live with their "oppressors" or, if not, they have close connections to men as fathers, brothers, and sons. To the extent that feminism changes women's own lives, it has an impact on the lives of intimate others (Litewka, 1978). No other movement holds so much potential power over its oppressor class. Thus the 1980s saw the continued growth of a men's movement that is strongly influenced by the feminist struggle. The goals of a core organization in the movement, the National Organization for Changing Men, include an end to the oppression of women and oppression that arises from homophobia, classism, and racism,

and a reexamination of those aspects of the male role that contribute to the oppression of women and other groups as well as to the emotional impoverishment of men.

Although the contemporary women's movement is increasingly diverse, decentralized, and loosely held together, during the 1980s efforts were made to set aside internal ideological disputes in order to mobilize in response to the growing backlash from the New Right. The feminist activist and writer Charlotte Bunch, once a proclaimed feminist separatist, suggested that the organizational task of the women's movement for the 1980s was not to build a "purer" feminism, as was the case in the 1970s, but to build a broad base by forming coalitions among feminist groups and other human rights movements. In the same vein, the feminist songwriter Holly Near, in her song "You Are Not My Enemy," in her 1981 album *Fire in the Rain,* urged radical feminist politics to be more warmhearted, stressing that the revolutionary process should bring people together, not make enemies of compatriots. Women indeed "came together" in March 1981, when 24 ideologically diverse women's groups, ranging from the League of Women Voters to the Women's Equity Action League, issued a joint statement charging that the Reagan administration's budget cuts were inimical to women's interests.

The women's movement, then, remained a vital force in American society throughout the 1980s, pursuing revolutionary objectives through an increased coalitional politics. Many would argue that it is presumptuous to use the term *revolution* for the activities of the contemporary feminist movement. In Western social thought *revolution* is usually reserved for sudden radical change in the political or economic order by means of a violent rebellion or overthrow (Paynton & Blackey, 1971). From a feminist perspective, however, much of what has been termed "revolutionary" change has been at best mere variation on the patriarchal theme and at worst no change at all. In revolutionary socialist societies, women still are subordinate to men (Dallin & Lapidus, 1977; Yedlin, 1980). The mere fact that American women are not employing traditional social movement tactics, such as marching in the streets, as they did so often in the late 1960s and early 1970s, or arming themselves for the defeat of the established political order, as male-led revolutionary movements have traditionally done, does not necessarily mean that feminism has been coopted by the established order—that it is not, in other words, a strong revolutionary force in contemporary society.

Feminism is revolutionary, first, because conversion to it involves fundamental change in a woman's identity and way of life. Second, feminism is revolutionary in terms of the effects it has had on established institutions, for it has confronted them not only with fundamentally new questions but with new ways of defining and solving a broad range of old problems, all the way from divorce to sexual harassment in the workplace. Third, the women's movement, in seeking ways to remedy the conditions that gave rise to the feminist challenge, has had major effects on all of our social, economic, and political institutions. The feminist analysis of the institutions that perpetuate and sustain patriarchy is thus more comprehensive today than any developed in an earlier period.

Institutionalization

At the same time that the women's movement has become more radical in its ideology, it has become more institutionalized. Although the movement failed to win ratification of the ERA by the 1982 deadline and, throughout the 1980s, fought an increasingly fierce battle over reproductive freedom, it has succeeded on a number of fronts in institutionalizing both organizations and goals. Feminists have become an important constituency of the Democratic party, and the party regularly seeks the endorsement of the National Organization for Women and the National Women's Political Caucus for its issues and candidates. Even groups that developed out of the radical branch of the movement have gained access to the established political structure and won support for their goals. Feminist antirape groups, for example, have received financial support from government agencies and private foundations to provide rape-prevention and -treatment services in public schools and universities. The widespread acceptance of the feminist analysis of rape as an act of violence and power rather than a strictly sexual act further attests to the impact of the feminist antirape movement on American society. Likewise, the movement to provide shelters for battered women has grown in less than ten years from a small group of radical feminists to a movement supported by such agencies as the United Way and, in some states, by a tax on marriage licenses.

The same kind of development is evident in almost every area of the women's movement: the growth of women's studies in colleges and universities and even in some secondary schools; the development of women's culture in alternative feminist publishing and music industries and its impact on the established publishing and music industries; and the success of feminist legal groups in expanding women's legal rights on a number of fronts. Evidence that the feminist movement has become a key factor in electoral politics can be seen in women's increased levels of electoral participation, the emergence of a women's voting bloc, the alignment of the feminist movement with the Democratic party, and the successful campaign to get a woman nominated as vice-president in 1984 (Klein, 1984; Mueller, 1987). The distinction between "working outside the system" and "working within the system," so important in the late 1960s, no longer has the same significance. Women who work to organize clerical workers, to educate children about sexual assault, to secure the licensing of midwives, to win legal recognition for the principle of equal pay for work of comparable value, to open previously all-male social clubs to women, and to organize a "Take Back the Night" march are all working toward the same goal of dismantling the complex structural base of patriarchy and ultimately transforming society.

The fact that collective action by the women's movement has both created new institutions and moved into almost every major institution of our society suggests that the feminist challenge today has a significant impact on every facet of social life and on the lives of many individuals as well. If this is the case, the decentralized structure and multiple and diverse strategies of the contemporary movement would seem to be effective in helping the movement to survive and to reach its ultimate objectives. At the same time, however, the movement has generated a countermovement that poses a serious challenge.

THE SOCIAL CONTEXT OF CONTEMPORARY FEMINISM: POLITICAL CONSERVATISM, ANTIFEMINISM, AND THE NEW RIGHT

The growth and direction of any social movement is always affected by the ebb and flow of sentiments it arouses, particularly the extent to which its goals and means are viewed as consistent with or counter to larger political activities, trends, and social norms (Zald & Ash, 1966; Turner & Killian, 1972). Of course, all social movements will encounter some resistance, since any effort to transform society inherently challenges the prevailing distribution of power and privilege in some way. In the 1980s the feminist movement existed in a political climate inhospitable to social reform movements generally and to feminism specifically. Indeed, so powerful were antifeminist sentiments and forces in American society that members of a major political party, the Republican party, were elected in 1980 on a platform developed explicitly to "put women back in their place." After forty years of faithful support of the ERA, the Republican party dropped it from its platform, called for a constitutional amendment to ban abortion, and aligned itself with the economic and social policies of a coalition of conservative organizations referred to as the "New Right."

In the 1970s the New Right, a highly organized movement with a broad program, took up the banner of antifeminism. It began as a coalition of groups opposed to busing, abortion, and the ERA, later took up opposition to gay rights and developed an interest in foreign policy issues, and by the 1980s included in its program a concern with economic policies and opposition to social policies designed to regulate business, such as affirmative action and health and safety programs.

The leadership of the New Right consists of a small cadre of professionals, mostly fundamentalist ministers and conservative politicians, who mobilize their constituency through preexisting institutional networks, primarily churches (Liebman & Wuthnow, 1983). With the exception of Phyllis Schlafly, the leaders of the New Right are men, though most of the foot soldiers are women. The women of the right are predominantly white, middle- to lower-middle-class homemakers with few employment options; they tend to be Protestant fundamentalists (Conover & Gray, 1983; Luker, 1984; Ferree & Hess, 1985). In joining the New Right, antifeminist women are in some ways responding to the same kinds of life experiences and changes that feminists are encountering, but they have fashioned a rather different response. Like feminists, they fear the consequences of abortion and divorce for women, but, unlike feminists, they want to end legalized abortion because they believe that the option to terminate a pregnancy has encouraged men to abdicate all responsibility for the children that women choose to bear (English, 1981; Luker, 1984). New Right women recognize, quite accurately, that the increase in divorce has contributed to family poverty because half of all divorced men default on child support within the first year and many single women cannot support their children on their own earnings (English, 1981; Weitzman, 1985). And antifeminist women deplore the sexual liberalism of the 1960s and '70s and trace the rise in divorce to an abandonment of traditional values; as a result, they are engaged in a battle that some feminists are also fighting but for different reasons, the crusade against pornography.

In short, antifeminist women sense that feminism has freed men and may never get around to freeing women. They see feminists as antifamily and antihomemaker, as self-centered narcissists who have contributed to the devaluation of their roles as homemakers, mothers, and wives; in other words, they blame the women's movement itself for the new complexities and hardships of women's lives (Klatch, 1987). Several scholars have pointed out that antifeminist women are in many respects more distrustful of men than are feminist women and that such antifeminist leaders as Phyllis Schlafly and Marabel Morgan, author of *The Total Woman,* prey on women's feelings of vulnerability and their fears that they will be left by their husbands for younger and more attractive women (Dworkin, 1983; Ferree & Hess, 1985; Richardson, 1988).

Ironically, participation in the antifeminist movement offers women opportunities similar to those offered by the women's movement. Women find here an opportunity to organize and work collectively in a female, almost sisterly setting where they can affirm their political power. Unlike the feminist movement, however, the New Right is almost exclusively led by men. Perhaps as a result, some noted antifeminists have raised feminist-like objections to the political policies of conservatives. Phyllis Schlafly, for example, protested Reagan's lack of women appointees in the executive branch during his first term (Mann, 1981); and the antifeminist and antigay activist Anita Bryant, when confronted by the breakup of her own marriage, admitted that not only feminists but perhaps even lesbians, a group even more despised by the leadership of the Right, might have a point (Jahr, 1980).

To achieve its goals, the right has employed strategies as diverse as the groups comprising it. Some are geared toward legal reform through such legitimate tactics as baking cakes or sending roses to state legislators on the day of a vote on an issue of concern to them, door-to-door canvassing, phone campaigns, and expensive television campaigns directed against liberal and pro-choice senators. In 33 states, a sophisticated voter identification program was launched by pro-life groups to survey voter opinion and sell or give the results to antiabortion and anti-ERA candidates to use in mail campaigns for fund raising. Pro-life advocates have also undertaken massive antiabortion and anti-ERA mailings to elected officials. The clear message of such mailings, in the words of a CBS reporter, is "vote our way, or we'll get you." Other New Right tactics are less legitimate—bombing abortion clinics, infiltrating state delegations to the Houston International Women's Year Conference, disseminating life-threatening antigay propaganda, and establishing organizations that "front" as abortion clinics but whose real purpose is to intimidate abortion seekers by showing slides of aborted fetuses and giving women false information about the dangers of abortion. In addition, camps have been established by the Ku Klux Klan to train explorer scouts in guerrilla warfare to "battle with communists and homosexuals" (Knedler, 1981).

Among the most effective tactics used by the New Right has been the deceptive use of labels that signify traditionally accepted American values and beliefs to lend legitimacy and credibility to the movement and its cause. One of the most visible early organizations that sought to build a mass following, for instance, was named the Moral Majority. Although the Moral Majority in fact represented a small but highly organized minority opinion (Yankelovich, 1981), it was so named because the term suggested, as one popular button of the day proclaimed, that the groups it sought to displace were an "immoral minority." Such words as *freedom, family, choice, human life, work,* and *peace* ring out in speeches at right-wing gatherings and flood their printed literature. However, as Jane O'Reilly (1980) pointed out in an insightful analysis of New Right language, what the right really means by *freedom* is free enterprise; that is, business free from environmental and other governmental regulation and taxes. *Family* means a working father, mother at home, and two children; in other words, 7 percent of all American households at the present time. *Human life* means the life of an unborn fetus, which is to be preserved at the expense of an adult woman if necessary, but ironically does not include the life of a criminal which is to be taken through capital punishment

to preserve the moral fabric of society. By *work,* the right means maintenance of "right-to-work," or anti-union, laws; a crackdown on "welfare chiselers" who do not work; and an end to affirmative action "quotas." Finally, *peace* refers to male leadership and machismo, that is, as the Reverend Jerry Falwell, founder of the Moral Majority, has put it, a foreign policy no longer "under the complete control of avid supporters of the women's movement" (O'Reilly, 1980). At the same time, the right uses negative labels to stigmatize its opponents and to blame them for the decay of society. Groups whose concerns are as broad as health care, the environment, poverty, world peace, and human rights, not to mention such groups as blacks, Jews, women, Hispanics, and gays, are termed "special interest groups" and are held responsible for the loss of morality and true Christian values.

Some scholars have argued that the New Right is attacking feminism as a means of returning the country to patriarchal and militaristic positions (Gordon & Hunter, 1977; Rupp, 1981; Dworkin, 1983; Ferree & Hess, 1985). Certainly women and their demand for equality have become the scapegoat for many of the problems confronting American society today. Whether it is the increase in divorce, the rise in teen-age pregnancy, unemployment among white men, the decline in "Christian" morality, the increased acceptability of homosexuality—which in turn has brought the AIDS epidemic to the United States—slower economic growth, the lack of a "tough" foreign policy, or the humiliations and defeats the United States has suffered both at home and abroad, the women's movement is blamed either directly or indirectly. Echoing the traditional conservative critique, the New Right ascribes to liberals the traits traditionally associated with women and disparaged by the larger society: liberals are "soft" on communism, "passive" in the face of military threats, "permissive" toward their children and the poor, and "submissive" in relations with Third World countries; their policies are guided by "emotion"—by the "bleeding heart" approach—rather than by reason. In the face of the broad challenges posed by the women's movement and the increasing acceptance of traditionally feminine as opposed to masculine values—egalitarianism rather than hierarchy, cooperation rather than competition, nurturance rather than rugged individualism, peace rather than conflict—masculinity rears its head and reasserts patriarchal forms.

From a social change perspective, the strong dis-

YES!

agreement between feminists and antifeminists about how to solve the major problems facing society today is less significant than the sharp rise in political activism by opposing groups focusing on the same set of central issues. The New Right, much like the movements to which it is responding, is a movement of self-affirmation. In the 1960s and 1970s, a variety of oppressed, devalued, and "deviant" groups in society "came out"—gays, blacks, Hispanics, women, the disabled, the aged—and organized collectively to demand recognition from the larger moral order, redress for the inequities they suffered, and equal access to insitutional resources. These movements set in motion at least the beginnings of a redistribution of societal rewards, not only of power and prestige but of access to economic benefits as well. To some extent, the New Right movement can be viewed as the collective efforts of a new set of "deviants" who perceive that the attempts of other populations to claim the legitimacy of their cultural values has forced upon conservatives a new kind of "deviant" status (Kitsuse, 1981). The right has even developed its own "oppression mentality." Thus, like all movements of oppressed groups, the New Right is in part a movement of self-affirmation which seeks to reassert the moral superiority of its own values and interests by, so to speak, coming out of the family room. The way to redress its grievances, however, is to "bring things back to normal," which means to restore the legitimacy of its own cultural values and lifestyles by rolling back the social and political changes that have already occurred, many of which it attributes to the success of the feminist movement. The right, then, is reacting to what it perceives as a cultural revolution already in progress which threatens its own social and economic advantage. The ability to mobilize disparate groups around the single issue of the importance of woman's role as family homemaker and childbearer demonstrates the success, not the failure, of feminists' efforts to bring changes to American society.

THE OUTCOME OF MOVEMENT-COUNTERMOVEMENT CONFLICT

This analysis has assumed that movements and countermovements are parts of a dialectical process centered on women's place in society. Feminist protest arose out of social conditions and in turn gave rise to antifeminist counterprotest, which, ironically, gained impetus from some of the same injustices that gave rise to feminism. I have also argued that feminism no longer is the liberal social reform movement it was in earlier periods of American history but, taken as a whole, has implications for the fundamental restructuring of the social order. The contemporary women's movement has a broad membership base, has established deep roots in society through both established institutions and the new structures it has created, and has developed a comprehensive ideology directed at changing all institutions that perpetuate patriarchy and other forms of social injustice. In short, the feminist movement has passed beyond the lift-off stage and has acquired a momentum of its own, almost independent of the generating conditions that gave rise to it. As we have seen, antifeminist opposition is also a powerful political force both within the established political system and outside it, in the form of a highly organized countermovement. The membership base of the antifeminist movement, however, is less diverse than that of the feminist movement (Huber et al., 1976; Tedin et al., 1977; Arrington & Kyle, 1978; Conover & Gray, 1983) and its goals and ideology are more particularistic, since they are, in essence, a reaction to feminist successes. Our task here is to examine the effect of movement and countermovement interaction.

It should be emphasized that opposition from the established order is a natural and expected part of any social movement. Ironically, one of the most effective ways to suppress a movement is for the established order, especially the media, to ignore it entirely (Molotch, 1979). Overt opposition can facilitate both the spread of a movement and the radicalization of its ideology and actions. Without opposition from dominant groups, there is, after all, no risk or bridge-burning associated with joining a movement and thus no firm basis for establishing commitment to its goals and ideals (Turner & Killiam, 1972).

Strong and overt opposition to the feminist movement was absent in the mid- to late 1970s. Elites in politics, education, and industry gave the appearance of supporting feminist aims through ineffectual affirmative action programs and the appointment of a few token women to high positions in their respective areas. Further, the popular image of feminism advanced by the mass media suggested that the women's movement had reached its goals. Every woman could now have a glamorous career, a happy marriage, and motherhood. If she was daunted by the prospect of juggling two, if not three, full-time jobs, she could go for the glamorous career and do without the burdens of marriage. More often what women got was neither of these options but a less attractive one—a divorce and a dead-end job in the pink-collar ghetto. Nevertheless, the image of the working woman became the feminine ideal of the 1970s and '80s; magazines emerged to appeal solely to the working woman, and hundreds of seminars, books, consulting firms, and businesses emerged to profit by the needs of the new liberated professional woman. By publicly reinforcing the idea of the "working mother," dominant groups were able to coopt and legitimate at least a narrow conception of women's equality which not only weakened liberal feminism as a protest movement but deflected the relatively more radical demands of feminists, such as passage of the ERA. The public discourse implied that since women had already achieved equality with men, they had no need for a protest movement, unless they happened to be lesbians and man haters.

The consequence of this propaganda was exactly what was intended, a dwindling of mass support for the feminist movement. By the end of the 1970s, the readiness of a large number of potential supporters of feminism to become involved in the movement had declined. Many of the early feminists who had been active in the late 1960s, although still sympathetic to feminist concerns, were by the early 1980s complacent; others, as Beverly Stephen (1980), a reporter for the *New York Daily News*, described them, decided it was safe to exchange their pants and sturdy shoes for dress-for-success suits and high heels. At the same time, many younger women were unaware that the women's movement had ever been about anything other than getting ahead. As Stephen put it, "they are so busy learning to play games mother never taught them that they are not aware that only a decade ago they would not have been allowed to play."

Certainly the women's movement has won new advantages for women, and increasingly a high percentage of women endorse such specific items on the movement's agenda as affirmative action, pay equity, reproductive rights, child care, the feminist analysis of rape and battering, and increasing numbers of women in positions of influence (Schneider, 1986). Yet despite growing levels of support for feminist goals, many young women especially do not identify themselves as feminists. Beth Schneider suggests that the reasons that so many women commonly say, "I'm not a feminist, but . . . [I believe in some goals of the women's movement]" is that the feminist as a person is stigmatized. In the course of interviews that she conducted, Schneider found that a large number of women who agree with the goals of the women's movement refuse to call themselves feminists because they view feminists as deviating from gender norms. First, they consider feminists to be "unfeminine," hostile, aggressive, and unattractive to men. Second, to be a feminist is to oppose marriage and motherhood; in short, to be antimale. A third stereotype is that feminists must be lesbians. Finally, feminists are viewed as women who want to become like men by doing and succeeding at the things that men ordinarily have done. Despite the apparent gains made by women in some areas, gender norms are still so rigid and deeply internalized that many women who otherwise support the feminist agenda experience failure to conform to them as undesirable and threatening. Laurel Richardson (1988) characterizes such women as "passive feminists" in order to distinguish them from the women who actually oppose the goals of the women's movement.

Through the 1980s, the more radical branch of the movement managed to draw strength from the growing opposition to feminism and to recruit some younger women, though in smaller numbers than in the 1970s. Among more politically radical feminists, conversion to feminism entailed risks, ranging all the way from being shunned by family, friends, and male lovers to losing a marriage, a job, or one's children, even the threat of physical violence. The director of a women's studies program at a major university was raped after appearing on a local television station to talk about women's studies. In the same community, five NOW members were arrested, convicted, and fined for writing pro-ERA and antirape slogans on a cement wall already covered with four-letter words and misogynist graffiti. In 1979 U.S. immigration officials used force to deny some women entry to the country to attend the Michigan Womyn's Music Festival. Others were allowed entry, but "Sexual Perversion" was stamped on their visas (Gillespie-Woltemade, 1980). In the same year the Ku Klux Klan threatened the lives of women attending a national NOW conference in Houston. Feminist collectives around the country reported taps on their phones, especially in communities where right-wing groups had set fire to pornographic bookstores and theaters. Attempts to suppress feminist interaction also occurred. Some universities have refused to establish women's studies programs, have dismantled existing ones in response to campaigns by New Right groups, and have denied feminist groups use of their facilities. The University of San Francisco refused to host the 1982 annual conference of the National Women's Studies Association (NWSA) on its campus because of the association's lesbian contingent. Ironically, this is the same university that held the founding convention of the NWSA in 1977. This method of suppression is in many ways more effective than outright physical force and violence, for it prevents movement interaction and recruitment of new members and does not attract public attention. Recruitment, of course, is essential to growth of any movement.

The established media rarely acknowledge the persecution of feminists. Such events are, however, a major topic of discussion in the feminist network. If opposition is an important factor in a movement's growth, then it can be argued that the ability to maintain a "psychology of persecution" helps to explain why radical feminism continued to flourish in the 1970s while liberal feminism declined. The escalation of opposition to feminism, then, as long as it falls short of complete suppression of the movement, can actually serve to increase commitment to feminist activism.

The actions of countermovements affect not only the spread and direction of the initial movement but the very changes the movement seeks to bring about. Tahi Mottl (1980) suggests three general types of consequences of movement–countermovement conflict. First, since the aim of a countermovement is to preserve the status quo, it may be successful in reversing at least some of the changes set in motion by the initial movement. Already this outcome has taken place. Government support for women's issues has decreased sharply through such policy changes as cuts in social welfare programs that affect women and children; cuts in funds for Title IX, which guarantees equal opportunity in education; cuts in grants for women-oriented programs such as nurses' training; cuts in Small Business Administration funding for women's programs; and the elimination of the women-in-science program.

When a movement has gained as much momentum as the contemporary feminist movement has, however, countermovement successes are not likely to terminate the process of change, but can instead serve to precipitate further action by the movement. Immediately after Ronald Reagan's election in 1980, feminist groups reported that formerly complacent women were swelling their ranks. Eleanor Smeal, then president of NOW, reported that new memberships began to roll in at the rate of 9,000 to 10,000 a month—two or three times the average in previous years (Charlton, 1981). By the end of the unsuccessful ERA campaign in June 1982, NOW alone had raised approximately $8 million, more than any political action committee spent in the 1982 congressional elections, and the organization had built a giant political machine with a staff of 300. While NOW continued to lobby at the state and national levels, the final campaign for ratification of the ERA witnessed a reintroduction of public demonstrations as a major strategy of the women's movement. Nonviolent protests on behalf of the ERA attracted as many as 100,000 supporters to Washington; several women began a hunger strike in Illinois during the last two months of the ERA campaign; and women chained themselves to a Mormon temple in the state of Washington and to Republican headquarters in Washington, D.C. (Mueller, 1987).

Second, if countermovements do manage at least to stabilize the process of change brought about by the initial movement, the outcome is likely to be an increase in political pluralism among the community of women rather than the suppression of the initial movement. This is, in fact, what has occurred throughout the 1980s. Feminist and antifeminist groups coexist as major forces, with feminists increasingly allied with the Democratic party and antifeminists with the Republican party. The fact that Reagan, who ran on an anti-ERA platform, appointed the first woman justice of the Supreme Court and appointed women to other key positions suggests that even political conservatives recognize that the female population is not a political monolith and that women can no longer be safely ignored.

The third effect of strong countermovement activities is that they provide justification for dominant groups to shore up and consolidate their defenses against the demands of the original movement, to "come out," so to speak, as antifeminist. We have seen this trend in budget reductions for affirmative ac-

THE ROCK WILL WEAR AWAY

MEG CHRISTIAN AND HOLLY NEAR

For someone who usually composes in total isolation, never uttering a public peep until every note, every word is perfectly polished and practiced, the experience of co-writing a song was fairly traumatic. But it was real wonderful to learn to share creative processes, and then to even like the result!

The theme of the chorus is a common one: many small, weak entities joining together to defeat a larger, stronger one. Holly heard the rock-water imagery in a Vietnamese poem, while I fondly recall the flies in the elephant's nose in Judy Grahn's poem. You haven't really heard this song until you've sung it yourself with a whole roomful of women. For me, that experience is one of those moments when I feel our growing collective strength and purpose, and I know we can win.

Sixteen-year-old virgin
Springtime takes her to the park
Where the moon shines down like the future
calling her out of the dark
But her nightmare finds her freedom

And leaves her lying wounded, worn from invasion
Light as a feather floating by
Landing, then covered with soot
Waiting now, watching now for rain
To wash clean her pain

CHORUS:
Can we be like drops of water falling on the stone
Splashing, breaking, dispersing in air
Weaker than the stone by far
But be aware that as time goes by
The rock will wear away
And the water comes again

Thirty-year-old mother
Autumn finds her pregnant once more
And the leaves like gold and copper reminding her that she is poor
And her children often are hungry
And she hungers too, for knowledge, time and choices

CHORUS:
Eighty-year-old poet
Winter keeps her home and alone
Where she freezes and darkness keeps her from writing her final wisdom
But she lights her last red candle
And as it is melting, tilting it, writing now

tion and women's studies programs, in the denial of welfare payments for abortions, in the reduction of aid to families with dependent children, in the Reagan administration's attempt to dismantle the Equal Opportunity Employment Commission, and in the denial of tenure to women's studies faculty at various universities around the country. This third outcome, however, only serves to make antifeminist opposition more visible and has served in many instances to increase feminist activism.

Liberal and radical feminist groups have joined forces in alignment with other progressive interests to block the efforts of the right to make abortion illegal and to eliminate social programs established largely to serve women and other minority groups. Women have been running in record numbers for political office since 1982, many on feminist platforms braced by anger over the defeat of the ERA, and feminists were part of the Rainbow Coalition that supported the presidental candidacy of Jesse Jackson in 1984 and 1988.

Several colleges and universities have instituted sweeping affirmative action programs to fill the void created by the Reagan administration's dismantling of federal programs. Even the established media have expressed alarm over the growing antifeminist backlash.

During the 1980s the women's movement confronted formidable challenges within its own constituency—the complacency of some women, the stigma that others attached to feminism, and the opposition of still others—as well as from a conservative political climate that has not been receptive to its aims and actions. Yet, as we have seen, the women's movement is not "dead," as the media have been proclaiming regularly since the late 1970s. It is true that its most active adherents are not young women but an older cadre of feminists who came to the movement in the late 1960s and early 1970s. In some ways these women can be compared to the small but dedicated band of feminists of the 1940s and '50s who had become involved in women's rights work during the suffrage struggle and continued to champion women's rights during the postwar years, which were so inhospitable to feminism (Rupp & Taylor, 1987).

Perhaps feminists today can take heart from the optimism of Alma Lutz, a feminist who remained active in those doldrum years, who remarked in a letter in 1950: "A new woman has been added to our family. On New Year's Day my niece's little girl was born. . . . I hope she won't still be asking for women's rights in 1970" (cited in Rupp & Taylor, 1987). Although Lutz's hopes were not fulfilled, we can share her optimistic view that the feminist struggle does not subside with the passing of an unfulfilled generation. As one generation fades from the scene with its ultimate goals unrealized, another takes up the challenge (Rossi, 1982). But each new generation of feminists does not simply carry on where the previous generation left off; it speaks for itself and defines its own objectives and strategies. As Myra Ferree and Beth Hess (1985:182) point out, "feminism is not simply a form of received wisdom" but something that evolves with each new cycle of feminist activism. Both continuity and change, then, will animate the feminism of the future.

ACKNOWLEDGMENTS

I am grateful to Leila Rupp for her extensive comments, criticism, and encouragement in the creation of this paper and to Laurel Richardson for inspiring me to write it.

NOTES

Acker, J. 1980. "Women and stratification: A review of recent literature," *Contemporary Sociology* 9: 25–35.

Arrington, T. S., & Kyle, P. A. 1978. "Equal Rights Amendment activists in North Carolina." *Signs* 3 (Spring): 666–80.

Atkinson, T. G. 1974. *Amazon odyssey.* New York: Links.

Beauvoir, S. de. 1952. *The second sex.* New York: Bantam.

Bernard, J. 1975. *Women, wives, mothers.* Chicago: Aldine.

Bunch, C. 1981. "Feminism's future." Paper presented at a Conference, Advancing Feminism: Strategies for the '80s, Columbus, OH, February.

Bunch, C. 1987. *Passionate politics.* New York: St. Martin's.

Cassell, J. 1977. *A group called women: Sisterhood and symbolism in the feminist movement.* New York: David McKay.

Chafe, W. H. 1977. *Women and equality: Changing patterns in American culture.* New York: Oxford University Press.

Charlton, L. 1981. "Sisterhood is braced for the Reagonauts." *New York Times,* June 1.

Conover, P. J., & Gray, V. 1983. *Feminism and the New Right.* New York: Praeger.

Dallin, D. A. A., & Lapidus, G., eds. 1977. *Women in Russia.* Stanford: Stanford University Press.

Daly, M. 1978. *Gyn/ecology.* Boston: Beacon.

Dworkin, A. 1983. *Right wing women.* New York: Putnam.

Eisenstein, Z. 1978. *Capitalist patriarchy and the case for socialist feminism.* New York: Monthly Review Press.

Eisenstein, Z. 1981. *The radical future of liberal feminism.* New York: Longman.

English, D. 1981. "The war against choice." *Mother Jones,* February/March.

Ferree, M. M., & Hess, B. B. 1985. *Controversy and coalition: The new feminist movement.* Boston: Twayne.

Firestone, S. 1970. *The dialectic of sex.* New York: William Morrow.

Freeman, J. 1975. *The politics of women's liberation.* New York: David McKay.

Freeman, J. 1979. "Resource mobilization and strategy: A model for analyzing social movement organization actions." In M. N. Zald and J. D. McCarthy, eds., *The dynamics of social movements,* pp. 167–89. Cambridge, MA: Winthrop.

Friedan, B. 1963. *The feminine mystique.* New York: Norton.

Frye, M. 1983. *The politics of reality: Essays in feminist theory.* Trumansburg, NY: Crossing Press.

Gerlach, L. P., & Hine, V. H. 1970. *People, power change: Movements of social transformation.* Indianapolis: Bobbs-Merrill.

Giele, J. Z. 1978. *Women and the future.* New York: Free Press.

Gillespie-Woltemade, N. 1980. "Feminism as an international metaculture." Paper presented at the Annual Meeting of the American Sociological Association, New York, August.

Goodman, E. 1981. "Struggle of the 1960's starts all over again." *Citizen Journal,* Columbus, OH, March 12.

Gordon, L., & Hunter, A. 1977. "Sex, family, and the new right: Anti-feminism as a political force." *Radical America* 12 (1): 9–25.

Griffin, S. 1978. *Women and nature.* New York: Harper & Row.

Hartman, H. 1981. "The family as the locus of gender, class, and political struggle: The example of housework." *Signs* 6 (Spring): 366–94.

Hartsock, N. C. M. 1983. *Money, sex, and power: Toward a feminist historical materialism.* New York: Longman.

Huber, J. 1973. "From sugar and spice to professor." In A. S. Rossi & A. Calderwood, eds., *Academic women on the move.* New York: Russell Sage Foundation.

Huber, J. C.; Rexroat, C.; & Spitze, G. 1976. "E.R.A. in Illinois: A crucible of opinion on women's status." Unpublished paper, University of Illinois, Urbana-Champaign.

Huber, J., & Spitze, G. 1983. *Sex stratification: Children, housework, and jobs.* New York: Academic Press.

Jaggar, A. M., & Struhl, P. R. 1978. *Feminist frameworks.* New York: McGraw-Hill.

Jahr, C. 1980. "Anita Bryant's startling reversal." *Ladies' Home Journal,* December.

Keuck, D. 1980. "Community action to prevent rape." A class presentation in Sociology of Women course, Ohio State University, Columbus.

Killian, L. M. 1973. "Social movements: A review of the field." In L. M. Killian, ed., *Social movements,* pp. 9–53. Chicago: Rand McNally.

Kitsuse, J. 1981. "Coming out all over: Deviants and the politics of social problems." *Social Problems* 38 (1): 1–13.

Klatch, R. 1987. *Women of the right.* Philadelphia: Temple University Press.

Klein, E. 1984. *Gender politics.* Cambridge, MA: Harvard University Press.

Knedler, B. 1981. "Klan to battle homosexuals." *News of the Columbus Gay and Lesbian Community,* Columbus, Ohio. February.

Liebman, R. C., & Wuthnow, R. 1983. *The new Christian right.* New York: Aldine.

Litewka, J. 1978. "The socialized penis." In A. Jaggar & P. R. Struhl, eds., *Feminist frameworks,* pp. 64–73. New York: McGraw-Hill.

Luker, K. 1984. *Abortion and the politics of motherhood.* Berkeley: University of California Press.

McCarthy, J. D., & Zald, M. N. 1977. "Resources mobilization and social movements: A partial theory." *American Journal of Sociology* 82 (May): 1212–1239.

MacKinnon, C. A. 1979. *Sexual harassment and working women.* New Haven, CT: Yale University Press.

MacKinnon, C. A. 1983. "Feminism, Marxism, method, and the state: Toward feminist jurisprudence." *Signs* 8 (4): 635–58.

Mann, J. 1981. "G.O.P. women are getting their act together." *Washington Post,* February 13.

Marshall, S. 1984. "Keep us on the pedestal: Women against feminism in twentieth-century America." In J. Freeman, ed., *Women: A feminist perspective,* pp. 568–81. Palo Alto: Mayfield.

Marx, G. T., & Wood, J. L. 1975. "Strands of theory and research in collective behavior." In A. Inkeles, J. Coleman, & N. Smelser, eds., *Annual review of sociology,* vol. 1, pp. 363–428. Palo Alto: Annual Reviews, Inc.

Millett, K. 1971. *Sexual politics.* New York: Avon.

Molotch, H. 1979. "Media and movements." In M. N. Zald & J. D. McCarthy, eds., *The dynamics of social movements,* pp. 71–93. Cambridge, MA: Winthrop.

Mottl, T. L. 1980. "The analysis of countermovements." *Social Problems* 27 (5): 620–635.

Mueller, C. 1987. "The life cycle of equal rights feminism: Resource mobilization, political process, and dramaturgical explanations." Paper presented at the Annual Meeting of the American Sociological Association, Chicago.

O'Reilly, J. 1980. "To fight them, we've got to understand what they're saying." *Savvy,* October.

Paynton, C. T., & Blackey, R. 1971. *Why revolution: Theories and analyses.* Cambridge, MA: Schenkman.

Rich, A. 1976. *Of woman born.* New York: Norton.

Richardson, L. 1988. *Dynamics of sex and gender.* New York: Harper & Row.

Rossi, A. S. 1982. *Feminists in politics.* New York: Academic Press.

Rubin, G. 1975. "The traffic in women: Notes on the 'political economy' of sex." In Rayne Reiter, ed., *Toward an anthropology of women.* New York: Monthly Review Press.

Rupp, L. J. 1981. "Can it happen here? Nazi Germany, homosexuality, and the right." *Sojourner,* Center for Women's Studies, Ohio State University, Columbus.

Rupp, L. J., & Taylor, V. 1987. *Survival in the doldrums: The American women's rights movement, 1945 to 1960s.* New York: Oxford University Press.

Ryan, B. 1987 "Changing orientations in ideology and activism: Feminism from the mid-1970s to the present." Paper presented at the Annual Meeting of the American Sociological Association, Chicago.

Schlesinger, M. B., & Bart, P. 1983. "Collective work and self-identity: The effect of working in a feminist illegal abortion collective." In L. Richardson & V. Taylor, eds., *Feminist frontiers.* Reading, MA: Addison-Wesley.

Schneider, B. E. 1986. "Political generations and the contemporary women's movement." Paper presented at the Annual Meeting of the American Sociological Association, New York.

Sparks, C. H. 1979. "Program evaluation of a community rape prevention program." Ph.D. diss., Ohio State University, Columbus.

Stephen, B. 1980. "This couldn't be happening to us." *Savvy,* October.

Tedin, K. L.; Brady, D. W.; Buxton, M.E.; Gorman, B. W.; & Thompson, J. L. 1977. "Social background and political differences between pro-E.R.A. and anti-E.R.A. activists." *American Politics Quarterly* 5 (3): 395–408.

Turner, R. H., & Killian, L. M. 1972. *Collective behavior.* Englewood Cliffs, NJ: Prentice-Hall.

Useem, M. 1975. *Protest movements in America.* Indianapolis: Bobbs-Merrill.

Weitzman, L. J. 1985. *The divorce revolution.* New York: Free Press.

Yankelovich, D. 1981. *New rules.* New York: Random House.

Yedlin, T. 1980. *Conference on women in Eastern Europe and the Soviet Union.* New York: Praeger.

Zald, M., & Ash, R. 1966. "Social movement organizations, decay and change." *Social Forces* 44: 327–42.

About the Authors

Laurel Richardson is a professor of sociology at Ohio State University. She received her B.A. from the University of Chicago and her Ph.D. from the University of Colorado. She is the author of numerous articles and two books: *The Dynamics of Sex and Gender: A Sociological Perspective,* which is in its third edition (1988), and *The New Other Woman: Contemporary Single Women in Affairs with Married Men* (1985), which has been translated into German, Portuguese, and Japanese. Her current research interests are in the areas of gender and intimacy, qualitative methods, and narrative forms.

Verta Taylor is an associate professor of sociology at Ohio State University. She received her B.A. in social work from Indiana State University and the M.A. and Ph.D. from Ohio State University. She is the author, with Leila J. Rupp, of *Survival in the Doldrums: The American Women's Rights Movement, 1945 to the 1960s,* and she has written numerous articles. Her teaching and research interests are in the sociology of gender and women's studies, social movements and collective behavior, and qualitative research methods. She is a recipient of the 1988 Ohio State University Alumnae Award for Distinguished Teaching. Taylor has been active in the contemporary women's movement and is a strong advocate of women's studies through teaching, lecturing to academic and community groups, and conducting feminist research.